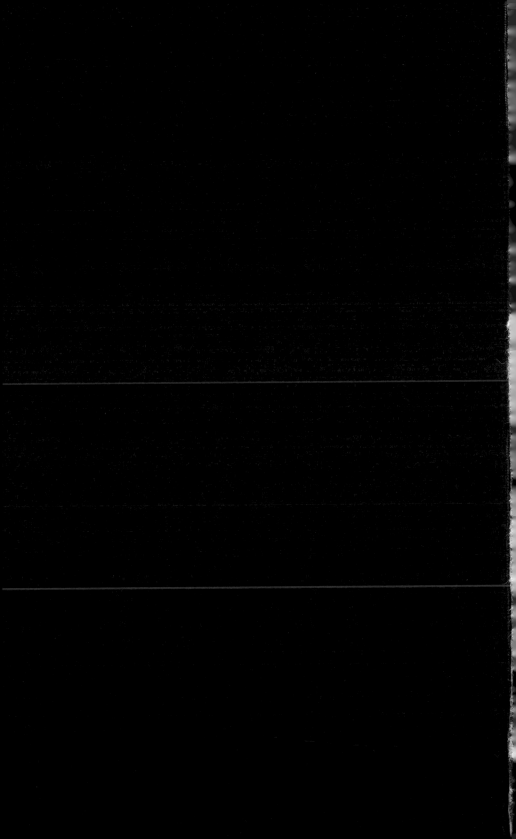

THE HONDA MYTH

THE GENIUS AND HIS WAKE

MASAAKI SATO

Translated by Hiroko Yoda with Matt Alt

Copyright © 2006 by Masaaki Sato

Published by Vertical, Inc., New York.

Originally published in Japanese as *Honda Shinwa: Kyoso no naki atode*
by Bungei Shunju, Tokyo, 1995.

ISBN: 978-1-932234-26-8 / 1-932234-26-8

Manufactured in the United States of America

First American Edition

Vertical, Inc.
1185 Ave. of the Americas 32nd Floor
New York, NY 10036
www.vertical-inc.com

CONTENTS

FOREWORD
By Paul Ingrassia

The names of the big Japanese consumer-products companies—Sony, Toshiba, Toyota and the like—are well known to virtually all Americans. But the men who built these world-class companies, and the stories behind how they did it, remain largely obscure in the world's largest consumer nation. Now Masaaki Sato, Japan's foremost automotive journalist, lifts the obscurity from the men who founded Honda Motor Co. during Japan's lean years in the wake of World War II.

There is, of course, Soichiro Honda, the engineering genius who gave the company his name. But equally as important, Mr. Sato brings to life Takeo Fujisawa, the financial and management genius without whose skills Mr. Honda would have been just another garage-shop tinkerer.

The two men were total opposites, yin and yang, and the polarity of their temperaments as well as their skills parallels those of the first Henry Ford and his top financial man, James Couzens. But there is a big difference between these two automotive odd couples. Messrs. Ford and Couzens had a falling out after Ford Motor rose to success, a phenomenon that happened more than once with those who were close to Henry Ford. In sharp contrast, when Mr. Honda was inducted into Detroit's Automotive Hall of Fame in October 1990, he flew back to Tokyo and placed his medal on the memorial tablet that commemorated Mr. Fujisawa, who had died two years earlier. "Takeo Fujisawa was the stalk that supported the gay flower Soichiro," Mr. Sato writes. "The stalk withered first, in the winter… The petals scattered in the summer."

Mr. Honda was a genius engineer and a born extrovert. He loved to party and he craved the spotlight. The reserved Mr. Fujisawa was a loner who often worked at home and rarely, if ever, drove a car, preferring instead to be chauffeured around. They met each other through a Japanese bureaucrat who knew Soichiro Honda needed money and also knew that Mr. Fujisawa could figure out how to raise it.

What Honda's co-founders had in common, as Mr. Sato tells it, were their explosive tempers—which earned Mr. Honda the nickname "Thunderer" among employees, who also labeled Mr. Fujisawa "Godzilla." But the two men also had an uncanny ability to command loyalty and to inspire their employees.

Honda Giken Kogyo, or Honda Motor Company, officially was incorporated as a motorcycle maker on September 24, 1948 in Japan's bleak, early post-war years. It was a year later that Messrs. Honda and Fujisawa met and formed their partnership, with the former handling engineering and manufacturing, and the latter handling financial affairs. Soichiro Honda was 42 years old, and Mr. Fujisawa was 38.

Expansion was frenetic in the early years. A young recruit named Satoshi Okubo got rude treatment during his job interview, which prompted him to ask the interviewer: "When did you begin working for Honda, sir." The reply: "Yesterday." Mr. Okubo later became chairman of the company.

By 1954, when the company went public, Honda was the dominant motorcycle manufacturer in Japan. But the company's sales soon plunged, partly due to quality problems. Mr. Honda responded by setting plans to enter the world's most prestigious and demanding motorcycle race: England's Isle of Man TT.

The goal rallied employees to improve quality, even though it took five years before Honda actually entered the race. The company's motorcycles placed sixth, but just two years after that Honda shocked the motorcycle world by sweeping the top five positions. Thus began a pattern: racing would inspire product advancements and generate publicity, both of which propelled Honda's increasing sales success.

All this inspired Mr. Fujisawa, despite his financial bent, to insist that the company's engineering research operations be set up as a separate entity, albeit affiliated, from the manufacturing business. His goal was "to isolate the new section's research budget from Honda's sales income," Mr. Sato writes. So Honda Research and Development Co. produced a string of engineering innovations, and also a string of Mr. Honda's successors as CEO. The setup remains unique among automotive manufacturers.

In 1955 Honda established stock options for employees, allowing each one to buy an unlimited number of shares for about 50 cents each—one-fourth of the market price at the time. Between 1959 and 1961 the price of Honda's shares surged 72-fold. The good times were rolling. Honda was a company of young people, many of whom met their spouses at work. If both husband and wife had purchased stock options, the couple was instantly well off. "Men who married within the company were the envy of the other staffers," Mr. Sato writes.

Then in 1961, as in 1954, Honda hit a financial crisis, but this time the cause was different. Instead of quality and production glitches, the new crisis began when production capacity surged beyond the capability of the company's sales and marketing network. Only emergency financing from Japan's Mitsubishi Bank allowed Honda to escape unscathed.

Just two years later, in 1963, Honda held lavish parties in Kyoto, Japan's cultural capital, to celebrate its fifteenth anniversary. The company booked virtually all of the nation's top entertainers and reserved the ballrooms of every major hotel in the city.

Most of these events occurred at the young company before it made a single automobile. Honda was a maker of motorcycles and motor scooters, pure and simple. And if Japan's strong-willed bureaucrats had had their will, Honda would have stayed that way.

Messrs. Honda and Fujisawa dreamed of going "big time" and entering the car business. But Japan's trade ministry planned laws that would "rationalize" the country's then-fledgling auto industry by limiting new entrants. Honda defied the bureaucrats and moved ahead anyway.

The Honda Sports 500 automobile, or "S500" for short, finally went on sale in October 1963. The car was derided as "just a four-wheeled motorcycle," and it never made money for Honda. But Honda was on its way to becoming the premier automobile manufacturer that it is today.

Mr. Sato introduces and portrays other key Honda personalities besides the two co-founders. One of the most vivid is Shoichiro Irimajiri, a talented engineer who oversaw Honda's first U.S. car-manufacturing factory in Ohio. Until Mr. Irimajiri and Honda came along, no foreign automaker ever had succeeded in making cars in America. Honda's brazen success seemed to give Mr. Irimajiri, known as "The Prince of Honda" for his outgoing personality and love of racing, the inside track to becoming CEO.

But it didn't turn out that way. While Mr. Irimajiri was overseeing Honda's American adventure, the more reserved Nobuhiko Kawamoto was closer to home and to headquarters—running Honda R&D, the company's engineering lab. Both men had joined Honda in 1963, had served on the company's Formula 1 engine-development team together and had been close colleagues and friendly rivals over the years. The winner, in the spring of 1990, was Mr. Kawamoto, who became Honda's fourth CEO thanks partly to Honda's "tradition of being led by those who do not seek to lead."

Mr. Kawamoto led Honda through another difficult period in the mid-1990s, when the Japanese yen rose in value and American consumers flocked to SUVs and minivans, catching Honda flat-footed. Ironically, part of his solution was pulling Honda out of Formula 1 racing, where both he and Mr. Irimajiri had cut their teeth.

Mr. Irimajiri, meanwhile, left Honda, and later was heavily recruited for a senior job at General Motors. But the man who had made automotive history at Honda declined the chance to do it again at GM.

The personalities, issues, crises and key decisions at Honda are portrayed in detail in *The Honda Myth: The Genius and His Wake*. The engineering innovations that spurred Honda's growth in its first quarter-century have given way to more conventional forms of success. No one can understand Honda, or the current state of the global automotive industry, without reading Mr. Sato's book.

PROLOGUE

Head of Section, Head of Department, Head of Company! Words, I say. It's so that chains of command don't get tangled up that we use those labels. They don't say a thing about our worth. Me, I never put my seal on anything as "The President." Maybe I should have been fired!

—Soichiro Honda

"President" is no more than the name of a post in an organization called the corporation. It isn't a rank expressing the greatness of a person. When some people become president, however, they start strutting about like they're field marshal. President is the most hazardous occupation known to man.

—Takeo Fujisawa

A quarter-century after total defeat, the Japanese were enjoying a period of unusual prosperity and hope in government. People spoke of a *showa genroku*, combining the calendric term for their emperor Hirohito's reign with another referring to some of Shogunate Japan's happiest days.

But the good times were growing oversweet in 1973. The name of warlord Toyotomi, the former footsoldier who unified Japan in the sixteenth century, was being mouthed in appraisal of Prime Minister Kakuei Tanaka and his inebriating plan to "Remodel the Japanese Archipelago." The leader of humble origins was yet to be exposed and brought down in a notorious corruption case, the Lockheed scandal.

The U.S. policy decision a couple of years earlier to suspend the dollar's convertibility into gold—the so-called Nixon shock—had generated a vast amount of excess capital in Japan. Companies seeking secure areas of investment were swamping the real estate and stock markets with their surplus funds. Land values skyrocketed, and ordinary people were robbed one after another of dreams of owning a home. Prices, indeed, were on the rise across the board. The Japanese economy was wading step by step into the perilous waters of inflation. The trade surplus reached nine billion dollars, and when the U.S. cut the value of its currency by a tenth in February, the yen's exchange rate was put on a floating basis, where it remains today.

It was early in 1973, too, that cars started to sell like hot cakes for reasons that aren't entirely clear. As summer approached, a number of explosions occurred at various petrochemical complexes in the western reaches of Honshu, the main and largest of the Japanese islands. A goods shortage, of which there had been warning signs enough, soon became a reality, particularly for oil-related products. Brand-new cars that weren't equipped with spare tires started to show up at the dealers.

Still, cars kept on selling. The word "bubble" had not yet assumed an economic meaning, but some balloon was surely swelling beyond control. What was in store just several months hence nobody foresaw: the first oil crisis, and panic in the developed world.

The annual rain season did not last long in 1973 and ceded to a long, hot summer.

The ninth of August was the hottest day of that hectic year, and the heat did not subside with nightfall. The cramped, patchy main lobby of Haneda International Airport was roiling with travelers returning to or fleeing the metropolis. The traditional *obon* holiday season was still a week away, but larger companies had begun staggering their employees' summer vacations. Local and federal agents on strict watch also inflated the crowd. Just that morning, thanks to a caller, police belatedly learned that around noon the previous day, former South Korean presidential candidate Kim Dae-jung had been abducted at gunpoint by five men, in broad daylight, from a hotel in bustling Tokyo. It beat gangster films.

Meanwhile, the special lounge on the second floor was no less stuffy despite the air-conditioning. Well over a hundred reporters awaited the arrival of a man. The soirée's impatiently anticipated star, Soichiro Honda, had turned a provincial factory called Honda Giken Kogyo (Honda Tech-research Industries) into the deservedly far-famed "HONDA" in just a quarter-century.

He had departed ten days ago on an inspection tour regarding the state of the auto industry in China, the Communist giant with whom diplomatic relations had just been restored. While Soichiro had left Japan on an All-Nippon Airways plane chartered by the Japan Amateur Sports Association, he was due back via Hong Kong on a regular service flight, "JL 62" (Japan Air Lines). The aircraft that bore the hero landed safely shortly after eight as scheduled.

The plane taxied to the passenger boarding bridge and docked. When the fore door opened, out came—first in line—a short man wearing a blue jeans jacket and no tie. Soichiro's trademark casual style.

"Hey, I made the papers, didn't I! Well, they got it right too this time. The world's too finely engineered for secrets, it's really a system against hiding anything. So let me just tell you. After I quit, I'll pass all my free time at a driving range, with an eye to becoming a pro."

Like some bully caught in the middle of his latest prank, now and then he shot his visibly scarred left hand up to scratch his balding head. His was an original Japanese, the dialect of his native Hamamatsu cropping up now and then amidst the tunes of working-class Tokyo.

After going through entry and customs, he appeared at the special lounge, the site of the press conference, where the bulk of the reporters waited. He repeated the same gesture but wore a less facetious expression as he elaborated upon his decision to retire.

"Ever since I was a young man I've liked to wear red shirts. Get past sixty, though, and people want to put you in a red *chanchanko*"—a sleeveless kimono, a sort of cardigan. "I'd like to think of myself as young and hale but I'm already sixty-six. Five, six years past that mark of sixty, you begin to lose your management sense, and you can't keep up with society's needs and your employees' demands anymore. In the hurly-burly world of business management, it's not easy to ignore those gaps, and I must say I've been feeling them acutely these days. And that's why I've decided to pull myself from the front line.

"You people call me a 'founder-president,' but a company doesn't belong to an individual or to his family. Honda Motor belongs to our employees and stockholders. Don't you all agree? The boss has got to be young to answer to them... We've found a successor that both insiders and outsiders like a lot. Well, now seems a good time.

"The vice president [Takeo Fujisawa] and I, we're half-good each. We're like apprentice geishas who count as one geisha together. We wouldn't have made it if either of us wasn't there. We're just applying the same logic to the business of quitting. One goes, the other does too.

"There's nothing in particular I want to take up. Anyway, I don't think the young executives would take to coddling me. I won't do more than I'm asked to, but I'm afraid it won't leave me any free time to speak of."

That so many reporters were there waiting for Honda was the result of media manipulation. It began on August 1 at the Federation of Economic Organizations assembly hall in Tokyo, where Honda Motor announced an additional public offering of twenty-six million stocks. There, executive director Michihiro Nishida suggested that a change in leadership was imminent.

"For the last few years, preparing the succession has been the number-one priority issue for the president and the vice president, and they have completed the task. Though no decisions have been made within the company, the two may privately be considering retirement."

Sharp journalists, catching on immediately, did not ask Nishida to clarify himself. They knew what the next step was.

The president, Honda, was out of the country. That meant they had to interview the co-founder of Honda Motor, Takeo Fujisawa. In Honda circles, Fujisawa was referred to as "Roppongi" after his home in Roppongi, Minato ward; likewise Honda was "Nishiochiai" thanks to his Nishiochiai address in Shinjuku ward. For those who had shared their joys and sorrows since the company's founding, Honda was also "Pop" or "Dad," while the more dignified Fujisawa was "Uncle" and sometimes "Master Roppongi." The president-to-be Kiyoshi Kawashima, who was for the others more a comrade-in-arms than an authority figure, went by "Bro" or even "Kiichan" (-chan is an affectionate version of the honorific -san).

Fujisawa was reputed to abhor journalists.

Media people are always looking for ways to spark up a fight between me and Nishiochiai. Don't ask me why they get such a kick out of it; what I do know is that they better look somewhere else for news fodder. I've considered holding a press conference and telling them, "We're terribly sorry, but we aren't after each other's throats," but that'd be too childish. Instead I avoid seeing them, period.

But the truth was that Fujisawa did not shun journalists. Whenever a reporter, heading for one of the bars in Roppongi, chose instead to take a turn towards the Defense Agency building at the main intersection, it was often because he knew that in the quiet residential district beyond was a living room where, in fact, he would be quite welcome. Generous with his stock of alcohol but nimble on the essential questions, Fujisawa took evident pleasure in getting a reporter to tell *him* about the goings-on at Honda Motor.

The night of the day Nishida dropped the hint, Fujisawa was fully prepared for the reporters—indeed, waiting for them. It was none other than he who had directed Nishida to hint, at the public offering, that Soichiro Honda was about to retire.

A fair number of "acute" newspapermen were lured to Roppongi that night to disturb Fujisawa's peace.

"I guess I don't have a choice, eh?" he mumbled, looking especially annoyed. He invited them all into his living room as usual. Having poured himself a liberal dose of expensive imported brandy, he proceeded to lay his heart bare in his lambent style.

"This autumn Honda Motor will be celebrating its twenty-fifth anniversary. I've already made up my mind to retire then, and I've conveyed my state of mind to Nishiochiai. How he'll respond to my message is a different matter. If he retires with me, his successor will probably be Kawashima. That, we have agreed on for some time now."

In the spring of 1970, Honda Motor made a virtual shift to group leadership by promoting four of its directors at once to executives with representative rights. Takao Shirai, Kihachiro Kawashima, and Michihiro Nishida were appointed heads respectively of general affairs, sales, and accounting. In charge of technology and overall coordination was Kiyoshi Kawashima, the president-to-be (no relation to the other Kawashima).

Honda and Fujisawa made a point of being absent at board meetings, leaving day-to-day operations to the new directors. A year after the rule of four was established, Soichiro retired as president of the subsidiary Honda R&D and began to devote himself to public relations. He did not show up at Honda headquarters unless he was needed. Likewise, Fujisawa, to whom the president's personal seal and control over the business side of things had long been entrusted, adopted a leisurely routine of coming in at eleven and leaving at two; Honda headquarters was where he had lunch. Once in a while, donning an expensive kimono—he preferred wearing it in the informal style—he would stroll across Tokyo, setting out from his home in Roppongi for a couple hours' walk, through Iikura, Shinbashi, and Ginza, finally on to the Honda headquarters in Yaesuguchi, only to communicate that he had no intention of helping out that day. But in accordance with an unwritten protocol, when there was an emergency, one of the four directors visited Fujisawa at his home and sought his sanction.

All was in place for the baton to be passed on to the successors. Since Honda and Fujisawa had just been reappointed to their posts at the stockowners' meeting in April, however, the prevalent view within Honda Motor was that the two would not retire until the spring of 1975, when their terms expired.

Among the Honda people who subscribed to that scenario was Soichiro Honda himself. Upon receiving a cue from Fujisawa early that spring via Nishida, Honda judged that it was indeed time and relayed back an okay. But he assumed that his co-founder meant two years hence.

It would be a lie to say that Soichiro Honda, great lover of festivities, did not wish at heart to preside as president at the diamond jubilee of the company named after himself. In March he had lost his second son Katsuhisa to illness and sorely needed a distraction from his sorrow. Work was it.

Hardly a year's gone by since we came out with the light car "Civic." When it comes to cars, I don't see our foundations as being secure yet. True, with the help of our low-emission CVCC engine, we overcame the "defective car" rep. But while the engine clears the Muskie law standard for 1975 easily, we're still in the labs for 1976. In fact, whether or not we'll make it in cars depends on where the Diet (the Japanese Congress) comes down on emissions. I've left day-to-day management to Roppongi, but it's my job as top dog to keep yapping at the tech boys. Kawashima is only forty-five. If I stay on for just a couple of years more, it isn't as though he wouldn't be replacing me as a "young leader."

When Honda departed for China—as much for pleasure as for business—he was not prepared emotionally for retirement. Japan's relations with China had been normalized in September 1971. Communications were still shoddy in that vast nation, whose inner reaches were yet to be connected to the rest of the world with radio waves, let alone phone lines. Meanwhile in Tokyo, the Nishida hint of the first of August had precipitated a kind of summer rain; the papers were soaked with news that Honda and Fujisawa were about to bow out. The press, however, were in the dark about what the duo's post-retirement status would be. Fujisawa, who had verified the simultaneous resignation rumor, adamantly refused to enlighten the media on this matter, insisting, "That's for the supreme head of management to do, and by that I mean President Soichiro Honda." The press were thus unable to give closure to their news story until they could interview Soichiro himself and turn his remarks to ink.

While he was in China, Soichiro did not have the slightest idea that back home his stepping down was the talk of town. When he picked up a Japanese paper in a hotel in Hong Kong en route to Tokyo and read the big news about himself, he felt as though he were reading the obituary of an alter ego named Soichiro Honda. Though the article was not framed in the customary black borders, there was a picture of his face and a lovingly detailed enumeration of his many accomplishments. The headlines were writ large:

HONDA MOTOR'S "PRIZE SON" IS C.E.O.; HONDA RESIGNS, KAWASHIMA PROMOTED; "MOVING BEYOND THE FOUNDING ERA"; GROUP LEADERSHIP BY YOUNG EXECS

The reason for his retirement was given as follows:

Mr. Honda, who has always been a step ahead of the times, faced his first great challenge since founding his company when the "defective car" issue exploded in 1969. "I wouldn't have admitted this back then, but those were really our darkest days," says Vice President Fujisawa, who announced officially yesterday that he will be resigning (*Mainichi Shinbun* morning edition, 4 Aug. 1973).

It was clear to Honda who was responsible for this "scoop." Fujisawa's face came to his mind immediately but he chose not to contact his co-founder just yet.

It must be for my sake that Roppongi had the news leak during my absence. He's arranged things so that I'll be able to deal with it privately, alone, before I deal with the press. Twenty-five years of working our heads off has really paid off; "Honda" is a bustling, world-renowned maker of motorbikes. Maybe he and I ought to leave the four-wheel stuff to the boys. No, there's no question about it, our days are over. Though Honda's named after me, it's actually always been "Honda Tech and Fujisawa Trading Co." Without my partner, how'd I ever have remained myself, not bothering my poor head about money? If the deputy resigns while the boss stays on, people will suspect a fire where there isn't any and feel licensed to speculate wildly about some internal strife. It'd be nasty of me to let the action of my dear old comrade cause that sort of stuff. What's more, it would stain my own last days as the head of Honda. The more I think of it, the more I agree I ought to go too.

While Soichiro, released by the press, headed home on a highway studded with officers on the lookout for Kim and his kidnappers, Fujisawa was meditating in the specially built tea room of his Roppongi home. How the press conference went was not known to him yet, but he could guess.

Soichiro and I've been married, so to speak, for more than twenty years; there's no way he wouldn't have understood. True, since the founding, all of the business successes have been my doing. But without Nishiochiai's engineering genius, Honda Motor wouldn't have become this big. It was by working on his talent that I made the company what it is today. Yet neither of us is going to be around forever and that's exactly why we've taken pains to fashion a management system amenable to group leadership. Our efforts have paid off, everything's on track.

As a person, Nishiochiai is full of flaws. It's not once or twice that we had serious fights. What's funny about him though is that his flaws are part of his charm. People love him because he's flawed, and, for all his flaws, he really knows how to ingratiate himself. "A flawful man!" I was the one who recognized his charisma. I worked on the press so they'd dress him up as a sort of guru. Guru of the Cult of Honda. There he's truly irreplaceable. Attempts to manufacture new Soichiro Hondas would be futile. Now's the time to liberate Nishiochiai from trivial tasks so he can devote himself to missionary activity as the guru of Hondaism. Today, that's how he'd best serve the interests of Honda Motor.

Our retirement drama will no doubt draw a standing ovation as "refreshing news." Right now, the structural defects trial of our small-sized car N360 is going into full gear; the courts will take at least ten more years to be through with it. When we're pestered by negative press about "Honda of the defective N360," there's only so much we can achieve by promoting "Honda of the low-emission CVCC engine." If we two resign now, just as our environment-friendly car goes to market, it'll divert the attention of the public. With luck, it'll turn things around reputation-wise.

Nishiochiai just can't sit still. He'll need no prodding to play the guru. And while Soichiro Honda is up and about, Honda Motor has really nothing to fear. As for me, I'll spend the rest of my days listening to Wagner and reading every-

thing Soseki and Tanizaki ever wrote. Maybe it won't disturb my peace too much if I begin a modest venture with my good-for-nothing sons.

The public rewarded Fujisawa with more kudos than he himself expected. Everywhere the media praised "The Honda Founders' Genial Exeunt" and denounced the gerontocracy of the rest of the Japanese corporate universe. Fujisawa's drama was sold indeed as a "refreshing breeze."

On September 24, just a week before the first oil shock hit the world, thirty thousand Honda employees and their families gathered at the Suzuka racing circuit for the company's twenty-fifth anniversary. There, the two men, endowed with such disparate gifts and personalities, alike in that they felt both reverence and enmity for the other, gave their farewell speeches. At the stockowners' meeting a month later on the thirtieth of October, Soichiro Honda, sixty-six years old, and Takeo Fujisawa, sixty-two, were appointed directors and supreme advisors and thereby retired from active duty as corporate leaders.

Their golden days began.

Soichiro decided that he "wanted to thank each and every employee who had worked hard for Honda Motor." Early in the following year, while the oil crisis still raged, he set off on "A National Tour of Thanksgiving" that took him all over Japan to factories, business offices, and dealerships, even to tiny repairing stations with merely a pair of workers. Once finished with that, he began hopping around the globe; in between trips, he kept himself busy serving the economic community and the public, sitting, for instance, on the Council for Administrative Reform. The activities of the Honda Foundation that he set up privately with his younger brother Benjiro brought him into contact with various national leaders. The foundation's mission was to spread the good news of "Hondaism." Soichiro's fame grew with every passing year.

Meanwhile, Fujisawa renovated his Roppongi home and turned it into a fancy shop. The signboard read:

Kokaido—General Store for the Modern Arts

The name "Kokaido" was specially coined by China scholar Tetsuji Morohashi, recipient of the emperor's Cultural Medal and father of Shinroku Morohashi, president, then chairman, of Mitsubishi Trading Co. Taken together, the three characters that comprise "Kokaido," which is not a word in Japanese, mean "a meeting-place for aesthetes." In other words, Fujisawa turned his hobby into his new line of work. As with his final years at Honda, however, he did not tamper with day-to-day operations, which he left to his wife Yoshiko and his two sons. Fujisawa embarked upon a life of magisterial leisure, surrounded by paintings, books, and music. He never appeared at any of Honda Motor's formal occasions.

In the fall of 1988, fifteen years after the Honda founders' "refreshing" abdication, there was melancholy in the air despite a roaring economy. Emperor Hirohito was declining. And it was on December 30 of that same year, late in the afternoon, amidst the flurry of the approaching New Year's Eve, that Fujisawa suddenly collapsed from heart failure. He had shown no serious signs of illness.

A professor of cardiac surgery from the Tokyo Medical University for

Women happened to be present. Yasuharu Imai, husband to Fujisawa's eldest daughter, had come by to say his end-of-the-year greetings. He applied CPR immediately, but Fujisawa's heart never beat again. Surrounded by family members, the man rested in peace. He was seventy-eight years old.

A regret tinged Fujisawa's last days.

Soichiro, you've played the role of "guru of Hondaism" to perfection. We put that icon on display for outsiders, but now some fools in the company are beginning to worship it as the real Soichiro. That's always alarming in an organization. When that false image gains a life of its own, it'll corrupt management at Honda. My last task—to help you down the seat of guru, to trim you down to your good old true self—it's become simply impossible, now that your false self's ballooned out like that. It's at bursting point already and the faintest needle prick spells chaos, unnecessary chaos. The real problem, though, is after you die. I worry, Soichiro: Is Honda Motor, too, subject to the law of flux, of transience, that all things that come...must go?

The company-sponsored funeral and farewell bidding for Fujisawa was a tranquil affair at Zojo Temple in Shiba park. Tadashi Kume, Honda Motor's third president, served as the event's chairman. It was January 27 of the first year of the Heisei reign; a couple of weeks earlier, Akihito had assumed the throne following his father's death. While eulogists praised Fujisawa's achievements, Soichiro was interrogating the flower-framed photo of the dead man.

Hey, Vice, Roppongi, what'd'ya think you're doing? You're four years younger than me, aren't you? You're cutting in, now get back in line! I've always done everything you told me to do. What's gonna become of my little company now? Hey, Roppongi, tell me! I'm begging you!

Soichiro and Fujisawa first met in the summer of 1949 through a common acquaintance, Hiroshi Takeshima, and struck up a partnership with eventual "separation" as a premise. They'd be a team all right, but when the time came, they'd split the spoils—and split. Indeed, after retiring, they left each other perfectly alone, a sign, perhaps, that each was satisfied with his share. The number of times they met since retirement could have been counted on either's hands.

In October 1990, the second year of the Heisei reign, Soichiro Honda was inducted into Detroit's Automotive Hall of Fame (it commemorates persons who have devoted their lives to the automobile and contributed to its development). To join the pantheon is to receive a Nobel Prize in car making and selling, and to have one's name inscribed alongside luminous ones like Henry Ford, Alfred Sloan, Walter Chrysler, Gottlieb Daimler, Karl Benz, and Ferdinand Porsche. Soichiro Honda, need it be said, was the first Japanese to be permitted into this elite institution.

Arriving back in Narita from Detroit, Honda headed straight to Roppongi, rather than to his own home in Nishiochiai. He leaned the medal, fresh from the receiving, against the mortuary tablet that commemorated Takeo Fujisawa.

I didn't win this medal alone. Roppongi, it was given to the two of us.

There was a gaping emptiness in him. It was about then that Soichiro's health started to decline visibly. Some of his spirit was gone too, as though his soul had already left him. In fact, hale though he had seemed, he had fought one illness after another ever since retirement. Liver malfunction, diabetes, cerebral thrombosis—he grappled with these and other maladies without showing the world anything but the vigorous and invigorating guru of Hondaism.

At long last, Soichiro Honda was running out of fuel. On July 22 the next year, shortly before the end of the rain season, he complained of stomach pains and took a room at the Juntendo University Hospital in Ochanomizu, Tokyo. Just two weeks later, on August 5—it was almost noon on the midsummer day— Soichiro Honda, eighty-four, gave up his hectic life. Only a month and six days prior to his death, he had attended a stockowners' meeting, despite his illness, to watch the fourth president Nobuhiko Kawamoto do a smooth, crisp job of moderating. The publicized cause of death was "hepatic insufficiency." The truth was that Honda had died of cancer of the liver.

Takeo Fujisawa was the stalk that supported the gay flower Soichiro. The stalk withered first, in the winter when wintry winds blew. The petals scattered in the summer, as the summer rains subsided.

It was left to "the kids" at Honda Motor to confront the beast, the myth of Honda, that their forefathers had begat.

CHAPTER ONE: HEADHUNTING

There are no rules for choosing one's successor. These days, no company has a fabulous system for that. But if you make a mistake in choosing your successor, the whole company is done for. This is no place for rigid, mechanical thinking.

—Soichiro Honda

If you are confident you are an expert, you have nothing to fear. If you become an expert, some other company is going to come looking for you. If Honda keeps developing the kind of people other companies come hunting for, then Honda's way of thinking will spread throughout the nation, and Japan will be a better place for it.

—Takeo Fujisawa

1

June 29, 1993. Japan's speculative economic bubble had burst. The early summer seasonal rain front hovered over the entire Japanese archipelago and a low-pressure system born in Kyushu had moved over Hiroshima and Osaka and was now heading for Tokyo. According to police data, 1,901 companies with fiscal years ending in March, most of which were listed on the Tokyo Stock Exchange, simultaneously held their annual shareholders' meetings on this day.

Honda, too, was among these firms. As every year, Honda's meeting took place in Sankei Hall, in Tokyo's Otemachi business district. The style of the meeting was still true to company founder Soichiro Honda's conviction that a company belonged to its shareholders and employees. Anyone who wanted to was always allowed to speak, whether they were ordinary shareholders or *sokaiya* extortionist thugs. That was the Honda way. The previous year, one shareholder had asked seemingly endless questions about automobile recycling and the meeting had taken a whole hour. Even when the result was a typical Japanese "clap-clap meeting"—so called because the attendees did nothing but applause at the end—Honda's general meetings always had some real content.

Honda could usually count on over 500 people to attend its annual meetings, but this year, perhaps because the weather forecast called for rain all day in Tokyo, only about 440 showed up. Among the shareholders who did were many former Honda employees. These people could be counted on to show up regardless of what the weather was like.

In keeping with Honda's tradition, former directors of the corporation, those paragons of social prestige, were invited at the start of each year to the head office, a gleaming white building on Tokyo's Rte. 246 in the fashionable Minami Aoyama district. There they would hear, directly from the president, his report on business conditions in the past year, and hobnob with the current directors, trading stories over drinks at the buffet reception that followed.

For those former employees who never rose to directorships, however, the annual general meeting was the only opportunity they had to hear directly from the president's own lips what was new at Honda, the company to which they had dedicated so much of their lives.

In the lobby of Sankei Hall, the attendees sipped tea and munched snacks as they chatted, happy to catch up with former colleagues and old acquaintances, filling the final minutes before the meeting started. It was almost as if they were at a Honda alumni gathering.

Company president Nobuhiko Kawamoto was up on the platform, nodding greetings to senior Honda retirees he had not seen since the previous year. He felt a pang of loneliness at not seeing Soichiro, who had sat in the front row until two years before. Soichiro had retired as president in 1973, the company's twenty-fifth year, but had stayed on as director and supreme advisor until 1983, when Tadashi Kume took the helm as the company's third president. Soichiro had then resigned his board seat and stepped down from the platform, taking his place in the front row of the audience at the annual meetings.

After retiring from active management, Soichiro opened a private office in Tokyo's Ginza district and made it his policy to stay away from Honda headquarters as much as he could. Even when he had business there, he would only briefly stop by the common boardroom and never used the supreme advisors' offices that the company had set aside for him and for Fujisawa. Of course, Soichiro said nothing in public about the company's management. Even when he ran into board members at launch parties for new cars, he would never do more than exchange small talk or crack a few jokes before quietly walking away.

The annual meeting, however, was a different story. The smile would vanish from Soichiro's face, to be replaced by the stern visage of a parent confronting the "kids" he had taken such pains to raise.

Honda's future rests on your shoulders. Keep going and persevere. It's your duty, as directors, to keep burning with passion until you burn out. With his intense gaze, Soichiro conveyed his support for the "kids" on the platform.

Kawamoto had risen to the president's post at the board of directors meeting in June 1990, so the following year's shareholders' meeting was his first as president of Honda. Perhaps Soichiro found reassurance in Kawamoto's no-nonsense way of getting things done; just one month later he passed on from this world.

On the dais, Kawamoto had no time to be lost in sentiment. Honda's earnings were not particularly good. For the fiscal year ended March 1992, sales had shrunk 7.5 percent to 2.69 trillion yen and the company's growth had come to a sudden halt, leaving Honda just shy of its target of making the three trillion-yen club. Net profit had fallen 7.7 percent to thirty billion yen. For the first time in thirty years, Honda was seeing a decrease in both revenue and profit.

On the street it was whispered that the "Honda myth" had collapsed. The earnings results seemed to provide quantitative proof. The yen was strengthening more rapidly than anyone had anticipated and the outlook for fiscal 1993 was that further declines in both sales and profits would be inevitable.

More than anything, Kawamoto had to reawaken the shareholders' trust at the outset of the meeting by providing a simple and convincing explanation of the earnings situation. At this year's meeting, however, one thing in particular weighed heavily on his mind.

Two months before, Shoichiro Irimajiri—a Soichiro disciple who had entered Honda Motor at the same time as Kawamoto, in 1963—had officially quit the company. Irimajiri, once known as "Mr. Honda," had washed his hands of the automobile world completely and gone to work for Sega Enterprises, the video-game maker that was hot on the heels of Nintendo.

Not so long before, Irimajiri had been regarded as the only real contender to become the fourth president of the company. One newspaper had been so confident of Irimajiri's prospects that, on the eve of the general meeting in which the final decision was made, it had printed an edition with a story on "Honda's New President Irimajiri," complete with photo and career history.

In the end, it was Irimajiri's rival Kawamoto who was given the president's seat and any possibility there may have been of a "President Irimajiri" disappeared forever. When Irimajiri suddenly resigned from his position as vice president in spring 1992 for health reasons, and later when he made his decision to join Sega, he had made no efforts whatsoever to consult with Kawamoto in advance. One could not truthfully say that there was nothing amiss between the two men.

How would Kawamoto respond if one of the shareholders were to stand up and ask whether he had not failed, as president, to make the most of Irimajiri's talent? The issue had naturally been covered in the mock Q&A his staff had prepared for him but, if it did come up, it would be the one point on which Kawamoto planned to depart from the prepared script to answer in his own words.

Still, as far as the reputation of Honda and Irimajiri are concerned, it won't do to tell the whole truth.

Kawamoto's concerns were unwarranted. Shareholders at the meeting were barely interested in finding out who was responsible for the poor earnings. There were no questions about Irimajiri and the meeting was over in twenty-five minutes. It had turned out to be, in fact, a real "clap-clap meeting."

At the very moment that the meeting at Honda was beginning, Irimajiri was at Sega headquarters, near the Tokyo International Airport at Haneda. The headquarters building was located on Kanpachi-dori, one of Tokyo's main ring roads. Due to the nearby railroad crossing for the Keihin Kyuko railway line for Haneda, the traffic along Kanpachi-dori in front of Sega headquarters was always bumper-to-bumper, making the area one of the most notorious places in Tokyo for traffic jams.

Next to the Sega building, casual family-oriented restaurants stood alongside convenience stores in a cluttered mix of business and industrial zones, providing a sharp contrast to the fashionable Minami-Aoyama district that was home to the Honda headquarters.

At a time when many Japanese companies were suffering post-bubble "hangovers," Sega's sales had nearly quintupled from 78 billion to 350 billion yen in the three years starting in fiscal 1990.

There could be no doubt that Sega's star was rising. As if to reflect the company's rapid growth, construction was already underway for a brand new headquarters building—complete with a full-scale studio—in the lot adjacent to the still new ten-story headquarters building. Just across the highway was an old five-story building—now marked as an office annex—that had been the company's headquarters in the days when Sega was still known as Nihon Goraku Bussan ("Japan Amusement Products").

Sega was also holding its annual shareholders' meeting at its headquarters on that day. In the main conference room on the third floor, twenty-five directors and nominees sat in front of a blackboard. A total of 144 people had shown up. Most were young men and women who appeared to be Sega employee shareholders. No identifiable *sokaiya* were present.

Irimajiri, who was a small man, sat quietly in his navy blue, double-breasted suit among those in the spotlight. A year earlier, he had occupied his place on the dais at Honda's annual meeting, pale and not yet fully recovered from his illness. This year he was the picture of health. With his neatly trimmed hair and tanned face, he appeared to have regained his former youthfulness. It was almost as if he were deliberately flaunting his resolution to start afresh. He gazed out at the crowd in the meeting room but, as could be expected, could not recognize a single face.

I wonder if I've made a mistake in choosing this new career, he thought to himself. He closed his eyes and imagined the choices he might have made, had it not been for pure chance.

Right about now, I would be at Narita Airport getting ready for boarding, saying good-bye to my family. Then I would be on a plane for Paris, my heart full of expectation and excitement.

When Irimajiri opened his eyes and came back to reality, Sega President Hayao Nakayama was proudly outlining the company's earnings and explaining how it had newly recruited three "heavy hitters."

"As Sega's sales have grown, so has our workforce. We now have 3,500 employees. In our long-term plan, we will be increasing this number to 6,000. With regard to mid-level managers, we have been, for some time already, actively hiring mid-career professionals. With all our efforts, however, we still lack experienced executives. That is why we have decided to ask the following gentlemen to join us: Mr. Irimajiri from Honda, Mr. Fujimoto from Daiei and Mr. Kinoshita from Sumitomo Bank."

The weather outside was gloomy and the sky looked ready to burst at any moment. The last item on the agenda was the nomination of directors. Irimajiri heard his name read aloud. He rose graciously and bowed. The meeting was over. The entire ceremony had taken all of twenty-two minutes. A board of directors meeting began at eleven o'clock in the same building and Irimajiri was officially made executive vice president in charge of R&D as well as production. From that day on, Irimajiri ceased to be "Mr. Honda." Instead he became "The Prince of Sega."

In the same third-floor conference room where the annual meeting had taken place, a press conference was scheduled for 2 p.m. Reporters from over fifty newspapers, magazines and television stations waited for the conference to begin. While Sega was dwarfed by Nintendo in terms of domestic performance, it was evenly matched against its rivals in Europe and the U.S. The presence of members of the foreign press was a reflection of Sega's success abroad.

Seated on the left side of Sega president Nakayama, the main speaker at the conference, were Irimajiri and Koichi Kinoshita. The latter had left a directorial position at Sumitomo Bank to join Sega as senior managing director. Keizo Fujimoto, former managing director at the Daiei supermarket chain now joining Sega as vice president—the same rank as Irimajiri—sat on Nakayama's right.

When the photographers had finished taking their shots, Irimajiri, encouraged by Nakayama, quietly began to explain his motives for coming to Sega. "For thirty years, I worked at Honda developing and manufacturing motorbikes and automobiles. Last spring, however, my health deteriorated, and I had to give up my position as executive vice president. Now, after a long recovery, I have regained confidence in my health. I had thought of myself as still young, but the truth is I am already fifty-three. I am not young at all.

"At the start of this year, though, I was overcome by a desire to try my hand in the business world once more, if possible something with a little excitement. It was around that time (only about two or three months ago) that I had the good fortune to be introduced to Mr. Nakayama by a mutual friend. We had a meal together and Mr. Nakayama asked me then and there whether I would be interested in joining Sega as head of development. At that time, I didn't take him seriously, but after we had met a few more times, Mr. Nakayama had convinced me that the amusement industry was worth committing one's life to. So I asked Mr. Nakayama in late May to let me start working at Sega.

"There are certainly big differences between the world of cars and the world of amusement. Nevertheless, both are manufacturing industries in the broad sense and have a lot of the basics in common. By making use of my thirty years of experience at Honda, I believe that I can make a contribution here."

After this dispassionate explanation, Irimajiri turned and looked out the window again. The rain was now really starting to come down.

Irimajiri folded his arms and closed his eyes as his mind went over the whirlwind of events that had taken place since the start of the year.

Until two months ago, it had never occurred to me that I might work for Sega. I didn't even have a clear idea what the company does. The fact that I am sitting in this chair is almost too strange to be true. The plan was that I would join General Motors, the world's biggest automaker. Right about now, I would be heading for Switzerland to start my new job.

By this time, my plane would have left the airspace over the Japan Sea. It would be flying over the desolate Russian countryside. In a few hours we would be landing at Charles de Gaulle Airport, in the suburbs of Paris. I would spend a night in Paris, and travel on to Zurich the following day. GM Europe President Lou Hughes would meet me at the airport. Hughes and I would discuss details at the hotel, and then there would be a press conference on July 1, where my appointment to GM would be formally announced.

Just then, a question came flying his way.

"I'd like to ask Mr. Irimajiri a question. Didn't you consider (before agreeing to join Sega, of course) going back to Honda once you'd regained your health?" It was a straightforward question, from a young *Wall Street Journal* reporter.

"I stepped down from my position as vice president of Honda on my own initiative. I did it because I believed my health, even my life, was at stake. In Japanese corporate society, one does not quit for personal reasons and then go back when one is feeling better. In my own mind, there was no question of returning to Honda even from the start." Irimajiri chose his words carefully, speaking in a detached manner, as if trying to convince himself of something.

I wonder. When I decided to quit Honda, I didn't consult with any of my senior colleagues who had looked after me since I was a young man. I wonder what I might have done if Soichiro Honda or Takeo Fujisawa were still alive. Surely I would have talked things over with them first. If those two had been around, they would have said something like:

"What do you think you're doing, sulking like a spoiled kid? Go cool your head. If you're not healthy, take time off from the company until you feel better. Take as long as you need and come back when you're all well again."

If the two founders had said something like that to me, I would have had no choice but to back down and say, "Of course."

On the other hand, if Irimajiri had joined General Motors, Lou Hughes, president of GM Europe and chairman of Opel AG as well as executive vice president of international operations for GM Corporation, would have given a speech like the following:

"The purpose of today's press conference is to introduce 'Mr. Iri,' former vice president of Honda, who has agreed to join us at General Motors as of July 1. Iri will be senior vice president of GM Corporation and vice president in charge of production for GM International.

"As you know, GM International, for which I am responsible, oversees production at all GM subsidiaries outside of North America, including Opel in Germany. Mr. Iri will, for the immediate future, act as my right-hand man, supervising and managing GM subsidiary factories, primarily in Europe. My own career has been mainly in finance and sales, and I am not that strong on technology. This means that, in effect, Iri will be GM Europe's top man for production and development. GM Europe is a major source of revenue for the GM Group, which makes the job all the more demanding. I have high hopes for Iri.

"Of course, Iri will have a seat on the board of directors of GM Corporation, and will therefore take part in management meetings in Detroit, taking an active role in management at the GM head office."

On the same day, GM president and CEO Jack Smith would also have held a press conference in Detroit formally announcing Irimajiri's move to GM.

Smith's aim would have been to demonstrate to the entire world the high expectations GM had for Irimajiri.

If Irimajiri had joined GM, it would have been one of the day's top business stories, not just for the automotive industry, but for the global industrial community as well. For the U.S. auto industry and car journalists, Irimajiri had been and was still a superstar; any career move of his would have been a major news story.

When Irimajiri had been president of Honda America Manufacturing Inc. (HAM) in Ohio, his policy had been to welcome all who knocked on his door. The Big Three were very interested in what was up at the Ohio plant, especially since it was the first Japanese auto plant in the United States. Irimajiri kept no secrets. Anyone who wished to visit was allowed to come in and see all the ins and outs of the plant, even if they worked for a rival company. What was more, whenever time allowed, Irimajiri took it upon himself to show his visitors around and provide explanations, making a conscious effort to integrate into American society.

Irimajiri worked hard to raise the ratio of locally produced parts used in Honda cars, and when it surpassed sixty percent, he decided that the timing was right to join the Alliance of Automobile Manufacturers. Honda was recognized as the number four U.S. auto manufacturer, both in name and in fact, after the Big Three: GM, Ford and Chrysler. This significantly widened Irimajiri's social circle. In Japan, the symbol of Honda was still Soichiro Honda, but in America it was "Mr. Iri."

Irimajiri's career attracted even more interest in the U.S. than it did in Japan. In the spring of 1992, when he suddenly quit his post, it was the *New York Times* and other American papers that gave prime coverage to the news, devoting more space to the story than the Japanese press. Former Prime Minister Kiichi Miyazawa once said GM was equivalent to "the stars and stripes." For Irimajiri to become a board member of the mega-corporation would have had major news value indeed.

The timing would have been good. In March, GM's executive vice president for purchasing José Ignacio Lopez de Arriortua had been poached by Volkswagen, leading even to legal action between the two companies.

No matter what the facts of that case, one could well imagine how eagerly the world's automotive trade press would have reported that GM had scouted Irimajiri from Honda as a replacement for Lopez, who in turn had been headhunted by VW. That would have been the second reason for Smith to hold his Detroit press conference: to deny that GM's hiring of Irimajiri had anything to do with the Lopez affair.

Had Irimajiri gone to GM, it would have made a considerable impact on the automotive industry in Japan as well. That is not to say that Japanese companies had been complete strangers to headhunting. When Nissan started making pickup trucks in Tennessee, it hired Marvin Runyon, then vice president in charge of production at Ford, and made him the first president of Nissan Motor Manufacturing Co. (NMMC.) As a matter of fact, in the fall of 1992, the same year that Irimajiri resigned from his position as Honda's vice president, the senior vice president and number two man at HAM, Al Kinzer, left the company for BMW. Kinzer was more than just senior vice president of HAM; he was the company's first American employee. From the very outset, he had been involved in building the facilities and hiring the American staff and had worked hand-in-hand with the Japanese staff through all the ups and downs of the plant's initial stages. He was a walking encyclopedia regarding the Ohio plant. BMW had caught wind of that wealth of experience and made him CEO of its U.S. manufacturing subsidiary. Having just lost its top executive at HAM, Honda turned around and hired Richard Colliver, vice president of Mazda's U.S. sales operation, as senior vice president of American Honda Motor Co., Honda's distributor in the U.S. In the American arena, the headhunting game was not uncommon even among Japanese-owned companies.

Nevertheless, as the world's largest automaker, GM was in a class by itself. In 1968, Ford's then-chairman Henry Ford II had shocked the U.S. auto industry by headhunting GM executive vice president Simon Knudsen and making him president of Ford. Lee Iacocca, the leading figure in Chrysler's revival and notorious for the "bashing" of Japanese cars, had concluded his term as chairman of Chrysler Corporation by successfully luring away Robert Eaton, Jack Smith's right-hand man in GM Europe, and making him his own successor at Chrysler.

Up to this point, GM's employees may have been subject to headhunting by other firms, but the company, in keeping with its image as the top dog in the industry, had never actively engaged in any headhunting activities itself. For proud GM to go to Honda—a Japanese company whose overseas cachet exceeded that of Toyota or Nissan—and seek to hire the man known as "Mr. Honda" or "The Prince of Honda" to be its senior vice president was truly an unprecedented move.

The global automotive industry was in flux. Behind-the-scenes maneuvers of players seeking a better position continued to intensify. In an industry shakeout, personal connections play a major role in determining which company will take the lead. Irimajiri's move to GM, if realized, would certainly have accelerated the pace of restructuring for the whole industry.

In its list of top U.S. auto industry news stories for 1993, *Automotive News* awarded first place to the GM-Lopez affair, with the difficulties faced by Japanese automakers coming in second, followed by Chrysler's revival, the NAFTA agreement and safety issues with GM pickup trucks. Had Irimajiri joined GM, that story would have undoubtedly been near the top of the list.

Irimajiri's sudden announcement to Kawamoto of his intention to resign as vice president of Honda and head of Honda R&D Co. for health reasons came on March 16, 1992, eight months after Soichiro Honda's death. It was mid-March, but there was no sign of spring anywhere; on the contrary, a developing low-pressure front had brought sleet to Tokyo on the night of the 16th, and on the 18th it snowed.

In the spring snow on the morning of the 18th, Honda's board met in a hastily assembled extraordinary session at the Minami Aoyama headquarters to discuss Irimajiri's resignation, which it accepted without objection. Honda told the press that Irimajiri had asked to resign due to "intense exhaustion of both body and spirit," which made it difficult for him "to keep up his strenuous schedule," adding that "President Kawamoto had tried to dissuade him from quitting, but that his mind was made up and the board had no choice but to accept his resignation." The press, however, placed no great faith in the company's comments, and the next morning, the newspapers were full of speculation:

"VP IRIMAJIRI RESIGNS / REASON: 'UNSTABLE HEALTH' / KAWAMOTO'S WOES MULTIPLY" (*Nihon Keizai Shimbun*)
"HONDA'S 'EXHAUSTED' FIFTY-TWO-YEAR-OLD ACE / VP IRIMAJIRI RESIGNS" (*Mainichi Shimbun*)

Within Honda, Irimajiri had consulted no one about his plans, not even the senior board members. With a reason as vague as "health problems," even the Honda spokesman had trouble coming up with an adequate explanation: "This is so sudden, his reasons for quitting are not entirely clear." Naturally, speculation fueled further speculation.

Every Honda watcher seemed to have his own theory.

"He quit because he disagreed with Kawamoto about the direction of the company's management."

"No, it goes deeper. The real reason is that ex-president Kume passed over him in choosing his successor."

"Not so. The problem was money."

Irimajiri himself checked into the Izu-Nagaoka Clinic of Juntendo University Hospital on the day after his resignation, so any opportunity of uncovering his reasons, whatever they may have been, was lost.

Kawamoto, for his part, was worried about how to deal with the media. Even if he told the truth, he could not expect to be believed. Precisely because they had no facts, the press assembled around Kawamoto's house in Tokyo's Nakano ward day and night, hoping for a scoop. Kawamoto invariably gave them the same answer:

"There is absolutely no truth to the rumors of a disagreement over strategy. In the thirty years since I joined the company, Irimajiri and I have been friends. It must have been his own strong sense of duty that led him to believe he could not maintain both his health and his demanding schedule."

3

Kawamoto and Irimajiri joined Honda in 1963, just as Prime Minister Hayato Ikeda's income-doubling plan was starting to bear fruit. In the spring of that year, Japan National Railways added special trains to transport 78,000 middle-school graduates from rural areas to Tokyo, Osaka and Nagoya where they would be starting their first jobs. The influx of young laborers to the cities helped to spur Japan's rapid growth.

In May of the same year, the first Japan Grand Prix for sports cars was held at the Suzuka Circuit. At the time, neither car nor tire makers had even been aware of the existence of special tires for racing. Still, Nissan's Fair Lady beat out many an experienced foreign competitor in the sub-two-liter class, boosting the confidence of Japanese manufacturers.

In July, Japan's first high-speed expressway was partially opened, linking Amagasaki and Ritto on a highway that would eventually run from Nagoya to Kobe. At long last, Japan would have roads on which it would be possible to zoom at speeds of one hundred kilometers an hour. Naturally, this drove up the national appetite for cars.

At the time young Kawamoto and Irimajiri joined the company, Honda was looking ahead to an era when owning cars would be the norm for most families. The same year, it began selling small sports cars and light trucks, finally achieving its long-sought goal of entering the market for four-wheeled vehicles. Its workforce had grown to over 7,000, and it was evolving from a medium-size company into a major enterprise.

Irimajiri's father was an aircraft engineer, and from childhood Irimajiri had been interested in machines. When he was in fourth grade, he decided that he too wanted to be an aircraft engineer. The idea came to him thanks to a science test. On the right-hand side of the paper were the names of mechanical parts like "piston" and "nozzle," and on the left were words like "steam turbine" and "jet engine." The objective was to connect the right words.

Irimajiri connected the word "nozzle" to "jet engine," but the correct answer was "steam turbine." Irimajiri complained, but his teacher would have none of it, insisting that jet engines do not have "nozzles." Not satisfied with the teacher's explanation, Irimajiri went to the public library, where he read hungrily through books on aircraft.

He found the word "nozzle" in a book entitled *The Wonders of Aircraft*, written by Hidemasa Kimura, the Nihon University professor best known as the designer of Japan's first civil passenger aircraft, the YS-11. This gave him great satisfaction and awakened in him an interest in airplanes.

"When I grow up, I want to be an aircraft engineer!"

Irimajiri held onto this dream throughout middle school and into high school. At that time, there were only three universities in the country that taught aeronautical engineering: Kyushu University, Osaka University, and the University of Tokyo. Irimajiri chose the University of Tokyo. The Aeronautics Department was divided into two sections: one for the study of engines and the other for the study of fuselages. Irimajiri didn't hesitate for a minute. He majored in engines.

In his third year of college, Irimajiri had an internship at Mitsubishi Heavy Industries' Oe plant, and in his fourth year at Kawasaki Heavy Industries' Akashi plant. Nonetheless, he had halfway abandoned his dream shortly after beginning college. Because of the U.S. Occupation's postwar ban on manufacturing aircraft in Japan, Japanese engine technology had fallen far behind the times, and it seemed a long way before complete domestic production of airplanes, starting with the engine and including the fuselage, could be resumed in Japan. No matter how much Irimajiri learned about aircraft engines at school, it meant nothing if there were no jobs in which he could put that knowledge to work.

At university, Irimajiri developed an interest in race car engines. He commuted on a 50cc Honda Super Cub his parents had bought for him, which no doubt led to an early affection for Honda. Irimajiri devoted his attention to tinkering with engines to turn them into high-rpm racing engines. Once, he even borrowed a 250cc motorbike engine from Honda and converted it for use in a hovercraft to exhibit at the annual campus festival.

When Irimajiri was a junior, he learned that Honda had made a clean sweep of the top five places at the Isle of Man Tourist Trophy Races. The news excited him like nothing else.

For his graduation project, Irimajiri chose to design a twelve-cylinder F1 engine. His faculty advisor was Ryoichi Nakagawa, a director at the Prince Automobile Company, eventually acquired by Nissan. In between his duties at Prince, Nakagawa lectured on engines at the University of Tokyo once a week and advised fourth-year engine students on their graduation projects.

Including Irimajiri, there were seventeen students majoring in engines in the Aeronautics Department. Eleven of them went to work for automobile manufacturers after graduation. In other words, eleven of that class became "car guys," scattering among the country's major manufacturers such as Toyota, Nissan, Isuzu, and Honda.

Yutaka Hirose, who became head of Mazda's R&D operations in North America, chose to join Mazda after reading an article in a new technical magazine on the strong future prospects of the rotary engine. It had been written by Mazda chairman and former president Kenichi Yamamoto, "the father of the rotary engine."

Irimajiri was one of three members of his class to join Honda. Another was Hiroyuki Yoshino. The reason Irimajiri opted for Honda rather than a bigger company like Toyota or Nissan was that only Honda took racing seriously.

"If I join Honda, I'll be able to work on racing engines."

Irimajiri didn't care if it was motorcycles or cars, as long as it was racing. Of course he was also a great admirer of Soichiro Honda. He had fallen in love with Honda, so much so that he couldn't even think of joining another company.

Someday, I want to build a racing car with my own hands, just like Soichiro Honda.

Irimajiri's dream came true, and in the coming years, the young man gave himself entirely to building motorbikes. Meanwhile, Honda continued to grow into a global enterprise. Before he knew it, Irimajiri was appointed to the board of directors at the young age of thirty-nine.

Kawamoto, meanwhile, was a graduate student at Tohoku University when he saw a film showing Honda's successes in the Isle of Man TT at the local movie theater and was deeply impressed. Although black-and-white television was already beginning to become common in households around that time, there were still no commercial video cameras. The scenes that had so impressed him could only be seen on movie theater newsreels.

Kawamoto was crazy about cars. From a very early age he knew he wanted to work for a car company. He studied precision engineering in the laboratory of

Yasushi Tanasawa, the very same professor who had taught Toyota Motor Corporation Chairman (currently Honorary Chairman) Shoichiro Toyoda. When it came time for Kawamoto to find a job, Tanasawa offered to write him a letter of recommendation for Toyota.

At one point Kawamoto seriously considered going to work for Toyota. The newsreel had gotten him interested in Honda, however, and from that point on, he quickly lost interest in Toyota. He followed closely all the news on Honda he could find. One day he came across a speculative story suggesting that after its outstanding performance in the Isle of Man TT, Honda might enter the Formula One World Championship.

Whether or not this was in fact true made no difference to Kawamoto, who could no longer hold back his desire to work for Honda. He went to his university's employment office, where an employment counselor told him that, by coincidence, he had just gotten to know a researcher from Honda on an overseas study tour. "It appears that Honda will be hiring a lot of technicians this year," the man told him. With an introduction from his employment counselor, Kawamoto took the exam at Honda. There was no written test, just an interview, but that interview was with Kiyoshi Kawashima himself (later Honda's second president). Kawamoto, like Irimajiri, was hired after a single interview.

In 1963, Honda hired a total of approximately eighty university graduates for technical and office positions combined. Of the technical personnel, those engineers who would work in product development were actually assigned to Honda R&D Co., a separate company. On Irimajiri's first day at work, two things astounded him. The first was an F1 cylinder block just lying around in the research center. That was when he first realized that Honda was readying a bid for the F1.

"Is Honda going into the F1?" he asked cautiously.

The leader of the F1 project replied with a rather self-satisfied smile, "We plan to be there starting next year. What kind of work would you like to do here?"

"I've always wanted to design racing engines. If I don't get a chance to do that, I intend to quit."

This made the other man laugh out loud.

"Young people these days have such modest dreams. If you wanted to send a rocket to the moon, Honda would be able to do it in just a few years. Honda can do anything, and it will let you do anything. Don't worry. You'll all get to do your dream jobs."

Kawamoto's first job was in the newly founded car engine design shop, which developed engines for passenger cars. Irimajiri landed a seat in the racing engine design section.

Irimajiri's section had only twelve or so staff members aside from the section chief. This small group designed the full range of Honda's racing engines, from 50cc motorcycles to 125cc, 250cc, and 350cc, as well as F1 and F2 racing cars.

Early on, Irimajiri was assigned to work on 50cc motorcycle engines. Kawamoto drew designs for passenger car engines. Although they worked in different sections, they were in the same big room, and they did similar jobs. Sometimes they sat at adjacent desks, drawing. Quite naturally, they became close enough to call each other by nicknames: "Iri-san" and "Kawa-san."

From their very first days in the company, the two men shared similar jobs and similar dreams. Both dreamed that a machine of their own design would rule the F1. Not long after they joined the company, Soichiro Honda's eldest son Hirotoshi introduced them to the racer Tetsu Ikuzawa. Hirotoshi and Ikuzawa were both born in 1942 and had grown up together. Both were still students, at Nihon University's College of Art.

In 1956, Ikuzawa's father, top-tier artist Rou Ikuzawa, bought his son a 50cc motorcycle, an Otsuki Dandy, which Tetsu rode in the Mt. Asama race.

Tetsu Ikuzawa was only fifteen at the time; in those days, fourteen-year olds could get driver's licenses for 50cc motorcycles. Still, no matter how brilliant a rider he was, there was no way he and his 50cc bike could win against the bigger motorcycles in the sub-125cc class. Ikuzawa started racing at fifteen because he dreamed of racing at the Isle of Man some day.

While still in college, Ikuzawa entered the first Japan Grand Prix, driving a Skyline GT for the Prince Automobile works team. This splashy debut as a race car driver quickly earned him a reputation as "the man behind the GT legend." Ikuzawa, however, was not one to stop at simply being a race car driver. In his spare time, he worked at remodeling the Honda S600 sports car as a racer, driving it in various races.

Kawamoto and Irimajiri were corralled by Hirotoshi Honda into helping his friend Ikuzawa. The dream shared by all three of them was for Ikuzawa to drive a car designed by Kawamoto and Irimajiri to victory in the Formula One.

As each weekend approached, they hurriedly wrapped up their R&D work, took out a few spare parts that were lying around, and headed to Ikuzawa's home in the Setagaya section of Tokyo where they set to work on souping up his S600. They would take the car for test runs on the newly opened Tokyo Expressway, driving at speeds well above the posted limit of eighty kilometers per hour. When that was done they stayed up until dawn talking about racing, sharing their dreams. By the time they got home, the eastern sky would already be light.

On weeks when there was a race, up to ten young technicians from Honda gathered at Ikuzawa's house. As soon as all the work was done, they piled into a bunch of cars, with the modified S600 in the lead, and head for the Suzuka Circuit where the race would be held. The Tomei (Tokyo-Nagoya) Expressway had not yet been completed, so they had to drive all night down Route 1, speeding all the way. Even then it took a full twelve hours. Honda Motor would have an official entry in the race, but Ikuzawa's hotrod always beat it.

The fact that Irimajiri, Kawamoto and other young engineers from Honda R&D were moonlighting for Ikuzawa did not remain a secret for long. In fact, it nearly cost them their jobs. At one point, Kawamoto casually sent Ikuzawa's car to a Honda "Service Factory" workshop in Saitama for repairs, where it was discovered that R&D shop parts had been used without authorization. Since it was Soichiro Honda's own son Hirotoshi who had gotten the whole thing started, the young employees were ultimately let off without penalty.

On Sundays when there was no race, the group rented cars from an agency in Ikebukuro that specialized in sports cars and drove up to the newly completed Ogochi Dam to try their hand at high-speed driving. Irimajiri and Kawamoto were always together, at work, and at play. Through sharing all of that work and play, they came to know pretty much what the other was thinking without exchanging words.

Despite this youthful intimacy, Irimajiri was the first to step into the media limelight. His promotion to the board at the age of thirty-nine in 1969, two years before Kawamoto's, was seen as a reflection of Honda's youthful corporate culture, a theme that was picked up by the mass media.

In terms of personality, Irimajiri was the flashy *yang* to Kawamoto's sober *yin*. Even as a board member, Irimajiri continued to commute to Honda headquarters in Aoyama in a leather jacket, astride a big 750cc motorcycle. He never was the shy type.

Kawamoto, on the other hand, was always plainer, and the expression on his face was difficult to read, making him difficult to approach. Once he had a drink or two, though, he would begin to speak in his own salty way and turned quickly into a cheerful fellow. The change in his personality was so great, in fact, that people mistakenly believed that the cheerfulness of the tipsy Kawamoto was a deliberate pose.

For Irimajiri, everything came naturally; nothing he did lacked style. His speech was logical, consistent, and articulate, and people found him charming. It was more than obvious why he should be the media's darling. At one point, the company deliberately promoted Irimajiri as the new "face of Honda," taking over Soichiro Honda's and Fujisawa's roles in this respect. Somewhere along the line, people both within the company and without started calling Irimajiri "Honda's Prince," and the name stuck.

The two friends were a study in contrasts, in all ways, from their personalities to the way in which they presented themselves. On the job, Irimajiri was closer to Honda's second president, Kawashima, than its third president, Kume.

Kawashima, a devout Christian, treated Irimajiri like his own brother. Whenever they had a few drinks, Kawashima would pound Irimajiri on the shoulder and say, "Listen. You will be president of Honda someday. In the future, you will take the tiller at Honda. That's why it's a good idea for you to experience as many different things as possible."

Kume, on the other hand, had a different view. When the press asked him for his opinion of Irimajiri and Kawamoto as potential candidates for his position, he answered, "Kawa-san, he's a very bad egg, a virtual Hitler. He's really messed up. Iri-san, on the other hand, he's a difficult man."

While Kume's opinion of Kawamoto may appear to be harsh, the words actually betray warmth and closeness. His opinion of Irimajiri, on the other hand, was curiously vague. In the spring of 1990, when it came time for Kume to choose his successor, he passed over Irimajiri, whom Kawashima had deliberately trained as a generalist, and chose Kawamoto, who had spent his entire career in Honda R&D. "Honda has a tradition of being led by those who do not seek to lead, as with myself," Kume replied enigmatically to those stubborn journalists who kept asking which of Kawamoto's qualities had led to his selection.

Objectively, the strengths of the two men were so well matched that former Honda board members familiar with both were prone to say, "The old man of

Roppongi held sway over Honda management long after he retired. If he were still alive, the results might have been different."

It would be false to say Irimajiri *wasn't* disappointed at not assuming the president's seat—the symbol of ultimate authority over the company's affairs. In Honda's tradition, the president was never chosen from among the vice presidents but from among the senior managing directors. At Honda, the next and only step up from vice president was chairman. Honda's chairman had the power to act as a representative of the company, but he was second to the president in terms of internal hierarchy. Irimajiri was promoted to vice president at the same time Kawamoto was made president.

Based on Honda's past history, that promotion killed Irimajiri's chances of ever becoming president of the company. The public, blissfully unaware of these subtle intricacies, simply thought Irimajiri was being positioned to succeed Kawamoto, who was, after all, four years older. Irimajiri himself, however, realized it was the beginning of the end.

If things go on as they are, Honda will be ruined. From now on I'll be Kawa-san's right arm and work to rebuild Honda from the ground up.

At the same time as Irimajiri's promotion, Yoshihide Munekuni, who had joined Honda mid-career, also became vice president. Those two men plus Kawamoto formed a kind of troika at the top of Honda. Irimajiri's resignation came just as the company was instituting a variety of bold management reforms aimed at reviving the company, including the introduction of an annual salary system for managers.

No matter what the rumors, it was true that Irimajiri's health was not good at that time. In 1985, one year after taking up his post as head of Honda America Manufacturing and the night before the groundbreaking ceremony for the new factory, he suffered a bout of heart arrhythmia. Having fallen violently ill in the middle of the night, he consulted his doctor the following morning; he was diagnosed as having had a mild heart attack. Irimajiri was told he should be hospitalized at once but could not bring himself to miss the groundbreaking ceremony. The governor of Ohio had been invited.

No doubt his heart condition had been caused by stress from overwork. Irimajiri had always been the sort to throw himself heart and soul into whatever he was doing, whether at work or at play. In terms of his job, he was never satisfied unless he gave his 100 percent and made sure that things went the way he had envisioned. He was a man of quick judgment, bold to a fault; some would say brash.

Luckily for him, that was the only heart attack he had in the U.S. As he grew used to things in America, life naturally became less stressful. His main outlet was golf, which he had taken up during his days as head of Honda's Suzuka Factory. In the U.S., Irimajiri worked himself half to death five days a week, and over the weekends forgot all his work-related troubles by being just as passionate on the golf course.

During the brief summer season, he was known to play three rounds in one day, each on a different course. He would eat his meals in the car on the way from one course to another, steering wheel in one hand, hamburger in the other. Such untiring efforts bore fruit and Irimajiri made remarkable progress. In no time at all, he had worked his handicap down to a single digit.

4

"I thought this might interest you."

After spending one month in the Izu-Nagaoka Clinic of Juntendo University Hospital, Irimajiri went home to recuperate. Soon after that, his wife Keiko handed him a book. The title of the book was *Ki, The Power of Life*, and it was subtitled *The Popular Nishino-Style Breathing Technique*.

The author, Kozo Nishino, was well known as the founder of the Nishino Ballet Company, which had turned out such talented stars as Katsuko Kanai and Kaoru Yumi. Later in life, Nishino concocted his own breathing technique, based in part on traditional Chinese *qigong* exercises. He then founded a school where his techniques could be put into practice.

Irimajiri read Nishino's book and became interested in the latter's ideas on *ki* energy. Without any introduction, he knocked on the doors of Nishino's school. Practice was difficult at first, but as he grew used to it, he was surprised at how quickly his health came back to him.

Early on, he was in the beginners' class and had little chance to talk with Nishino himself. As he continued to attend classes, however, he and Nishino eventually grew close enough to share with each other their views on life. It boiled down to this: more than anything, people who are ill need to cure what ails their minds before they can cure their bodies.

"Mr. Irimajiri, everything in life is a game. The only truth is life itself. Many people believe their work is their life. Some people even think life is about honor, or status. We should let our dreams and our fantasies bloom large. But we must not forget that it is the fact that we are alive that is the only truth. All else is fantasy."

Listening to Nishino speak these words, Irimajiri felt as if the scales had fallen from his eyes. A new kind of ambition welled up from deep inside him.

Now that I think about it, I'm still only fifty-two. That's too young to dry up and blow away. Sure, my pension as a retired Honda director would take care of us, but I won't be able to stand just hanging around the house. I have to do something...

Even if it were to be some time before he took another job, Irimajiri decided that, while he was restoring himself to full health, he could occupy himself with an inquiry into the strengths and weaknesses of Japan's manufacturing industry. Walking the floors of Japan's factories on his own two feet, he could take it all in with the trained eye of a technician and write a book. Japan's economic bubble had burst, and the country had been thrust into a severe recession. Japan's manufacturing industry had been the engine of its rapid growth, but now it was starting to show signs of fatigue.

How had the birth and expansion of Japan's manufacturing industry come about? What was the secret of its strength? Would this strength last? Or had the bursting of the bubble secured its perpetual decline?

At the annual shareholders' meeting in late June, Irimajiri formally relinquished his post and was made standing counselor. In Honda tradition, anybody who had served as executive vice president or above was made "advisor" after he retired, while those who retired as managing directors or senior managing directors become "counselor." The company gave a rather unconvincing explanation of its treatment of Irimajiri:

"It's true that Mr. Irimajiri rose to the level of executive vice president; however, he resigned before his term was over. His last title before retiring was member of the board of directors, so he has now become 'standing counselor.'"

Irimajiri did not complain and simply accepted the title the company had given him. The thing that would have an impact on his future plans—his executive pension—would be calculated based on his former salary as vice president. "Advisor" or "counselor," he still had an office in Honda's former headquarters building near Tokyo Station, which he could use as he wished. He would be able to work as he pleased.

Soon after his resignation at the annual meeting, he departed on his tour of Japan's factories. He traveled to Osaka, Nagoya, Hiroshima, and Kyushu among other cities and regions. He deliberately avoided large companies and sought out the founders and managers of smaller firms with unique technologies—the kind that formed the foundation of Japan's manufacturing industry.

Irimajiri knew every inch of every Honda factory and research center, and he also knew all of the primary parts suppliers, but little about the secondary and tertiary suppliers. Now he was greatly enjoying getting to know this world firsthand. Whenever there was anything he did not understand, he went to the National Diet Library or to the Tokyo Metropolitan Library to investigate.

He continued his twice-weekly visits to the Nishino breathing school. His health improved so much that it was hard to believe that only six months before, he had been teetering between life and death. In early autumn, people started talking to him about possible job opportunities. Most of these offers came from U.S. auto parts makers. The British company Rover, with which Honda had a capital and business tie-up, also offered him a position.

Honda had a tradition that directors did not take up posts at other companies after retirement; they were supposed to have burned themselves out working for Honda. In return, retired executives were given generous pensions that allowed them to live comfortably without needing to work at all. Going to a Honda competitor was out of the question. The one acceptable occupational route for a former executive was to take up teaching at a university or some other educational institution.

Only one man had ever broken this unwritten rule: Yuhei Chijiiwa, who had joined the company in 1953, the year it began hiring university graduates on a regular basis. After retiring from his post as managing director of Honda, Chijiiwa had become president of HondaLand, an affiliated company that operated an amusement park in Suzuka. This, however, had led to his being headhunted by another amusement-park company in Okayama that had taken note of his performance. The development caused a great ruckus among Honda executives. Chijiiwa, disgusted, gave up his pension out of spite and severed all ties with Honda.

Irimajiri was well aware of this tradition—i.e., that those who had entered the corporate pantheon at Honda did not go looking for other jobs. He politely turned away all offers from U.S. auto parts makers, without even hearing them out.

Going to Rover, Honda's tie-up partner, would have been even more difficult since it raised issues of loyalty. The offer, however, had come through an old friend who was a senior executive at Rover, so Irimajiri met him in person, explained to him how things worked at Honda, and persuaded him to give up.

Still, the idea of casting aside all his worldly ambitions and living on his pension at his age—he was, after all, only a little over fifty—was just too dreary. As his health and strength returned, he could feel his ambition beginning to swell.

In November 1992, Irimajiri began to make efforts to interact with the outside world with the idea of getting back into the game. He was invited to speak at a campus festival at Hitotsubashi University, where he gave a talk on "The Qualities of an Internationally-Minded Person and University Education." Irimajiri, who had recruited local college graduates to work in the Ohio factory, pulled no punches with the audience: "American collegians have more confidence in what they've been taught than Japanese students."

In December, he was guest speaker at Alliance 92, a meeting of major U.S. and Japanese companies aimed at fostering strategic cooperation beyond traditional boundaries. There he unveiled the major thesis he had derived from his six months of wool-gathering: "Japanese high-tech—the kind that can be used by ordinary people—has entered a mature phase. Manufacturing is also in a bottleneck. Only alliances that go beyond traditional frameworks, including national boundaries, can achieve breakthroughs."

As he grew confident that his health was indeed restored, and as his public activities began to occupy more and more of his time, Irimajiri realized he needed to get serious about what to do with the rest of his life. Now and then, some newspaper journalist who had known him for many years would visit him at home, but when asked about his plans for the future, Irimajiri would always answer, "I've received offers from many companies, but I want to spend some more time thinking about what I can still do for Honda and for Japan's manufacturing industry."

Before long, rumors of Irimajiri's return to health had made their way into the halls of Honda headquarters. He had been a hero there, and the younger engineers, unaware of the circumstances of his departure, began to talk openly of "Irimajiri's reinstatement."

Far from taking a turn for the better, the company's performance seemed to be stuck in the mud. Honda had pinned its hopes on the U.S. market, but results were not measuring up. The atmosphere at the company was bleak. All the more because earnings were so poor, the board grew extremely sensitive to any rumors of Irimajiri's reinstatement. Naturally, talk of this state of affairs made its way to Irimajiri, but his mind was made up.

I left my position as executive vice president for my own reasons. Since I did leave, the chances of my returning to Honda in a management position are

*zero. I realize that some people who used to work under me have heard that I'm
healthy again and are hoping I'll come back to work, but that's no more than
wishful thinking. Even though I'm just a counselor, the fact that I still can park
my briefcase at Honda is rubbing salt in old wounds. The only way to heal those
wounds would be for me to go away altogether, and the sooner the better.*

Irimajiri decided to sever his ties to Honda by the following spring at the
latest. To do so, however, he had to find another job, notwithstanding Honda's traditions and unwritten rules.

One offer he gave serious thought to came from a private university that
had asked him to serve as president. If he were to work for a university, there
would be no conflict with Honda's interests or its unwritten rules. Through his
research into the strengths of Japan's manufacturing industry, he had come to
keenly appreciate the importance of education. His experience lecturing at a
campus festival, where he came into contact with students his own children's
age, only reinforced his belief, which grew stronger with each passing day.

*The great strength of Japanese industry has always been its ability to refine
existing technologies. Basic technology, now and in the past, has always been the
province of the United States. Japan imported that technology after the war and,
with typical dexterity, layered refinement upon refinement to create the foundation of what we see today. Meanwhile, the well of U.S. basic technology has
begun to run dry. When the U.S. develops important new technology, it won't be
so cavalier about sharing it with Japan. Japan must get more involved in developing basic technology; university education will be more important than ever.*

Irimajiri's passion for education grew and grew. He made repeated visits to
the university that had made him the offer. He would take a seat in the back row
of a classroom and listen to a lecture, or talk to the board chairman about management and philosophy. *I'll dedicate my second career to education*, he said to
himself.

That was where Irimajiri stood as of mid-December 1992 when, suddenly,
an old friend, well acquainted with the overseas auto industry, made a most
unexpected proposition. As they made small talk over sushi in the Garden Court
at the New Otani Hotel, Irimajiri's friend asked, "Iri-san, have you heard of a guy
at GM by the name of Lou Hughes? He is part of Jack Smith's innermost circle,
and a really capable guy, in charge of the whole European market. He's president
of GM Europe as well as chairman of Opel. Hughes will be coming to Japan just
after New Year's. I'm not quite sure what his motives are but he's expressed
interest in meeting you. Would you care to meet with him—on an informal
basis?"

Of course Irimajiri knew Hughes's reputation from his own time in the U.S.

*He's still only about forty-three, nine years younger than me. Why would
he want to see me? And why now?*

Irimajiri was puzzled. He had all but narrowed down his employment
prospects to one—the university. But that didn't mean he had no regrets whatsoever about leaving the automotive industry.

"I would have nothing against meeting him."

That was the answer he gave, but at the time, the idea that GM might be trying to sound him out did not cross his mind.

Hughes would be arriving in Japan just after the New Year's holiday to attend a ceremony commemorating the first shipment of Opel cars to importer Yanase, an event scheduled to take place on January 9 at Yanase's headquarters. Adam Opel AG was a GM subsidiary that made cars in Germany, and its management came under the GM Europe umbrella.

In Germany, Opel was a contender with Volkswagen for dominance in the mass-market segment, but in Japan few people were familiar with the brand or its lightning logo. Meanwhile VWs, imported by Yanase, the top importer of cars in Japan, boasted many passionate fans since the days of the Beetle. In fact, VW's success in Japan owed much to Yanase's efforts. Not satisfied, however, VW began to build a separate sales network, tying up with Toyota to reach even more dealerships. This was too much for Yanase President Jiro Yanase, who, after a bitter quarrel with VW, cancelled his contracts for importing VWs and Audis.

At the time, VWs and Audis together accounted for half the cars Yanase sold. By relinquishing its rights to sell them in Japan, Yanase had cut its own sales in half. This was when it turned its attention to Opel.

The rights to import Opel cars had originally been held by Isuzu, which had a capital tie-up with GM, but Isuzu's focus was trucks and Opel cars failed to sell well. In the end, Isuzu gave up the import rights.

Yanase had cut ties with VW; Opel was looking for a strong sales partner in Japan. The interests of the two companies were perfectly aligned. Yanase, the president, badly wanted to make VW suffer. GM Europe president Hughes was visiting Japan in support of the importer right as it started selling Opels.

For executives at the American Big Three automakers, Europe was the gateway to top posts. GM president Jack Smith had been ribbed as a "country boy" since his younger days; yet, after wrapping up joint-venture negotiations with Toyota, he became head of GM Canada and later of GM Europe, where he got Opel and all other GM units to adopt Toyota's *kanban* production methods, helping transform Europe into a money-spinner in the process. Flush with this success, he returned to Detroit in triumph, becoming vice president of international operations, and then president and CEO in 1992.

It was on a visit to the Opel factory in Rüsselsheim, Germany, that Smith met the Spanish-born J. Ignacio Lopez de Arriortua, who at that time was working in the Opel plant's purchasing department. Lopez's purchasing policies and strong track record at Opel were highly valued, and when Smith returned to Detroit to come to head all of GM, he took Lopez with him, making him chief of GM's worldwide purchasing. In time, Lopez would come to be known as Smith's right-hand man and GM's top cost-cutting czar. Lopez was the very model of an employee who had worked his way up through the ranks of GM.

Chrysler chairman Bob Eaton had also worked for Smith in Europe and had become head of GM Europe upon Smith's return to the U.S. But because Eaton was close to Smith in age, he felt he had little chance of ever becoming top dog at GM. When Lee Iacocca invited him to Chrysler, he accepted.

Likewise, as executive vice president of Ford Motor Co., former chairman Harold "Red" Poling had led Ford Europe for a time. Chairman Alex Trotman, an

Englishman and the first foreigner to head one of the Big Three U.S. automakers, had entered Ford in the U.K. and won recognition for his achievements in Europe.

Hughes, a trusted Smith aide who succeeded Eaton as head of GM Europe, had long served in GM's finance department, at one point as treasurer in charge of Isuzu. Hughes had also been on the task force that negotiated GM-Toyota cooperation. When those two giant companies decided to combine their production operations in Australia, he was the chief negotiator for GM. After that, he was transferred to overseas marketing, but he remained familiar with the Japanese car industry and had many friends and acquaintances at Isuzu, Toyota, and Suzuki.

For three years in a row, GM Europe had been highly profitable, sending money back to Detroit even as the parent company was showing losses. Despite a European market slump in 1991 and 1992, GM Europe managed to send 1.5 billion dollars in profit back to GM. While GM returned to profit in the fourth quarter of 1992, European dividends remained a vital lifeline as the company struggled to thoroughly restructure its operations. The important market was Hughes's responsibility.

The European market suffered from chronic oversupply. Further rationalization and higher productivity looked to be the only means to maintaining high profits.

GM Europe had been profitable despite the recession thanks to Lopez's tight purchasing policies and a new factory in Eisenach—in the former East Germany—which had come into full working capacity. Smith had introduced efficient Japanese manufacturing techniques at the factory by bringing over U.S. technicians who had learned Toyota production methods at the GM-Toyota joint venture NUMMI (New United Motor Manufacturing, Inc., in Fremont, California). Shop-floor personnel were handpicked from existing Opel factories.

Japanese manufacturing's origin was the "Just-In-Time" production system proposed by Toyota founder Kiichiro Toyoda before World War II. In order to be able to deliver just the parts needed, in the quantity needed, at the time needed, to the assembly line each day, it was essential to eradicate inefficiency.

Toyoda had worked out the principles, but it was Taiichi Ohno who put them into practice, making a name for himself as "the man who created the Toyota Production System (TPS)." Ohno realized Toyoda's dreams by using *kanban*—mere rectangular pieces of paper in plastic bags.

A *kanban* was a kind of order form, and every box of parts had one attached to it. When the parts were used up, the *kanban* was removed from the box and placed in a special collection box. These *kanban* were then picked up at specified times, and new directions were written in. Looking at these, parts makers produced the exact quantity needed. Following the plan eliminated overproduction and the need for inventory.

While the *kanban* were the key to realizing the Just-In-Time production system at Toyota, every company in Japan had come up with its own way to achieve an efficient production system. At heart, all were based on the same principles as Toyota's *kanban*.

Opel wanted to follow these Japanese production principles at its Eisenach plant, but there were limits to what Americans and Germans could accomplish in this area without assistance.

Hughes was getting impatient. No matter how well he understood the Japanese production methods in principle, he was not an engineer and could not take a hands-on role in overseeing productivity improvement and rationalization at the factory.

When Hughes first began his stretch in Europe, he was senior vice president of GM Corp. and president of GM Europe. In April, when Smith was promoted to president of the parent company, Hughes became its executive vice president, and in November, when Smith was made CEO, Hughes was given responsibility for all of GM's international operations.

GM Europe's headquarters were in Zurich, but its factories were spread across Germany, Britain, Spain, Belgium and elsewhere. The company also had a capital stake in Sweden's Saab; Hughes also had to pay attention to management there. On top of all this, he was now responsible for all of GM's international operations. He moved GM's international headquarters from Detroit to Zurich, but even so, the job was too big for one man.

The work seemed to pile up from month to month. While this demonstrated the trust Smith had in Hughes, living up to it meant finding the right number-two person for GM Europe. He or she needed to have a strong technical background—Hughes's weak point—in addition to sound business sense. Just as Smith had made GM Europe into a highly profitable company by making use of Lopez's abilities, Hughes needed someone with talents that supplemented his own.

If it were simply a matter of implementing Japanese production methods, Hughes could have asked his friends at Toyota or Isuzu to send in some experts through existing official channels. The name that came to Hughes's mind at that stage, however, was Irimajiri. His resignation had been big news in Europe as well as the U.S.

Hughes had never met Irimajiri face to face, but "Iri" was highly regarded even in Europe for his success in getting the Ohio factory on its feet. GM technicians who had visited the Ohio plant had nothing but respect for what he had accomplished. No matter how bad the earnings picture got for GM, it had a proud tradition stemming from its long years at the top of the auto industry of not trying to spirit away an active executive from a rival company. Things were different, though, if the executive in question had already pulled back from the front lines. Irimajiri, at fifty-two, was the same age as Lopez, and had many good working years left in him. There was no way Hughes could overlook him.

I may not understand the Japanese decision-making system very well, but there should be no problem with Honda if we scout someone who has retired from the front lines of management. I would like to meet this man Irimajiri, and if he has any interest in coming to GM, I'll make him an offer.

Hughes sensed great possibility in Irimajiri, whom he'd never even met. Of course, he had no way of knowing that Honda tradition didn't allow former executives to take up new employment after retirement. For Hughes, what seemed to be the biggest issue was simply whether he and the man he intended to make his own lieutenant would be on the same wavelength. That was why he had to meet Irimajiri and size him up for himself.

To keep the meeting confidential, he extended the invitation through a mutual friend, and not through GM Japan. Hughes and Irimajiri would meet for breakfast at 7:45 on January 6, the day after Hughes's arrival in Japan, at the Hotel Okura where Hughes would be staying.

5

Just after receiving the confidential fax confirming the meeting with Irimajiri, Hughes received another fax—from GM Japan. This one said, "Honda President Nobuhiko Kawamoto is eager to meet you while you are in Japan. How would you like us to reply?"

GM Japan had made no formal announcement that Hughes would be visiting Japan, but neither was it a secret. It was not at all strange, therefore, that the top people at Honda had somehow learned of his visit. Hughes had no idea what Kawamoto was after, and for a second he was not sure how to respond. He could just say no, but if Irimajiri did eventually join GM, Hughes would have to say something to Kawamoto formally in due time. So he asked GM Japan to send the following reply: "My trip to Japan this time will be very short. As of now, I'm afraid I am only available for breakfast on the 7th."

I don't know President Kawamoto at all. I remember, though, that former GM president Lloyd Reuss had nothing but praise for a Honda engineer named Kawamoto. I remember him saying, "There's this fantastic engineer named Kawamoto at Honda. If I'm not mistaken, he'll be president of Honda some day. Honda is setting trends in the global market for small cars. If you have a chance to go to Japan, meet Kawamoto. He'll teach you a thing or two."

Reuss and Kawamoto were both engineers. That's why they were on the same wavelength. Why in the world would Kawamoto be trying to meet me, though? I haven't even said anything yet to Jack Smith in Detroit about trying to grab Irimajiri for GM. There is no way Kawamoto could have found out. If this is about the Isuzu business, I'm the wrong person for him to talk to, because I'm not in charge.

The "Isuzu business" was the cooperative agreement between Honda and Isuzu that had sent a shockwave through the industry when it was announced on December 19, 1992.

In the U.S., pickup truck-based recreational vehicles (called sport-utility vehicles (SUVs)) were the hot product of the moment, but Honda didn't have one to offer, which was causing problems for its dealers. To support its sales network, it had to come up with some sort of an SUV, and fast. Honda itself, however, did not have the basic technology for light trucks, so it was not in a position to make an SUV even if it wanted to. The fastest way would be to set up an arrangement to buy vehicles from another manufacturer. Honda had chosen to approach Isuzu and had been conducting negotiations behind closed doors since summer.

The secret talks had finally produced a consensus in mid-December. Honda would buy the SUVs on an OEM basis from Subaru Isuzu Automobile, a joint venture between Isuzu and Subaru manufacturer Fuji Heavy Industries located in Illinois.

In return, Honda would supply Isuzu with cars in the Japanese market. Passenger cars were Isuzu's Achilles' heel—the entire reason for its difficulties turning a profit. Kazuhira Seki, taking over as president of Isuzu in January 1992, decided right away to cancel development of the Gemini compact car and was trying ever since to get out of passenger car manufacturing altogether.

It was at that point that the idea of cooperation between Isuzu and Honda came up. Of course, the negotiations had the approval of GM president Smith, but since it was primarily a matter of negotiations between the U.S. and Japan, Hughes, as head of international operations, had little direct involvement. Hughes had been informed of the details of the cooperation by Smith in a board meeting and had given his support, saying there was no problem as long as the cooperation would be a good thing for Isuzu.

If this is just a matter of Honda's top management wanting to make a report to GM as Isuzu's parent company, it shouldn't come to me, it should go to President Smith in Detroit.

As planned, Hughes arrived in Tokyo on the evening of January 5, even before the first week of the new year was out. Five automotive industry groups, including the Japan Automobile Manufacturers Association (JAMA) and the Japan Auto Parts Industries Association (JAPIA), wrapped up their annual New Year's gathering in the large reception hall at the Hotel Okura, where Hughes would be staying, just a few hours prior to his arrival. Given the economic slump, the party was less lively than usual, but Yoshiro Mori, who at that time was Minister of International Trade and Industry (later prime minister), gave a hortatory speech, predicting the economy would turn upward again in the spring.

At the event, an acquaintance surprised Honda President Kawamoto by saying, "I hear you're going to meet with Hughes from GM soon." Rather than lie about it, Kawamoto gave a noncommittal reply, saying that it would just be a courtesy call.

In fact, Kawamoto really did plan on making a simple courtesy call. Honda executives, including Kawamoto, had a rather limited social sphere, mainly because they had always left such matters up to Soichiro. Their assumption of top posts at a young age also contributed to their tendency to act much more modestly in the outside world than back at Honda.

Kawamoto was no exception. He had been busy developing automobiles since joining the company right after college. Having spent most of his career in R&D, his only foreign friends were engineers or from the F1 circuit. The only person in Europe with whom he could exchange information was BMW's Eberhard von Künheim. Künheim, however, had stepped down as president the year before to become chairman of the supervisory board. Kawamoto had recalled then something former GM president Lloyd Reuss had told him years before: "We have a young vice president named Hughes. He is a finance guy, but he is the kind of person who someday will carry GM forward, no doubt about it. I would be happy to introduce you, when I have the chance." Reuss had been demoted and had left GM before following through on his offer. But now Hughes was coming to Japan, and Kawamoto put in a request for a meeting through GM Japan.

On the morning of January 6, 1993, Irimajiri drove his own car from his home in Koganei in western Tokyo to Hotel Okura. The Chuo (central) Expressway was wide open, so soon after New Year's, and the city center was also devoid of traffic, as if it were a Sunday. Ordinarily the drive would have taken at least an hour, but on this day Irimajiri arrived at the Okura in less than forty minutes.

He was somewhat early for his meeting, but when he went up to the Chelsea Room on the twelfth floor of the hotel annex, Hughes was already there waiting for him.

Their mutual had advised, "The important thing, in this kind of meeting, is to see whether there's any rapport. It's best if just the two of you get together without any intermediaries."

Irimajiri was small even for a Japanese man, but Hughes was also on the small side for an American. Hughes presented his business card, rushed through the preliminary greetings and launched into a rapid-fire monologue about GM as he started breaking up his breakfast roll.

"Mr. Iri, GM was in the red in 1990 and again in 1991. 1992 will be even worse. But while earnings may be down, we'll get back on our feet again. Restructuring is proceeding faster than people realize. Improving profitability at GM Europe will play a key role in helping Detroit operations rebound. My job is to boost GM revenues in the European market. To do that, productivity needs to go up, and there has to be increased rationalization."

Irimajiri had no aversion to talking about work, but he thought it rare that a foreigner was launching right into such a detailed discussion when they'd only just met. Irimajiri listened quietly, occasionally interrupting Hughes to ask a question.

In 1989, GM had turned a profit of 4.2 billion dollars, but in 1990 this turned to a gigantic loss of 1.98 billion dollars, followed by an even bigger 4.45 billion dollar loss in 1991. For 1992, the company was expected to show the largest loss ever for any American company—24 billion dollars—because of medical insurance costs and factory closures due to restructuring. Calculated at one hundred yen to the dollar, GM's loss amounted to about 2.4 trillion yen, the equivalent of Mitsubishi Motors Corp.'s entire annual revenue.

Hughes maintained that demand was already beginning to show signs of revival in the U.S. market. He told Irimajiri that the Big Three automakers were shaping up at a quick pace. GM had been at the tail end, but under Smith's leadership it had gotten serious about rationalization, and the results were beginning to show. The company was expecting a profit in all quarters of 1993, returning to the black for the first time in four years. The European market had lurched into a slump after the unification of Germany, and GM had no choice but to undertake a restructuring that went beyond national borders.

The question was how could GM take the lead amid the massive transformation that was gripping the world? And how could he, as president of GM Europe, boost productivity at Opel plants in Germany, Vauxhall plants in the U.K., and elsewhere? Hughes went on and on, barely allowing the other man to slip in a word.

At first, Irimajiri listened, smiling rather indulgently as Hughes, nine years his junior, rambled on passionately about the global auto industry. As time passed, however, he felt his own expression growing sterner.

There were not many men in the world who were so obviously passionate about their work. As long as GM had men like the one before him, its recovery might actually turn out to be speedier than expected. Irimajiri was awed at GM's depth and the fact that it had put a man just over forty in charge not only of the European market but of its entire international operations. The man was the genuine article, no matter how you sliced it. For the first time in a while Irimajiri had encountered a real American businessman. Frankly, he was surprised to find such a fabulous specimen working for GM. GM was not to be written off lightly.

Once Hughes started talking there was no stopping him. Whenever Irimajiri asked a question, the answer he got was more than he'd hoped for. Irimajiri got excited just listening to Hughes go on. Hughes never came right out front about his headhunting mission, but Irimajiri understood—mind and body—what was being left unsaid.

Hughes went on: "Under Jack Smith, GM Europe introduced not only Japanese manufacturing systems, but all aspects of the Japanese system from parts procurement to product development, in all its European factories. As you know, Smith was responsible for our negotiations with Toyota, and he put a lot of effort into establishing NUMMI, our joint venture with Toyota.

"GM set up Saturn in Tennessee, an independent division for manufacturing small passenger cars. All-too-sure that Japanese cars' success owed to automation, robots and all that, Roger Smith, GM chairman at that time, set up a state-of-the-art high-tech factory.

"GM also invested huge amounts of capital and bought Ross Perot's Electronic Data Systems and aerospace company Hughes. It started a robot-making joint venture with Fanuc of Japan. Roger Smith hoped that by stressing high-tech, GM could develop a production method that would outstrip Toyota's *kanban* system.

"Unfortunately, that plan collapsed. Roger Smith's assumption that high-tech could conquer all was a delusion. Meanwhile, Jack Smith brought members of the NUMMI crew to Europe and succeeded in transplanting Japanese production methods there, turning GM Europe into the main source of revenue for all of GM.

"GM has been the slowest of the Big Three to show an earnings rebound because Robert Stempel, Roger Smith's successor as chairman, was irresolute in his policies. Stempel took an optimistic view of the situation and, early in his tenure, let people know that he expected GM to pull through on teamwork alone, without any major restructuring. This brought down the wrath of the company's external directors, and ultimately, in the summer of 1991, the company was forced to hammer out a major restructuring plan.

"The plan called for the closing of twenty-one factories and layoffs of 74,000 employees in North America by 1995. GM's external directors came to the conclusion that Stempel would never be able to pull off such a major restructuring, so he was ousted and one of the external directors, Procter & Gamble chairman John Smale, personally took over as chairman, appointing Jack Smith CEO.

"Today, Japanese production methods are in use at GM Europe, not just in our car assembly operations but also at our suppliers. The initiative is being directed by people who've been to Japan on short-term training programs or who've worked for joint ventures with Japanese partners. Still, I don't think GM has completely mastered the Japanese production system. For GM to emerge as a leader in Europe, we have to be more thorough in our adoption of Japanese production methods. Unfortunately, my own background is in finance. I don't have that firm a grasp of technical issues. Germans are very proud and confident about their own technology, and they don't appear to be anxious to implement Japanese methods. Opel is the same way. That's where I need to make a breakthrough."

Quickly finishing his breakfast, Hughes wrapped up his summary of the situation at GM.

It was already nearly nine o'clock. Soon Hughes would have to be on his way. The meeting had come to a close, but at the very end, Hughes came up with a proposition: "Mr. Iri, this meeting has been very meaningful for me. If you ever come to Europe, I hope we have a chance to continue this conversation. I would like to show you our factories, and I would appreciate your advice."

Irimajiri could see what Hughes was getting at. But if Hughes was not going to put it out in the open, Irimajiri was not going to be the one to broach it, either.

This man is serious about trying to lure me to GM. If that's the case, there would be no harm in going to see the plants that might be my future workplace. There's no need to force any conclusions before that.

"In fact," said Irimajiri, "IBM will be holding a conference on production technology in London in April. A friend has asked me to be a guest speaker, comparing production technology in Japan, the U.S. and Europe. I know the situation in Japan almost too well. I think I also have a pretty good grasp of the U.S. situation, from my time in Ohio. There are a lot of things I don't know about Europe, though, including the current state of technology. I'm spending three weeks in February to look into this, checking out representative factories in Europe."

Hughes pulled his planner from his jacket pocket. "When would that be, exactly?" With a serious expression on his face, Hughes began leafing through his organizer and adjusting his schedule.

Irimajiri had told Hughes the truth about his reason for planning a trip to Europe, but there was more. He also wanted to see if his health had recovered well enough to stand up to an extended business trip overseas.

The next day, in the same room at the same time, Hughes had breakfast with Honda President Kawamoto. Hughes had told Irimajiri about the date with Kawamoto, to see if Irimajiri knew what the president's intent might be. Irimajiri had simply tilted his head, looking thoughtful, and not given a precise answer.

At this stage, Kawamoto had no idea that GM had made contact with Irimajiri privately. Hughes, for his part, did not know what Kawamoto was after, so he was a little on the defensive. At the breakfast, Kawamoto asked questions, which Hughes answered. It was all very formal. Hughes let slip nothing about his meeting with Irimajiri the previous day. Kawamoto was just following up on a thread left dangling by former GM president Lloyd Reuss. In the end, the meeting amounted to very little for both sides.

That afternoon, Honda held its usual New Year's party for former executives, at its headquarters in Aoyama. Naturally, Irimajiri was there. This was the only opportunity of the year for current and former board members to mingle and enjoy chatting with each other.

Only three of Honda's retired executives had ever risen to the rank of supreme advisor: company founders Soichiro Honda and Takeo Fujisawa, and the company's second president Kiyoshi Kawashima. Not all past presidents of the company advanced to the position. Former president Tadashi Kume, for example, was given the title board director and counselor.

There were no clear internal rules on who could become supreme advisor, but one top executive offered the explanation that only those former presidents who had doubled the company's sales during their tenure would make the grade. The two founders were in a class by themselves, and Kawashima had boosted annual sales from 336 billion yen to 1.846 trillion yen in ten years, by a factor of 5.5. Under Kume, by contrast, this figure rose just fifty percent in seven years, to 2.8 trillion yen. The difference in these growth rates was reflected in the post-retirement titles of the two men. Both advisors and counselors had full use of the company's Yaesu offices.

Former executives, or "friends" of the firm, came together for lunch at the Yaesu building on the second Tuesday of each month. A current board member was always invited as guest speaker, to keep the group abreast of company affairs, but it was rare for the president to address this group, and so the annual New Year's party was the only occasion for these Honda "friends" to talk with the president.

It was an iron rule that retired executives did not intervene in the management of the company, no matter what their post-retirement titles might be. Former vice president Michihiro Nishida once joked bitterly, "This was true in my case as well, but at Honda, no one seeks advise from the advisors."

At the New Year's party, Kawamoto described the business environment surrounding Honda as increasingly harsh and then followed up by saying, "As you all know, our cooperative agreement with Isuzu has been very much in the newspapers recently. This cooperation was realized at Isuzu's request. Honda has grown so strong that the rest of the automotive industry now relies on us. This would never have been possible without the long years of effort by our predecessors."

Kawamoto's intention was to brag to the assembled VIPs by pointing out how Honda's status in the industry had risen so high that Isuzu had come begging for help. But many interpreted his words in a different way and were disappointed.

Honda has no strategy these days. It is the passive player in the Isuzu alliance. In the old days, Honda would have been the instigator in such a deal.

Kawamoto summed up the events of the past year at Honda, and the group moved on to the buffet. Kawamoto and Irimajiri avoided one another. Chairman Koichiro Yoshizawa casually approached Irimajiri with a whiskey glass in one hand and whispered into his ear, "Let me know when you've decided what you'll be doing next."

6

Hughes and Irimajiri had had a meeting of the minds at that breakfast in Tokyo that January day. Hughes was completely taken with Irimajiri. *Mr. Iri was even more amazing than I expected. If GM Europe can make use of his knowledge and experience, Opel can knock out Volkswagen to become Europe's most powerful automaker.*

Irimajiri also had the feeling that Hughes was a man in whom he could entrust his future. *Hughes is even more of a workaholic than any Japanese. He never once came out and said that he wanted me to come work for GM, but still my heart raced just listening to him speak. Somehow, I couldn't help feeling that I'd like to help him. I can see myself working for him, even if he is younger than I am. Still, jumping to GM is really very much a leap in the dark. Honda will do everything it can to prevent me, calling attention to the internal rules for former directors. I'll also have to convince my family first. But none of these problems are unsolvable. I've just turned fifty-three this month. This will probably be the last exciting job I ever do.*

Keeping his promise to Hughes, Irimajiri headed for Europe in early February. His plan was to first go to Britain, where he would tour automobile, auto parts and electronics plants, and then to proceed to France, arriving in Germany on the 22nd to meet up with Hughes at Opel's headquarters so that they could spend three days touring the company's most modern plant at Eisenach. Finally, he would visit GM's European headquarters in Zurich.

In Britain, Irimajiri made the rounds mostly of smaller companies in Wales that made molds, radiators and other auto parts. The racer Tetsu Ikuzawa, who had moved to London, volunteered to act as Irimajiri's driver and guide. After he had finished touring each factory, Irimajiri expressed his appreciation to the manager by offering a few tips on improvements that might be made.

Ikuzawa was astounded by Irimajiri's skill as an engineer. *I don't know what reasons Irimajiri had for leaving Honda, but his passion for automobiles has changed not one iota since the days when he used to come to my house to work on the S600. This is a man who has no business leaving the auto world.*

Hughes intended to accompany Irimajiri personally during his time in Europe as a way of demonstrating his own sincerity. Irimajiri, too, knew that even if he were to postpone making any final decisions until he returned to Japan, he would still need considerable resolve if he was going to visit GM Europe at all.

Irimajiri was enthralled by the idea of taking the experience he had built up at Honda and seeing what he could do with it at one of the Big Three U.S. automakers, on a scale several times larger than what he had experienced in Japan.

In order not to let his enthusiasm run away with him, he disciplined himself to study the German language. If he was going to work for GM, he hoped to work directly with the staff at the Opel factory, addressing them in German instead of through interpreters, in order to save time.

Irimajiri was well aware of his own nature. *I will be like a storm troop leader. There's no point to just sitting around in a fully air-conditioned office and talking about boosting productivity. If GM Europe will leave production to me, I'll go straight into the factories, just like I did at Suzuka and Honda America, and go the whole hog. Otherwise, I'll never be satisfied.*

One of Irimajiri's old nicknames at Honda had been "Iri-san, the *kachinko* (clapper-loader) man." For thirty years, Irimajiri had worked at Honda R&D Co., and even after he had become a director, he had always been the first to take the lead on the shop floor. He insisted on checking everything personally, with his own eyes, and was never satisfied until he took a product in his own hands and rapped on it with his knuckles to see if it was as it should be. Irimajiri was a walking picture of Honda's *sangen-shugi*—the "Three Actualities Principle" of going to the actual site, focusing on the actual situation, and making decisions based on actual facts.

From his long years of experience on the shop floor, both at Honda R&D Co. and elsewhere, Irimajiri could tell at a glance what was good or bad about a factory. Indeed, when Hughes took him through the Eisenach plant, which was a two-hour drive from Frankfurt on the *Autobahn*, he saw almost immediately what needed to be done.

Opel has implemented Japanese production methods in form, but not in spirit. It's only natural that productivity remains low. That shouldn't be so hard to change. The Germans, however, take great pride in themselves. That's going to be the hard part—changing the attitudes of the people working here. The only way this can be done would be for me to go into the factory myself, and instruct people first-hand, in German.

After Irimajiri had seen the Opel plant, he accompanied Hughes to GM Europe's headquarters in Zurich, where he was introduced to the company's top executives. Hughes's position as vice president in charge of international operations meant that the means to control all of GM's overseas business were concentrated in Zurich, making Zurich effectively GM's international headquarters. Hughes introduced Irimajiri as someone who would soon be a member of the club.

The day before Irimajiri's return to Japan, he had dinner with the GM Europe executives. After dinner, Hughes waited until the two of them were alone before he finally broached the issue. The expression on his face was all seriousness.

"I have shown you everything there is to see at GM Europe. I have introduced you to everyone. We need what you've got. How would you feel about coming to work with us? I'll be sending someone around to talk to you soon. We will do what we can to meet your needs in terms of conditions and compensation. You can let me know where things stand when you come back to Europe in April."

After spending roughly three weeks abroad, Irimajiri returned to Japan on

February 26. On overseas business trips during his days at Honda, he was accustomed to spending his plane rides hastily looking over materials and preparing for the following day's meetings. This time it was different.

In the plane on the way home, Irimajiri was overwhelmed by a sense of fulfillment at having successfully completed two major tasks. First, he had seen with his own eyes the foreign factory where he planned to work in the future and had satisfied himself that he could handle the job. And he had dispelled any worries he might have had about the effect that spending three weeks abroad would have on his health.

After returning to Japan, he went to the hospital for a thorough physical examination and got a clean bill of health. The doctor was pleasantly surprised at the progress of his recovery.

Irimajiri had given his heart to GM. *The work at GM will be both exciting and rewarding. My younger daughter just entered high school, so my wife will have to look after him for a while. I won't be able to take them with me. For the first year I'll be on my own, but as long as I have no worries about my health, my daily life should not be that complicated. Japanese companies are starting to become more and more internationalized now. Even if I do go to GM, it will probably be for five years at most. Those years will not be a negative experience, in terms of the things I want to do with my life. On the contrary, they should make it easier to do something more with my career after that.*

In March, Irimajiri met with representatives from GM to talk about terms and conditions of his employment. GM expressed the hope that Irimajiri would work for them until age sixty-five, as was the rule for its executives, but binding him to such strict terms presented some difficulties since Irimajiri was Japanese. He himself saw five years as a goal, and so the two sides agreed to set the initial contract term at five years. The contract could be extended if both sides agreed.

The next issue was compensation. Honda's executive pension plan was head-and-shoulders above ordinary Japanese companies. The exact figures are not publicly disclosed, but according to a former executive, counselors and advisors are guaranteed payment equal to their final salary prior to retirement. Later, they are paid approximately thirty-five percent of their former salary, up to the age of eighty. The pensions are indexed to a measure of consumer price, so there is no need to worry about inflation. If the executive dies before reaching eighty, his immediate family receives sixty percent of his pension.

Take, for example, the case of an executive who retires from Honda at age sixty, making forty million yen a year. That person would collect two hundred million yen over the next five years as either a counselor or an advisor. For fifteen years after that, until age eighty, he would get about fourteen million yen a year, adding up to a total pension of four hundred and ten million yen over the twenty-year period. Inflation adjustments would make the figure even larger.

Irimajiri, who had stepped down as vice president at age fifty-three, still stood to earn well over five hundred million yen in his post-retirement career, if he followed Honda's retirement path.

If he were to violate Honda's internal rules by defecting to a rival company, however, he stood to lose his executive pension. He would receive just a one-time payment in reward for his service as director. If Irimajiri went to GM, he would be making a big sacrifice in financial terms.

The two parties agreed that GM would pay Irimajiri a hefty signing bonus, a guaranteed salary equal to what he was making at Honda, and an additional bonus linked to the company's earnings performance. In addition, GM would match the pension benefits Irimajiri would be giving up at Honda.

Irimajiri would be given the title of vice president in charge of production for GM International, the division responsible for all of GM's business outside North America. The division was headed by Hughes, executive vice president of GM as well as president of GM Europe.

For the time being, Irimajiri's main task would be to raise productivity at GM's factories in Europe, but since his official title was vice president of GM International, he would also be responsible for factories in Latin America, Africa and Southeast Asia.

Irimajiri feared that Honda might bring a lawsuit against him, using as a pretext the internal rules prohibiting directors from taking on new jobs after retirement. If it ever came to that, it was agreed the GM would take on the case on behalf of Irimajiri.

Regarding the plans for his rank and compensation, Irimajiri had nothing to complain about. If he had any reservations at all, it was simply that, in all of GM, Hughes was the only one with whom he could be sure of being on the same wavelength. What would become of Irimajiri once Hughes left GM Europe? GM was a mammoth corporation with six hundred thousand employees worldwide, so Irimajiri had reason to be concerned.

As if fully aware of Irimajiri's concerns, GM addressed the issue head-on: in addition to the title of vice president in charge of production for GM International, he was offered the title of senior vice president of the parent company, GM Corporation. As senior vice president, Irimajiri would be a member of the board of directors in Detroit. This would mean that even though, in matters of production, Irimajiri would be primarily responsible for European factories, his views would also be sought on U.S. operations.

This settled it for Irimajiri, clearing the last clouds of doubt from his mind. He had already politely declined the offer from the private university. He had indeed given his heart wholly to GM.

Lawyers for GM and Irimajiri immediately went into action to draft a contract. Irimajiri was scheduled to speak at the IBM-sponsored conference on production technology in London in April. Before that he wanted to visit the Honda factory in Ohio, and say his farewells to the people he had worked with there. Then he would be moving to Europe.

He sent a copy of his travel itinerary to Hughes so they could arrange a date to get together again in Switzerland. The reply he received from Hughes exceeded his expectations.

"President Jack Smith in Detroit has approved all points regarding your move to GM. Smith is very happy, and says he would like to meet you himself beforehand. The appointment as senior vice president of GM Corp, however, will require the approval of the board and the finance committee.

"These two meetings will take place on Monday April 5, at the GM Building in New York. Smith wants to consult with these two bodies about the matter of your move to GM. If at all possible, would you be available to meet President Smith on April 6? We would like you to sign a provisional contract at that time. Of course, the formal contract can be signed at a later time."

GM had its own reasons for wanting to make him senior vice president of the parent company in addition to vice president of GM International.

On March 12, just after GM and Irimajiri had gotten down to details in their talks, Volkswagen announced that it had lured international purchasing vice president J. Ignacio Lopez de Arriortua away from GM.

Rumors that Lopez would go to VW had been circulating since early in the year, but auto industry watchers in Detroit had thought the chances were slim. Lopez had been a run-of-the-mill manager at GM Spain before he was discovered by Smith. Lopez had not failed Smith in his expectations, and in Detroit he had implemented a drastic reduction of GM's parts purchasing costs. Every chance he got, Lopez openly professed: "Everything I have today I owe to President Smith. For him I would cut off my right arm." That was how strong the bond was between the two men.

As a rule in the U.S., component prices were fixed when a new car model was launched, and automakers continued to pay the same prices for the entire production life of that model. In Japan, by contrast, automakers negotiated productivity-based price cuts with parts suppliers on an annual basis. Lopez introduced this practice in the U.S., demanding steep price cuts of ten percent each year from GM's suppliers. This was harsh medicine, but it did start letting in some fresh air to GM's bureaucracy-encrusted corporate culture.

On March 10, out of the blue, Lopez handed in his resignation to Smith. Smith had considered Lopez to be an indispensable part of his plans for reforming GM. In a last-ditch effort to persuade him to stay, Smith offered Lopez the title of executive vice president, making him the number two in all of GM, as well as the post of president of North American Automotive Operations (NAOO), a position held by Smith himself. Lopez initially accepted this offer and decided against going to Volkswagen, but on March 12, he changed his mind once again and decided to go to VW after all.

On that day, Smith was supposed to hold a press conference announcing his new management structure. At the same time, however, Lopez was scurrying off to catch a flight to Frankfurt from Detroit's Metro Airport. The press conference took place as scheduled, but the main subject ended up being the announcement of Lopez's departure.

A few hours later, Volkswagen CEO Ferdinand Piech held a news conference announcing that Lopez had joined VW. For Smith, it was as if he had been bitten by his own pet dog. It is believed that Lopez defected to VW, betraying Smith's trust, because VW had promised to build an auto plant in his native Spain, in the Basque region Lopez was originally from.

GM was a bureaucratic company, but since Smith had taken over as president, it had deliberately taken a variety of actions on the personnel front to break out of that rut. This included promoting young, capable managers and bringing in fresh talent from outside the company. Hughes himself, in charge of international operations at forty-three, was a prime example of this. Another was thirty-nine year old chief financial officer Richard Wagoner. The move to make Lopez executive vice president, as well as the hiring of Irimajiri, was part of this same strategy.

Hughes may have been the first to spot Irimajiri, but Smith had fully supported him in the plan. In the days before Smith became president, no one at GM would ever have thought of hiring a Japanese manager and making him a senior executive of the corporation. Hughes had high expectations for Irimajiri as his own right-hand man, but with the departure of Lopez, Smith had bigger plans to use his skills and experience for the benefit of the GM Group as a whole.

"Mr. Iri was, after all, the second most important person at Honda. This means that it would be embarrassing for GM to offer him anything less than what he deserves."

With that word from the top, Irimajiri's appointment to senior vice president of GM was all set.

7

Irimajiri, meanwhile, had no way of knowing GM's hidden agenda. His original plan had been to go to the IBM conference in London in late April, and then stop by at GM Europe in Zurich, where he would convey his decision to Hughes.

In reality, however, things moved faster than he had planned. GM had asked him to sign a contract at his meeting with Smith in New York on April 6, the day after the board of directors and the finance committee approved his appointment.

Irimajiri had had no objections to signing the contract at the time of his meeting with Smith, assuming it was ready by then. The details, however, were still being discussed by the lawyers, so it would only be a provisional agreement, not the formal contract, which would require some more time. Irimajiri was pragmatic about this point: he would sign the provisional contract in a personal meeting, and the formal contract could be sent through the mail. What concerned him more was that rumors of his move to GM might get out before he had completed the procedures for his formal departure from Honda.

Regardless of when the contract was to be signed, both sides had basically agreed that Irimajiri would start his new job on July 1. Irimajiri planned on informing Honda President Kawamoto of his move to GM about one week before that date, and then spending a few days making the rounds of Honda people who had been important to him during his career, before leaving Japan on June 29, the day of the Honda shareholders' meeting.

On this schedule, the press conference he and Hughes would hold at GM Europe in Zurich would take place after the Honda shareholders' meeting. Irimajiri had also begun to prepare an article for a monthly magazine, tentatively titled "Farewell to Honda: Why I Am Going to GM," to be released in July.

Still, if he were going to sign even a provisional contract with GM on April 6, he could not afford to take his time. Protocol dictated that he formally resign from Honda before officially signing on with GM. But Irimajiri would only be getting back from Europe on April 23, a Friday.

That would mean meeting with Kawamoto on April 27 or 28th, before the Japanese "Golden Week" holidays, to tell him of my intention to resign from Honda. Even if I am not going to join GM until July 1, I would still have to take my family to Zurich in late May or early June to look for a place to live. Actually, it might even be a good idea to hold the press conference with Hughes about my appointment to GM while I'm there.

Irimajiri had not discussed his plans to join GM with anyone outside his family. He knew that if he talked about it with current or former Honda managers, they were bound to take a dim view. Company Chairman Koichiro Yoshizawa had asked, whenever he had the chance, to be kept informed of Irimajiri's future intentions, and promised that Honda would do everything it could to help him. At one point, Irimajiri had told Yoshizawa about the offer to become president of a private university. Yoshizawa had actually encouraged him, saying, "That would be perfect for you. It would be good for Honda's public image. And it would not run afoul of Honda's internal guidelines, either."

I'm beginning to wonder if I'm making a big mistake.

As the time approached for him to leave for New York, Irimajiri found that he could no longer contain the urge to talk to someone about his decision and make sure that his judgment had not been impaired. The only person who had nothing to do with Honda and in whom Irimajiri could confide about personal matters was LDP legislator Masaharu Gotoda.

Irimajiri's family was originally from Kochi Prefecture, while the Gotoda family was based in the neighboring Tokushima, on the same island of Shikoku. Gotoda had been close friends with Irimajiri's late father and when Gotoda's second son Yusuke applied to work for Honda, Irimajiri had recommended him, strengthening Irimajiri's own ties with the elder Gotoda. When Yusuke got married, Irimajiri, together with Soichiro Honda, was invited to give a speech as guest of honor at the reception. After Irimajiri's own father died, he looked to Gotoda as a father figure for advice on personal issues.

It was late March, only a week before his departure for New York, when Irimajiri went to see Gotoda at his office in the Diet building in Tokyo's Nagatacho political district.

"I don't know much about the inner workings of the business world," Gotoda said to him. "Your decision is not for me to approve or oppose. In the end it's up to you to decide whether to go or not. You must be prepared, however, as a member of Japanese society, to be shut out of that society if you defect to a rival company, and a foreign company at that."

To some extent, Irimajiri had anticipated Gotoda's reaction. At least it was some consolation that this father figure had not strongly opposed his plans.

At this point, however, Irimajiri started feeling anxious about another aspect of his plan. When he had worked at the Ohio plant, he had achieved a lot, and to many people in the U.S. he was something of a hero. Therefore, when chief executives of U.S. auto parts suppliers were in Japan, they would often come to see him, even after he had retired as executive vice president of Honda. Once Irimajiri had made up his mind to move to GM, he made it a point to ask these people about the latest developments at GM and its chances of getting back on its feet. Eight or even nine times out of ten, their response was negative.

"GM's organization is rotten to the core. Rebuilding would be impossible, no matter who tried. The only hope for GM will be to file for corporate reorganization."

More than a few times, Irimajiri heard extreme views such as this, and his heart began to waver. *Will I really be able to achieve anything in a big, bureaucratic organization like GM?*

Irimajiri had made up his mind to go to GM, but the gods were toying with him, as if they could see he was beginning to have doubts. In fact, both Irimajiri and GM would end up victims of this "game of the gods."

On the evening of March 26, Irimajiri received a phone call at his home in Tokyo from his friend Koichi Hori. Hori was head of the Boston Consulting Group in Japan, which acted as Honda's consultant. "Are you free tomorrow? It's Saturday, and I was wondering if you have time to play golf. We need a fourth. The other guys are Hideki Sakai, president of Hirose Electric, which is a client of mine, and Hayao Nakayama, president of Sega Enterprises."

Irimajiri had no important appointments, and he had the time, so he readily agreed to go along.

He had never met Sakai or Nakayama, but the golf game went well. As they approached the eighteenth hole, Irimajiri casually whispered to Hori, "I've been doing a lot of thinking, and I've decided to move to GM. The week after next, on April 6, I'm going to New York to meet GM President Smith and sign a provisional contract."

Hori's reaction was swift and loud. "Iri-san, don't get ahead of yourself here. Let's finish this golf game and then we'll talk, just the two of us." Irimajiri immediately regretted that he had said anything, but it was too late to take it back.

After the game, the foursome chatted in the clubhouse for a while, and then when Sakai and Nakayama had gone, Hori and Irimajiri went back to their seats and got down to the serious discussion. Irimajiri summarized the whole story for Hori, and told him about the job description, conditions and compensation. Then Hori launched into his tirade:

"Iri-san. In Japan it is our custom to observe the first anniversary of someone's death. When someone dies, we mourn him for a year. It was mid-March of last year when you stepped down as vice president of Honda, so it has been over a year. But you were still a director at Honda until the end of June, and it hasn't been a year since then.

"Even today, you receive a stipend from Honda. The shareholders' meeting will be in late June. Even if nothing can persuade you from leaving Honda for GM, you should at least wait until after the shareholders' meeting to announce the fact. You should know, though, that if you do go to GM you will be losing your friends at Honda."

The time was now past 6 P.M. Outside, it was getting dark. Irimajiri and Hori were the last two guests in the clubhouse. Closing time came and the two had to leave. Hori was not yet finished talking, though.

"Let's go to a quiet hotel in the city where we can continue our conversation."

Each got into his own car, and drove back to the city, where they met up again at a hotel a little past eight. Hori did all the talking, and Irimajiri just listened.

"Iri-san, I know this because I myself have hitched my wagon to a foreign company: let me tell you no matter how qualified and talented a Japanese person is, he doesn't have a chance in Caucasian society. Take a look at these foreign companies. Even if people do well at their Japan offices, they can never make it at the parent company. We are seen as disposable.

"If I thought you had even a fifty percent chance of succeeding at GM I would not stand in your way. I look at your case, though, and even though English may not be a problem for you, we are talking about GM here, the world's largest manufacturing company, and those white people aren't going to understand your way of thinking.

"I don't know what sweet nothings GM has been whispering to you, but in all likelihood it will chew you up and spit you out. Why can't you see that? I can see it before you even go. As your friend, if I can see that you're bound to fail, I can't just let you go off like that.

"I will think hard about your future too. We're running out of time, so I just want you to promise me one thing. If you go to New York in April, don't sign anything, even if they call it a 'provisional' contract..."

The two said goodnight. Irimajiri's head was spinning.

Even as Irimajiri wrestled with his inner turmoil, Hori called Sega president Nakayama the following Monday, on the 29th, only two days after their golf game together.

"Nakayama-san. You know Iri-san, who played golf with us on Saturday? If he should somehow be in need of a job, could you take care of him at Sega?"

"The Prince of Honda? If someone like that were to consider joining Sega, well, I'm sure I couldn't ask for anything more. Of course we would find a place for him. He could name his own price."

Nakayama hung up, and immediately called Irimajiri at home. They chatted about Saturday's golf game for a minute, and made a date to meet the next day.

As they shared a meal, Nakayama came right out with it: "Irimajiri-san. It's not that Mr. Hori asked me a favor, but how would you feel about coming to work for my company?"

Irimajiri was taken aback at this.

"Your offer is very flattering, but frankly I know little more about your company than its name. I don't even know what you make. Now all of a sudden you're asking me to come to work for you... As a matter of fact, I am already entertaining another offer..."

"Yes, yes. I can see that you believe Sega to be not much better than a big toy store. I understand. Our research lab is near Haneda. Why don't you come down with me now and see for yourself what we're up to? If you find it interesting, you can take some time and think about it."

Nakayama practically picked Irimajiri up and dragged him down to the lab, which was a renovated warehouse on Kanpachi-dori. There, Irimajiri, who until then had thought that Sega was something like Nintendo, making computer games for kids, had his first encounter with something completely unexpected: a virtual reality machine for a commercial arcade.

Irimajiri looked at the contraption, which consisted of a huge, bare metal body bearing the letters "AS1."

"Please, climb up and get in."

Following Nakayama's instructions, Irimajiri entered the machine. Inside there were eight full-sized seats. At the front of the room was a large, widescreen video monitor. He sat down and fastened his seatbelt. The door closed and he was in total darkness. The machine began to move, its movements matching the picture on the screen.

It was as if the entire metal capsule had been transformed into a spacecraft, lifting off from the earth and heading for the void. Irimajiri could use the buttons at his fingertips to shoot down the invaders that appeared on the screen. Though the science fiction plot was quite simple, the fact that the AS1 allowed humans and images to communicate with one another was a most convincing display of virtual reality.

"How do you like it? This amusement machine allows people to experience a virtual world with all their senses. The special effects software is interactive. You can change the program, and find out what it's like to actually be in a natural phenomenon like an earthquake or a storm, or even a car accident."

The two men left the lab and went to another lab in the main building, where Nakayama handed Irimajiri a headset that looked like a pair of goggles with liquid crystal displays in each eye.

"Try these on." Irimajiri put on the headset, and a race course appeared before his eyes. As he turned his head, the scene changed as if he were really in a racing car, with his own two hands on the steering wheel.

"This is a racing game. It lets people taste the Formula One world in their own home, or anywhere. How about this now? This one's a helicopter flight simulator. Add some software, and you can fight off attackers sneaking up from behind. It's a video game that makes you the center of the action, with full command of the space around you: up, down, left, right, 360 degrees.

"It will take a little more time before the products you've just tried will be available commercially, but all of them will be playable at home. In the future, we're also planning to develop software for sports games like tennis, golf and soccer."

Irimajiri, looking at one virtual reality game after another, felt that he had arrived at the polar opposite of Honda's "Three Actualities Principle" of sticking to actual places, things and facts, in which he had been such a firm believer. This made the shock all the stronger.

Coming as it did just as he had begun to lose faith in the idea of going to work for GM, Irimajiri's experience at Sega had a powerful impact on him. That did not mean it changed his mind immediately; it was, he felt, after all too late in the game to cancel his decision. His departure was imminent: three more days.

The next day, on the 31st, he met again with Hori at the Palace Hotel, and once again Hori warned him:

"Iri-san. Automobiles are not the only business in the world. There are lots of other things to do and see. Why don't you give serious thought to Sega's offer? In any case, you certainly should not sign anything while you are in New York, not even a 'provisional' contract. Promise me just this one thing."

8

On Saturday April 3, Irimajiri boarded JAL Flight 6 leaving Narita at 11:30 a.m. for New York. On the 6th he was to have lunch with GM President Jack Smith at the company's office building in midtown Manhattan. GM Europe President Lou Hughes would be there, along with executive vice president William Hoglund, chief financial officer Richard Wagoner and a host of other senior executives. GM was already treating him like a member of the club.

Only ten days before, he had confirmed his intentions and had notified GM that he would sign an informal, provisional contract. Just before leaving Japan, however, he had contacted GM again, saying that he would not be able to sign the contract while in New York because he wanted to have it revised to include coverage for his family's health insurance. This put him a little at ease for the time being, but the real problem was that he was unable to sort out his own thoughts. His experience at Sega had been a powerful awakening. But he had not lost interest in GM. As Irimajiri boarded the JAL jet, he felt himself stuck in the middle.

Due to the time difference, he arrived at New York's JFK airport at 3 p.m. the same day. Apart from the rest of that Saturday, which he planned to use resting and getting over his jet lag, he still had two more days, Sunday and Monday, with no particular plans.

The New York Auto Show opened Sunday at the Jacob Javits Convention Center. He thought about going, but decided against it since the last thing he wanted to do was to draw attention to himself. He stayed in his hotel room the entire day and tried to sort out his thoughts. But despite racking his brains the whole day, he was still torn and indecisive: which would it be, GM or Sega?

GM of course had no way of knowing of the turmoil brewing in Irimajiri's mind. GM's board of directors, including the external directors, met according to schedule on Monday April 5 in New York and approved Irimajiri's appointment to the company. The finance committee meeting, which directly followed the board meeting, approved the compensation package he would receive as executive vice president. Everything was set: Irimajiri had only to sign the contract on the 6th and even as soon as that very day, he would be vice president of GM Corp.

On the 6th, Irimajiri had breakfast at his hotel, the Essex House, which was owned by JAL. After breakfast, he got into the limousine GM had sent round to pick him up and headed for the GM Building.

He was shown to the board members' lounge, where Hughes greeted him warmly and then introduced him to Smith. Smith was not so tall for an American, but he had a powerful build. His hair was cropped short. From any angle, he looked more like a Midwestern farm boy than a New York businessman.

When Irimajiri was at the plant in Ohio, Smith had been president of GM Canada. Later he became head of GM Europe, so the two had never met.

Smith was born in 1938, making him two years older than Irimajiri. The GM managers Irimajiri had gotten to know during his time in Ohio had all been more or less cookie-cutter bureaucrats, but Smith was nothing of the kind. *Judging from the top management, one might say that by now it's Honda, rather than GM, that's become bureaucratic.*

Hughes reassured Irimajiri that his move to GM had been officially approved by the board the day before. Irimajiri, in turn, honestly apologized for not being able to sign the provisional contract at this time.

With the other board members in attendance, lunch got under way. Irimajiri's behavior remained stiff and formal. Hughes tried to break the ice with some small talk.

"What gave you the hardest time when you were working at the plant in Ohio?"

Irimajiri relaxed a little and began to talk about the troubles he had faced in Ohio. The luncheon conversation wandered aimlessly, but GM's main goal was to get Irimajiri comfortable with the board members, so he could get a sense of how they operated.

From the very first time I met Hughes, it was plain to me that GM has begun to change. I could definitely get along with people like these.

Irimajiri's determination once again began to waver, but not enough for him to change his mind and decide to sign the provisional contract after all. Lunch ended and Smith stood up and left, looking satisfied. Irimajiri was left to talk with Hughes alone. If they stuck to small talk, Irimajiri's move to GM would be like an established fact. Even though he had postponed making his final decision, Irimajiri still felt he needed to set a few things straight.

"Lou, about the provisional contract. The reason I couldn't sign today is that, frankly, I haven't yet been able to convince my family it is the right thing to do. I'm going to need a little more time."

"That's all right. Circumstances are different for every family. At GM, all the internal procedures are now complete. We only ask that you sign the contract by the end of June. No need whatsoever to worry about talk of this getting around before then. We'll be putting a stern gag order in place. You can relax about that."

Hughes was one hundred percent confident that Irimajiri was going to come to work for GM as his own right-hand man. Irimajiri was aware of this, and felt a twinge of irritation at his own words; still, there was nothing he could do.

He had not completely made up the story about needing to convince his family either. When the subject of moving to GM had first come up, no one in his family had shown much opposition to the plan. But since the possibility of working for Sega had come up, the situation had taken on an entirely different aspect.

For Irimajiri's family, of course, the question of his health was of primary importance. Working for GM would mean that he would have to spend extended periods of time abroad on his own, so naturally they preferred Sega. Most vigorously opposed to GM were his mother in Kobe and his younger brother, who was a doctor.

Irimajiri left the GM Building feeling a little guilty and headed straight for LaGuardia Airport. A few hours later, it was Smith's turn to be flying out of New York. Smith was going to Washington, D.C. to meet with Toyota Motor Corp. President Tatsuro Toyoda. The main topic of discussion between the leaders of GM and Toyota was the volume of exports to Japan of the next model of the J-Car, the compact car developed by GM.

On April 23, Irimajiri returned to Japan after having first visited Honda's Ohio factory, followed by some time spent touring Europe. The entire time he was in Europe, he had continued to waver, but more and more he found himself beginning to lean toward Sega. No matter which he chose, he would have to formally resign from Honda beforehand.

Three days after his return to Japan, Irimajiri went to his office in the former Honda headquarters building in Yaesu, near Tokyo Station, to take care of the paperwork for leaving the company. He asked for an appointment with Kawamoto through the secretarial section so he could personally hand him his letter of resignation. The response from the secretarial section was curt: "From now until the 'Golden Week' holidays, the president is busy, and has no time."

There was nothing else to do but hand in his resignation to Chairman Yoshizawa. As for his future plans, he was deliberately vague: "I will decide in the next month or two. I will inform President Kawamoto as soon as I have made up my mind."

And so Irimajiri left Honda for good, quietly and without ceremony.

Irimajiri planned to hold a family conference with his mother, younger brother, wife and two children during the "Golden Week" holidays to decide his fate. Ultimately, however, as Gotoda had said, it was up to Irimajiri himself to make the final decision. *My entire family is concerned for my health. I cannot ignore this. If only I were ten years younger, or even five…*

Irimajiri comforted himself with this thought, but still he could not help feeling some regret. No matter how sorry he felt, it was too late for him to fly: his wings had already been clipped. In the end, Irimajiri could not break free from the ties of human society which had developed around him over the fifty-three years that was his life.

The decision was made even before the family conference began. His family members had only to stamp their approval on Irimajiri's choice. Irimajiri had decided on his own accord to throw away his chances of making it big on the world stage as an executive in the world's largest corporation.

Although he had made up his mind to turn down GM's offer in favor of Sega's, before he could tell Nakayama of his intention, he would first have to write a letter to Hughes. That was the order of things.

Irimajiri drafted a long letter to Hughes, based on the outcome of the family conference. He explained that he could not join GM after all, due to his health problems and the opposition of his family. He apologized for all the inconvenience he had caused GM. He knew that his plan to go to Sega would become public before long, but he decided to say nothing about it at this point. If he mentioned it, it would seem like a half-baked excuse. And he did not want Hughes to think he had been playing GM off against Sega.

At the end of his letter, he wrote: "Dear Lou, I regret very much that we will not have the opportunity to work together. I am truly sorry about this. I enclose a report on the GM Eisenach plant, based on my own observations, and the specific restructuring remedies I would recommend. Please show it to your most trusted factory manager. I guarantee that if you do as I recommend, Opel's restructuring will be successful."

Irimajiri offered the report as a token of his sincerity. It was seven pages long, tightly handwritten in English. He had thought out the remedies believing that he himself would be going to GM, and they were very much to the point.

It was after the "Golden Week" holidays when Irimajiri met Nakayama and told him of his intention to join Sega. Nakayama could hardly believe it. Although he had been asked to look after Irimajiri by Boston Consulting's Hori, he never imagined that Irimajiri would actually decide to join Sega in so short a span of time.

It would take at least two weeks to settle the outstanding questions of Irimajiri's conditions, compensation, job responsibilities and title. No public announcement could be made until an agreement had been reached on these points. Under ordinary circumstances, companies decide on new directors when the board meets to discuss and approve the annual financial results; however, Sega's fiscal year ended in March, and the board would be holding their meeting in just a few days. There was no way an agreement would be ready by that time. If, however, a decision could be reached before the end of May, there would be just enough time left to allow an announcement to be made at the annual shareholders' meeting at the end of June.

A few days after Irimajiri's meeting with Nakayama, Hughes received the thick envelope. Hughes read it and was baffled. He had been one hundred percent certain Irimajiri would come to work for GM. Now he was genuinely confused. What had happened to Irimajiri in the course of one short month? Why had he changed his mind? Hughes couldn't make heads or tails of the situation.

Health? GM had the most advanced medical facilities in the world. Family matters? As a vice president, Irimajiri would be managing his own schedule and could afford to go home to his family in Japan every month if he wished. On top of that, the fact that he would also be senior vice president of GM Corp. meant that his compensation would be more than he could hope for.

There was still time before July. Hughes thought about changing his schedule and flying to Japan to see Irimajiri face-to-face to convince him to change his mind. Just as he was thinking such thoughts, on Saturday the 19th, the first speculative articles about Irimajiri's move to Sega began to appear in the Japanese press.

"HONDA COUNSELOR IRIMAJIRI / LIKELY TO JOIN SEGA" (*Nihon Keizai Shimbun*)

"SEGA SNAGS HONDA'S IRIMAJIRI" (*Sankei Shimbun*)

Neither article was conclusive, but both hinted that the possibility was strong. Foreign news wires picked up the story and relayed it to the world.

Now that it's in the newspapers, I suppose I should call Hughes and tell him myself.

On Sunday, the day after the story appeared in the papers, Irimajiri called Hughes at his home in Zurich. Irimajiri apologized that he had been unable to keep his promise to Hughes, but the latter still had not given up hope.

"I understand your reasons for not coming to GM. Let's forget about your becoming vice president of GM. Just as my own personal proposal, though, how about if you were to be a part-time technical advisor to GM Europe? If that's too much, couldn't we think about some kind of technical consultant's contract? We could set a certain number of times per year you could come and give us advice."

Irimajiri stood firm.

"Lou, it won't work. In Japanese society, once you join a company, you have a moral obligation not to become a technical advisor to another company, even in a different industry. I am not cut out to be a consultant. If I set out to do something, I do it all the way. That's my personality. If I were a consultant, I would just be trouble for you."

The international call lasted all of ninety minutes. The conversation went round and round in circles, failing to bring the two any closer to each other, and didn't reach a conclusion. Irimajiri tried to wrap it up.

"Lou, I just can't go to GM right now. Take the restructuring proposals I sent you the other day, and see what you can do with them. In two years the situation could be different. Let's have another look at the issue then."

Hearing those words, Hughes gave up chasing after Irimajiri. Even without seeing Irimajiri's face he knew he was just paying lip service to the idea of checking back in two years and that it probably meant nothing.

The official announcement that Irimajiri had joined Sega came on May 28. Irimajiri paid a formal visit to Honda President Kawamoto to tell him this in person.

"Iri-san. I want you to do your best at your new company," Kawamoto uttered this one sentence, and left the conference room.

At Honda, people responded to Irimajiri's move with mixed feelings. In June, Irimajiri traveled with his wife to Hokkaido, avoiding the rainy season in Tokyo. He spent the intervening time paying calls on former company presidents Kiyoshi Kawashima and Tadashi Kume and the other people at Honda who had meant the most to him.

Rumors that Irimajiri was being headhunted by both GM and Sega had already been circulating among the former directors as early as the Golden Week holidays. At their meeting, Kume addressed Irimajiri in a tone of voice that could be construed as either encouraging or sarcastic:

"Iri-san. Sega was the right choice. If you had gone to GM, they would have just used you and tossed you aside. I bet Toyota was behind GM's attempt to pluck you. If GM had really wanted you, they should have come to us first. If you had abandoned Honda for GM, you would have lost a lot of friends here..."

Honda co-founder Takeo Fujisawa, who had pioneered modern corporate structure in the early 1950s, had predicted: "If Honda's employees truly become experts [in their fields], other companies will try to lure them away."

As Fujisawa had foreseen, Irimajiri had indeed become an expert. Recognizing this, the world's largest automaker GM had offered to make him executive vice president. But the response of the "Honda kids" who had worked frantically under Fujisawa to make Honda a world-class company was a far cry from what one might expect of a world-class company.

After retiring, Honda executives automatically become members of an elite corps known as "friends" of the firm, but Irimajiri did not take steps to join this group. He gave up his executive pension and cut his ties to Honda of his own free will.

The book on Japanese manufacturing that he had been researching would remain unfinished. It had been intended as a parting shot at the Japanese manufacturing industry, which he had resolved to leave, and so he had been more than free with his criticisms. Now that he had decided to continue working for a Japanese company, however, he could not afford to have his own comments come back and hit him in the face. The book would have to go unpublished.

CHAPTER TWO: ONE PART, TWO PLAYERS

Our company's motto is the Three Delights: the delight of a maker creating a product; the delight of a distributor selling the product, and the delight of a customer purchasing the product. Ensuring all three sides are delighted encourages production and the development of new technology, which allows our business to grow.

—Soichiro Honda

The "Three Delights" may be Honda's corporate motto, but they must be prioritized properly if Honda is to succeed. We must place the delight of the customers first, for that feeds the delight of the distributors. And delight of the customers and distributors feeds that of the maker. That is the only proper order.

—Takeo Fujisawa

1

The sudden resignation of Irimajiri, Prince of Honda, left the public with the distinct impression that the company was facing a crisis. For a long time, the Japanese public had associated "Honda" with four specific images: "Soichiro Honda, genius engineer," "F1 racing," "overseas success" and "youthfulness." The company's rapid success and continued growth added to the legend. As performance fell, these key impressions became diluted, and before long, people began to whisper of the collapse of the Honda legend. Both Soichiro Honda, founder of the "Cult of Honda," and Takeo Fujisawa, the man behind the scenes, have passed away. And with the burst of the Japanese economic bubble, sales had slumped low enough to force Honda to retire from its longtime "running advertisement" of the F1.

There is no doubt that Honda will continue to be revered as a pioneer in doing business outside of Japan. But the strengthening of the yen that accompanied the 1985 "Plaza Accord," the agreement among the financial ministers and central bankers of the then G-5 nations, began to tarnish Honda's once almost untouchable reputation as a global success story. With the exchange rate plunging below one hundred yen per U.S. dollar, Japanese industries were practically obliged to run their businesses abroad. In fact, if left unchecked, the current trend towards globalization could well lead to a "hollowing out" of the Japanese economy.

By the mid-nineties, the average age of a Honda executive, once considered symbolic of the company's youthfulness, was fifty-four years and three months. While this was younger than that of other Japanese manufacturers, the company's youngest executive was forty-six: Honda could hardly boast of its youthfulness any more. Similarly, the average age of the Honda employee, once the lowest in the industry, had risen to thirty-seven years and two months—fifth place among Japanese automobile manufacturers.

The first public inkling of the problems facing Honda came in the form of the sales figures announced for the fiscal year ended March 1993. For the first time in the twenty-six years since the fiscal year ended February 1967—when Honda had been in the midst of its struggles to break into the automobile market and weathering a slump in foreign sales of their motorcycles—the company suffered a drop in both income and profits. For the first time in Honda's history, ordinary profit and net profit after taxes were lower than the previous year for the third year in a row. Profits at the end of the fiscal year ended March 1994 dropped by half, the worst loss in Honda's history.

Of course, it hadn't always been smooth sailing for the company. Honda overcame one crisis after another on the path to building its reputation as a world-class manufacturer of motorcycles. Making inroads into the automobile marketplace had been no easy task, either. Honda had faced crises more than a few times during its history. In every case, however, the company overcame the obstacles facing it and even managed to grow in the process. Indeed, this perseverance in the face of adversity was one of the major reasons for Honda's rise.

Honda's co-founders put on, as it were, one of those stage tricks where two men play a single part. Soichiro Honda took the forefront, addressing the audience passionately with his hands behind his back. Crouched behind him and hidden under the kimono, Takeo Fujisawa quietly proffered his hands in front of Soichiro, as if attached to his partner's body. Their seamless collaboration proved so deft that the audience gradually began to forget that two people were actually playing the role and started to believe that Soichiro was the sole player in the act.

Many people believe Soichiro played the main role, while Fujisawa was a supporting character. Nothing could be further from the truth. While Soichiro may have been Honda's president, the day-to-day business affairs of the company were under Fujisawa's total control. In fact, until the day he retired, every check and every bill issued by Honda bore the name of "Takeo Fujisawa, Representative Director."

Although Fujisawa may have run the Honda business behind the scenes, Soichiro was far from being a puppet. Soichiro took great pride in thinking, "I founded Honda." Fujisawa, for his part, fully respected Soichiro's role and poured his effort into playing the man behind the scenes—acting as scriptwriter for the Honda myth, ensuring that Soichiro had a stage where he could fully utilize his talent for playing the lead, and doing his best to keep the press and public on the house's side. Fujisawa's skill in doing so cemented Soichiro's place as the charismatic leader of the Cult of Honda. This talent of Fujisawa's would become more apparent than ever during the recall scandal over defective cars and the resignation of the two founders that ensued.

Soichiro Honda was born the son of the local blacksmith in the village of Komei (now Tenryu City) in the Iwata district of Shizuoka prefecture. Soichiro's rise to fame from such humble beginnings was entirely due to his great "stage director," Fujisawa. Meeting Fujisawa allowed Soichiro, who would otherwise undoubtedly have ended his career as president of a medium-sized corporation, at best, to instead utilize his considerable engineering skills to the fullest.

The reverse is true for Fujisawa as well. While he possessed an amazing knack for business management, he never would have gotten his chance to shine behind the scenes without the talented "actor" that he found in Soichiro.

Soichiro and Fujisawa were opposites in nearly every respect. Everything about them was different: the way they saw the world, the way they thought about things, the way they spent their time on their personal hobbies. The one similarity the two men did share was the lack of any formal higher-level education.

Kihachiro Kawashima, former vice president of Honda, often used Yaeko Nogami's work *Hideyoshi and Rikyu* to characterize the relationship between Soichiro and Fujisawa. In his words, the novel "describes the friendship and conflict between two highly talented individuals. I saw that it bore more than a little similarity to the relationship between Mr. Honda and Mr. Fujisawa. Each had an absolute sense of rivalry and respect for the other. That's the reason for Honda's growth and success."

Soichiro and Fujisawa may have had an ideal relationship, but things didn't begin particularly smoothly. In fact, according to Fujisawa, their relationship got off to a rather rocky start when they first met. It was the summer of 1949, when the scars from the flames of World War II could still be seen across the nation.

The man who introduced Soichiro and Fujisawa was Hiroshi Takeshima, an official at the Ministry of Commerce and Industry (later MITI/METI). Before taking his job at the Ministry, Takeshima had worked for the Nakajima Aircraft Company and had also taught classes as a part-time instructor at his alma mater, the Hamamatsu School of Technology (now the Faculty of Engineering at Shizuoka University).

After graduating from Futamata Ordinary and Higher Elementary School in 1922, Soichiro was taken to Tokyo by his father, Gihei, and apprenticed at an auto repair shop called "Art Shokai" ("shokai" means "Co."). Gihei had changed professions and opened a bicycle shop, and it was an advertisement in his favorite magazine, *World of Wheels*, that had led to the apprenticeship.

"Don't return to Tenryu until you can set up your own Art Shokai franchise!"

With his father's words echoing in his ears, Soichiro, just fifteen years old at the time, worked hard for the next six years. After another year of service as a token of gratitude to his master, Soichiro, at the age of twenty-one, opened a Hamamatsu branch of Art Shokai in 1928. He even put out an English sign, the height of fashion at the time: "ART, Automobile Service Station." Although one could say he returned home in glory, Soichiro's auto repair shop comprised a grand total of two employees, including himself.

Black Monday in 1929, arriving only one year after Soichiro began his own business, signaled the beginning of the Great Depression and sent Japan too into financial turmoil. Soichiro's local auto repair shop, however, was completely unaffected. On the contrary, it earned a good reputation and fared well during this time, eventually growing to a total of fifteen employees.

Soichiro's breakthrough came in 1931 when he invented an automobile wheel with cast-iron rather than wooden spokes. His creation caught quite a bit of attention at the National Industrial Exhibition, which even led to licensing offers abroad. Before going independent, Soichiro had dreamed of saving a nest egg of one thousand yen by the time he retired. No sooner had he struck out on his own than he found himself receiving royalty checks in excess of one thousand yen every month.

Elated, Soichiro tore around town on a new Harley Davidson. He built several motorboats with which he cruised the lakes of Hamana and Sanaru. In the evenings, he held luxurious parties with geisha entertainers. Soichiro's penchant for spending his royalties on parties and playtime made him a local legend in Hamamatsu.

Soichiro's auto repair shop continued to grow, year after year, but it left him dissatisfied. In fact, if anything, he was getting tired of it. As long as he worked in his repair shop, there were limits to what he could do and where he could go. Meanwhile the act of inventing something new was a different story, with near-endless opportunities. Soichiro founded the Art Piston Ring Research Institute and began manufacturing piston rings on the side.

I can build anything if I can just see it once. Soichiro brimmed with confidence in his engineering skills. Given his history of successful inventions, he was sure that he could easily manufacture piston rings.

Without a firm educational background, however, Soichiro found it impossible to make quality cast-iron piston rings; his many attempts inevitably ended in failure. Realizing that what he lacked was a basic knowledge in metallurgy, Soichiro decided to go back to school. He enrolled as an auditing student at the Hamamatsu School of Technology, where he met Takeshima. The sight of Soichiro, already thirty at the time, making his way to class in his tight-collared school uniform and hat astonished everyone.

In 1939, while still a "student," Soichiro resigned from the Hamamatsu branch of Art Shokai, handing the reins to employee Sueo Kawashima. He then joined Tokai Seiki Heavy Industries, a relatively well-known manufacturer of piston rings in Hamamatsu, immediately assuming the post of president.

At the end of his second year at the school, Soichiro was expelled for ignoring all of his exams. However, he simply decided that he would become an "unregistered student" and continued to attend classes for yet another year. For Soichiro, it was not the exams that mattered. He was there to learn what he needed for his work. After a long struggle, Soichiro learned what he needed about piston rings. He ended up being awarded a total of twenty-eight patents on the subject.

Fujisawa, on the other hand, was a true Tokyoite, born and raised in the Koishikawa section of the city. After graduating from high school, Fujisawa led an easygoing life, paying the bills by doing office tasks such as copying documents and the like. In 1934, Fujisawa began an apprenticeship at Mitsuwa Shokai, a small retailing company of ten employees that dealt in steel. As things turned out, the owner was drafted for the war, and Fujisawa gradually came to be entrusted with the management of the company.

In 1939, the same year that Soichiro completed his studies at the Hamamatsu School of Technology, Fujisawa pulled together 100,000 yen in capital and founded a tiny company with the grand-sounding name of Nihon Kiko Kenkyujo—the "Japan Mechanical Research Institute." Fujisawa's new company specialized in manufacturing blades for cutting tools, and one of their customers was the Nakajima Aircraft Company. Takeshima, who worked in Nakajima's procurement department, paid frequent visits to the company's subcontractors to check the quality of the parts they supplied and to advise on quality improvement. It was on one of these visits that Fujisawa and Takeshima first met.

Even in his young and carefree days, Fujisawa had dreamed of putting his own talents to the test by teaming up with an unrecognized genius. He knew that his own talents lay in securing capital and selling products, and so he intended from the very outset to remain a behind-the-scenes player rather than take center stage himself.

In 1942, during WWII, Tokai Seiki Heavy Industries became a munitions factory, manufacturing piston rings for ships, trucks, and aircraft, which it supplied to Toyota Motor Corporation and Nakajima Aircraft Company. As Tokai Seiki grew, Toyota Motor Corporation increased its investment in the company to forty percent. At the same time, Toyota's Taizo Ishikawa took over as president and Soichiro withdrew to the position of managing director.

In any event, Tokai Seiki grew into a large corporation with twelve million yen in capital and some two thousand workers, including draftees. Alas, just nine months before the end of the war, the Tokai Seiki factory was leveled in the Tokai Earthquake of December 1944 that claimed a total of some 1,000 lives in Hamamatsu and neighboring regions. Soichiro became fed up with the business, and in September 1945, one month after the end of the war, sold all of his shares to Ishida's company Toyota Industries for 450,000 yen, and became unemployed.

Soichiro called it his "human holiday." He spent a year doing nothing in particular. He purchased a drumful of medicinal alcohol, which he converted into synthetic *sake* and served to all his friends. During the day, he learned to play the traditional Japanese bamboo flute, or *shakuhachi*, and built machines for making salt and popsicles. He traded the salt he made with his electric-powered salt-processor for rice. He even spent some time as an instructor in science and technology for the Iwata Police Department. The nights, he usually spent drinking and partying.

Just as he had planned, Soichiro ended his "human holiday" a year after it had begun. In September of 1946, he founded a small business, which he called Honda Gijutsu Kenkyujo, or the Honda Technical Research Institute. The business specialized in manufacturing internal combustion engines and textile machinery. He built a small, shed-like factory on the spot where the Tokai Seiki factory had stood before it was razed during the war. Inside there was an old belt-driven lathe, and outside ten machine tools. The company started out as a typical small backstreet workshop, with a total of ten employees including Soichiro. The fact that Soichiro called it a "Research Institute" symbolized Soichiro's pride as an engineer.

The same year, Masaru Ibuka and Akio Morita joined forces to found Tokyo Tsushin Kogyo K.K., or the Tokyo Telecommunications Engineering Corporation, later to be known as Sony. Japan's two most famous post-war corporate successes were born at almost the exact same time.

Soichiro's secret ambition was to develop the world's first mechanical rotary loom. Hamamatsu had traditionally been known as the center of Japan's textile industry and Soichiro's mother, Mika, had been a master weaver, fully capable of repairing a loom on her own. Soichiro's passion for gadgets ran in the Honda family.

As the seat of the textile industry, Hamamatsu flourished after the end of the war thanks to what people referred to as the "gacha-man boom" ("gacha" signified the sound of a loom's shuttle, while "man" means ten thousand, the amount of money that could be made per run.) Soichiro saw a huge business potential in creating a rotary loom for the textile industry. But he quickly abandoned the idea after realizing just how much time and capital the process would require.

The "gacha-man boom" made quite a few people rich, but the public transportation system, on which the average citizen relied, remained a shambles from the war. People had a hard time just going shopping for food. Soichiro's attention was drawn to the engines used to generate power for the Mark 6 radio sets used by the Japanese Army during WWII. After the war, these radio sets had been abandoned and simply left to waste in the burnt-out ruins of the city. Soichiro came up with the idea of collecting these engines and modifying them so that they could be attached to bicycles. For a man who had started out by running an auto repair shop, the modifications were a piece of cake. As for fuel tanks, Soichiro made do with hot-water bottles.

Once the modifications were finished, Soichiro attached the engine to an old bicycle for testing. The engines, however, lacked precision. Moreover, due to lingering effects of wartime government control, Soichiro had no choice but to use a raw pine-resin fuel, which naturally didn't burn very well. As a result, the engines took well over a half an hour to get started.

Each motorized bicycle took a full day to build. Yet as unsatisfactory as they were, they still sold reasonably well as a means of civilian transportation. After Soichiro had made about five hundred or so of them, however, the free supply of engines, which were essential to their production, simply ran out.

By that time, Soichiro was completely obsessed about building motorized bicycles. He invented his own engine, which had an outwardly projecting cylinder head. Attached to a bicycle frame, it looked awkward, but it ran surprisingly well. Encouraged by this success, Soichiro next developed a rear-drive V-belt 2-stroke engine, which he dubbed the "A-Type."

The engine came to be known as the *bata-bata*, after the sound it made. The main customers were bicycle shop owners and shady black market dealers. The former put the *bata-bata* engines on their bicycles. Black market dealers, on the other hand, attached the engines to any sort of frame they could find, slapping on a pair of wheels taken from a trailer cart, and sold as many of these makeshift vehicles as they could. Even such precarious-looking vehicles could reach a speed of ten or twenty kilometers per hour, accompanied at all times by its loud and unmistakable "putt-putt" sound.

As products of their time, the *bata-bata*s were an astounding success, literally selling as quickly as they could be rolled off the assembly line. Soichiro's factory remained chronically out of stock. At the time, no single company produced both frames and engines. Soichiro decided he wanted to make a serious effort at creating a real motorcycle entirely on his own. And the place to do it, he knew, was Tokyo.

The slow-paced Hamamatsu lifestyle had never suited Soichiro's impatient disposition. Ever since his days at Art Shokai, he had spent his nights out on the town racing around in foreign cars and motorcycles with his young employees in tow, wearing his characteristic red shirt and shop overalls. The inevitable complaints from the neighbors didn't faze Soichiro in the slightest although they did embarrass his family.

Soichiro had saved some money, but it wasn't anywhere near the amount he would need to found a new motorcycle company from scratch in Tokyo. Around this time, Takeshima, who'd left his previous job after the war to join the Ministry of International Trade and Industry, came to Hamamatsu on business and unexpectedly dropped in on Soichiro. It was 1947, a year after Soichiro had founded his Research Institute.

"I'm great at building things," said Soichiro, "but what I need is money. I've had a few offers from the *gacha-man* crowd here in Hamamatsu, but these people invariably want a say in the business. I can't partner with people like that. I wonder if there's anyone in Tokyo who might be willing to put up the money." While filling Takeshima in on the latest developments of his business, Soichiro seized on the occasion to mention what was on his mind. He didn't harbor high hopes but figured he had nothing to lose by asking.

For his part, Takeshima didn't take the request particularly seriously either. But two years later, after running into Fujisawa in the still war-scarred streets of Tokyo's Shinbashi district, Takeshima remembered what Soichiro had said.

At the height of the war, Fujisawa had closed down his company and evacuated to the city of Nihonmatsu in Fukushima prefecture. A doctor had advised Fujisawa that the clean air of the countryside would be good for his ailing wife, and so Fujisawa had remained in Fukushima even after the end of war. He ran a small sawmill there.

Nevertheless, Fujisawa couldn't get the idea of making it big in Tokyo out of his mind. He went often to Tokyo for no particular reason and haunted the black markets in the Shinjuku and Shinbashi districts, eagerly looking for his chance. Even though Fujisawa didn't have any money of his own, Takeshima knew that Fujisawa possessed a unique talent for getting it from others. And since he had heard Fujisawa mention his dream of partnering up with a talented man more than once in the past, Takeshima suddenly remembered Soichiro and brought up the subject.

Soichiro knew nothing of Fujisawa, but Fujisawa, who had managed his own small machine factory before the war, had heard rumors of Soichiro, the "genius engineer" of Hamamatsu. And when Fujisawa had dealt with the Nakajima Aircraft Company, he remembered Takeshima telling him of "an interesting man in Hamamatsu called Soichiro Honda" whom "I'll introduce you when I have the chance."

"Count me in," Fujisawa had replied immediately on hearing about Soichiro again from Takeshima. "It's true that I don't have any money of my own, but you can rely on me to get Soichiro Honda whatever he needs."

By this time, however, Soichiro had all but forgotten his conversation with Takeshima and was concentrating on looking for ways to manufacture motorcycles without outside assistance. When it became possible to mass-produce the A-Type *bata-bata* engine, Soichiro began to think about incorporating his business. On September 24, 1948, when production reached two hundred units per month, Soichiro's factory officially became Honda Giken Kogyo (Honda Motor Company). The company was capitalized at one million yen and the number of employees had increased to twenty. Honda's father Gihei helped raise the necessary money by selling his nest egg, nearly ten thousand square meters of mountain timberland.

Soichiro named Honda's engines in alphabetical order, starting with the A-Type and followed by the B- and C-Types. The D-Type engine, completed in 1949, was a 98cc, chain-driven, two-stroke engine with a two-speed transmission. At the same time, Honda also designed and manufactured the motorcycle's frame. When the first complete prototype was unveiled, someone remarked that it was really "like a dream" to see the frame, tires, and engine all in one machine. Inspired by the comment, Soichiro named his newest product—a symbol of his own dreams and hopes—the Dream D-Type.

The prototype was an instant sensation wherever it was shown. But the consequences of the U.S. Occupation's fiscal austerity program, known as the Dodge Plan, were sweeping the country, and the Japanese economy continued to slide further and further into recession. Massive cuts in spending and inflation squeezed the money markets. Honda's engine sales slipped drastically. The company began to miss payments to suppliers and to have problems paying its employees, eventually having to resort to paying them in installments. It was at this time that Takeshima proposed to Soichiro that he meet a man by the name of Fujisawa.

Soichiro's company may have been small, but he was a fiercely independent man and the owner of his own business. Yet Soichiro had once run a company with some two thousand people working under him, albeit under the wartime government-controlled economy. Under such circumstances, Fujisawa would normally have been the one making the trip, to Hamamatsu, to see Soichiro. However, the younger man deliberately avoided doing so. If they met in Hamamatsu, Soichiro's home ground, it could tip the balance of power between them in favor of Soichiro from the very outset. Despite not having any money of his own to invest, Fujisawa was determined to become nothing less than a full and equal partner.

Soichiro, for his part, couldn't care less where the meeting took place. He knew that his company was running out of money and that if he didn't get an infusion of capital soon, it would be all over. Soichiro was eager to meet with anyone who could provide the necessary funds or, failing that, had a talent for bringing in other investors. If that person wanted to meet on his own ground, Soichiro was ready to oblige.

In the end, Fujisawa and Soichiro's first meeting took place in August 1949 at Takeshima's home in Tokyo.

"The transportation system may change in form, but it will never disappear," Soichiro told Fujisawa. "Even if we form a partnership, I'm the engineer and I don't want you meddling in my decisions about what to make. But in return, I'll leave everything having to do with money firmly in your hands."

"Understood," replied Fujisawa. "I'll take full responsibility when it comes to money, and I'll leave you to your work. I'm only interested in creating the best possible working conditions for you. You're the president, so I'll follow your lead. But promise me that you won't be short-sighted when it comes to making decisions."

And so Soichiro and Fujisawa pledged from the start to maintain a hands-off attitude about their respective domains. Fujisawa respected Soichiro's engineering genius, while Soichiro accepted Fujisawa as a quick-witted financial strategist. Soichiro was forty-two years old; Fujisawa was thirty-eight. It could hardly be called an early start for either of them. But a deal was struck that very day, and Fujisawa joined the ranks of Honda.

It was not long before the two men visited each other's homes and discovered that they were near-total opposites in every respect from their backgrounds and previous careers to their personalities and individual characteristics.

Soichiro was a rather small man with thinning hair. Fujisawa, on the other hand, was tall, sturdy, and featured a bushy head of hair. Soichiro's classmates had dubbed him "Black-Nosed Weasel" when he was in elementary school, as he was fleet of foot and his nose perpetually blackened with soot. Fujisawa couldn't stand anything having to do with athletics.

Soichiro was frank, sociable and extroverted. Witticisms poured from his mouth like bullets from a machine gun. No matter how rough the man's words, he never seemed to ruffle his listeners. Somewhat paradoxically, however, he was also a shy man, perhaps not only by nature but also as a result of his going independent at such a young age and handling so many rough experiences along the way. In a sense, he knew how to run a business better than many a man of business.

On the other hand, Fujisawa, who prided himself on being a businessman through and through, was a meticulous, logical thinker who always had a severe air about him. He made it his policy to avoid public notice whenever possible. Whereas Soichiro was loved all the more for exposing his weaknesses to the world, Fujisawa kept his weak points hidden from public view as much as he could.

Had the relationship between the two been hierarchical, Soichiro would have undoubtedly chosen Fujisawa as his successor at an early stage. Yet, Fujisawa had chosen not to aspire to become president of Honda but rather to be Soichiro's business partner; his ambition was to realize his own dreams through the genius of Soichiro. That was essentially why a limit was placed initially on the period of their cooperation.

If Fujisawa had merely been supporting Soichiro, Honda would have turned out far differently than it did. In the end, it was Soichiro and Fujisawa's deftness at blending their two independent performances into a single role that led to the creation of the Honda myth.

In October 1949, two months after his first meeting with Soichiro, Fujisawa sold his sawmill business in Nihonmatsu and came to Tokyo to begin working for Honda. In November, Honda doubled its capital to two million yen. Fujisawa put up half of the new money, 500,000 yen, and, with a twenty-five percent stake in the business, became a major shareholder in the company. From that moment on, Honda was no longer a family business run by the Honda family; it had become a joint enterprise that might have been called "Honda Tech and Fujisawa Trading Co."

1949 was a turning point for Japan. Swimmer Hironoshin Furuhashi set a new world record in the 1,500-meter freestyle at the U.S. National Swimming Competition, and scientist Hideki Yukawa received the Nobel Prize in physics. These events restored pride to a Japanese people who had been crushed by the shock of defeat in WWII. Singer Ichiro Fujiyama's jaunty tune *Aoi Sanmyaku* ("The Green Mountains") became a major hit, symbolizing the country's emergence from the turmoil of the post-war era. Before the war, Fujiyama had driven a Renault—which was at the height of its popularity at the time—and made a point of stopping by Art Shokai for a tune-up whenever he had a concert in Hamamatsu. It has been said that the streets outside Art Shokai used to be crammed with people hoping for a glimpse of the famous singer.

Upon joining Honda, Fujisawa immediately became "managing director," which meant he had the authority to represent the company, and which put him in the same rank as Soichiro's younger brother Benjiro. Benjiro, six years younger than Soichiro, was Soichiro's right-hand man. After graduating from elementary school, Benjiro moved to Tokyo and, following in his brother's footsteps, begun an apprenticeship at Art Shokai. Once he had completed his training, he moved back to Hamamatsu and helped Soichiro at the Art Shokai branch there.

Fujisawa's first task at Honda was to establish a sales office in Tokyo for the company. In the spring of 1950, he rented an old house in the Kyobashi area with a total floor space of around fifty square meters and achieved this long-sought goal. The Tokyo office was charged with developing new markets in the Kanto, Koshinetsu, and Tohoku regions of Japan. Fujisawa bought some used desks and installed a phone line. The next thing he needed to do was to look for sales staff, but since he couldn't spare the money to put want ads in the newspapers, he relied on the free public employment office.

Soichiro remained in Hamamatsu with Honda's forty-six other employees to focus on improving the Dream model. Soichiro remained the idea man, but it was the young Kiyoshi Kawashima, his assistant, who now drew up the plans and blueprints.

Kawashima had joined Honda in 1948—when it was still called a "research institute"—directly upon graduating from the Hamamatsu College of Technology (formerly Hamamatsu School of Technology and now the Faculty of Engineering of Shizuoka University). Jobs were scarce at the time. Kawashima's father was the chief official at one of Hamamatsu's hospitals, and it was through a friend of his that he had landed his job at the early incarnation of Honda. Kawashima had known of Soichiro's reputation as the "local inventor" but knew nothing about the Research Institute itself. He had no idea whether it was a corporation or a personal enterprise or even what type of research went on there. The friend of Kawashima's father, who had helped him get the job, ran an automobile repair shop near the family house, and it was there that Kawashima found out that Soichiro's house was only about 200 meters away from his own. The truth was that Kawashima and Soichiro lived virtually around the block from each other.

Kawashima's interview was held at Soichiro's house, rather than at the factory that was the Research Institute. The two men sat across from one another over a *kotatsu*, a traditional Japanese heater-table.

"I can't pay you much right now, but I promise you that one day we'll make our own motorcycles!" said Soichiro, launching into a passionate speech outlining his hopes and dreams for his company. Kawashima was hired on the spot. He became Honda's twelfth employee.

Fujisawa had been convinced that Honda had a hit on its hands the moment he had set eyes on Soichiro's Dream D-Type, and it was this conviction that had driven him to open a Tokyo office. Fujisawa managed to secure two million yen in loans from the Japanese government's U.S. Aid counter fund, and, using this as seed money to expand the factory and purchase more equipment, set up a production plan for the D-Type. Although the engines would still be made in Hamamatsu for the time being, Soichiro and Fujisawa planned to open a factory in Tokyo to assemble the final product. In fact, Soichiro was itching to leave Hamamatsu as soon as possible.

The end of the war signaled the break-up of the industrial clans known as *zaibatsu* and the privatization of the Japanese economy. However, Japanese corporations continued to struggle through the after-effects of the deflation policy advocated by the Occupation's Dodge plan. The return of pre-war labor leaders from the battlefield led to frequent labor disputes across the country. In 1949 and 1950 alone, more than 1,100 companies, mostly in the manufacturing industries, went bankrupt and 510,000 people lost their jobs.

In May of 1950, the year following the opening of Honda's Tokyo sales office, Toyota Motor Corporation conducted a mass layoff of a thousand employees, exacerbating labor woes and causing their labor union to launch an indefinite strike. Founder and president Kiichiro Toyoda took responsibility and announced his resignation, and the union finally gave in and accepted the layoffs. The responsibility for the company's future fell squarely upon Taizo Ishida, loyal supporter of the Toyoda family and former president of Toyoda Automatic Loom Works, who took over in Toyoda's stead. In the end, the bank agreed to finance Toyota on the conditions that the founder resign and that the company's manufacturing and sales operations be separated, and Toyota only narrowly missed bankruptcy.

As Honda was still a tiny company that no one could be sure would still be in business the next day, such goings-on at the larger corporations held little interest for Soichiro and Fujisawa. They usually worked separately in Hamamatsu and Tokyo, but Fujisawa impatiently waited for Soichiro to visit the Tokyo office, and whenever he did, the two inevitably stayed up all through the night discussing the future of their company. This was the first time they began joking about a "Honda cult."

"Honda-san, you're really good at convincing others to go along with your schemes, no matter how far-fetched they may be. I mean, you're a genius. I don't know how you do it, but you've sure got the charisma. If our company doesn't make it, we should start a cult instead. I'll get the money. You can be the leader. And you know, I think we might actually make more money from prayer offerings than from sales. Who knows? It might be easier than running a company!" joked Fujisawa.

"Making money off of religion is wrong!" Soichiro countered. "But if I did start a cult, I wouldn't be your average guru. I'd advocate thinking logically about every aspect of life. Instead of preaching about the mysteries of life, I'd offer ideas with universal validity that any modern person could understand."

Whenever the two met, Soichiro always told Fujisawa that he wanted to make Honda the world's top motorcycle manufacturer. Fujisawa didn't pay much attention at first, passing it off as a mere dream of Soichiro's. But the more Soichiro talked about it, the more realistic it began to sound. Eventually, Fujisawa began to feel that Honda really did have a shot at becoming the world's best. *My job is laying the tracks for the locomotive that is Soichiro's dream. If I make them strong enough, all he'll need to do is shoot down the rails at full speed. We can't lose!*

The Korean War broke out on June 25, two weeks after Toyota president Kiichiro Toyoda's resignation. The U.S. military immediately placed orders for nearly 10,000 heavy trucks with Toyota, Nissan, and Isuzu, lifting Toyota out of the red. America's special procurement demands for the war effort were like a ray of light for the Japanese economy. Naturally, this also meant an increased demand for motorcycles.

Fujisawa seized this opportunity. In the fall of that same year, and without even telling Soichiro, Fujisawa purchased an old, 1,485-square-meter sewing-machine factory in Tokyo's Kita ward to start up a Tokyo factory for the Honda Motor Company. Money was always in short supply at Honda. Fujisawa secured 400,000 yen in government subsidies from a MITI fund for bicycle manufacturers in October, and another 100,000 yen for promoting innovations in bicycle engineering in December. Even then, Fujisawa lacked the capital to put the business into full swing.

Fujisawa secured more money by canvassing his extensive black market connections. As Kiyoshi Kawashima would later recall, Fujisawa resorted to everything short of outright fraud and thievery to secure funding. Traditionally, Honda was supposed to invest in the shops that dealt in their products. Fujisawa instead squeezed them for more money, using Honda stock as security. He borrowed extensively from shady black market brokers and even from Chinese merchants he'd met through his contacts from his days as a broker. Honda began exporting the Dream series to Okinawa, the Philippines, and Taiwan as early as 1952—less out of a sense of globalism than out of a necessity to clear its debts.

During this time, Tokyo Telecommunications Engineering Corporation (now known as Sony) also faced a financial shortfall. But the founder Masaru Ibuka had a patron, a man by the name of Kodo Nomura, author of the phenomenally popular *Zenigata Heiji* detective series. Nomura had been the go-between in Ibuka's marriage and had also contributed a considerable sum towards the establishment of the company, so whenever Tokyo Telecommunications Engineering Corporation found itself in trouble, Ibuka turned to Nomura for help. Honda, unfortunately, had no such patron. The responsibility for anything having to do with money lay squarely upon Fujisawa's shoulders.

Honda workers moved engines from the Hamamatsu factory to Tokyo, where they began to assemble the Dream motorcycles starting in November at a rate of 300 units per month. In 1952, Soichiro finally realized his dream of moving both his home and main office to Tokyo. He locked himself away with his assistant Kawashima in a tiny room not much larger than four square meters in a corner of the Tokyo factory. When they emerged, they had created an all-new four-stroke OHV (overhead valve) engine with an integrated transmission.

Soichiro's OHV engine was as much of a breakthrough as the CVCC (compound vortex controlled combustion) engine would be for Honda's automobiles years later. Up to that point, motorcycles and automobiles used flathead engines, with cylinders mounted on the sides. But it was impossible to improve the compression ratio of the engine with this design. The OHV, on the other hand, offered a boost in compression ratio, allowed the combustion chamber to be designed in any shape, and promised double the horsepower to boot. It was a true stroke of genius.

Whenever Soichiro finished building a prototype for a new product, he inevitably called Fujisawa into the factory to ask for his opinion.

"What do you think of this latest invention?" asked Soichiro.

Fujisawa took a seat atop the prototype and gripped the handlebars. "This looks great! Our customers have been waiting for a motorcycle like this. I can already see the smiles on their faces! This is going to be a hit—you just leave sales and marketing up to me!" Fujisawa lavished praise on the design. Only after satisfying Soichiro's vanity did Fujisawa begin to make suggestions. "But, Honda-san, looking at it from the customer's point of view, if you improve this part, I think we'll sell even more. I know you can do it. I have faith in you."

Fujisawa knew just how to talk to Soichiro. Now it was a matter of pride. Soichiro found himself compelled to meet Fujisawa's demands.

As expected, the Dream D-Type was a hit. In 1951, Honda unveiled a new-model Dream based on Soichiro's 146cc OHV engine. Demand and production only increased as Soichiro designed improved models with larger displacements of 175 and 200cc. The Dream series featured high torque and horsepower as their selling point.

Fujisawa's sales philosophy could be summed up in a single sentence: make a higher quality product, and customers will buy it even if they have to wait a while for it.

"Every Honda motorcycle is designed by the president himself. Every aspect of our company's products outshines those of our competitors. I know our customers will understand!" Fujisawa exhorted his salesmen, encouraging them and sending them all over the country to cultivate new sales routes. The salesmen created their own pamphlets for Honda products, received business travel expense accounts equivalent to four or five months of their normal salary, and stayed out "in the field" for extended periods of time. Each salesman personally met the owners of motorcycle and bicycle shops in their sales areas, negotiating face to face to build up Honda's customer base dealer by dealer.

Whenever owners agreed to sell Honda motorcycles in their shop, the salesman asked for a down payment on the spot and immediately contacted the main office to have the products sent out. Then, the salesman would extend his business trip by applying the down payment toward his travel expenses. Thanks to the tireless efforts of its sales force, Honda eventually managed to establish a system capable of selling a thousand motorcycles a month, despite having very little money at the time.

While his salesmen crossed the islands of Japan, Soichiro poured his efforts into making an improved powered bicycle. The result was the 50cc "Cub F-Type," which featured a white fuel tank mounted atop its rear fender and a bright red engine at the center of the rear wheel. Red and white were Soichiro's favorite colors.

Soichiro's first creation, the A-Type engine, used a rubber V-belt in the center of the bicycle frame, which often led to complaints of stained clothes. Needless to say, these vehicles were totally unsuitable for women. For the Cub, Soichiro solved the problem by moving the engine to the rear of the frame.

At the time, some 120 separate manufacturers of engines for bicycles, most located in and around Hamamatsu, competed for market share in Japan. Honda's rapid success in this sea of competitors can be attributed to the undeniable uniqueness of Soichiro's products. The Dream was the first serious motorcycle to be produced in Japan.

Although the Dream series allowed Honda to establish a firm marketing base, big, showy foreign motorcycles, such as those made by U.S. manufacturers Harley-Davidson and Indian, continued to dominate the Japanese marketplace. The foreign products were lavishly made using abundant amounts of material and were resistant to dents. However, they were also too large to pass through the narrow streets in many Japanese towns. While they may have looked like the perfect vehicle for police officers to use in tracking down traffic violators, they were all but unusable for people like the local *soba* noodle deliveryman who had to make his way through narrow alleys. In addition, they were extremely expensive, making them status symbols that were simply beyond the means of the average Japanese consumer.

What Soichiro wanted was a motorcycle for everyone, a machine suited to the latest trends and designed to meet actual demand. The Cub was his answer. Technology has always been Honda's main selling point, and Soichiro's innovations were always directly linked to people's work-a-day needs. In this respect, the ideas were actually quite simple and proved that Soichiro was an engineer who knew how to "bring in the dough."

Because the Cub was simply a bicycle with an auxiliary engine, it was not intended to interest those who craved speed and excitement. Fujisawa's hope was that it would become popular as a means of transportation for the general public. Since it was inexpensive and easy to handle, there was no reason why it shouldn't sell well. But of course, good products alone did not guarantee good sales.

Fujisawa dreamed of using the Cub to realize Honda's great leap to the next level. The first Cubs hit dealerships in May of 1952. In the two months of June and July, Honda shipped a total of 5,000 units, of which complaints were received from consumers for only three.

Japan was enjoying a consumer-spending boom as a result of the U.S. military's Korean War-driven procurement orders and increased production. Fujisawa was convinced that the boom would continue for a while. *If we can expand our assembly line and marketing outlet, we should be able to move at least 10,000 units a month.*

If Honda relied solely on its operant marketing routes, however, there was no way it could sell 10,000 units a month, no matter how great the potential demand. In order to dramatically increase their marketing outlets in a short period of time, Honda needed to mobilize an enormous sales force to reinforce the company's sales networks. But that would involve huge sums of money, which Honda, having just made the transition from a tiny cottage industry to a medium-sized business, just didn't have. Even Fujisawa, with all his money-making prowess, couldn't possibly raise all the necessary capital in one go.

How might Honda sell large quantities of its products without spending excess money in the process? Fujisawa hit upon the idea of using direct mail to contact each of the some 55,000 bicycle shops scattered throughout the country. The letter he composed read as follows.

"After the Russo-Japanese War (1904-05), instead of meekly repairing chains and fixing flat tires, your ancestors courageously decided to sell imported bicycles. That was the origin of your business. Now that World War II is over, things have changed. Your customers are looking for bicycles with engines. We at Honda have made just such an engine. We fully guarantee the quality of our products. Please reply if you are interested."

A surprising number of shops—some 30,000, in fact—responded. Fujisawa replied with another letter.

"We thank you for your interest in our products. To begin with, we will be distributing one motorcycle per shop. The wholesale price is 19,000 yen and the suggested retail price is 25,000 yen, which should yield a profit of 6,000 yen. We request, however, that you make your payment first, via either postal transfer or transfer to our designated bank."

Because Honda was still virtually unknown, Fujisawa knew it would be difficult to convince shopkeepers to pay in advance, even if they were interested in the new product. In order to address this issue, he persuaded the Kyobashi branch of Mitsubishi Bank, Honda's principal lender, to help by sending out a letter signed by the manager guaranteeing Honda's credibility and requesting customers to send their remittances to Honda through the bank's Kyobashi branch.

Thanks in part to the bank's letter of support, Honda immediately received replies from 5,000 shops and, in the end, 13,000 shops sent in their payments. By the fall of 1952, Honda had built an assembly line capable of manufacturing 6,500 Cubs per month. Honda's market share had grown to seventy percent. It was undeniable that the Cub had uncovered a broad base of demand and had established a firm foundation for make-to-stock manufacturing as well as the mass production of motorcycles in Japan.

Every Cub was purchased in advance, so there was money coming into Honda's account every day. Payments for the Dream were received, on the average, about two months after the products were shipped from the factory. Honda's payments to its parts suppliers, on the other hand, were on a five-month cycle. Fujisawa finally had some money in his hands.

Soichiro was making steady progress developing new products as well. Designs were completed for the Benly, an all-new 90cc motorcycle with an OHV engine, and the Juno, a scooter whose frame incorporated plastic components. Thanks to the combination of Soichiro's engineering skills and Fujisawa's marketing acumen, Honda found itself well on the way to becoming a major manufacturer.

"Would you believe, Honda-san," said Fujisawa one day, "my six-year old son seems to think I'm some master counterfeiter! My wife tells me it's easy enough for him to understand what *you* do, since you made the Dream and the Cub. But he just can't figure out what I do at Honda. Every morning when I leave the house I tell my wife, 'I'm off to the bank to produce some money!' and my son actually believes I print fake bills or something."

In those days, Fujisawa was on such an incredibly busy work schedule that even his young son had noticed.

By 1953, Honda was a medium-size manufacturer with sales of four hundred million yen a month. The company bought roughly 325 square meters of land in Yaesu, near Tokyo station, where it built a two-story office building with a total floor space of around 580 square meters. Honda's headquarters was also transferred from Hamamatsu to Tokyo. The number of employees increased from 216 in 1952 to 1,337 in 1953—more than six times in a single year.

Even in the brand new office building in Tokyo, the only Honda employees who wore suits were those who worked in administration. The rest of the employees, including the salesmen, wore the same overalls as any shop worker. The main reason for this was that motor shop owners in their overalls and their wives with scarves wrapped around their heads would often visit the office in person to make their payments, taking advantage of the opportunity to see the new Honda headquarters.

Sometimes new employees, who had dreamed of wearing smart business suits to work, expressed reluctance to wearing overalls. Whenever Fujisawa came into contact with such workers, he blew his top.

"Just who do you think you are? Honda's core clients are the shopkeepers who sell our products to customers. They wear overalls, so it's only natural that you wear them too. If the wife of a client sits Japanese-style on her knees on the sofa, you do the same!"

Michihiro Nishida and Takao Shirai joined Honda in 1950, followed by Kihachiro Kawashima in 1951. Together with Kiyoshi Kawashima, the four would later be known as the "big four" who collectively managed Honda after Soichiro and Fujisawa's retirement.

Nishida had been a technical officer in the Imperial Japanese Army. After the war, he had taken a job at Nasu Aluminum, which manufactured pots and pans under the Nigiriya label, but had found that he didn't get along with his fellow workers. Nishida quit and founded a small aluminum-finishing factory on his own. It eventually grew into a company with seventy employees, but in the end money troubles led to bankruptcy. Unemployed at the age of twenty-seven, he swallowed his pride and turned in an application at the local public employment office.

It was the first time Honda had actively looked for new talent. Fujisawa conducted the interview himself. Nishida was the only applicant considered, and he was hired at once. He was the first employee to join the company without having any private connections.

The next batch of employees—Shirai, Kihachiro Kawashima, and Oka-mura—however, were basically recruited through personal connections. This was because the want ads Honda had placed in newspapers and at the public employment office had failed to turn up enough attractive prospects, and the company had no choice but to make use of its personal networks. Hiroshi Takeshima, who had introduced Soichiro and Fujisawa to one another, also joined Honda as managing director in 1953.

Shirai came on board right after Nishida. After graduating from college, he had worked first for the Toyo Steel Corporation and later for the Japanese National Textile Corporation. Kihachiro Kawashima had been employed at Toshiba and the Tokai Petroleum Corporation. Noboru Okamura, who would become Honda's second chairman, worked as an English teacher in his hometown on the island of Shikoku before joining Honda in 1951.

After becoming chairman many years later, Okamura actively sponsored meetings with securities analysts in the U.S. and Europe to explain Honda's value, in an attempt to secure low-cost funding. On those occasions, he would read out loud a summary of Honda's rise to world-class manufacturer. But Okamura, who had joined Honda when it was still a fledgling company, could barely manage to choke back tears, overcome by just how far the company had come from its humble beginnings.

Hideo Sugiura, who would become Honda's first chairman, joined the firm in 1953 after responding to a want ad in the newspaper. After graduating from college, Sugiura had difficulty finding employment and joined his father's 150-employee company. The work didn't suit him, however, and Sugiura soldiered on an unhappy employee for some time before finally deciding, at the age of twenty-eight, to leave the family business for something new. He didn't care what kind of company the new one would be. It was purely by chance that Sugiura happened across Honda's want-ad looking for "high-level hires." It was only a small ad—not much more than the standard three lines—and the truth was that "high-level" simply meant having a university degree, but Sugiura found himself sufficiently intrigued to apply for the position.

Sugiura traveled to Honda's factory in Shirako in Saitama prefecture without having any clue as to what Honda really did. He saw men clad in overalls with license plates strapped to their waists barreling past on motorcycles in the direction of the Kawagoe Highway.

"Is Honda a motorcycle manufacturer?" Sugiura asked the interviewer sheepishly.

"You came here without even knowing that? Well, it's okay, I guess. I just started here a month ago myself. Our company is still too small to have its own test course. So we use temporary license plates and take our products for a spin on Kawagoe Highway for final testing."

After a tour of the factory, the interviewer asked Sugiura if he would be interested in joining the company. Sugiura, quite taken with the factory's energetic atmosphere, replied "Yeah" without giving too much thought to the matter. He was hired on the spot.

Honda began hiring university graduates on a regular basis in 1953, but even then there was no official recruiting procedure. Due to a job shortage, Satoshi Okubo (third chairman) and Yuhei Chijiiwa (later managing director) were having a difficult time finding employment. With their graduation dates rapidly approaching, both of them managed to secure introductions through personal contacts such as the local motor dealer and ended up knocking on Honda's door.

In those days, there was no written exam. Applicants merely went through a simple interview with Honda's head of administration, himself a recent addition. New recruits were told then and there that they were hired and to start working the next day, if they could. Okubo later recalled that when he was being given his tour of the factory floor, the interviewer had acted so boastful and self-important that he had asked the man how long he had been working for Honda. The interviewer, much as in Sugiura's case, replied: "Since yesterday." In contrast to the rest of the country, which had sunk back into recession after the temporary boost due to the Korean War, Honda was doing so well that it actually suffered a shortage of employees.

Honda finally introduced an official recruitment procedure for university graduates, consisting of a written exam and interview held in a rented office, in the fall of 1953. Based on this procedure, twenty-eight university graduates joined the company in the spring of 1954. Among them were Tadashi Kume, who would become Honda's third president, Koichiro Yoshizawa, later Honda's fourth chairman, Kazuo Nakagawa, who would become vice president, and Takao Harada, who would become a senior managing director of the company.

Kume loved cars and had unsuccessfully tried to land a job at Toyota and Nissan. In light of the poor economy, and reasoning that there really wasn't much of a difference between cars and motorcycles, he decided to take Honda's exam. It was held at a later date than the others.

Yoshizawa too was fascinated by major manufacturers, but like Kume, hadn't succeeded in securing a position at one before he was accepted at Honda.

3

Soichiro always gave the same personal welcome speech to the newcomers: "Other companies may not appreciate you so much at first because you're young and have little experience in the working world. But Honda is different. We have high hopes for you. And just remember, if you ever want to leave Honda, you're free to walk away at any time."

In those days, Honda had not yet established a place for itself in Japan's corporate world and Soichiro and Fujisawa were still practically unknown as businessmen. More than a few workers took positions at Honda because they hadn't been able to find employment at the larger companies or hadn't enjoyed the working conditions at the more established firms. Some of these newly hired employees, however, quickly left Honda, unable to adjust to its distinct "apprentice" culture. Tougher youths, however, quietly dedicated themselves to their work, watching and learning from the founders.

Fujisawa's direct mail approach had established a solid sales network. Production for the Dream had increased to over 1,000 units a month, for the Cub to over 5,000 units a month. Even then, the motorcycles sold like pancakes. Some industry experts believed that the motorcycle was nothing more than a fad and would eventually disappear. Fujisawa paid no mind to such naysayers and continued his aggressive sales and marketing tactics.

2.4 million motorcycles in West Germany, 1.5 million each in England and Italy, but only 200,000 in Japan. That's raw potential. We have 1,400 employees at Honda and we own eight cars, six three-wheeled vehicles and 132 motorcycles. We built the motorcycles ourselves, but they're worth more than twenty million yen. If they didn't generate more value than that, we wouldn't still be owning them. Honda grew because our salesmen put those motorcycles to good use. There's no way we'd have gotten this far if they'd been on bicycles. Automation, speed—that's the trend. If we can keep making products that meet the needs of the times, and if the public recognizes it, there won't ever be a dip in demand for motorcycles. They aren't fad items.

Soichiro also diligently kept up his efforts to develop new products. Once on the market, these products promised to bring in revenues of over one hundred million yen a month. Cash flow was improving. Honda had more engineers and salesmen than ever, thanks to its aggressive recruitment of mid-career workers, and the company was now hiring university graduates—the prospective leaders of Honda—on a regular basis as well.

The one remaining challenge was how to expand Honda's manufacturing facilities. Honda's sales were flying high at the moment thanks to the Cub, but competition at the retail end was as fierce as ever, and Fujisawa knew that if Honda relaxed for even a second, it would lose market share. The only way that Honda would be able to establish a solid business foundation was for it to invent products so unique that they couldn't be duplicated by rival companies and to cut costs through mass production and through use of the latest in cutting-edge equipment, while increasing the company's competitiveness in the process.

At the time, Japanese machine-tool technology was ten or fifteen years behind that of the United States and Europe. If Fujisawa wanted the latest in cutting-edge equipment, he was going to have to import. Not only did Japanese machine tools perform poorly, they also cost a small fortune, so using them wouldn't help cut costs at all. In terms of both efficiency and cost, Honda would never be able to compete on the world market. This was no time to adhere to the old adage "a talented man isn't particular about what tools he uses." Fujisawa decided to "buy time with money" and made Soichiro a bold proposition:

"Honda-san, now's the time to expand our facilities in a big way. You could personally visit the United States and look for good equipment there. Buy as much as you need. I'll take care of the money."

Around the same time, in April 1952, Soichiro had received a Blue Ribbon Medal of Honor—given to individuals who have made prosperous efforts in the areas of public welfare and education—for the contribution that his various inventions, including his compact engines, had made to Japanese society. Soichiro, who was only forty-five years old, was elated. If Soichiro and Fujisawa had been employed by a large corporation, they would still have been section chiefs at their age. Instead they were competent entrepreneurs and owners of their own mid-sized corporation.

Following Fujisawa's advice, Soichiro left for the United States, the "land of machines," on his own, six months later in November 1952. During his month-long stay, Soichiro spent three hundred million yen and purchased a hundred high-tech machine tools. For some reason, his purchases included a spiral bevel gear cutter from the Green Corporation, a piece of equipment not required for manufacturing motorcycles. In January of the following year, Kiyoshi Kawashima, who had been promoted to engineer, flew to Germany and Switzerland and spent another one hundred and fifty million yen on additional pieces of equipment.

Back in Tokyo, Fujisawa took action as well. After establishing a Honda branch in Nagoya in February 1952, he opened offices in Takamatsu prefecture in Shikoku, in Osaka, and in Fukuoka prefecture in Kyushu, the southernmost of Japan's main islands. He also took out a loan to purchase a used factory in the town of Shirako in Saitama prefecture. When Fujisawa consulted Soichiro about the renovations, Soichiro made only one comment.

"We'll use the factory as is, but do me a favor and put in flush toilets. If you don't make the places people have to use on a daily basis nice and clean, we'll never be able to create beautiful products."

As the man in charge of the company's budget, Fujisawa knew there was a limit to what he could spend and certainly had other priorities in mind, but, of course, he couldn't refuse such a relatively small request from Soichiro when the latter seemed to consider it so important to his work as an inventor.

In January 1953, Fujisawa bought more land in Saitama prefecture—nearly 100,000 square meters in the city of Yamato—for construction of a second factory. In July, he bought another 66,000 sq.m. parcel of land, a former military airbase in Hamamatsu, for yet another factory. Construction on the three factories began at roughly the same time. By the end of it, Honda had invested a total of some 1.5 billion yen in their plants and equipment, an astounding sum in an era when major manufacturers such as Nissan and Toyota spent an average of only five hundred to six hundred million yen a year.

Honda had just increased its capital in 1952 from six million to fifteen million yen. It had, in fact, spent a hundred times the value of the company in capital investment. If anything at all had gone wrong with Fujisawa's strategy, it would have spelled immediate bankruptcy. Fujisawa had staked the life of his company on the investments.

The shipments of machine tools that Soichiro and Kiyoshi Kawashima had purchased abroad arrived in Japan in the first few months of 1953. Fortified with the new equipment, the new factories opened one after the other over that summer and fall. The production lines for the Dream and the Cub were moved from Tokyo to the three new factories, while the old Tokyo factory in Jujo was converted into an employee training facility.

Finally, after thorough preparations, the Benly scooter hit the marketplace in August that year, and, in December, Honda increased its capital four-fold to sixty million yen. The following January, 1954, around the same time that the new Juno scooter went on sale, Honda made a public offering of stock on the Tokyo Stock Exchange. It was glorious time for the company. Not a single employee doubted that Honda had a bright future ahead of it.

In October 1952, just after he and Fujisawa had decided to make the massive investment in equipment and facilities, Soichiro had climbed atop an old orange crate to deliver his manifesto to the Tokyo factory workers.

"Good products go beyond national boundaries. 'The best in Japan' means nothing when you are only comparing yourself to others in the Japanese market. The minute a better foreign product is imported that kind of 'number one' no longer means a thing to anyone. If you're not 'number one in the world,' you can't be 'number one in Japan.' That's why we have to become the top manufacturer of motorcycles in the entire world!"

Soichiro expanded on the same ideas in the March 1954 issue of Honda's corporate newsletter, published just months after the opening of the three new factories:

"Today, Honda has become the focus of attention in the motorcycle industry. I strongly believe that, within the next few years, we will become the world's top manufacturer of motorcycles." It was an astonishing thought, but neither Soichiro nor Fujisawa had any doubt that once their enormous capital investment began producing results, Honda would become not only number one in Japan, but one of the world's top motorcycle manufacturers, if not actually number one in the world.

Soichiro had been raised as a blacksmith's son. In the world of apprenticeships, young apprentices spent years of long, hard training under the direction of their masters, slowly mastering the required skills through repeated practice. There, a person's value was measured only by the skills he possessed. When Soichiro ran the Hamamatsu branch of Art Shokai, he had always kept a careful eye on his workers, and if he ever caught one slacking off, he didn't hesitate to throw a wrench or a hammer in his direction. Soichiro's severe and even violent style had resulted in a huge employee turnover back then.

Soichiro's attitude at Honda was hardly any different. Clad in his blue overalls, he personally prowled the conveyor lines to keep an eye on his employees. He rarely hesitated to hurl epithets—or objects—if he found workers using their tools in a careless manner. In one of his fits of rage, he was known to have hit a worker in the head with the corner of a triangular ruler, or even to have hurt an employee on the receiving end of the spanner he had thrown. Such stories, as well as the fact that Soichiro constantly told his employees that they should "work for themselves, not the company," reveal that he looked upon his relationship with his employees as being not much different from that of a master and his apprentices.

Soichiro's weak point was his short fuse and tendency to fly off the handle; he could barely control himself once he got angry, and things often spiraled out of control. Whenever he got really upset at an employee, he would inevitably end up shouting, "I want your letter of resignation! Get out of here!" Confused by the sudden leap in logic, some factory workers even took his words at face value and brought their letters to his office. By that time, however, Soichiro would have cooled off and have forgotten his own words, so he would offer a direct apology and that would be the end of the affair. While Soichiro's fiery personality led to his being dubbed "Thunderer" by fearful employees, he was at the same time frank and approachable, even to the newest and youngest workers in the factory. And so it wasn't at all uncommon to hear his employees refer to him affectionately as the "Old Man."

Despite his seeming spontaneity, however, Soichiro had his own personal philosophy when it came to yelling at employees. When it was a single employee he was chewing out, and if the employee had potential or else was really incompetent, he always left the target a way out. If there were two or more people who needed disciplining, Soichiro knew that the rest of the plant would hear of his outburst by the end of the day and calculated his words and actions accordingly. He picked the easiest targets and reprimanded them for making the types of mistakes that anyone could make. Those unfortunate employees who were targeted were simply chosen as examples for all to take note of.

Fujisawa, for his part, scared the workers just as much as Soichiro. Employees practically ran in terror when they saw his angrily bulging eyes and wide-open mouth. They nicknamed him "Godzilla."

Fujisawa visited Honda's branches in Nagoya, Osaka and other major cities at least once or twice a month. His visits always began with a roar. The reason for the explosions hardly mattered. If he happened to find a disorderly desk, he would throw everything on it, one by one, to the floor. Then he would launch into a lecture about what marketing was really about. After that, he'd listen to the reports from the sales staff. If Fujisawa discovered his salesmen taking an easy way out, he'd chew them out for it—even if sales were better than before.

Once they got used to it, Honda's salesmen realized that the yelling and shouting was simply Fujisawa's personal style of training them. After a while, the workers, catching on to Fujisawa's real motives, would start taking notes while listening to his tirade. This would prompt Fujisawa to flare up all the more and shout, "A salesman's job is to grab the attention of his customer! How can you expect to do that without looking into their eyes? If you keep taking notes all the time, you'll never sell a thing." At that, the workers would put down their notes and nervously fix their eyes directly on Fujisawa's, listening attentively. Without so much as a pause, Fujisawa would continue, "Honda isn't a funeral home. Come on, show me your smiles. Smile, everyone."

Whenever Fujisawa exploded, the news inevitably spread throughout the entire company, not just the sales branches but even in the factories, within a single day. Like Soichiro, Fujisawa was aware of this fact, so he never yelled about the same subject twice, even at different offices. Commiserating over drinks after work, salesmen grumblingly compared Fujisawa's reprimands to a bell at a Buddhist temple for its tendency to continue resonating inside people's minds for a long time. Everyone knew that the impact of Fujisawa's words would only grow larger as the hours passed by. So the salesmen always wound up drinking a great deal on such evenings.

Fujisawa's goals were to promote a fertile atmosphere for Soichiro's ideas, while at the same time building a solid framework for the organization so that Honda would be able to keep up the vitality it enjoyed as a medium-sized company. His way of training the employees through explosive lectures were all a part of this scheme.

Soichiro and Fujisawa shared the same goal: making Honda ever larger. Both used "world-best" as their keyword. Neither Soichiro nor Fujisawa had yet gotten around to the concept of corporate social responsibility.

Reality, however, turned out to be considerably harsher than they had anticipated. The huge investment in plants and equipment all but backfired. If, at this stage, Honda had not been able to make its payments and had gone bankrupt, Soichiro Honda and Takeo Fujisawa would never have gone down in industrial history as heroes of one of the biggest success stories in post-WW II Japan.

The financial crisis of 1954 was a turning point for Honda. It was Soichiro and Fujisawa's chance to transform a company characterized by old-fashioned apprenticeship ideals into a truly modern corporation.

The crisis hit Japan at the beginning of the year. Due to a backlash from the high consumer spending in 1952 and the investment boom in 1953, international payments dropped into the red. The Bank of Japan responded by instituting its tight-money policy. This prompted the first inventory cycle-based downturn in the Japanese economy of the post-war era.

These events affected Honda as well. Sales of the Cub, Honda's main moneymaker, took a sudden plunge. Had other companies simply copied the Cub and produced their own rear-engine designs, Honda would have easily maintained its dominant position. But Honda's rivals instead engineered motor systems that fit inside the bicycle's triangular frame, which gave the motorcycles more stability and made them easier to steer. No matter how much Soichiro went on about Honda's destiny of becoming world class, retailers would only move products that customers actually wanted to buy, especially in the middle of a recession. And the Cub's market share was shrinking before Soichiro's eyes.

Unfortunately for Honda, things got even worse. Immediately after the Dream's engine was updated from 200cc to 220cc, complaints began pouring in. The OHV-equipped Benly scooter suffered from reliability problems and had earned a bad name. And the Juno's plastic engine cover—an innovation intended to let it operate in all weather conditions—caused the engine to constantly overheat, causing Juno to be widely regarded as a failure from the moment it hit stores.

By March of 1954, Soichiro and Fujisawa were tearing their hair out. They had based their investment on projections that sales of the Cub and Dream would quickly and smoothly rise to a billion yen per month. But in reality, sales reached a plateau at three hundred and fifty million yen a month. Because the projections had turned out to be inaccurate, Honda quickly ran into cash flow problems. If things didn't improve shortly, the company would inevitably go bankrupt. Honda had just gone public on the Tokyo Stock Exchange, but already rumors had begun to spread that "even a loan shark wouldn't accept a check from Honda," casting doubt on the company's credibility. Employees started becoming nervous about the piles of inventory in the warehouses.

To get through the crisis, Soichiro and Fujisawa needed to tackle the money issue, develop better products, and raise company morale—all at the same time. On the cash flow side, Fujisawa managed, with considerable difficulty, to secure financial support from Honda's main bank, Mitsubishi Bank. He personally visited and begged Honda's suppliers to extend the due dates of their outstanding invoices. He also negotiated a new payment plan that would allow Honda to pay thirty percent in cash up front, with the balance to be paid when Honda recovered. Some suppliers stopped doing business with Honda, but the majority accepted Fujisawa's request and stayed on board. No matter how far Honda's reputation had sunk, when it came to financing, Fujisawa was fully confident in his ability to survive a crisis.

Soichiro's responsibility was improving Honda's product line. He cloistered himself in the R&D headquarters, which was now located in the Shirako Plant, and literally worked day and night tracking down the sources of the problems. It didn't take long for him to realize that the culprit for all the complaints regarding the new, updated Dreams was the carburetor; carburetor technology in those days simply couldn't keep pace with Soichiro's other improvements to the engine. Honda stopped manufacturing the 220cc Dream, and built more 200cc versions to satisfy their contracts with retailers. Honda also introduced a new version of the Cub to keep its market share. In addition, Soichiro personally took charge of improving the Juno and Benly designs to win back some of their lost reputation. Thanks to Soichiro's efforts, Honda managed to pull itself out of its difficulties on the technology front, at least for the time being.

The remaining issue was company morale. Early that year, Soichiro had proudly declared in Honda's corporate newsletter that "Honda will become the number one motorcycle manufacturer in the world." Such declarations were all very well as long as Soichiro was voicing them atop crates in the factory, where employees would simply think, "There goes Pop again with his dreams." Once the words were in print, however, the company couldn't expect to get away with passing the idea off as a mere dream or vision of its founder. If he backed down, Soichiro would lose the trust of his employees, and company morale would fall even lower. This was where Fujisawa decided to take a big gamble: he decided to cast Soichiro in the role of a cult leader, who would act as a living demonstration of Honda's vigor and potential, both to Honda employees and to the outside world. Fujisawa's plan was that Honda publicize its entry in the Isle of Man Tourist Trophy Races in England—the "Olympics" of motorcycle racing.

Originally founded in 1907, the Isle of Man TT was renowned as the world's most demanding road race. It required racers to make seven full laps of the island, a total of 420 kilometers. A hundred thousand spectators would be watching. A victory at the Isle of Man would cement Honda's reputation as the world's top motorcycle manufacturer once and for all.

"Honda-san, how about giving the Isle of Man TT a shot? If you're game, I'll write up a PR statement for you," offered Fujisawa.

In the early days just after they had founded Honda, Fujisawa recalled, Soichiro had talked incessantly about his desire to build a motorcycle that could win a world-class race. True, it was little more than a desperate shot in the dark, but Fujisawa believed that linking the names of Honda and Soichiro to international motorcycle racing would help ease the crisis the company faced. *If we can pull this off*, thought Fujisawa, *Soichiro really will become the leader of the Cult of Honda.*

At the time, Japanese motorcycles were still far behind the world in terms of technology. To get a feel for Honda's ability to compete on the international scene, the company had already entered a small race in Sao Paulo, Brazil that January. As minor as the competition was, the Honda team only managed to finish thirteenth out of twenty-two participants.

More than anyone else, Soichiro knew there was a long way to go before Honda's designs were accepted as international contenders. Nevertheless, he grandly replied:

"The Isle of Man TT? That's the best in the world! What a fascinating idea. Let's do it. We may not win right away, but sooner or later, we'll become world champion and astonish the entire world!"

Although Soichiro had left financial matters fully in Fujisawa's hands and focused only on engineering, he was not indifferent to the danger facing his company. He had seen through Fujisawa's designs and made up his mind to fulfill his co-founder's expectations by becoming the leader of the Cult of Honda.

On March 20, while desperately struggling over cash flow issues, Fujisawa wrote a statement in Soichiro's name.

"Since I was a small child, one of my dreams has been to compete in motor vehicle races all over the world with a vehicle of my own making. However, before I can become victor over the whole world, I must first, of course, assure the security of the business, obtain precision machinery and equipment, and create superior designs. I have, therefore, been devoting myself entirely to these points, and working to present superior practical vehicles to our customers in this country. Consequently, I have not had any free time for turning my energy to motorcycle racing until today… Now that we are equipped with a production system in which I have absolute confidence, the time of opportunity has arrived. I have reached the firm decision to enter the Isle of Man TT Races next year… We must gauge the true worth of the Japanese machine industry, and raise it to a point where we can display it proudly to the entire world. The mission of our Honda Motor Co. is to shed light on Japanese industry. With this, I announce my determination, and pledge that I will put my entire heart and soul and turn all my creativity and skills to the task of entering the TT Races and winning them. This I affirm. Soichiro Honda, President, Honda Motor Co., Ltd."

Although written in concrete language, Soichiro's words resonated like a manifesto. Just as Fujisawa had expected, Soichiro's declaration lifted the spirits of Honda's workforce and made them forget the fact that the company was actually on the brink of bankruptcy. Fujisawa had another trick up his sleeve as well. He sent Soichiro to Europe to observe the Isle of Man TT Races in person. He carefully timed the trip to make sure that Soichiro would be out of the country on June 10, when payment was due for outstanding invoices. Fujisawa didn't want to burden Soichiro with financial worries. But more importantly, he figured that sending the company president abroad at such an important time would reinforce the perception, both within Honda and among the public, that there couldn't possibly be anything seriously wrong with Honda's operations.

On June 10, Fujisawa somehow managed to make Honda's payments, averting the financial difficulties for the time being. Honda had weathered its financial crisis. Soichiro, however, couldn't shake his sense of unease after returning from Europe. He had been absolutely flabbergasted by what he had seen at the Isle of Man. The race demanded unbelievable amounts of speed and horsepower. Soichiro marveled at the sheer ferocity of the competition. Honda could never expect to win against such competitors. He even began to wonder if he had made an enormous mistake. But it was too late to turn back. Not only had he declared Honda's entry, he had even claimed that it would win. Ready or not, Honda was heading to the races.

4

Soichiro may have sworn to participate in the Isle of Man TT Races the following year, but Honda's employees knew full well that the company was far from ready for the competition. The crisis had passed for the moment, but the company still owed significant amounts of money to its suppliers. Fujisawa continued to adjust the production runs. Honda employees, and in particular the factory workers, began to feel that it was only a matter of time before there was a lockout—or even layoffs.

Honda's employees were undoubtedly aware of the labor issues facing the Nissan Motor Company. Nissan laborers had requested a raise to 20,000 yen per month, basing their calculations on a "market basket" of representative goods and services that the workers need to live. In an era when the average entry-level university graduate earned less than 10,000 yen a month, however, paying every worker a monthly salary of 20,000 yen was simply out of the question. Even in light of the money Nissan had made from Korean War procurement demands, the company still couldn't afford such a raise. Nissan's management rejected the request, stating, "No work, no payment." The workforce went on strike, and the company responded by instituting a lockout of workers who participated in union activities. In the end, Ichiro Shioji, leader of the Second Labor Union and Katsuji Kawamata, then Nissan's managing director in charge of labor management, reached a settlement and created the basis for a working relationship between

Nissan's labor union and management.

The workforce at Honda's Saitama factory had formed a labor union in July 1953, a year before the financial crisis hit the company. It had been organized by Tetsuya Kuze, who had joined the company the year Honda first began hiring university graduates on a regular basis. At the time Kuze was hired, all new employees, including university graduates, had to work a stint in the factory. New trainees naturally were slow at their work and during his training period, Kuze had been berated by Soichiro for his inefficiency. Soichiro, not being able to tell the difference between a management trainee and normal factory workers, had simply yelled in his usual style at any worker he found to be slow. Kuze felt humiliated nonetheless. He devoted all of his all spare energy thereafter towards organizing a labor union.

At the end of 1954, Honda's labor union demanded a considerable company-wide bonus. Unsure of Honda's future, the workforce took action to get as much money as they could before what they saw as an inevitable meltdown. The company responded with a bonus of 5,000 yen per worker, far lower than what the workers had expected. In fact they would have been disappointed with three times that amount. Negotiations were in a deadlock and the workforce only a step away from going on strike. Fujisawa headed alone to the Saitama factory to bargain with the workers, one man against 1,600 employees.

"How does the company feel about this bonus?" asked the leader of the union.

"5,000 yen is embarrassingly low," replied Fujisawa. "But if the company pays more than 5,000 yen, it will go bankrupt. If the company goes bankrupt, everyone will pay the price. As the manager of the company, I have a responsibility to provide you with job security. I believe the economy will recover and motorcycle sales will pick up by the time the cherry trees bloom next spring. I'd like to return to the negotiating table when Honda is back on track again."

Fujisawa's sincere approach worked. As he finished delivering his passionate address, the union members actually applauded, shouting, "We're counting on you!" Fujisawa had succeeded in averting the worst-case scenario, where a labor strike would lead to the closing of factories and a layoff of workers, and eventually bankruptcy for the company. Shortly thereafter, the labor union split into three groups: Chuo, Saitama, and Hamamatsu. In 1955, the groups united again, with Kuze as the second leader.

In reality it took not one but five years from Soichiro's proclamation for Honda to enter the Isle of Man TT. It had been no easy task. The first technical hurdle was increasing the torque of Honda's engines from 3,000 to 10,000 r.p.m. Ten thousand r.p.m. was a fantastic number for a motorcycle engine in those days—double that of engines used in aircraft. Soichiro realized that even if he did manage to build a prototype, the high-performance parts needed to maintain it could not possibly be procured in Japan. He flew to Europe on his own again and spent every yen he had purchasing as many components as he could. In fact, he ended up buying so much that he was stopped at the airport in Rome for exceeding the allowable weight limit.

In its first attempt in the Isle of Man TT Races, Honda placed sixth in the

125cc class. It was a respectable outcome for a first trial, but Honda team leader Kiyoshi Kawashima saw it as nothing less than total defeat. The way he saw it, Honda had lost because their engine wasn't capable of putting out even half of the horsepower of the winning design.

"Horsepower! We've got to do something about the horsepower, or we can't win," said Soichiro. Consumed with the idea, he mumbled about horsepower and engine specifications from morning to night.

Soichiro's dream would come true two years later, in 1961, shocking motor sports enthusiasts and industry people the world over, Honda's motorcycles swept first through fifth place in both the 125cc and 250cc classes in the Isle of Man TT Races.

"Honda's engines run with clockwork precision," enthused the British *Daily Mirror*. Soichiro's dream had come true.

Soichiro had calculated that focusing on winning the race, cost be damned, would kick Honda's technological know-how to the next level so that the company could offer even higher quality products to its customers. In addition, the victory would undoubtedly attract better and more unique engineering talent. Soichiro was right. Honda's work on the races resulted in new technological breakthroughs, and a new crop of "Honda kids," including Kawamoto and Irimajiri, would eventually lead the next generation of management at Honda.

Fujisawa, on the other hand, hoped that the victory would open up a foreign market for Honda's products. The idea of participating in the Isle of Man TT had started simply as a way to boost morale and to divert the employees' attention from the company's financial difficulties, but the win happened to be a tremendous boost for the "Honda myth" as well.

After averting the management crisis in 1954, Soichiro and Fujisawa completely divided their work. Soichiro shut himself away in the Shirako factory, devoting his time to designing cutting-edge motorcycles for the races. The production team at Shirako was moved to the new Wako factory, but Honda's heart and soul, the R&D section, remained in Shirako. It was there that Soichiro built his office to establish his base of strategic operations.

Honda's headquarters were located in Yaesu, Tokyo. But the president's office was miles away in the Shirako factory in Saitama prefecture. This arrangement was unique in the Japanese business world, to say the least. It was as if the headquarters of Soichiro's "Honda Tech" was located in Shirako, while the "Fujisawa Trading Co." part of the company was in Yaesu. This two-headquarters system would continue until the day Soichiro and Fujisawa retired.

Although Fujisawa ran the headquarters in Yaesu, he did not appear in the office every day. He rented a thirty meter square room in the Echigoya building in the Ginza district, decorated the entire office in black, carted in a tremendous amount of business documents and books, and spent most of his time there alone, reading through the materials. Whenever he felt tired, he would either meditate quietly in his room or take a stroll around Ginza to refresh himself. Fujisawa and Soichiro barely saw each other during this time, sometimes as little as several times a year. When they did meet, it was not at the company offices but at a restaurant, where they would discuss recent developments with one another over *sake*.

In 1956, the Japanese government stated in its Economic White Paper that "the postwar period is over," announcing the official end to the economic restoration efforts. The country now faced an entirely different challenge. From that point on, the future of the Japanese economy would depend not on restoration but on modernization, the paper proclaimed. Fujisawa watched the changes around him and began to think long and hard about the future of his company.

Before anything else, however, Fujisawa knew that he needed to analyze exactly why Honda had fallen into financial crisis. The technical issues were already defined. In addition to the effect of the recession, the sales of the Cub had dropped off when rivals introduced new products that featured engines in the triangular frames of bicycles. The real problem, however, was that the engine Soichiro had designed had far too much horsepower for the bicycle frames then on the market. The carburetor for the Dream was a prime case in point. It simply had not been able to keep pace with the performance of Soichiro's engine.

Another factor was that Honda had switched from make-to-order to make-to-stock manufacturing. The company also suffered from a lack of cost consciousness. It was a fact that the better the product, the better the sales. And the more a product sold, the more a company could invest in factories to satisfy the demand. Anticipating a cost savings from mass production, a new and inexperienced company would tend to leave things at that. But in reality, it was just as important to invest in an efficient inventory-management system; without one, there was no way to achieve true success.

Any number of factors contributed to the crisis. But the bottom line is that there was a lack of balance in our management. I put all our hopes on Soichiro's engineering capacities. So what do I need to do to keep our management well-balanced?

Fujisawa remembered a book that he had read when he was running his own business, the Nihon Kiko Kenkyujo, during the war. The book, by Kiyoshi Kiyosawa, was entitled *A History of Japanese Diplomacy*. One part in particular had left a deep impression on him.

"Military strength and diplomacy are like the wheels on a car. Both sides need to be balanced to achieve stability. A perfect example can be seen in 1933, when the Japanese government played strong-arm diplomacy and left the League of Nations in spite of the fact that the nation's actual military power was quite small. Once this occurred, Japan's fate was sealed, its fall only a matter of course. The Japanese withdrawal from the League of Nations is a typical example of placing overly large wheels on one side of a vehicle while those on the other remain too small to keep up, throwing off the balance of the entire machine."

Fujisawa saw the same logic applying to his own business. In his case, technology was military strength, while management was diplomacy. Technology and management should have been carefully balanced against each other. Instead, Fujisawa had increased his distribution network based on nothing more than a blind faith in Soichiro's engineering skills. From the creation of the Cub to the 200cc Dream, the company had based its entire management strategy on the prospects outlined by Soichiro and had encountered no problems. What had pushed them over the edge was the fifteen billion yen investment, which, looking back on it, had clearly been excessive. There was the trap. Fujisawa had been so focused on expanding the company that he hadn't realized that the balance between management and technology had gone awry.

In his rented office in Ginza, Fujisawa undertook a business analysis of Japan's top-ranking companies, including rivals Toyota and Nissan, but also unrelated firms like Toray, in an attempt to learn how to maintain the necessary balance. By looking at the figures for these companies, he hoped to find a way to build Honda into a large enterprise without losing sight of its strengths.

When Fujisawa joined Honda, it had only thirty-seven employees. By now, however, that number had increased to more than 2,500. *So long as Honda remained small, all we needed were my management skills and Soichiro's inspiration*, thought Fujisawa. *But if we want to become a large corporation, there is a limit to what our two-man leadership model can accomplish. We need to reorganize ourselves into something that's more appropriate for a modern corporation. An organization that has no choice but to rely on Soichiro cannot last…*

In 1956, Fujisawa instituted a one-year guarantee for all Honda products. One purpose of this was to address the company's sagging reputation, tarnished by near continuous returns and service claims. The other aim was to regain some of the balance between technology and management by lighting a fire under the research and development department.

Fujisawa took another step as well. He sent those members of the engineering staff with university diplomas to a hotel in Hakone for a week to study how to read a balance sheet. Fujisawa said:

"Engineers such as yourselves need to understand money, too, or you'll be at a disadvantage when you rise to the factory manager level. As good engineers, you have the privilege of understanding the exact value of your products. But if you want to be good managers, you must understand the relationship of that value to your company's cash flow."

While Fujisawa was searching for answers to the questions facing Honda, he suddenly remembered something that he had read in the pre-war writings of Kiyoshi Hiraizumi, a professor of Japanese history at Tokyo Imperial University and the father of politician Wataru Hiraizumi. His book, *All Things Are in a State of Flux*, taught that everything inevitably changes—and that anyone or anything that thrived was also destined to decline. *It's a given that all power and prosperity will wither in time. It is thanks to this rule that we were able to found Honda, that it expanded the way it did. But followed to its logical conclusion, this also means that once Honda becomes large, it's destined to fall to the innovations of newcomers.*

At the same time, however, another idea occurred to Fujisawa. *It's not destiny. Once a company becomes large, it has the advantages of abundant capital and labor. Not to mention the trust of society. But absent such a law, small companies will never have a chance to grow…*

One day, Fujisawa accosted Kiyoshi Kawashima, then factory manager of the Saitama Plant.

"Kawashima. Do you think Honda will last forever?"

"Of course. It'd better, or we'd be in trouble," replied Kawashima.

"Do you really believe that, though? If corporations grew forever, Japan would be swamped with them before long."

"Does that mean you think that corporations have a lifespan?"

"Put that way, it would seem Honda is destined to die. I want you to think about how we can avoid that."

The more Fujisawa tried to attack the problem with logic, the more cornered he felt. He wrote of his worries in Honda's corporate newsletter in April 1956:

"Everything inevitably changes. Honda will undoubtedly face this rule of nature in the future. I have put a great deal of thought into how Honda can avoid this fate and continue to flourish forever. Competition in the business world is incredibly fierce. We have seen that even a large company, which everyone believed would last forever, could come falling down in the end. Even excellent facilities, a devoted labor force, and abundant capital cannot protect a company forever. How, then, can we continue to flourish? So long as Honda relies on others—other things, other people—we will never be able to boast true stability. I want everyone to be aware of the changes in the world around us, and to keep a progressive mindset to allow us to continue to grow."

The "large company" referred to in Fujisawa's article was Tokyo Hatsudoki, known as "Tohatsu." Tohatsu, which had manufactured motorcycles, water pumps for fire extinguishers, and electrical generators, was once Honda's main rival. When Honda had fallen into its financial crisis in 1954, economic magazines such as the *Weekly Diamond* and *Weekly Toyo Keizai* had rushed to praise Tohatsu as the superior manufacturer based on the company's impeccable balance sheet.

Tohatsu had 671 employees at the time. It had invested two hundred and ten million yen in facilities and machinery, less than a fifth of what Honda had spent. Tohatsu boasted net sales of two hundred million yen a month, which broke down to 300,000 yen per employee. Honda's net sales, on the other hand, were five hundred million yen a month, or 200,000 yen per employee. Tohatsu's ratio of profit to net sales was ten percent, whereas Honda's was only one percent. In other words, in spite of having a smaller scale of facilities and fewer employees, Tohatsu had higher sales and was more profitable than Honda. Tohatsu's notes payable were one-fourth of Honda's, their accounts payable one-third, and their debt only one-tenth.

Within only a few short years, however, Tohatsu went bankrupt, while Honda survived and thrived. The main difference between the companies was the presence of genius engineer Soichiro Honda, who could not be tallied as an asset on any balance sheet. Tohatsu, of course, did not have Soichiro.

Soichiro Honda is a genius. He founded Honda and I turned it into a decent-sized company. The key to our success was my ability to exploit Soichiro's hidden potential. But even he has limits. If Honda was full of people who are as good as Soichiro, could the organization survive even after Soichiro runs out of ideas and retires from the front lines?

Fujisawa's conclusion was that he had to make his organization strong enough to survive the loss of Soichiro in the future.

If Soichiro had joined a large corporation, he would have undoubtedly wound up as nothing more than another underling. That the Honda Motor Company existed at all was thanks to Soichiro's personal drive and foresight. But he had a natural gift; Fujisawa knew it wasn't realistic to expect to find another like him. Instead, Fujisawa hit on the idea of creating an environment that recognized and maximized the personal expertise of individual employees so as to foster the growth of Honda as a whole. It was the only way, Fujisawa thought, to ensure Honda's continued development as a unique company.

Fujisawa began by placing a notebook in each factory. He instructed the factory workers to feel free to write anything that was on their mind, whether it be a concern, the report of a mistake, or a suggestion for improvement. Employees were free to read and write in the notebooks at any time. Fujisawa saw these notebooks as the basis for an "expertise system," which would be adopted companywide in 1968. This unique method for encouraging employees to share original ideas would play a major role in improving and refining Honda's production techniques.

Honda wasn't the only company to promote the input of individual employees. Toyota is famous for its "suggestion system" that Honorary Chairman Eiji Toyoda developed based on his experience as an intern at Ford Motor Company in the United States. Unlike Toyoda, however, Fujisawa had come up with the concept entirely on his own.

Next, Fujisawa devoted a great deal of time and effort to developing Honda's organizational chart. Up to that point, Honda lacked a real official corporate structure. While unprofessional, it had been a deliberate move on Fujisawa's part. The outward reason Fujisawa gave for this was that he feared that employees would see "structure" as "boundaries," sapping the company of its vitality. But the real reason for the delay in instituting an official structure was that Fujisawa had a hard time figuring out where to place Soichiro. The normal pyramid structure simply would not work with him in the picture.

When a labor union was organized in 1953, Fujisawa had drawn up a structural chart out of necessity during the negotiating process, but even then, he always told people that the hierarchy he had created "only existed to be destroyed." No matter how innovative the structure, there could be no avoiding a pyramid shape. Yet, Honda had become a corporation of several thousand employees and it was becoming unfeasible to run a company of that size without some kind of corporate structure.

To this day, Honda is skeptical of the idea of structure. For example, unlike most large Japanese companies, Honda does not shuffle its employees through different positions at regular intervals.

Fujisawa began his career at Honda as a managing director. He was "promoted" to senior managing director in 1952 and then vice president in 1964. Usually, a company's president handled the promotion of directors. Honda was different. Fujisawa made decisions independently and then told Soichiro after the fact. "I'm going to use the title of 'senior managing director' on my business cards from now on," he would say, or, "by the way, I'm promoting somebody else to 'senior managing director' so I'll be 'vice president' now." Soichiro never complained. He knew it really didn't matter which title Fujisawa used. Fujisawa's real responsibilities never changed at all.

Fujisawa saw his title as nothing more than a tool to make his presence felt inside and outside of Honda. Even with the title of vice president, his real position and responsibilities were equivalent to that of CEO. Fujisawa had Soichiro's presidential seal, an official stamp used to sign documents in Japan, but he never actually used it. All checks and bills were issued under the name of "Takeo Fujisawa, Representative Director," clearly showing Fujisawa's pride as the manager of the company. For Soichiro, on the other hand, the title of president was a way of indicating to those outside of Honda that he was the man who had founded the company. His real responsibility was head of research and development, and if he was actually president of anything it was of the Honda Research and Development Company, which would be established some years later. Fujisawa and Soichiro's relationship was unique in the Japanese business world. It wouldn't change until the day they finally retired.

Until the day he passed away, Soichiro retained his pride as the founder of Honda. But as far as Fujisawa was concerned, Soichiro only called himself president because he had founded the company, and there was never anything more to it than that. Now, Fujisawa began to feel that the time had come to clarify Soichiro's role within the company, whatever title the latter might use.

Nobody knows how talented an engineer he is as well as I do. But if I just put him atop the usual corporate pyramid, Honda's uniqueness as an organization will go out the window. We're not going to take the company to the next level unless I can come up with a structure capable of maximizing Soichiro's talents. What I really need is an army of Soichiros.

5

To create his army of Soichiros, Fujisawa came up with the idea of spinning off Honda's research and development section as an independent entity.

He took a hint from one of his favorite books, Soseki Natsume's *I Am a Cat*, a novel set in Japan at the turn of the twentieth century. One scene in particular stuck out in his mind. Amidst the turmoil of the Russo-Japanese war, a young scholar, Kangetsu, toiled in a basement laboratory at a university, polishing glass balls to study the electrical characteristics of frog eyeballs. The character had supposedly been based on the famed scientist Torahiko Terada.

Perhaps our engineers would benefit from Kangetsu's isolation—a place so serene that they can conduct their research even when society is in an uproar around them. That way, the engineers can focus on their work without worrying about anything else. If we can beef up our engineering department that way, we'll have hit after hit on our hands.

Fujisawa decided to give the engineers the isolation they needed by completely splitting the R&D section off from the factories. The only problem was organization; it would be self-defeating to apply the same pyramid structure to the research and development section as used for the factories. The factories necessarily prioritized profits and the streamlining of production techniques over the development of new ideas. If the research and development section remained part of the factory organization, the research agenda would inevitably be driven purely by sales results. This would not only tie the engineers' hands by forcing them to focus on short-term goals and results, but it would also undoubtedly create engineers with a simple profit-based mindset. The research and development section needed to stand on its own, so as to allow the engineers the freedom to dedicate themselves to long-term projects without worrying about demands for higher profits from the sales and production sections.

What the engineers needed was an environment where they could conduct their research freely while still receiving appropriate recognition of their status within the corporate organization as a whole. Yet a pyramid structure necessarily limited the number of managers.

Fujisawa's idea was to use a "flat organization"—or "paper weight" as it would later come to be known—structure, rather than a pyramid-shaped one. This way, Honda could have many engineers with the same status as section or department chiefs under one leader. In addition, if the new section's research budget could be isolated from Honda's sales income, the engineers would be free to focus on whatever research subject they liked.

As the Shirako factory was already beginning to feel crowded in 1956, Fujisawa purchased land and prepared a new facility in the neighboring city of Wako in Saitama prefecture. Here he moved the plant and the core sections of the company's technical division—the engineering design team in charge of drafting designs and product testing—that would later become the Honda R&D Company. A handful of engineering employees took the opportunity to leave the labor union and create a new one of their own.

Fujisawa suggested his new organizational plan to the unions the following year in 1957. Surprisingly, however, it was met with fierce resistance. The employees had interpreted it as a scheme to further divide the unions.

Without an independent research and development section, thought Fujisawa ruefully, *Honda has no future. When I joined Honda, we had nothing but a handful of old belt-driven machine tools and a few pieces of manufacturing equipment. We barely had forty employees. I didn't even have any collateral to offer the banks. We really started from nothing. Nothing, but Soichiro's talent. Even in those days, Soichiro and I always claimed that we would make Honda the world's top manufacturer of motorcycles, although no one ever took us seriously.*

We may have started from scratch, but we really did it. And it took us only ten years. Looking back, there's no way we could have made it this far if Japan's economy had been stable and healthy; the chaos of the post-war era actually turned out to be an advantage. But the real challenge starts now, when dozens of smaller companies try to beat Honda at its own game. If we only focus on defense, we'll stop developing as a company. What we need are more Soichiros and a larger, more aggressive research network to maintain our superiority. If we lose our edge in technology, we'll have nothing left.

The more Fujisawa thought about it, the more he knew he was right. But he also knew that forcing the issue would destroy his relationship with the labor unions. He backed down temporarily, but never stopped working on his plan in private. The need for an independent research and development section became all the more apparent after Honda instituted an "expertise system" with Fujisawa's "notebooks." *Even if we do have an army of experts in reserve, they won't thrive within a pyramidal hierarchy. Just like Kangetsu and his frog eyeballs, we've got to create an environment where engineers can focus, if we want to create more Soichiros.*

Whenever Fujisawa had a chance, he talked to the leaders of the labor unions and explained why he thought having an independent research and development section was so important. Eventually Fujisawa's efforts paid off as he slowly began to persuade the union leaders.

The real problem lay with Honda's management. In June of 1960, Fujisawa gathered a hundred and fifty of Honda's managers and delivered a fiery speech promoting his plan. "Unless we make the research and development section independent," he warned, "we won't make the rapid progress our company requires, and that means no future for Honda." In spite of Fujisawa's passion, however, few seemed enthusiastic about the prospect.

Running out of patience, Fujisawa pushed his idea through one month later without waiting for a consensus within the company. He founded the Honda Research and Development Co., Ltd, a subsidiary wholly owned and operated by Honda Motor Company. The new company's president was Soichiro. Fujisawa was vice president, and Kiyoshi Kawashima took on the role of non-executive director. The company's mission statement read as follows:

"Maintaining an indivisible relationship with Honda Motor Company, we will employ a unique system that meets the needs of advanced research in a wide range of fields. We will freely promote originality and talent to sell product blueprints that are the fruit of such efforts."

That being said, at the time, Honda R&D focused more on the development of products for sale than on developing fundamental technologies. As such, in spite of being an independent entity, the research and development section worked closely with the Honda Motor Company's marketing section to develop products for sale. In those days, Honda R&D had to conduct their research at the same time as working on actual products for sale.

Fujisawa then set to work tackling the myriad issues facing the new company. He needed to streamline the process from development to production and look at their guarantee and customer service policies. Even though Fujisawa had succeeded in spinning off the research and development section as an independent company, he knew that he could not immediately apply his "paperweight structure." He used a loose pyramid structure in the meantime as a transitional measure.

All organizational changes result in a certain amount of confusion. No one was more surprised by the new structure than Soichiro. He made rather provocative remarks about "the strange thing that our senior director has created"—not that it influenced any of his actions. Whenever he encountered problems in his factory, he didn't hesitate to point them out, and if any of the engineers failed to do just as he demanded, he thundered at them in his usual explosive manner.

When informed of Soichiro's bewilderment, Fujisawa just smiled and said nothing. After all, it wasn't for Soichiro's sake that he had set up this structure; he was creating a system that would ensure a future for Honda after Soichiro's inevitable retirement.

Even with an independent research and development center, Honda still had far fewer researchers than companies like Toyota or Nissan. It was enough for a company that produced nothing but motorcycles. But the small size of the research staff would prove a liability in the event Honda began to manufacture cars, let alone participate in the F1 races.

Fujisawa's expertise system proved an effective device for addressing such issues. It allowed engineers to be shuffled about with a high degree of flexibility. For example, an expert in engines for two-wheeled vehicles could easily adapt their same skill set into developing engines for sports cars or race cars. As many engineers as necessary could be moved to a new project. And as an added bonus, the engineers would learn new skills in the process.

The budget for contract research started as 2.5 percent of the sales of the Honda Motor Company. This was later raised to three percent and then to five percent where it remains to this day. When Honda's sales reached 2.5 trillion yen in the fiscal year ended March 1994, the R&D section's budget hit one hundred and twenty-five billion yen, seventy-eight times their initial budget of 1.6 billion yen. Even today, Honda is the only automobile manufacturer in the world with its own independent research and development company. Furthermore, Honda is the only manufacturer besides Mercedes-Benz in Germany—which is known for its emphasis on quality—to expand its R&D budget in proportion to its sales revenue.

Today, having been president of the Honda R&D Co. is an actual prerequisite for becoming president of the Honda Motor Company. Not all R&D presidents have become president of the parent company but all of the first four heads of Honda Motor—Soichiro, Kiyoshi Kawashima, Tadashi Kume, and Nobuhiko Kawamoto—also served a stint as president of the Honda Research and Development Company.

The role of the president of the Honda Motor Company is to use the latest technologies to give people dreams. Therefore, the president should be someone with a background in engineering. In that respect, it's preferable for him to have had the experience of running R&D. Honda's day-to-day business interests can be left to someone on the administrative side, an expert on the money and sales aspects of the business, like myself, thought Fujisawa. He strongly believed that Soichiro's successor needed to share his background in engineering to inherit his ideology.

By the mid 1950s, the Japanese economy had begun to grow at an increasingly rapid pace. Fujisawa had rented an office in Ginza to spend time thinking out ways to guide Honda on the path to becoming a modern corporation, but now he moved his private office to a building right next to Honda headquarters. Furthermore, in 1960, when the riots and protests against the U.S.-Japan Security Treaty broke out, Fujisawa followed the advice of his friend Fukuzo Kawahara, then vice president of Mitsubishi bank, and built a traditional Japanese tearoom in his new house in Roppongi and began to use this space for reflection and meditation. Kawahara later became a special advisor to Honda in 1961, and the company's auditor in 1964.

Around this time, Fujisawa began to tell his colleagues at Honda that "business is art." He engaged in as much contact with the arts as he could. Whereas Soichiro spent practically seven days a week at Honda R&D, Fujisawa took things easier. Every summer, he traveled with his wife to Germany to see Wagner's works performed at the opera. Before long, Fujisawa was able to discuss music—be it classical, opera, or modern jazz—as intelligently as any critic. Fujisawa even took up lessons in *tokiwazu* ballads, said to be the most difficult type of traditional Japanese music to learn. Fujisawa studied directly under Mojitayu XV, head master of the *tokiwazu* school, reaching accredited master status within a short period of time. When other directors at Honda became interested in learning *tokiwazu* themselves, Fujisawa advised them, "If you're serious about learning, start with something that's difficult. As long as you are going to study at all, study under the best master you can find."

Fujisawa's interests were not restricted to music. He rapidly expanded his hobbies to include the *kabuki* theater, paintings, sculpture, metal craft, traditional crafts, furniture, interior design, jewelry, architecture, and gardens. Fujisawa saw art as a means for sharpening his taste, which would also benefit him in the business world. He strongly believed that coming into contact with many different types of artwork would make him more sensitive, and thus more insightful, longsighted and innovative.

In addition to Fujisawa's personal philosophy that work did not necessarily have to be done in the company offices, the main reason he could act as he pleased was that business was going well for Honda.

In 1958, Honda began production of the Super Cub, a small 50cc motorcycle based on Fujisawa's initiative. Fujisawa had felt for some time that the original Cub, being only a bicycle with an auxiliary engine, had reached the end of its growth phase. Meanwhile in Europe, a new type of lightweight 50cc motorcycle called a "moped" had already hit the market.

Customers' disposable income has been on the rise. It's only a matter of time before they start losing interest in the Cub, especially since they're not attractive to women. Unless we come up with a product that pleases a wide variety of people, Honda's future is lost.

In 1956, two years after recovering from their financial crisis, Soichiro and Fujisawa traveled in Germany and Italy together. On the airplane ride back to Japan, Fujisawa casually suggested developing a new small-sized motorcycle to Soichiro.

"Honda-san, those 'mopeds' that the German company Kreidler and the Italian Lambretta make are interesting, but you know, I don't think they're very good as products. First of all, they're not convenient to use. If we can improve on them, though, I think the moped has a chance in Japan. It'd be nice to see Honda selling a product like that…"

"You aren't an engineer, so it's no surprise that you don't see things the way I do. But take my word for it: those aren't real motorcycles. Let me tell you what real motorcycles are all about," replied Soichiro, brushing off Fujisawa's suggestion.

Fujisawa let Soichiro talk about "real motorcycles" for as long as he wanted. Once Soichiro had talked himself out, Fujisawa tried again.

"If you can design a small motorcycle, say 50cc, with a cover to hide the engine and hoses and wires inside, I can sell it. I don't know how many *soba* noodle shops there are out there in Japan, but I bet you that every shop owner will want one for deliveries. No one in the world but you could build something like that, Honda-san."

Soichiro remained quiet. This time, he wasn't ignoring Fujisawa. In fact, Soichiro had realized the need for smaller motorcycles long before Fujisawa had even brought it up. But even if there was a market for such a motorcycle, Soichiro couldn't accept Fujisawa's suggestion right away.

There were large differences in the way that Soichiro and Fujisawa saw product development. Fujisawa was making his request simply from the standpoint of the user, i.e., the consumer. But as an engineer, Soichiro lacked confidence in the safety of the concept, and so he held his tongue.

As an engineer and a user, respectively, Soichiro and Fujisawa looked upon the issue of safety quite differently. For example, although Fujisawa had gotten his motorcycle license after joining Honda, he rarely rode one. In fact, he used the laminated license as a shoehorn. Fujisawa never used taxis—which people at the time mockingly called "kamikaze"—to go anywhere, preferring instead to use chauffeured cars operated by companies that advertised their safe-driving policies. And when Fujisawa took trips to visit Honda offices in other parts of the country, he never rode in cars driven by the local office employees.

Soichiro, on the other hand, drove everywhere himself. He had no problem riding in cars driven by employees; he would jump in the passenger seat and excitedly talk all the way to his destination. Fujisawa avoided riding in cars driven by employees because he knew that his very presence would make them nervous. As one of the heads of the company, Fujisawa would feel the need to say something to the employee, but he knew the person would undoubtedly take it as some reprimand, tense up, and forget to pay attention to his driving. Life was barely any easier on his chauffeurs, however. Woe betide the man who stepped on the brakes too suddenly. "If your company really believes in 'safe driving,' you'd damn well better pay more attention to what you're doing! Keep your eyes to the right and left, and you'll always be able to deal with someone jumping out suddenly!"

Soichiro, on the other hand, saw the brakes as his best tool for avoiding an accident. His personal philosophy was to jam on the brakes at the first sign of trouble, regardless of the impact on the passengers. As in so many other things, when it came to driving, it was clear that Soichiro and Fujisawa represented opposite ends of the spectrum.

Fujisawa's specific request was for a mini-motorcycle that could be driven with one hand while balancing trays of *soba* noodles in the other. Such a motorcycle would indeed be an asset to any *soba* shop. The driver would be able to drive the vehicle using only his one hand and two feet—and even the feet would need to be free to act as a kickstand to prevent the motorcycle from tipping over when starting. And with only one hand available for operating it, the clutch would need to be automatic. In short, Soichiro would have to come up with something that was easy to control, safe to ride, and inexpensive to manufacture.

"A motorcycle for a *soba* delivery boy, for a noodle-shop..." mumbled Soichiro, once he had returned to his dark office in the Shirako factory.

After several efforts, Soichiro finally unveiled his prototype in the fall of 1957. It was basically a cross between a motorcycle and a scooter, but taken to the next level. In keeping with Fujisawa's request, it was designed so that it could be driven with one hand.

Soichiro placed a call to Fujisawa at headquarters in Yaesu and told him to come and take a look. Fujisawa couldn't hide his excitement once he saw the "Super Cub" prototype, with its 50cc engine, automatic clutch, three-speed transmission, and automatic ignition.

"Honda-san, you did it! This is amazing. You managed to keep the appearance similar to a bicycle, and the open frame is a real plus, too. Now we can attract female customers as well. It's a masterpiece, among the best work you've ever done!"

"I met your every request," agreed Soichiro, as proudly as a kid who had scored an "A+" on his exam. "Now, tell me how many you think we can sell!"

"This is a great product. It'll move for sure. I say we can sell at least 30,000 of them," replied Fujisawa.

Soichiro could hardly conceal his disappointment. Thirty thousand a year meant only a little more than 2,000 a month. That was less than half the sales of the Cub.

Fujisawa saw Soichiro's expression and grinned.

"I think you misunderstood me. I meant 30,000 a month. That's 360,000 a year. If we include exports, I bet we can break 400,000."

"W-What?" stammered an engineer who had overheard the conversation. Soichiro was speechless. In those days, the total sales of the entire motorcycle industry added up to 20,000 units a month. Fujisawa seemed to feel that Honda could exceed that number, easily, with just a single product.

One thing Soichiro and Fujisawa did have in common was setting the goal high, as if to hoist an ad balloon into the sky, to gauge reactions before forging ahead to meet that goal. Fujisawa had tossed off the 30,000 figure as an off-the-cuff guess, but it buoyed the spirit of the engineering staff immensely.

The year was 1957. Japan was enjoying the greatest economic boom it had ever known. At the same time, it was also being rocked by tumultuous change.

6

The 50cc Super Cub went on sale in June of 1958 and practically sealed Honda's fate as the world's top motorcycle manufacturer. Still, it wasn't easy going at first. The timing was poor, as the nation happened to be in the midst of a lingering recession. And within three months, Honda began to receive a steady stream of complaints about clutches slipping on the Super Cubs. At the end of the year, the salesmen and factory workers gave up their holidays to visit each and every customer with a service claim and repair the clutches in person. Interest in the Super Cub didn't take off until the latter half of 1960, nearly two years after it first went on sale.

To reach his promised sales of 30,000 units a month, Fujisawa adopted a two-fold strategy: establishing a large-scale factory dedicated to producing motorcycles, and beginning to export to the United States. He took advantage of the Japanese economy hitting rock bottom in 1959 to purchase approximately 694,000 square meters of land in the city of Suzuka in Mie prefecture. Fujisawa then invested six billion yen to build his new facility. It was with the building of this facility that Honda started calling its factories "manufacturing plants."

Before the birth of the Super Cub, Soichiro and Fujisawa's vision for Honda's future had been for the company to join the ranks of celebrated British and Italian manufacturers such as BSA, Triumph, Norton, Moto Guzzi, and MV Agusta. When they made their tour of German and Italian motorcycle companies in 1956, however, Soichiro and Fujisawa discovered that these famous European manufacturers were actually not large, mass production factories but small, "cottage industry" workshops, which assembled their motorcycles by hand, in small quantities.

When Soichiro first heard Fujisawa's estimate of 30,000 Super Cubs a month, his thoughts turned to a Ford Model T that he had repaired as a grease-covered apprentice long ago. As a child, he had dreamed of becoming the Japanese Henry Ford. Ford's greatest achievement had been to establish a full-scale production line for his Model T automobiles. Soichiro decided to follow in Ford's footsteps by implementing a make-to-stock, mass production system for the Super Cub.

Fujisawa, of course, had no objections, as mass production had significant potential for lowering costs. At that time, however, no factory in Japan—not even those of automobile manufacturers—was capable of producing more than 10,000 vehicles of a single model a month. Soichiro and Fujisawa wanted to produce three times that number of their motorcycles. Honda found itself treading into an area no Japanese manufacturer had ever explored.

One of the biggest questions was how to supply the staggering quantity of parts that would be required. Honda did not have a *keiretsu*, a hierarchy of affiliated suppliers. Seventy percent of the necessary parts were procured via outside suppliers. Fujisawa took a businesslike approach to placing orders. *From now on, it'll be up to the suppliers themselves, not Honda, to enhance their volume of business with us. In other words, the amount of effort that suppliers make will be the deciding factor in the amount of orders that Honda places with them.*

With this policy in mind, Fujisawa approached members of Takarakai and Kyohokai, the supplier associations for Nissan and Toyota, respectively, and invited them to supply parts to Honda. The strategy worked, and Honda was able to buy quality parts at lower prices, even though it had no *keiretsu* suppliers. Others in the industry decried Honda's new policy as "self-serving and self-centered," but Fujisawa paid them no mind.

Exports were also a must if Fujisawa wanted to reach sales of 30,000 units a month. But the export cycle then was intermittent and unreliable. Honda would have to offer a diverse lineup of products and establish its own marketing network to achieve the stability it required. Mass-producing a limited variety of products is, naturally, more efficient but also carries greater risk. If sales stagnated, the entire factory would grind to a halt. The ideal situation, therefore, would be to mass-produce a variety of products at the same time. Once Honda established an export cycle with large quantities of multiple product lines, prices would drop and Honda would find itself in a superior position from a competitive standpoint. MITI officials, eager to promote export, had often sarcastically remarked, "Honda only imports machinery; it doesn't make the slightest effort to export." With the development of a product as broadly appealing as the Super Cub, Honda at last was in a position to start exporting.

But where to begin? "Due to geography, our top priority should be Southeast Asia," said Kihachiro Kawashima, head of export sales. "Our victory in the Isle of Man TT Races has brought Honda quite a bit of recognition in Europe. Unfortunately, however, the European market is already entering a mature phase. Honda remains unknown in the United States. Who can expect people to buy products from a manufacturer they've never heard of? We need to start by conquering the Southeast Asian market, then Europe. I say we should leave the United States for last."

In the United States at the time, the word "motorcycle" was associated with rough riders in black leather jackets, an image largely created by Marlon Brando's portrayal of a motorcycle gang leader in the hit film *The Wild Ones*. Only some 50,000 to 60,000 motorcycles were sold annually. America was considered something of a dark continent for the motorcycle industry.

Fujisawa, however, saw things differently. Southeast Asia would undoubtedly bring in large revenues in the short term, but it wouldn't provide the breakthrough necessary to become "world class." The United States sat in the center of the global economy, and Fujisawa felt that if he could open up demand there, the rest would follow naturally.

We must make an effort to conquer the most difficult market first. If we can succeed there, we can definitely succeed in Europe. And besides, tackling the most difficult tasks first is the Honda way, thought Fujisawa. In July 1959, Fujisawa overruled opposition and established American Honda just outside of Los Angeles. Ironically, it was Kihachiro Kawashima, the same man who had proposed tackling the American marketplace last, who was chosen to be its first president.

At that time, exporting durable consumer goods from Japan to the United States meant selling the products by bulk to American trading companies and distributors. This kept the risk to the Japanese manufacturers at a minimum. For their part, the American distributors usually demanded exclusive distributorship on the product being sold, so the system generally worked well for both sides.

As usual, however, Fujisawa didn't follow the accepted way. He decided to sell Honda's products directly to retailers, just as he had done when cultivating the market in Japan. First he would use the 50cc Super Cub as a trial balloon. Watching the sales figures carefully, he would then go on to add the 64cc and 90cc models to the American line. For a change, Honda now had some extra money, which allowed Fujisawa to invest in the creation of a sales and marketing network.

Because of the sheer vastness of the United States, it wasn't practical simply to rely on sales staff traveling all over the country to sell the products. Kawashima came up with the idea of launching a major advertising campaign. He established a contract with Grey Advertising and spent five million dollars placing advertisements in popular magazines such as *Time*, *Look*, and *Life*. The tag line read, "You meet the nicest people on a Honda."

The cheerful pitch had been patterned on that used for the increasingly popular Volkswagen Beetle. With the unprecedented small size of the machines and Honda's unique ad campaign, the motorcycles rapidly gained popularity as "two-wheeled Beetles."

Honda's success had the side effect of invigorating the American motorcycle market as a whole. In fact, the Honda brand name was rapidly replacing the image of leather-clad riders. Honda had succeeded in taking the next step towards establishing world motorcycle dominance by entering the American market.

In Europe, on the other hand, Honda followed up its victory in the 1961 Isle of Man TT by snatching first place in the World Motorcycle Grand Prix. The multiple victories firmly established Honda's name as a top-level motorcycle manufacturer and gave it the confidence it needed to start manufacturing its products in Europe. Honda built an assembly plant for small-sized motorcycles in Belgium, which began operation in May of 1963.

The Suzuka manufacturing plant was completed in April of 1960. By November, the assembly line there had become capable of producing 60,000 motorcycles a month. There could be no doubt in anyone's eyes that the Super Cub would be the greatest success in the history of motorcycle manufacturing. The problem was that the production line began turning out finished products more quickly than anticipated. Once the money was invested and the factories built and put into operation, production could begin at a regular pace almost right away. Establishing a decent sales network, on the other hand, invariably required a certain amount of time.

Rather than borrowing from the banks, Fujisawa planned to foot the six billion-yen construction costs for the Suzuka manufacturing plant by first increasing sales, and then increasing Honda's capital to cover the rest. The reason for this was that the outlay was simply too large to ask of any bank, even Mitsubishi, Honda's main bank. Fujisawa knew they would refuse to provide the money.

When Fujisawa had made the decision to build the Suzuka plant in 1958, Honda's capital had been only one hundred and twenty million yen. Anticipating that the Japanese economy would make a quick recovery once the lingering recession ended, Fujisawa increased Honda's capital to seven hundred and twenty million yen, a six-fold increase, and used the money to buy land for the new plant. In May of 1959, he once again increased Honda's capital, this time doubling the amount to 1.44 billion yen.

Of course, this still wasn't enough. So, Fujisawa tripled the amount in January 1960, and then doubled it again in May 1961. By that time, Honda's capital had grown to 8.64 billion yen. Just as Fujisawa had expected, the capital markets made a rebound. Fujisawa had to shorten the time for his plan.

Honda's capital had increased by an incredible seventy-two times in three years. By all accounts, it appeared totally reckless. But the Japanese economy was growing at a breakneck pace, riding sky-high with no end to the growth in sight, and Honda was riding this "rising wave." In the end, total capital investment in the Suzuka manufacturing plant came out to over ten billion yen. Honda had managed to pay for the bulk of this by increasing its capital.

Even so, Honda still needed to continue paying a dividend to its shareholders. If this stopped, the company's reputation would be irrevocably tainted as people would criticize Honda for bilking them out of their money. Until the 1959 capital increase, Honda had been paying a dividend of thirty percent. This was reduced first to twenty-five percent, and finally to twenty percent in August of 1960. However, due to the rapid pace at which the capital increases were carried out, as well as the fact that the amount of the dividends skyrocketed after each increase, the company's moves were actually welcomed by the shareholders.

Crisis hit at the beginning of 1961. Sales simply could not keep up with production. Before long, piles of stock began to fill every available amount of space in the plant. By March, the number of units in stock rose to over 40,000, and Honda began running out of space to store it all. There was no way around it: the production runs would have to be adjusted. Knowing that the company intended to double its capital once again in May, more than a few Honda workers resisted the call to adjust production. Nevertheless, Fujisawa went ahead and made the decision to suspend operations at the Suzuka manufacturing plant for five days.

Fujisawa kept the reason for the shutdown from the public. Instead, he told those outside of the company that Honda had temporarily suspended production at Suzuka in order to move in some new equipment from the Hamamatsu factory. As a result, the newspapers gave the shutdown only minimal press and the public remained unaware that Honda was facing yet another crisis.

Just before the five-day shutdown, Fujisawa turned to Mitsubishi Bank and requested a cash infusion to offset the reduced production run. A company in financial crisis usually attempted to hide the extent of the problem by asking for just enough money to settle its current accounts, while anticipating asking for additional funding to cover the rest later. Of course, banks were more than familiar with the tactic and usually rejected such requests as a matter of course. Fujisawa, however, was fully aware of the bank's worries and addressed them up front.

"Sales of the Super Cub will recover this summer," insisted Fujisawa. "Once sales pick up, we'll begin mass production again. The amount of money that Honda has requested includes the amount we will need to re-start production."

He made a grand presentation before an assembly of close to ten Mitsubishi bank executives, including the president, vice president, director of finance, and the manager of the branch that dealt with Honda's account, assuring them that there would be no further need for funding. Addressing the worry of an additional request for funding up front convinced Mitsubishi that Honda was doing well enough to continue running its business. Fujisawa managed to secure five billion yen in emergency funding from Mitsubishi Bank. Once again, Honda had overcome its crisis.

The 1954 crisis had been precipitated by technical problems. This time, it was because the production line was doing far too well for sales and marketing to keep pace. Once again, Honda had failed to balance production and marketing. Although Fujisawa had managed to establish a Ford-style mass production line for Honda's motorcycles, he had also learned a harsh lesson in the risks of make-to-stock production. In the end, plant operations were only suspended for five days, but the sense of impending crisis continued to spread within the company.

Honda continued to strengthen and tune its marketing network. Once the marketing network inside Japan kicked into high gear, achieving the balance between production and marketing would be only a matter of time. Sales of the Super Cub were booming in the United States. By the time Honda finished paying for the May capital increase, however, Honda found itself facing a shortage of inventory. In August, Honda set a new record by selling 100,000 units of the Super Cub in a single month. It goes without saying that Honda paid back the five billion yen that it had borrowed from Mitsubishi even before the end of the summer.

The profit margin for a Super Cub was only about ten percent. This wasn't particularly high, but the skyrocketing popularity of the motorcycle allowed Honda to pay a large dividend even in spite of the rapid capital increase and having to repay its debt.

In 1962, Honda produced 1,055,000 motorcycles, and its share of the motorcycle market grew to sixty percent. Sales of the Super Cub, however, had grown to dominate 93.6 percent of the small motorcycle market. Honda was quickly building a monopoly position within the industry.

The explosive popularity of the Super Cub revitalized spirits within Honda as well. Honda derived its energy as a company from the youth of its employees. Although Honda's workforce had swelled to more than 5,000 employees, the average age of its employees at the time was just twenty-four years and nine months. When older recruits—those who had spent several years attempting to get into university before succeeding, or people with graduate degrees—were assigned to a factory, the manager would often joke, "Thanks to you, the average age around here will go up a bit."

Honda's managerial staff was relatively young as well. Although Usami Masafumi, section manager for general affairs, was slightly older at fifty-one, Nobusuke Harada, manager of the Hamamatsu manufacturing plant, was forty-five, and Kihachiro Kawashima, president of American Honda, was forty-four years old. Sumio Kobayashi, section manager for the marketing division, was forty-one; Noboru Okamura, general manager for Honda Europe, was thirty-seven; and Kiyoshi Kawashima, manager of the Saitama manufacturing plant, was just thirty-five years old.

Honda's factories, headquarters, research and development section, and marketing section were practically bursting with energy. Youthfulness aside, high salaries did wonders to raise sprits inside the company as well. Honda did not discriminate between white-collar and blue-collar employees; all were placed on the same pay scale. Whether or not they had college degrees, Honda employees were promoted based on their personal skill and ability. The average monthly salary for a high school graduate was 75,000 yen after two years, whereas the average monthly salary for a university graduate was 130,000 yen after three years. And in summer 1963, every employee received a bonus equivalent to six times their base salary.

On September 23, 1963, a year before the 1964 Olympic Games were held in Tokyo, Honda gathered its 7,500 employees and held a ceremony in Kyoto to celebrate the company's fifteenth anniversary. Following the suggestion of a young employee, Honda also spent one hundred million yen to place reservations at every hot nightclub and restaurant for the evening of the ceremony. The party was called "International City Expo: A Night in Kyoto."

The scale of Honda's celebration shocked the people of Kyoto. Honda reserved the ballrooms of Kyoto's major hotels and concert halls, and held musicals, popular song concerts, traditional dance shows, and dance parties. Honda footed the bill for the performances of famous singers such as Haruo Minami, Hideo Murata, Mie Nakao, Yukari Ito, and Mari Sono, popular comedians such as Makoto Fujita, Frankie Sakai, Norihei Miki, and Junsaburo Ban, and even the celebrated magician Tenko Hikita. Nearly all of Japan's top show business talents found themselves in Kyoto that day.

Honda employees were provided with commemorative gifts and special coupons called "Night of Kyoto Invitations" that allowed them to enjoy as much free food and drink as they wanted all night long. It was a celebration of both Honda's youthfulness and its spectacular rise from a local workshop to an international corporation.

The most impressive event of all, however, was the elaborate party held at the Kyoto Kokusai Hotel. Honda had invited every geisha in Kyoto to attend. It was here that Soichiro, clad in his quilted kimono-coat, poured his heart into his version of Hideo Murata's hit song "Osho" (the Shogi King):

"Put my whole life into a *shogi* board / Pieces so small they'd blow away at a single breath / You think it's funny, you go ahead and laugh..."

Neither Soichiro himself, nor Fujisawa, who stood listening nearby, could help but recall how far they had come. *We grew out of the ruins of the war. Honda started out so tiny, you could have blown us away with a single breath, just like in the song. But we did it. We made it this far.*

Kaname Kasai, executive manager of the Suzuka manufacturing plant, who joined Honda in 1964, said ruefully of the celebrations, "I received an informal job offer from Honda in the summer of 1963. I leafed through the corporate newsletters that the company sent us every month and read about the big party in Kyoto. I thought prospective employees would be invited too, but we weren't. It was like only getting to enjoy the aromas of a delicious banquet. Later on, I heard from other employees just how great it had been." Even today, Kasai regrets not having joined Honda a year earlier.

It was also around this time that business magazines began to carry articles featuring titles like "Honda's many female millionaires." Honda had begun offering stock options to its employees in January of 1955, just after overcoming its first crisis. The price of a Honda share was around 200 yen on the open market, but Soichiro and Fujisawa sold them to employees at the par value of fifty yen. They placed no limits on the sale; any employee, male or female, could purchase as many shares as he or she wanted. Practically all the employees opted to buy.

Soichiro and Fujisawa knew that the employees could simply turn around and sell their shares on the next day's stock market for a healthy 150-yen per share profit. Nevertheless, as might be expected, not one of the employees sold any of their stock during the first year. Between the years 1959 and 1961, the number of shares issued by the company increased seventy-two times. Honda's method of raising capital had been entirely through rights issue. Unless shareholders paid up, the company would end up with forfeited shares. To prevent this, Honda introduced its employee shareholders to Mitsubishi Bank, which provided them with loans so that they could pay for their shares. Male employees sold their shares on the market once the prices went up in order to raise the money for Honda's capital increases. Most female employees, however, elected to pay up, as requested.

The large number of young employees led to many marriages within the company. Whenever this happened, employees would inevitably ask about the bride's "fixed assets," i.e., the amount of company stock she held. Men who married within the company were the envy of the other staffers. "Fixed assets" aside, Okubo, Kume, and Yoshizawa, who would later become top executives at Honda, all met their spouses in the company.

The more factories Honda built, the more the number of executives increased. Still, the company had fewer than ten directors on its board. As a result, aside from Soichiro and Fujisawa, even managing directors wore multiple hats as plant or section managers in addition to their directorial duties. In Fujisawa's eyes, however, all the directors seemed to be doing was stamping seals on official documents.

Managing is more than just paperwork. If I don't do something, Honda's going to become mired in bureaucracy. I need to define exactly what it is that an executive should do. An executive needs to look to the future. Every executive should be an expert of some kind. Making them deal with the miscellany of daily business life is a waste of their talents. I'll set them free from paperwork and put them all together in one room. It's the only way they'll be able to tackle the issues facing our company together.

The "directors' room" was Fujisawa's answer to the "law of transience." Just as spinning off the research and development section had been his attempt to create an "army of Soichiros," the aim of the collective directors' room was to create an "army of Fujisawas." Fujisawa was an expert in business management, whereas Soichiro was an expert in technology. What distinguished a person as an expert was the ability to make the right decisions based on intuition and instinct. Even if Honda succeeded in creating a second or third "Soichiro," the company would stagnate without more "Fujisawas" to respect and support their skills.

Fujisawa had never experienced the "salaryman" lifestyle and preferred to work alone, rather than as part of a rigid organization. This mindset undoubtedly played a major role in helping him connect with Soichiro, who, despite the differences in personality, shared his fiercely independent attitude.

The system for creating a second or third "Soichiro" was, of course, the "paperweight structure" of the Honda R&D Company. To avoid throwing off the balance between management and technology, its counterpart had to have some sort of structure as well. A tip in the balance would certainly mean the financial crisis of 1954 all over again. To avoid such a scenario, Fujisawa decided to introduce a collective management system.

Fujisawa put his plan into motion in 1964, immediately after Honda entered the market for four-wheeled vehicles. He brought every executive except Soichiro to Honda's Yaesu headquarters and placed them into a single room. The "collective directors' room" system was born.

At roughly the same time, Soichiro finally purged any appearance of nepotism from his company by pressuring his younger brother Benjiro to resign. Benjiro was past his prime as an engineer and had lost his ability to keep pace with new developments in technology. But he had also worked tirelessly alongside Soichiro ever since their Art Shokai days and had played as much of a role in Honda's success as anyone, so naturally, he held a high position in the company. Even Fujisawa couldn't bring himself to tell Soichiro that Benjiro's presence was holding the company back.

Witnessing Fujisawa's struggle, Soichiro swallowed his tears and made the move to fire his own brother. Once the deed was done, Soichiro and Fujisawa promised one another that they would not allow their children to work at Honda, thus preventing the company from turning into a family concern.

In September of 1963, a year after Benjiro had resigned as director of Honda, Soichiro established a foundry company to provide cast parts to Honda and installed Benjiro as the president. This company would eventually grow into the Honda Foundry Co., Ltd. Fujisawa, who owned one share in the new company and lent his name as the first president, supported Benjiro by acting as a behind-the-scenes advisor.

Next in line after Soichiro and Fujisawa as top directors at Honda were Hiroshi Takeshima, who had introduced Soichiro and Fujisawa to each other, and Kensuke Takahashi, an executive who had been scouted from the Mitsubishi Corporation. Takeshima was also manager for the Saitama manufacturing plant, while Takahashi oversaw the procurement and distribution of parts and materials for the company. Both had been born in the Meiji era and were of the same generation as Soichiro and Fujisawa.

Kiyoshi Kawashima, Kihachiro Kawashima, and Michihiro Nishida all became directors in 1962, replacing Benjiro, in a step towards their eventual role as collective managers of Honda after Soichiro and Fujisawa's retirement. They were young, being only in their thirties. The other member of the "big four," Takao Shirai, had risen to director some years earlier, in 1959.

At first, the directors openly resisted Fujisawa's "collective directors' room" system.

"When I was doing paperwork and putting my seal on documents, I had an actual job," said one. "Now I don't have anything to do. What on earth am I supposed to do here from now on?"

"Sales is all I know how to do," said another. "That was my job, and that's what I plan to keep doing. How can I market anything when I'm stuck in this room?"

"At the factory, I was responsible for so many employees," remarked another director. "It was because I took the reins myself that we were able to increase production. The factory will fall to pieces without a leader."

Fujisawa ignored the complaints. He replied:

"Let me remind you that you're all top management at Honda, the world's top motorcycle manufacturer. Being top management means you don't have to do anything. Look at me, I don't do anything. I only even come in to the office a couple of days a week. The real job for a company's top management, if there is one, is to start with a clean slate and come up with a vision for its future. Leave the paperwork to your staff, and put your minds into what really matters: the future of Honda. You directors should just meet here every day and chat among yourselves or something."

Another objective for the collective directors' room system was to nip factionalism in the bud by fostering mutual trust. Isolating the directors in one room without giving them any actual responsibilities made it difficult or impossible to rally underlings to their personal causes. And with their newfound free time, the executives found themselves actually talking and listening to one another for the first time, generating interest in areas of the business that had been previously unknown to them.

Fujisawa made the directors take turns dealing with the labor union to further heighten their sensitivity to business and management concerns. Regardless of their previous experience, each and every executive had the chance to represent Honda's interests in a negotiation with the labor union.

Just as Fujisawa had expected, those directors with engineering backgrounds generally had more difficulty adjusting to the system. However, the more time the directors spent with one another, the more they began to understand exactly what it was that Fujisawa was trying to accomplish. A director who had managed a factory received impromptu lessons in marketing and accounting. The director from the procurement and supply section got a crash course in the development of new technologies. Before long, the directors found that they had managed to establish equilibrium, a shared perception about the state of the company. Indeed, the fact Soichiro and Fujisawa's retirement occurred so smoothly ten years later was due in very large part to the success of Fujisawa's collective management system.

The establishment of the "collective directors' room," where all Honda directors except the president and vice president sat together every day, fostered an atmosphere of free discussion where anyone could voice his opinion on any topic, no matter how far removed from his own specialty. The unique system eventually developed into the *waigaya* for which Honda became famous. The term, a contraction of "*waiwai-gayagaya*," the Japanese onomatopoeia for chatter in a crowded room, was coined by Satoshi Okubo, later to become Honda's third chairman, and began to catch on around 1970.

In a reflection of Soichiro's frank and debate-loving personality, Honda's environment began to prioritize freedom of both speech and time spent at work. Fujisawa's "expertise system" had helped crystallize the new way of thinking, while the "collective directors' room" system had taken it to the next level. Meanwhile, conservatives criticized Honda as being "après-guerre," a term used in Japan at the time to mean the self-indulgence and irresponsibility of the young generation of the post WWII era.

Soichiro maintained his office at the Honda R&D Company in Wako and stayed out of day-to-day management concerns. Fujisawa, too, spent as little time as possible at headquarters, while the rest of the directors shared the same room at all times. It soon became accepted practice, therefore, that whenever there was a problem, the directors would first discuss the issue with each other until they reached a consensus, and then approach Fujisawa for the final decision.

In order to reach a conclusion within a reasonable period of time, it was necessary to make sure that the directors were basically on the same wavelength with one another at all times. Repeating this process on a daily basis allowed them to reach a group consensus. The *waigaya* provided a great opportunity for anyone to express himself or herself without worrying about formality. But total openness was a double-edged sword. A step in the wrong direction could also lead to a flippant exchange of personal opinions without any constructive consequences.

Soon, employees in other sections began employing *waigaya* in their own offices. Eventually, the *waigaya* concept, as well as the term itself, spread to Honda's foreign facilities and factories.

Back in 1961, just as Honda struggled with production adjustments at the Suzuka manufacturing plant, another major problem was brewing in the industry. In preparation for an upcoming liberalization of the Japanese marketplace, the Ministry of International Trade and Industry (MITI) proposed its Draft Law on Temporary Measures for the Promotion of Specified Industries, also known as the Specified Industries Bill.

Japan had joined the General Agreement on Trade and Tariffs (GATT) in 1955 and was scheduled to move over to Article 11 status under the Agreement, which would prohibit it from imposing import quantity restrictions due to balance-of-payment reasons, in 1963. The government, therefore, made a Cabinet decision in 1960 and drew up its Outline of Trade Liberalization to increase the import liberalization rate from forty to ninety percent within the next three years. Once the markets opened, liberalization of capital transactions would follow.

At the time, the Big Three U.S. auto manufacturers—General Motors, Ford, and Chrysler—were seen as the "elephants" of the industry. Compared to such massive American companies, Japanese automobile manufacturers were mere ants. The number of automobiles, including both passenger cars and trucks, produced in Japan in 1960 was only 480,000. General Motors alone manufactured more than that number for just a few of its vehicle lines. Even if every Japanese manufacturer cooperated to form a united front, their combined total output barely reached a tenth of the production of General Motors.

The Japanese automobile industry had only developed the means to stand on its own feet as a result of the "special procurement" orders placed by the United States in 1950, during the Korean War. Before that time, not a few people believed that there was no need for Japan to manufacture passenger cars domestically.

A strong advocate of this approach was Bank of Japan Governor Hisato Ichimada, who was so influential he was known as the "Pope." During his eight years in office from June 1946 to December 1954, Japan saw six cabinet reshuffles, and nine finance ministers. The purge directive had left only a handful of influential people in the financial world, and Ichimada took full advantage of the chaos and exercised his powers to the fullest.

"Even if we build factories for passenger cars in Japan, they won't be able to survive," insisted Ichimada. "We should focus on manufacturing trucks, and import our passenger cars from the United States and Europe. What could be a better example of the international division of labor?"

Ichimada based his thinking on two factors. One was that passenger cars at the time were a luxury that few outside of the upper crust could afford. The second was the massive investment required for manufacturing passenger cars; each unit comprised more than 20,000 components, from the engine to the body frame. Ichimada believed that consumer demand for cars in Japan was too soft to make producing them profitable.

After the end of World War II, the GHQ had imposed restrictions on the Japanese production of passenger cars, which were only lifted in October of 1949. That year, Japan manufactured 25,000 trucks, 2,000 buses, and a meager 1,000 passenger cars. The machinery in Japanese factories was severely antiquated. It was evident that they would have to be replaced before Japan could start manufacturing passenger cars in any great quantity.

The outbreak of the Korean War, however, led to an unexpected demand for trucks. Finding itself profitable once again, the industry was able to begin developing new automobiles for consumers. At last, MITI also began to support the manufacture of passenger cars as well. Japanese auto makers, however, lacked the technological know-how.

In 1952, Nissan joined forces with the British company Austin to design and manufacture a new passenger car called the "A40." The following year, Isuzu partnered with another British company, Rootes, to produce the Hillman Minx, while Hino Diesel industries (now Hino Motors Co., Ltd.) worked with the

French Renault to create the Renault-4CV. In these cases of licensed production, the foreign companies not only provided technical support to their Japanese counterparts, but also supplied parts for the vehicles as well. Toyota had also approached Ford to discuss licensed production but the outbreak of the war in Korea made it difficult for Ford engineers to travel to Japan, and in the end, the plan fell through.

The cooperative strategy began to pay off for the Japanese companies. In 1954, the first All Japan Motor Show, later to become the Tokyo Motor Show, was held in Tokyo's Hibiya Park.

By the mid-1950s, most engines and mechanical components for passenger cars were being produced domestically, although the cars themselves continued to be manufactured under licensed production agreements. The highest demand was from businesses, mainly taxi companies; sale for commercial use by businesses accounted for almost eighty percent of total demand for passenger cars.

The first phase in the "motorization" of Japan began in 1958, just as the market found itself slowing down again. Only some 50,000 passenger cars were produced domestically that year, but the percentage of vehicles owned by businesses for commercial use had dropped by nearly half to forty-four percent, while forty-six percent of all automobiles in Japan were privately owned (although used for business). It was the first time in the history of the Japanese automotive industry that the number of privately owned vehicles exceeded that of business-owned vehicles.

In the United States and Europe, motorization had occurred when the average price of a passenger car came to more or less equal the average national income per person. In other words, the trend had been triggered by the growing demand for personal-use vehicles. In Japan, however, the trend towards motorization was due entirely to the advent of privately owned vehicles for business use.

The big question was: just when would the market for personal-use automobiles take off in Japan? In 1955, the national income per person in Japan was 81,000 yen; by 1960, this had increased to 142,000 yen. Meanwhile, the retail price for a Toyota Corona or Nissan Bluebird, marketed as Japan's first personal-use vehicles, had only just dipped below one million yen.

Drastic reductions in price were still necessary to bring about true motorization in Japan. While Japan adhered to the licensed production of foreign cars, however, there were limits as to how far prices could be reduced. Unless companies began to manufacture and market smaller cars that were more appropriate for Japan's narrow roadways, there would be no way to increase consumer demand or to bring down costs.

The Japanese auto industry was clearly at a crossroads. With the timely resignation of Prime Minister Nobusuke Kishi, who had stepped down to take responsibility for the riots against the Japan-U.S. Security Treaty, Hayato Ikeda stepped in with his plan to double the annual income of Japanese citizens. If the growth of the economy continued to gain momentum and national income really did double, the number of cars produced in Japan in ten years' time would exceed one million per year and make Japan one of the world's most advanced nations for automobile production and ownership.

The future of the Japanese automobile industry appeared rosy. But it was also apparent that once the restrictions on international trade were lifted, the Big Three U.S. manufacturers would swoop down upon the Japanese marketplace, using the full weight of their immense capital to their advantage. The Japanese viewed the coming of the Big Three as another version of Commodore Perry's "black ships" that had sailed into Japanese harbors the century before. To minimize the impact, Japanese manufacturers had to band together and enhance their capacities. In terms of international competitiveness, however, the automotive industry, along with the machine tool industry, was among the weakest in Japan. Nevertheless, two years was very much the limit that liberalization could be postponed.

Anticipating the impact of the liberalization of trade on the Japanese automotive industry, as well as the approaching wave of motorization, MITI began working up a plan to promote the development of a "people's car" in the mid-1950s. This led Toyota to open negotiations in 1960 with Ford for joint production in Japan.

At around the same time, New Mitsubishi Heavy Industries (now Mitsubishi Motors Corporation), which had in 1953 successfully produced its "Jeep" with the support of Willys Overland Corporation, began planning a new licensed production contract based on a technological tie-up with the Italian company Fiat. Both Toyota and Mitsubishi realized that trade liberalization would soon be followed by liberalization of capital transactions, which could threaten the very existence of Japanese manufacturers, and therefore poured all their effort into pursuing licensing agreements with foreign manufacturers.

MITI had relatively little problem with the joint production contract between Toyota and Ford, as the result would be the Toyota-designed 800cc "Publica" passenger car. But Mitsubishi's case was another matter altogether. Mitsubishi's plan consisted of a simple knockdown production of Fiat's automobiles in Japan and would hardly support the growth of the native Japanese auto industry. Debate raged within MITI as to whether to allow Mitsubishi a permit.

In fact, MITI itself was at a crossroads as well. The ministry had divided into two camps, each advocating an opposing position for the future of Japanese trade policy and the liberalization of trade. The nationalists, led by Heavy Industry Bureau Director Shigeru Sahashi, fought endlessly with the internationalists. By the time the deadline for the lifting of the restrictions arrived, however, Sahashi's nationalists' had gained the upper hand.

MITI raced against time to bolster the competitive edge of the Japanese industry before new regulations took effect in 1963. The ministry announced plans to take a two-pronged strategy: closing the auto marketplace to new manufacturers in an attempt to prevent excessive competition, while reorganizing the remaining manufacturers to streamline production.

Catching on to what was going on at MITI, Japanese vehicle manufacturers eagerly sought to get a toehold in the marketplace before they were shut out. The Toyo Kogyo Company (now Mazda) and the Daihatsu Motor Company, which had mainly specialized in motor three-wheelers, the Suzuki Motor Company and Fuji Heavy Industries, manufacturers of motorcycles and scooters, respectively, all immediately announced plans to begin manufacturing automobiles.

In 1959, Toyota completed work on a dedicated automobile manufacturing facility in the city of Motomachi, in Aichi Prefecture. Following Toyota's lead, Nissan immediately laid the groundwork for a factory capable of producing 20,000 cars a month in the city of Oppama, Kanagawa Prefecture. The remaining member of the Japanese "big three" automakers, Isuzu, also broke ground for a new factory dedicated to manufacturing passenger cars in Fujisawa (also in Kanagawa). It was akin to Japan's *sengoku* ("warring states") period—only this time, rather than shogun and samurai competing for territory, auto companies jostled to position themselves before the markets opened to foreign imports.

At the time, k-cars, or *keijidosha* (light automobiles), with 360cc engines were by all means the gateway into the world of automobile manufacturing. Tokyu Kurogane Kogyo, Aichi Machine Industry, and Hope Jidosha had already begun manufacturing light trucks and had started something of a boom among small- and mid-sized shops and businesses.

A hit television drama, *Mr. Manager and Apprentice Boy*, reinforced the image of automobiles in the public eye. Consumers came to associate small, three-wheeled vehicles such as Daihatsu's "Midget" with an apprentice, whereas the manager would drive a k-car instead. In other words, the public was already seeing four-wheeled automobiles as being "classier."

By this point, Honda found itself the only company in the vehicle industry that had not yet committed to manufacturing a passenger car. It was evident that developing automobiles was the only way to ensure the future growth of the company. Now that Honda was indisputably a world-class manufacturer of motorcycles, Fujisawa knew that Soichiro wanted nothing more than to win an F1 race to establish Honda's reputation as a major auto manufacturer as well. Still, both felt that the timing wasn't quite right yet.

In fact, Honda had been working on its own automobile for the past several years. Fujisawa and Soichiro knew, however, that no matter how superior the design of their vehicle, the real key to success centered on the marketing network and after-sale service system. Fujisawa had only just put the finishing touches on his nationwide marketing network for motorcycles. He knew it would take an incredible amount of money and effort to establish a similar system for automobiles.

True, Honda had conquered the world with motorcycles. From a technological and investment standpoint, however, the motorcycle industry was child's play in comparison to the auto industry. Soichiro may have been a genius when it came to motorcycles, but his knowledge of cars was largely based on the old Fords that he had repaired while working at Art Shokai. In fact, Soichiro's hands-on knowledge ended with the 1920s vintage Model T.

The market for automobiles in the United States and Europe had already matured. It was often said that the last successful entrant into the industry had been Walter P. Chrysler, who had founded Chrysler in 1925. Any number of gung-ho "car guys" from Hudson, Studebaker, Packard, and Willys to former GM vice president John DeLorean, who started the DeLorean Motor Company in 1975, tried their hand at founding their own automotive companies. All had been unsuccessful in the end.

Competing in the automotive manufacturing industry was not for the faint of heart. Even if a company did possess spectacular engineering prowess and large amounts of cash, there was no guarantee of success. Fujisawa knew that this meant Honda couldn't treat its entry into the auto industry as just an extension of its motorcycle manufacturing business. If he did, he would not only compromise Soichiro's dream, but the company could easily find itself too financially wounded to carry on in any form.

In any event, Fujisawa and Soichiro were more than aware that Honda possessed neither the cash nor the appropriate technology to have a chance for success in the automotive industry. They also knew that entering the business properly meant the difference between life and death for Honda. And so Soichiro and Fujisawa had bided their time, carefully watching and waiting for the most appropriate timing for Honda to make its move.

Honda may have waited, but society did not wait for Honda. MITI, led by Sahashi and his nationalist supporters, began to take measures to raise the Japanese industry's competitiveness on the international market by drafting a law on Temporary Measures for the Rationalization of the Production of Automobiles.

The idea was to divide Japanese passenger car manufacturers into three groups: a first group consisting of companies capable of manufacturing more than 10,000 automobiles a month, such as Toyota, Nissan, and Mazda; a second group that focused largely on specialty vehicles including sport, diesel, and luxury cars, such as Prince, Isuzu, and Hino; and a third group consisting of k-car manufacturers such as Fuji Heavy Industries and Mazda. Under the proposed policy, newcomers would be required to apply for a permit from MITI before being allowed to enter the marketplace. Sahashi's plan was to authorize a rationalization cartel to reorganize the industry and quickly streamline the manufacturing process, thereby strengthening Japan's competitive edge.

In the roughly ten years since Honda's founding, both the company's sales and profits had grown to nearly half that of Toyota and Nissan. The enormous success of the Super Cub cemented Honda's position as the top manufacturer of motorcycles in Japan. And the glorious victory at the Isle of Man TT Races had given Honda a tremendous boost abroad, resulting in a major increase in exports. Honda was rapidly gaining a reputation as "world best" both inside and outside of Japan.

There's no question that our motorcycle business will continue to thrive, thought Fujisawa. *And if we continue at our present pace, we can close the gap with Toyota and Nissan even further. But MITI is serious about its new law. If Honda doesn't take a stand in the auto industry before the bill is passed, we'll never establish a position there. I know we aren't even close to being ready, but we'll have to at least announce our intentions of entering the market, and then I'll try to buy as much time as I can while we get ready.*

Fujisawa and Soichiro made their decision immediately after the five-day suspension of the Suzuka factory. It was very much as difficult a decision to make as the one to participate in the Isle of Man TT Races in the midst of the 1954 financial crisis.

Soichiro and Fujisawa aimed high. Without worrying about feasibility studies or detailed cost-and-profit analyses, they would start by setting a high goal. If there was even the slightest chance that it could be achieved, they presented it as nothing less than a fait accompli to their employees. And if they didn't have the necessary technology in the beginning, well, they would just come up with it as they went along. Over the years, this approach even earned its own name: "Hondaism."

Although the strategy was the R&D equivalent of a "banzai charge," the fact was that Honda largely accomplished the tasks that it set for itself. This was due in no small part to the clear division of responsibility at the top of the company: Fujisawa fully trusted Soichiro's engineering skills, and Soichiro gave Fujisawa full responsibility over financial issues. Soichiro and Fujisawa were famed throughout the industry for talking big, but they also had a reputation for making their outlandish claims a reality. The cornerstone of their success was the full and complete confidence that the two founders proudly placed in one another.

Honda had been quietly developing automobile technology even before Fujisawa had spun the research and development section off as an independent company. The secret research project was overseen by Yoshio Nakamura, a former aviation engineer who had worked for the Nakajima Aircraft Company after graduating from Tokyo University in 1942. While at Nakajima, he had helped design engines for fighter aircraft at the Imperial Army's Second Aviation Technology Facility in Tachikawa. When Nakajima had been dissolved at the end of the war, Nakamura joined a company called Fuji Sangyo, later to become Fuji Heavy Industries. From there he switched companies to Nihon Nainenki Seizo, later known as Tokyu Kurogane Kogyo (Kurogane). And in 1957, at the age of thirty-nine, he left Kurogane for Honda.

Nakamura had been introduced to Honda by the same man who had brought Soichiro and Fujisawa together—Hiroshi Takeshima, who had left his post at MITI to join Honda a short while earlier. Takeshima was head of the Wako plant in Saitama Prefecture when he brought Nakamura to the company's attention.

At the time, Honda had already announced its intention to enter the Isle of Man TT Races, and speculation in the industry raged as to whether manufacturing automobiles would be next. Nakamura had no interest in motorcycles; in fact, he often professed to hate them, saying that they were "for barbarians." In fact, Nakamura didn't even think it would be worth his while to work for Honda if the company wasn't planning on manufacturing automobiles, if not sometime soon, then at least in the future. Furthermore, Nakamura wasn't simply interested in designing consumer automobiles; he wanted to take his designs to the F1 races.

Nakamura pushed the issue directly during his interview with Soichiro at the Shirako factory.

"Does Honda have any plans to participate in the grand prix for automobiles after winning the Isle of Man TT?"

Soichiro's answer was straightforward: "Whether or not it's possible, I have no idea, but yes, that's what I want to do. The F1's the fastest race on the planet, you know."

Hearing these words, Nakamura made up his mind to join Honda. His first assignment was to the engineering department, which consisted of less than one hundred employees working directly under Soichiro. The department was further subdivided into three divisions: research, testing, and administration. And the design division was further broken down into four sub-sections plus a dedicated "design room." The first section worked on engines for motorcycles. The second section designed motorcycle frames. The third section, which handled automobile design, was founded upon Nakamura's arrival. The fourth section focused on agricultural machinery and other types of all-purpose equipment.

Each sub-section consisted of roughly ten members. There were eight working in the automotive section. Half had been transferred from the Honda Motor Company, and the other half had followed Nakamura from Kurogane to Honda. Only those from Kurogane knew anything about automobiles, so Nakamura, being the oldest of this group, soon found himself taking on the role of project leader.

At the time, Soichiro was completely focused on the development of the Super Cub, and didn't make any specific requests to Nakamura about the kind of automobiles to design. The development of automobiles was still far removed from Honda's mainstream corporate culture. Still, Nakamura knew time was of the essence.

Nakamura drafted plans for a k-car with a V4 engine and a FF (front engine, front wheel drive) layout. The "A120," as it was called, had a 360cc air-cooled engine under the hood, and used a hypoid gear to drive the front wheels.

The "A" in A120 referred to "automobile," while the "120" meant that Nakamura aimed for a top speed of 120 kilometers per hour for the vehicle. The chief characteristic of Nakamura's design was that the technology could be applied to any type of frame, whether that of a car, van, truck, or sports car. Based on the fact that Honda's technical experience began and ended with motorcycles, and considering the scale of its dealership and service networks, Nakamura felt that Honda's first car should be a k-car.

After finishing the Super Cub, Soichiro poured his entire effort into building the new Suzuka factory. As such, he paid scant attention to the A120 on his occasional visits to the third section. That being said, Soichiro took issue with only one aspect of the A120—the fact that it was a front wheel drive design. For one thing, it was unprecedented in the auto industry. And for another, he had grave doubts about the design's ability to climb steep inclines.

Meanwhile, Fujisawa, who had taken a ride in the A120 prototype, felt that while he appreciated the multi-purpose nature of the chassis that Nakamura had developed, it would be more realistic for Honda to focus on the light truck for its first automotive design.

By 1960, anticipation of the upcoming MITI legislation had led one company after another to sell new k-car designs. Fuji Heavy Industries unveiled its famed "Subaru 360," Mazda sold the "Carol," Daihatsu had its "Hijet," and Suzuki sold its "Suzulight."

Taking a cue from Fujisawa, Nakamura stopped work on the A120 and began developing a light truck instead. Dubbed the "A170," It featured an air-cooled, horizontally opposed V4 engine and a semi cab-over design. A prototype was made, and workers began dissecting its various problems.

That was when Soichiro paid another visit to the third section.

"Okay, everyone, listen up!" yelled Soichiro as he walked into the room. "We're doing a sports car. Ditch the truck! It's going to be a sports car, no matter what!"

Not long afterwards, rumors spread like wildfire through the R&D center.

"I hear Fujisawa-san gave his go-ahead on the sports car after all."

"Fujisawa-san agreed with the president that Honda's first automobile should be a passenger car."

At that time, it was well known that Soichiro and Fujisawa were in the throes of an intense argument over Honda's first automobile. Nobody knew exactly what words were exchanged between the two, but it was easy for anyone to guess that Soichiro favored sports cars while Fujisawa preferred trucks. Due to MITI's attempts to enact their policy to rationalize the auto industry, however, Fujisawa backed down and agreed to develop passenger cars.

Even after reaching a tenuous agreement to develop cars rather than trucks, Soichiro and Fujisawa remained at odds over the type of passenger car to develop. Soichiro argued for a serious sports car, designed around an engine normally used in a Curtiss aircraft. Fujisawa, on the other hand, didn't mind the car looking sporty, but wanted a small "business car" with two seats and a tight turning radius. Fujisawa pictured an automobile version of the "Dream" motorbikes that had so contributed to Honda's early growth. At the same time, while he had backed down for the moment, Fujisawa had far from given up on his idea of developing light trucks.

That being said, Fujisawa knew that Honda simply wasn't big enough to develop sports cars and trucks at the same time. Nakamura's team in the third section drew up plans for a sports car, but the concept was actually closer to Fujisawa's vision in that the engine could be "re-purposed" for use in a truck later.

Soichiro admitted the necessity of developing truck designs, but strongly felt they should work out the technology in sports cars first and apply the lessons to trucks later.

"We can use a DOHC (double overhead camshaft) engine for the truck, just like a sports car. Now *that* would be a truck!" said Soichiro.

Without waiting for Soichiro and Fujisawa to reach a consensus, the automotive section kicked off a new project, called the "A190."

On April 21, 1962, Fujisawa casually mentioned that Honda would manufacture automobiles at a national retailers' conference that was being held along with the ribbon-cutting ceremony for the Suzuka Racing Circuit. It was a month since Fujisawa had shut down the Suzuka factory for five days.

"Honda has completed a prototype for a 360cc k-car with a top speed of 120 kilometers per hour," said Fujisawa.

Although the audience consisted of Honda's top dealers, Fujisawa made the comment with the full knowledge and expectation that his words would reach the officials at MITI.

On May 31, a month after the Suzuka conference, MITI convened a meeting to discuss funding for support of the rationalization of the auto industry. Heavy industry section chief Sahashi indicated his desire to see his nation's capital grow as a whole and unveiled the Specified Industries Bill as the cornerstone of his plan. By all appearances, Honda had made its announcement in the nick of time.

8

On July 7, 1961, the Ministry of International Trade and Industry announced that Corporate Bureau Director Hisatsugu Tokunaga would be promoted to Deputy Minister and that his post, generally seen as a stepping-stone to becoming the next Deputy Minister, would be filled by Heavy Industry Bureau Director Shigeru Sahashi. Sahashi's appointment marked the first official step towards addressing and minimizing the effect of trade liberalization.

Sahashi firmly believed that the automotive industry needed to be consolidated in some way before the Japanese marketplace opened to foreign competitors. From his standpoint, therefore, a policy of shutting off the market against new entrants so as to reduce excessive competition was a natural choice.

Honda had expressed an interest in manufacturing automobiles via Fujisawa's casual comments to dealers in April. MITI did not take the announcement seriously. At a time when it was doubtful whether even industry leaders like Toyota and Nissan could survive liberalization, entering the fray as a newcomer was regarded as reckless and ill-advised.

In addition, MITI had a long history of distrust towards Honda. Back in 1950, when Honda first launched its Tokyo factory in an old sewing-machine factory converted to Honda's purposes, the government was still in the business of rationing and distributing gasoline. This meant that the number of motorcycles that could be manufactured was actually controlled by MITI. In other words, the ministry essentially held the lives of Japan's manufacturing companies in its hands. Honda had applied for a permit to produce three hundred motorcycles a month. At a time when only some one thousand motorcycles were being manufactured a month industry-wide, this was a stunning figure. Honda was an unknown quantity at the time, a company without any capital or marketing network. The ministry officials had shaken their heads and said:

"How in the world could a tiny company produce that many units a month without any capital, marketing ability, or experience? Is Honda trying to pad out its production plan in a bid to get more gasoline?"

Furthermore, Honda showed complete disregard for Japan's shortage of foreign currency and lavishly spent what little there was purchasing machine tools abroad. And yet, the company showed no interest in exporting the products that it made. In fact, nearly everything Honda did upset the ministry officials in one way or another.

Of course, Soichiro saw things differently. *Japanese motorcycles were able to conquer the world market mainly because the industry was not protected by the government. If the government steps in with some kind of far-reaching indus-*

trial policy to prop up the corporations, it's going to have the exact opposite effect. The best way to tackle the liberalization of trade is open competition. The auto industry has been crippled ever since the end of the war. And why? Because of the government restrictions on importing foreign cars. Companies need to hone their technology through competition. No matter how hard the government tries to stop it, better products will certainly keep entering the country.

Thus began the battle between Honda, which did everything it could to make its entry into the automotive marketplace a fait accompli, and the Ministry, which was bent on ignoring Honda's efforts. Soichiro and Fujisawa began to work out tactics to block the approval of the new policy.

Soichiro advocated a rough and direct approach. He infiltrated the front hallway of the Ministry with a huge bottle of sake in his hand and pretended to be drunk.

"The Ministry! Ministry of What? You're a bunch of morons! You're the reason the Japanese industry is so damn weak!"

Soichiro even snapped at Sahashi at a banquet one day.

"Government employees are supposed to dedicate themselves to the public good, but every time we try something new, all we get are complaints and rejections! If you've got a problem about Honda's policies, why don't you become a stockholder first? Buy some stock and then I'll listen to what you have to say."

Soichiro's protests hardly mattered, however, as Honda hadn't even set an exact timetable for manufacturing a car. MITI had its hands full bolstering the manufacturers it had already officially approved. Honda wasn't even on its radar screen.

Fujisawa may have bragged informally that the company had completed a prototype, but Honda had yet to produce even a single automobile for sale. In fact, the company hadn't even made an official announcement. How could it? The directors still hadn't reached any sort of decision as to the type of car to manufacture yet.

Honda finally revealed an outline for its plan to enter the auto industry just after the New Year's holidays the following year, in 1962.

"Until now Honda has devoted itself to manufacturing motorcycles," Fujisawa explained to the reporters at his newly built home in Roppongi, Tokyo. "But now, with our share of fifty percent of the motorcycle market, we have more freedom to focus on research and development. The Honda R&D Company has been working in secret on a prototype for an automobile, and we have completed the necessary testing and research. The prototype is for a 360cc k-car. It has a water-cooled V4 engine, the first of its kind for a vehicle of its size. We plan to unveil the finished test vehicle to our dealers and the press in May, with manufacturing to begin shortly thereafter. We aim to sell the first cars by year's end. We'll announce the retail price and production run after we have everything else worked out."

Fujisawa emphasized that Honda would sell cars rather than trucks. Considering Honda's capacities, Fujisawa still felt that it would be better for Honda to sell a truck as its first auto product. He had, however, changed his mind and thrown his full support behind Soichiro's plan after realizing that the proposed

MITI bill specifically targeted passenger cars.

What Fujisawa had left out of his announcement was the fact that the first Honda automobile would be a sports car. Of course, a sports car was still a passenger car, but sales expectations were far lower. No matter how Fujisawa ran the numbers, he couldn't see selling more than a dozen or so a month in Japan. If Fujisawa had announced that Honda was making a sports car, the Ministry would have undoubtedly rejected Honda out of hand again. "You can't call those numbers 'entering the industry,'" they would have said. "You aren't even going to produce a hundred units a month!" Fujisawa knew better, so he kept his mouth shut. *Even if our first product is a sporty two-passenger vehicle, we should be able to get around the Ministry's complaints if we emphasize that it is a 'business car.' In fact, we might even be able to expect reasonable demand if we market it well.*

On January 16, both Soichiro and Fujisawa took part in Honda's New Year's press conference, where Honda finally announced its plans to enter the auto industry. They were still deliberately vague as to the type of automobile Honda would manufacture, but told the assembled reporters that production would be split among the Saitama, Hamamatsu, and Suzuka factories. Honda's dream of entering the auto industry was rapidly becoming a reality.

The development process was not without its travails. With the company's two top executives unable to fully agree about the type of car they wanted to make, head of development Nakamura found himself caught between a rock and a hard place. Nakamura hadn't even finished building a clay model when Fujisawa made the unofficial announcement to the dealers. In the meantime, Honda had hired more experienced engineers to tackle a full-scale prototype, but there was no way to expect prompt results.

The persistent effects of production adjustments at the Suzuka manufacturing plant caused Honda to miss its opportunity to recruit new university graduates in 1962. Spirits were high throughout the company after Soichiro's New Year's announcement, but the automotive development team was anything but excited. More than anyone else, they knew that if Honda failed to show substantial progress by the specified deadline, the media would skewer Soichiro as a blowhard.

The clock was ticking and the promised May deadline was approaching. No matter how hard the managers at Honda R&D urged the engineering team to apply the old "Honda spirit," it appeared next to impossible to meet the original deadline.

Is Honda really going to enter the automobile market? As time went by, whispers of doubt spread not only through the press but among auto dealers as well. Following Fujisawa's policy, Honda always announced its profit and loss figures before accounting adjustments, which meant they were likely to show sharp fluctuations. This was reflected in the company's stock price, which also fluctuated considerably.

Traders at the Tokyo Stock Exchange usually just shrugged when they heard "Honda." Those in the auto industry reacted in much the same way. Even though both top executives appeared in the New Year's press conference to announce the company's entry into the market, more than a few industry insiders saw it as nothing more than grandstanding for PR.

Soichiro paid absolutely no heed to the rumors. He locked himself away in the plant, taking personal command of his development team. Since automobiles were a totally new playing field for Soichiro, he left the engineering aspects, including the engine, entirely up to Nakamura, who had some experience with them at Kurogane. Soichiro himself focused instead on designing the car's body.

Encouraged by its sweeping victory at the Isle of Man TT Races in 1961, Honda went on to win the World Motorcycle Grand Prix, organized for the first time by the International Motorcycling Federation (FIM) that same year. Furthermore, both the first Japan Grand Prix for motorcycles and the Suzuka National Road Race—Japan's first international road race—were scheduled to be held in Suzuka in 1962. Honda had hoped to sweep the winners' circles in its native Japan and to cement its position at the top of the international motorcycle marketplace once and for all. But such ambitions were a luxury Honda could no longer afford. Honda had no choice but to transfer its motorcycle engineers to the automobile project to bring it into full swing.

On May 23, with only ten days of so to go before the deadline, Honda suddenly announced that the unveiling of the test vehicle would be postponed until the fall Tokyo Motor Show. The official line was that Honda didn't want to leave such a long period of time between the presentation of the vehicle and the day the actual product went on sale. The real reason was, of course, that Honda hadn't managed to build a working test vehicle yet.

Usually, a delay in the unveiling of a test vehicle meant a delay in the day it would go on sale. Honda's case was no different. The best Fujisawa could do was to offer a lame apology:

"It appears we will not be selling our first automobile this year. We assure you, however, that development is proceeding according to plan. We plan to have an unofficial showing of a 'half-way test vehicle' at the dealers' conference on June 5."

The concept of a "half-way test vehicle" was quite unheard of, but Fujisawa had no other choice. He explained the measure as being due to "wanting to incorporate last-minute suggestions from our dealers into the design."

The June 5 dealers' conference was held in a meeting room at the Suzuka Circuit. True to Fujisawa's promise, a sporty-looking car with large headlamps sat on a stretch of the brand new short-course track outside. Honda did not allow the press to enter the exhibition area. Instead, it distributed handbills titled "Information on our light automobile (k-car) and light truck," listing only displacement, maximum power, and maximum speed. Nevertheless, any industry expert could tell from the specifications that the "light automobile" was in fact a sports car. That Honda was simultaneously developing a light truck with the internal development name "AK" attracted quite a bit of attention. Within Honda, "A" referred to "automobile," while "K" designated a truck design.

The "half-way test vehicle" was that of the car. Nakamura, however, remained unsatisfied with the design. It looked like a sports car, but the 360cc engine didn't provide nearly enough torque for it to drive anything like a real sports car.

Soichiro had designed the stylish, cutting-edge look of the car himself. But in keeping with regulations for k-cars, the full length had to be less than three meters. This was too small to incorporate the "business car" features and functions that Fujisawa hoped for. Fully aware of the shortcomings of the 360cc design, Nakamura and his team were developing a 500cc version as well. But it wasn't ready by the date of the conference, so Honda had postponed its public unveiling until a later date.

The production model was finally unveiled on September 24, a month before the Tokyo Motor Show. It was a sports car with a water-cooled, 45 horsepower V4 engine and a top speed of 140 kilometers per hour. It was called the "Honda Sports 500," or "S500" for short. The S500 was a roadster, and its performance was equivalent to that of a compact with a 1000cc engine.

"The S500 is intended for export," boasted Fujisawa at the unveiling. "For the domestic market, we're planning to manufacture a 360cc version, which will fall within the category of k-cars, but that would be unsuitable for sales abroad. We will be showing three types of vehicles at the Tokyo Motor Show: the S360, the S500, and a light truck: the T360. We will introduce the new lines of cars and truck one by one, basing our timing on consumer demand, starting this coming spring, both domestically and internationally."

Fujisawa felt that in order to generate demand, Honda needed to position the new cars as being perfect for commuting to work. He therefore regarded the 500cc sports car as an export model, and planned to focus on selling the 360cc "business car" in the domestic market.

Both types of car went on display in Honda's booth at the Tokyo Motor Show. Staff manning the booth had to be particularly careful: when Soichiro came to examine the booth before the show opened to the public, he was shown the sports car side. On the other hand, when Fujisawa appeared, he was taken to the business car side. Soichiro and Fujisawa knew perfectly well what was going on, but kept their mouths shut for the time being.

As it turned out, the development team only built several test versions of the S360 before eventually deciding to abandon the project. The S500, however, went on sale in October of 1963, just as Honda had promised. People in the industry derided the S500 as simply being "a motorcycle with four wheels," but Soichiro paid the critics no mind.

In preparation for the October release, Honda had undertaken a massive marketing campaign starting four months earlier in June, to make its presence as an automobile manufacturer known in Japan. The campaign included a "guess the price" contest that was an immediate hit with the Japanese public. More than 5.7 million people sent in their entries—the largest number of entrants ever recorded by the Tokyo Central Post Office for a mail-in campaign.

Shortly after the sale of the S500, Honda released the S600 and S800 sports cars. The bodies were identical to that of the S500, but the cars used 600cc and 800cc engines. Although these managed to gain a passable reputation abroad, the interest they had received at the Tokyo Motor Show was not reflected in domestic sales figures. The sports cars hardly sold at all in their home country.

The main reason for the poor domestic sales was the state of Japanese roadways at the time. The Japanese economy may have been booming, but the under-developed Japanese highway system simply wasn't suitable for sports cars. And Fujisawa's idea of marketing the cars for business use didn't meet with much support from Japanese consumers either.

The light truck fared just as poorly. As with the S500, high speed and raw horsepower were the main selling points of the new trucks. However, Honda lacked the resources to build two separate types of engines and had been forced to incorporate the sports car engine into the truck design as well.

Honda tried to spin the sports car engine as a unique sales point for the trucks but power and ease of handling were the things that mattered to truck users. The only people who would purchase a truck with a racing car engine were either passionate Honda fans or special users who drove in first or second gears only, even when the trucks were overloaded.

There was no way to export a truck like the T360. And what was more, since the engines were intended for sports cars, they were expensive to manufacture. No matter how sturdy Soichiro thought a truck based around a sports car engine might be, the only thing that really counted was sales. From that standpoint, the design was a total failure.

While the sport cars clearly demonstrated Honda's drive to pioneer new technologies, domestic sales—as Fujisawa had feared—didn't even reach a hundred units per month. The car made absolutely no contribution to Honda's bottom line. The same could be said of the trucks.

As things turned out, the Specified Industries Bill that had spurred Honda to enter the automotive marketplace never even made it as far as the Diet and was formally abandoned in 1963. Anticipating that the bill would lead to government-imposed controls on the types of vehicles manufacturers would be allowed to market, automakers had announced one new product after another, making it impossible for MITI to apply its notorious practice of "administrative guidance."

Shortly thereafter, Corporate Bureau Director Shigeru Sahashi found himself out of favor with MITI Minister Hajime Fukuda. Rather than being promoted to Deputy Minister as he had hoped, Sahashi was transferred to another section. Such developments only escalated the dispute within the Ministry and in the end, it was decided that the manufacturers should work out strategies for dealing with liberalization themselves.

Of all the tools that humans have ever created as means of transport, none has evolved as much as the automobile. This is undoubtedly what Soichiro had in mind when he said to Fujisawa at their first meeting: "Transportation may change in form, but it will never disappear." With the crushing weight of the Specified Industries Bill lifted from his shoulders, Soichiro could finally devote himself to developing automobiles at his own pace.

CHAPTER THREE: A DOUBLE SUICIDE

The key to a company's success is ideas that are ahead of their time. Without good ideas, it doesn't matter how much money you've got in your pocket—you'll always miss the bus. Our era of rapid progress has inverted the values of capital and idea. As the Buddhist sutra tells us, "Form is emptiness; emptiness is form."

—Soichiro Honda

I am where I am, not because I have experience in the job I do, but because I have total confidence in myself. No matter how great your past achievements, the only way to stay at the top is by achieving in the here and now—and having the potential to continue doing so in the future.

—Takeo Fujisawa

1

Like a storm long brewing on the horizon, an economic recession descended upon Japan just after the 1964 Summer Olympic Games in Tokyo. In March of 1965, Sanyo Special Steel Company filed for protection under the Corporate Reorganization Law, meaning that it had, in effect, gone bankrupt. Its staggering debt of fifty billion yen was the largest ever recorded in post-war Japanese history.

Only two months later, in May, Yamaichi Securities found itself in hot water. When the Japanese economy peaked during what was known as the "Olympic boom," Japanese citizens had said goodbye to banks and hello to investment companies. Even housewives had proudly carted their cookie-jar funds to Kabutocho, home of the Tokyo Stock Exchange. When the Kyushu-based newspaper *Nishi Nippon Shimbun* broke the story about Yamaichi Securities, however, customers all over Japan rushed to their local branches in a desperate bid to cancel their trusts and withdraw their deposits. Within three days, some 40,000 Yamaichi Securities customers canceled seven billion yen worth of contracts with the company.

The run didn't stop with just Yamaichi Securities customers. It expanded to swallow all of Kabutocho and then Kitahama, home of the Osaka Stock Exchange. Stock prices tumbled. Following Yamaichi, competitor Ohi Securities was also reported to be facing financial difficulties. The multiple crises rocked public trust in the securities marketplace. The Ministry of Finance and the Bank of Japan knew they could no longer sit back and watch quietly; on May 28, one week after the Yamaichi crisis had been brought to light, the Bank of Japan announced that it would provide uncollateralized "special loans" as needed to ensure that the failed financial institutions could repay deposits.

The tactic put the brakes on the run for the time being, but stock prices continued to fall. It was a serious setback for the Japanese markets; nevertheless, the motorization of Japan continued unabated. Financial crisis or not, it was clear that Japan was poised on the brink of a new era of private car ownership.

Back in 1960, Hayato Ikeda had successfully campaigned for prime minister on a platform of doubling national income within the decade. At that time, the Ministry of International Trade and Industry had predicted that Japanese auto production would exceed one million units per year within the same timeframe and place Japan squarely in the top ranks of automobile-producing nations.

In reality, however, the auto industry's growth far exceeded MITI's forecast. One million eight hundred and seventy thousand automobiles were manufactured in Japan in 1965. By the following year, the number had soared to 2.2 million, surpassing the United Kingdom and elevating Japan to third-largest auto manufacturer behind the United States and West Germany.

The rapid growth of the automobile marketplace was supported by a rise in national income. By 1965, average national income per person had grown to 265,000 yen, an eighty-seven percent increase over five years. Nearly every financial expert predicted that it would break the 300,000-yen mark by sometime the following year. It appeared Ikeda's campaign promise would come true, four years earlier than expected.

In 1966, Toyota produced 590,000 automobiles, which was 110,000 units more than the entire nation had made in 1960. Toyota suddenly found itself the ninth largest auto manufacturer in the world, the first time it had ever broken the top ten. Toyota had manufactured a cumulative total of two million automobiles by 1965. As soon as April of 1967, the number reached three million.

The Japanese auto industry marked 1966 as year one of the era of motorization. The boom was led by Japan's top two automobile manufacturers, Nissan and Toyota.

It is a widely known fact that both companies had started developing cars with 1000cc engines around the time of the Tokyo Olympics in 1964. Nissan was the first to market, and advertised heavily to create a buzz in preparation. The campaign was almost identical to the one Fujisawa had for the Honda S500. Nissan launched a contest to allow the public to name the new product and held presale events at dealers throughout the country. From among the eight million entries received, the name "Sunny" was chosen for the new product, which went on sale in April 1966.

Unfortunately for Nissan, however, President Katsuji Kawamata had made two critical errors in his approach to motorization. First of all, Kawamata had judged, based on the national income at the time, that Nissan would be able to meet the growing public demand with used specimens of its small car, the "Bluebird." Nissan's failure to develop a new car specifically tailored to the public's needs caused it to get off to a late start in stimulating early demand for a "people's car."

Worried about the situation, Nissan's engineering team had gone ahead developing the Sunny without telling the president. The question was: how could they show it to Kawamata without upsetting him?

According to company tradition, every year, after the annual ceremony marking the anniversary of Nissan's founding on December 26, the president visited the Yokohama factory that was the company's birthplace. With help from the labor union, the engineers decided to trick their president. They placed a clay model of their new car design in a hallway of the Yokohama factory and covered it with a sheet. A strategically placed team member then casually removed the sheet when Kawamata happened to walk by. The ruse worked.

"Wait. What's this?" asked Kawamata, pointing at the clay model.

"I don't know," answered someone innocently. "I suppose the development team made it for fun."

"It's not bad," replied Kawamata thoughtfully. "You know, I think we can sell this."

Just as Nissan appeared to have gotten back on track by adopting the new design, however, Kawamata made his second critical mistake. He misjudged the pace at which the public's appetite for cars was growing, and decided simply to reconfigure the line at Nissan's Oppama factory to produce the new design. The factory was only capable of manufacturing 5,000 of the automobiles a month.

Head of Marketing (and future vice president of Nissan) Masayuki Komaki, on the other hand, took an aggressive approach. He felt that sales of 15,000 units a month were well within the realm of possibility. The labor union, led by Ichiro Shioji, agreed. Emboldened, Komaki took the initiative and laid plans to quickly build a dealers' network for Sunny over a short period of time.

Just as Komaki had expected, public demand for the new car skyrocketed. Nissan immediately stepped up production at Oppama, but it wasn't enough. In the end, Nissan decided to build an all-new assembly line in their Zama factory. Nissan just barely managed to surf its way through the dawn of the era of motorization, but production costs spiraled during the process. The tremendous expenditures incurred during this time period continued to affect Nissan's business a few decades later.

Toyota, meanwhile, was well prepared for the growth in public demand for automobiles. It had kept a close eye on the situation at Nissan. They created their own car, dubbed the "Corolla," with an engine 100cc larger than that of Nissan's Sunny; it went on sale six months later in October. Anticipating the speed of Japan's motorization, Toyota built an engine factory in Kamigo and an assembly plant in Takaoka. At a time when the company's total manufacturing capacity was 40,000 cars a month, Toyota designed its new factories to be capable of producing 20,000 Corollas a month. The company had indeed staked its fortune on the new era of private car ownership.

Nissan and Toyota jostled for the top position, taking out American-style advertisements that openly attacked their rival's products. The Japanese economy was experiencing yet another boom by now, and public interest in owning cars was increasing on what seemed to be a daily basis.

Eiji Toyoda, president of Toyota at the time, describes the expectations the entire company had for the Corolla as follows:

"The reason that Toyota exists today isn't because Toyota responded to motorization, but because Toyota actually created motorization with the Corolla. If motorization hadn't occurred when it did, Toyota wouldn't be here today."

The differing approaches reflected the personalities of the heads of the two companies. Eiji Toyoda's background was in engineering, while Katsuji Kawamata had risen from the financial world. Kawamata's banker-like aversion to risk led him to miss critical opportunities to take advantage of the rapid changes occurring in the automotive marketplace.

Kawamata's decision to address motorization with used Bluebirds rather than new cars had been based on the average national income of the early 1960s. It wasn't an unreasonable position. But Eiji Toyoda, looking at growth rate trends, had predicted that average national income would exceed the retail price of a mass-market car by the early 1970s. This had turned the tables in Toyota's favor.

Buoyed by rapid economic growth, the Japanese GNP grew to second largest in the free world behind the United States in 1968. The country had only just eclipsed Canada to take fifth place in 1960, France to take fourth place in 1966, and England to become third in 1967. In 1968 it finally knocked West Germany out of second place.

Even then, average national income per person remained at twentieth place in 1968. The wide gap between GNP and average national income was largely due to low productivity. But it also indicated that there was great potential for increasing productivity and that the Japanese economy could very likely see a period of extended, high growth.

Honda, too, had not been idle during this period, but the company still lacked technical expertise when it came to automobiles. Going toe-to-toe with major players like Nissan and Toyota was akin to a suicide mission.

Honda raised the displacement of its S series sports car by increasing the pitch of the engine's bore, but the adjustment did little to increase the car's popularity. Honda did manage to maintain production capacity through exports, but this wasn't enough to make the car profitable. Honda couldn't tolerate the situation forever.

Enthusiasm for motorization surged like a rising tide, yet Honda found itself dying by inches. If the company did nothing to change, it would find itself forced out of the auto industry before long.

Fujisawa and Soichiro were at their wit's end. They decided to go back to the basics and reanalyze Honda's marketing network and after-service system. This led them to conclude that the k-car market remained the only appropriate target for the company.

Unfortunately, the initial surge in interest in k-car designs had given way to larger compact designs. The k-car market had taken a nosedive with sales dropping to just 4,000 of the vehicles a month. Fujisawa took a closer look at the market slump. He quickly discovered that in addition to having low horsepower and being too small to carry four adult passengers comfortably, k-cars remained saddled with high prices.

Automobile critics expressed doubt about the future of k-cars, taking the view that these mini-vehicles, having fulfilled their mission, would "quickly disappear once the mass-market cars developed by Nissan and Toyota come out on the market."

But Fujisawa saw things differently. *It's true that motorization is soaring,* but with the current national income levels, it will still take some time before the average citizen can afford even a "people's car." If we can create a 360cc k-car with 30 horsepower, a trunk, and enough room to accommodate four adults comfortably, and we set the retail at roughly the same as average national income, say between 300,000 and 400,000 yen, I think we can move 10,000 of them a month.

Generally speaking, manufacturers first analyzed the market, set a goal for market share, and only then decided on a type of automobile. Fujisawa was different. He settled on an idea about the type of automobile first and then chose a market in which to sell the new design. Fujisawa's big success with the Super Cub had convinced him that the same strategy would work with the k-car.

As always, it was up to Soichiro to turn Fujisawa's ideas into actual products. Only Soichiro knew the details about what type of product would be made, and what factory would be used to manufacture it. From the very first days of Honda's existence, Soichiro had taken full responsibility for the development and production of every one of the company's products. The engineers at the Honda R&D Co. were little more than extensions of Soichiro himself.

The development of the S500 was the sole exception. As Soichiro lacked the basic expertise when it came to automobiles, Yoshio Nakamura, originally from Kurogane, had taken the lead with the S500. Nakamura, however, had since moved to England to focus on Honda's nascent F1 program. So Soichiro had no choice but to take over as team leader himself. He was eager to apply his motorcycle expertise to the challenge of creating a satisfying car.

The role of establishing a marketing network for the new car naturally fell to Fujisawa. In the case of the Super Cub, production at the Suzuka plant had taken off so quickly that it had outstripped the ability of marketing to handle the products, leading to a five-day shutdown of the Suzuka plant. Responsibility for that fiasco lay entirely with Fujisawa.

Fujisawa convinced Soichiro that Honda would be able to sell 10,000 k-cars per month and had him begin work on the new automobile. At the same time, Fujisawa knew that preparing the marketing network would not be an easy job. Organizing bicycle shops had worked for selling motorcycles. Automobiles were a different story. Even if Fujisawa decided to use Honda's existing network of motorcycle dealers, there was no way they could provide the necessary after-service and maintenance on their own. Unexpected malfunctions could, and would, happen.

Something had to be done. Fujisawa's first idea was to create facilities that specialized in handling maintenance issues, after-care, and spare parts. He envisioned a nationwide network of five hundred of the facilities, called "Service Factories," directly operated by Honda, so that dealers would be able to focus their full attention on selling the product rather than making repairs.

In April 1966, six months before Honda planned to unveil its new automobile, Fujisawa established three new companies: Honda Eiken, a support company for dealers new to car sales; Honda Chuhan, which specialized in used cars; and Honda Shinpan, a credit company. Together they would provide the much-needed support for Honda's dealers, all of which were complete novices when it came to selling automobiles.

Honda Eiken's specialty was sales analysis. Fujisawa had set the company up as a sort of counterpart to the Honda R&D Company, which, of course, specialized in technology. Honda Eiken was unique in that its five hundred employees were not organized in any hierarchy and that it didn't concern itself with administrative or financial matters.

Satoshi Goto, the eldest son of Tokyu Group chairman Noboru Goto and later president of Tokyu Construction Company, entered Honda straight out of college to gain basic working experience. He was immediately assigned to Honda Eiken. Honda had also started hiring mid-career professionals, but it still wasn't enough. Some employees were transferred from the factories into the new marketing section. Others were transferred from the Honda R&D Co. to the factories. The re-shuffling was the largest reorganization in Honda's history.

As soon as the new marketing system was in place, Fujisawa began another direct-mail project. He drafted a letter of inquiry to motorcycle shops, bicycle shops and repair shops throughout Japan, asking if they would be interested in selling Honda's new k-cars. From among those that replied, Fujisawa chose 25,000 to create a unique marketing network that clearly differentiated between wholesale merchants and retail dealers. Honda's entry into automobile manufacturing, brought on by the Specified Industries Bill, had been rushed and unprepared, without even a basic agreement between the two founders. This time around, Honda was fully prepared.

Honda's new "N360" was a cutting-edge light automobile. The "N" stood for new, while "360" referred to its engine displacement. It was a front engine, front-wheel-drive car with a 33 horsepower, air-cooled, two-cylinder engine and a top speed of 105 kilometers per hour. The trunk was large enough to accommodate two golf bags, and the interior spacious enough for four adults to sit comfortably. It achieved mileage of twenty-eight kilometers per liter of gasoline. Marketing stressed the car's fuel efficiency and high performance.

The N360 debuted in October of 1966, but sales were far more sluggish than anticipated. In addition, sales of Honda's steady moneymaker, the Super Cub, had dropped off sharply in the United States. American inventory began to pile up. By August, American Honda found itself facing 300,000 units of dead stock, including at the distribution stage, and a forty-four million dollar shortfall.

At the time, Fujisawa was in Germany with his wife, mainly to enjoy live performances of Richard Wagner's operas. Upon hearing the news, he immediately cut short his vacation and flew to Los Angeles to take a firsthand look at the problem. The major cause of the slump was that American customers had tired of the Super Cub. After the American debut of the 50cc Super Cub, Honda had introduced 60cc and 90cc versions there as well. But there was no denying that all of the motorcycles were fundamentally the same. And the higher the displacement, the higher the retail price.

Immediately after returning to Japan, Fujisawa made arrangements to halt exports of the Super Cub and to send money to cover American Honda's shortage of funds. He also ordered Honda R&D to come up with a more stylish version of the Cub that would appeal to young customers. The Suzuka manufacturing plant bore the brunt of the sales slump, significantly reducing the size of its production runs.

The effects of the economic slump of 1965 still lingered, while inventory continued to pile up in the U.S., Honda's main export market. On top of it all, the burden of developing new automobiles weighed heavily on Honda. It was obvious that Honda would be announcing a drop in income and profits in their statement for fiscal year 1966. In spite of it all, Honda's two founders took an optimistic view of the situation.

The time came for Fujisawa to announce the unveiling of the N360. His comments turned out to be almost eerily prescient.

"We will announce the retail price in December. We believe that it may throw the auto industry into chaos," said Fujisawa.

The Sunny and Corolla had retailed for 410,000 yen and 432,000 yen, respectively. The price of an N360, on the other hand, was 313,000 yen delivered at the Saitama manufacturing plant—roughly 100,000 yen lower than the competition. This allowed Honda to add "low price" in addition to "fuel efficiency" and "roomy interior" to the N360's advertisements. In short, the N360 was everything that Fujisawa had asked for.

Even with its smaller 360cc engine, the N360 handled remarkably well, almost matching the Sunny and Corolla. Like Nissan, Honda had decided to start with 5,000 of the cars a month. Honda was every bit as enthusiastic about their new car as Toyota had been for the Carolla. And like Toyota, Honda aimed for nothing less than to use the N360 to create its own wave of motorization.

The N360 went on sale in March of 1967. Just as Fujisawa had expected, the N360 created a sensation the moment it hit the dealerships. In May, just three months after kicking off sales, Honda sold 5,500 N360s, exceeding the sales record of Fuji Heavy Industries' Subaru 360, and making Honda Japan's top manufacturer of k-cars.

The N360's main claim to fame, in addition to its roomy interior, was its air-cooled two-cylinder engine, the design of which was a direct extension of Honda's motorcycle expertise. The N360 also included a heater, albeit a simple one, as a standard feature.

At the time, most automobiles used water-cooled engines that relied on radiators. But this design had the shortcoming of occasionally leaking water or developing cracks in the radiator. For the S500, Soichiro had left the design entirely up to Nakamura. Nakamura followed industry convention and employed a standard water-cooled engine, but the problems inherent to the design had given the engineers no end of trouble. Soichiro, with his experience running a repair shop, was more than familiar with the annoyance of repairing a broken radiator.

On the other hand, all an air-cooled engine needed was for the car to be driven at a normal speed, which allowed the natural flow of air to cool the engine. Air-cooled engines were somewhat louder than water-cooled designs, and had a tendency to overheat if the car was driven at slow speeds for a prolonged period of time, but they were simple and reliable. And as far as the customer was concerned, the most attractive feature of the air-cooled engine was its lower cost, which in turn lowered the retail price for the car.

More than a few critics had predicted that sales for k-cars had reached a plateau before the N360 hit the marketplace. In fact, k-cars were widely known as *gamansha*—"patience cars," bought and used by those who couldn't afford anything better but hoped to eventually upgrade to a "real" car. The arrival of the N360, however, touched off a price war as manufacturers fought tooth and nail to reduce the price of their vehicles. By September of that year, combined monthly sales in the k-car category for all manufacturers had reached a new high of 70,000. The k-car marketplace had made a miraculous recovery in almost no time at all.

The smashing success of the N360 seemed to know no bounds, and, by the end of the year, Honda had expanded its facilities to be capable of manufacturing 20,000 vehicles a month. Sales of the N360's "sister vehicle," a light truck based on the same chassis and called the LN360, were brisk as well. In 1967, Honda manufactured a grand total of 150,000 k-cars and light trucks. In comparison, Toyota had manufactured a total of 160,000 Corollas altogether. Considering that the Corolla had gone on sale in October the year before, it was clear that, seen on a monthly basis, the N360 had overwhelmed the Corolla.

The Saitama manufacturing plant (also known as the Sayama Factory) had been running at full capacity since the day it had opened in April of 1965. Fujisawa came up with an aggressive plan to manufacture a minimum of 400,000 automobiles in 1968. According to Fujisawa's plan, capacity at the Sayama Factory would be increased to 40,000 automobiles a month by the end of the year. If realized, the plan would ensure that Honda's production capacity and marketing network for a single model—albeit a k-car, as opposed to the compacts produced by its rivals—exceeded not only that of Nissan but of Toyota as well.

Nevertheless, not everything was smooth going for Honda. Immediately after the debut of the N360, Honda's second largest dealer, Fukuoka Honda Hanbai, made the decision to abandon Honda for Suzuki. Then, in August, five months after the N360 went on sale, top dealer Honda Hanbai and three other major dealers in the Kansai region also relinquished their dealers' rights in favor of Suzuki. This turn of events was a major shock for Honda. Several of the dealers had even provided loans to Honda when it had run short of money in the earliest days of the company.

The reason for the defections was basically due to the dealers' growing frustration with Fujisawa's marketing strategies. In a bid to reduce distribution costs for the N360, Fujisawa had skipped over the main dealerships and had conducted business directly with smaller sub-dealers. Fujisawa felt that it was too late in the game for Honda to rely purely on local distribution systems as Toyota and Nissan did. In his unceasing drive to make Honda world-best, Fujisawa had decided to risk alienating specific dealers in an effort to establish a totally new marketing network. He had anticipated some ruffled feathers during the transition. As it turned out, however, his decision would have a major impact down the road during a scandal involving defects in the N360s.

Fujisawa, for his part, had never intentionally adopted a harsh or merciless policy towards the dealers. In fact, when quite a few of the dealers found themselves in dire conditions due to irresponsible management, Honda had presented them with a restructuring plan. If they accepted and worked hard to achieve their goals, Honda actually paid off their outstanding loans or, if they had borrowed directly from Honda, forgave the loans altogether. More than ten companies across the nation took advantage of these benefits. One such dealer in Nagoya received notice just before the New Year that Honda would forgive his debt and decided to celebrate—unfortunately, he dropped dead of a heart attack in the midst of his celebration!

In the end, it took a total of six years from the time Honda first announced that it would start manufacturing automobiles until it managed to get the business running along the right lines. The advance into the auto marketplace had temporarily diverted Honda's attention from the international motorcycle racing scene but once their automotive business had stabilized, Honda had returned with a vengeance, setting a world record by sweeping first place in every category (50cc, 125cc, 250cc, 350cc, and 500cc) at the 1966 World Motorcycle Grand Prix. When it came to motorcycles, Honda was second to none.

Once he had secured a foothold with k-cars, Soichiro began to focus on creating "serious" automobiles. Honda's S series, which featured water-cooled engines, may have sold sluggishly but the air-cooled N360 had been a massive success. Emboldened and eager to make Honda into a world-class automotive manufacturer, Soichiro ordered his team to develop a "basic car" called the H1300. "H" stood for "Honda," while the 1300 referred to the 1,300cc engine around which the automobile would be designed.

The Japanese economy had overcome the worst of the 1965 recession, ushering in the era of post-war prosperity. Motorization was finally taking off in earnest. The Japanese auto industry had survived the liberalization of the Japanese marketplace. Now, however, a new threat loomed on the horizon: the liberalization of capital transactions. The industry had dodged the bullet of government-mandated reorganization with the death of the Specified Industries Bill. But by the mid-1960s, calls for reorganization began to rise once again—this time, from within the industry.

The first proponent of reorganization was Nissan. In March of 1965, Nissan acquired k-car manufacturer Aichi Machine Industries, and, in August 1966, merged with Prince Automobile. Toyota reacted to the merger by forming a capital tie-up with Hino Motor Company in October of 1966. Isuzu created a technological partnership with Fuji Heavy Industries in December. In November of 1967, Toyota engaged in another capital tie-up, this time with Daihatsu. The "Big Three" American companies—GM, Ford, and Chrysler—watched the situation vigilantly, waiting for their opportunity to move into the fray.

Honda, too, could not afford to be indifferent to the situation. The fiercely independent Soichiro and Fujisawa had no interest in partnerships or mergers with other companies. But unless Honda strengthened its foothold on the automobile market, there was no way it would be able to resist getting caught up in the wave of reorganization sweeping the industry. Moreover, it was not out of the question that the government may come up with another version of the Specified Industries Bill.

Soichiro was a staunch believer in free competition and an open market-place. *Everything depends on competition,* thought Soichiro. *The only reason Honda has become the world's top motorcycle manufacturer is that we took all the top places in the Isle of Man TT. Just because the N360 was a hit, it doesn't mean that Honda's position as an auto manufacturer is secure. We need to develop real cars and make sure that they too are a hit, and then we will have established a firm base for ourselves. A series of victories in the F1 championship would definitely give Honda an edge. It would also give us a chance to begin exporting. It's only by winning against the competition in both business and in the races that we can make our contribution to society.*

Fujisawa was just as aggressive about competing as Soichiro. His personal motto was "carry your own torch." *A torch is a great help to the person carrying it, but not so much for those that follow. If the holder of the torch decides to put it out, only he will know which way to go. You've got to carry your own torch to make your way.* Fujisawa hadn't been taught his motto. He had learned it the hard way, through experience.

While Soichiro and Fujisawa may have appeared to share their basic outlook, they had, in fact, completely opposite ideas when it came to the subject of how to transform Honda into a major auto manufacturer.

2

Once again, the threat of reorganization had thrown the auto industry into chaos. But morale was as high as ever at Honda, thanks to the overwhelming success of the N360 and sweeping the winner's circles at the World Motorcycle Grand Prix. Honda salesmen were in high spirits as well, knowing that Fujisawa was just putting the finishing touches on Honda's new 40,000 vehicle-a-month marketing network. Not a single employee doubted that sales of the N360 would soon exceed those of Toyota's Corolla and Nissan's Sunny, making it the single most popular car model in Japan.

In reality, however, from a corporate standpoint, a huge gulf remained between Honda and the major automobile manufacturers of Toyota and Nissan. The difference was akin to that between a heavyweight and a welterweight boxer. Just as a heavyweight would never face a welterweight in the ring, Toyota and Nissan didn't see Honda as a serious competitor. It didn't matter how well Honda happened to be doing; k-cars were a totally different ballgame from compact and mid-sized cars. As far as Toyota and Nissan were concerned, k-cars were out of their league.

Honda, however, saw the marketplace strategically. The company eagerly awaited its chance to dominate the welterweight class before bulking up to face off against the heavyweights.

Thanks to Honda's freshly established direct distribution system, Honda Eiken salesmen benefited from immediate feedback from their customers. Honda's plants were running every day, seven days a week. The production and marketing teams were working at full tilt. All the employees had their eyes on the same dream.

The most active and energetic area of the company was the Honda R&D Company, which was busy developing an F1 race car and the H1300 compact car at the same time. Honda director Michiyoshi Hagino, currently also managing director of Honda R&D, describes the situation at the time:

"I joined Honda in 1966 because I loved cars. After my training period, I was lucky enough to get assigned to the automobile design section of Honda R&D, just as I had hoped. Before joining Honda, I had envisioned an R&D section as being like a laboratory in a university, with everyone quietly focusing on his subject of research. But I was totally mistaken. Everyone worked at their own desks without saying a single word to anyone else, but the tenacity and ferocity was palpable. The entire office was like a crucible. The workers had almost forgotten about eating, sleeping, and holidays. The 'Old Man,' Honda-san, prowled around every day, and pity the employee who wasn't working up to his standards; Honda-san wasn't afraid to let him know at the top of his lungs. The office was full of experts on engines, but the people in my group working on automobile design were all amateurs. Apart from the engines, no one had any experience building a car, so we had to copy other companies' designs. The Old Man would yell at us again to use our heads more, to come up with our own ideas. That was what the environment was like."

Hagino had initially wanted to work for Toyota or Nissan. But Honda had come through with the first job offer, and Hagino had taken it. When Hagino went to tell his university professor that he would be starting work at Honda, his professor had said, "It's okay to work for Honda, but for god's sake don't work in their R&D section! It'll kill you for sure." The Honda R&D Company's penchant for overworking their staff was notorious throughout Japan's universities.

In terms of profit, Honda was by this time making enough to be seen as a large company. As prospective employers, however, Toyota and Nissan, with their solid business foundations, remained far and ahead the most popular choices for mechanical engineering graduates. Most new hires at Honda, and especially at Honda R&D, had either come to Honda because of their personal admiration for Soichiro, or, like Hagino, had hoped to work at Toyota or Nissan but had been led by circumstance to Honda's doors.

Once the collective directors' room was in place, Soichiro and Fujisawa began to consciously avoid participating in board meetings, letting Kiyoshi Kawashima, Takao Shirai, Kihachiro Kawashima, and Michihiro Nishida take the reins of leadership for the company instead. Sharing the same room at the Honda headquarters in Yaesu, the four men had naturally become experts at discussing things to reach a collective decision. And whenever they had time, they shared their views about the future of Honda with one another.

As Shoichiro Irimajiri would later recall, the entire company maintained itself in a "state of chaos," prioritizing freedom over order. General manager Hideo Sugiura oversaw the day-to-day affairs at Honda R&D. He had worked on the N360 directly under Soichiro. Just after the first shipment of the finished cars, he stopped by for a routine medical check-up.

Oddly enough, the higher an employee rose in the company, the more they looked forward to their periodic check-ups. The tests usually took an entire day, and that meant an entire day of not being yelled at by Soichiro. The check-ups became precious break time for Honda's employees. Sugiura had swallowed an endoscope almost happily.

But several days later, after the results of the various tests came through, Sugiura was told that he had stomach cancer.

"It's still in the early stages," the doctor told him. "If you have surgery right away, there's a ninety-nine percent chance you'll survive. Otherwise, it's a ninety-nine percent chance you won't."

Having just turned forty, Sugiura was in the prime of his life. He elected to have the surgery at once. To ease the financial burden on his wife and young child, Sugiura asked the doctor to arrange for him to have the surgery at the University of Tokyo Hospital, which had relatively low hospital fees. This incurred Soichiro's wrath.

"Why on earth did you pick the University of Tokyo? The doctors may be good, but they don't have any air-conditioning and you won't have a private room. Summer's coming and it'll be so hot that you'll get an infection the minute they cut you open. Look, pick a hospital with air conditioning. You're an invaluable engineer for Honda. You're going to cripple the company if you go off and die in a cheap room! Let me take care of it. Just leave everything to me."

Before Sugiura could protest, Soichiro cancelled Sugiura's appointments at the University of Tokyo and personally arranged for him to stay instead at Juntendo University Hospital, which was Soichiro's regular hospital. Juntendo University had both private rooms and an air-conditioning system.

Then, on the night before Sugiura went into the hospital, Fujisawa took him out to dinner at the Chinese restaurant in Hotel Okura. Afterwards, Fujisawa invited Sugiura to his house in Roppongi and gave him a present of some genuine English tea, which was still a rare and precious commodity in Japan at the time.

"After the surgery, drink it cold," instructed Fujisawa. "You'll feel it spread through your stomach, and it'll give you a new lease on life. Don't worry about the company, or your family. I'll take care of them while you're in the hospital."

Sugiura lost two-thirds of his stomach, but the surgery was a success. He left the hospital, recuperated at home for a while, and then went back to work. The atmosphere at Honda R&D, however, was as tense as ever.

The fact was that Soichiro had been locked into a fierce debate with the younger engineers over the type of engine to be used in the H1300, Honda's first compact car. Soichiro wanted an air-cooled engine like the one he had used for the N360; the engineers, on the other hand, were in favor of a water-cooled type. Meanwhile, behind the scenes, a new conflict had arisen between Soichiro and Fujisawa over the F1 and the direction of development for compact cars.

"Winning the F1 race at any cost is the only way to prove the superiority of Japanese automobile technology to the world," was Soichiro's view on the subject.

At the time, Soichiro was wholly consumed by the F1. It hadn't always been that way; in fact, he had been quite hesitant at first. After Honda had swept the Isle of Man TT in 1961, Nakamura—who had joined Honda in 1958 firmly believing that Honda would not only start making automobiles but that it had a good chance of entering the F1 races—had actually floated the idea to Soichiro but the latter had refused to reply. It was obvious, he felt, that the F1 was beyond his reach at the time. A motorcycle had two wheels. Keeping it stable while moving was up to the rider. An automobile, on the other hand, had four wheels, and was naturally stable even when not in motion. Keeping it stable on the racetrack required knowledge of machines and electronics. Intuition and experience were key to developing winning motorcycles; automobiles were a different story. A race car engineer needed a solid understanding of physics, of power, of energy, to even get a grip on the mechanical design.

Soichiro's hands-on, craftsman-like approach to technology was based on his time spent as an apprentice at Art Shokai. He was extraordinarily adept with any machines that were visible to the eye but needed a long time to come to grips with "invisible" concepts such as electricity. The relatively simple machinery of a motorcycle was the ideal medium for Soichiro to make the most of his practical, experience-based skills and unique intuition.

Whenever he devised a new motorcycle design, Soichiro patiently explained its inner workings to Fujisawa. No matter how complex, Soichiro was able to provide an explanation that even a layman could understand. He also described, in simple terms, how the product was made. Moved by Soichiro's tutorial bent, Fujisawa at one point made efforts to have a book published on Soichiro's contributions to the field of mechanical engineering.

Fujisawa's idea was that the book should demonstrate, through Soichiro's personal experiences, just how much Soichiro himself had achieved as well as how far Japanese engineering had come in the post-war era. Properly made, it would be an informal history of the development of the Japanese machine industry. Arrangements were made with a publisher and a writer was hired to transcribe the interviews with Soichiro. The interviews went well, and Fujisawa looked forward to seeing the book in print.

Published in 1962, the book was titled *Raise the Sail With Your Stronger Hand*. It became an instant bestseller. But when Fujisawa cracked open his copy, he could hardly believe his eyes.

Rather than the serious historical text Fujisawa had expected, the book was a comedic take on Soichiro's life, even down to the chapter titles: "Devotion to one's parents as explained by an 'undevoted son'," "The roots of all my ideas: Troublemaking," "You never know how your life will turn out until you live it," "Life is a horserace: young people today," "Poverty and hardship are what make you strong," and "Six messages for young people today: spending your youth without regret."

What a motormouth! thought Fujisawa. *I should've known he'd get carried away and go off on some totally irrelevant topic every chance he got. The man has no concept of business. He's a genius at developing technology, but he mistakes that technology for a management strategy. It amuses the mass media, so they treat him like a star. The dangerous thing is that all the flattery could lure Soichiro into feeling too satisfied with himself. But what can I do? If I say something that sounds reproachful, he might look on it as sour grapes, and that wouldn't be good for the company at all. It's sad that it turned out this way, but*

Soichiro has completely missed his opportunity to systemize and categorize his understanding of technology for future generations.

Soichiro didn't say as much, but he was beginning to realize that he was reaching his limits as engineer. Despite Nakamura's urging him to participate in the F1, Soichiro had held back because he still felt that his knowledge of automotive engineering was incomplete.

Regardless of Soichiro's thoughts on the matter, European motorsports journalists saw it as only a matter of time before Honda entered a design in the F1. For European automakers, a success in the Isle of Man TT usually meant that the company would go on to participate in the F1 as well.

It was in 1962, just after the decision had been made to push into the automobile industry, that Soichiro began to show a renewed interest in the F1. Meanwhile, Nakamura steadily exhorted the engineering team at Honda R&D to prepare themselves.

"Now that we're moving into the auto industry, we should be more aggressive about participating in the F1. It doesn't matter if we win or not at first. The important thing is getting our foot in the door," he exhorted.

One day, Nakamura invited Editor-in-chief Günther Molter of the Swiss magazine *Auto-Jahr (Automobile Year)* to the Tokyo Motor Show to interview Soichiro.

"Are the rumors in Europe that Honda will participate in the F1 true?" asked Molter.

Nakamura interpreted the question, fully expecting Soichiro to brush it off. The response took him by surprise.

"Yes, we are," answered Soichiro quickly and firmly.

It was the first Nakamura had heard of it. He even felt the need to confirm that Soichiro was serious before interpreting the comment. Soichiro nodded his assent. It didn't take long for the article—complete with Soichiro's photo—to hit the newsstands. From that point on, Europeans took Honda's participation in the F1 as a given.

Taking Soichiro's words at face value, Nakamura began drafting blueprints for an F1 race car, in parallel with the S500 consumer sports car he was working on at the time. Once the news about Soichiro's announcement reached Japan from Europe, there was no turning back.

Soichiro's sudden decision stemmed from a renewed passion for automobile racing. The first auto race that Soichiro had been involved with was back in 1922, when he had just started working at Art Shokai. The Nippon Automobile Race Club had been established in the spring of that year. Japan's first automobile race, the "Great Car Race," was held that November in Suzaki—Tokyo's first patch of "reclaimed land" created by infill of soil and waste into Tokyo Bay.

Art Shokai had modified a foreign car and entered the race, but Soichiro, still low on the totem pole, found himself babysitting the factory manager's children. The traditional Japanese master-and-apprentice relationship meant that a young apprentice like Soichiro wasn't allowed to touch the car, let alone take it for a test spin. Soichiro wouldn't get his first chance to drive one until just after the Great Kanto Earthquake of 1923.

In 1924, Soichiro participated as an engineer on the "Curtiss" project, an all-new automobile designed around a V-8 engine repurposed from the Curtiss aircraft. In 1925, Soichiro got his first taste of victory when he drove the car in a race held on Tokyo's Yoyogi Parade Ground.

Soichiro retained his passion for auto racing even after going independent. Soichiro and his brother Benjiro adapted a Ford engine and chassis for use in a race car, which they called the "Hamamatsu." Soichiro entered it in the Japan Motor Vehicle Competition at Tamagawa Speedway, sponsored by *Hochi Shimbun*, and drove it himself.

Soichiro had spent the twenty years since leaving the Hamamatsu branch of Art Shokai immersed in work completely unrelated to the sport. But Honda's complete and total victory at the Isle of Man rekindled his passion and ambition for auto racing once again. Now he wanted to be world champion not only in motorcycle racing but in the world of car racing as well. The first step on the way to fulfilling his ambition was to build a racetrack.

"I'm the king of hotrodders," he joked. "I'm going to build a real track, so our kind won't have to tear around the city anymore."

From around this time, Soichiro poured his entire soul into auto racing. His passion bordered on the obsessive.

America had the Indy 500, and Europe the F1. Soichiro dedicated himself to building a racing circuit that would make it possible to hold a world-class race in Japan as well. In doing so, he sought both to fulfill his own dream and to elevate the Japanese industry as a whole.

Soichiro spent 2.5 billion yen building what came to be known as the Suzuka Circuit on a plot of land right next to Honda's Suzuka manufacturing plant. The circuit opened for racing in 1962. The inaugural race was for motorcycles, but six months later, it became the venue for the first Japan Grand Prix for automobiles. The successful completion of the speedway fueled Soichiro's passion for winning the F1 all the more.

Now that Honda's entry in the F1 was seen as an established fact, both abroad and in Japan, Soichiro and Nakamura devoted their entire effort to the development of an F1 racing machine. Fujisawa, on the other hand, showed next to no interest in the project. He had his hands full dealing with sagging exports of the Super Cub, for one thing, and with Honda's future in the consumer auto industry, for another. At the time, Fujisawa saw Soichiro's interest in the F1 as nothing more than "the president's hobby."

Soichiro, on the other hand, treated the F1 challenge not as a spur-of-the-moment decision, but a virtual requirement for Honda to succeed in the consumer industry. It was no accident that Soichiro had chosen a sports car design for Honda's first car.

Winning the Isle of Man TT was our chance to prove we were world-best in motorcycles. The F1 is the pinnacle of automobile racing, the ultimate test of speed. If we're going to sell sports cars, we've got to prove ourselves in the F1. The short lead-time means the young engineers are going to get a crash-course in race design, which won't hurt either. But now that it's decided, we've got to aim for the top. Winning's all that matters.

In reality, there is more than a little doubt as to whether participating in the F1 was a real necessity for Honda at the time. The Motorcycle Grand Prix had indeed been a gateway to success for Honda as a motorcycle manufacturer, boosting exports and moving the company up to join the ranks of the world's top firms. But Honda lacked even a prototype of an automobile at the time. Under such circumstances, there really was no immediate need for Honda to participate in the F1. It would have made far more sense to build up some actual experience with consumer cars before venturing into the world of auto racing. In the end, it was only because Honda had a president, whose passion and pride simply would not let him back down until his company had won the race, and an engineer, who had joined the company with the single hope of living out his passion for car racing, that it managed to venture into the world of F1 when it did.

As Honda's top financial executive, Fujisawa knew more than anyone about the staggering expense of participating in the F1. Soichiro and Nakamura waged a constant war of persuasion to bring him over to their side. Soichiro insisted that the whole enterprise was good training for the engineering staff, while Nakamura exploited the PR angle.

"Fujisawa-san, simply entering the F1 will be a great advertisement for Honda. I guarantee you we're going to get worldwide press coverage for it. It's precisely because we don't have a compact car yet that we need to enter the races now."

Fujisawa finally relented after extracting a grudging promise from the pair that Honda would only develop an engine, which cost far less than developing an entire car. Nakamura dutifully opened negotiations with several famed F1 teams, including those run by Britain's Lotus and Jack Brabham. In the end, however, the discussions came to nothing. It was finally decided that Honda would form its own team and build its own F1 machine.

Honda officially announced its participation in the F1 in January of 1964. In June 1965, only six months later, Honda unveiled its prototype, called the RA271, to the mass media. It boasted a 230 horsepower, 1500cc V-type twelve-cylinder engine that was capable of 1300 r.p.m. and a top speed of 271 kilometers per hour. For the car's debut, Honda selected the England Grand Prix, which would be held on July 11. The reason for this choice was simple: Honda already had a London branch, and the team felt that English would be an easier language in which to communicate. In spite of the fanfare, however, the development team couldn't make the deadline. The RA271 made its actual debut three weeks later in Germany.

In the 1960s, the F1 did not enjoy the widespread popularity it does today. In Japan, only die-hard automotive fans were even aware of the race. The race cars lacked the flashy sponsors' logos with which modern competitors are emblazoned. Instead, each car was painted in a color that corresponded to the country of its origin. England's official color was green, France's blue, Italy's red, and Germany's silver.

"We should be gold," Soichiro, unaware of the rules, had exclaimed. "Gold! Wait! I've got a better idea—we can plate it in actual gold!"

Unfortunately, gold-rich South Africa had already registered the color for its own country. Soichiro had to settle for metallic gold (which was used on the prototype R270 but later changed to ivory white for the R271), with a vivid red circle painted on its hood, symbolizing the Japanese flag.

Honda had yet to export its first automobile to Europe, and so the company's participation in the race barely registered on the radar of European manufacturers. As such, the European teams welcomed Honda with open arms.

The British and Italians were particularly devoted fans of the F1. Some races featured nothing but green and red colored cars. There was a preliminary heat, but it was only for show. In those days, every official participant was guaranteed a slot in the actual race.

In 1964, the year of Honda's debut, a grand total of ten F1 races were held across the world. Honda participated in the sixth—the Grand Prix in Germany—and in the Grand Prix races held in the United States and Italy. Honda came in thirteenth in Germany, but was forced to retire early from the other two races. The following year, Honda participated in a total of eight races. Honda entered two cars in six out of the eight, and managed to come in first at the Mexico Grand Prix.

Yoshitoshi Sakurai, who, as chief supervisor of Honda's F1 team, led Honda to become world champion in 1986 and 1987 recalls that watching a newsreel of Honda's victory at the Mexico G.P. was key to his deciding to join Honda in 1967.

Soichiro firmly believed that winning races was all that mattered. Fujisawa expected Soichiro to turn away from F1 racing, since his dream had come true, but he was wrong. Now that he had tasted the thrill of competition, there wasn't a chance Soichiro would quit.

"Our next goal," said Soichiro on nearly every occasion he met with Fuji-sawa, "should be winning consecutive races to secure our position as world champion for the year." Seeing Soichiro so passionately devoted to this goal, Fujisawa found himself unable to throw cold water on the man's plans.

Soichiro's ambitions were temporarily sidelined in 1966, however, when the F1 regulations were amended to require participants to use engines with a minimum displacement of 3,000cc. It was a frustrating time for Honda. Had the requirement remained at 1,500cc, the company would have been in a position to aim for the top spot. Instead, Honda found itself having to start from zero again.

Honda's engineers began working on a new race car, the RA273, right after Honda's victory at the Grand Prix in Mexico in 1965. In Honda nomenclature, "R" stood for "racing," "A" meant "automobile," and the number indicated the maximum intended speed. Honda's first F1 car was the RA271, reflecting the engineers' expectations that the car would reach a maximum speed of 271 kilometers per hour.

Irimajiri, who at this point was in his fourth year working for Honda, drew up the blueprints for the RA273. He was an "engine man" through and through. In his first year at Honda, Irimajiri had developed a 50cc engine intended for use in Honda's racing motorcycles. At the time, Honda was having trouble trying to secure a victory in the 50cc World Motorcycle Grand Prix. Irimajiri speculated that the problem was the horsepower of their engines, and tuned his design to turn out 10.8 rather than the previous 10 horsepower. As a result, Honda won first place at the next year's World Motorcycle Grand Prix in 1964. That same year, Irimajiri also created a 250cc engine. His designs impressed all his colleagues, and soon enough he had developed a reputation for excellence throughout the auto industry.

Irimajiri's first brush with engines had come when he was still in elementary school. His thesis project at the university was designing a theoretical engine for an F1 racer. Whether for automobiles or motorcycles, engines formed an integral part of Irimajiri's life. All he needed was a request: Irimajiri was confident enough in his skills that he felt no design was beyond his abilities.

Irimajiri nourished a secret resolve as he drew up the blueprints for the RA273. He could not forget that Honda's failure to complete the Grand Prix in England the August before had been due to a design error on his part.

Irimajiri had been responsible for the piston rings in Honda's 1,500cc racing engine, but they had overheated on the speedway, causing an engine fire that forced the team to retire from its first race. Soichiro had been furious. The car was hauled back to Honda R&D for analysis. Soichiro took the lead in the investigation. It didn't take long to discover the cause of the problem.

"Who made these piston rings?" shouted Soichiro at the engineering team.

"I did, sir," replied Irimajiri, trembling with fear.

"Did you design them to burn?" pressed Soichiro mercilessly.

"None of my calculations indicated the rings would burn," replied Irimajiri cautiously. "Perhaps there may have been other factors at play…"

"I'm an expert in piston rings!" shouted Soichiro, his face turning purple with rage. "Before the war, I ran a company that made nothing but piston rings. I've got patents on piston rings. And you're trying to lecture me? This is why I can't stand university graduates. Your heads are all swollen, but you still don't know a damn thing!" Soichiro turned to the chief engineer, Kazuo Nakagawa. "Nakagawa! I want this guy out. Have him bring his letter of resignation on my desk first thing tomorrow morning."

"I'm not going to quit," answered Irimajiri. "I'll apologize if I made a mistake, but I won't quit."

In hindsight, Irimajiri had an idea as to why his piston rings had failed: he had applied a piston ring designed for a motorcycle in the engine for a car. From a theoretical standpoint, Irimajiri's decision had been sound. But the conditions of an actual F1 race, where vehicles operate at nearly three hundred kilometers an hour, had proven too harsh for the design.

"Okay then, go and apologize to everybody!" Soichiro shouted back. "It's your design that got us in trouble. I'll go with you as you apologize to every member of the team for your stupidity."

Clutching a burned-out piston ring in his hands, Irimajiri had made the rounds of each member of the F1 team. "I apologize for the trouble my mistake caused," he had repeated over and over. Soichiro followed him the entire time. Although the Cultural Revolution in China would not occur until approximately six months later, it was as if Soichiro was a Red Guard soldier forcing a "revisionist"—Irimajiri—to march through town wearing a dunce's cap. Irimajiri never forgot the humiliation. Soichiro knew it—and that was precisely why he gave Irimajiri a second chance.

None of the engineers at Honda had any hands-on experience with large engines. All they had going for them was sheer willpower, which obviously was not enough. Each and every day was a struggle. The racing season came and still the RA273 engine wasn't ready. The team barely made it to the last three races in Italy, the United States, and Mexico. Development time was so tight for Honda that they hadn't even been able to run a decent test lap. Needless to say, the results showed it. Honda's biggest win was fourth place at the Mexico Grand Prix.

In spite of the underwhelming showing, a British racing annual by the name of *Autocourse* profiled Irimajiri and his work on the RA273 engine. The article included a photograph and introduced him as "a twenty-seven year old chief engineer in his fourth year at Honda." In Europe, only well-established and highly experienced engineers had the chance to design engines for the F1. Irimajiri found himself the envy of nearly everyone in the world of F1 racing.

3

Struggling with the new regulations, Honda didn't fare any better at the 1966 F1 races. The separate F2 circuit, however, was another matter. Honda had teamed up with Jack Brabham for the F2, where the engine requirement was 1000cc, and had secured a one-two finish in most of the races, sweeping eleven consecutive victories—a first in the history of auto racing. Honda engineer Tadashi Kume, who later became the third president of Honda, was responsible for the winning engine design.

"And next year, we'll do it at the F1!" crowed an overjoyed Soichiro.

For Fujisawa, however, this was a source of major anxiety. Honda's sales figures were terrible. The U.S. market, Honda's main source of revenue from motorcycles, suffered from excess inventories, and Fujisawa had to divert large sums of money to address the problem. The S500 had yet to break even. And the N360 k-car was just about ready to hit the marketplace. The company wasn't making nearly enough money to survive challenges.

Fujisawa's duty as financial manager of Honda wasn't to satisfy Soichiro's vanity—it was to decide on the successor to the N360. Soichiro had already begun work on the H1300, another small sports car, but Fujisawa could tell right away that it wouldn't be a major moneymaker for the company. In fact, it could very well end up another S500.

Market research had convinced Fujisawa that the N360 would be a big hit. Fujisawa hoped to extend that success to a new mass-market car so as to firmly establish Honda's reputation as an automobile manufacturer. For that to happen, Honda needed a family car, just as Toyota had its Corolla and Nissan its Sunny. The problem was getting one to market.

Fujisawa, who regarded the F1 as nothing more than "the president's hobby," had wanted to pull the plug after the 1965 win in Mexico to allow the engineers to devote themselves to creating a winning compact car design. Fujisawa was convinced that Honda could come up with a product to rival anything of Toyota and Nissan's, if only the R&D team would devote its full attention to the project.

Nevertheless, Soichiro's beaming enthusiasm had made it difficult for Fujisawa to pull the rug out from under the team after the 1965 season as he had planned, and so Honda was still in the races in 1966. As it turned out, however, although Honda's results in the F1 were poor, the team had racked up victory after victory on the F2 circuit. And unlike the F1, F2 regulations specified a design that was much closer to that of a consumer car. The results caused Fujisawa to smile in spite of himself.

When it comes to motorcycles, we're invincible, thought Fujisawa as he watched Soichiro's successes. *But k-cars are not enough to solidify Honda's position as an automobile manufacturer. The only way to do that is to create a car that appeals to the mass market, one that will generate tremendous demand. Motorization has only just begun. We've still got a chance. After all, we've got a secret weapon up our sleeve.*

Fujisawa's "secret weapon" was the 148 horsepower, 1000cc engine used on the F2 racing chassis. In fact, Fujisawa was earnestly planning out a strategy to knock Toyota out of their dominant market position.

Honda started out as a maker of engines, rather than of motorcycles, reflected Fujisawa. *We've produced engines for motorcycles, automobiles, and other vehicles. By this point, we must have manufactured more engines than any other company in the world. In this field, Honda is second to none, not even GM or Ford, let alone Toyota. We were able to produce such brilliant results at the F2 because of our immense reserve of skills, and it would be a waste to let those skills go unused. If we make use of our experience with engines to develop a consumer car, we will certainly be able to make a compact car that would beat Toyota's Corolla.*

When Fujisawa and Soichiro had first agreed to work together, the two leaders had promised never to meddle in each other's area of responsibility. In reality, however, Honda had only managed to expand as it did because Fujisawa had provided the ideas, while Soichiro made them into actual products. It was how they had created the Super Cub and the N360. Soichiro's pride as an engineer usually led him to dismiss Fujisawa's ideas at first, but once he was convinced of the need, Soichiro poured his entire being into creating the product. The two were a perfect match for each other in this way.

Immediately before the N360 went on sale, Fujisawa, as always, casually mentioned his idea to Soichiro.

"I'm absolutely convinced the N360 is going to be a major hit, and it's all thanks to you, Honda-san. Now the time has come to consider the kind of car our customers will want to drive next. I know you'd like nothing better than to make another sports car. But I believe our next step should be to create a family car, something to rival Toyota's Corolla or Nissan's Sunny. You know we have a marvelous engine—the one that gave us all the victories in the F2 last year. Now that's an engine! If we built a family car based around that engine, it would definitely sell. We could really give Toyota and Nissan a run for their money."

"Vice president," began Soichiro, "you're not an engineer, so you might not understand this. But there's a big difference between engines for racing and engines for consumer cars. Besides, the F2 engine is a water-cooled engine. Our products are unique, and that means using air-cooled engines. I hate to say this to you, but I have no interest in building a car around the F2 engine. Just leave the car-making side of things to me. Once we secure a string of victories in the F1, we'll be able to take on Toyota and Nissan any time we want."

Soichiro dismissed the idea out of hand, as usual. Fujisawa, of course, was prepared for the response. He knew it would take time to bring Soichiro around. From that moment on, Fujisawa seized every available chance to suggest the family car idea to Soichiro. This time, however, there was no compromise. Soichiro dug in his heels and focused on the development of H1300.

Even in his final years, Fujisawa still regretted his decision to back down. He saw it as a missed opportunity: Honda's chance to pull ahead of Toyota once and for all. *I should have stopped Soichiro from working on the H1300, no matter what it took. If only we had built a consumer car around the F2 engine, we'd probably be bigger than Toyota today.*

But work on the H1300 had already begun, and it was next to impossible for Fujisawa to convince Soichiro to abandon the project. The Honda R&D Company was like Soichiro's personal citadel. The organization wouldn't budge without his direct order. Being in charge of the company's finances, Fujisawa knew he still needed something to make up for the sales deficit. Unprofitable ventures were not to be left alone. The real problem was the F1 project.

What Fujisawa really wanted was for Soichiro to quit the F1, but he knew the man was simply too crazy about the races to abandon them now. So Fujisawa used the back door. He called Yoshio Nakamura, supervisor of the F1 team, and told him that they needed to drastically cut costs if they wanted to continue participating.

Nakamura believed as strongly as Soichiro that Honda's technological edge depended on the F1. He struggled with the question of how to satisfy Soichiro's ambitions to become world champion while fulfilling Fujisawa's order to keep expenses down. After mulling it over for a while, he realized the only choice was to move the F1 team from the R&D headquarters in Wako to England. It would reduce the costs of transporting the cars and equipment, not to mention customs duties. And it would be far cheaper and easier to hire engineers on the scene than to bring them over from Japan.

London was the undisputed capital of the F1. The city brimmed with shops and garages that sold nothing but parts for F1 race cars. The Italian Ferrari and French Renault teams had their headquarters in London. Honda needed to follow their lead. It would be far cheaper to develop a race car in London, England than in Wako, Japan. Thanks to the more efficient use of time and labor, Nakamura calculated, Honda would be able to maintain the same level of productivity with far lower costs. With Fujisawa's permission, Nakamura built a headquarters for the Honda Racing Company, a wholly owned subsidiary of Honda, on the outskirts of London.

The move wasn't entirely without repercussions, however. Moving the base of operations to England meant taking day-to-day control over the F1 operations away from Soichiro. Neither Fujisawa nor Nakamura were yet aware of the implications of this. It would turn out to be, in fact, one of the events foreshadowing the eventual "double suicide" of Soichiro and Fujisawa.

Now that Fujisawa had decided to allow the F1 project to continue, he could no longer dismiss it as the president's little hobby. He could use the image of the F1 to sell sports cars, if Honda had a serious sports car. But the N360 was a vehicle designed for practical use.

"How can we use the F1 as an advertisement to boost sales?" asked Fujisawa of Nakamura.

Nakamura came up with the idea of calling the F1 Honda's "research laboratory on wheels."

"We can spin it that the extreme conditions in the races are key to studying how to get cars to run fast—and more safely," explained Nakamura.

Fujisawa loved the suggestion. He began using the phrase as often as he could to strengthen Honda's appeal to the public. Ironically enough, however, the tactic would later backfire when Honda became embroiled in a dispute over defects in the N360. The Japan Automobile Users Union cited the phrase as proof positive that Honda had used the N360 as a test bed on unwitting consumers.

By this time, the workforce at Honda R&D had swelled to 600 employees. Nearly half of them were involved in the F1, including Irimajiri and Kawamoto—who had completely forgotten the concept of profits or market share. They firmly believed that their job was to create an invincible engine for the F1, whatever the cost.

Moving the F1 team to England reduced some of the stress on the Honda R&D Company. One day, while Soichiro was away, Fujisawa stopped by at the R&D offices.

"We may be continuing to participate in the F1, but we aren't going to be making the cars here in Wako. The team will be based in London. We didn't create Honda R&D for racing. We separated it from the parent company so that it can develop products to sell. But look at you! You haven't created a single thing! A company can't survive if it doesn't make money. From now on, you'd better start focusing on cars we can sell!" he roared at the assembled R&D staff. Immediately thereafter, Irimajiri and several other engineers from the F1 project began developing a light truck version of the N360.

No sooner had Honda moved its F1 base to London than a famed British driver by the name of John Surtees came calling. He wanted to join the team.

Surtees had driven a Ferrari to victory in 1964, but had left the team shortly thereafter. He had founded his own team, Team Surtees, but hadn't had any luck in finding a winning car design. In the midst of his struggles, Surtees heard about Honda Racing's move to London and decided to give them a call.

Moving their base of operations to London had proven Honda's dedication to the sport. For his part, Surtees was interested in Honda's RA273, which used a powerful but heavy, water-cooled V8 engine.

Surtees had only one request when he approached Honda: to keep Nakamura as the team supervisor. The proposition appealed highly to Honda. Surtees' participation would certainly validate Honda in the eyes of the British racing world and would also reduce both the technical and financial burden for Honda. Honda jumped at the opportunity. In 1967, a part of Team Surtees, located on the outskirts of London, was branched off to become a part of Honda Racing, now a joint venture between Surtees and Honda. The new company recruited British engineers, and Honda's F1 team made a fresh start as a Japanese team with a base in the center of Europe's racing culture.

Honda used a modified version of the RA273 in its fourth season at the F1. The car was about forty kilograms lighter than its previous version, but at 700 kilograms, it was still quite heavy. The engine turned out enough power, but the team couldn't manage to squeeze any more speed out of the design. The best result it managed to achieve was third place; the championship was completely out of reach. In fact, it was mainly due to Surtees top-notch driving skills that the team was able to enjoy a decent showing throughout the season.

If the team wanted a shot at the championship, however, Honda needed a lighter engine. The team began work on a new car called the RA300. The engineers aimed to increase the top speed to 300, twenty-seven kilometers per hour faster than the previous design. They employed a Lola chassis to reduce weight. And they threw as much British know-how into the car as they could muster.

Honda participated in a total of nine races in the 1967 season. The RA300 made its debut in the sixth race, the Italian Grand Prix, taking first place in its very first outing. It was a precious second victory for the team, and the first victory for Honda since the maximum engine size had been changed to 3000cc. The RA300 retired early from the eighth race, the U.S. Grand Prix, but placed a respectable fourth in the Mexican Grand Prix, the final race of the season.

Thanks to the RA300, world championship finally appeared to be within Honda's grasp. The team knew they needed to reduce the weight even further to make their dream a reality. Other teams were also concentrating their efforts on reducing total car weight, so that in spite of being far lighter than the RA273, the RA300 remained nearly 100 kilograms heavier than rival designs. Nakamura began work on a new car, dubbed the RA301, to bring the weight of Honda's car in line with the competition.

Nakamura had already stepped down from the forefront as an engineer. He no longer drew up blueprints on his own. Instead, he focused his skills as a technology consultant. Nakamura lured Tadashi Kume from Japan to England and locked him in the offices at Honda Racing until he had drafted the blueprint for the new car. Kume's engine designs had a reputation for being fast. If they could manage to indeed bring the weight in line with the competition, Kume's touch would undoubtedly give the RA301 an edge in top speed.

Kume had designed every one of Honda's consumer automobile engines: the S series, the N360, and the H1300. The N360 had originally been designed by someone else, but Soichiro hadn't liked the preliminary layout.

"A car like this isn't going to run fast enough!" yelled Soichiro. "Give it to Kume. Let him work on it."

Soichiro trusted Kume completely. Normally, Nakamura should have spoken to Soichiro before using his treasured engineer to design the RA301. But Nakamura had been afraid that Soichiro would not only insist on putting in his own two cents, but even shoot the idea down if given the chance. Nakamura waited until Kume had drawn up the blueprints in London before sending him back with an explanation.

"What are you guys doing out there in London? You can't design the engine in London and the chassis in Japan! Engines and chassis are integrated—you've got to design them together," growled Soichiro at Kume. "And look at these blueprints: this is water-cooled. We're going to use an air-cooled engine! If you're so desperate to design a water-cooled engine, you can modify the one from the RA273. I'm going to be developing an air-cooled one on my own."

Soichiro said the exact same thing to Nakamura, who made a short trip to Japan some time later. Nakamura flushed with anger. He patiently explained to Soichiro exactly why air-cooled engines were out of date. Soichiro, of course, refused to listen.

Nakamura knew he was fighting a losing battle. Sooner or later, Soichiro would play his trump card and say, "It's my company. If you can't deal with it, get out." Nakamura also knew that Honda Racing would collapse if he left. All the dreams, all the hopes pinned on winning the championship would be lost. He was between a rock and a hard place. If Nakamura backed down and used an air-cooled engine, Honda would be the laughingstock of the F1 world. If he forced his idea through, it would poison his relationship with Soichiro. *Damned if I do and damned if I don't,* thought Nakamura. *Best not to argue with Pop. If we want to keep racing, we'd better suspend work on the RA301 and re-work the 273 to make him happy.*

Nakamura began exploring ideas for lowering the weight of Irimajiri's RA273 engine. He decided to use chassis that had been designed for the RA301 as-is, and charged Nobuhiko Kawamoto with redesigning the engine.

Nakamura had conceded to Soichiro's demands because he simply didn't believe the latter was serious about attempting an F1 with an outdated air-cooled engine. But it was no joke to Soichiro.

Soichiro was absolutely convinced that the key to victory was using air-cooled engines. And this wasn't limited to the racing world. When the time had come to design the H1300 for the consumer market, the engineering staff had unanimously voted to use a water-cooled engine. Soichiro vetoed it from the get-go, insisting on an air-cooled design. He had his favorite engineer Kume draw up the blueprints. Kume harbored strong doubts about the air-cooled concept, but could hardly disobey a direct order from his president.

Every one of the motorcycles that Soichiro had designed used an air-cooled engine. Honda's first car, the S500, had used a water-cooled engine, but had not been all too successful. The N360, on the other hand, developed under Soichiro's direct supervision, had used an air-cooled engine and was a big hit. This had cemented Soichiro's belief in air-cooled engines.

And so Soichiro specified an air-cooled engine for Honda's next project, the H1300. President or not, however, Soichiro needed to explain to his staff exactly why air-cooled engines were better.

"No matter the type, engines radiate heat into the air," lectured Soichiro. "So it goes without saying that an air-cooled engine is more efficient. You know how Rommel defeated the British in North Africa during World War II? His tanks used air-cooled diesel engines! England lost because theirs relied on water-cooled engines. And it's no coincidence that both American and Japanese aircraft use air-cooled engines."

The story about Field Marshall Rommel was famous in the United States, thanks to a hit ad campaign for the Volkswagen Beetle, run by the VW president Heinrich Nordhoff as the company commenced export to America. "No need for water even in the desert" had been the tagline. Soichiro had heard about it and used it to try and justify his views on the superiority of the air-cooled engine design.

"I hate to say this, sir," one engineer spoke up, "but in the end General Rommel was defeated by Americans driving 4WDs with water-cooled engines. And these days, more and more aircraft are also using water-cooled engines."

The comment didn't bother Soichiro in the least. He simply went on to cite the success of his motorcycles.

"There's no question that air-cooled engines were the secret to your motorcycles' success," piped up another engineer. "But engines for motorcycles are small and are exposed to the wind. Automotive engines are housed under hoods and generate tremendous amounts of heat. It's impossible to cool them simply with airflow."

No matter how hard his engineers attempted to explain, Soichiro turned a deaf ear to the benefits of the water-cooled engine. And the more they detailed the problems inherent in using air-cooled engines, the more Soichiro insisted that it was their job to fix them. Soichiro was a firm believer in the concept that there was nothing a little research and inspiration couldn't overcome in the end.

"Even if ninety-nine percent of your experiments are failures, the remaining one percent can change everything," explained Soichiro. In the end, he always brought out his theory that all humans are lazy.

"Keep an open mind and listen. People are born procrastinators. They're lazy. Look, it's like when you have to pee when you're driving. You always hold out to the last minute, right? Or if you're hungry, you might put off stopping for a while until you reach the next service area. Who's going to check the water in their radiator every day, or watch their hoses? Nobody! That's why air-cooled engines are better—drivers can forget about them. What can't you understand such a simple concept?"

At roughly the same time, Honda's rival Mazda acquired the rights to a rotary engine from a West German company called NSU. Now they were rushing to manufacture automobiles using the new engines. Rotary engines were attracting a lot of attention for their quietness and high horsepower.

Soichiro now felt that it was a question of honor. If Honda could not create a unique engine that was both unlike those made by Toyota and Nissan and at least as good as those made by Mazda, he would lose face. In fact, Soichiro saw it as his duty—his fate—as an engineer and the president of the company. At the same time, his stubborn sense of pride prevented him from even considering importing technology from abroad.

For Soichiro, the only automotive engine worth developing was the air-cooled model, which he had been familiar with from his experience with motorcycles, and which had been such a success in the N360. Although air-cooled engines were seen as completely old-fashioned not only within Honda R&D but in the industry as a whole, Soichiro banked everything on the "one percent chance" that research would lead to a better air-cooled design.

The most effective way to prove the superiority of air-cooled engines, reasoned Soichiro, was winning the F1 championship. Now that Honda's F1 team had moved to England, however, Soichiro couldn't control them as closely as he once did. *Fujisawa may be running things,* thought Soichiro. *But I'm the one who founded the company. If I want to run the damn company into the ground, that's my decision! I don't care what they say. We're going to take on the F1 with an air-cooled engine, and we're going to win!*

While he never said anything directly about it, Soichiro remained furious about Fujisawa's decision to cut expenses, and even more so with his decision to move the F1 team to England. So when Kume had come to show him the blueprints for the RA301, his anger and resentment had finally boiled over.

In the end, the modifications Soichiro had ordered for the 273 proved unsatisfactory. After countless hours, the team had no choice but to abandon the project.

The tremendous delay meant that Honda was forced to use the older RA300 model in the season-opening for the 1968 South African Grand Prix. The result was a dismal eighth place, barely enough for the team to save face in the racing world.

The team rushed to ready the RA301 for the next race of the season, the Spain Grand Prix. The car weighed in at 530 kilograms, eighty kilograms lighter than the RA300, and the engine put out 450 horsepower in comparison to the RA300's 420. In spite of having to forego testing at Honda's Suzuka track, the RA301 managed to place third position in the qualifying session. Disappointingly, however, engine trouble forced an early retirement from the race proper.

The RA301 made a good showing at subsequent Grand Prix qualifying sessions in Monaco, Belgium, and the Netherlands, raising hopes for a shot at a first-place victory. In the end, however, a series of minor problems and troubles, largely due to the lack of time for testing the car, contrived to dash the team's dreams. Nevertheless, Nakamura believed that, with a little more time and development, Honda Racing would be seeing the light at the end of the tunnel.

The next race was the France Grand Prix, scheduled to start on July 2. But no sooner had Nakamura begun preparations than he received unexpected news from Honda headquarters in Tokyo. It said, "President Soichiro has completed his RA302 with an air-cooled V8 engine. It has already been entered in the France G.P. via Honda France."

Nakamura had heard that Kume was designing an air-cooled racing engine for Soichiro, but hadn't taken it seriously. Now it appeared that not only had they managed to create an engine but a chassis as well. And they would actually be joining the race.

Soichiro wasn't just frustrated with the choice of engines but also the styling of Honda Racing's cars. The way Soichiro saw it, a race car needed to be sexy as well as speedy.

Soichiro's RA302 certainly fit that bill. The lack of a radiator allowed the position of the cockpit to be moved forward The car was sharply modern-looking and featured an aerodynamic, closed nose.

The question remained as to whether the car could get enough air to cool its engine. If not, it would overheat almost instantly. When Porsche had once experimented with an air-cooled race car, they had mounted a large fan in the chassis to assist in cooling. Betting that the high speeds and long runs of the F1 would produce enough airflow, Soichiro placed tube-like ducts on either side of the car's body to guide air into the engine. In essence, it was the same structure employed in his motorcycles.

After its presentation to the mass media at the Suzuka circuit, the RA302 was transported to London without any further testing.

4

Soichiro was satisfied with his RA302. The only thing he needed to do now was to sit back and wait for the results of the France Grand Prix. Even if it failed to win, so long as it placed respectably, the RA302 would undoubtedly remove the stigma of air-cooled engines being old-fashioned—and would once again spread Soichiro's fame throughout the world. In addition, there could be no better advertisement for the H1300, Honda's first serious compact car.

Soichiro had insisted on using an air-cooled engine in the H1300 in spite of the strong opposition from all the younger engineers on his team. The engine did indeed provide more torque and horsepower, but the engineers were racking their brains to figure out a way to keep it cooled. On Soichiro's orders, the engineers experimented with the concept of inducting air behind the pistons, but it was obvious that, even if successful, the method would prove quite expensive to implement in the finished product. Unlike the F1 group, which had something of a flexible budget, the engineers for consumer cars could not ignore the cost of their finished product. But for Soichiro, cost analysis took a backseat to proving that air-cooled engines were suitable for the F1. It was as if proving the validity of air-cooled engines was his personal cross to bear.

The RA302 arrived in England for a final checkout. The minute he saw it run, Nakamura turned pale. Even with a professional F1 driver like Surtees behind the wheel, the engine invariably overheated and sprayed oil across the track once the car reached a certain speed.

"I can't communicate with this car," said Surtees. "The RA302 just isn't ready for the F1 yet. It won't endure a race at all. The engine temperature jumps as soon as I open the throttle. We can't run it in an F1. Not only will it have no chance of winning, it'll be dangerous."

After listening to Surtees' honest impressions, Nakamura seriously considered withdrawing the RA301 from the France Grand Prix, if that was what it would take to convince the RA302 team to stay out. That way, Honda Racing and Soichiro would be even. But it was already too late. The RA302 had already gone through the official registration process. What was more, Soichiro had signed a contract with French F2 racer Jo Schlesser to drive the car. Although Schlesser had been professionally driving sports cars for some time, it was his debut in the F1. He had waited a long time for this opportunity, and it meant everything to him. Schlesser felt honored just participating in the F1 Grand Prix, regardless of outcome.

All of these arrangements had been made without Nakamura's knowledge. The role of supervisor for the RA302 team had been given to Kume, who had designed the engine for Soichiro.

Nakamura's hands were tied. All he could do was give Schlesser a full rundown as to the characteristics of the RA302's air-cooled engine and advise him not to push the limits. *So long as it finishes*, thought Nakamura, *Soichiro will be satisfied.*

The qualifying session was held on July 2 in Rouen. The Rouen circuit was notoriously full of curves and bumps; it was enough to make even experienced drivers nervous. Eighteen cars were entered in all. Jochen Rindt of the Brabham team took pole position. Surtees' RA301, two seconds behind, would be starting seventh. Schlesser came in eight seconds behind, relegating the RA302 to seventeenth place, second from last. Nakamura was hardly surprised. He was just relieved that the RA302 had managed to complete the course.

As a rule, in the F1, the qualifying sessions and the races are held one after another. The France Grand Prix, however, was an exception: traffic conditions at Rouen dictated that public roads in the vicinity be shut down for the race. Therefore, at Rouen, the race proper was held several days after the qualifying session.

The tragedy occurred during the main race, which was held on the 7th. It was raining in Rouen when the race began, making the track extremely slippery. The weather was both a worry and a source of relief for Nakamura: the RA302 was starting next to last in the race, and if the bad conditions forced it to retire after the first few laps, it wouldn't make the course any worse by spraying engine oil everywhere. *Once the air-cooled engine is proven useless, this whole headache will be over and done with,* thought Nakamura. In fact, Nakamura was praying harder for the RA302 to retire than for his RA301 to win. Unfortunately, however, the scenario that unfolded before his eyes was beyond anything Nakamura had expected or imagined.

Tadashi Kume, supervisor of the RA302 team, also had his eyes fixed intently on the car as it completed its first lap.

Please just let this race end safely, he prayed.

Then, just as RA302 finished its second lap and entered the downhill curve at the far end of the course from the pit, its tires slipped on the wet road surface and Schlesser lost control. The RA302 crashed into a three-meter-high embankment, bounced off, and was hurled outside the course boundaries. For a moment, Kume's mind went completely blank. *This can't be happening,* he thought.

Kume barely had time to take in what had happened when the RA302's fuel tank burst. Two hundred liters of high-octane gasoline ignited in a fireball that enveloped the RA302 and raised a cloud of oily black smoke into the sky. In contemporary racing, when cars are involved in an accident, a red flag is waved, temporarily halting the competition. At the time, however, nothing short of a total blockage of the course—not even accidents resulting in the death of the driver—stopped a race.

The rest of the cars screamed ahead through the smoke and flames, splashing their way through the fire extinguishing foam. But course conditions continued to deteriorate, and one after the other, the cars were forced to retire. In the end, only two cars completed the full sixty laps: Ferrari, the winner, and the RA301, which placed second.

The RA301 had only narrowly missed first place. The Ferrari, running directly ahead, had kicked up a puddle of extinguishing foam onto Surtees' goggles, forcing him to pit the RA301. Exchanging his goggles for a new pair, Surtees made it back to the course, but he never managed to make up for the time he had lost.

Nakamura watched the accident unfold before his eyes with horror. The RA302 burned fiercely, raising a pillar of black smoke into the sky. He prayed for Schlesser to emerge from the flames. But, after several minutes, it was obvious that he could not have survived. Schlesser had burned to death.

You're a murderer, thought Nakamura, fixing Kume with a cold glare. But his real venom was directed at the man he considered to be the true culprit: Soichiro Honda. That night, Nakamura could hold himself back no longer. After having a few drinks, he directly addressed Kume:

"No matter how I look at it, I still think you're a murderer, Kume. You'd better hope and pray there's a way to atone for what you've done."

All Kume could do was lower his head in shame.

Schlesser and his wife Annie had been staying in the same hotel as Kume. Now he prayed that he wouldn't run into her. Dealing with Nakamura had been bad enough. Kume was at a total loss as to what he might say to Schlesser's wife.

As fate would have it, Kume ran into her in the lobby the very next morning. Kume tried to speak but the words simply wouldn't come from his mouth.

"It was an accident. It couldn't be helped. It was an accident…" Annie Schlesser said, tears streaming down her face as she recalled the events of the previous day. Kume found this far more difficult to deal with than being yelled at.

News of the horrific accident in France reached Honda's headquarters in Tokyo almost at once. Even after hearing of the tragedy, Soichiro did not change his mind one bit about using air-cooled engines in the F1.

Deadly accidents were quite common in the racing world of the 1960s. Three months before the France Grand Prix, at an F2 race held in Hockenheim, Germany, driver Jim Clark had died when his car skidded on a wet course. Clark had widely been hailed as a racing prodigy, and his death at such an early age elevated him to legendary status. At the time, other drivers saw the death of a colleague as one of the inevitable costs of a life of racing.

Soichiro's indifferent, seemingly heartless attitude was largely due to not having seen the tragedy with his own eyes. The only Grand Prix race he had seen in person was the American Grand Prix of 1966. And what was more, fatal accidents—even during test runs—were an annual occurrence. To Soichiro, Schlesser's death was just another statistic.

Nakamura and Kume ordered their colleagues to do their best in the wake of the tragedy. Soichiro, on the other hand, barreled ahead with his pet project as if the accident had never happened. Instead of halting work on the air-cooled engine, he ordered his engineers to perform new modifications on the RA302 engine. Far from realizing the limits of the engine, Soichiro's thoughts were focused on finding ways to overcome the weaknesses that led to the failure at the France GP with an eye towards using the improved design in the upcoming H1300.

Soichiro's callousness frustrated and angered the employees at Honda Racing. It was no longer just Nakamura; a feeling of distrust for the parent company gradually spread throughout the racing team. The more Soichiro insisted on working on air-cooled engines, the larger the gap between him and Honda Racing grew. Increasingly disenchanted, the members of the racing team not only stopped working on developing the next model of race car, but also lost all motivation to make any modifications on the RA301. After the France GP, Honda participated in the races in England, Germany, Italy, the United States and Mexico, but only managed to place a maximum of third, in the American Grand Prix. The 1968 season ended without another victory, putting an end to Honda's aspirations for world championship.

Soichiro had ordered the modifications to the RA302 engine for a simple reason. He placed his F1 machine on the same level as any of Honda's consumer automobiles, and he was utterly convinced that his choice for an air-cooled engine was correct.

The Honda Racing staff felt cornered. Although Honda Racing hadn't designed the RA302, the team still felt the burden of responsibility for the accident. Separate entity or not, the public saw Honda Racing as inextricably connected to the Honda Motor Company of Japan. Given the situation, there was no way they could justify participating in the F1 any more. There was nothing to do but withdraw from the competition.

Feeling that an official statement from the Honda Motor Company would be too shocking to the public, Nakamura discussed things with Surtees and had Honda Racing Company make the announcement instead. They further couched the issue by framing it as temporarily "suspending" the project rather than "withdrawing" from the world of racing.

Nakamura had chosen the word "suspend" to express his chagrin, as well as his frustration with Soichiro. It was a bitter end to Honda's hard-fought, five-year project to take on the F1. To take responsibility for terminating the project, Nakamura submitted his resignation, which he addressed to Soichiro, but Fujisawa and Kiyoshi Kawashima persuaded him to stay on. Nakamura remained in London and, instead of the F1, devoted his time and effort to trying to establish a foothold for Honda's business activities. The man who had joined Honda because of his passion for the F1 had come to the end of that chapter in his life. Honda's F1 project entered a long period of hibernation from which it would not emerge for some fifteen years, until the 1983 Grand Prix in England.

Soichiro quietly accepted Honda's withdrawal from the F1. The main reason for this was because the social environment in which the company operated was going through drastic changes. In later years, people would say that Honda withdrew from the F1 so that it could focus on modifying its engines to comply with stricter laws governing automobile exhaust in America. At least that was the commonly accepted explanation, but it was not entirely true.

While the issue of automotive exhaust had indeed taken on a new prominence in the United States, in Japan, Honda's N360 found itself in the midst of a growing controversy over defective cars. Sales had dropped dramatically. At the same time, Honda's first automobiles, the S series sports cars, were also nearing the end of their commercial lifespan. Soichiro, being an engineer himself, knew that in order to survive as an automaker in Japan, Honda needed to concentrate all its efforts into bringing the air-cooled H1300 to market as quickly as possible.

As director of the RA302 team, the experience in France had been a tremendous shock to Kume. Kume attended Schlesser's funeral, held at a church near the Place Étoile in Paris, and returned to Japan. Once he was back at the R&D headquarters in Wako, Kume realized just how little had changed. Soichiro continued to yell and shout at the young engineers as they all worked diligently on his air-cooled engines. Kume couldn't bring himself to forgive Soichiro for what happened at the France Grand Prix.

Kume had managed to get hold of a Super-8 film of the accident that had been shot by a spectator. He replayed it over and over again, his eyes fixed on the screen. The film lacked the detail of a professional job, but clearly showed Schlesser losing control on the slick track at the bottom of the slope before slamming into the embankment.

Why did Schlesser have to die? Kume asked himself. *Was it the car? It must have been. If so, I've got to atone for my sin.* Although he was still as angry as ever at Soichiro, the more Kume thought about it, the more he was overcome by the urge to make some form of atonement. Shortly thereafter, he told his family that he was going on a business trip and headed to Haneda Airport. He didn't even let the office know he was taking the time off; he simply had to get out of Tokyo.

"I'd like to board the next plane out," said Kume at the airline ticket counter. "I don't care where it goes."

The clerk issued Kume a ticket to Kochi, located on the southern coast of Shikoku, the smallest of Japan's main islands. Upon reaching the city, Kume took a bus to Cape Muroto. He selected a simple inn and spent his days watching the ocean at dawn and at dusk. Still, Kume couldn't purge his sense of guilt.

Having nothing better to do, Kume visited a nearby Buddhist temple, one of eighty-eight in Shikoku representing a famed traditional pilgrimage. An old sign stood on the grounds: "If you have the resolve, please help us by moving as many to the temple as you can." Under the sign sat a large pile of roof tiles. Day after day, Kume toiled away, hauling the tiles up the stone steps to the temple. He finally felt as though he had found something that would let him make amends.

Around ten days later, while carrying his usual armload of roof tiles up the stairs, it came to him. *Life is like a staircase, climbing upwards step by step, day by day. Even the Old Man, who everyone says is a genius, must have slowly worked his way up, one step at a time. And even today, he and all the members at R&D are still climbing, striving, step by step towards their goal.* It was as though a weight had been lifted from Kume's shoulders. Kume was overcome by a desire to return to Tokyo immediately.

Finally coming back to his senses, Kume returned to Honda R&D, somewhat embarrassed about his absence without leave.

"Hey, you look great," exclaimed Soichiro, as if nothing had happened. "Where have you been? I haven't seen you around for a while. Anyway, we'll keep at it together, right?"

Soichiro's treasured H1300 hit the market at the end of May 1969, just before the storm of controversy over defective cars swept Japan. The sales point was the relative quietness of the air-cooled engine. While the engine was indeed fairly quiet for an air-cooled type, from a financial standpoint, the product was an albatross around the company's neck. Unexpected production costs meant Honda was taking a 50,000-yen loss on every sale. The more H1300s that sold, the bigger a financial hole they created for the company.

What was worse, the car could never be exported to the United States. Along with the rapid increase in private car ownership in the United States came a drastic increase in the number of motor vehicle accidents. In 1967, the National Highway Traffic Safety Administration addressed the growing problem by issuing a set of twenty Federal Motor Vehicle Safety Standards (FMVSS). One of these standards required cars to have an adequate windshield defrosting system, which would allow the car's windshield to be defrosted within a certain time limit after starting the engine. The time limit was no problem for a car with a water-cooled engine, but it proved an extremely difficult task for one with an air-cooled engine. The only way for the H1300 to meet the standard would be to install a supplementary oil-driven heater unit into each car.

The most popular import car in America at the time remained, as it had been for some time, the Volkswagen Beetle. The Beetle also featured an air-cooled engine, which made it next to impossible for the car to meet the new standards. Volkswagen took the opportunity to begin work on an all new, front-engine, front-wheel-drive car with a water-cooled engine: the Rabbit. Air-cooled engines were beginning to fall out of vogue in the United States as well.

The only way to export the H1300 would be to drastically modify it. Soichiro rode his engineers mercilessly in an attempt to get the job done lest Honda lose market share. Times were changing, however, and Soichiro, with his fixation on air-cooled engines, was about to find himself left behind.

5

1969 marked the first year that the Japanese public began to see motor vehicle accidents as a major societal problem. The number of traffic deaths had broken 1,000 within just the first twenty-eight days of the year. Estimates suggested that some 15,000 people could die by the end of the year—higher than the total number of soldiers killed during the entire Russo-Japanese War of 1904—and that the number of traffic-related injuries could exceed one million.

One million six hundred and sixty thousand automobiles, including k-cars, had been sold in 1965. In the next three years, the number jumped up to three million. The Tomei Highway was set to be completed by May 26, 1966, escalating Japanese motorization all the more. Increasingly concerned about the growing number of traffic accidents, the Ministry of Transport sent a letter of request to the Japanese Automobile Manufacturers Association (JAMA) and other automobile industry organizations. The letter read, in part:

"We request that you make the utmost effort to refrain from listing in your advertisements information on maximum speed and other information that may encourage drivers to violate speed limits. For sports cars in particular, we ask that you provide information that will lead to the safety of the driver, such as acceleration and braking characteristics."

The following day, JAMA called together the vice presidents of its member companies for an emergency meeting. The members agreed to voluntarily refrain from carrying out advertising campaigns that placed emphasis on the speed of their vehicles. While the arrangement did not set any penalties for violators, the Fair Trade Regulations, announced earlier by the Japan Fair Trade Commission, did. Any company not following the rules would indeed be penalized.

The new trend proved a major headache for Honda. The H1300 was set to go on sale at the end of May. Soichiro had poured his blood, sweat, and tears into the sports car. The sales target was 2,000 vehicles a month, but expected to be gradually increased as time went by.

The selling point of the H1300 was the high speed and horsepower provided by its highly tuned air-cooled engine. The industry arrangement meant that there would be no way to advertise these characteristics openly. Soichiro and Fujisawa felt as though their hands had been tied. But it was a direct request from the ministry; there was nothing they could do.

The number of traffic-related deaths showed no sign of decreasing. Fatalities reached 6,000 by the end of May, twenty-three days earlier than the previous year.

According to a report prepared by the Prime Minister's Office, the number of "traffic orphans"—children who had lost one or both parents in traffic accidents—had reached close to 30,000 for elementary and junior high school students alone. Most of these children were receiving welfare benefits or some other form of subsidy from the government to support their school studies. In order to provide another level of support for the children, Shigeo Nagano, president of the Japan Chamber of Commerce and Industry, organized the Foundation for Orphans of Traffic Accidents.

Nagano aimed to gather 1.6 billion yen for his foundation in the first year. He issued a request to the auto industry, asking for one billion yen in contributions. The industry's response was limited to one hundred million yen donated by Toyota, to commemorate the company's having reached the five million mark in cumulative production, and another one hundred million from JAMA.

Incensed at the weak response, Yoshiomi Tamai, the managing director of the Society for Educational Aid to Traffic Orphans, sharply criticized the auto industry. "Auto manufacturers have traditionally laid the blame for traffic accidents on drivers and passengers, and have become rich off of the 'killing machines' that they produce, under the overprotective policies of the government. And yet, they begrudge contributing to the Foundation for Orphans of Traffic Accidents."

On June 1, just as public opinion began to look critically at auto manufacturers as villains in the "traffic war," The *Asahi Shimbun*, one of Japan's largest newspapers, ran a story with the following shocking title: "PROBLEMS WITH JAPANESE AUTOMOBILES / WHY DO MANUFACTURERS HIDE DEFECTS? / AMERICAN NEWSPAPER CRITICIZES NISSAN AND TOYOTA / REPAIRS CARRIED OUT IN SECRET / MANUFACTURERS PLACE PROFITS BEFORE SAFETY."

The article, which quoted a *New York Times* article by John Morris and also included two photographs of cars condemned as being defective, was the top story on the newspaper's local news page. The lead read as follows:

"The *New York Times* criticized Toyota and Nissan for secretly recalling defective products without notifying the public, a practice it described as common in the Japanese auto industry. Both manufacturers said that they were taken aback by the criticism, commenting, 'The number of units sold in America was minimal, which is why we didn't announce the defects. We have contacted the concerned customers directly through the mail.' However, the same models of car are also sold and out on the streets in Japan. Not only have Nissan and Toyota not sent out any mail to their customers, the companies have even endeavored to hide the defects from their own employees. Other manufacturers besides Nissan and Toyota have also been recalling defective cars in large quantities, but only the Ministry of Transport and the manufacturers themselves know the true state of affairs. In short, it appears that the safety of consumers has taken a backseat to marketing and profits in the eyes of Japan's auto manufacturers."

This article, the first of many on the topic, triggered a full-blown scandal that rocked the entire Japanese auto industry. As the passage above indicates, however, Japanese manufacturers did not take the issue very seriously at first.

The concept of a "defective car" was coined by Fumio Matsuda, the secretary-general of the Japan Automobile Users Union, who would later emerge as a major player in the growing scandal. With Matsuda's advice, *Asahi Shimbun* used the term for the first time in the article. Despite being a new term and concept, "defective car" came to be widely used by the public, even appearing in court rulings for civil trials against manufacturers.

The scandal kicked into high gear when, on June 6, the Ministry of Transport ordered Toyota and Nissan to re-examine the allegedly defective cars. The issue was also raised in the Committee on Commerce and Industry in the Diet. The *Asahi Shimbun* was especially zealous in its campaign to expose the manufacturers' wrongdoings and followed the story closely:

"MINISTRY OF TRANSPORT ORDERS TOYOTA AND NISSAN TO EXAMINE DEFECTIVE CARS" (June 6, morning edition, front page)

"NISSAN SECRETLY RECALLS DEFECTIVE MICRO-BUSES" (June 6, evening edition, local news page)

"NISSAN BLUEBIRD CATCHES FIRE AGAIN / EXPLODES ON ENTRY INTO GARAGE / TUNED ONLY THREE MONTHS EARLIER" (June 7, morning edition, local news page)

"CORRECTIVE MEASURES FOR DEFECTIVE CARS IN OTHER

COUNTRIES" (June 8, morning edition, business page)

"TOYOTA'S POLICY ON DEFECTS: 'PUBLIC ANNOUNCEMENT IF SITUATION IS URGENT'" (June 8, morning edition, local news page)

"NISSAN BLUEBIRD / '69 MODEL ALSO CATCHES FIRE / MITI MINISTER OHIRA ISSUES STRONG WARNING TO JAMA" (June 10, evening edition, local news page)

"DIET COMMITTEE ON PUBLIC TRANSPORT SUBPOENAS PRESI-DENTS OF TOYOTA AND NISSAN TO TESTIFY" (June 11, morning edition, local news page)

"PRESIDENTS OF TOYOTA AND NISSAN ADMIT DEFECTS: 'SOME CARELESSNESS IN MANUFACTURING'" (June 11, evening edition, local news page)

"ANNOUNCEMENT BY TOYOTA AND NISSAN: NINETEEN ADDI-TIONAL MODELS WITH DEFECTS / IMMEDIATE RECALL OF 470,000 CARS / A BLIND SPOT IN TRANSPORT MINISTRIES' ABILITIES EXPOSED / AU-TOMOBILE EXPERTS AGREE ON POTENTIAL FOR SERIOUS TRAFFIC AC-CIDENTS IN THE FUTURE" (June 11, front page)

"WHIPLASH VICTIM SUES CAR MANUFACTURER" (June 12, morning edition, local news page)

"TOKYO METROPOLITAN POLICE DEPARTMENT RE-EXAMINES TRAFFIC ACCIDENT CASES INVOLVING DEFECTIVE CARS / SAYS THAT CRIMINAL CHARGES ARE NOT OUT OF THE QUESTION" (June 12, morning edition, local news page)

Scarcely a day went by without news related to defective cars appearing in the *Asahi Shimbun*; the morning and evening editions, the front page as well as the local news page all brimmed with condemning articles. Although the newspaper claimed that it was the duty of journalism to investigate and expose scandals, the coverage was rapidly taking on the character of a witch-hunt.

"Why do the Japanese media have to follow the lead of an American newspaper, when all it amounts to is harassment, pure and simple, of the Japanese auto industry?" confided Katsuji Kawamata, president of Nissan and chairman of JAMA, to a newspaper reporter who came to see him late one evening. It was obvious that Kawamata lacked a full understanding of just how serious the dispute was becoming.

The media offensive showed no signs of winding down. On June 13, a Japan Socialist Party politician by the name of Tetsuya Nakatani dropped a bombshell at the Diet's Committee on Judicial Affairs.

"There are rumors that Honda's cars are even more defective than those of Toyota and Nissan," he said.

"We've heard them too," answered Ministry of Transport deputy minister Murayama. "We're conducting an investigation as we speak, and, when we have the necessary information, we will take all appropriate measures regarding the matter."

Based on this exchange in the Diet, the evening edition of *Asahi Shimbun* on the same day made Honda the target of their attacks. "IS HONDA NEXT? /

TRANSPORT MINISTRY INVESTIGATES / GOVERNMENT DRAFTS RELIEF MEASURES FOR AFFECTED DRIVERS / REPLY BY MINISTER OF JUSTICE / ACCIDENTS DUE TO DEFECTS LISTED BY COMPANY"

It became apparent the following day that the defective car in question was Honda's N series, including the N360. The *Asahi Shimbun* reported dutifully: "HONDA N SERIES: CONSUMERS USED AS PRODUCT TESTERS / HIT PRODUCT RUSHED TO MARKET / DEFECTS FOUND IN 280,000 CARS"

The article, which ran as the top story on the local page of the morning edition, began as follows:

"Defective cars sold by the Honda Motor Company were discussed at a Committee on Justice meeting held at the Diet on June 13. As a result, the Ministry of Transport launched an investigation into the matter and found that Honda's popular k-car series often suffered from malfunctions related to design or structural defects, leading to frequent traffic accidents. *Four Wheel News*, a Honda magazine distributed only to dealers, carries a list of methods for dealing with the defects. The question has been raised as to whether Honda has been using consumers as test subjects, since the measures listed in the newsletter imply that Honda, in an effort to rush the products to market, had not run enough tests on the cars.

"Michihiro Nishida, managing director of the Honda Motor Company said that the N series had problems related to steering, leaking, and noises. However, he continued, Honda workers have put their full effort into addressing the problems, and that the automobiles rolling off the line now should be close to perfect. Mr. Nishida also described Honda as having originally been an engine maker, meaning that few staff members had experience with automobile frames; the manufacture of automobiles was a totally new field for his company. Mr. Nishida stated, however, that he has a high degree of confidence in the structure of Honda's automobiles. Furthermore, he continued, Soichiro Honda, president of Honda Motor Company, considers safety as his highest priority and would never do anything as foolish as using consumers as test subjects. Honda still needs to make one or two final repairs and will make an official announcement in this newspaper on June 17."

That evening, Honda publicly announced the existence of nine defects: low quality material used in the brake lines; a defective gearbox; overly loose front brakes; inferior air filters; inferior shock absorbers; inferior brakes; over-tightened bearings on the camshaft; inferior carburetor; and an overly loose steering column. On the same day, Isuzu also publicly disclosed the defects of its buses and trucks, bringing the total of auto manufactures that had admitted to selling defective cars to four.

On the 16th, JAMA turned in a report on the defects to the Ministry of Transport, the Ministry of International Trade and Industry (MITI), and the Tokyo Metropolitan Police, and also disclosed its findings to the media.

JAMA's announcement that day revealed that nine companies—in addition to Nissan and Toyota, which had already been reported on—sold defective cars, meaning that every auto manufacturer in Japan was responsible. According to JAMA, a total of 2.45 million defective cars had been sold industry-wide. Of these,

1.3 million had neither been recalled nor fixed. With 12.48 million cars in private hands by the end of 1968, the statistics meant that one out of every five cars in Japan was defective, counting those cars that have been recalled or fixed. And one out of ten still presented a potential danger to drivers and passengers.

JAMA promised the Ministry of Transport that it would make voluntary public announcements concerning defective cars and take immediate measures to recall and repair them. Furthermore, JAMA immediately agreed in a unanimous decision by its members to pay the eight hundred million yen balance of the funds that Nagano had requested for the Foundation for Orphans of Traffic Accidents. Now that it had taken action, all JAMA could do was wait quietly in the hopes that the coverage of the defects would die down.

As promised, on June 17, Honda took out a five-line newspaper ad asking customers to bring their defective cars in for check-ups and servicing. It estimated that some 200,000 cars were affected.

The next day, Honda took out another ad—this time covering a full page— stating that Honda "Service Factories" were now fully equipped with the necessary replacement parts. Toyota and Nissan had also taken out five-line advertisements on the same day as Honda, but Honda was the only company to run a second ad, and a full-page ad at that.

In the late 1960's, the newspaper was still far more popular than television as a medium for mass communication. The economic boom at the time meant that it wasn't easy to secure ad space at the drop of a hat. What Honda had decided to do was to sacrifice space already reserved for H1300 advertisements and run announcements about the recall instead.

"I want you to focus on recalling the defective cars, even if it means sacrificing the production of new cars," said Soichiro to his workers.

Soichiro dispatched seven hundred workers from the Sayama factory, where the N360 was being manufactured, to provide on-the-spot maintenance at two hundred Service Factories around Japan. In spite of the growing scandal, customers continued to purchase N360s, and Fujisawa had intended to produce 34,000 N360s a month in June, July, and August. The loss of the workers, however, meant that actual production only reached 30,000 a month.

Honda's rapid response created a buzz in the industry and was a tremendous help in shoring up its damaged reputation. But an incident shortly thereafter put the brakes on the recovery process. An organization consisting of former Honda dealers had requested special protection from MITI and the Ministry of Transport. They also held a press conference at a Tokyo hotel, where they displayed a defective brake drum to the assembled reporters.

The organization's complaints against Honda basically addressed two points. First, it claimed that when a manufacturer directly controls both the sales and maintenance network for its products, as Honda was doing, the disclosure of defects ends up being one-sided and self-serving. Second, the organization accused Honda of hiding additional defects. They claimed to have discovered a grand total of forty-two defects in the trucks, vans, and Honda's N series of k-cars, only five of which had appeared on Honda's official list. Honda was keeping silent about the remaining thirty-seven defects, the organization said, even though the company was currently working on measures to address them.

Honda immediately responded by issuing a comment by Nagao Yoshida, chief engineer for Honda's maintenance division:

"There are no additional defects necessitating a recall, apart from those announced on June 14. While the issues raised by the organization have been a problem in the past, they have already been addressed and fixed."

The campaign against defective cars had resonated with the public for several reasons. One was the fact that motorization, largely led by Nissan and Toyota's consumer cars, had developed far faster than anyone had expected. Auto manufacturers rushed to build factory lines to meet the demand, but mass-production technology simply hadn't been able to keep pace. The large number of defective products was proof enough.

The other reason centered on the relative inexperience of Japanese drivers. According to a test conducted by the Tokyo Metropolitan Police Department and the National Research Institute of Police Research in 1969, one in five drivers were dangerously unskilled. The public blamed the explosive increase in traffic accidents on the manufacturers. In reality, however, the poor skills of Japanese drivers played a significant role as well.

The public outrage over the defective cars can also be interpreted as a reaction to the rapid growth of the Japanese economy. By the late 1960s, Japan had grown into the world's second largest economic power. At the same time, however, the nation found itself wracked by social problems, including the high price of consumer goods, pollution, and urban crime. People had begun to doubt whether growth of the economy necessarily led to increased standards of living, and had started calling for a review of Japan's "growth-first" policies. As one of the main pillars of Japan's economic growth, the auto industry made a prime target for this growing frustration.

The *Asahi Shimbun*, which had led the campaign against the auto industry, ran ninety-seven articles on the subject in June alone. By the next month, however, the furor had largely died down.

The recall proceeded smoothly. Ninety-six percent of the 2.47 million cars labeled defective, i.e., 2.37 million cars in total, were processed and repaired. Half of the remaining four percent consisted of unrecoverable cars that had already been scrapped, and the other half those for which no owner could be located. Considering that the average number of cars actually serviced in a recall campaign in the United States at the time was seventy percent, the Japanese auto manufacturers can be commended for doing better. In any case, the defective car scandal appeared to be over for the moment.

Owing largely to the impact of the scandal, Honda's new H1300 got off to a miserable start. In addition, the new restrictions on advertising prevented the company from advertising the capabilities of the new car as desired. As a result, sales fell far short of the predicted 2,000 per month. Fujisawa was forced to curtail production of the vehicle by that fall. The N360 k-car had created a sensation when it had gone on sale. But the defective car scandal had effectively spoiled the launch of Honda's first compact car.

6

The scandal over defective cars in 1969 forced Honda to undergo a major change of direction. Left unchecked, Soichiro's one-man crusade for air-cooled engines would not only have tainted Honda's reputation, it could well have driven the company itself into the ground.

As Fujisawa had dreaded, the scandal had a major impact on sales of the H1300, which were as low as they could be. Honda found itself facing a slump with no relief in sight. The American FMVSS regulations precluded exports of the car for an indeterminate time. It was becoming rapidly obvious within Honda that the H1300 wasn't the breakthrough product the company needed.

Looking over the situation, Fujisawa resisted the urge to bury his head in his hands. The best way out of the slump, he knew, would be to develop a new compact car to replace the H1300 as soon as possible. Naturally, this would require the full support of the Honda R&D Company.

"We need to know why the H1300 failed," Fujisawa told the R&D staff, ordering them to prepare a secret report on the subject.

Irimajiri took charge, quietly convening a meeting of Honda R&D managers one day in early summer, at a hotel in the city of Karuizawa, safely out of Soichiro's sight.

Fujisawa waited, giving Irimajiri and his team enough time to discuss all the necessary points, before showing up at the meeting. The R&D staff briefed Fujisawa on their findings, but the conclusion had been obvious even before the investigation had begun. As far as Honda R&D was concerned, the air-cooled engine was the root of all evil. Fujisawa listened and nodded. He had expected as much.

"There are other reasons as well," said another young engineer. "The complaints began pouring in from almost the first day the H1300 went on sale. We lack a good test-course for our cars. We're using a vacant stretch of land alongside the Arakawa River for the time being, but the makeshift course simply isn't enough to uncover everything that's wrong with a design. And so we're only able to fix the defects after receiving the complaints from the customers. If Honda had a test course like GM…"

As soon as Fujisawa heard these words, he flared up. "Don't you deceive yourselves," he roared. "This isn't GM. We don't have that kind of money. I spun off the R&D section because I wanted you to focus on your research. If you made products that sold, you'd have more money to work with. If there isn't a test course nearby, why can't you use the one in Asama? The auto manufacturers didn't all pitch in and build it for nothing. It's slack attitudes like that that's leading to all the defects. If Honda R&D goes under, it'll take all of Honda with it! I won't tolerate that last remark. Take it back, now!"

All the more because he was irritated by the defect scandal, Fujisawa had zero tolerance for such a coddled and spoiled attitude, even from the younger employees. Especially when the person responsible for the coddling and spoiling was none other than Soichiro himself.

I've got to make Soichiro realize that the H1300 is a failure, thought Fujisawa. Soichiro showed no signs of abandoning his crusade, however. He continued to order his engineers to work on one air-cooled engine project after another. *I've got to put a bell around this cat's neck*, groaned Fujisawa to himself. The more time he lost, the higher the chance that Honda would miss the opportunity to ride the wave of motorization that was sweeping the country.

Completely unrelated to the problems within Honda, but compounding the situation nevertheless, was the clamor surrounding Senator Edmund Muskie's bill to regulate automobile exhaust in the United States. By the 1960s, environmental pollution had emerged as a serious issue in America. In fact, smog had troubled California since the early 1940s. The outbreak of World War II had postponed research into the cause of the problem, but once the war ended, research was resumed. Scientists discovered that the smog was the product of a photochemical reaction of carbon monoxide, hydrocarbons, and nitrogen oxides.

A rise in citizens' movements had led to the passing of the Clean Air Act in 1963. Muskie's bill was a revision of the original act, specifically dealing with the regulation of car exhaust fumes. Automobile exhaust contained a large amount of toxic substances, so the bill aimed to control air pollution by obliging manufacturers to significantly reduce exhaust gases. The aggressive plan called for a reduction of carbon monoxide and hydrocarbon emissions to one-tenth of their 1970 levels by 1975, and the same for nitrogen oxides by 1976.

The demands stunned the American auto industry. American manufacturers were enjoying the height of their prosperity, thanks to the popularity of their large-sized cars. Considering the state of technology shared by the auto industry at the time, eliminating ninety percent of the specified compounds from car exhaust within a timeframe of only five to six years was quite impossible. The Big Three—GM, Ford and Chrysler—fought the bill tooth and nail.

In spite of the not inconsiderable political influence of the Big Three automakers, however, there was no way to buck the public's growing interest in environmental issues. If the companies stubbornly opposed the law, sooner or later the public would turn against them, and consider them to be "enemies of society." And if any one company managed to meet the regulations, the rest would be completely ignored by the consumers. As awareness of environmental issues continued to grow, auto manufacturers found themselves rapidly losing their previous status as the darling of the times.

The proposed Muskie Act would also have a tremendous impact on Japanese automakers. The Japanese automotive industry relied on exports to the United States to support itself. Toyota and Nissan had started exporting their products back in the late 1950s. While sales had been sluggish at first, they had taken off as manufacturers introduced larger designs that appealed to the average American consumer. In 1965, Japan had exported only 22,000 automobiles to the United States, but by 1968, the number exceeded 200,000—a tenfold increase.

Nevertheless, Japanese manufacturers still lacked full-scale marketing networks in the United States. The previous year, when the *New York Times* had carried the story about the defects of Japanese vehicles, manufacturers feared their exports would take a tremendous hit. In the end, they survived the crisis. But this time, things were serious. If Japanese manufacturers failed to meet the new regulations, they would find themselves forced out of their most lucrative new market once and for all.

Japan was at the height of its rapid economic growth, and pollution from car exhaust, together with traffic accidents, was starting to gain recognition—though gradually—as a social problem. If Muskie's bill was passed, it was a near certainty that similar regulations would be drafted in Japan. Following the new regulations was a prerequisite for the future survival of the Japanese auto manufactures.

That being said, Japanese manufacturers faced the exact same technological hurdles as the American Big Three. For the moment, the regulations appeared quite impossible to meet.

Soichiro alone was surprisingly enthusiastic about the situation.

"Now's the chance for Honda to take over the world marketplace," Soichiro told his engineers excitedly when he first heard that Muskie's bill had been submitted to Congress. "Every manufacturer is facing the exact same problem. We're all at the same starting line. You can't buy the technology. This is a rare chance. A chance for Honda to pit our ideas and technology against a score of world-class contenders! When it comes to developing new technologies, we can't lose. Let's focus our abilities and create an engine that meets the Muskie standards!"

Soichiro seized on the pollution-free engine as his chance to clear Honda's name of the disgrace of withdrawing from the F1, to absolve his company from the scandal surrounding the N360, and to make up for the low sales of the H1300. Besides, Soichiro loved nothing more than a challenge—and he desperately wanted to give his rivals a scare by developing the new engine first.

Still, no matter how much Soichiro wanted to develop an environmentally friendly engine, he had a bigger issue to settle first. Would Honda focus on air-cooled or water-cooled engines? The new project couldn't begin until the debate was laid to rest.

Air-cooled engines were famed for their high torque and horsepower. But the drastic temperature gradients within the engines made it extremely difficult to regulate the discharge of toxic substances in their exhaust. The key to reducing emissions was to precisely control the air-fuel mixture ratio, which had proven a difficult task in air-cooled engines. The process was far easier in a low-torque, water-cooled engine. Of course, using water-cooled engines didn't automatically guarantee environmentally friendly cars, but they did at least promise some potential for meeting the regulations.

Even before the proposal of Muskie's bill, R&D Chief Manager Hideo Sugiura and his fellow technology managers, including Tadashi Kume, had repeatedly requested Soichiro's approval to work on water-cooled designs. Soichiro had dismissed them out of hand. As a matter of fact, he even tried to tackle the emissions problem with air-cooled engines.

This time, however, a team at Honda R&D, led by Shizuo Yagi and Kazuo Nakagawa, had secretly, without Soichiro's knowledge, begun working on a new water-cooled engine called the "AP."

The only reason that the H1300 had made it to market in spite of its old-fashioned, air-cooled engine was because cutting-edge electronics had been used to cool down the engine. But there were limits to what could be done. The AP project team quickly concluded that the longer it took Honda to make the switch from air-cooled to water-cooled engines, the more difficult it would be to meet the new emission standards.

In spite of his dedication, it was becoming apparent that Soichiro's very presence was the greatest stumbling block to creating a low-emission engine at Honda.

Sugiura, Kume, and the other head managers realized that the entire R&D Company would have to band together and confront Soichiro. They decided to enlist the aid of the only person capable of reasoning with him on a one-to-one level: Fujisawa, vice president of both the Honda Motor Company and the Honda R&D Company.

Actually, Fujisawa had been waiting for this opportunity for quite some time. The sense of crisis at Honda R&D stemmed from a technological problem, but Fujisawa had long sensed the growing crisis in Honda's management. For the moment, Fujisawa was able to use the profits from Honda's motorcycle division to make up for the deficit in automotive sales. But sooner or later, he would have to come up with a more radical means of addressing the problem, some paradigm shift based on a long-term goal, lest Honda find itself forced out of the auto industry.

Fujisawa still believed that Honda had missed a major opportunity in not developing a consumer model of the F2 engine. Had they done so, Fujisawa felt, Honda would be as big as Toyota or Nissan. As it turned out, with the failure of the H1300, not only had Honda fallen way behind these two companies, but rumors also began to circulate that Honda's prowess in manufacturing automobiles stopped at k-cars.

R&D is in an uproar, but is simply getting Soichiro to abandon air-cooled engines really going to solve the problem? pondered Fujisawa. *We've always been driven by technology. If we lose that edge, our growth will grind to a stop. I'd better listen to what the managers have to say and spend some time thinking seriously about Honda's future. It's the only way I'll be able to come up with a coherent marketing strategy.*

With the fallout from the defect scandal finally settled at the end of the summer, Fujisawa invited his R&D managers to a hotel in Atami. Sugiura and Kume saw it as a prime opportunity to make their case to Fujisawa. Kawamoto stayed up all night preparing the technical documents for the meeting.

Kume opened the discussion in a trembling voice. "Honda has focused its entire effort on developing an air-cooled V4 engine and on using its high torque and horsepower as a sales point. This is how the company managed to grow so far. Now, however, the only way to meet the emissions regulations is to focus on the exact opposite type of engine." Kume launched into a detailed technical explanation of exactly why air-cooled engines were old-fashioned.

"Well, then," asked Fujisawa, "are you saying the companies that have traditionally manufactured water-cooled engines with low torque and horsepower have an advantage?"

"Not at all, sir," replied Kume. "As their research has up to now focused purely on low torque and horsepower, we believe they haven't grasped our theory yet. We only managed to figure it out this quickly because of all the research we've done on the limits of combustion in air-cooled engines."

That's it! thought Fujisawa. *It doesn't matter what technology we use. If we can come up with a low-emission car first, it'll be a first-class ticket into the world's markets for Honda. We built our reputation as an automaker on the S series, but it was a total failure from a marketing standpoint. The N360 is not doing badly, but not well enough to pay for the investment we made in it, and there isn't much of a chance to export them, even if we do increase the displacement. My dream of creating a car around the F2 engines didn't go anywhere, either. But creating a low-emission engine...it's our chance to clear the whole slate at once.*

Hiding his excitement at all the marketing prospects, Fujisawa kept a calm face and asked, "So Honda can create a low-emission engine. Is that what you're saying?"

Now that Fujisawa had come to the point, it wasn't enough for the R&D managers to inform him of how Honda's technological foundations were starting to crumble. Their immediate mission was to get Fujisawa to put an end to Soichiro's air-cooled engine projects. The only way to do so was to persuade Fujisawa that the only chance for meeting the emissions regulations lay with water-cooled engines.

"We're afraid that we can't guarantee it one hundred percent," answered Kume. "But we do believe that we stand a chance. The only way to ensure that chance, however, is to cancel the air-cooled engine project and pour everything into developing a new water-cooled engine. The president believes that air-cooled engines can meet the regulations, but we believe that's one hundred percent impossible."

The R&D managers concluded with a direct request to Fujisawa for permission to develop automobiles with water-cooled engines.

I've nagged and nagged at the R&D section, but it's paid off, thought Fujisawa. *I've got my army of Soichiros. Spinning off the R&D section was the right thing to have done.*

"I understand your points. I'll speak to the president on your behalf," he promised.

The report from the managers had given Fujisawa his epiphany, but it had also been something of a shock. Fujisawa had established Honda R&D to create a legion of Soichiros that would ensure his company's future. And now the "Honda Kids," whom Soichiro had raised with such care, had come to tell Fujisawa, in essence, that their "captain," the Old Man, Soichiro, was turning into a cancer that was eating away at the company.

Upon returning to Tokyo, Fujisawa locked himself in the tearoom in his home in Roppongi. *Even geniuses have their limits, and that's just what I've been sensing with Soichiro lately. It's time for Soichiro to step down from running R&D. The longer he stays, the more his presence will taint its reputation. How can I get him to resign without hurting him? And comply with requests of the R&D at the same time? For the sake of the company, I've got to do this properly. I must protect Honda. Even if it means death for Soichiro and myself at each other's hands.*

The following day, after pulling his thoughts together, Fujisawa headed to Soichiro's office at the R&D headquarters in Wako.

"Honda-san. Your staff tells me that water-cooled engines are the key to beating the Muskie Act. Why don't you let them give it a try?"

"I don't think you'd understand even if I gave you the detailed explanation, but you'll just have to trust me on this. We can meet the regulations with an air-cooled engine as well. I'll make sure that we do," Soichiro answered firmly.

Fujisawa knew it was now or never. If he backed down as he had before, he would be shutting the door on both water-cooled engines and the prospect of creating low-emission engines. But changing the mind of a staunch believer like Soichiro would be no easy task. Fujisawa prepared for the worst.

"Honda-san, do you remember our first meeting? When you told me never to meddle in the technical side of the business? I'm no engineer, so I've stayed out of your way, and I promise that I'll continue to do so in the future. But there is one question I'd like you to ask yourself. Which path are you planning to take, Honda-san? Are you the president, or an engineer? I believe the time has come to clarify your position, and I'd like to know what you think." It was the first time Fujisawa had ever confronted Soichiro directly during their twenty-year partnership. He knew it would be the last.

Soichiro flinched. He knew exactly what Fujisawa meant from the expression on his face. He knew it was a serious question, and that once a decision had been reached, there would be no turning back. Soichiro looked up at the ceiling and closed his eyes. *I entrusted my presidential seal to Fujisawa and let him manage Honda. But I am the president of the company. I founded it. If I say I want to remain as engineer, it would mean resigning my post as president. On the other hand, staying on as president means giving up day-to-day control over engineering. It'd be the end of my career as an engineer.*

Fujisawa fully intended to force Soichiro to resign as president if he insisted upon remaining an engineer. If Soichiro stepped down, who would become president of Honda? Considering age, experience, and expectations within the company, it would certainly be up to Fujisawa to step in to fill the gap. But Fujisawa knew more than anyone that he was not cut out to be president. He believed that the president of Honda should be an engineer. And what was more, no matter how the public perceived it, there would be no doubt that what he'd done was to stab his old partner in the back. It was a critical moment. Everything depended on Soichiro's answer.

"I suppose I'd better stay on as president," said Soichiro, finally breaking the silence.

Soichiro was, by this point, over sixty years old, and beginning to feel limits on his physical strength. Starting with his first bicycle engines, Soichiro had worked tirelessly, developing Honda's motorcycles, the N360, an air-cooled engine for the F1, and the H1300. He hadn't taken a break since the company had been founded. Seeing his "kids"—whom he had raised with such care—grow further and further away from him each year tore him apart.

If only I were still in my fifties, thought Soichiro. *I'd take the reins just like I've always done; I'd take on any project, whatever anyone said, even if there's only a one percent chance of success! It may be easier to meet the regulations with water-cooled engines, but air-cooled engines still have potential. All the top cars, the Volkswagens and Porsches, have air-cooled engines. Even GM, the largest automobile manufacturer in the world, used one recently in their Corvair. Air-cooled engines have so much unexplored potential. If only I were younger...*

Soichiro was a rare genius with an unshakable confidence in his work. But it hadn't been enough to convince his partner or his "kids." Soichiro's life as an engineer was effectively over. At the same time, Fujisawa also took pains to nip in the bud any possibility of ever becoming president himself.

"It's all right with you then, if the staff work on water-cooled engines?" he pressed. Then he added, "Honda-san. I want you to know that I'll quit when you quit."

This is the way it should be, thought Fujisawa. *From now on, my job is to protect Soichiro's reputation as genius engineer. And the only way to do that is to exit together. It'll be our "double suicide."*

There was no need to say anything else. The critical moment was over. Soichiro and Fujisawa both knew that resigning together was the only way to keep Honda alive.

The next day, Fujisawa made a phone call to Sugiura.

"I talked to the president, but I want you to talk to him again to confirm everything yourselves," said Fujisawa. He kept the details of last night's conversation to himself.

Sugiura met with Soichiro in a dark, prototype assembly room at Honda R&D.

"Times have changed, Mr. Honda. Everyone knows how you poured your soul into air-cooled engines. I feel terrible saying this, but there's no way that they can meet the U.S. regulations. Please let us work on water-cooled engines. If we spend every waking hour we've got working on them, we may be able to make it in time."

Soichiro listened quietly, then got up and turned his back to Sugiura. "Do what you need to do..." he said and walked to the door, keeping his back to the younger man. Before leaving the room, he turned to look back at Sugiura once more, and Sugiura thought that he saw tears in Soichiro's eyes. Fujisawa's "coup d'état" involving all of Honda R&D had been a success.

7

The chance to freely work on water-cooled engines breathed new life into the Honda Research and Development Company. The first car designed around a water-cooled engine was a k-car called "Life." It had taken only six months to build the prototype from the day Soichiro had finally relented. The engineers asked Soichiro to be the first to test-drive it.

"So this is your car with the water-cooled engine," said Soichiro. "It's much better than I expected."

Soichiro's positive comment came as a great relief to Sugiura and the rest of the engineers at Honda R&D, but many issues remained to be tackled before the Life could reach the market. Even with their previous experience with water-cooled engines for the F1 and F2, the Life was Honda's first commercial car to feature one. The development team was determined to make it a success at any cost, but they also needed to use it as a test bed for creating a low-emission engine. The environmental demands would mean giving up some of the speed and horse-power that had traditionally served as Honda's sales points.

The reason that the R&D engineers were able to complete the prototype in so short a time was largely linked to the "legacy" left behind by Yoshio Naka-mura, who had left R&D for an assignment at Honda's London subsidiary in the wake of the F1 tragedy. During the time that Soichiro devoted himself to the N360, Nakamura had designed the "BS," a front-wheel, front-engine compact car with a 1100cc, water-cooled, V4 engine. A modified version of the BS would form the basis of the groundbreaking Honda Civic.

Nakamura had created his car to compete head to head against the Toyota Corolla and Nissan Sunny. But when he had finally shown his blueprints to Soichiro, Soichiro had rejected the design out of hand.

"It's too tame for a Honda. And it's got a water-cooled engine. What I want is a sports car with an air-cooled engine!" said Soichiro, and Nakamura's design was shelved indefinitely.

When the Life project began, Sugiura revived Nakamura's BS design. He modified it from a V4 to a V2 and narrowed the bore to fit a k-car chassis. Up until that point, Kume had always overseen the development of automotive en-gines at Honda. For the Life, however, Kawamoto took charge.

As far as the public was concerned, the best thing to come out of the defect scandal was the establishment of an official system for dealing with defective cars in Japan. When a defect was identified, a manufacturer was now obliged to report it as such to the Ministry of Transport, as well as to the consumer, and to recall and repair the vehicle. With the establishment of the new system, stories related to defective cars all but dropped off the front pages.

In the summer of 1970, however, another major automobile defect came to light. On August 6, Toyota, Japan's largest manufacturer of automobiles, reported cases of defective accelerators and brakes to the Ministry of Transport. Eight hundred and forty thousand of Toyota's compact cars, including the Corolla, Pub-lica, Corona, and the Mark II, had to be recalled.

The major factor driving the recall was the Japan Automobile Users Union, which had been founded on April 20 that year. The objective of the union was to mobilize the one million or so reported car owners in the country and form a lobby group that could effectively lay pressure on manufacturers and the ministry to make sure safer vehicles were produced. The founders were a powerful bunch: Shigeri Yamataka, chairman of the National Federation of Regional Women's Or-ganizations; Isamu Akashika, former vice president for the Japan Federation of Bar

Associations; Masuo Shimoizaka, a former Supreme Court judge; and Yoshihiko Okubo, director of the traffic department at the National Research Institute for Police Science. Jushiro Komiyama, a former politician with the Liberal Democratic Party, acted as chairman. Fumio Matsuda, an outspoken automotive critic, became managing director and secretary-general. Haruo Abe, a lawyer and former public prosecutor, acted as organizer.

"The only way for us to stand up to the manufacturers and their experience is to harness the combined strength of the automobile consumers," said Matsuda on the occasion of the union's launch. "If we don't speak out, the manufacturers will simply keep raking in enormous profits, while continuing to sell their defective cars. MITI has pledged their full support of our role in protecting the consumer."

In the United States, the activist Ralph Nader was causing a furor with his reports exposing defects in cars and his crusade against environmental pollution. At the Users Union, the two men effectively in charge, Matsuda and Abe, aimed for nothing less than to become the Japanese Naders. They launched a union magazine called *Jack* and spent the profits from it on a variety of consumer services, including car testing and legal counseling for those who wished to lodge complaints or take action against manufacturers.

The first public action taken by the Japan Automobile Users Union was to lodge an objection to a June traffic safety report issued by the Tokyo Metropolitan Police Department. The department had spent a year investigating twelve traffic accidents from the first half of 1969. The accidents involved five models of cars from four automakers: Toyota, Nissan, Mazda, and Honda. The two accidents attributed to Honda vehicles both involved the N360.

Their official report concluded that "the manufacturers of the automobiles in question bear full responsibility for the accidents. However, only the case involving Nissan's Echo microbus, which injured twenty people in Kyoto, can be seen as a criminal case. The remaining eleven cases cannot be seen as legally actionable."

The Japan Automobile Users Union decried the report as being "skewed towards the manufacturers." The Union ran an extensive list of defects in the July issue of *Jack*, and it was this list that had proven instrumental in forcing Toyota to institute its brake and accelerator recall of over 800,000 vehicles.

On August 18, two weeks after Toyota initiated the recall, the family of an individual from Kyoto who was killed in an accident involving an N360 filed a suit at the Special Investigation section of the Tokyo District Public Prosecutors Office. Basing its claims on statements by the survivors, the family asserted that the accident was a direct result of a defect in the car, and accused Soichiro Honda of murder through willful negligence. Haruo Abe of the Japan Automobile Users Union represented the plaintiffs in court.

The case wasn't the first brought against the N360. Others had been filed in the Osaka and Nagoya district courts, as well as the Hachioji branch of the Tokyo District Court, but these cases had simply involved drivers claiming that defects in the N360 had caused their accidents.

The newest case was shocking in that it directly accused Soichiro of murder.

And what was more, the suit was fully backed by the Japan Automobile Users Union. It wasn't actually the first case directly naming the president of a manufacturer; in the automobile industry, Nissan's Katsuji Kawamata had been named earlier in a suit involving the Echo. The Echo was manufactured by Aichi Mechanical Industries, a company that had been acquired by Nissan in the late 1960s. As Kawamata was the head of the entire Nissan *keiretsu* hierarchy, the plaintiffs had targeted him directly.

Unlike Nissan's case, however, at Honda, the development of the N360 had been carried out under the direct leadership of its president Soichiro. What was more, Soichiro enjoyed a degree of celebrity status with the media as the flamboyant president of a highly visible company. That the charges were for murder only attracted more attention from both the media and the public.

Legally speaking, the concept of "willful negligence" means that even an unintended accident could be seen as intentional if there was even a chance the accused could have predicted the outcome. In the case filed against Soichiro, the prosecution alleged that although Soichiro and his company may not have intended to cause the accident, they should have known that a failure to address the defects of the N360 could well have led to one.

The same concept would be used (ultimately unsuccessfully) in the famed suit involving industrial mercury pollution in Minamata. The idea of using this reasoning as grounds to sue the president of a manufacturer was unheard of even in the United States, which was far more advanced than Japan when it came to motorization.

The case came as an utter surprise to the Honda Motor Company. The most it could do was issue a comment on the newspaper reports.

"We have no official comment on the allegations for the time being, as we do not yet know the details involving the accident. But if we are asked by the court or Public Prosecutors Office to give evidence, we will take full responsibility and prove that the N360 is not a defective car."

Earlier that year, in May, Honda had promoted the four managing directors, Kiyoshi Kawashima, Kihachiro Kawashima, Michihiro Nishida, and Takao Shirai, to senior managing director, bestowing upon each the right to represent Honda. The collective directors' room management system was working smoothly, the defect scandal of the previous year had died down, and the endless arguments over air-cooled versus water-cooled engines had finally been settled. Honda R&D was making steady progress in developing a water-cooled, low-emission engine.

The lawsuit came just as the company was regaining its breath. Before the news hit, Fujisawa had just started thinking about his retirement. In fact, the promotion of the four directors had been the first step in his plans.

Soichiro's fiery personality was a source of worry for Fujisawa. It was entirely possible that Soichiro would say something damaging in front of reporters, throwing oil onto an already growing fire. On the other hand, Fujisawa fully sympathized with the man. Soichiro had poured his blood, sweat and tears into the N360. He had ensured every aspect of the car's quality with his own eyes and hands. It was like his baby. A judgment acknowledging Soichiro's car to be a "weapon on wheels" (as the prosecution alleged) would be an affront to everything for which the man had lived and worked.

Whenever Soichiro overheard an employee casually referring to "the defective car issue" of the N360, he blew his top.

"The N360 isn't a 'defective car'! If it was, we'd be no better than murderers. The only reason we've been able to work so hard is that we know our cars aren't defective. I will not tolerate you calling the N360 a 'defective car', ever again. If you think it is, I'm more than happy to accept your resignation and see you pack up and leave for good!"

Before long the term "defective car" had become taboo within Honda. Even today, employees refer to the N360's "problems" rather than "defects."

"I want the directors, in particular the four of you, to handle this case," said Fujisawa to his four executive directors. "The president and I will stay behind the scenes on this one."

All was quiet for three weeks after the indictment. Then, on September 8, secretary-general Matsuda of the Japan Automobile Users Union appealed to the Diet Committee on Public Transport to conduct a national investigation into the N360. According to the Users Union's own investigations, there had been a total of ninety-one accidents related to defects in the N360 over the previous three years, resulting in forty deaths and 114 injuries. The majority of the cases involved a phenomenon called "sudden drift."

"We cannot allow the number of victims to increase. We request that the Ministry of Transport and the Tokyo Metropolitan Police Department cooperate to analyze the accidents and recognize the defective nature of the cars," said Matsuda in front of the National Diet, obviously relishing his role as a self-styled protector of justice.

The Committee on Public Transport could hardly ignore such allegations. The members discussed the issue with each of the political parties and concluded that, as the House of Representatives was out of session, the subject would be officially raised at the Special Committee on Traffic Safety in the House of Councilors scheduled to convene on the 11th. Once again, the representatives of the auto industry were called to testify.

That the Diet had been so quick to take up the issue was undoubtedly influenced by the report presented on the 10th by the Tokyo Metropolitan Police Department to the National Public Safety Commission. "The Honda N360 had a known defect of lateral vibrations when driven at high speeds. As such, the Tokyo Metropolitan Police Department has launched a reinvestigation into thirty-eight traffic accidents involving the car."

The four Honda directors discussed at length how best to represent the company before the Diet. Eventually, they decided that Honda needed to take a do-or-die stance of resisting the charges. Michihiro Nishida, who was responsible for the company's public relations, was chosen to represent Honda before the committee.

Looking back from the present day, the defects in the N360 could be interpreted as the result of pushing the limits of Honda's still-developing automotive technology. At the time, however, the concept of product liability had yet to be established. Certainly none inside Honda, from the president down to the youngest employee, were aware of it.

Honda began as a manufacturer of engines. The company entered the motorcycle industry with its *bata-bata* engine, turned a profit, and eventually used their success as a springboard into the automobile industry. The problems experienced by Honda's early motorcycles were due to the fact that other components, such as carburetors, simply couldn't keep pace with the engines that Soichiro created. The N360 may have been a similar victim of Soichiro's engineering success. The difference, however, was that motorcycles generally didn't kill riders unless driven at high speeds, while automobiles had a good chance of becoming "coffins on wheels."

The problem was that Honda didn't have a manual for manufacturing its automobiles. Had the company ever tried its hand at licensed production of foreign brands, it could have copied its partners' manuals to make one of its own. Unlike its rivals, however, Honda handled everything on its own. Building automobiles was a hands-on learning process for the employees. The engineers didn't even know how extensively they needed to test their products. They basically called a car complete at whatever point they felt that they had conducted enough tests to satisfy themselves.

Honda's first car, the S500, was practically handmade, and as such, was relatively free of defects. The N360 was another story. Thanks to motorization, it was produced and sold in mass quantities. But the bottom line was that none of Honda's engineers truly believed they had created a defective car, no matter how much evidence the Users Union produced to the contrary. Their pride and ignorance blinded them to the reality of the situation.

The Special Committee on Traffic Safety convened at eleven o'clock in the morning on the 11th. In addition to Nishida, Toyota director Shoichi Matsuo and Nissan vice president Tadahiro Iwakoshi were called in to testify. At the beginning of the session, each made a brief statement and then answered the questions put to them.

Matsuo and Iwakoshi did their best to avoid upsetting their inquisitors, while making sure that they got their point across in the end. Nishida took the opposite tack. He was aggressively defiant in his responses.

"The allegations of our N360 being defective are utterly unfounded. We find the manner in which this issue is being treated to be regrettable. It does nothing but promote unnecessary anxiety on the part of the consumer." The gloves were off. Honda would go head to head against the Japan Automobile Users Union.

"Honda's attitude is arrogant and unconvincing," began one committee member before being cut off by Nishida.

"The N360 is designed to be suitable for export. It is mechanically stable even at speeds approaching 120 kilometers per hour. The committee member has accused us of being arrogant, which is not Honda's intention at all."

Nishida was asked to explain Honda's confidence.

"From 1967 to April 1968, Honda sold 135,351 N360s. It is true that problems were identified in nine of these, but almost all of these cars have been recalled by the end of last year. As for the current models now in question, we have run several types of tests on them on a closed course. Even under the same conditions as those in which accidents have been reported to occur, we have not encountered any cases of lateral vibration," answered Nishida.

Another politician asked Nishida for his reaction to the report prepared by the Japan Automobile Users Union.

"With regard to the lateral vibration issue, the fourteen cases raised by the Users Union in the press unfortunately did not involve normal driving situations," replied Nishida. "The union also claims a total of ninety-one accidents involving our car, but we were dismayed to find that they were unable to provide any further information when we contacted them for details. At any rate, the results of our research and testing indicate that there are absolutely no mechanical defects in the N360."

The conversation continued on these parallel tracks for some time. Finally, an increasingly irritated committee member asked, "Are you willing to prove that there are no defects, then, with a public test?"

"We would welcome it," replied Nishida confidently. "We can tune a car to reflect specifications used in our cars at the time of the accident. If the test is fair, we can assure you of the proper result."

The television, radio, and newspaper coverage roundly criticized Nishida's aggressive tone and Honda's arrogance, while heaping praise on the Union of Japanese Automobile Users. The evening edition of the *Asahi Shimbun* on the 11th carried the following analysis of the session.

"[The root of the defective car problem] lies in the fact that auto manufacturers fail to respond with sincerity to customers who have suffered accidents with their products. In the case of accidents involving Honda's N360, not only does the company refuse to listen to the owner's claims, it immediately collects the damaged cars, which could well be interpreted as destruction of evidence. If the owner has not fully paid their loan at the time of the accident, the car dealer retains ownership of the car. Even if the accident was clearly not the fault of the driver, it cannot be proven as such if the evidence has been taken away... The Japan Automobile Users Union should be commended for its role in expressing the anger of consumers. Since the union's magazine *Jack* was launched this May, the union has received accounts of suspicious accidents from all over Japan. More than 2,000 reports have been made by telephone and through the mail. It is thanks to the collective efforts of consumers nationwide that, for the first time ever, enough data has been accumulated to be able to refute the manufacturers' arguments. Indeed, one might say it was the anonymous consumers in various parts of the country that were the true key players in today's Committee meeting."

Nishida had perfectly expressed Soichiro's thoughts to the public, but in the end, Honda ended up being shunned by consumers. Sales of the N360 dropped dramatically.

Honda had manufactured 960,000 N360s in the three and half years since March 1967, when the product first went on sale, until the lawsuit was brought against Soichiro. Nine hundred and thirty thousand of these were sold inside Japan, while the remainder were exported abroad. Even after the 1969 defect scandal, Honda had managed to sell more than 200,000 of the cars within Japan, but the number dropped to 40,000 in 1971. No matter how passionate Nishida's testimony was, the suit and reports of accidents were obviously damaging public confidence in the safety of Honda's products.

Business slumped as Honda tried one unsuccessful marketing strategy after another. When calling at customers' homes, Honda's salesmen found themselves having to engage in lengthy attempts to persuade customers that the N360 wasn't really a defective car before they could even start to make their sales pitches. Before long, people had even stopped visiting Honda dealerships to pick up Honda's catalogs and pamphlets, let alone check out a prospective purchase.

Soichiro's beloved H1300 suffered as well. The H1300 factory line had been designed to manufacture 10,000 cars a month, but actual sales had plunged, even dropping below 1,000 units a month for some months. Consumers were running from Honda's automobiles in droves. Although the motorcycle division continued to turn a profit, it was only a matter of time before Honda went bankrupt. Action needed to be taken—and soon.

8

It was the lowest point in Honda's history. Meanwhile, the Tokyo District Court investigations swung into full gear and ordered a ten-day full investigation into "suspicious" cars beginning on December 10, 1970. The tests would be held at the closed course of the Japan Automobile Research Institute (JARI) in Tsukuba, Ibaragi prefecture. Cars to be tested included eight N360s (four "problematic" cars provided by customers via the Japan Automobile Users Union, four provided by Honda), and six k-cars in the same class, such as the Subaru 360, from other manufacturers. Eleven people would test the cars, including Wataru Murata, chief prosecutor of the Tokyo District Public Prosecutors Office, and Kenzaburo Ishikawa, head of the Automotive Safety Office at the Traffic Safety and Nuisance Research Institute. Fumio Matsuda, secretary-general of the Japan Automobile Users Union, and Hiroshi Hayano, chief engineer at Honda who had been responsible for testing the N360, would also be present. Judging would be handled by Atsushi Watari, a professor in the School of Industrial Science at the University of Tokyo. The battle between Honda and the Union of Japanese Automobile Users was on.

The fourteen automobiles had been brought to the Ministry of Justice by the afternoon of the day before the test, where they were loaded onto trailers for transport to the test course.

Even before the test, a fierce battle raged behind the scenes. The Users Union took the first potshot. The union complained that the Public Prosecutors Office had asked a Honda subsidiary to transport the "problematic N360s" collected by the union to Tokyo and that Honda had loaned new cars, when requested, to consumers who had given theirs up for testing.

"The Public Prosecutors Office is receiving special favors from Honda. Letting Honda transport the cars for free actually amounts to having Honda bear the test fees. How can we ensure impartiality?" cried the union.

What really concerned the union wasn't transport per se, but the potential for Honda secretly pulling into a factory and repairing the cars before the test. To settle the matter, the Public Prosecutors Office paid a fee to the Honda subsidiary responsible for the transport and pledged to fully supervise the process to ensure that Honda did not touch the automobiles.

The tests began as planned. Along with meters to measure drift and steering angle, each car carried a driver and passenger in the front seats and two test dummies weighing sixty kilograms each during the tests. One sat in the driver's seat, another in the front passenger seat, and two were placed sitting in the back seats. Tests were undertaken in eight categories, including driving on straight and curved roads, free control stability, steering characteristics, and overall stability while driving. When asked in the Diet in September if Honda was ready for a public test, Nishida had answered with confidence. In the end, however, the tests were closed to the public due to Public Prosecutors Office policy.

The second round of testing took place in January of 1971. A third involving early versions of the cars in question was undertaken in March. From what could be gathered about the tests, nearly every one of them reflected poorly on Honda. Once the N360 began to drift, it was difficult for the driver to recover, and the cars displayed an obvious lack of stability. One car flew off the test course. Others revealed a tendency for the rear wheels to "float" when the car was driven on a curve. The more time they spent with the cars, the more the testers began to feel that Honda had made serious errors in the design of the N360.

Every time Soichiro heard the rumors about the test results, he flew off the handle. He would barge into the R&D offices and shout at anyone who happened to be there, "The results can't be right. Not about our N360!"

Fujisawa did his best to keep Soichiro away from the mass media. Fujisawa knew Soichiro's emotional comments would serve no purpose other than to create misunderstandings. Any judgment on the issue now rested with the judicial authorities. No matter how much information leaked to the public, Honda's directors refrained as much as possible from commenting. That is not to say that they stood around with their hands in their pockets.

More than anything, Honda needed to find a way to restore its tarnished reputation. The business slump was nearing a critical point. The N360 had tumbled from its position as Honda's top seller almost immediately after Soichiro's indictment in October 1970. Honda unveiled the upcoming Life, with its water-cooled engine, to the public, but refrained from advertising too openly for fear of damaging sales of the N360 any further.

While the Japan Automobile Users Union busied itself prosecuting automobile manufacturers, a debate over the environmental impact of car exhaust finally erupted in Japan as well. In May of 1970, study results were announced indicating that residents living near a busy intersection in the Shinjuku area of Tokyo had unusually high levels of lead in their blood. Then in July, high school students in Tokyo's Suginami ward were sickened by a cloud of photochemical smog. Within two days, the Ministry of Transport had drafted a Basic Plan on

Measures for Automobile Exhaust Gases. By the end of the month, the Cabinet had decided to establish an official headquarters for dealing with the growing pollution problem. Starting on August 2, certain areas in cities all over Japan were designated "pedestrian-only precincts" and closed off to traffic—another sign of the growing public opposition to automobiles.

The debate over car exhaust intensified with each passing month. In November, an extraordinary Diet session was convened to discuss pollution. In the United States, Muskie's bill was passed in early December and signed by President Nixon on the 31st. Japanese auto manufacturers could avoid the issue no longer.

Although saddled by the defect investigation, Honda found the development of the low-emission engine was proceeding more quickly than expected. On February 11, 1971, Soichiro, Fujisawa, and Kiyoshi Kawashima held a press conference to publicize two cutting-edge engines: one that was suited to the use of unleaded gasoline, and another that featured an exhaust gas purification system.

The gasoline of the day contained lead to prevent engine knocking. Studies indicated that the additive was a major factor in environmental lead pollution. MITI addressed the problem by mandating the use of unleaded gasoline by 1974. It was an easy enough directive to follow for oil and petroleum companies, who could simply stop adding lead to gasoline, but automobile manufacturers had to re-design their engines to address the knocking problem. Honda worked together with Sumitomo Electric Industries to create a thermally resistant sintered alloy based on glass fibers and copper. When incorporated into an automotive exhaust system, it prevented knocking even when unleaded gasoline was used.

For the exhaust gas purification system, Honda modified the shape of the combustion chambers and improved the fuel-supply devices and ignition systems of conventional reciprocating engines to produce a new combustion system. Other manufacturers, including Toyota and Nissan, believed that modifications to the engine itself would not be enough and had incorporated supplementary equipment such as thermal reactors and catalyst systems into their cars. Only Honda's engineers remained confident that they could meet the coming standards with their engine modifications alone.

Honda called its new creation a "compound vortex controlled combustion engine," later to be shortened simply to "CVCC." It boasted emissions eighty percent lower than that of a standard engine. Honda's testing indicated that the level of emissions handily beat the Ministry of Transport regulations for 1975. That meant Honda was within a hair's breadth of meeting the Muskie standards, which called for a ninety percent reduction.

In spite of the fact that they were still prototypes, Honda's two new engines rekindled the public's confidence in Honda's technology. The defect tests conducted by the Public Prosecutors Office were nearing to a close. Meanwhile, Fujisawa quietly worked on his own scheme. Since the press conference on the new CVCC engine dealt with a technological issue, it was natural that Soichiro be there. But Fujisawa meant to ensure that the occasion marked Soichiro's final public appearance as Honda's chief executive. *Honda has managed to develop the new low-emission engines, which could ensure the future of the company as an automobile manufacturer without Soichiro's direct involvement. The expertise system has taken root. Our company is full of Soichiros now. Automotive technology grows more and more complex every day. It's time to let the young ones take over the business. Honda-san, the low-emission engine is the perfect cap to your engineering career.*

In addition to the fact that Honda was well on the way to completing its low-emission engine, it was his shock at seeing the final prototype of the Life, finished just after the press conference, that prompted Fujisawa's decision. Fujisawa found the car design to be completely incompatible with recent trends in the market.

At the time the new low-emission engines were announced, the Life, which would go on sale in May of 1971, was undergoing the final round of endurance tests. For Honda, the Life would serve as a bridge in the market until the company could come out with its next generation of compact cars using the new, environmentally friendly engines.

The Life's specifications, however, were not at all what Fujisawa expected for such a car. Its top speed was 120 kilometers per hour, even higher than that of the N360. The appearance of the N360 had indeed escalated competition over the speed of k-cars. Some manufacturers even introduced k-cars capable of 125 kilometers an hour—fast enough to outspeed sports cars. In spite of the legal speed limit for k-cars at the time being only eighty kilometers per hour, manufacturers aggressively wooed customers with promises of top speeds exceeding 100 kilometers per hour. Driving at top speed in a tiny k-car was bound to increase the risk of having an accident.

"The top speed's too high for a k-car. You've got to cut it down. This isn't the N360. The selling point of the Life is not its speed," yelled Fujisawa at the project director.

Fujisawa reminded the engineers that the Life concept was one of a "town car," a car for daily use. A high top speed simply wouldn't be one of the sales points. And reducing the top speed would allow engineers to improve the utility of other areas as well. To be fair, the engineers were more than aware of the points already. But their hands had been tied by Soichiro's personal thirst for speed. It was Soichiro's habit to constantly push his engineers to increase the horsepower and raise the top speed.

Even though Soichiro had not played a direct role in designing the Life, so long as he remained head of Honda R&D, he still exerted a major influence on all the R&D staff. In an unconscious effort to please Soichiro, the engineers automatically brought up the speed of their designs, even if it was meant to be a "town car."

Times were changing. The defective car scandal had been a turning point for the auto industry. The new environmental regulations were the nail in the coffin for the era of speed. Some American manufacturers even began citing a low top speed as a sales point. Soichiro's personal tastes were falling behind the times.

Fujisawa knew that openly suggesting retirement would deeply upset Soichiro. To ease the pain, Fujisawa sent his message through the board of directors instead, gently suggesting that Soichiro cede his title of president of the

Honda R&D Company to Kiyoshi Kawashima now that a stable line of succession had been established. Fujisawa himself had been vice president of Honda R&D ever since it was first established. He made it clear that he would give up this position when Soichiro left. It worked. Soichiro immediately accepted the suggestion.

Soichiro's quick decision had been facilitated by his memory of Fujisawa's question from the previous year as to whether he intended to remain the president or an engineer at Honda. In fact, he had already made up his mind at that time to retire as president of Honda R&D. That was why he had intentionally refrained from having anything to do with the new compact car Honda planned to introduce after the H1300. He wanted to watch and see what his "kids" could do on their own. Soichiro and Fujisawa retired simultaneously from Honda R&D on April 1. Fujisawa's "double suicide" scheme had begun to take shape.

Now that Soichiro had officially ceded his position as the head of the Honda Research and Development Company, he became, in effect, simply president of the Honda Motor Company. This meant he no longer needed to commute to the Honda Research and Development Company in Wako on a daily basis, but he found he wasn't quite used to going to headquarters in Yaesu. Every morning, he set out in his H1300, only to find himself heading to the R&D headquarters in Wako. More than a few times, he realized his mistake midway and turned his car around to go back the way he came.

Under Fujisawa's direction, the Life was unveiled to the press on May 11 at the Akasaka Prince Hotel. Its top speed, at Fujisawa's request, had been reduced to 105 kilometers per hour. Certain models even topped out at 90 kilometers per hour. The Life would be Honda's first step in its 180-degree change from high-speed, high-performance cars to the world of family cars.

Fujisawa initially worried about how consumers would react to the new cars, which were so obviously devoid of the traditional Honda-like characteristics. But his fears proved groundless. The Life was hailed as a vehicle that was "ahead of the times." The success of the Life signaled a turning point not just for Honda but for the entire industry. Other manufacturers also began to question the previous era's mindless penchant for speed. Shortly thereafter, Japan's k-car industry made a joint decision to set a new standard of 110 kilometers per hour as the highest speed for vehicles in that category.

Professor Watari from the University of Tokyo handed in his report on the N360 to the Special Investigations section of the Tokyo District Public Prosecutors Office at the end of July 1971. The report had reached two conclusions. One was that the early N360s exhibited unusual handling characteristics at speeds exceeding eighty kilometers per hour, making it potentially difficult for inexperienced drivers to control. Thus, the N360 was not suitable for use as a consumer automobile. The second conclusion stated that there was no way to determine with certainty whether the handling characteristics in question were, if fact, the direct cause of the accidents. There was simply not enough evidence, as the drivers were deceased and the cars severely damaged. In short, although the report acknowledged the inherent instability of the N360, all it said of the relation between the problem and the accidents was that it was "not known." The Watari report completely avoided the issue of criminal liability, leaving that decision in the hands of Tokyo District Public Prosecutors Office.

Honda took Watari's report very seriously. If the Tokyo District Public Prosecutors Office convicted Honda, the N360 would be branded a "defective car," and the company could expect a slew of civil suits to follow. The demands for compensation would be colossal. Soichiro would be treated as a murderer, the public perception of his many achievements ruined. It could well mean the end of Honda.

Hideo Sugiura, who had been directly responsible for the N360 project under Soichiro, recalls his resolve at the time.

"After the Watari report came out, we expected the Tokyo District Public Prosecutors Office to make a final judgment in early August. Even if it was Soichiro who had been indicted, the person who would be going to prison would have been me, as I was the one who had been in charge of the project. It was a sweltering summer and I remember making a mental note to take some mosquito repellent incense with me if I had to go to prison."

On August 5, ten days after the report had been submitted, the Special Investigations section of the Tokyo District Public Prosecutors Office, after discussing the matter with the Supreme Public Prosecutors Office and the Supreme Tokyo District Prosecutors Office, issued its official judgment. None of those involved in the N360 affair, from the president who was accused of murder and professional negligence leading to death, to Sugiura and the others, were subject to criminal liability and therefore would not be prosecuted. The stated reason was that the death of the drivers precluded the Tokyo District Public Prosecutors Office from obtaining enough evidence. There was no way to prove whether the accidents were a result of the instability of the N360 coupled with the drivers' inexperience, or due to other factors, such as careless driving due to fatigue. The theory of "willful negligence" alleged by the Japan Automobile Users Union was not endorsed.

In spite of finally being let off the hook, Honda could not freely rejoice in its situation. The judgment contained enough gray areas to raise the specter of a civil suit from the Japan Automobile Users Union. All in all, it was a hollow victory for Soichiro, Fujisawa, and the engineers at Honda.

CHAPTER FOUR: SOLIDARITY OF THE ORDINARY

Society is full of ignorant old people. I believe that when people grow old, they should step down as quickly as possible. Not so long ago it was the young who were seen as lacking in wisdom. Now that's been reversed. Old people simply cannot keep pace with the rapid changes of modern society.

—Soichiro Honda

I managed Honda's business affairs, and every Honda employee knew it. But there was no way I could have taken on the role of president. A president needs a flawed personality. It engenders feelings of superiority in others, which has the effect of breeding a sense of affinity. A perfectly logical approach doesn't work at all.

—Takeo Fujisawa

1

The foundations of former *zaibatsu* conglomerates like Mitsubishi, Mitsui and Sumitomo, as well as may other major corporations existing today, were laid out by founders whose entrepreneurial spirit, resourcefulness, and tremendous effort were key to their later success.

The first Japanese steam-driven automobile was built in 1896. Three years later in 1898, engineers under the direction of Shintaro Yoshida at Tokyo Jidosha Seisakujo (Tokyo Automobile Factory) created Japan's first gasoline-driven automobile. In 1936, the Japanese government enacted the Automobile Manufacturing Industry Law, which led to the establishment of two companies dedicated to the manufacture of automobiles: Toyota and Nissan.

The Toyota Motor Corporation started out in 1933 as the automobile department of Toyoda Automatic Loom Works, a manufacturer of weaving machinery founded by genius inventor Sakichi Toyoda. Sakichi's son Kiichiro used royalties from licensing of the firm's loom technology as the seed money for the auto manufacturing business.

Nissan was founded in 1933 as a joint venture between the Tobata Foundry Company, which owned the brand name of Datsun, and Nihon Sangyo (Japan Industry Company). The company, originally called Jidosha Seizo (Automobile Manufacturing Company), was owned by Yoshisuke Aikawa, president of the Nissan *zaibatsu*, and was renamed the Nissan Motor Company the following year.

The foresight and ambition of these pioneers, who dared to venture into the world of domestic automobile production in pre-WW II Japan—a time when demand for automobiles was limited and future prospects uncertain—is indeed worthy of admiration. Like the former *zaibatsu* groups, Toyota and Nissan owe much to the drive and untiring endeavors of their founders for establishing the very basis on which their present-day success rests. One aspect that Nissan and Toyota have in common is that both companies were blessed with a relative abundance of capital when they were first starting out.

Honda, on the other hand, was born from the ashes of World War II. The only "capital" its founders had was Soichiro's engineering skills, Fujisawa's talent as a manager, and the shared ambition of making Honda the greatest motorcycle company in the world.

In a little over two decades, Soichiro and Fujisawa would realize their dream. Honda did grow into the world's top manufacturer of motorcycles. As Fujisawa himself pointed out, Honda's birth and subsequent growth had only been possible because of the turmoil into which Japanese society was thrown after WWII. At a time when, in the Western world, both motorcycle and automobile industries were considered to have matured to the point of excluding any further competition, Honda had dared to make an entry. Under normal circumstances, it would have been unthinkable. But the economic climate in Japan, which saw the people's main mode of transportation rapidly evolve from bicycles to motorcycles to automobiles, matched Honda's moves and propelled the company's amazing growth.

The driving force behind the 1950s consumer revolution in Japan had been household electronic devices: the black and white television, the washing machine and the refrigerator, known collectively as the "three sacred artifacts." By the late sixties they had ceded their place as the most highly desired commodities of Japanese households to the "three Cs": cars, coolers (air conditioners), and color televisions. The prices of the three Cs were higher than that of the "artifacts," and subsequently had even stronger repercussions on the Japanese economy.

Of the three Cs, it was obvious that cars topped the list. In 1965, just before the arrival of "Year One" of Japanese motorization, the number of automobiles manufactured in the country had been 1.87 million. By 1970, the number had reached 5.29 million: an increase of 2.8 times in a period of only five years.

Over the same five-year period, the production of passenger cars increased 5.8 times from 700,000 to 3.18 million units. The growth of the Japanese automotive industry was obviously led by the popularization of passenger cars, in particular, privately owned cars for personal use. Only 5.7 percent of households in Japan owned cars in 1965, but only five years later, the number had increased to 22.1 percent. Among households with salaried workers, including office workers and civil servants, the numbers went from 3.4 to 20.8 percent. Cars were no longer luxuries for the rich. The rapid growth of the economy propelled car sales to the point where one in five working households owned one.

In the summer of 1970, Japan hosted its first World Exposition in Osaka. Although December 1969 had marked the end of the "Izanagi boom"—fifty-seven straight months of economic growth and the longest economic expansion since WWII—the positive aftereffects still lingered. This phase of prosperity for Japan came to be known as the "Showa Genroku period" after the Genroku era (1688-1706), a period in Japanese history particularly known for its flourishing culture and economic development.

Now that cars were no longer the exclusive provenance of the rich, auto manufacturers sought to woo consumers by presenting them with a diverse selection of models to choose from, introducing one new model after another. At the same time, they strove to build market share by restyling and modifying former models.

Motorization had only just gotten off to a start when Honda, drawing confidence from its success at becoming No.1 in the world of motorcycles, took its first steps onto the auto scene. The company introduced its first k-car, the N360, at precisely the right timing to ride the wave of motorization sweeping the country. Although neither dared say it aloud at the time, Soichiro and Fujisawa set their sights on a new goal: becoming No.1 in the auto marketplace.

In spite of their shared ambition, however, the two took completely different approaches towards making the dream a reality. When it came to expanding Honda's influence in the auto industry, Soichiro's passion for F1 racing informed his every decision. He saw a victory in the F1, the world's fastest race, as an ideal stepping-stone towards dominating the consumer auto marketplace. On the other hand, Fujisawa, who had absolute faith in Soichiro's engineering abilities, hoped to develop a mass-market passenger car using the F2 racing engine, which he believed would allow Honda to overtake Toyota.

At it turned out, the defect scandal and impending regulations to make car exhaust cleaner ended up derailing both approaches. Not only did these issues shatter Soichiro and Fujisawa's dreams, both had a direct and negative impact on Honda's bottom line. As more and more attention needed to be devoted to fulfilling the new exhaust requirements, Honda had less and less time to spare for the F1. And in spite of Honda's previous treatment as a darling of the press, fallout from the defective car dispute in the mass media nearly put the company out of business.

In fact, it would be no exaggeration to say that unless Honda reorganized its automotive division immediately, the company could be forced into bankruptcy. In 1970, Honda had manufactured a total of 393,000 automobiles—only a step away from reaching the 400,000 mark. The following year in 1971, however, at the height of the defect scandal, the number had dropped dramatically to 308,000. Domestic sales fell from 364,000 to 294,000.

During the same period, Toyota, which Fujisawa at one time secretly considered Honda's main rival, was making steady progress in establishing itself as a full-line automobile manufacturer. The best-selling Crown, which had first gone on sale in 1955 and had cemented Toyota's position as a world-class automotive manufacturer, had been successfully updated twice to secure nearly sixty percent of the market for mid-sized cars.

In the early 1960s, Toyota had only two other cars in its lineup besides the Crown: the Corona and the Publica. But by the late sixties, Toyota had introduced a series of new cars, including the Corolla, the Sprinter, and the Mark II. Furthermore, in 1970, the company introduced two additional sports models, the Carina and the Celica, in response to consumers' growing hunger for stylish, higher-quality cars. Toyota simultaneously invested fifty billion yen to build a new factory in Tsutsumi, its third in addition to those already in Motomachi and Takaoka. Toyota successfully laid the groundwork to make itself competitive on a global scale.

When the Diet approved new laws liberalizing capital transactions in October of 1969, Eiji Toyoda, who had taken over as president in fall 1967 after the sudden death of Fukio Nakagawa, addressed Toyota's assembled employees.

"The path to success for Toyota is clear: mass production. By the time capital transactions are liberalized in 1971, I want our company to be capable of producing two million automobiles a year," he ordered.

Toyota's total production had just reached one million units a year in 1968. Toyoda planned to double that number in only three years. It was a remarkably aggressive plan, particularly in light of the fact that there were only two companies in the world, General Motors and Ford, that were capable of manufacturing more than two million automobiles a year at the time.

Toyota former chairman Taizo Ishida, considered to be the "savior of Toyota," often used the expression "defend your castle yourself" to emphasize the company's policy of independence and self-reliance. In order to defend Toyota against foreign competitors, Eiji Toyoda opted for mass production. Toyota's plan to increase production capacities proceeded smoothly, easily boosting Toyota's production over two million cars a year by 1972.

Although the number of Japanese people purchasing automobiles increased on a yearly basis, capital liberalization was just around the corner. Medium-size companies without the resources to build massive assembly lines desperately sought other ways to ensure their survival. Mitsubishi entered into a capital tie-up with Chrysler in February of 1970, and Isuzu likewise announced a tie-up with General Motors in July 1971. Mazda was close to closing a deal with Ford. Honda alone, clinging to its flag of independence but lacking the actual cars to sell, was in danger of being left behind.

In April 1971, Soichiro ended his engineering career by ceding the title of president of the Honda R&D Company to his favorite "disciple," Kiyoshi Kawashima. Since Soichiro and Fujisawa were not in the habit of participating in Honda's board meetings, day-to-day management of both the parent company and Honda R&D fell entirely into the hands of Honda's four executive directors.

Honda had put all its hopes of regaining lost ground into its new k-car, the Life, which was selling tolerably well. It wasn't enough to fully compensate for the drop in sales from the N360 controversy, but it was enough for the company to keep its head above water. Development of the new low-pollution engine was proceeding smoothly, and Honda appeared on track to meet the environmental standards set by the Muskie Act (Clean Air Act of 1970) in America. And although it could hardly be termed a victory for the company, all charges from the defect scandal had been dropped. For the moment, it appeared that the dark clouds hanging over Honda were lifting.

Our time is over, thought Fujisawa. *We've got to leave the automobile business to Kawashima and the young generation.* Still, Fujisawa and Soichiro couldn't retire just yet: the drama of the defect scandal, which had been left to the four directors to deal with, wasn't entirely over. And as it turned out, the aftermath ended up leading to some very unexpected consequences.

On November 2, 1971, three months after the Special Investigations section of the Tokyo District Public Prosecutors Office dropped the case against Honda,

Japan Automobile Users Union secretary-general Fumio Matsuda and chief manager Haruo Abe were placed under arrest. The two were charged with attempted extortion of Honda, and the police searched through both Union headquarters and Abe's personal office in a hunt for evidence. It was a startling reversal of fortune for "the Japanese Ralph Naders." Up to that point, the union had enjoyed almost universally favorable coverage in the media. Things quickly changed after the arrest, however. An *Asahi Shimbun* story appearing on January 24, 1971 quoted the former managing director and secretary-general of the Users Union secretariat as saying, "Although Matsuda claims to have specialized in internal combustion engines at technical school, he in fact possesses no more engineering knowledge than that of an entry-level garage mechanic. Understanding the handling and stability characteristics of the Honda N360 requires a high level of specialized knowledge. Matsuda's grasp of these concepts is on par with that of a child."

Haruo Abe also suffered a fall from grace. Prior to the arrest, Abe's profile in the *Who's Who* directory had highlighted his illustrious career, citing how he had successfully established in 1963 the innocence of Ishimatsu Yoshida—a man who had been imprisoned for nearly fifty years on false charges of robbery and homicide (he was dubbed "Japan's Count of Monte Cristo"). The profile also mentioned his publication of a sharply critical exposé on the backwardness of the Japanese criminal justice system, as well as his role in seeking the retrial of Sakae Menda, a thirty-four-year inmate of Japan's death row. Abe was transferred in June 1963 from the Tokyo District Public Prosecutors Office to the Hakodate District Public Prosecutors Office and later to the Fukuoka Supreme District Public Prosecutors Office. He then went on to become a prosecutor in the Fukuoka High Public Prosecutors Office before retiring in January 1967.

After retiring as a prosecutor, Abe became a lawyer and began to champion private clients instead. During this time, the media idolized him as a "rebel prosecutor" and an anti-establishment hero.

The arrest, however, completely upended the mass media's treatment of Abe. "His ability to control the mass media is well-known," stated a former colleague prosecutor in another *Asahi Shimbun* story printed on the same day as the article commenting on Matsuda. "Behind his grandiose actions lie the hidden aim of generating publicity for himself. Ego and a hunger for fame are at the root of everything the man does."

The story of the extortion allegations goes back to the time immediately after the case against the N360 was dropped. The evening edition of the *Yomiuri Shimbun* on November 2, 1971, described the case as follows:

"According to the arrest warrant, Abe and Matsuda plotted to extort a large sum of money from the Honda Motor Company under the name of 'compensation' for accidents caused by what they claimed were defects in the N360. Between September 3 and 27, Abe and Matsuda met with Director Kiyoshi Kawashima and other representatives of the Honda Motor Company several times at restaurants, including 'Hatsuhana' in Shibuya, Tokyo. The two stated that they planned to file multiple criminal and civil suits involving the N360 and take full advantage of the mass media to promote the cases. They further stated that they had fodder for at least ten years of litigation, claiming that they could bankrupt even Nissan if they seriously pursued the truck issue. Abe and Matsuda suggested that the Honda situation could be settled out of court with a payment of 1.6 billion yen.

"Honda requested a list of alleged victims and confirmation that Abe and Matsuda were authorized to represent them, but Abe and Matsuda refused to comply. Around October 5, the two met with Honda representatives at the Grand Hotel Hamamatsu in Hamamatsu, Shizuoka Prefecture, where Honda again asked them for more details on each case. Abe and Matsuda began to threaten the men, saying, 'There's no time for that. This is a critical time for your company. If we don't resolve this before the end of the year, you'll have a war on your hands.'

"Furthermore, on the 18th of the same month, in a meeting in Abe's office, Abe and Matsuda told Honda that 'a politician has obtained an expert's report detailing defects in the N360 and intends to bring the matter up before the National Diet to seek a complete recall of every N360 ever sold,' and demanded that Honda pay the 1.6 billion yen by the end of October. Abe and Matsuda reportedly reiterated their threats to file lawsuits and hold press conferences if Honda refused to pay. In the end Honda representatives refused and instead filed a report against Abe and Matsuda with the Tokyo District Prosecutors Office…

"It is true that Mr. Abe and Secretary-General Matsuda have visited us numerous times, claiming to be representatives of the victims of accidents involving the N360, demanding an excessive amount of money from us,' stated Takayuki Hattori, a director and head of public relations for the Honda Motor Company. 'We see consumer rights movements as a reflection on the auto industry itself and plan on maintaining an open dialogue with our consumers. However, demands for money made by a few individuals acting as go-betweens simply for their own benefit is another story.'"

Abe and Matsuda had initially been arrested on charges of attempting to extort 1.6 billion yen from Honda. During their interrogation, however, it was found that they had previously extorted eighty million yen from Honda over a traffic accident that had occurred in Nara prefecture. Furthermore, the two had also sought to extort several hundred million yen from Toyota during the same time period.

Twenty days after their arrest on November 23, the Special Investigations section of the Tokyo District Public Prosecutors Office formally charged Abe and Matsuda with two additional counts of extortion and attempted extortion. In the end, Abe and Matsuda were charged with attempted extortion of one hundred and eighty million yen and of extortion of twelve million yen from Toyota in addition to the two cases involving Honda.

"We fully support the rights of consumers to make claims against manufacturers," asserted Yusuke Yoshinaga, a public prosecutor with the Tokyo District Public Prosecutors Office, during his testimony explaining the reasons for Abe and Matsuda's arrest. "However, the Japan Automobile Users Union masquerades as a benign consumer-rights organization but is actually a malevolent group of blackmailers. The Special Investigations section will continue its investigation into this organization to clarify its true form and aims."

While Honda's day-to-day affairs were handled by the four executive directors, it was Fujisawa who had the final say. Fujisawa's management policy was based on making sure that logic and reason prevailed at all times. Why, then, had he acquiesced to Abe and Matsuda's initial demand for eighty million yen? Fujisawa, of course, had his own reasons.

According to Matsuda, the whole incident was a "set-up" engineered by the Honda company, "a major plot yet to dodge the criminal charges brought against it" and "an outright attempt to use state authority to oppress consumers." To this today, Matsuda continues his crusade for a retrial. Honda, on the other hand, saw the incident as nothing more or less than a case of extortion, a loathsome incident, which the company was eager to put behind itself.

The charges of homicide filed against Soichiro by the Japan Automobile Users Union may have been dropped, but Honda's problems were not yet over. Along with the criminal charges, the union had organized 140 victims in a collective suit against the company, a rarity at the time, and was claiming total damages of 1.6 billion yen.

Honda found itself in a difficult position. It had to deal with the official criminal investigation, and at the same time negotiate an amicable settlement with the victims. After the criminal charges were dropped, the negotiations should have turned in Honda's favor, but, as might be expected, the acquittal itself wasn't enough to satisfy the victims. Honda proposed a settlement of three hundred million yen; the victims continued to ask for much more. Negotiations stalled. Increasingly frustrated, the victims had turned to Abe and the Users Union for redress.

At first, Abe met with Honda representatives in a small Tokyo restaurant. Both sides quickly realized that this attracted far too much attention. At one point, reporters even managed to uncover one of the arranged meetings and rent the adjacent room in an attempt to listen in on and tape the meeting.

To avoid the public eye, Honda suggested an old and prestigious restaurant called Hatsuhana for the next meeting. Hatsuhana was a traditional establishment, which had, in the past, served as the venue for *shogi* (Japanese chess) championship tournaments, but which now looked more like a deserted old temple than a restaurant. The meeting room was adjacent to a large Japanese garden; there would be no way for anyone to eavesdrop, even if voices were raised.

According to the arrest warrant, Abe and Matsuda came to the restaurant on September 3. In reality, however, only Matsuda showed up. Honda's Kiyoshi Kawashima was accompanied by Kiyoshi Mori, who had overseen the design of the N360's chassis.

Mori had left Kurogane for Honda in 1958, at the age of twenty-eight. Soichiro had handled the interview personally.

"So I hear you worked for Kurogane. What's your specialty?" Soichiro had asked.

"Anything and everything," Mori had shot back.

Mori joined Honda at roughly the same time as Yoshio Nakamura, who would make a name for himself in the F1 project. Mori's first task at Honda was to design a welding jig for the Super Cub. He moved on to help develop the chassis for both the S500 and the N360. On account of his bold personality, Mori was selected to help with addressing the N360 defect scandal right from the very start. Mori commuted to the Public Prosecutors Office in Tokyo on a daily basis. In fact, his visits became so routine that guards there mistook him for another prosecutor and began saluting him. Mori knew more about the details of the scandal than anyone else in R&D and was quickly appointed as the main negotiator in the civil suit. Mori had come to know Abe and Matsuda quite well during the proceedings.

"Matsuda-san, you've got a temper as terrible as our Soichiro's. If you worked for Honda, you'd be at each other's throats every day," laughed Kiyoshi Kawashima one day in an attempt to break the ice.

The first meeting went smoothly. Neither side brought up money issues and conversation focused on benign subjects. Things only started getting tense when Abe appeared for the actual negotiations.

Honda and the union changed venues several times for the negotiations, from Hatsuhana, to the Hamamatsu Grand Hotel, to Abe's law firm. In the course of the negotiations, the union began to demand 1.6 billion yen as compensation. Each time the demand was made, Kiyoshi Kawashima asked for a list of the names of the individual victims and an official letter from the victims delegating the union's authority to negotiate on their behalf. Abe and Matsuda stubbornly refused.

Matsuda later explained his reasons for rejecting Honda's request. "Try to see it from our side," he said. "We were negotiating with a large corporation. If we had simply handed over the list of the names, they would have started negotiating privately with the individual victims, using the people's ignorance of technical and legal matters to the company's advantage."

To say that Abe and Matsuda harbored a deep mistrust of Honda would be an understatement. At the end of August, just before the start of actual negotiations, Mori invited Matsuda out to a small restaurant. The moment the waitress left, the young engineer who had accompanied Mori to the unofficial meeting spoke up.

"Matsuda-san, money must be a big concern for you," said the young engineer in a trembling voice, unbuttoning his suit jacket to reveal a money belt stuffed with cash. "Please feel free to take this."

Mori sat with his back turned to them, quietly listening to the proceedings.

They want to buy us off, thought Matsuda. When the young engineer had shown the cash, Matsuda had also noticed the edge of a tape recorder tucked in just behind the belt. *That means evidence,* thought Matsuda. *Taking the money now would be seen as accepting a bribe. That'd be it for me as far as society's concerned.*

It was entirely on Fujisawa's orders that Honda had resorted to such an act of near-bribery.

"There are two kinds of business negotiations," Fujisawa used to explain. "One is offensive, which means taking a spear and charging the target. The best way is to give the spear to someone who doesn't know anything about the plot. The other is defensive. In that case, the person in charge needs to be fully aware of the situation, and play as many cards as he can to confuse the opponent."

Based on this negotiation strategy, Fujisawa had selected Mori, who was fully aware of the situation from the beginning, and a young engineer who didn't know a thing about the scandal, to carry out the tactic. He also figured that since Matsuda had once been an engineer for Nissan, sending in another engineer could help ease the discussion; perhaps the fellow engineers could come up with an alternate solution. But what Fujisawa really wanted to know was if Honda's opponent was simply interested in money.

The young engineer, clutching cash and a tape recorder instead of a spear, had "charged" Matsuda. The only question had been whether Matsuda would take it.

The incident with the cash and the tape recorder only served to escalate the tension between the two parties. Honda tried every means at its disposal to get hold of the list of victims. The union, on the other hand, dug in their heels in an attempt to defend themselves from Honda. Both sides exploited the mass media and practically spied on one other. After several unfruitful meetings, Abe and Matsuda took off the kid gloves. Finally, they began to use language that bordered on outright threat.

"Because of your refusal to honor our requests, this situation has gotten totally out of hand," Abe and Matsuda said. "We can finish our discussions in front of the National Diet. We're more than happy to take this up with the media and begin filing civil suits."

Indeed, the defect scandal would rear its head again, and it was largely thanks to the union. Not only did they carry out their threat to file a suit at Tokyo District Public Prosecutors Office, they directly petitioned the National Diet to re-examine the issue. The attitude at headquarters quickly turned to fear as the four executive directors charged with resolving the issue realized the true extent of the union's political influence. The directors truly believed that they were in danger. Although the government had dropped the criminal charges against Honda, they knew the company's image would be irreparably tainted if the issue came up before the Diet a second time.

The directors appraised Fujisawa of the situation and asked for advice. *Soichiro poured his heart and soul into the N360*, reflected Fujisawa. *It couldn't possibly be defective. But there's no upside to dragging out this scandal any longer. It's already a burden on our salesmen. Ever since this whole affair began, the four directors, Soichiro and I have all been going through hell. If we have to take more, we'll start tasting blood. I knew how to deal with the financial crises in 1954 and 1962 since I could pin down their causes. But this time, I'm pretty much stumped. We are going to fall if things keep up like this. If money is what it takes to solve the problem, maybe we should pay.*

It was the first time Fujisawa, the man of logic and reason, had ever even considered caving in to what he believed in his heart to be unfair demands.

"I'm not fully comfortable with paying them, but if that's what you say has to be done, we'll do it," Fujisawa told the board of directors. "Since you're all in agreement about this, I can only assume the situation is critical. I will only say that if we pay now, it will open the way for others to squeeze us as well. We must prepare for that."

Fujisawa desperately wanted to put the defective car scandal behind. During the criminal investigation, a large number of Honda engineers had been summoned to the Tokyo District Public Prosecutors Office on a regular basis, virtually paralyzing the Honda Research and Development Company. If a civil suit started, the engineers would be taken from their offices once again. The engineering staff was focused on developing the low-emission engine, a critical project that would affect the future of the entire company. Fujisawa wanted to avoid a time- and labor-consuming trial at any cost.

The biggest mistake that Honda made in the entire affair was that they had judged the Japan Automobile Users Union to be a malevolent group of blackmailers rather than a benign consumer-rights organization, based on the rough language used by Abe and Matsuda. If that were truly the case, there would be a good chance that Abe and Matsuda would split the money without giving any to the victims. Honda actually believed this was likely.

"According to the Hoffmann calculation, the settlement should be around thirty million yen," said a Honda representative at one of the many negotiating sessions. "We'll add to that and pay you fifty million yen. What do you say?"

Time and time again Abe and Matsuda rejected these offers, reiterating their demand for eighty million yen in compensation for the accident in Nara prefecture. They knew that any sign of weakness on their part would play directly into Honda's hands. On September 25, Abe and Matsuda gave Honda a final warning, threatening to suspend negotiations if the company refused to pay the full amount. Four days later at the Keio Plaza Hotel in Tokyo's Shinjuku district, Kiyoshi Kawashima handed Abe a check for eighty million yen bearing Fujisawa's signature, while Matsuda looked on. It was a bitter pill for the Honda Motor Company.

Honda had deliberately made the payment under the name of "sympathy money." Even at this stage, Honda was firmly convinced that Abe and Matsuda planned to embezzle the eighty million yen. If they did keep it for themselves, it would all but prove that the union had been founded with blackmail in mind. And if the sum was satisfactory, it would stop the threats. Even if it didn't, at the very least it would make a strong case for extortion.

Contrary to the hopes of Honda's directors, the matter did not end there. Honda may have described the payment as "sympathy money," but as far as the union was concerned, it was compensation. Seeing the payment as an admission and acknowledgement of Honda's responsibility in the affair, the union continued to demand an additional 1.6 billion yen in compensation. As for the eighty million yen they had received, Abe and Matsuda, after deducting expenses, actually did distribute the sum to the families of the victims of the accident in Nara prefecture.

At the beginning of October, Honda learned from a reliable source that a pair of dealerships selling products made by Honda's rival Suzuki was quietly bankrolling the union's activities. Fujisawa prepared for the worst.

The two dealers in question were Suzuki Hanbai in Osaka and Kyushu

Suzuki Hanbai in Fukuoka. Both had once been among Honda's top dealers but had switched over to Suzuki when Fujisawa had launched the new sales system for N360. And what was more, the two had sued Honda for four hundred million yen of what they described as profits "stolen" by the new policy. The defections had generated quite a stir in the media at the time. The incident came to be known variously as the "Spring Battle of Osaka" and the "Ten-Year War."

When the defect scandal first came to light in June of 1969, an organization of former Honda dealers wasted no time in holding a press conference to publicize the defects of the N360. The conference was led by Suzuki Hanbai president Yutaka Nagao. In its former incarnation as Honda Hanbai, Suzuki Hanbai had been Honda's largest dealer. After leaving the Honda fold, Nagao had organized the other dealerships that had left Honda to form the "Society of Former Honda Dealers."

Honda conducted intensive research into the matter and found that the majority of cases which had come up in the N360 defect scandal were centered in and around the Kansai region—the same area, incidentally, where several major dealers had followed Nagao's suit and had switched flags from Honda to Suzuki. It was too suspicious to be coincidental.

Even if the basic problems in the N360 had been caused by insufficient engineering skills on the part of Honda, it was still highly likely that, behind the scenes, the former dealers were intentionally escalating the situation in some way or another. These were the same dealers that, at one time, had worked tirelessly under Fujisawa selling Honda's products. Some of them had actually helped Honda out in its earliest days by lending money to the company, taking Honda stock as collateral. Others had been helped out, in turn, by Honda, as Honda forgave their debts and supported their recovery in times of financial difficulty. Nevertheless, in spite of the strong relationship Honda had built with these companies, they had chosen to defect in anger as a result of Fujisawa's new hard-line sales policy for the N360.

One could, of course, simply say that Fujisawa had made his own bed, but the potential loss to Honda was simply too large to swallow. Left unchecked, the situation would undoubtedly begin affecting not only Honda but also the entire industry. And so, after describing everything that had occurred between Honda and the Users Union to the Tokyo District Public Prosecutors Office, Fujisawa proceeded to file his own suit against the Japan Automobile Users Union.

It was at this moment that Fujisawa fully realized the only way to address the collective anger of the dealers towards his company was to retire from the front lies of management, together with Soichiro. The trial would drag on for months, perhaps even years. So long as Soichiro was helming the company, he would inevitably be called to testify in court. While Soichiro had already testified once during the criminal proceedings, that trial had been held behind closed doors. Soichiro's very public appearance this time around would make a far different impression than his previous testimony.

He may be president of the Honda Motor Company, thought Fujisawa, *but I've been running the business. I can't let Soichiro testify; he simply doesn't have enough of a grasp of our business situation. But that being said, I'm growing tired of dealing with such trying times. Perhaps a quarter of a century is the maximum length of time that two people with such vastly different personalities can continue working together. It's about time to put an end to it. My final job will be ensuring that Soichiro can retire without tarnishing his glorious past. I'll make the four directors understand this first. Soichiro may be the last person to know, but I think he'll understand in the end.*

The trial against the Users Union began on July 4, 1972. Predictably, it got off to a rough start. It took the prosecutor a solid forty minutes to read the indictment, which included a full background of the case. No sooner had he finished than the union's lawyer requested that the prosecution be dismissed.

"There is some question as to the legality of the investigation," insisted the union's attorney. "The written indictment was crafted specifically to bias the judges. With the incendiary commentary removed, it's apparent that there isn't a case here."

Just as Fujisawa had expected, the trial dragged on for years. President Kiyoshi Kawashima, Vice President Kihachiro Kawashima, Director Michihiro Nishida, and other top executives took turns testifying. The final judgment was handed down on August 12, 1977, five years later.

There were three points at issue in the trial. One centered on whether the vehicle was truly defective, and whether the defendant had recognized it as such. The second centered on the appropriateness of the defendant's actions as an auto-consumer authority. And the third centered on the appropriateness of Abe's actions as a lawyer.

"The defendant claims that out-of-court negotiations were legitimate, but there is no conclusive evidence indicating that the N360 was a defective car. Furthermore, the amount of money demanded exceeded the amount that could be considered legitimate for consumer compensation. Abe's actions are not in line with what may be considered permissible behavior for a lawyer," concluded the judge, agreeing with nearly all of the prosecutor's claims. The judge sentenced Abe and Matsuda to three years and two years in prison, respectively, with no stay of execution. The judge ruled that while the union's motivation and purpose may have been legitimate, their means could not be justified.

Abe and Matsuda immediately appealed the decision to the Tokyo High Court. In the meantime, they were taken to the Tokyo Detention Center, where they posted eight million yen each in bail and were released that same evening. They immediately held a press conference at the judicial press club in Kasumigaseki, Tokyo, where they openly expressed their frustrations.

"The ruling simply parroted the written indictment and indicates laziness on the part of the judges."

"This is a total miscarriage of justice. We may have lost the first round, but you can bet we'll make our case heard in the second and third."

Naokazu Takeuchi, representative of the Consumers Union of Japan, also strongly criticized both the judgment and Honda's actions in the matter. The Consumers Union was something of a headline-grabber itself in those days. Takeuchi, a former official at the Ministry of Agriculture, Forestry and Fisheries, as well as the Economic Planning Agency, had founded the organization to fight against corporate activities that he considered "anti-consumerist."

"The judgment is utterly unreasonable," said Takeuchi in the August 12, 1977 evening edition of the *Mainichi Shimbun* newspaper. "The judges seem to lack any sort of understanding of the needs and desires of the consumer. So long as people have actually been injured in defective cars, consumers should have the right to make their voices heard on the matter, even if there are some doubts regarding the exact cause of the accidents. If Honda truly doubted the legitimacy of Mr. Abe and Mr. Matsuda's requests, why didn't they file suit before making the payment? Their going to court after paying seems to be nothing but an attempt to silence the consumers' movement."

Honda, for its part, refrained from comment on the victory. The newspapers reported the incident on the front and local news pages but not on the business news page. In terms of impact on business, the case had all but lost its news value.

The judgment on the appeal was finally handed down another five years later, on June 28, 1982. Of the three extortion charges filed against Abe and Matsuda involving Honda, Toyota, and Hino Jidosha Hanbai, the chief justice ruled that Abe and Matsuda were innocent of the charges of extortion of Honda, which involved the highest sum of money. His judgment read in part:

"The negotiations with Honda were undertaken with the aim of pursuing compensation on behalf of the victims of traffic accidents. The two defendants were convinced that the car was defective. As such, they had the right to demand compensation for the damages resulting from said defects."

Acknowledging the Users Union's claims for compensation as legitimate, the judgment not only reversed the decision of the lower court and found Abe and Matsuda to be innocent of the charges related to the extortion of Honda, it also found the strong language used in the negotiations by Abe and Matsuda to be "a part of the bargaining process," and denied the validity of the charges altogether.

"While it is true that the pair took a disagreeably coercive approach to the negotiations, their behavior was a direct result of their desire to assist the victims of these tragic accidents. In light of the fact that Honda failed to respond to their initial requests with sincerity and did not make sufficient efforts to prove that their product wasn't defective, the defendants' actions can be seen as socially acceptable," said the judge.

However, the justice declined to overturn the judgment against the pair involving Toyota and Hino Jidosha Hanbai. He sentenced Abe to two years in prison, suspended for four years, and Matsuda to one year and six months in prison, suspended for four years. Even though the overall outcome still resulted in a conviction for the defendants, Honda received a severe comment from Chief Justice Tsuneo Niizeki, who pointed out that the company had shown a lack of sincerity towards its consumers and had not fulfilled its social responsibility in addressing their concerns.

"Safety concerns must be treated as strictly as possible in cases where there is any doubt. The Honda Motor Company has a responsibility to society to address any doubts about the safety of its products and to actively prove that they are not defective."

Although the high court had shown a certain degree of understanding for the consumer movement and had come out with a decision that was more sympathetic towards the defendants than the lower court, and had reduced their penalties, Abe and Matsuda were not at all satisfied. They filed a final appeal with the Supreme Court of Japan, stating, "This is a black and white issue. We fully expect a full acquittal."

On January 24, 1987, two years before Fujisawa passed away, the Supreme Court of Japan dismissed Abe and Matsuda's appeal, upholding the judgment and sentence of the Tokyo High Court. From start to finish, the Users Union case had taken all of sixteen years to settle.

While the final judgment wasn't particularly favorable to Honda, neither was it mortally damaging. There were three reasons for this. One was that the public had largely lost interest in the case over the sixteen years it had taken to reach an official conclusion. For another, Honda representatives had stubbornly kept their silence regarding the case during this time, preferring instead to allow courtroom findings to speak for themselves. And finally, Abe and Matsuda had spared no occasion to argue their case, never hesitating to call press conferences or make public statements whenever they encountered perceived mistakes or negative speculation in the mass media. Eventually the press grew tired of the story, so that even when they ran a story on Honda, they intentionally avoided touching on the N360 defect issue.

The scandal, touched off by the *New York Times* article of June 1969, was a tragic result of the motorization boom, which had occurred before automobile manufacturers could achieve a firm enough grip on mass production technologies. At the same time, the scandal revealed the immaturity of the nascent consumer movement.

At the time, the main course of action undertaken by consumer-rights organizations was simply to sue the government and related manufacturers whenever problems occurred. While these early campaigns did result in advances such as the enactment of the Product Liability Law, consumer activists have since begun to question whether simply dumping the responsibility for problems on the government and corporations really improved society. In fact, the Japanese consumer movement has faced a new turning point as it wrestles with this very issue.

During all the years of the trial, rather than using the mass media to gain the public's sympathy, Honda put its efforts into trying to avoid making enemies and prevent potential opposition groups from forming. Ironically enough, it was Abe and Matsuda's unceasing and stubborn attempts to justify themselves that gave Honda the chance to re-cast its corporate image. It thus contributed to the making of the "Honda myth."

Honda never gave an inch during the courtroom battles, but the experience did allow the company to mature. The most important lesson learned was that the directors finally realized that maintaining an active dialogue with the public went a long way towards legitimizing the company in the eyes of society. Until then, like other owners of mid-sized corporations of the day, both Soichiro and Fujisawa had kept their heads down and focused totally on making Honda as large and successful as possible. They simply hadn't made time to engage in exchanges with the public.

Nishida's heavy-handed replies during his Diet testimonies on the N360 were a prime example. In essence, his argument had been that the car couldn't possibly be defective because it had been built by genius engineer Soichiro Honda. This sort of arrogance infuriated not only politicians, but the mass media and the public as well. Just before the scandal had broken, Honda's revenues had exceeded four hundred billion yen, making the company one of the top thirty manufacturers in Japan. In terms of net profit, Honda ranked even higher on the scale. Although the company had grown into a major corporation in both name and fact, its representatives were still too inexperienced and unseasoned to realize the need to take on the responsibilities associated with a company of that size and status.

Honda wasn't a small company anymore. The public now looked on the company with quite a different set of expectations than it had when Honda was just starting out with little more than a million yen in capital. The problem was that although people knew that Honda was by now a large corporation and that it was founded and run by Soichiro Honda, they knew next to nothing about what kind of activities Honda was involved in or what contribution the company made to Japanese society. If, by some unfortunate twist of fate, a second, or third scandal should break out, it was obvious that Honda would be even more severely criticized.

This didn't mean the company had been resting on its laurels when it came to social causes. In 1961, Fujisawa had drastically increased Honda's capital to build the Suzuka manufacturing plant. The capital increase had involved issuing rights to shareholders to purchase additional stock, so that, in the end, it resulted in considerably enhancing Soichiro and Fujisawa's fortunes. Not only did they own more shares, they were receiving dividends on those shares, which meant that their earnings only continued to grow. The investment made them rich men many times over, and finally Fujisawa began discussing ways for he and Soichiro to return a portion of their profits to society.

Fukuzo Kawahara, a former vice president of Mitsubishi Bank and Honda's main financial advisor, guided the pair to invest a total of six hundred million yen between them to found the "Sakkokai." The foundation was designed to support developments in science and technology by sponsoring research projects and study-abroad programs for scientists and engineers. At a time when the salary for new employees fresh out of college fell short of 20,000 yen per month, and even research assistants who had successfully completed graduate work on a doctoral level received less than 30,000 yen a month, those who qualified for foundation assistance received a monthly stipend of 15,000 yen. There was no expectation of having to pay the money back, and it was given with no strings attached other than that it be used for research. And what was more, the foundation made no attempt to intervene or otherwise influence the outcome of a sponsored project. The scholarship system gave young Japanese researchers an incredible degree of freedom.

The Sakkokai remained active until 1983. During the twenty-two years of its existence, more than 1,735 individuals received scholarships, including Mamoru Mori, who went on to board the Space Shuttle Endeavor as NASA's first Japanese astronaut.

The most unique aspect of the foundation was that Fujisawa and Soichiro requested to have their names kept secret. They didn't want to worry the recipients over the source of the funds. This meant that Mori, for example, received a scholarship to study for his Ph.D. in the United States, as well as enough funds to get by on for some time after his return to Japan, without ever knowing that his sponsors were the founders of the Honda Motor Company. Fujisawa and Soichiro saw their involvement in the Sakkokai as pure volunteer work, meaningful only as long as they contributed privately. The pair went to great pains to avoid contact with the scholarship recipients. Their involvement was only made public at the farewell party thrown when the Sakkokai was finally disbanded.

Honda's first public contribution came with the Honda Driving Safety Promotion program. During Nishida's testimony before the Diet, a politician had commented, "Honda should pay more attention to consumer safety education." By October 1, 1970, two weeks after the comment, Honda had created a new section charged with providing information about safety issues and promoting driving-safety campaigns. Honda was the first Japanese auto manufacturer to establish any sort of consumer safety division, although there is an argument to be made that the company should have acted more quickly considering the central involvement of its products in the defect scandal.

The company's attempts to engage society at large didn't stop with simply establishing a foundation or actively promoting driver safety. Starting with the four executive directors, Honda directors began putting serious thought into how they could contribute to society on an individual level. It was a realization and acknowledgement of the fact that understanding the public's expectations for the company played a direct role in creating successful products.

The base of demand for cars was far broader than that of motorcycles. Exhaust regulations would soon be taking effect, and the development of a low-emission engine was proceeding smoothly. In fact, it appeared that Honda would be first to market with the new type of engine. Still, the directors knew that even if they managed to beat other manufacturers to market, unless they had engaged in sufficient dialogue with the public, Honda's philosophy would never gain mainstream status.

The defect scandal had been a hard lesson for Honda's four top directors. Venturing out of the sphere of their individual competence, the men began to actively socialize with politicians and officials from MITI, the Ministry of Transport, the Science and Technology Agency, and other relevant government offices.

The success of the N360 appeared to have cemented Honda's reputation as an automobile manufacturer. But the sluggish sales of the H1300 and the aftereffects of the defect scandal had caused Honda to miss a critical window of opportunity to take advantage of the motorization boom. Fujisawa's dreams of defeating Toyota had faded away. The k-car Life had essentially been a modified version of the N360, so that now, the engineering department needed to start from scratch to create a new car. So long as Soichiro stayed on the front lines of management, it would be difficult or impossible to effect the change necessary to rebuild Honda's automotive section. Soichiro and Fujisawa's era was coming to an end.

The machinery for the founders' retirement had been set into motion the moment the lawsuit was filed against the Japan Automobile Users Union. Fujisawa secretly set the date for their retirement to coincide with the ceremony in the fall of 1973 commemorating the twenty-fifth anniversary of Honda's founding. He timed it to avoid the height of the trial, which would not come until later, and perhaps more importantly, in the expectation that Honda's new low-emission engine would be ready by then. An engine that met the Muskie standards would not only help repair the company's tainted image, it would serve as a perfect cap to the career of Soichiro Honda, the greatest engineer of Japan's post-war era.

3

The first step towards setting the stage for Soichiro and Fujisawa's retirement was on the launch of a new compact car called the "Civic." The name had been carefully chosen to showcase Honda's "basic car for the citizens of the world."

The concept for the Civic was entirely based on a review of the weaknesses of the H1300. The design was as simple as possible, and the vehicle was lightweight and inexpensive. Needless to say, it was built around a water-cooled engine. On July 11, 1972, six months after the Winter Olympic Games in Hokkaido, Honda unveiled the Civic to the press at a hotel in central Tokyo.

At first glance, the new car appeared quite odd. It had a front-mounted four-cylinder 1200cc engine and front-wheel drive. Most surprisingly from a design standpoint, the rear of the car did not swell out to accommodate the customary trunk space. At the time, most cars utilized a "three-box" layout—engine, passenger compartment, and trunk. The Civic was a two-box arrangement with a trapezoidal shape described by the designers as being like a clenched fist. Unorthodox though it may have appeared, Honda engineers were confident in the utility of their new creation. The initial reaction of customers, however, was almost uniformly negative.

"This is an ugly car. There's no way anyone's going to buy it."

"It's just a scaled-up Life!"

Before long, the Civic found itself saddled with the nickname of "Big Life." In fact, it wasn't an altogether inaccurate description. The Life had been built by adapting the basic design used in the Civic—known as the BS—into a k-car. So, to put it more precisely, the Life was actually a miniature version of the Civic. Although the Civic appeared quite small, the front-engine front-wheel layout made it roomy enough to accommodate four large individuals comfortably.

The sales price was reasonable as well. The standard model retailed for 425,000 yen, while the four-door custom model of the Life sold for 443,000 yen. By this time, the average annual national income per person had reached 710,000 yen, making the cars readily available to nearly anyone who wanted one.

Two months later in September, Honda added a hatchback version to the Civic line. Although the term "hatchback" was starting to gain popularity in the United States, it remained alien to Japanese ears. To avoid creating a negative impression, Honda's marketing staff described the car as being a "three-door" design. But the term proved even more confusing to consumers. In fact, Honda reportedly had prospective customers calling to ask, "Which side of the car has two doors?"

Although the unusual design of the car led to negative advance reviews and caused it to be regarded as something of a "misfit" in the industry, it eventually turned into one of the auto industry's great success stories. Consumers were cautious at first, but gradually came to understand the inherent user-friendliness of the vehicle. Automobile critics also began to praise the design. Only 21,000 Civics were sold in Japan in 1972, but the number increased to 86,000 the following year, and to 160,000 in 1974. In 1975, Honda sold 176,000 of the cars, an all-time record for the company.

Before long, the Civic's hatchback design had come to be recognized as the standard for two-box cars with front-engine layouts. As it turned out, the Civic was not a "misfit"; it was simply ahead of the times. At the end of 1972, the same year that the Civic went on sale, the number of Volkswagen Beetles sold reached 15,007,033, finally beating the record set by the Ford Model T. Soon, people were calling the Civic the "Japanese Beetle."

While auto magazine journalists were, as always, mainly interested in the Civic's handling and mechanical characteristics, questions asked at a press conference for the mass media tended to focus on the development of the company's upcoming low-emission engine.

"We've completed all the necessary tests at the Honda Research and Development Company," said Soichiro proudly, anticipating the reporters' questions. "We're now in the middle of a 50,000 mile durability test."

Two months later, on September 19, 1972, Honda completed its low-emission engine. The engine met both the standards set by the Muskie Act and the 1975 standards of the automobile exhaust regulations established by the Central Council for Environmental Pollution Control (known as the Japanese version of the Muskie Act).

On the morning of the same day, in the presence of officials from the Ministry of Transport, MITI and the Tokyo Metropolitan Police Department, Honda conducted a public test of the new engine, dubbed the CVCC—for "Compound Vortex Controlled Combustion"—at the Suzuka manufacturing plant. The data showed that the CVCC engine successfully cleared both the American and Japanese regulations. Two days later on September 22, Honda brought a Civic equipped with the CVCC engine to the Nagoya Land Transport Office for official inspection and registration. With that, the first "low-polluting" car was born.

The CVCC version of the Civic entered a month of intensive open road testing. On October 20, one day after the tests were completed, Soichiro held another press conference at a hotel in central Tokyo to show off the car and the official exhaust data.

At the press conference, Soichiro began by proudly announcing that Honda would begin sales of CVCC-equipped Civics in the fall of 1973. Furthermore, he stated that Honda would not be applying to the U.S. Environmental Protection Agency for an extension of the compliance date for the 1975 requirements, now that it was likely to be able to meet both the American and Japanese standards. He then went on to add:

"Honda will offer its patents and know-how for the CVCC engine to other manufacturers as well."

Honda's press conferences traditionally were held jointly by Soichiro and Fujisawa, and usually ended with an amusing back-and-forth exchange between the two. After Kiyoshi Kawashima became president of Honda R&D, Fujisawa had Kawashima join the pair onstage as a way of indicating to the media that the company considered him to be the next president of Honda. On this day, Kawashima had acted as MC for the press conference, but the assembled media also found themselves looking at a host of unfamiliar faces.

"The development of the CVCC engine was possible through the combined efforts of the twenty-one engineers from the Honda Research and Development Company you see here today," explained Kawashima. "In particular, head researcher Tasuku Date, managing director Tadashi Kume, and chief researcher Shizuo Yagi have been central to the team's success. Needless to say, the twenty-one also includes our president Soichiro Honda, who guided us with his unceasing belief that it was possible to create a low-polluting engine without using any additional devices."

Kawashima went on to introduce each member of the engineering team, one at a time, to the press. It was his way of rewarding them for all the hard work they had put into the project over the last several years. It was also the first glimpse the media got of the next generation of Honda managers. The group not only included the aforementioned Tadashi Kume, who later became the third president of the Honda Motor Company, but Nobuhiko Kawamoto, who would become the fourth, and Shoichiro Irimajiri.

At the conference, Kawashima had mentioned Date's name before Kume's for a reason. It was Date who had come up with the fundamental principle behind the CVCC engine: purifying the exhaust by effecting a controlled explosion of a lean fuel-air mixture.

Date realized that the energy generated by the spark plugs was too small to ignite the lean mixture. He suggested using a small supplementary engine rather than spark plugs to create a flame of the size necessary to effect combustion. Date's proposed method promised the possibility of creating a low-emission engine entirely with the available technology. It formed the foundation for all of the research that had followed.

The final design split the combustion chamber into two parts and used the carburetor to supply separate mixtures into each of the combustion chambers— a rich fuel-air mixture for the small prechamber, and a lean mixture for the main combustion chamber. The spark plug was attached to the prechamber.

The new standards specified a reduction in the amounts of three substances in automotive exhaust: nitrogen oxides (NOx), carbon monoxide (CO), and hydrocarbons (HC). The temperature differential between the two combustion chambers greatly reduced the amount of NOx produced during the combustion process.

The higher oxygen content in the lean mixture fed to the main combustion chamber reduced the amount of CO produced there. Modifications to the exhaust pipe produced an oxidation reaction that resulted in the reduction of HC.

The CVCC engine will give new direction to Honda's future, thought Fujisawa, watching a young engineer struggling to explain the intricacies of exhaust reduction to newspaper reporters who lacked any sort of background in engineering. *The stage for our retirement is now set.*

Just as Fujisawa had expected, the CVCC engine created a sensation. Not only were other manufacturers surprised to find that the youngest contender in the industry had beaten its more established rivals to the punch with a reduced-emission engine, they were stunned by the fact that Honda had decided not to apply for the extension of the compliance date on the Muskie standards. At the same time, these companies—who previously had barely taken note of Honda's existence—began regarding the company as a serious adversary.

The Muskie Act (Clean Air Act of 1970) consisted of a set of standards to be met by 1975 and an additional requirement on NOx reduction to be met by 1976. The Act also stated that if, after making all possible efforts, no manufacturer was capable of meeting the standards, the U.S. Environmental Protection Agency (E.P.A.) would grant an extension on the deadlines. But the provision was conditional. If at least one company could prove that it was capable of meeting the regulations, the provisions would apply.

The Japanese auto industry was split over the interpretation of the phrase "at least one company." Large corporations such as Toyota and Nissan conveniently construed the phrase to apply to one of the U.S. Big Three, or a company of equal size. By insisting on this interpretation, they intended to say that even if Honda had achieved a breakthrough, it was too minor of a player to prevent the extensions from taking effect.

Yet, the decision to grant the extension lay with the E.P.A. and not the Japanese automakers. It was clear that Japan's Environment Agency would simply follow the E.P.A. decision. Support for stricter emissions regulations was growing among the American public day by day. Public opinion held that so long as the CVCC passed the E.P.A. tests, it was highly unlikely that there would be an extension of the 1975—if not also the 1976—regulations.

Until the advent of the CVCC engine, most bets for the first reduced-emissions engine had been on Mazda's RE (rotary engine), developed after much difficulty using technology licensed from NSU and Wankel in West Germany. The RE featured a sharply angled combustion chamber with a crescent-shaped cross section. It reduced NOx by retarding the combustion efficiency. Although the RE had the downside of extremely high fuel consumption due to the low combustion efficiency, it would only need a thermal reactor to reduce HC and CO, as NOx levels were already low.

The world's largest automaker, General Motors, had also secured a license with the West German companies and with Mazda—to which it paid fifty million dollars in licensing fees—and was preparing to introduce the technology in its sports car "Vega." Toyota had entered into negotiations to purchase RE engines from Mazda, and Nissan had also licensed the basic technology and was rushing to bring its own rotary engine to market. Even the large manufacturers realized that if they didn't want to be left behind they needed to swallow their pride, and began shamelessly spending tremendous amounts of money on any engine that appeared to have potential.

Kohei Matsuda, president of Mazda, was doing his best to create a fad of sorts by licensing RE technology to auto manufacturers across the world. Mazda had spent the last three years negotiating for a capital tie-up with Ford, but had called off the negotiations entirely in March of 1972. The reason for this was that Mazda had balked at Ford's request for a fifty percent stake, worried that the latter would take over.

While such an attitude might appear to show a reckless disregard for the company's future, Matsuda had in fact had shrewdly calculated his actions. *The RE is our ace in the hole*, he thought. *Every auto manufacturer is going to need it to beat the regulations. We have the application patents for its use. That means we can survive on our own without the protection of a foreign company.*

The appearance of the CVCC drastically changed the playing field. Although all the manufacturers took out licenses on the basic technology for the RE as a precaution, they found that its actual use was only suitable for special cars like sports cars. It also required massive capital investment. The CVCC, on the other hand, merely required modifying the standard reciprocating engine, allowing manufacturers to continue using their current equipment and factories.

The first company to try and license the CVCC was Ford, which had just broken off its negotiations with Mazda. Ford was in the process of developing a new type of engine called PROCO, which utilized separate lean and rich air-fuel mixtures. Similar to the CVCC, the PROCO was a stratified charge combustion system. It relied on a computer-controlled fuel-injector rather than a carburetor to time the spark plugs to spark just before the fuel and air mixed, with the aim of achieving combustion at the moment the fuel and air formed a rich mixture.

PROCO stood for "programmed combustion." The project had been developed with the support of the U.S. Army and had already been a success at the experimental stage. Although the engine was only one step away from practical application, Ford engineers had nonetheless run up against a major stumbling block due to limitations in computer technology of the day.

Thanks to their experience on the PROCO project, the Ford engineers fully understood the implications of the CVCC innovation. Judging that it would be far cheaper to license the CVCC than to develop new computer technology, Ford approached Honda almost as soon as the test results for the CVCC engine were publicized.

Toyota was also investigating the potential of licensing the CVCC technology. Toyota's attempts to surmount the 1975 regulations centered on engine modifications combined with the addition of new equipment such as catalytic converters. Experiment results implied that, with these changes, Toyota might just be able to clear the 1975 regulations. However, the company lacked any prospect for clearing the 1976 regulations, especially since it had so many models of cars in its lineup. That was when Toyota heard about the CVCC engine, which, according to the technical explanations Honda offered, had the potential of meeting both the 1975 and the 1976 standards.

Eiji Toyoda, president of Toyota, visited Soichiro at the Honda headquarters in Yaesu in person to request a license on the CVCC technology. The technology encompassed some 230 patents in Japan and abroad, designs specifications, and engineering know-how regarding the engine's production. Honda would provide the technology to Toyota for a fee, and retain the right to offer the same technology to other manufactures. The two companies reached an agreement in November.

Only a year or so earlier, Honda had been facing a major crisis stemming from the defect scandal, which had threatened the continued existence not only of its automotive department but of the entire company. But now, in terms of technical capability, the company had grown powerful enough to make even Japan's top manufacturer come begging for help.

Toyota's decision to license production of the CVCC raised public opinion of the design to new heights. MITI started to consider granting an exemption on automobile taxes for low-emission vehicles in order to help popularize the vehicles among consumers. If the decision were finalized, there was no doubt that CVCC-equipped cars would be the first to benefit. Honda expected a Civic with a CVCC engine to retail for somewhere between 500,000 and 600,000 yen. A tax break would reduce that price by 70,000 to 80,000 yen.

In the beginning of December, the U.S. E.P.A. contacted Honda with a request for several CVCC equipped cars for testing. Honda agreed and sent two factory-fresh CVCC cars and one CVCC car with 50,000 kilometers of mileage, together with relevant data on the CVCC. The tests were conducted in Ann Arbor, Michigan. The Muskie Act standards for 1975 required a car to emit less than 3.4 grams of CO, 0.41 grams of HC, and 3.1 grams of NOx per volume of exhaust generated in a mile of driving. The new CVCC cars easily cleared the requirements, emitting 1.9 grams, 0.21 grams, and 0.81 grams of the substances.

The E.P.A. presented the results to the public on December 18, officially certifying that Honda's CVCC met the standards for low-polluting engines. As promised by Soichiro at the press conference in Japan, Honda turned in a written document stating that it would not apply for an exemption from the 1975 regulations. This virtually guaranteed that the 1975 standards would be applied according to schedule. Public attention shifted to the regulations for 1976.

The 1976 standards stipulated less than 0.4 grams of NOx per volume of exhaust generated in a mile of driving. Even the CVCC generated twice this amount of the substance. In spite of the difficulties, the Honda R&D team remained in high spirits.

"We are confident that we can clear the 1976 standards without using any exhaust after-treatment devices like platinum catalysts," the R&D staff reported to Fujisawa. "With the CVCC, it can be done."

The report strengthened Fujisawa's resolve. Just after the New Year's holidays in 1973, Fujisawa informed Soichiro through the board of directors, as planned, of his intention to retire from the front lines of management. Now he sat and waited for Soichiro's agreement.

4

Soichiro enjoyed almost universal recognition as a genius, especially in the field of mechanical engineering. Fujisawa had finally persuaded him to back down during the debate over water-cooled versus air-cooled engines, but no one thought any less of his abilities as an engineer for it. In fact, more than a few engineers at Honda R&D believe, even today, that Soichiro could have coaxed an air-cooled engine to pass the regulations, had he been ten years younger. Soichiro's natural charm and charisma not only made him a hero with the engineers but also instantly attracted everyone who came into contact with him.

Fujisawa wasn't a friendly man, but he made up for it through his outstanding skill as a business manager. Seeking to further the aims of the company by giving Soichiro the perfect environment in which to shine, Fujisawa had taken Honda from zero to a large and successful corporation in only a quarter of a century. Not only that—along the way, he had also taken numerous steps to ensure Honda would survive the "law of transience."

Both men had fiery dispositions and each was a genius in his own way, but otherwise, their personalities were not at all alike. It was only because of their shared goal of making Honda as large and successful as possible that they had managed to work together for so long. Despite such talents, neither Soichiro nor Fujisawa possessed the ability to turn back the clock, to overcome their own age. Both were exhausted, having "burned themselves out" in addressing the defect scandal and overseeing the development of the CVCC engine.

Yet if only one of the two were to retire, people would talk and speculate, to the detriment of both their reputations. The choice, then, was already made: Soichiro and Fujisawa had to step down in tandem. Although the two initially did not see entirely eye-to-eye as to the exact timing of their retirement, in the end, Soichiro and Fujisawa anticipated each other's thoughts and came to an implicit agreement.

The new management system took effect at the board of directors meeting held immediately after Honda's shareholders' meeting on October 29. Unlike the geniuses that had founded the company, the "Honda kids" who took over were only ordinary people. The retirement of the founders posed the danger of diluting the corporate ideology, leading the company off course. Ensuring momentum in their absence would not be an easy task.

For Kiyoshi Kawashima, the new president of Honda, and his three executive directors, Takao Shirai, Kihachiro Kawashima, and Michihiro Nishida, Honda had not been their first choice jobs. They had joined Honda in the turmoil of the post-war era, when the company was little more than a tiny cottage industry, simply because they needed to put food on the table. They weren't alone. Several other directors, including Hideo Sugiura and Noboru Okamura, had been in a similar situation. Yet whatever their reasons for joining the company, all worked furiously year after year under Soichiro and Fujisawa's leadership until one day, they looked up and realized that their company had earned worldwide recognition.

For managerial level staff like Tadashi Kume and Koichiro Yoshida, the first choice of employer had been Toyota or Nissan. Failing to get in, they had come to Honda. It was only with the next generation of employees—people like Nobuhiko Kawamoto and Shoichiro Irimajiri—that working for Honda had been a wish, arising from an admiration for the company's reputation with regard to motorcycles, racing, or Soichiro himself.

None of the successors, from Kawashima to the entire management team, were as talented as the founders. The only way that these "ordinary people" could continue to protect what the founding geniuses had built up from scratch and ensure the company's further growth, was to work together in solidarity. Fortunately, all of the directors had grown under Soichiro and Fujisawa's strict leadership so they all shared an ideology. President Kiyoshi Kawashima decided to maintain the collective management system to ensure the company's momentum.

Although they were no longer active in managing the company, Soichiro and Fujisawa remained the company's largest shareholders and enjoyed perfect health. Furthermore, they still held positions as directors, if only part-time, so there was actually little chance that Honda's corporate identity would start to falter immediately.

The directors' first task to ensure Honda's momentum was to complete negotiations with Ford, the world's second largest auto manufacturer after General Motors. It was the first time Honda would be forming an alliance with another company. And this was no run-of-the-mill company, either. Ford was a multinational cooperation that was notorious for being a corporate raider. The company was also known throughout the industry for its outstanding negotiation tactics.

In the early afternoon of October 31, two days after Kawashima took responsibility as president, Ford president Lee Iacocca arrived at Tokyo International Airport in Haneda in his private jet. The plane had a white body, upon which were painted two lines in Ford's corporate colors, blue and orange.

Iacocca was in good humor as he answered the various questions put to him by reporters. He explained that he was in Japan to expand Ford's business, that he was looking forward to discussing cooperation with Honda, and that while there was not yet any discussion of a capital tie-up, he was certainly interested in pursing the possibilities. Iacocca planned to stay in Japan until November 4 so as to give him the maximum amount of time to focus on negotiations with Honda.

By this time, the industry had all but forgotten about the defect scandal. Interest had shifted to technological developments related to the exhaust regulations, and the potential of cooperation between Honda and Ford. Ford had spent the last three years in negotiations with Mazda before going back to square one. Honda, thanks to the sales of the Civic and the incredible success of the CVCC engine, had, for the first time in the ten years since creating the S500, finally found the opportunity it needed to build its reputation in the auto industry. Ford and Honda's interests were a perfect match, and the prospects for an alliance of some kind appeared quite high.

Ford had expressed interest in Honda for the first time the previous year, in September of 1972, during the final stages of the 50,000-mile durability testing of the CVCC. At the time, Ford had adopted a two-step approach. First, it had dispatched an executive of the Morgan Guaranty Trust Company, a bank with close ties to Ford, to meet with Honda executives at the company's headquarters in Yaesu and deliver a personal letter from chairman Henry Ford II. The letter suggested that, Ford and Honda, both being internationally-minded companies, should discuss possibilities that may lead to potential benefits for both sides. Immediately after the visit, Iacocca followed up with an official letter of inquiry from the Ford Motor Company.

The reason Ford had gone through so much trouble in approaching Honda was that it was interested in using cooperation over the CVCC as a stepping-stone towards a full-blown partnership and alliance. It was a timely proposal. Honda had just decided to begin licensing CVCC technology to auto manufacturers all over the world. Taking a long-term perspective, Honda judged that responding to a proposal from Ford would give it an edge in the negotiations and accepted.

The first order of business was the signing of mutual non-disclosure agreements to ensure secrecy. Kihachiro Kawashima, executive director of sales, acted as Honda's representative, while Ford was represented by chief engineer Hen Nichol. Ford indicated that it was interested in discussing not only technological cooperation, but also tie-ups in production, sales, financing and any other area that might hold potential benefits for both sides.

In fact, Ford was itching to reach an agreement. General Motors and Chrysler had already established bases in the Japanese market through capital tie-ups with Isuzu and Mitsubishi, respectively. But Ford, though far more aggressive in its attempts to enter the Japanese market, had lost its foothold when negotiations with Mazda had collapsed. Ford was feeling the pressure of having to rebuild its Japanese strategy at such a late date.

In 1970, the number of cars produced in Japan broke the five million mark. Estimates indicated that this number would increase to seven million within the next three years. Analysts predicted that annual domestic sales would also reach five million by 1973. The number of cars produced in the United States exceeded ten million when the economy was prospering, but fell to around eight million in a slump. At least as far as production volume was concerned, the Japanese motor industry had grown to be only a few steps away from reaching the level of the United States.

Although they had designed the PROCO engine, Ford engineers had no clue as to when, exactly, it would be ready for practical use. Rival General Motors, on the other hand, had announced that it had designed an "epoch-making invention" that would allow them to meet the Muskie standards. GM was also but a step away from selling cars equipped with rotary engines.

Ford had licensed the basic technology from two German companies and was struggling to make a workable RE of its own, but, unfortunately for Ford, the improvement patent was owned by Mazda. Ford couldn't bring itself to beg Mazda for further assistance so quickly after negotiations had fallen through.

Adding to the stress of the company, Ford had made a serious blunder regarding the emission standards for its 1973 line of cars. The E.P.A. had accused Ford of negligence regarding its anti-exhaust measures. Ford was facing a crisis. Something needed to be done to fix the situation, and quickly, lest it begin to seriously affect the bottom line. Just as things were looking their worst and Ford executives were scrambling for a solution, the company got wind of Honda's new engine.

Ford chairman Henry Ford II had been in charge of negotiations with Mazda, while president Lee Iacocca, who had been trained as an engineer, oversaw developments relating to car exhaust regulations. The two were still in their "honeymoon period," and when the negotiations with Mazda fell through, both seized upon Honda as the best way to atone for their previous failures. Considering that Honda was a personal concern like Ford, Henry Ford II was confident that, as long as Iacocca paved the way by licensing the CVCC, a meeting between the two top men would be enough to push the alliance beyond a mere business cooperation into a capital-tie up.

For his part, Soichiro had made his own calculations of the risks and benefits the moment Ford first approached his company. *The Muskie Act has given Honda a rare opportunity. We used it to arm ourselves with the powerful weapon of the CVCC. Now we're in a position to go face-to-face with anyone, even foreign companies. No matter what people say, the CVCC is an earth-shattering, history-making development in automotive technology. Our suitors will beg before we even need to ask.* Soichiro was deeply satisfied with the success of the CVCC technology. His confidence, which stemmed from his massive ego, led him to adopt a brazen attitude towards the larger company. Before he knew it, his pride had turned into arrogance. He had convinced himself that Honda's technology was far superior to that of any other company.

On the other hand, Fujisawa, ever the rational business manager, remained calm about the potential of the CVCC. He knew that the actions of the Big Three were guided by the logic of capital and investment and relied on this knowledge to predict Ford's behavior. *Ford won't be satisfied with licensing the CVCC technology,* thought Fujisawa. *Sooner of later, they'll suggest a joint venture to produce engines or perhaps even compact cars together. It may not even be a bad idea, depending on what they bring to the table. Honda could use their marketing network to sell its products and quickly make up for lost ground. But Honda could never consider a capital tie-up with Ford. If they so much as mention the word "capital," that's where the negotiations will stop.*

Just as Fujisawa predicted, Ford had already prepared plans for an alliance on a scale far exceeding technical cooperation. Ford's scenario began with the licensing of CVCC technology and the importing of engines and continued to include the sales of Civic in the U.S. market under Ford's brand name, then co-production of new compact cars, a capital tie-up, and potentially even more. Ford was anxious to leave no possibility unconsidered.

Accepting Ford's offer in its entirety would mean Honda becoming, in essence, a subcontractor. It was an unthinkable scenario for the fiercely independent company. But rejecting Ford out of hand could well be a deal-breaker for licensing the CVCC, which wouldn't be good for Honda, either. Licensing production to Ford was essential to establish the value of the CVCC in the industry. Behind the scenes, the two sides engaged in a fierce battle of wits, each furiously trying to out-negotiate the other.

At the time, Honda was also proposing a CVCC license to General Motors. If GM followed Ford's suit in licensing the technology, Honda's reputation would be assured. True, Honda was making a large profit on its motorcycle sales; nevertheless, Honda's future depended on expanding its automobile business. Licensing the CVCC to foreign manufacturers would be just the thing needed to pull the company out of the fire.

Meanwhile, in terms of exports to the United States, Honda had quickly abandoned the H1300, with its air-cooled engine, and had focused on modifying the N360 with a larger 600cc engine. But the N600, as the improved version of the N360 was called, was still only a k-car; it lacked the power that Americans demanded for highway driving.

Honda had therefore pinned its hopes for American exports entirely on the Civic, which was scheduled to be introduced to the market early the next year. The company planned to eventually manufacture 20,000 of the cars a month; however, there was no question that Honda still lacked hands-on know-how about the U.S. market.

In return for allowing licensed production of the CVCC, Honda wanted to get its Civic into the sales and marketing networks of one of the Big Three, which would allow the company to make a major leap forward in the automobile market. But Honda had no desire to become just another OEM supplier for the American companies. Just as it did in Japan, Honda wanted to sell its own product under its own brand name in America.

That Honda had been so successful in exporting motorcycles to the United States without assistance from other companies was largely due to the lack of any serious competition. Car sales were a different matter altogether. World-class manufacturers, including the Big Three, jostled for position there. Jumping into such a crowded and well-developed marketplace was not a matter to be taken lightly.

Although Honda called itself "world-class," in reality this referred to nothing more than its status as a motorcycle manufacturer. As an automaker, Honda was the youngest competitor in the industry. It would take tremendous amounts of time and money to establish an American marketing network on its own.

Ford had contacted Honda almost as soon as the latter had announced its success at developing the CVCC. In contrast, General Motors remained silent even in the face of Honda's repeated inquiries. Honda's directors came to the conclusion that they needed to prove the CVCC to General Motors in a more direct manner. They came up with the idea of overhauling a GM car themselves to accommodate a CVCC engine, thereby proving that the technology was applicable to large cars as well.

Two-thirds of the three hundred Honda dealers in the United States were also affiliates of General Motors; obtaining a GM car would pose no problems for the company. Successfully convincing General Motors to license the CVCC would definitely turn negotiations with Ford in Honda's favor. Which meant that, if Honda played its cards right, it would be able to choose from between two major venues for selling the Civic in the United States.

On October 30, 1972, Honda publicly announced that it would be entering into negotiations with Ford.

"Ford has suggested the potential for cooperation on technologies, marketing, and other areas," said Kihachiro Kawashima to a journalist who came to see him that evening. "Honda has decided to accept their offer for negotiations and has sent an official written reply indicating as such." Knowing that his comment was sure to reach the ears of Ford's executives, Kawashima deliberately phrased his words to seem as optimistic as possible. "Negotiations will begin without any preconditions. We are confident that some form of agreement can be reached."

Negotiations began in earnest in early of 1973, as planned. From time to time, Ford made occasional hints about a capital tie-up. Honda smoothly dodged them, insinuating that the talks would be deadlocked if Ford brought the issue up again.

Ford approached the negotiating table cautiously, mindful of the bitter failure it had suffered by tenaciously clinging to its demand for a fifty percent stake in Mazda. Ford also knew that they would get nowhere by discussing the tie-up issue at the working level. Talks proceeded gingerly.

Soichiro and Fujisawa had ambitiously and aggressively expanded their business after founding Honda, but the defect scandal had taken a large toll on the company. Although outwardly Honda looked and acted as tough as ever, the company's management had taken on a timid and almost passive stance ever since the incident. The passing of the baton to the "Honda kids" only served to reinforce the attitude. Since Honda's new management consisted of "ordinary people" working together in solidarity, their approach to management was, naturally, one of consensus. Kiyoshi Kawashima, Kihachiro Kawashima, Nishida, and Shirai knew that they weren't geniuses. And so they ended up opting in every case to take on only tasks in which they were confident of success.

The negotiations with General Motors were a perfect example of this passive approach. As Honda had hoped, General Motors expressed interest in licensing the CVCC technology in the spring of 1973. Hideo Sugiura, who had just recently been promoted to Honda's board of directors, flew to Los Angeles to negotiate with GM directly.

The General Motors negotiator opened discussions by stating that his company had been experimenting with different methods of reducing exhaust emissions for each car model. He continued that GM was considering mounting CVCC engines in its Vega sports car, and was interested in purchasing between 200,000 and 400,000 of the engines from Honda.

Sugiura had not expected this. As far as he knew, GM intended to use a rotary engine for the Vega. Sugiura realized at that moment that the development of the RE must have stalled. But filling an order for such an enormous quantity of engines would require a huge investment in capital and new infrastructure. It was a risky proposition.

General Motors declined to propose an exact timeframe for purchasing the engines. In any case, Honda wasn't interested in supplying engines, but rather in licensing the technology to build its reputation. Furthermore, Ford had broached a similar subject in their negotiations with Honda as well. Even if Honda had been interested in supplying the engines to GM, it would be have been a breach of faith with Ford to proceed with the negotiations.

"I understand that you're interested in using our CVCC engine in your 1975 Vega. With the numbers involved, however, even if we began investing in new facilities at once, we wouldn't have enough time to supply the engines. What's more, Honda is not interested in supplying engines at the moment. I would ask that you please consider licensed production instead," replied Sugiura, declining General Motors' suggestion.

The negotiations had naturally been carried out in secrecy. Ten days later, however, GM chairman Ed Cole disclosed Honda's refusal to supply the engines at a Senate subcommittee hearing on air and water pollution. Cole's aim was to use the Honda negotiations to prove to the Senate that his company had been working seriously to address the exhaust regulations.

Meanwhile, negotiations with Ford continued. After on-again, off-again progress and hard bargaining, the two companies managed to strike a deal over licensed production of CVCC engines in the beginning of July 1973. The contract was officially signed on the 13th of the same month. The agreement was almost identical to the one Honda had made with Toyota.

Even then, Ford was not convinced that the CVCC technology could be easily adapted for use in their large eight-cylinder engines. Honda addressed their concerns by dispatching engineers to Ford. First, Shoichiro Irimajiri spent three months at Ford sketching out a detailed framework of the program. Then, two younger engineers, Yoshitoshi Sakurai and Hiroyuki Nishimura, who had been directly involved in developing the CVCC engine, took over and spent a year coaching Ford's engineers in the new technology.

Irimajiri flew to the United States in the fall of 1973. Everything he saw and heard in Ford's research facility was completely new to him. One of his most eye-opening experiences was encountering the Ford safety manual, which was a full fifty centimeters thick and contained several hundred checkpoints. The thoroughness of the manual stunned Irimajiri. It was a wake-up call as to just how far behind Honda really was as an auto manufacturer. *What an amazing company!* marveled Irimajiri. *The Big Three are really remarkable. Compared to them, Honda is like an amateur in so many respects. We don't even have official safety standards. And not having any standards leads to easy compromises; when problems arise, no one knows where the responsibility lies, so no one can take responsibility, even if they wanted to. It's nothing short of reckless—although it may be precisely because we were reckless that we dared enter the industry when we did and that we were able to create the CVCC. I see now how amateurish Fujisawa-san's old idea of creating a car around the F2 engine was. Even if we had the world's best engine, there's no way Honda could have created a mass-market car to rival Toyota's at that time.*

During the three months Irimajiri spent at Ford offering technical advice to the American engineers, he sent every Ford manual he could get his hands on, including the safety manual, back to Honda headquarters. Ford hadn't yet started to see Honda as a serious competitor, so it saw no problem providing the materials. The treasure trove of documents Irimajiri sent back home proved tremendously helpful. Today, engineers at the Honda Research and Development Company agree that Honda's automotive business only exists today thanks to the knowledge gained through cooperating with Ford.

In any case, a relationship had now been established between Honda and Ford. The next step was to broaden the range of cooperation between the two companies. An executive-level meeting would be required to decide the specifics. Soichiro remained in charge of Honda until the 29th of October. Fujisawa may have been taking care of the business side of things, but if the president of the second largest auto manufacturer in the world visited Honda, Soichiro, as president, could hardly avoid meeting him. As it turned out, however, Soichiro retired two days before Iacocca arrived in Japan. All he did was welcome Iacocca as supreme advisor of his company. Did Honda executives deliberately arrange for the meeting to take place after Soichiro's official resignation or was it pure coincidence? The answer remains unknown.

The ostensible reason for Iacocca's first visit to Japan had been to inspect the state of Ford's business in the Asia-Pacific region. But Ford's love affair with Honda had already become common knowledge in the world auto industry.

Ford's enthusiasm for establishing an alliance with Honda was more than strong. But there was still plenty of time for negotiation. As a gift for Soichiro, Iacocca brought with him a Mustang II, the latest version of the massively successful Ford Mustang sports car originally designed by none other than Iacocca himself.

5

"Honda Civic: What the World Is Coming To," read the first American advertisements for the car.

Just as with the "You meet the nicest people on a Honda" campaign for the Super Cub, Grey Advertising took a unique tack with the Civic. Ads for cars usually focused only on price and functions. The Civic campaign was crafted to appeal to Americans' sense of whimsy.

The U.S. retail price for a Civic was 1,800 dollars. It was an aggressive move for the company, considering that the similar Volkswagen Golf sold for 1,480 dollars. But Honda's instincts were correct. In spite of the higher price, customers flocked to the Civic from the moment it appeared on the market. Career women in particular loved the "cute" two-box design, which was as uncommon in the United States back then as it was in Japan.

Honda exploited the popularity of the Civic to officially announce that the 1974 model of the car would come equipped standard with the new CVCC engine, in preparation for the soon-to-be-adopted 1975 Muskie standards. The similarity between the names of the car "CIVIC" and the "CVCC" reinforced the car's environmentally friendly image. The Civic soon became a favorite, not only among female consumers, who are generally the most environmentally conscious in the market, but also among young people in general.

The young executives at Honda began to regain confidence in their company. They started to believe that Honda actually could maintain its independence by establishing its own marketing network in the U.S. market without any help from American partners, just as it had done for motorcycles. Although only 4,000 Honda cars were sold in the U.S. in 1970, the number continued to double every year so that 9,500 were sold in 1971, 20,000 in 1972—the year the CVCC Civic went on sale—and 39,000 in 1973. The rapid growth of the U.S. market for the cars instilled Honda's youthful workforce with hope.

When he arrived in Japan for his second visit, Iacocca could hardly conceal his excitement about the potential for cooperation with Honda. Honda, on the other hand, was rapidly losing interest in the deal. The unexpected success of the Civic in the U.S. further cooled the urgency of forming alliances with foreign automakers.

In fact, the more time Honda and Ford spent locked in their secret negotiations, the more differences emerged between them. The subject over which their views differed most sharply was how to sell the Civic in the United States.

Even if Honda utilized the Ford sales network, it remained adamant about selling the Civic under the Honda name. Ford, on the other hand, wanted to rebrand the car as a Ford, essentially relegating Honda to the role of an OEM supplier. Such an arrangement would benefit the supplier by increasing production quota, but it also came with the risk of hampering the supplier's chances for developing its own brand name in the long term.

It was in the spring of 1973, at around the same time Fujisawa began informally telling those close to him of his intentions to retire, that Honda's board of directors had made an official decision to maintain Honda's independence in the industry.

"Our company's future depends on the success of the Civic. In both the United States and Japan, exhaust regulations are set to take effect, which is a favorable development for Honda. The CVCC is our 'trump card' in this respect. We'll establish our own marketing network for cars as we did for motorcycles. Even if it will be tough, it will, in the long run, offer more opportunities to us as a manufacturer of compact cars."

"Maintaining independence" meant not only rejecting any outside stake in the company but avoiding becoming an OEM supplier as well. But clearly announcing such policies could cause negotiations with Ford, including those concerning technical cooperation on the CVCC, to go back to square one. Honda needed to convince Ford to agree to licensed production, and it needed to maintain a friendly relationship with the company. Making an enemy of Ford had the potential to create serious problems for Honda in the U.S. market. Although Honda was seeking independence, it had to avoid isolating itself in the auto industry at all costs.

In the end, Honda's efforts bore fruit in the form of a licensing agreement with Ford. The contract dramatically increased Honda's standing in the global automotive industry. Honda owed Ford a large debt of gratitude.

Honda's corporate policy was to always return a favor. How could Honda repay Ford? After discussing the issue, the board of directors came to the conclusion that Honda could help Ford sell its products in Japan.

Just as expected, Ford began pushing for a stake in Honda almost as soon as the licensing contract had been signed. Honda's representatives parried the subject, giving noncommittal answers, and then presented the offer to sell Ford cars in the Japanese market.

Needless to say, Honda's directors were fully aware that assisting Ford in the Japanese market would have positive implications for them as well. Although the Civic remained popular both in Japan and abroad, the fact remained that it was the only compact car in Honda's lineup. The company's k-cars did little to improve Honda's standing as a full-fledged automobile manufacturer. Honda had no idea how much of a market there might be for Ford's large cars in Japan, but at least they would add variety to the company's lineup and go a long way towards making the showrooms of Honda dealers more attractive to customers.

President Richard Nixon's decision to abolish the gold standard for the American dollar in the summer of 1971 led to the yen being revalued from 360 to 308 yen to the dollar. In succeeding months, the yen remained strong and a floating exchange rate was adopted in February of 1973. Simultaneously, the Japanese government lowered import duties and taxes on automobiles. The number of foreign automobiles imported into the country had hovered around 30,000 a year for the past several years, but this figure was expected to increase dramatically with all the favorable conditions in place. Selling Ford's automobiles in Japan would mean benefits for Honda as well as Ford.

At roughly the same time that the licensing agreement with Ford was signed, Honda engineers completed modifying a 1973 GM Chevrolet Impala to accommodate a 5700cc V8 CVCC engine and sent the car to the American E.P.A. for testing. The results showed that the CO, HC, and NOx generated by the engine successfully cleared the 1975 Muskie standards.

Until that point, the applicability of CVCC technology to larger automobiles had been an open question. Some critics held that such an application would be technically demanding. Now Honda had proved that it worked. Honda had declined to supply engines to GM, but had left the possibility of licensed production open. Honda wanted to avoid focusing too closely on Ford lest it ruin the chance of building a relationship with General Motors. On the other hand, Honda didn't want to upset Ford, either. Honda's executive directors found themselves walking on thin ice.

Ford president Lee Iacocca arrived in Japan on the afternoon of October 31. He took the day off to prepare for negotiations. On the early morning of November 1, a rested and prepared Iacocca came to the Honda Research and Development Company in Wako, Saitama prefecture. He paid a courtesy call on Soichiro, who was now supreme advisor, and then toured the facility. After that, Iacocca returned to Tokyo for secret negotiations in a private room at a French restaurant in the Shiba district.

President Kiyoshi Kawashima, Kihachiro Kawashima, Hideo Sugiura, and several others represented Honda at the negotiating table. It was after five o'clock when the meeting ended. Even considering the time spent over lunch, it was far later than anyone had expected. Outside, it was completely dark.

By the end of the meeting, the smiles had evaporated from the faces of both parties. The two delegations pushed stiffly and silently past the press waiting outside of the restaurant. The Honda team did not return to their homes but stayed in a nearby hotel so that no information slipped out of the negotiating room.

The following morning, Iacocca paid a courtesy visit to the official residence of Prime Minister Kakuei Tanaka, followed by a visit to the U.S. Embassy and meetings with various financiers, Ford dealers, and other individuals and groups representing American interests in Japan. Ostensibly, he had no meetings with Honda on this day.

It was apparent, nevertheless, that the first round of negotiations had not gone well for either side. In fact, Iacocca met secretly with Honda that afternoon for a second round of talks, which did nothing to improve the situation. That evening, when Iacocca held a press conference at a hotel in central Tokyo, he kept word of the deadlock under his hat.

Iacocca reported that the idea of a capital tie-up did not come up during the negotiations, but that both sides planned to discuss the details of cooperative sales and marketing sometime within the next four to six weeks. He explained that Ford's decision to focus on a sales cooperation, rather than a capital tie-up, was due not to a change in Ford's policy towards the Japanese market but simply to the fact that favorable conditions—floating exchange rate, lowered tariffs and taxes—now made it easier to sell Ford vehicles in Japan. Iacocca told the press that Ford would soon be establishing a sales subsidiary, Ford Japan, to increase Ford's sales in Japan but that he looked forward to Honda's assistance in selling the cars.

Iacocca shortened his itinerary, leaving Japan a day early. Honda declined to hold a press conference about their meeting. The negotiations between Honda and Ford had begun with much excitement and fanfare but had resulted in very little payoff.

In his press conference, Iacocca had claimed that the issue of a capital tie-up hadn't come up during the meeting and that he had no intention of discussing such an alliance with other manufacturers either. The truth was that Ford had suggested it indirectly, and Honda had firmly rejected the idea. Furthermore, it is believed that Honda also openly stated its policy of independence in the U.S. marketplace by refusing to supply the Civic to Ford on an OEM basis. The negotiations had almost broken off completely at that point. However, Honda still felt that it owed Ford a favor for agreeing to license the CVCC. In the end, Honda barely managed to save face by proposing a plan to establish a new company dedicated to selling Ford products in Japan.

The idea of selling Ford products in Japan was, for Honda, simply a business-like proposition through which Honda would be able to return the favor it had received. Ford, on the other hand, saw it as the first step towards a capital tie-up with Honda. Iacocca, a true negotiating pro, knew enough not to expect a favorable answer during their first visit. He was aware that upsetting Honda now would only hurt Ford's cause in the long run. So he decided to shorten his trip and return a day early to the United States.

Honda and Ford signed a cooperative sales agreement on January 9, just as the prices of consumer goods began skyrocketing due to the oil crisis. The contract specified that Honda Chuhan, the used-car arm of the Honda Motor Company, would change its name to HISCO—the Honda International Sales Company—and begin selling Ford products starting with the 1975 line, focusing mainly on the Mustang II. The two sides agreed on an annual sales goal of 10,000 cars. Immediately after signing the contract, President Kiyoshi Kawashima issued a statement to the public that Honda was not considering any form of capital tie-up with Ford, but that there had been other offers made by Ford, which both sides would consider. Iacocca took the comment at face value.

Soichiro was planning to visit Detroit in May to attend an award ceremony where he would receive an honorary doctorate from Michigan Technological University. When Ford executives got wind of Soichiro's trip to Detroit, they began a campaign to get him to stop by their offices. Ford even offered to ferry Soichiro from New York to its headquarters in Dearborn via the chairman's private jet.

Soichiro readily accepted the offer. He had idolized Henry Ford and his company ever since working on Ford cars as a young apprentice. And now that Sakurai and Nishimura had taken over from Irimajiri, they were in Dearborn working with Ford's engineers as part of the CVCC licensing agreement. Business conditions at Ford had rapidly deteriorated as a result of the oil crisis and had thrown the company's technological development policies into turmoil, making Sakurai and Nishimura's work more difficult. Soichiro wanted to drop by in person to cheer them up.

The company rolled out the welcome mat for Soichiro and gave him the royal treatment. In the afternoon, Ford II invited Soichiro to his office at headquarters for lunch, while Iacocca threw a dinner party in Soichiro's honor at his own house in the evening. Ford II and Iacocca were convinced that wining and dining Soichiro would pave the way for a capital tie-up with Honda.

Soichiro was touched by Ford's hospitality. But he had retired from the front lines of the business, even if the company still bore his name, and would never even think of pressuring his "kids" into a tie-up. In fact, perhaps no single other person wanted to see Honda remain independent as much as he did. The company was and always would be Soichiro's baby. In the end, Ford's "war of hospitality" came to nothing.

The HISCO arrangement wasn't going particularly well, either. Ford's automobiles sold sluggishly in Japan. Honda had estimated that it could sell 10,000 Ford vehicles a year, but actual sales came nowhere near that figure. Ford high-handedly expected Honda to follow its instructions in specific aspects of the sales campaign from the dealers' signs to the layout of showrooms, which Honda resented. Judging from the high popularity foreign cars enjoy in the Japanese marketplace today, Honda's problems in this area appear largely due to the decision being twenty years ahead of its time.

Because the cooperation had faltered right at the outset, the subsequent stages in the plan never materialized. Ford had been preparing to implement CVCC engines in both its Pinto and Mustang lines but had run into financial difficulties accompanying the oil crisis. In addition, the compliance date for the 1976 Muskie Act standards had been extended.

The cooperative sales agreement between Honda and Ford also eventually evaporated as Ford successfully reopened negotiations with Mazda through intermediary Sumitomo Bank and established a capital tie-up with the company. GM also abandoned the use of CVCC engines in its cars for the same reasons as Ford.

The negotiations with General Motors and Ford were Honda's first experience with foreign companies. The Honda kids learned that negotiating with Westerners was far more difficult than initially anticipated. For one thing, Western negotiators tended to press the attack at the slightest sign of weakness. Even though Honda's founders had stepped down from the company's management, so long as their influence still prevailed, it was unthinkable that Honda would enter into an alliance with a foreign company. Nor would such an alliance be necessary.

Honda had realized that, however difficult it might be, the path of independence was still much easier to follow than any other option. At the same time, the company became painfully aware that it would always need to stay one step ahead of its competitors to keep things that way.

People both within Honda and outside the company sometimes mockingly referred to the Honda kids as a school of fish or flock of birds—small fry who clung to one another to protect themselves from predators. There was no doubt that they were maturing rapidly and eager to leave the protection of their "nest," but the oil crisis cemented their solidarity more than ever before.

Signs of the impending crisis began to appear just before the summer of 1973. Automobiles were selling like hotcakes, and manufacturers were suffering from a shortage of both products and workers. Toyota only barely managed to meet planned production quota by getting dealers to send their sales staff to help with work in the factories. The dealers had little choice, since securing enough cars to sell took priority over any form of sales effort. By the fall, the shortages of parts and materials had reached a critical level; it became more and more difficult to keep the rising costs from influencing product prices by rationalization alone.

In keeping with the ability of mass production to lower the cost of goods, the price of automobiles continued to drop every year during Japan's period of rapid economic growth from the late 1950s to the early seventies. The trend is clearly illustrated in the following statistics regarding changes in annual national income and average automobile price (Toyota Corona, list price in Tokyo). Based on an index of 100 in 1965, the average national income had grown to 215 in 1970, while the index for average automobile price had fallen to 83. In 1973, the year of the oil crisis, the indices for average national income and average automobile price were 320 and 100, respectively.

Furthermore, during the age of motorization, improvements were made in engine displacements, performance, decorations, and other features with each new model of car so that the actual price of a new car was an even better deal than the figures above suggest. Considering the rapid increase in average national income, one could say that it was inevitable that motorization occurred when it did. Before long, consumers began to believe that the prices of cars were subject only to downward revision.

The oil crisis, which brought about a major turning point not only for Japanese automakers but also for economies and industries all over the world, was triggered by the October War (Yom Kippur War), which broke out on October 5, 1973. The morning edition of the *Nihon Keizai Shimbun* on October 6 reported the following story: "MORE FIGHTING IN THE MIDDLE EAST / EGYPT ADVANCES PAST SUEZ / ISRAEL INVOLVED IN HEAVY FIGHTING AT SYRIAN AIRPORT."

On October 18, only twelve days later, the evening edition of the same newspaper carried news directly related to the oil crisis. "ARAB NATIONS DECIDE TO REDUCE OIL PRODUCTION IN AN EFFORT TO INCREASE ADVANTAGE IN MIDDLE-EAST WAR / REDUCTION OF 5% EVERY MONTH / FRIENDS OF OAPEC (ORGANIZATION OF ARAB PETROLEUM EXPORTING COUNTRIES) TO RECEIVE PREFERENTIAL TREATMENT."

The article explained how the Arab nations had begun to use their oil as a bargaining chip to gain an advantage in armed conflict. OPEC (Organization of the Petroleum Exporting Countries) had already been engaged in negotiations to raise oil prices with the seven international oil majors when the Arab countries among them belonging to OAPEC decided to cut down production.

As many had expected, the negotiations between the oil majors and OPEC fell through. Oil-producing countries began raising prices significantly, one after the other. At the beginning of the year, a barrel of oil had cost two dollars and seventy-four cents. By the end of the year, it had jumped more than four times to over eleven dollars. The impact on the Japanese economy—which had promoted the development of its heavy and chemical industries based on an estimated oil price of around two dollars a barrel—was tremendous.

On November 1, Nissan was the first automaker to present its statement for the fiscal year ending September 1973. On that occasion, Nissan director of accounting Haruhiro Saku presented his outlook that the company could well have to raise the price of its cars within the present term without making any improvements to the current models.

Saku's gloomy prediction became reality on November 15, when Nissan instituted an across-the-board price increase without changes for its cars on the marketplace. Nissan's action had a snowball effect on the entire industry, as other manufacturers scrambled to raise the prices of their cars as well. Mazda committed an embarrassing blunder when it announced a price hike across its entire range of cars, including two new reduced-emission cars, the Grand Familia and Savanna AP, which had just been put on sale the day before on November 21.

As for Honda, less than a year had passed since the Civic had first been unveiled, so the company wanted to avoid raising prices if at all possible. Still, it couldn't afford to sit back and do nothing either. Honda needed to sell 20,000 Civics a month including exports to break even. A price increase could lead to a drop in sales, which would make the car unprofitable. Honda kept its markup on all cars to an average 5.7 percent (roughly 27,000 yen), which was the lowest in the industry. Honda also made sure that the raise would take effect only after all the other Japanese automakers had finished raising the prices on their goods.

The reason for Honda's reluctance to increase its prices was due in part to the management's guilt over having already done so in the recent past. On May

16 of that year, just as the price of raw materials had started to skyrocket, Honda had quietly raised the price of the Civic by 15,000 yen, attributing it to "upgrades" in the upholstery and engine space. At the time, Honda had avoided announcing the raise and had simply distributed a one-page document listing the new price. More than a few journalists didn't realize the price had been raised and Honda was later frowned upon for using "deceptive" tactics. Ever since the defect scandal, Honda's management had endeavored to be more open to the public, but the directors were still inexperienced, and occasionally slipped up. The secret price hike had been just such an embarrassing mistake.

The price of consumer goods skyrocketed as the oil crisis reached its peak. Consumers began to panic, at one point even causing a run on toilet paper. In the midst of this economic turmoil, Honda launched the low-polluting CVCC Civic on December 12. While credit for marketing the first low-polluting car had gone to Mazda, the new Civic boasted the same fuel economy as that of other cars, in spite of its low-emission CVCC engine. And while the engine added 45,000 yen to the base price of a car, tax exemptions largely insulated consumers from the price difference.

"In this day and age, it's not good enough to sell products that turn a profit," said Kiyoshi Kawashima confidently at his first press conference as president of the Honda Motor Company. "We have to create products that answer society's needs, the kind of products that we have a duty to sell. We have a firm hold on the low-polluting car, which is just such a product. We plan to fully develop our strength in this area."

A month and a half later, reacting to the public opinion that "restylings of existing models are a waste of resources," Kawashima publicly announced that Honda would no longer be introducing any new modifications on the Civic.

"We have fully exploited the potential of the Civic. It's easy to use, economical, and low-polluting. As such we will not be offering any further restylings of the car."

Kawashima's statement indicated, if only indirectly, that Honda planned to take a different path from Nissan, Toyota, and the other Japanese manufacturers.

1973 had been a big year for Honda. It was the company's twenty-fifth anniversary. The two founders resigned. The oil crisis presented new challenges. Negotiations for cooperation with Ford led to new experiences. And the first cars featuring the CVCC had finally gone on sale. All in all, it had been a roller coaster of a year for the company.

6

Japan entered the New Year, but still, the oil crisis showed no signs of easing. If anything, it appeared to be escalating. The price of oil-related products continued to rise with no end in sight. On January 10, the four major business organizations—Keidanren (Federation of Economic Organizations), Keizai Doyukai (Japanese Association of Corporate Executives), Nikkeiren (Federation of Employers' Associations), and Nissho (Japan Chamber of Commerce and Industry)—issued a collective statement declaring their decision to voluntarily refrain from raising prices during the crisis. Based on this joint declaration, Keidanren chairman Kogoro Uemura issued a direct request to the eighteen major trade associations under its umbrella, including the Japan Iron and Steel Federation, the Japan Automobile Manufacturers Association and the Japan Petrochemical Industry Association, to exercise restraint with regard to price hikes.

Despite these efforts, only four days later Nissan, whose president Katsuji Kawamata also served as vice chairman of Keidanren, announced an average ten percent price increase for its entire line of cars. It was barely a month since Nissan had announced its previous price hike. Soon, Keidanren's core corporate members began raising prices and the effect spiraled tornado-like through the entire financial world. The appeal for voluntary restraint had collapsed in a shockingly short period of time. Teizo Horikoshi, executive vice chairman of Keidanren, pleaded for understanding for his colleague's company, saying, "Nissan's price increase was an unavoidable decision and not an attempt to take advantage of the general trend." Horikoshi's statement, however, did nothing but add fodder to the growing fire.

In December, domestic sales of automobiles, which until that time had been strong, dropped by twenty-three percent in comparison to the same month the previous year. Although the mounting oil prices brought about by the crisis also played a role, the price hike was undoubtedly the primary cause for this drop. It was more than obvious that increasing the prices any further would simply reinforce the trend. Sales were bad enough already; if things got any worse, the manufacturers would all be faced with severe financial difficulties.

Nevertheless, like lemmings following their frontrunner over a cliff, Toyota and the other manufacturers rushed to follow Nissan's example and implement price increases without any improvements to the cars. Many in the auto industry came to believe that a full thirty percent drop in sales was inevitable.

The Honda kids fretted over how to cope with the situation. Honda had sold 8,766 Civics in December, a 9.9 percent increase over the same month the year before. The only reason that there was an increase at all was that sales had been sluggish the previous year; in any case, the price hike had taken its toll and sales targets had not been achieved. Honda's new low-polluting cars had only just gone on sale. Another increase in prices now could well put the brakes on the popularity of the cars. Toyota's latest sales figures were thirty percent lower than the previous year, but the company managed to sell more than 100,000 automobiles. As manufacturers of automobiles, Toyota and Nissan were in a different league from Honda.

Should Honda raise prices now? Or sit tight for a little longer to ride things out? The debate raged among the directors. When Fujisawa had been running the company, one of the staff had inevitably gone to his home in Roppongi to ask for his advice. But now that he had officially resigned, the Honda kids were reluctant to seek out his opinions.

"I know Fujisawa-san has retired from the front lines," said one director during a *waigaya* session in the collective directors' room at headquarters in Yaesu. "Even so, as supreme advisor, he's still nominally on the board of directors, and what's more, he's one of this company's largest stockholders. I don't think it would be out of line to ask for his advice about how to deal with this difficult situation."

And so director of sales Kihachiro Kawashima headed to Roppongi.

"It's your decision as to whether you should raise prices or not. What kind of decision have you come to in the directors' room?" demanded Fujisawa almost immediately.

"I'm afraid we haven't reached a consensus yet. Personally, I believe it would be better for Honda not to raise prices," answered Kihachiro Kawashima cautiously.

"Well, so do I. I guess it's all up to how the president, Kawashima, makes the executive decision then," replied Fujisawa.

Some three months had passed since Fujisawa's resignation. Little had changed in his life aside from the fact that, while his dear "kids" still visited him as regularly as they had always done, they had stopped asking for his advice on business matters. Fujisawa saw their not asking for advice as meaning that the company was free of major problems. While this was of course a good thing, after so many years he could hardly help feeling somewhat lonely about it. Yet, he couldn't just walk into headquarters and start offering advice. He wanted to avoid pulling strings behind the scenes at all costs.

Fujisawa had long been frustrated about what he saw as the Honda kids' slow response to the oil crisis. Around the time that Nissan had implemented its second price hike, the skyrocketing prices had reached a peak. Since then, Fujisawa sensed, something had begun to change; the trend was reaching a head.

From his experience working on the black market in the turmoil of post-WWII Japan, Fujisawa could see as clear as day how speculators seeking to capitalize on the oil crisis were now eagerly waiting for the right moment to start selling. Although oil prices were still on the rise, the prices of consumer goods had begun to stabilize around the 20th of the month—a possible sign that those who had stocked up on goods in the hopes of turning a quick profit were losing patience and had started holding clearance sales.

It was at this moment that Kihachiro Kawashima had shown up at Roppongi, asking for advice. Fujisawa contemplated the situation, imagining that he was still vice president of Honda.

Honda has successfully launched its CVCC-equipped cars, thought Fujisawa as he listened to Kawashima. *But it doesn't mean we've totally made up for the damage to our reputation from the defect scandal. If Honda decides to raise prices again in step with the other manufacturers, people will see us as just another large corporation, with nothing to differentiate us from Toyota or Nissan. On the other hand, if we announce publicly that we won't raise prices, it will set us apart from the competition, as well as put a damper on the current trend of inflation.*

In fact, Kiyoshi Kawashima had already made up his mind. He had, after all, made it clear that Honda would be following a different path from Toyota and Nissan. On January 31, Kawashima stated in the company's annual New Year press conference at Keidanren that Honda would not raise the prices of either its automobiles or motorcycles for some time. Kawashima gave as his reasons the fact that inflation seemed to be easing with regards to the price of parts and raw materials, and that the favorable exchange rate provided for the possibility of raising export prices.

The other auto manufacturers, having just raised their prices, greeted Honda's announcement with bitter dismay. But just as Fujisawa had expected, the public applauded Honda's decision. The statement improved the reputations of both Honda and president Kawashima. Fujisawa took a long breath of relief.

Kawashima did well. The kids can stand on their own now. All I need to do now is iron out a system that will support the kids from behind the scenes— by re-casting Soichiro as the guru of the Cult of Honda. Business relies on youthful energy for success, but Honda has a responsibility to society as well. That's where Soichiro will come in. He can carry some of that burden for the kids.

On January 28, three days before Kiyoshi Kawashima's announcement at the press conference, Soichiro embarked on a countrywide tour of Honda manufacturing plants, dealers, and affiliates. Making full use of his private helicopter and cars, Soichiro planned to visit roughly fifteen places a day for a total of 700 stops altogether, and shake hands with everyone related to Honda to personally thank them for their work. After that, there were plans to tour Honda's facilities abroad. All in all, the worldwide tour would take some three years to complete. During that time, the Honda kids led by the four executive directors worked to set the stage for Soichiro's new role—something Fujisawa had been urging them to do for some time.

While president of Honda, Soichiro's "outside activities" had been more or less limited to his professional sphere: he had served variously as board member of the Japan Automobile Research Institute (JARI), trustee of the Foundation for Orphans of Traffic Accidents, vice chairman for the Japan Motor Industrial Federation (JMIF), board member for the Japan Automobile Federation as well as the Japan Aeronautic Association, and slightly more unconventionally, vice chairman for a supporters' association for the Japan Self-Defense Forces and a member of the program examination board for the TV Asahi Corporation.

After their dual resignation, Soichiro and Fujisawa split the cost of establishing a new foundation called the International Association of Traffic and Safety Sciences (IATSS). In contrast to the secrecy of their involvement with the Sakkokai foundation, the IATSS was founded from the beginning as part of Honda's social investment plan. Furthermore, in 1977, Soichiro and his brother Benjiro spent four billion yen in private funds to establish the Honda Foundation. These two foundations went a tremendous way towards increasing Honda's popularity among scholars, journalists, and politicians.

Soichiro's frank yet charming personality attracted far more offers for honorary public office than he could realistically handle. Soichiro had an innate ability to attract positive attention. As president of Honda, even with people whom he met for the first time at a party, Soichiro would always lead the conversation by talking away at them for the first half-hour, going from one topic to another, from automobiles to racing, golf and even dirty jokes. If his listener expressed interest in any of the subjects he brought up, Soichiro quickly switched gears to focus on it for his listener's sake. Before long he would have made another admirer. Soichiro had the gift of being able to charm people without their even realizing it.

"You look so serious in your pictures," people would often say. "But after meeting you in person, I see that you're really different from what I expected. I feel like we've known each other for years!"

In 1974, perhaps because of their approval of Honda's decision not to raise prices, the Prime Minister's Office asked Soichiro to participate in its council on price issues. The following year, Soichiro became a member of two other government councils: one on issues related to civil servants and another on reform of the national railway system. He also became director and president of the board of examiners for the Venture Enterprise Center, chairman of the Tokyo Council Maintenance Foundation for the Boy Scouts of Nippon, and director of Boy Scouts of Nippon (now the Scout Association of Japan).

As a rule, it was unusual for people appointed to these kinds of positions to attend all the meetings on a regular basis. Soichiro, however, tried to participate as often as possible. Generally, only a business trip abroad or something similarly unavoidable could keep him away.

Soichiro's comments sometimes lacked consistency, but his approach of basing everything on his personal experience often succeeded in getting his point across. For example, when the Tokyo Gas Company decided to raise customer charges, its employees visited various industry professionals and business leaders to explain the situation as a part of the usual consensus-building process. Soichiro, on account of his participation on the price issues council and the board of the Tokyo Chamber of Commerce and Industry, also received a visit. After listening to the employees' explanation for some time, Soichiro said in his typical straightforward style:

"That was a pretty complex explanation, but you know what? I still have no idea why you have to raise the charges. How can you expect the average resident of Tokyo to understand if you can't even convince me? You'll have to come up with a better explanation than that, or you're not going anywhere."

As Soichiro's reputation grew, so too did his titles: vice chairman of the Japan Automobile Manufacturers Association (JAMA); vice chairman of the Tokyo Chamber of Commerce and Industry; member of the Small and Medium Enterprise Agency's council on a future vision for SMEs in the 1980s; honorary chairman of the Defense Technology Foundation; vice chairman of the Association for the International Science and Technology Exposition; chairman of the Japan-Belgium Society; chief organizer of the National Forum for the Promotion of Administrative Reform (now the Citizens Forum for Renewal); member of a Tokyo Metropolitan Government council on free access to information; advisor to the Provisional Council for the Promotion of Administrative Reform; advisor to the governor of Saitama prefecture; temporary member of the Aviation Industry Council; visiting professor at Nagaoka University of Technology; chairman of the National Health Council of the Ministry of Welfare; chairman of the Europalia Japan Committee, and many others. And as time went on, Soichiro's number of job titles only continued to grow.

Not all of Soichiro's titles were directly business- or industry-related. Occasionally, some opportunist would conspire to use Soichiro's name for some money-making scheme, and such offers were practically the only ones he declined. Some of the more atypical positions Soichiro held were: chairman of the Prime Minister's Office's Council of Measures Against Prostitution, advisor to the Japan Youth Hostel Association, board member of the Japan Boxing Commission, honorary advisor of the Professional Golfers' Association of Japan, board member of the Forest Culture Association, chief secretary for the Criminal Victims Aid Fund, and board member of the Tokyo YMCA Supporters Organization.

In 1981, Soichiro, at age seventy-four, was awarded the First Class Zuiho Order. Ironically, the basis for the award was not his achievements in the motorcycle and automobile industry but his contribution as chairman of the Council of Measures Against Prostitution. In addition to his not having held a public position of a rank considered suitable for recipients of first class awards, there can be little doubt that the N360 defect scandal and trial had contributed to his receiving such an award only so late in life.

Since Soichiro began enhancing the scope of his activities outside Honda, his circle of connections also grew much wider. Soichiro's only close friend in the business world was Masaru Ibuka, founder of Sony. Honda and Sony shared quite a bit in common, both belonging to that group of outstanding companies that had flourished in the rough-and-tumble of the postwar economic boom.

Soichiro and Ibuka shared an "engineer's mentality" and both were full of ambition. As their companies developed, their roles as engineers-turned-presidents began to attract the attention of the mass media. The two had met for the first time during a joint interview for a magazine article and had immediately hit it off, becoming fast friends.

When outspoken critic Soichi Ohya described Sony as a "guinea pig firm," Soichiro had furiously countered, "Corporations are nothing like laboratory animals! Corporations are a combination of labor and management working together to provide inexpensive and high quality goods to society."

Soichiro took an insult against Sony as an insult against himself. He saw Ibuka, who was two years younger, as a rival and an inspiration.

When Ibuka and Soichiro retired at around the same time, each promised never to turn down a request from the other. In fact, it was on Ibuka's request that Soichiro had accepted the position of chief organizer of the National Forum for the Promotion of Administrative Reform.

The major difference between Honda and Sony was the way in which the founders chose their successors. In Honda's case, the two founders resigned together. In Sony's case, Ibuka's partner and co-founder, Akio Morita, became the next president.

When Ibuka and Morita had launched Sony, Morita's family had helped finance the company. Even today, the Morita family remains Sony's major shareholder. Moreover, Morita spent many years in office as president and chairman of the company, and, unlike Fujisawa and Soichiro, allowed his brother-in-law, children, and other family members to join the company, leading some critics to deride Sony as a Morita family operation. In November of 1993, however, Morita fell ill and resigned as chairman and CEO to become simply founder and honorary chairman. Signs of major upheavals at Honda first became apparent in the early 1980s, after the two founders retired from the board of directors; Sony may very well be following a similar path.

The breadth and variety of Soichiro's interests and qualities can be seen in his friendships with the Japanese imperial family and with well-known authors. He came to be on good terms with Prince Takamatsu (Nobuhito) through a mutual interest in golf and was interviewed together with Prince Mikasa (Tomohito) on several occasions by magazines. Soichiro always had an interesting story to tell, and his comical gestures made people laugh. These qualities attracted popular writers like Saburo Shiroyama and Jiro Nitta into his circle of friends.

Soichiro's social skills weren't all instinctive. In fact, he made a dedicated effort to charm those around him. Soichiro knew that acting more unaffected and frank than people expected of him would break the ice and improve Honda's reputation as well. Whenever he attended a party or gave a lecture, Soichiro made sure to find out what he could about the intended guests or audience beforehand so as to better tailor his performance to their interests.

When Soichiro's lecture tours took him to far-flung locales, he would switch seats with his chauffeur just before reaching his destination. His hosts would invariably marvel that Soichiro had driven himself so far just to see them.

Soichiro made a point of punctuality as well. Whenever unavoidable circumstances such as a traffic jam threatened to delay him, he would get out of the car and use a public phone to alert his hosts that he would be late. If he happened to arrive too early, he would kill time around the area, making sure he arrived at precisely the specified time.

"It goes without saying that you should tell someone you're going to be late," Soichiro would say. "But showing up too early causes problems, too. The organizers are usually working on a tight schedule and still getting ready."

When he talked to members of the imperial family, he deliberately focused on common, plebian topics. Rumor had it that Prince Mikasa changed his official car to a Honda as a result of his friendship with Soichiro. Fans of Soichiro became fans of the company he had built and purchased Honda products.

As president, Soichiro had directed his staff at the top of his lungs. Although his attitude towards his dear "kids" hardly changed even after his retirement, he adopted a softer approach with younger employees who did not know him well.

After finishing a lecture, Soichiro would proceed to an elevator or other quiet space and open the envelope containing his payment. Without fail, he would give half of it to the employees who had arranged the event or had taken care of him during his stay.

"Everyone seemed to enjoy my lecture today. But that's because you let me know who would be here and what they wanted to hear ahead of time. Half of the success is due entirely to you."

Eiji Toyoda, honorary chairman of Toyota, once remarked enviously:

"People say that working as a contractor for Toyota is harsh and that our purchasing policies are tough. In reality, things are far worse at Honda, but you don't hear anyone criticize them. The reason is that Soichiro Honda always has a ready smile, anywhere he goes, and charms the hell out of everyone he meets. Honda is a very fortunate company to have such a man. We at Toyota don't have that luxury."

If anything, Soichiro's schedule after his resignation became even more packed than it had been as president. His only hobby was painting, which he had taken up at the prodding of his friends and family. In classic dedicated Soichiro fashion, he started with the very basics under Okitsu Gyoshun, a master of the Japanese style. Whenever he found time, he went on sketching trips. Once he got started, he would became so absorbed that he would stay locked up in his home studio, working on his painting the entire day and even forgetting to take his meals.

Just as Fujisawa had planned, Soichiro was well on his way to becoming the guru of the Cult of Honda. Every year in July, around the end of the rainy season, Soichiro released live *ayu*, Japanese sweetfish, into an artificial stream on his property and invited friends and acquaintances to his home for a two-day-long fishing party. Fujisawa never attended, claiming it wasn't to his taste. Fujisawa was busy enjoying his own leisurely retirement—keeping a sharp eye on Honda and the "kids" all the while.

7

The Japanese Environment Agency officially announced its 1975 regulations, known as the Japanese version of the Muskie Act, on January 21, 1974, at the height of the first oil crisis. The law was set to take effect on April 1, 1975. As Fujisawa had predicted, the oil crisis began to ease that spring. But thanks to manufacturers having raised prices twice already, auto sales stagnated at a level far lower than the previous year. In the midst of this glum news, it became apparent that Mazda, whose rotary engine had competed with Honda's CVCC as the key technology in the race to produce the first low-emission vehicle, was facing a management crisis.

The crisis was, in a sense, self-inflicted. Kohei Matsuda, president of Mazda, was famous for his dictatorial style of leadership. Predicting that the shortage of goods brought about by the oil crisis would continue for some time, Matsuda had ordered his company to significantly step up production even though other manufacturers had slashed the size of their production runs. At almost precisely the same time, however, the U.S. E.P.A branded the rotary engine a "gas guzzler." Sales immediately dropped off in the United States, followed, before long, by a dip in Japanese sales as well.

In the blink of an eye, Mazda found itself facing massive quantities of dead stock. Its Hiroshima factory was jammed full of unsold automobiles. A rumor in the U.S. held that Mazda had deliberately sunk shipments of cars in the Atlantic to deal with the problem.

As stock rapidly continued to pile up both in Japan and abroad and it became virtually impossible to ignore the crisis, Matsuda was finally forced to slash production and move surplus factory workers into sales positions. Day after day, the Hiroshima station was filled with Mazda employees seeing off fellow workers as they left for their new destinations at Mazda dealerships. The scene resembled families sending their sons off to war. The press covered the situation extensively.

Mazda's crisis was a valuable lesson to the auto industry. A manufacturer simply could not survive unless they managed to achieve both reduced emissions and fuel efficiency. Mazda wasn't the only one suffering. Nissan found itself in the position of having to temporarily lay off factory workers as well. Only Honda appeared to be making any headway.

Honda reported gross sales of two hundred and forty-five billion yen for the fiscal term from February to August of 1974—Honda settled accounts twice a year at the time—a 40.8 percent increase over the same term the previous year. Profits declined due to an increase in corporate tax rates, but according to the National Tax Agency's records, Honda's net declared income was 14.5 billion yen—a 78.4 percent increase over the previous term, and a 13.8 percent increase over the same term the previous year.

Needless to say, it was the highest reported income of any automobile manufacturer in August of 1974. At least in terms of its balance sheets, Honda appeared not only to be weathering the oil crisis but doing almost as well as it had in the era of rapid economic growth. The oil crisis had been bad news for the industry, but for Honda, now that the company had taken the lead in actually marketing a low-emission vehicle, it had actually been a blessing.

In those days, the car industry consisted of a number of rivals vying for supremacy. In 1973, Toyota had topped the list of manufacturers by producing 2.31 million vehicles, closely followed by Nissan with 2.04 million. These were the two giants of the industry. Mazda with 740,000 vehicles came as a distant third, followed by Mitsubishi with 560,000. This was the second group. Then came Honda with 350,000 and Daihatsu with 310,000 vehicles. Slightly further behind, Suzuki, Isuzu and Fuji Heavy Industries, practically bunched together, produced 240,000, 220,000, and 210,000 vehicles, respectively.

Although Honda had risen to become the top manufacturer of k-cars, it was still a newcomer to the compact car market. Honda barely manufactured 160,000 compact cars in 1973, which was lower even than Suzuki. Even with the widespread respect the CVCC had garnered in the industry, large corporations like Toyota or Nissan simply didn't see Honda as a full-fledged manufacturer, let alone rival.

That being said, the impending exhaust regulations combined with the effects of the oil crisis were precipitating a tectonic shift in the auto industry. The oil crisis had had a tremendous impact, causing the first downturn in Japanese automobile production since the start of motorization. National production as a whole dropped by 7.5 percent, with Nissan, Mitsubishi, Daihatsu, Suzuki, and Fuji Heavy Industries all recording double-digit decreases in production.

Only Honda, thanks to the success of the CVCC, recorded a major increase of 20.8 percent in performance over the previous year. Production shot up to 430,000 vehicles as Honda joined the group of manufacturers vying for third place after Toyota and Nissan.

The oil crisis shaped and determined Honda's rapid growth, particularly with regards to the U.S. market. The United States had managed to transform itself into an economic superpower in the twentieth century, not so much because it had a ready domestic supply of crude oil, but rather because of the development of an automobile industry that relied on that oil. Thanks to a highly developed rail system, the Japanese people could live without cars. In the United States, on the other hand, cars were a fundamental and indispensable part of daily life. A shortage of gasoline in the U.S. was as shocking a prospect as not having electricity or water in Japan. Furthermore, the American auto industry supported some four million laborers and spent roughly forty billion dollars annually on the purchase of equipment and raw materials. The United States depended on automobiles for both the daily life of its citizens and the success of its industries.

When Americans woke up on the morning of October 5, 1973, they learned that they were facing something far worse than a price hike: an actual shortage of gasoline. Gasoline had long been so cheap that it verged on being free; when the prices had tripled, it was still a matter of money. But a shortage of supply was another story altogether. Initial panic gave way to resignation as time went on, but the issue remained unresolved. Lines of cars stretched from every pump as people searched for gas stations with fuel to sell.

Fuel tanks on new cars featured modified openings that only allowed the use of fuel pumps that dispensed unleaded gasoline. Honda's new 1500cc CVCC-equipped Civic allowed the use of both types of fuel pump, which meant the owner could line up for whichever type of gasoline was more readily available at the moment.

Advertisements for the Civic stressed the inexpensive, highly fuel efficient, and low-polluting CVCC engine that permitted the use of both leaded and un-leaded gasoline. With sales points like these, there was no way the car would not be a smash hit.

The American media had nothing but praise for the Civic. The December 1975 issue of the *Reader's Digest* carried a five-page feature article under the head-line "Japan's New 'Clean Cars' Economize on Gasoline." The article outlined Honda's struggle to develop the CVCC. It further explained that while the new engine cost 170 dollars more to produce than other engines, in the end it actually saved consumers roughly 180 dollars because it didn't require the usual 350 dollars worth of additional components such as catalytic converters to meet emis-sion standards. It also pointed out that the fuel economy of the car improved the more it was driven. In other words, initial costs were low because the CVCC engine relied entirely on modifications to the engine itself, as were running costs, thanks to fuel-efficiency improvements. The explanation clinched the reputation of the CVCC. The *Reader's Digest* article had backed Honda's ad copy of being "gas-saving" with hard facts and figures.

Soon both automotive magazines and general magazines were singing the praises of the CVCC "miracle engine." American Honda, Honda's sales arm in the U.S., made photocopies of every article on the CVCC to be published and sent them to major dealerships. Honda's fame and popularity skyrocketed in the United States. Dealers rushed to American Honda to make contracts.

Honda's rise to fame in the U.S. had been far from smooth. Although the company had conquered the American market for motorcycles in almost no time at all, its entry into the auto business had been plagued with difficulties from the start. Honda had applied know-how from the Japanese marketplace to sell its motorcycles in the United States. But Honda had next to no track record with cars, even in Japan. Efforts to convince Honda motorcycle dealers to sell cars met with cold resistance. In the United States, the sale of automobiles and motorcycles were handled completely separately.

Honda was at a distinct disadvantage from another standpoint as well. Prior to the Civic, the company had only offered a single car on the American marketplace, a k-car called the N600, essentially an N360 with a 600cc engine. It had only gone on limited sale in the states of Hawaii, Oregon, California, and Washington and had been poorly received.

"Honda just scaled-up a motorcycle to create a miniature car," went a common refrain. "It's not much more than a sidecar with a roof." It was obvious that the U.S. market didn't see Honda as a serious auto manufacturer.

Toyota and Nissan first began exporting cars to the United States in 1958. Their first products couldn't even be driven on the highway with any reliability; when drivers pushed the envelope and drove at high speeds, the engines would die. In the end, it took Toyota and Nissan more than ten years to overcome the engineering issues and establish a name for their companies in the United States.

Even with the improved engine displacement, there was no question that the N600 remained a k-car, and the reception was much the same as for Toyota and Nissan's cars fifteen years earlier. Nevertheless, the salesmen at American Honda under the leadership of Kihachiro Kawashima patiently visited every Chevrolet and Ford dealer that would see them to persuade them to handle Honda products. It was like spraying water in a desert; the amount of time and effort to establish a decent sales network was mind-boggling.

Truth be told, with only one model of car to offer, building an independent sales network was more of a dream than a business strategy. The best they could hope for would be convincing a GM or Ford dealer to give some corner display space to a single N600. Despite the initial difficulties, however, the hard work of American Honda's salesmen paid off. By the time the Civic was ready to roll onto the American market, the staff had organized some 300 dealers—mostly GM dealerships—that agreed to give space to Honda's products.

It was around that time that Ford first approached Honda about a possible tie-up. While American Honda saw Ford's offer as highly attractive, in the end, Honda drew confidence from the positive reception of the Civic and its CVCC engine in the United States and elected to remain independent. The oil crisis had all but plunged the Big Three into a bottomless pit, but for Honda, it was a window of opportunity to join the ranks of the world's leading auto manufacturers.

The big question was: how could Honda improve its channels of distribution for the Civic? Were Fujisawa still in charge, he would probably have poured money into building new factories, even if it meant going back into debt. Honda under Kiyoshi Kawashima was a different and less aggressive animal. Kawashima and his directors made the decision to completely suspend k-car sales in order to establish a foothold in the compact car market. It was an unexpected and shocking decision.

Although the N360 defect scandal had put a major dent in Honda's sales, the company eventually managed to stage something of a comeback, as introduction of the new "Z" and Life models proceeded smoothly. By November 1971, domestic sales had reached 24,000 vehicles per month.

Annual demand for k-cars in Japan had peaked at 720,000 units in 1969 and continued to drop over the next several years, hitting a low of 396,000 units in 1973. That year, Honda's share of the k-car market was 28.5 percent—larger, albeit by a slim margin, than any of the other smaller manufacturers such as Suzuki, Daihatsu, Mazda, Mitsubishi and Fuji Heavy Industries—restoring the company to a dominant position in this area.

Thanks to the popularity of the Civic, Honda's balance sheet in August of 1974 boasted a large increase in revenue. However, Honda still sold close to 100,000 k-cars annually, which made a major contribution to the bottom line. Even if the Civic continued to sell well, withdrawing from the k-car market would mean an inevitable drop in overall sales. The new management at Honda was well aware of the implications of such a move as they decided, nonetheless, to abandon their position as top k-car manufacturer.

There were two reasons for the decision. For one thing, the Civic was selling far better than anyone had expected, both in Japan and the United States, creating an urgent need to increase production capacity to 30,000 Civics a month. The other reason was that Honda just didn't have enough engineers to spare for the work needed to make the k-cars compatible with the exhaust regulations.

If Honda invested in new facilities for the Civic, it would take at least two to three years to complete the entire process of purchasing land, building the factory, and starting to manufacture the products. The Suzuka manufacturing plant could accommodate a new assembly line, but even that would take a year to build. Neither option would allow Honda to produce additional Civics quickly enough to meet the immediate and sensational demand for the cars.

Although the number of Civics sold and registered monthly was around 10,000, Honda was receiving orders for more than 15,000 every month. The company planned to put a "Civic van" on the market in December. And in January, Honda would add to its model line in the United States—which at that time consisted solely of the 1200cc version—the 1500cc Civic CVCC. All signs pointed to the distinct possibility of combined domestic and international automobile sales of 30,000 units a month in the near future.

K-cars did have certain advantages, such as low vehicle taxes and the fact that buyers did not have to prove they owned a parking space before purchasing one, as was required for larger vehicles. At the same time, strict government regulations dictated the maximum engine displacement and chassis dimensions for k-cars. When national income was low, consumer demand for k-cars had skyrocketed. But as the economy matured, buyers gradually started turning to luxury models instead. The target market for k-cars shifted away from the young generation to older, middle-aged car owners, and the vehicles themselves had come to be known by the unwelcome nickname of *gamansha*, "patience cars" to be abided by people who could not afford a better car.

The biggest problem, however, was making the cars compatible with the new exhaust regulations. Honda R&D built a prototype 360cc CVCC engine for use in k-cars, but discovered that given the small displacement of the k-car engines, additional low-emission measures resulted in low performance, undermining the marketability of the products. Before long, rumors spread throughout the industry that while the CVCC technology could be applied to bigger cars, it was unsuitable for k-cars. Honda lobbied JAMA, the Japan Automobile Manufacturers Association, to expand the specifications for k-cars, without success.

If Soichiro had still been president of the Honda Research and Development Company, there can be no doubt that he would have taken things into his own hands and spurred his engineers to adapt the CVCC technology for use in k-cars. His pride would simply not have let him rest without proving that he could produce k-cars with CVCC engines that were still marketable and attractive as products. At the same time, Fujisawa too, would undoubtedly have aimed at both the compact car and k-car markets, as long as Soichiro could solve the technical problems and as long as he himself was convinced of the future potential of the k-cars. Such ambitious plans, if successful, would have given Honda a truly unique position in the world of automotive manufacturing, as a manufacturer dealing in the full range of consumer vehicles: motorcycles, k-cars and compact cars. In terms of sales figures, such a strategy might not have been enough to allow Honda to take on Toyota, but it would have at least given the company an opening to knock Nissan out of second place.

When Soichiro and Fujisawa agreed on something, no one could possibly challenge them. Their charisma and power of conviction overwhelmed the employees, who felt confident that a decision made by the two genius founders—one an expert on technology, the other on business—couldn't possibly be wrong. But president Kiyoshi Kawashima knew that he and the other Honda kids had neither the charisma nor the talent of Soichiro and Fujisawa. They had no choice but to play it safe.

A decision based on the "solidarity of the ordinary" could only mean one thing: making the best of limited resources. In this case, that meant focusing everything on the compact car division so as to build it into a world-class operation while the marketplace still favored Honda. The future of k-cars was far from certain. Re-tooling the k-car assembly lines to manufacture compact cars would be an easy and reasonable investment.

Superficially, giving up the title of the top k-car manufacturer may appear to be quite a bold move. In reality, however, it was a carefully calculated choice and the one carrying the least amount of risk. Honda manufactured its last k-car at the end of October 1974. The seven-and-half-year saga that had begun with the launch of the hit product N360 in the spring of 1967 was over—for the time being.

Honda's withdrawal only served to escalate the increasingly negative image of k-cars. National sales topped off at 157,000 in 1974, a fifth of what they had been during the peak.

On the other hand, the decision only enhanced Honda's corporate image all the more. In November 1974, the low-polluting Civic CVCC, launched at the height of the oil crisis the previous year, won the Car of the Year Japan award. Shortly thereafter, the 1500cc version of the Civic received official E.P.A. recognition as a low-polluting car.

The E.P.A. had also conducted fuel efficiency tests on the Civic CVCC. The results were a certified mileage of 27 m.p.g. in city driving and 39 m.p.g. on the highway. Previous tests on cars sold in 1975 had proved Nissan's Sunny (B210), which used a catalytic converter, to be the world's most fuel-efficient car. The results for the Civic exactly matched those for the Sunny.

Newly touted as the most fuel-efficient car in the world, the Civic proved that fuel efficiency and low-emission technology were perfectly compatible. Honda's reputation as an auto manufacturer in the United States soared. The Civic was a tremendous hit and the CVCC engine received the Society of Automotive Engineers Award for 1974. In March 1975, *Motor Trend* magazine selected president Kiyoshi Kawashima as their "Man of the Year."

In the end, the decision to withdraw from the k-car market turned out to be all for the best. Although Honda's February 1975 financial statement reported a drop in the total number of vehicles sold, the sale of compact cars—which sold at higher retail prices—was stronger than expected, resulting in not a decrease but rather an increase of 11.7 percent in sales over the previous quarter. In terms of profit, the growing popularity of Honda's large-size motorcycles had a very positive effect, and the figures were the highest in Honda's history. In the following term ending in August 1975, Honda saw a slump in motorcycle exports but was able to cover for it with the increased sales of its automobiles, so that, once again, the company was able to announce increases in both sales and profit.

Honda's rapid advance picked up even more speed in the late 1970s, thanks to its "trump card," the CVCC engine. But even the CVCC had an Achilles' heel. Although the E.P.A. had guaranteed the Civic CVCC to be fuel efficient as well as low-polluting, the engine still consumed roughly ten percent more fuel than an unmodified reciprocating engine.

The difference in efficiency hadn't been a problem when gasoline was cheap. But the cost of crude oil had tripled during the oil crisis, and consumers were now growing increasingly concerned about what they would have to pay for their fuel. The Big Three, lacking any definitive low-emission measures of their own, wasted no time in taking advantage of the situation. They argued that, while anti-pollution measures were also important, priority should be given to fuel efficiency in an era of limited natural resources.

The American exhaust regulations for 1975 and their Japanese equivalent both took effect on schedule. Application of the 1976 regulations, however, were delayed for two years in both countries; as the automotive industry suffered from the effects of the oil crisis, no company managed to create an engine that produced less than the specified 0.25 grams of NOx per volume of exhaust. An interim measure raising the allowed NOx limit to 0.6 grams per volume of exhaust for the years 1976-77 was adopted; even so, the Big Three claimed that the figures were still unrealistic, and petitioned the E.P.A. for an extension.

If the growing awareness of fuel efficiency caused the exhaust standards to be repeatedly postponed so as to eventually render them toothless, Honda would lose its competitive edge in the marketplace. Honda engineers had managed to tweak the CVCC design to meet the 0.25 gram-per-volume standards at an early stage in their test labs, but had not yet found any way to circumvent the resulting drop in fuel efficiency. Unless they brought the CVCC's fuel consumption more in line with that of an unmodified engine, there was always a risk that application of the regulations would be postponed once again. This was the new challenge that Honda now faced.

Honda's engineers finally began making headway on the technical aspects of the efficiency issue in 1975. Improving and adjusting the valves, ignition system, carburetor and other aspects resulted in a CVCC engine with its fuel economy improved ten to thirty percent over previous models and up to twenty percent over an unmodified reciprocating engine.

Shortly thereafter, the E.P.A. held a hearing to discuss the Big Three's request for extension on the 1977 regulations. Hideo Sugiura attended from Honda.

"Honda can meet the 1977 regulations without a loss in fuel efficiency," he announced confidently.

On April 2, 1976, Honda officially announced that they had not only achieved technology capable of lowering NOx emissions to the specified 0.25 gram level, but that they had developed the technology to mass produce the new engines. Mazda, Mitsubishi, and Fuji Heavy Industries also took the opportunity to announce that they had achieved similar results, but only Honda boasted the ability to begin manufacturing and selling cars equipped with the new engines right away. Although the Japanese Environment Agency's decision wasn't due until the fall, Honda's statement virtually guaranteed that the regulations would indeed take effect when the two-year extension period expired.

The Civic continued to sell well both domestically and abroad. For the fiscal year ended February 1976—the first year Honda introduced an annual settlement of accounts—Honda had predicted domestic and international sales of compact cars to total 300,000 units. As it turned out, the annual statement reported actual sales of 345,000 units.

Honda's sales in the U.S. in 1975 finally cleared the 100,000-unit mark and reached 102,000, ranking Honda fourth among foreign automakers in the U.S. after Toyota, Volkswagen, and Nissan. Meanwhile, domestic sales dropped to 248,000, fifteen percent lower than the previous year, influenced by Honda's withdrawal from the k-car market. Still, the drop was less than the company had expected. Although Toyota and Nissan remained far ahead of Honda as far as domestic sales were concerned, Honda boasted an equity ratio of 31.7 percent, higher than Nissan's 26.9 percent, and an ordinary income to total assets ratio—used as a measure of a company's earning power—of 6.6 percent, which also trumped Nissan's 3.3 percent. The numbers were evidence that Honda had finally earned some respect as an automobile manufacturer.

Spirits were high in the collective director's room where president Kiyoshi Kawashima and directors Kihachiro Kawashima, Nishida, and Shirai gathered to make their joint decisions. All decisions that would have an impact on the company's future were managed by consensus, from the withdrawal from the k-car market to the timing for increasing production of compact cars, the allocation of cars for domestic and export sales, and the timing of the company's official statement about clearing the new exhaust regulations. The collective decision-making system had already been in place before Kawashima became president, but since the resignation of the two founders, it had become even more firmly established as the basic mode of getting things done.

The collective decision making system was based on the *waigaya*, Honda's unique "brainstorming" system that encouraged participants to bring up and discuss any topic they liked. The *waigaya* system proved invaluable in reaching a consensus among the directors, who actively encouraged its use throughout the company. Before long, the concept had spread not only to all corners of Honda's headquarters but also to branch offices, the Honda R&D Company, and factories.

The ACT Group was a venture-capital business that had emerged as a result of *waigaya* sessions among the directors. Named after the English word "action," ACT consisted of four companies established between 1972 and 1974: ACT-A, ACT-L, ACT-TRADING, and ACT-B. The objective of the ACT Group was to find business opportunities in new fields.

ACT-A and ACT-L focused upon the development of recreational products. ACT-A, which focused on aquatic recreation, marketed the "Amenboat" (a play off the name of an insect called *amenbo*, the water strider). The product was based on a winning entry in a contest for ideas held by Honda. ACT-L, which focused on land-based recreational activities, developed a scooter-like riding toy called the "Roller Through GO GO." The scooter became a huge hit among Japanese children, so that at one point Honda found itself producing some 100,000 of the toys a month.

ACT-TRADING focused on promoting imports. It was founded in an effort to ease the imbalance of international payments, given the fact that Honda's business relied heavily on exports. ACT-B involved running farms. In addition to motorcycles and automobiles, Honda also manufactured engines for a wide variety of farming equipment. ACT-B gave Honda the hands-on farming experience it needed to create better products for the industry.

The ACT companies assisted each other as well. For example, ACT-B raised cattle, made beef jerky, and sold it through ACT-TRADING. ACT-TRADING imported animal feed and sold it to farms through ACT-B. In short, the symbiotic matrix formed by the ACT companies allowed Honda to kill not two but many birds with a single stone.

The idea of creating the ACT companies had in fact grown from an increasing desire to escape the confines of the structure that had been created by and for Fujisawa and Soichiro.

"Honda's remarkable growth to date is a testament to the amazing leadership of the two men who founded the company," said Kiyoshi Kawashima in a discussion for the company's newsletter just before the founding of the ACT group. "Generally speaking, management loses influence as a corporation increases in size. It becomes more difficult to reach decisions and act quickly. Honda may be a large corporation, but I don't want to see it growing old and stubborn. We must strive to make our company as flexible as possible... A company can survive so long as its management responds appropriately to the issues facing them. But waiting for problems to come to us isn't the way to achieve long-term success in this day and age. A successful corporation needs to anticipate future trends and establish a system to avoid problems before they happen. I am absolutely convinced that Honda has the potential to do just that."

Kiyoshi Kawashima completely shifted Honda's management style from a two-man system to one of collective decision and consensus. Although the ACT companies, being based more on ideals than actual business calculations, would not actually survive in the long run, their foundation demonstrated to Honda's employees just how enthusiastic their leaders were about taking on the challenge of creating new types of products, new methods of distribution, and whole new markets for the company.

8

In an era of rapid change, thinking ahead is the only way to achieve long-term success. And so the Honda kids, led by president Kiyoshi Kawashima, began looking ahead, focusing on luxury cars and export to the United States as the next step in Honda's quest to become a world leader in the production of automobiles as well as motorcycles. Now that Honda had abandoned k-cars and had finished reinforcing its Civic line, entry into the luxury car market was the only logical choice.

By the end of 1975, Honda was already producing some 35,000 Civics a month, including both cars and vans, which put the model in the same league as Toyota's Corolla and Nissan's Sunny. In a ranking of the world's top automobiles of 1975, the Civic came in an impressive eighth.

That the Civic sold so well in such a short period of time was partly due to the "clean" image of the CVCC, but also to the roughly one million owners of Honda products such as the N360 k-car, who now turned to the Civic for their next purchase. With such an established consumer base, Honda was able to ensure a decent level of sales for the Civic simply by targeting those who already owned Honda's k-cars. But one hit product alone was not enough to ensure Honda's reputation as a respectable auto manufacturer. Even though the Civic had great sales potential, sooner or later consumers would grow tired and turn to the luxury designs of other manufacturers.

This was also a problem for the dealerships. Dealing exclusively in light trucks and Civics certainly provided for efficiency, but also put limits on potential growth. If Honda didn't introduce a compact design with more "class" like Toyota's Corona or Nissan's Bluebird, the company would soon find itself up against a wall. Ford vehicles were being handled exclusively by HISCO, so they weren't going to be of any use in adding variety to Honda's lineup. Honda would have to come up with something of its own.

The success of the N360 had led Soichiro to chase his dream of creating a sports car. Unlike the N360, which had been marketed as easy to drive even for novices, Soichiro's H1300 was made to seduce racing fans with its high speed and sport-handling characteristics. Even if it had succeeded, it would never have been the next choice for N360 users to move on to.

The H1300 had arisen purely out of the personal desire of one of the founders. There was no way the current Honda leadership would even consider such a risky proposition. Designing a car based on nothing but personal whim was totally out of the question.

When Kiyoshi Kawashima became president of Honda, the "kids" decided to adopt a new development system. It was dubbed SED: sales, engineering, and development. The SED system provided for salesmen, engineers and R&D research staff to work together from the beginning to the end of the product-development cycle. It was designed to channel information from the sales side directly to the R&D section, eliminating complacency and arrogance on the part of R&D and instilling the engineers with a new sense of marketing and cost-awareness. The greatest benefit this sharing of information offered was that it would allow the company to build cars that conformed to the precise needs of customers at a low cost and in the shortest possible period of time.

The most certain way to retain current Civic owners who might "graduate" to luxury cars later was to create a luxury car that embodied the key concepts of the Civic. The first goal established through the SED system, therefore, was to create a scaled-up version of the Civic.

Honda's image in Japan was initially one of speed. This had started with motorcycles, and had carried over to the automotive side of the business with the creation of the S series of sports cars, the N360 to a certain extent, and the H1300. But the exhaust gas regulations had prompted the company to start marketing restrained cars with lowered maximum speeds like the "town car" Life and the Civic. These cars ended up being a huge success and, as a result, Honda's image was beginning to change. In the United States, Honda was seen from the start as specializing in family cars—the antonym of speed.

One day, just as the oil crisis was finally starting to ease, Masami Suzuki, executive director of domestic sales, paid a visit to the Honda Research and Development Company.

"Do you think you can make a slightly larger version of the Civic in a short period of time? You can use the Civic as the base," said Suzuki to Nobuhiko Kawamoto, who headed engine development.

This was the beginning of the "bigger Civic" project. For this project, the team had decided to gather as much information as possible about the needs and wants of American consumers. They had just gotten started developing a basic concept for the car, which would determine the size of the engine. Developing the engine would take another two years. But Suzuki wanted the car to be ready within a year.

"That's impossible, Suzuki-san. We don't even have an engine for it," Kawamoto flatly refused.

"I know I'm not an engineer," replied Suzuki, refusing to back down. "But wouldn't it be possible to scale up the engine used in the Civic?"

The idea of simply making a pre-existing engine larger didn't sit well with

Kawamoto's pride as an engineer. But Suzuki's question wasn't his own—it was a collective request from headquarters. And what was more, it came from the sales department, which had the closest working relationship with Honda's customers. Kawamoto had no choice but to agree.

"All right. Let's give it a try," said Kawamoto in resignation. Hesitantly, he set to work increasing the bore of the existing Civic engine.

The Civic used a 1200cc engine. The engineers had already stretched the design to make a 1500cc version for vans. Now Suzuki wanted Kawamoto to raise it by another 100cc.

The result of Kawamoto's efforts—the Honda Accord—went on sale in May of 1976. It featured a front-mounted 1600cc engine and front wheel drive. Like the Civic, it was hatchback. Headquarters set a monthly sales target of 4,000 cars each in Japan and abroad.

"The Accord is an extension of the Civic. The fundamental themes are space, environment, and harmony," said Kiyoshi Kawashima in description of the new automobile.

The larger size made the Accord more comfortable both for the driver and the passengers. But externally, it was nothing more than a scaled-up version of its predecessor. Ignorant of Honda's SED system, Honda's rivals could hardly contain their mirth.

"They must have been really desperate to have to whip up something like that," they said. "There's no way they can hope to win over rivals' customers with that car. The best they can possibly do is sell the car to Civic owners who are looking for an upgrade."

"The price of a luxury car is more than a million yen. The only way to sell such expensive cars is to build a strong and healthy sales network. Every other luxury manufacturer has bent over backwards to attract customers to their 1600cc cars. I guess Honda hasn't figured that out yet."

Honda may have indeed rushed the Accord to market, but that didn't mean that it took the matter lightly. Fully aware of the fact that the sales of the Accord would all but determine the fate of their company, Honda's employees were doing everything in their power to bolster the sales network.

At the time, Honda had two separate networks for selling cars. One utilized fifty Honda sales branches that worked together with 2,500 Honda-affiliated dealerships. The other consisted of 2,000 specialized dealerships. The total number of sales staff in the dealerships was 4,500—an average of only one salesman per dealership. This meant that Honda couldn't rely on a huge network of door-to-door salesmen to go out and sell the cars like Toyota or Nissan. Honda would have to get customers to visit the dealers and make their purchases there. The problem was that although Honda had a large number of dealerships, the average number of sales at each location remained quite low.

For the Accord, Honda decided to cut out the specialized dealerships, selecting instead 500 of the larger affiliated dealerships to handle the new car. Honda then asked the selected dealers to hire additional sales staff—an average of two new staff per dealer—promising in return to help the dealerships secure loans to expand their businesses.

Honda also invested thirty billion yen to expand its factories in Sayama and Suzuka. The company's annual manufacturing capacity at the end of 1975 had been 500,000 vehicles. Over the next six months, Honda increased the number to 600,000.

Of those manufacturers vying for third place after Toyota and Nissan, Mazda was the first to reach a production capacity of 700,000 vehicles a year, turning out 740,000 vehicles in both 1973 and 1974, although the numbers would come back down again to 640,000 vehicles in 1975 as a result of a drastic drop in both domestic and export sales after the first oil crisis. Mitsubishi also raised its capacity to 600,000 vehicles a year. The manufacturers in this group found themselves standing at roughly the same starting line. The stage was set for a vicious competition.

The Civic had taken off in the United States before Japan. The Accord, on the other hand, defied expectations and became a sensation in Japan first. Honda had set a preliminary goal of selling 4,000 Accords a month, but in May, the company found itself sitting on orders for 9,000 of the cars. In June, this figure had increased to 10,000. Honda shifted some of the products intended for export to domestic dealers to try and meet the demand, but it wasn't enough. A hasty decision was made in June to increase production by fifty percent.

Still, it wasn't easy to raise the production run by such a large number. Not only were employees working seven days a week, a large number of seasonal workers were hired in August—a time when production was usually slow—to work exclusively on the Accord assembly line. This allowed Honda, for the first time in its history, to add a third shift to keep the line running twenty-four hours a day. Even with the changes, the company only barely managed to keep pace with the orders.

The reason that Honda put so much effort into its domestic sales, even cutting down the number of cars intended for export to transfer the products to domestic dealers, was that the company had still not managed to establish a firm base for sales in Japan. Meanwhile, Honda was fully confident that the Accord would prove a hit in the United States even if sales began there slightly later than anticipated.

The confidence came from the solid respect that the CVCC enjoyed in the USA. The fact that the CVCC was a system for reducing exhaust emissions to the level of the Muskie standards using only modifications to the engine itself and without the use of catalytic converters was already known to the general consumer. American consumers weren't necessarily interested in the technical details of the engine; what they wanted was an engine that cleared the new environmental regulations without sacrificing fuel efficiency. As for the mechanism used to reduce emissions, the simpler the better. And of course, the car should also be reasonably priced. The Civic had been the first to satisfy all of these demands at once.

Forty-three thousand of the 1974 model Civics had been sold in America. The 1975 model was due to go on sale in the fall of 1974 and a meeting was held between Honda and its American sales arm to decide on the number of vehicles to be shipped to the U.S. Yoshihide Munekuni, vice president of marketing at American Honda, spoke up.

"Based on the current situation, I believe we can sell 150,000 Civics in the U.S. alone."

Kiyoshi Kawashima and the other directors looked at Munekuni in amazement. The U.S. market was indeed huge, and with a little help from the media and word of mouth, it wasn't out of the question to sell 100,000 of a new model in a year. The difficulty was in maintaining and expanding sales in the following years, once things cooled down.

Kiyoshi Kawashima and the rest of the Honda kids also worried about the fact that the Civic had originally been designed for the Japanese market. It was an open question as to how long the topic of the CVCC would remain on the lips of American consumers. If the interest in the CVCC waned like a short-lived fad, Honda's efforts would be totally squandered. The Honda kids had to move cautiously.

For his part, Munekuni wasn't simply talking big. He had used Honda Research of America (HRA), the U.S. subsidiary of the Honda R&D Company, to do his homework. Immediately after the launch of the Civic, Munekuni had taken teams of Honda salesmen and HRA employees on a tour of American dealerships. While the salesmen discussed business concerns with the dealership, the HRA team would head to the garage to get first-hand information from the service staff about the kinds of cars customers wanted to buy. Everything Munekuni had seen and heard led him to believe that the customers' demands matched the overall concept of the Honda Civic. This was the basis for his prediction that Honda could sell 150,000 Civics a year.

During this time, American Honda increased its capital from fifty million to seventy-five million dollars. The company's annual sales were at five hundred and ninety million dollars, resulting in a profit of twenty-six million dollars after taxes. Calculated at an exchange rate of 300 yen to the dollar, this translated into 7.5 billion yen, which was almost on the same level as half a year's worth of operating profits at the Honda Motor Company itself (8.5 billion yen).

"If we spend the raised funds on enhancing our sales network," said Munekuni, running the calculations in his head, "I don't think 150,000 units a year is unreasonable."

American Honda's profits weren't due to the impressive sales of the Civic. Generally speaking, no matter how well an automobile sold, a good part of the profits had to be used to pay for various sales promotion activities—marketing, advertising. American Honda's profits were being driven by the incredible popularity of Honda's large-size motorcycles. The motorcycles had a higher profit margin than the cars, and they were selling like hotcakes.

While Honda's Super Cub had completely changed and softened the image of motorcycles on the U.S. market, the trend did not last. Before long, American consumers began to return to medium and large motorcycles with displacements of more than 250cc, and the leather-clad "rough rider" image also staged a comeback as well. In the days before the oil crisis, Nixon's decision to depart from the gold standard had slowed down the American economy, resulting in an extreme slump for the entire motorcycle industry. At its lowest point, the total amount of dead stock industry-wide exceeded some one million units—roughly equivalent to the total number of motorcycles sold in a year.

The oil crisis, however, dramatically changed the playing field. In 1974, sales of 750cc motorcycles jumped. The gasoline shortage showed no signs of letting up, and it appeared that Americans were turning from cars to the more fuel-efficient motorcycles for their daily transportation needs.

In both Japan and America, large motorcycles had a reputation for belonging to the younger generation. They also had a reputation for being dangerous, making it difficult for fathers and husbands to justify riding them. But in light of the gasoline shortage, the fact that they were significantly more fuel-efficient than automobiles made them an attractive alternative. Now, at the height of the crisis, large numbers of people, in particular those in the middle-aged group, were turning to large-sized motorcycles instead of cars as their main tools for transportation. Thanks to the oil crisis, the one million units of dead stock disappeared almost at once.

The retail price for a 750cc motorcycle in the U.S. was $1,800, roughly the same as a Civic. But the cost of manufacturing a motorcycle was less than half of the cost of manufacturing a car, making the former far more profitable to sell. The fact that they shared a similar price range should not be seen as proof that automobiles were particularly inexpensive, but rather that motorcycles were expensive products at the time.

Unlike automobiles, motorcycles were generally seen more as niche products for hobbyists than an actual form of transportation. Lowering the price wouldn't necessarily result in increased sales. Motorcycles were a product for which consumers were willing to pay up to get exactly what they wanted.

As a result of the oil crisis, American Honda not only managed to establish a firm base in the auto industry, it was also able to move its dead motorcycle stock and turn a high profit. Honda decided that it had benefited from a windfall, and that, rather than send the money back to Japan where it would be taxed, the company would use it to increase capital in Honda America.

No matter how confident and optimistic Munekuni may have been about the Civic, however, there was no way Kiyoshi Kawashima and the other directors would agree to raise the number of exports to 150,000 units on the spot. But Munekuni's confidence did play a major role in helping headquarters make the decision to abandon k-cars in favor of larger cars.

In the end, the Honda kids agreed to send 103,000 units of the 1975 model Civic to the United States, all of which sold. The following year, Honda increased the number to 150,000, but still couldn't meet the incredible demand for the car. Honda had long been unpopular among car dealers, but no more. At dealerships across the country, acquiring the right to sell Hondas was a new "American dream."

"The Accord gave Honda its foothold in the U.S. market," reminisces current HRA vice president Norimoto Otsuka, who joined Honda in 1963 alongside Irimajiri and Kawamoto. "The Civic sold well thanks to the market for low-polluting cars during the oil crisis. As other manufacturers introduced their own low-polluting cars, the sales of the Civic started to drop off. But the Accord was different. As a staff member here at HRA, I helped develop the first version.

I knew it would be a big hit even from the early stages of the design process. I know it just looked like a larger version of the Civic, but we used data we had collected directly from the dealers to tailor the Accord to the needs of our consumers."

A second oil crisis in 1979 brought on by the Iranian revolution proved another stroke of luck for Honda. Thanks to their previous experience, consumers didn't panic this time around. But it was a wake-up call to Americans who came to accept for good that oil was a limited natural resource. Just as before, lines of cars stretched from nearly every gas station. For the most part, consumers were resigned to the situation. Their one small attempt at resistance consisted of trading in their inefficient "Big Three" cars for smaller, more economical Japanese versions.

At the time, some thirty-four percent of the oil used in the United States was consumed as fuel for automobiles. The appearance of the Accord, which anticipated and catered to the needs and desires of American consumers, was perfectly timed to take advantage of the public's reappraisal of automobile-based society.

Inventory shortages would prove the main thorn in American Honda's side for the next ten years. While this may sound like an enviable problem, in fact it was severe enough to cause a scandal for the company. At the height of the shortage, an American executive at American Honda began asking dealers for under-the-table "kickbacks" in return for preference in the supply of the cars.

The main reason for the success of Honda's cars in the United States can be attributed to the simple fact that the company had managed to create, before any of its rivals, a product that addressed the growing demand among consumers for a low-polluting vehicle. Honda had demonstrated that simply following the cardinal rule in the business—listening to the customers and tailoring to their needs and desires—was the way to prosperity.

Although the first models of the Accord did use a modified Civic engine, the Accord was in fact the first car ever to be "tailor-made" based on customers' needs and requirements. It proved so successful that the American automobile magazine *Motor Trend* selected it as import of the year for 1976.

"When I visited Ford's R&D facility on business," recalls Kawamoto, "I spotted a new Accord in the employee parking lot one day. I overheard the staff talking about it, saying that 'the new Honda car is really amazing.'" When he heard the praise, Kawamoto knew that Honda had finally achieved its goal of becoming one of the world's major auto manufacturers.

All of Honda's early products had depended on Soichiro's engineering genius and inspiration. The Accord made it clear that the Honda kids had successfully harnessed the "solidarity of the ordinary" to create a hit product all on their own.

CHAPTER FIVE: THE WEIGHT OF THE DONS

The Honda Motor Company is a public corporation, and it's a pity that people tend to think of it as a private enterprise, just because I named it after myself. You can bet that if I had the chance to do things over, I wouldn't make the same mistake again. I've always drawn a clear line between my private and business lives.

—Soichiro Honda

An executive should notice things. It's men with an eye for detail that become executives. A man who simply rides herd on his subordinates is a field supervisor. A man who sticks to making sure they're on the right track is a manager. It's only the man who can look at the same problem from many different aspects that will make a true leader.

—Takeo Fujisawa

1

The 1973 oil crisis was a turning point for the Japanese economy, bringing about the end of the period of rapid growth and the dawn of a new era of stable growth. The wave of motorization, which had swept the country over the past ten years, had now reached a plateau, as a result of the crisis and the exhaust regulations. It seemed as if the Japanese auto industry would finally reach maturity. In fact, however, an unexpected increase in exports actually triggered another major growth spurt.

In 1973, just before the oil crisis, the Japanese auto industry produced 7.08 million vehicles. The following year, the number dropped 7.5 percent to 6.55 million, marking the first negative figure in the country's high-growth period. Domestic Japanese sales during this time fell 21.6 percent from 4.91 million to 3.85 million. On the other hand, exports increased from 2.07 million to 2.62 million vehicles and it was only this 26.7 percent increase in foreign sales that kept the plunge in overall production figures below the ten percent mark.

Domestic sales wouldn't exceed the record set in 1973 for another six years until 1979, and exports only continued to rise during this period. Finally, in 1980, export sales exceeded domestic sales at 5.67 million and 5.01 million vehicles, respectively.

The year 1980 also marked the first year that total production broke the ten million mark, rising to 10.04 million, an 11.4 percent increase over the previous year. In the United States, on the other hand, which had long dominated the world market for automobiles, production dropped to 8.01 million, a thirty percent decrease over the previous year. Almost overnight, Japan became the world's top manufacturer of automobiles by a three million-vehicle wide margin.

The first Japanese automobiles on the American market had been sold as inexpensive "budget cars." Ever since the oil crisis, however, they had gained a great deal of popularity as fuel-efficient "economy cars." Their reliability, features, and low price only served to cement the impression. With such a sterling reputation, it was no wonder that the cars sold like hotcakes.

These "economy cars" weren't just popular in America but also in Europe which had always been a major market for compact cars. Exports to Europe rapidly increased throughout the 1970s. Furthermore, demand for the cars increased in oil-rich countries in the Middle East as well.

Japan had exported only 420,000 vehicles to the United States in 1970. By 1975, this had ballooned to 920,000 and, in 1980—the year after the second oil crisis broke out—2.41 million vehicles were sent to America. The Japanese auto industry had managed to increase the number of exports by 5.7 times within just ten years. The two oil crises acted as "divine wind" in the sails of the Japanese auto industry. There can be little doubt that the tremendous growth in the Japanese automobile industry in the late 1970s owed largely to the rapid and intensive increase in exports to the U.S. At the same time, however, this rapid growth also brought with it a serious side effect: trade friction.

Today, Honda's strategy is to manufacture on-site to meet local demand, but this hadn't always been the case. Honda's reasons for manufacturing its motorcycles locally in twenty-eight countries around the world were mainly due to the political and economic circumstances in these countries, for example, high customs duties, or a ban on imports altogether. Cases where Honda opted for local production for purely economic reasons—such as to save on shipping costs by introducing a system known as "knock-down" production, in which unassembled parts are shipped to and assembled at the local destination—were rare.

Honda's experience in the motorcycle business gave it an advantage over competitors such as Toyota and Nissan when it came to foreign production. It allowed Honda to conduct on-the-scene market research and apply it directly to the automobile business. Knock-down production of motorcycles required only a fraction of the investment in capital and labor necessary for automobiles production.

Honda's venture into building facilities for local production of automobiles in the United States dates back to September 1974, when Ford first approached Honda about a business alliance.

"There's a growing trade imbalance between Japan and the United States," said Kihachiro Kawashima to Shigeyoshi Yoshida, who was working in procurement at the time. "If things continue, it's going to develop into outright friction. We can help address the problem by purchasing parts from the United States. I want you to go to the U.S. for three months and find potential parts suppliers for the Civic."

After graduating from university, Yoshida had joined Jidosha Kiki Co. (now Bosch Corporation), a company that supplied parts to Isuzu. Realizing the limitations of working for a second-tier supplier, however, he switched to Honda in 1962. Yoshida's prior experience at the parts supplier and his duties handling procurement at Honda made him an expert when it came to American parts and components.

Kihachiro Kawashima's order came as a shock to Yoshida. The U.S. automobile industry at that time was infatuated with large automobile designs; none of the Big Three had even so much as introduced a single compact car. What was more, it had been only two months since the Civic had gone on sale in Japan. Plans for exporting the car to the United States were still totally up in the air. Yoshida feared that the outcome of his trip to the U.S. was a foregone conclusion.

What could Kawashima be thinking? wondered Yoshida. The hierarchical nature of the Japanese company left Yoshida no room to openly question his orders. And so, in September, he packed his bags and spent three months in the United States, meeting with as many parts suppliers as he could. Just as he had expected, however, he couldn't manage to find a single part that was suitable for use in the Civic.

Yoshida turned in his report to Kihachiro Kawashima that December. Kawashima was not convinced.

"There must be something we can use there," he said. "I want you to go back over to America after the New Year and spend another three months there."

Kawashima's zeal for procuring parts from the United States wasn't based simply on the grand purpose of making a contribution to easing trade friction between Japan and the U.S.; he was thinking ahead and preparing for the eventual negotiations with Ford. If Honda decided to enter into a joint venture with Ford in the United States, local procurement of parts would be inevitable. Unaware of the drama behind the scenes, Yoshida flew to the Unites States and tried again with similar results. Still Kawashima would not let Yoshida drop the matter.

"I understand that there aren't any parts we can use in the Civic. But we're going to start exports to the United States this year. And once we do, we're going to have to source spare parts for repairs locally. We're going to found a new company in the U.S. called Honda International Trading. I'd like you to set up shop over there and establish a parts supply network for us in America."

Yoshida would end up staying in the United States for nearly twenty years. By the time he retired in 1992, he had obtained a green card and decided to stay in Los Angeles. He founded a consulting company called Yoshida & Associates that offered support to Japanese and American corporations.

Another turning point for Honda regarding local supply involved allegations of dumping. In August of 1975, the Union of Automobile Workers (UAW) filed a claim with the Department of the Treasury over what they felt were clear cases of European and Japanese auto manufacturers dumping their products on the U.S. marketplace. The list of companies accused even included subsidiaries of GM, Ford, and Chrysler.

In the beginning, the Japanese manufacturers largely underestimated the gravity of the situation, believing European manufacturers to be the real target of the allegations, with the Japanese simply being implicated by association. In May of 1976, however, when the Department of the Treasury concluded their preliminary investigation, only four manufacturers—Toyota, Nissan, Porsche, and Rolls Royce—were completely cleared of any wrongdoing. Other manufacturers, including Honda, were categorized as falling into a "gray area," where there was suspicion of dumping although the point would not be pressed in that particular instance.

Underlying the Department of the Treasury's decision to drop the case was Volkswagen's sudden decision to build a factory in the United States. Of all the companies that the UAW had accused of dumping, Volkswagen had been most likely to be found guilty. But it had successfully appeased the UAW with its decision to build a factory in the U.S., which promised employment opportunities for American autoworkers.

Of the Japanese automakers, Honda experienced the greatest shock. Up until the last minute, Kihachiro Kawashima, then vice president of sales, had prided himself on the legitimacy of Honda's business methods, declaring proudly, "Honda's sales in the U.S. are good but we've never given any discounts." Even within the auto industry, it was generally believed that Toyota and Nissan would be far easier to prosecute for such claims than Honda. Why then had Honda been lumped into the "gray area?" The most likely reason was because the company had not raised the price of its 1976 model automobiles by as large a margin as the other manufacturers.

Honda's directors gathered in the "collective directors' room" for a *waigaya* session. They concluded that although the United States generally had a tolerant trade policy, the auto industry was top on the list of the country's key industries and played a role in national security there. There would be no problems for foreign competitors so long as the Big Three were doing well. But in times of trouble, the U.S. government would undoubtedly step in and impose restrictions on imports, using dumping allegations as a pretext. The Department of the Treasury report was a message from the United States to foreign manufacturers that it wished to keep imports under control.

If Honda played ball with the U.S. government and reduced the number of cars it was exporting to America, it would cripple the development of the company. Honda's cars were selling well domestically, but the company still had a long way to go in order to catch up with Toyota and Nissan. The only way to survive as an independent auto manufacturer was to establish a firm base in the U.S. marketplace, where the Civic was achieving outstanding sales.

Honda's products only continued to gain popularity in America, and the company could expect to grow exponentially, as long as it managed to keep up the supply. If the pace kept up, Honda executives predicted that they would be able to catch up with, and possibly even overtake, Toyota and Nissan within five years. Restricting exports at this stage would cut off the company's future. The only conceivable way to avoid the tightening noose of import restrictions was to produce the cars locally. In other words, Honda needed to start building factories now before the trade friction got any worse.

At the time the exchange rate was 300 yen to the dollar. The average wage of a Japanese worker was far lower than that of his American counterpart. Furthermore, Japanese workers were known for their loyalty and dedication to quality and also enjoyed a good relationship with their employers. Given such conditions, it was almost unthinkable for any manufacturer, automotive or otherwise, to move production from Japan to the United States.

Honda had only two automobile factories, in Sayama and Suzuka, and both were rapidly approaching full capacity. Meanwhile, Mazda and Mitsubishi, who were vying with Honda for third place in the industry, had already bought land in Yamaguchi and Aichi prefectures, respectively, for new plants. Although Mazda had totally suspended exports to America in the wake of the failure of the RE, and Mitsubishi's capital tie-up with Chrysler had a restrictive impact on the company's exports to America, it was obvious that once Honda's rivals finally ironed out their problems, they would immediately start building the new factories. Honda would be left behind if it didn't take action.

The easiest way to increase production capacity was to follow the competitors' lead and build a new factory in Japan. But it came with a risk. If the U.S. government started restricting imports to protect the Big Three, the extra capacity would be of no use at all.

As had been the case with motorcycles, the U.S. market was rapidly growing into Honda's main source of income for the automobile business when the company was hit with the dumping allegations. Although none of Honda's directors dared to openly voice their conclusion, their minds were already made up at an early stage: they had no choice but to go back to Honda's basic philosophy of manufacturing on-site to meet local demand. As long as Honda stuck to this principle, it could avoid being shut out of the local market, no matter what circumstances arose.

The success of the Civic had filled American Honda's coffers. Normally, any profits made abroad would be transferred back to headquarters in Japan as dividends; under Honda's policy, however, instead of sending the earnings back to headquarters, the money was used to strengthen and expand local capacities. This policy not only applied to American Honda, but also to all Honda subsidiaries outside of Japan.

American Honda president Koichiro Yoshizawa was a strong advocate of striking while the iron was hot lest Honda lose a precious opportunity. He also maintained that profits made in the U.S. should stay in the U.S. and be used there, which coincided well with Soichiro's views on leaving profits to the subsidiary that had generated them. The fact that American Honda would bear the greater part of the costs for setting up a local production system made his position all the stronger.

Yoshizawa had joined Honda at the same time as Kume. He had started in accounting, but Fujisawa had spied a talent for business management and promoted him to sales. While Kihachiro Kawashima oversaw Honda's sales both domestically and abroad, it was widely assumed that Yoshizawa was next in line for his position.

When it came to designing a factory, the most important decision was production capacity. Conventional wisdom dictated that an automobile factory should have an output of between 200,000 and 250,000 vehicles per year. But such calculations didn't apply to Honda.

Both the Sayama and Suzuka factories had been originally built to manufacture motorcycles. After a series of extensive modifications, the factories were upgraded to manufacture automobiles as well. Apart from the N360, Honda hadn't created a car that was successful enough to warrant a dedicated factory, so the layouts of the manufacturing plants were changed freely to accommodate whatever design was being produced at the time.

For the U.S. factory, Honda decided to establish a "half-line," capable of manufacturing 100,000 vehicles per year. Because of the smaller production capacity, there would be less initial investment involved. But reducing the size would not completely remove the risk.

It went without saying that Honda lacked any sort of experience when it came to manufacturing goods in the United States. *Would Honda be able to ensure the quality of its automobiles, even when they were made by American workers?* This unspoken concern was the reason that, even though all the Honda executives were aware of the urgency of establishing a local production facility, none dared to openly broach the topic.

Meanwhile, in the factories of the Big Three, morale was at a nadir. American automotive workers commanded salaries of over twenty dollars an hour, the highest in any industry in the country. Even so, efficiency was low and workers staged frequent strikes. There were even cases of outright negligence, such as a Coca Cola bottle left in an engine compartment, or workers being caught smoking marijuana on the job.

In 1976, Honda hired an American consulting company, Fantus Consulting, to undertake a feasibility study for local production in the United States. Honda told the firm it was looking for land for a factory within a one-hour drive of a major airport. The company would use roughly one million square meters for a motorcycle factory at first, but expected to eventually expand the facility to manufacture automobiles, so the site needed to include ample room for expansion. The idea was to manufacture 100,000 Civics a year. Honda further specified that the land be somewhere in the southern portion of the American Midwest, so as to better serve the market on the east coast. For the time being, Honda planned to keep serving west coast customers with cars exported from Japan.

In addition to the consulting company, Honda organized a secret project team, led by Shigeyoshi Yoshida, who by then had been promoted to vice president of American Honda, to look into potential locations on their own as well.

Honda wasn't alone in its endeavors. At almost the same time, Nissan was working behind the scenes to establish a local manufacturing facility in the United States as well. The UAW had approached Ichiro Shioji, chairman of Jidosha Roren (federation of automobile workers' unions associated with Nissan), with a request for the company to build a factory in America, and Shioji had in turn approached Nissan. The president of the company, Tadahiro Iwakoshi, was enthusiastic about the idea and not only dispatched his own secret research group, but also visited the United States personally in spring 1977 to inspect potential factory sites. Although Iwakoshi's top priority was ensuring strong sales, he was also interested in local production as a way of giving an added dimension to the business. After visiting the U.S., Iwakoshi retired from his position of president to become vice chairman and was succeeded by Shun Ishihara.

Neither the new president Ishihara nor chairman Katsuji Kawamata, however, were optimistic about the payoff of establishing an American factory. They saw the costs as being too high and the reliability of the workers being too low, and decided against the idea. In fact, these were exactly the same issues facing Honda's executives.

In April of 1976, just before the Department of Treasury made its official decision regarding the dumping problem, the Ohio newspaper the *Columbus Citizen-Journal* carried a brief news agency report from Tokyo citing that Japanese auto manufacturers were considering building factories in the United States as a possible way of getting around the anti-dumping issue. Needless to say, the article did not name any specific companies.

Noticing the article, James Duerk, chief of the Ohio Department of Economic and Community Development, passed it along to governor James Rhodes.

The state of Ohio had been more active in attracting auto factories than any other state in the Midwest. The state had recently been working to sign a preliminary contract with Volkswagen when Pennsylvania successfully courted the company away. It had been a bitter pill for Ohio, and Rhodes and Duerk were determined not to let another opportunity slip through their fingers. Rhodes got to work at once.

"Let's go to Japan," he said.

Rhodes and Duerk asked the State Department to arrange appointments for them with Japanese auto manufacturers. In fact, they were so anxious to get the ball rolling that they left for Japan even before receiving a concrete answer.

The State Department successfully arranged meetings with Toyota, Nissan, and Honda. Rhodes and Duerk thoroughly explained Ohio's benefits, including its labor, geographical, tax, and transportation advantages, to the assembled executives of each company. In the end, however, Rhodes and Duerk were unable to discern which company was actually considering establishing a plant in America. Not one of the companies contacted them upon their return to the U.S.

The two had all but given up when, a year later in 1977, vice president Yoshida of American Honda contacted Rhodes out of the blue with a request for a personal meeting.

Fantus, the consulting company hired by Honda, had raised Ohio and Tennessee as high-potential candidates for factory sites. Honda had also conducted its own investigation, looking into Michigan, Illinois, Indiana, Missouri, and Kansas. The results of feasibility studies carried out on these seven states pointed to Ohio as the best choice for Honda's needs.

Honda employees scoured the Ohio countryside by helicopter and small airplane for potential sites. Whenever they found a likely spot, they rented cars and headed to see the area for themselves. For all their effort, however, there seemed to be no one site that clearly met the company's demands. Honda was at a complete loss for how to proceed. In the end, Yoshida decided to contact the governor to inform him unofficially of Honda's interest in building a factory and to ask for his advice, even though such a move risked giving away Honda's plans to rivals.

All that remained to be done now was the selection of the site for the factory. Taking the topography and the socioeconomic background of the area into consideration, Honda finally settled on open farmland bordering the Transport Research Center (TRC), about ten kilometers west of Marysville, which was a small town near Columbus with a population of 8,400. The area surrounding the site was state-owned land, meaning that Honda would be able to expand the facility as much as it needed to. The site also had easy access to Route 75—a highway connecting Detroit with cities to the south—and to a rail line. Together with senior managing directors Masami Suzuki and Kazuo Nakagawa, Shigeyoshi Yoshida finalized the decision in a hotel room in Columbus in June of 1977. President Kiyoshi Kawashima visited the site himself that summer, and a formal decision was taken by the board of directors shortly thereafter.

Governor Rhodes's wish had come true. Once the decision was made, Honda lost no time in advancing its plans. The state of Ohio also offered to give preferential treatment in the form of subsidies amounting to five million dollars to be used to improve nearby roads and public facilities, to bring the railroad close to the factory, and to set up the water supply and sewer systems. The contract was officially signed on October 11, 1977.

The plans called for Honda to purchase 870,000 square meters of land from the state of Ohio. Honda would spend 31 million dollars to build a 24,300-square meter factory, and then hire 500 workers and manufacture sixty thousand motorcycles per year. The factory was due to open in the middle of 1979. American Honda and the Honda Motor Company, investing ninety-five percent and five percent, respectively, would jointly establish Honda of America Manufacturing (HAM), which would be responsible for managing the new factory.

The contract also included the option to purchase another million square meters of land for an automobile plant in the future. The signing ceremony was held at a hotel in Columbus, with Honda vice president Kihachiro Kawashima in attendance.

"The exact timing will depend on demand, the exchange rate, and import regulations, but we hope to break ground on the automobile factory within no more than four years," Kawashima told Rhodes, somewhat optimistically.

For Honda, there wasn't a huge economic advantage to manufacturing motorcycles locally. But the company had taken the bold step because it looked upon the new factory in Ohio as a test for the next stage of Honda's plan: the production of automobiles in America.

2

Once the dust had settled over exhaust regulations, the U.S. government came out with a new requirement for the automakers: increasing fuel efficiency. Manufacturers would be required to bring up the average mileage for their cars to 27.5 miles per gallon—the level maintained by Japanese cars—by 1985 or they would be charged a penalty.

The bulk of the Big Three manufacturers' product lines consisted of large cars. The only way to meet the new regulations was reducing the size of the automobiles. The Big Three decided to spend a total of eighty billion dollars—3.5 times the cost of the Apollo project that had put man on the moon—in their quest to develop small cars. General Motors alone had budgeted fifty billion dollars to the project. Ford chairman Philip Caldwell described the efforts of the Big Three to create compact cars as the "largest and most extensive peacetime industrial project in human history."

All signs pointed to an inevitable economic showdown between the Untied States and Japan over compact cars. The American auto industry had a broad base and was even linked to national security. American manufacturers of consumer electronics such as color televisions had already lost the battle to Japanese manufacturers. While New York's Wall Street was still thronged with automobile and steel analysts, the number of domestic consumer electronics analysts had dwindled to almost nothing.

It was obvious that the U.S. government would try to turn the tables on the Japanese via import regulations once it became clear that the Big Three were losing ground. The Japanese companies most adversely affected by such regulations would be those with the highest export-sales ratios, and that list included Honda. Honda exported more than sixty percent of the products it produced. The only way to avoid friction would be to start local production the U.S. before the market giants Toyota and Nissan did. The new motorcycle factory in Ohio would be a test bed for the production of automobiles in the United States. Construction on the factory began in the middle of 1978 and was completed according to schedule a year later. Production began in September of 1979.

Yoshida had thought that his duties in America would conclude with the decision for the site for the factory. Upon returning to headquarters, however, he was told to return to America to study the feasibility of automobile production.

What Honda had not counted on was that the Iranian revolution in the spring of 1979 would trigger a second "oil shock" in the U.S. and plunge the American auto industry into another crisis. Once again, long lines stretched from American gas stations. Highly fuel-efficient Japanese cars and trucks began selling at premium prices.

The demand for Japanese cars had exploded into a full fad in the United States. All a dealer had to say was "made in Japan" to close a deal. The automobiles of the Big Three, on the other hand, were all but ignored. Exports from Japan to the U.S. shot up dramatically. It was only a matter of time before the growing trade friction escalated into a full-blown political issue. Japanese automakers realized that they needed to exercise self-control or risk facing an even more aggravated situation.

Honda found itself in a tight spot. In the U.S., it was common practice to maintain a stock of four months worth of products, including those in circulation. Honda had less than two months worth on hand. Some car dealers even threatened legal action against the company, claiming that they were losing both customers and profit because Honda was failing to fulfill its responsibility as a supplier. American Honda's standard contract with the dealers stated that Honda was obliged to provide as many units as the dealer deemed necessary unless doing so would harm Honda's business as a whole.

Honda, for its part, was not restricting the number of automobiles it shipped to the United States in order to avoid friction; the company was simply having difficulties keeping pace with demand. But the United States is a contract-based society, and American dealers weren't particularly sympathetic to Honda's excuses for failing to fulfill its obligations.

Amidst the controversy, Honda's directors made the decision to move forward with plans to produce automobiles in the United States. As planned, Yoshida oversaw the feasibility study. With the help of the people in charge of procurement and supply at headquarters, Yoshida and his team made thorough calculations based on local parts supply. The results were miserable. There was no way to break even. In fact, sourcing the parts locally promised a deficit that would continue to grow at a rapidly accelerating rate every year.

Al Kinzar, HAM's first local hire, looked over the results glumly. *I joined Honda because they were planning to manufacture automobiles in the United States. But now it looks like it simply won't happen.*

On Christmas Eve, president Kiyoshi Kawashima and the senior managing directors at Honda sequestered themselves in a Tokyo hotel to discuss American production. Kiyoshi Kawashima had barely slept since he had given orders to begin the feasibility studies. He felt the urgency for local production more than anyone. But in the end a feasibility study, even one as thorough as Yoshida's, was just that—a study. There was no way to determine the exact risk facing the company. In the end, everything rested on the president's decision.

At times like this, Kiyoshi Kawashima often reflected upon an Indian philosophy that Fukuzo Kawahara, the former vice president of Mitsubishi Bank who acted as Fujisawa's mentor, had described to him. It said life was too complex to divide into simply "yes" or "no" answers and that there were actually four fundamental solutions to a given problem. These were "yes," "yes and no," "neither yes nor no," and "no." Kawahara had advised using this set of four potential conclusions when facing a difficult decision. While the use of such a method may appear to the uninitiated as an expression of indecision, Kawashima was convinced that by applying this strategy, he would arrive at the right conclusion.

Applying the four possible outcomes to the question of whether or not to build an automobile factory in the U.S., Kiyoshi Kawashima had reached a personal conclusion of "yes and no." Naturally, he kept this choice to himself as he allowed the discussion to begin at the hotel. Just as he expected, the debate quickly grew heated.

"It's true that the studies conducted in the U.S. make it clear that we're facing an uphill battle. But if we don't move now, we'll never be able to build factories in the United States," said one director.

"Right now we're looking at getting everything locally, including major components like engines and transmissions. This is what is making the issue so difficult. If we send the main parts from Japan and assemble the rest in Ohio, we might very well be able to ensure that the products have the same quality as those we make in Japan," said another.

The discussion continued.

"The quality of labor issue is the real crux of the matter. But judging from the results from our motorcycle factories, I don't think there is such drastic difference between American and Japanese workers."

"The study says we'll be in the red. But what about cutting back production to just one model? Could we break even that way?"

"If we are looking to make a profit, we should be producing the Accord. There's more of a margin there than on the Civic."

"The locally manufactured products should counted as an addition to our exports from Japan. That means aiming for production of around 10,000 per month. If sales go up, we expand the facility. So we'll need to leave some extra room for future expansion needs."

"If we do that, we'll only need to put up between two hundred to two hundred and fifty million dollars in initial investments."

"If that's all we'll need, American Honda should be able to handle the entire amount."

"There might be a need to build engines locally in the future as well. Ideally, we'd put the engine factory adjacent to the assembly line. But is that possible? I guess we should settle for the assembly line first. We can talk about expanding it later."

"Are we going to register with the UAW? I suppose it would be up to the employees to make the final decision."

"We should start laying the groundwork as soon as possible so that we can start construction within a year. Two years should be enough to complete the factory. That means it can go into operation at the end of 1982."

The *waigaya* continued, the directors exchanging thoughts and ideas from their own areas of expertise. Towards the end of the discussion, someone jokingly said, "Building an automobile factory is a relatively small investment. Even if it failed, it wouldn't be a mortal blow to the company. If things don't work out, we can just close down the factory and sell off the machines as scrap."

Finally, president Kiyoshi Kawashima came out his decision of both "yes and no."

"Building an automobile factory is risky," said Kawashima. "But Honda has been known to take big risks at crucial moments in the past. Besides, we're only talking of an investment of two hundred million dollars. That's less than it would cost to build a new building for headquarters. A new building won't generate profits, but our new factory will, if we play our cards right."

Tension over Japanese automobile imports in the United States continued to grow on a daily basis. Toyota and Nissan continued to drag their feet over local production. Although Honda's feasibility study predicted that Honda might well end up in the red with the project, the company directors knew that they could use the new factory to turn the growing trade friction to their advantage.

The directors finally made the decision to go ahead with the project on Christmas Eve. A few days later, on the last day of 1979, a newspaper journalist came to see vice president Hideo Sugiura at his home.

"Sugiura-san, we're going to be running an article in tomorrow morning's paper about Honda's decision to build a factory in the United States. It will, of course, be the top story on our front page. I have a reliable source. I just wanted you to know beforehand," said the journalist.

Sugiura couldn't believe it. *How did this leak so quickly? True, we reached a positive conclusion in last week's meeting, but still... Not that it makes any difference now*, he thought. In a few hours, the New Year would begin. The countdown to the tumultuous eighties had already begun.

"We've been discussing the possibility within the company for some time," said Sugiura, wearing his best poker face. "But we haven't made an official decision yet. I'm afraid this isn't quite the scoop you think it is."

The issue had not yet been brought before any of the official decision-making bodies at Honda, such as the executive council or the board of directors. In fact, Honda had not even conveyed the directors' decision to Yoshida and his team who were responsible for the feasibility study. With trade friction already becoming a political problem, Honda also needed to signal its intentions to the Ohio state government beforehand as well. Everything had been arranged to start after the New Year holidays. If the newspapers disclosed the plans at such a sensitive stage, it would throw everything into turmoil. All the preparations the directors had so carefully made would amount to nothing.

In the end, the story appeared at the top of the front page of the *Nihon Keizai Shimbun* on January 11.

"HONDA DECIDES TO MANUFACTURE ITS CARS IN THE USA / MONTHLY RUNS OF 15,000 / PLANT TO OPEN IN 1982 / OVER 2,000 WORKERS TO BE HIRED LOCALLY / PART OF COMPANY'S EFFORTS TO PREEMPT TRADE FRICTION " (*Nihon Keizai Shimbun*, morning edition, January 11, 1980)

The news traveled around the world at lightning speed. Quoting the *Nihon Keizai Shimbun*, the *New York Times* ran the article among its top news stories.

The directors of Honda often based their decisions on principles. For example, when a reporter once questioned him about personnel matters, Soichiro told him:

"If we can't find any good successors within the company, there are still billions of candidates out there in the world. We will just choose the most appropriate one."

Soichiro had made the comment to emphasize that Honda was not a family enterprise.

The decision regarding local production in the United States was based on another principle: that of manufacturing on-site to meet local demand. Kiyoshi Kawashima's final decision of "yes and no" had stood for "no" in terms of profitability, but "yes" in terms of principle.

"Really, building a factory in America was the only choice we could have made," said vice president Sugiura, responsible for the U.S. factory project. "Of course, it would be cheaper and easier to ensure quality in Japan. But if we built the factory here, just when the trade friction issue was heating up, we were sure to be severely criticized. It may be more difficult for a Japanese manufacturer to make products in the United States, but there is steady demand there, and building a factory creates jobs and brings benefits to the local area as well. We do business in the United States, so we see it as a duty to help the United States in some way. This is precisely why Honda hired a local company to build the factory as well. Other companies used a Japanese construction company and brought workers over from Japan. We at Honda feel that we simply did the right thing, something that we were supposed to do. There was nothing heroic or praiseworthy about it."

Sugiura was surprised at the outpouring of public support he received, from both within and outside the company.

Soichiro also applauded the Honda kids' decision:

"Kiyoshi Kawashima made the decision not because the Americans asked us to come, but rather because it would benefit Honda in the future. Running a business has nothing to do with politics or relations between countries. I don't trust either the Japanese or the U.S. government. If you simply rely on the government or the ministries, you're not being a good business manager. In this respect, Kawashima did well."

At the same time, Soichiro's competitive spirit was also sparked.

General Motors was small once, too, he thought. *Now Honda might even stand a chance of beating GM one day. The Ohio factory is the first step. When I started the company, I had no money. I could only build a tiny and cramped little factory that gave the "kids" no end of trouble. The United States has something Japan never will: large amounts of open space. And it comes at a low price. It's incredible! The kids should take advantage of this vast land and build a factory they can be proud of.*

Meanwhile, Nissan had arrived at a decision, which was almost the direct opposite of Honda's. At the beginning of February, just after Honda had made its decision to build its U.S. factory, the Jidosha Soren (Confederation of Japan Automobile Workers' Unions), led by Ichiro Shioji, invited Douglas Fraser, chairman of the UAW, to Japan. Fraser pressed the other Japanese manufacturers to build factories in the United States as well, and met with various government officials to address the growing issue of trade friction.

In response, Nissan made the decision to open a compact truck factory in the United States. Toyota, for its part, did no more than hire the Stanford Research Institute, Arthur D. Little, and Nomura Research Institute for a combined one million dollars worth of feasibility studies.

Shun Ishihara, president of Nissan, explained to the public that compact trucks were the logical choice because of the relatively long period between model changes and the fact that the vehicles didn't require as many parts as passenger cars. While this was all true, the real reason lay in the fact that Ishihara was far more interested in circumventing customs duties on his company's compact trucks than in resolving the trade friction.

In the early 1970s, West Germany had raised customs duties in response to a rapid increase in poultry imported from the United States. In response, the United States raised duties on compact trucks by twenty-five percent. This was the so-called "chicken war," and it had the effect of virtually shutting Volkswagen's trucks out of the U.S. marketplace.

Since these duties affected Japanese auto manufacturers as well, the Japanese manufacturers came up with the idea of detaching the cargo beds from the trucks' chassis, exporting them separately, and re-assembling the trucks in the United States. The unassembled trucks were called "cab chassis" and taxed at the lower rate for auto parts; the gambit allowed Japanese manufacturers to pay only four instead of twenty-five percent in customs duties on their products.

American customers found small Japanese trucks convenient, as they could be used not only for leisure purposes but also for commuting to work and for hauling loads. Demand for the compact trucks skyrocketed in the U.S. almost from the moment of their introduction. In 1975, a total of 250,000 trucks had been shipped from Japan to America. By 1980, the number had jumped to 580,000. This was still smaller than the number of passenger cars exported to the U.S.A., but compact trucks grew into a reliable source of profit for the Japanese manufacturers.

In May of 1980, however, the Department of Treasury made a sudden decision to revamp the schedule for customs duties so that cab chassis would be treated as unassembled trucks, rather than auto parts. The Japanese manufacturers filed a case with the U.S. tax court, and made preparations to also press a complaint before the General Agreement on Tariffs and Trade (GATT). Still, President Carter declined to intervene and the new duties took effect as planned, as soon as the ninety-day notice period expired on August 21.

Customs duties on cab chassis jumped from four to twenty-five percent, undermining the price competitiveness of the Japanese compact trucks overnight. The Big Three, who had long been waiting for just such a chance, took the opportunity to increase their shares in the compact truck market.

Under the circumstances, Nissan's decision was not unreasonable. But one thing is clear: if Nissan kicked off local production efforts in America with automobiles rather than trucks, it would not have ended up trailing behind Honda in the U.S. marketplace.

The issue of local production also caused Nissan's labor relations to grow more intense and confrontational. The situation reached a head when, in January of 1981, Nissan announced plans to begin local production in the U.K. It wouldn't be until four years later that Nissan finally made the decision to modify its American truck assembly line to manufacture automobiles. Today, Nissan has yet to recover from its late start. Looking back, Nissan's decision to delay local car production was a major miscalculation. And Honda exploited it to push ahead of Nissan in the U.S. auto market.

3

Honda's youthful image stemmed mainly from the fact that its two founders had resigned at the ages of sixty-six and sixty-two, and that the new president, their successor, was only forty-five years old. Even in the late 1970s, the average age of a Honda director was slightly over fifty. At the same time, the youthful atmosphere at the company wasn't simply due to the directors' age. Honda's top executives were also deeply sensitive and curious about current trends.

Automobiles are essentially fashion products, and understanding fashion requires sensitivity above all else. This "sensitivity" requirement doesn't simply apply to the individuals designing the cars. In fact, such qualities were most necessary in the top managers, the decision-makers of the company. When the mass media began reporting the need for increased attention to consumer needs in the auto industry, one manufacturer had its managers get together and take a bus tour through the city to "brush up on their sensitivity." Learning of the incident, the Honda directors burst into laughter in their "collective directors' room" at headquarters.

"They must really be desperate," said one. "Do they really think that a bus tour will be of any use in 'brushing up' their sensitivity? All of us here, we commute to work by train; I suppose you could say that we're 'brushing up' our sensibilities every day!"

Unlike other companies, Honda did not use chauffeurs to shuttle directors to and from the office. In fact, this tradition continues to the present day. President Kawashima drove himself in to work. Most of the other directors, who lived in the suburbs of Tokyo, commuted by train. At one point, the Secretarial Office had proposed a chauffeuring system for managing directors and higher-ranking executives, but the idea came to nothing.

"Certainly not. If I have a chauffeur pick me up, I'll have to get up an hour earlier than if I come in by train. It'd be a big hassle. One should be able to come to the office whenever one wants," said one director.

Another suggestion from the Secretarial Office also met with flat rejection: breakfast meetings. "It'll just cause more stress for everyone," the directors said.

At Honda, the higher one's title, the later one came to the office. Ten o'clock in the morning was an average arrival time for a director. The directors showed up according to their own schedules; some, for example, Noboru Okamura, Honda's second chairman, occasionally took things even further.

"When I got on the train yesterday morning," he is known to have said, "I suddenly realized just how beautiful the weather was. I flipped through my schedule book and saw I didn't have any meetings scheduled for that day. The idea of heading to the office seemed almost absurd, so I got off, took a nap in the park, and went back home."

Skipping work was also part of president Kiyoshi Kawashima's routine. When he didn't have any meetings to attend, he sometimes stayed at his home in Nerima, Tokyo. In the early summer months, he sunbathed naked in his yard. If a journalist happened to drop by that evening, he would say:

"I've been playing golf with clients all day today. I suppose that's why I look so tanned! The sun's rays are very strong at this time of year, you know?"

Honda's directors firmly believed in taking breaks whenever they could, because their responsibilities meant late nights and working weekends and holidays whenever there was a problem. In addition, they knew that if they showed up on days without previously scheduled meetings, the Secretarial Office would inevitably set some up just to kill their time. It was far more effective to work from home.

Honda's directors were known for their independent spirit. When the directors had a golf tournament, those who wanted a few drinks afterwards would come by train, golf bags in tow, while those with more stoic inclinations would drive their own cars to the gathering spot. Generally speaking, the directors didn't socialize after business hours. They were in the same room together every day where they could discuss everything they needed to at any time. It made more sense for them to use their free time to get together with people outside the company to broaden their horizons. Honda's freedom-loving corporate culture originated from Soichiro's love of parties and Fujisawa's hands-off style of managing his subordinates. Honda's system was built up in such a way as to make sure that the business kept going even if the top management came in a few hours late or even took a day or two off. An invisible discipline ran through Honda's directors and down into the company as a whole.

Honda's supreme decision-making authority rested in the executive council, which consisted of the seven men at the level of senior managing director and above with representative rights. Those at the managing director level and below were organized into three specialized groups, which focused on personnel, products, or finance. Honda had begun to implement a system where all information gathered from inside and outside of Honda was categorized into one of the three specialties and discussed according to certain set standards.

As a matter of principle, members of the executive council were not assigned any specific responsibilities. The managing directors below them also did not take on responsibilities as representatives of a particular department or office, but simply belonged to one of the three specialized groups. A good part of the actual responsibility in each department was delegated to the middle management, while the executives were expected to make appropriate decisions based on a broad view of carefully screened information. The "collective directors' room" system carefully crafted by Fujisawa was now coming into full operation.

Rather than physical youth, being a Honda director demanded having a youthful mind. That being said, physical age could hardly be ignored either. How could Honda maintain the actual youthfulness of its executives? The traditional "first come, first go" system of enforced retirement couldn't be applied at Honda, as too many of the company's top men had been recruited mid-career rather than being lifetime hires straight out of high school or college. The only way to be fair about it would be ousting the oldest first.

Kihachiro Kawashima—the sales guru responsible for making HONDA a household name around the world—announced his own retirement at a board meeting in May of 1979. The statement of accounts for fiscal 1978 was excellent. Thanks to strong U.S. sales, Honda was enjoying the highest sales and profits in the history of the company, and all signs predicted sales of more than one trillion yen for the following year. At the time in Japan, there were about eleven manufacturing companies that boasted sales figures of more than a trillion yen, but Honda would be the first company founded in the post-war era to join their ranks.

Kawashima took the opportunity to leave Honda on an upbeat note. His retirement at such a relatively young age shocked the industry. Of the original four senior managing directors working under Soichiro and Fujisawa, Takao Shirai had retired young as well, at the age of fifty-five in 1975. But Shirai had a quiet personality, and his responsibilities had been in general affairs, which meant that he rarely appeared in front of the media, so his retirement hadn't drawn nearly the level of attention that Kawashima's had.

Although unrelated to one another, two of the upper echelon at Honda shared the last name of Kawashima: president Kiyoshi Kawashima and vice president Kihachiro Kawashima. To distinguish between the two, employees called Kiyoshi "Euro-Kawa" since Europe had been his first foreign assignment at Honda. Kihachiro, on the other hand, was called "Ame-Kawa" ("American-Kawa") because of his time spent for Honda in America.

Kihachiro Kawashima, or "Ame-Kawa," was only fifty-nine years old. Soichiro believed that his directors should work as hard as possible until they "burned out." The tradition changed over time, however, and it became more popular instead to leave the company while one still had some energy left for a fresh start and while one's co-workers still were sorry to see one go. Kihachiro Kawashima believed that this new trend should become the company standard. In order for that to happen, he himself, as the oldest of the directors in the front line of the business, would have to take the first step. It was the right time to make his exit.

This was the conclusion Kihachiro Kawashima had arrived at after much deliberation. Needless to say, the prospect of leaving his work saddened him. Even though it was his own decision to retire, he still felt that there was so much more he could do. But as difficult as it was, he knew the decision was the right one.

Kawashima was able to overcome his feelings of wanting to do "so much more" for the company because he had a secret dream. After retiring from Honda, Kawashima planned to establish a new business in Los Angeles, which he considered a second home.

Kihachiro Kawashima had first moved to Los Angeles in 1959 under orders from Fujisawa to establish American Honda and had remained there for over ten years. When America Honda started taking off, Kawashima brought his family over from Japan and bought a house in the suburbs, thinking that he could well end up living there for the rest of his life.

Kawashima's family loved life in the U.S. even more than Kawashima himself. Still, even though he was a director, Kawashima was first and foremost a Honda employee; if ordered by the company, he would have to return to Japan.

"Why don't you quit and start your own business in L.A.?" his family suggested.

As long as Kawashima worked for Honda, however, he knew he couldn't do anything that might harm the company. All the same, the more time he spent time in Los Angeles, the stronger his desire became to start a new business there. Each time he felt such an urge, he told himself that it wouldn't be too late to start again after he retired from Honda.

Kihachiro Kawashima's dream centered on starting his own automobile dealership. Naturally, he would sell Honda's products. By doing so, he wanted to become a role model for Honda dealerships across the United States. He also saw it as a wonderful way to show his gratitude to the company.

Working as a dealer would mean working under his former subordinates, but

Kawashima didn't mind. And although Honda had a rule barring Honda directors from working for rival companies after their retirement, Kawashima believed that working as a dealer in the U.S., and what's more, a part of the Honda dealership network that he himself had toiled to set up, should pose no problems whatsoever.

In preparation for his future plans, Kihachiro Kawashima chose not to sell his house in Los Angeles even after he was ordered back to Japan. Traditionally, Honda vice presidents acted as an advisor for a certain period of time after their retirement. Kawashima planned to spend the time preparing for the new business.

Kawashima openly discussed his dream with those around him. He knew that if he were to actually, he would have to obtain permission from Fujisawa. The best way to find out how Fujisawa felt about the plan, figured Kawashima, was to talk to as many people as he could so that Fujisawa would eventually hear about it. One day, Kawashima learned exactly what Fujisawa thought. According to an employee, Fujisawa had said:

"Honda isn't the small backstreet workshop it used to be. It's a large corporation now. The vice president is second to the president as the top manager. What would happen if this new business went wrong? It would hurt Honda just as badly as it would hurt Kawashima. What's more, not only was Ame-Kawa former president of American Honda, he was the one who established the foundations of the company. Ame-Kawa is also a big name in L.A. If such a man founded a dealership there, the employees at American Honda would feel pressured to support him no matter what. Even when supplies run short, they would make sure that Ame-Kawa will get what he needs. If Ame-Kawa received such beneficial treatment, you can bet it would upset the other dealers. On a personal level, I wish I could help him make his dream a reality. But not with this sort of plan."

Learning of Fujisawa's views on the subject, Kihachiro Kawashima gave up his dream. The last thing he wanted to do was bite the hand that had fed him for so long.

At roughly the same time, Ichiro Isoda, president of Sumitomo Bank, was readying a secret plan to recruit Kihachiro Kawashima for the presidency of Mazda. Isoda was working to improve Mazda's failing performance, acting as the middleman as the company secretly re-opened the negotiations with Ford on the capital tie-up that had been called off under Kohei Matsuda's presidency. Under Isoda's direction, Mazda and Ford had finally agreed to the tie-up and a public announcement was made in May.

Although the nominal president of Mazda was Yoshiki Yamazaki—a Mazda man from the start who had worked his way up the ranks—actual power resided in vice president Tsutomu Murai and managing director Hiroshi Mineoka, who had been sent to Mazda from Sumitomo Bank. The first oil crisis had sent Mazda into a business slump, from which the company still had not completely recovered. Feeling that Mazda wouldn't be able to continue on its own in the long term, Isoda had arranged the alliance with Ford.

In order to conduct business on equal footing with Ford, however, Mazda needed to bolster its top management. It wasn't healthy from a business stand-point to allow people closely tied with Sumitomo Bank to control Mazda's busi-ness interests forever. And Mazda's head office was located in Hiroshima, where Sumitomo Bank's history of mass layoffs and transferring workers to dealerships had made it unpopular with the people of the region so that sending one of its own men to act as president was next to impossible. The ideal solution was to head-hunt a capable successor from a rival.

The most pressing needs at Mazda were achieving higher domestic sales and reconstructing its American sales network. Kihachiro Kawashima was an expert in both. On top of this, Kihachiro had been in charge of Honda's negotia-tions with Ford and had a good perspective of the American company. Although Philip Caldwell had replaced Lee Iacocca as president of Ford, the company's top executives, including chairman Henry Ford II, thought highly of Kawashima's business management skills. And at fifty-nine, Kawashima was just the right age: in a typical Japanese company, he would still be just be beginning to mature as a top manager. Isoda saw him as a perfect fit for Mazda in every way.

In the end, however, Isoda's headhunting plan never came to fruition. After quietly investigating, Isoda learned that scouting Kawashima would be not only lead to a full-scale war between Mazda and Honda, but also potentially cripple re-lations between Sumitomo Bank and Mitsubishi Bank, which acted as Honda's main bank. The final deciding factor was Isoda's realization that even in retire-ment, Fujisawa still exerted a fair amount of influence behind the scenes at Honda.

Isoda would need Fujisawa's blessing to scout Kihachiro. While he had never met Fujisawa face to face, Isoda had heard through acquaintances at Mitsubishi Bank that he could be a tough man to win over. As long as Kawashima was a disciple of "Don" Fujisawa, it would be no use approaching Honda with customary courtesy. Perfect match or no, trying to headhunt Kihachiro would be a losing battle. It would be best to give up before the plan came out in the open and brought about any hard feelings or embarrassment. Isoda abandoned the idea.

And so Kihachiro Kawashima gave up his dream of starting a dealership in L.A., just as Isoda gave up his hopes of recruiting Kawashima for Mazda. Kawashima retired, as planned, to become an advisor at Honda. In the world of the Honda Motor Company, however, the post of advisor was a nominal one and those filling the position were not expected to actually do any work. When cor-porate headquarters became cramped and was moved from the Yaesu building near Tokyo Station to the Yashica building in Harajuku in 1974, the advisors took up residence in the old Yaesu building together with Honda's subsidiaries and affiliated organizations such as the Honda Foundation. It became very rare for re-tired directors to appear at the new headquarters in Harajuku. Once a month, an active director would be dispatched from Harajuku to Yaesu, where he briefed the advisors as to the current state of the business over lunch.

Former directors received generous pensions, which made sure that they could live comfortably without ever needing to take another job. Kihachiro Kawashima thought about moving to back to Los Angeles with his family and living in leisure there, but felt it was too early to cut ties and go into complete retirement.

In 1984, five years after retiring from Honda, Kawashima was offered the presidency of the Shinyou-jouhou Center (currently the Credit Information Center Corporation), which had been founded under the auspices of the Ministry of International Trade and Industry (MITI). Toshio Nakamura, a former MITI official and then executive director of Japan Automobile Manufacturers Association, Inc. (JAMA), had recommended Kawashima for the job.

"Sounds like they're making a solid contribution to society," said Fujisawa when Kihachiro asked for his advice. "I would say go ahead."

The same year, Kihachiro received an award for outstanding contribution to business from the University of California. It was the closure he needed to finally let go of his business plans. He sold his home in L.A., putting down roots in Japanese soil once and for all.

Kihachiro Kawashima's retirement from Honda at the young age of fifty-nine had been big news in the auto industry. The year after his retirement, Michihiro Nishida, the first vice president to have joined the company without any personal connections, retired at an even younger—fifty-six—to become advisor. After retiring, Nishida made it his new lifework to become a sort of storyteller for Honda, spreading the tale of Honda's history and the business management practices of its founders through books and speaking engagements.

The main reason that had led Kihachiro Kawashima, Shirai, and Nishida to early retirements was the knowledge that they were all older than president Kiyoshi Kawashima. When they had all been directors together, they could speak to each other as equals on almost any topic; now that Kiyoshi Kawashima was president, however, things were different and they felt obliged to treat each other with a certain amount of reserve. The three men wanted to take the initiative and step aside in favor of creating a favorable environment for the younger leader.

Honda's "out with the old, in with the new" approach, which had started with the retirement of the two founders, became a tradition at the company. After the retirement of Kihachiro Kawashima and Nishida, younger directors were brought in and the average age of a full-time Honda director fell below fifty.

That being said, Fujisawa didn't hesitate to call in an older man as an outside advisor to keep the balance. One such man was Takezo Shimoda, Japan's former ambassador to Belgium and the United States. Shimoda had been ambassador when Honda had built its motorcycle factory in Belgium. This had led to Shimoda's appointment as chairman of the board of directors of the Honda Foundation, which was founded by Soichiro. Another outside advisor was Toshio Nakamura, chairman of Mitsubishi Bank, Honda's main bank. Fujisawa aimed to use the men as a check and balance against the youth of Honda's directors.

4

The retirement in rapid succession of Kihachiro Kawashima and Nishida, Honda's two most well known vice presidents, served to maintain Honda's youthfulness and, at the same time, marked the end of the era of collective decision-making by the four senior managing directors and of the "troika system," consisting of President Kiyoshi Kawashima and directors Kihachiro Kawashima and Nishida, which succeeded it. Decisions were still made collectively, but the system now included a younger executive, one who would lead the next generation of Honda's top management. This new director, appointed in 1979, was only thirty-nine years old, which caused waves throughout the auto industry.

The new director was none other than Shoichiro Irimajiri, who had joined Honda in 1963. It wasn't common for such a young man to work at such a high level in a trillion-yen corporation, and the story attracted much attention from the media. And since he was not related to either Soichiro or Fujisawa, the public viewed his promotion as purely merit-based.

At Honda, which was a relatively young company being only established after WWII, young executives were hardly uncommon. President Kiyoshi Kawashima had been promoted to an executive position at the age of thirty-four, and Michihiro Nishida became an executive in his eleventh year at Honda at the age of thirty-nine, like Irimajiri. But the difference was that they had all been promoted when Honda was still a small company. In fact, because of the size of the company and the lack of human resources, the founders had had no choice but to use talented young men.

When Fujisawa and Soichiro were still on the front lines of the business, Fujisawa had applied a strict system of punishment and reward to his employees. If an employee had the skills, he would be promoted to executive regardless of age. But the sword cut both ways. If it turned out that an executive wasn't capable, he would not even be allowed to serve out the usual term of two years but be replaced after, in some cases, only six months or a year. That being said, even after firing an executive, Fujisawa made sure to take care of him by placing him in a Honda subsidiary. Fujisawa's style of managing his executive personnel was clear and easy to understand.

Kiyoshi Kawashima maintained Fujisawa's system and even took it a little further. He set the mandatory retirement age for executives at sixty—the same age as for regular employees—and also pledged that no one person would hold the same title, i.e., director, managing director, senior managing director, or vice president, for more than ten years. This meant that if Irimajiri, for example, after being promoted to director remained where he was without receiving any further promotions, he would automatically retire at the age of forty-nine. Kihachiro Kawashima and Nishida's voluntary retirement served to cement the early retirement system all the more.

As expected, the mass media almost immediately began to look upon Irimajiri as a future candidate for president of Honda. When Kiyoshi Kawashima promoted Irimajiri, he did so with strict orders for Irimajiri to avoid direct contact with the mass media for a solid year after his promotion. Before Irimajiri, several other young employees had been promoted to executive positions while still in their thirties. Some couldn't handle the pressure at their age, or had turned arrogant and overly self-confident, leading to their early dismissal and transfer to subsidiaries. To avoid another such situation, Kiyoshi Kawashima completely isolated Irimajiri from the mass media. Irimajiri kept his promise to Kawashima and never appeared once in the media spotlight during his first year as a Honda director.

Why was Irimajiri promoted to director at such a young age? True, Kiyoshi Kawashima had always looked upon him as a younger brother, as any of the Honda R&D employees knew. But if that were the sole reason behind his promotion, Kawashima would indeed be guilty of favoritism.

According to Tadashi Kume, who had been Irimajiri's direct superior at Honda R&D, and who was also promoted to executive at the same time, Irimajiri had been chosen because the management was seeking to train an engineer who would be able to look at the entire business from a broad perspective. In other words, Honda was looking for a generalist. If that were the only reason, however, Kawashima could just as well have chosen Nobuhiko Kawamoto, who had earned a postgraduate degree in engineering before joining Honda, instead of Irimajiri.

What, then, were the factors that divided Kawamoto's and Irimajiri's careers? Kawamoto had focused on automobiles, and more particularly on the development of engines, ever since joining Honda. Soichiro had acted as president of Honda Research and Development Company until 1971, but day-to-day management had been totally in the hands of Kiyoshi Kawashima. In preparation for Soichiro's impending retirement, Kiyoshi Kawashima had begun making efforts to implement a new system, ordering Kume to split the R&D section into independent research and development departments. His aim was to make sure that the R&D Co. would still continue to function smoothly without the genius at the helm.

The younger engineers rebelled against the decision. They felt that their freedom had been taken away. Kawamoto had taken it particularly hard when his "baby," the F1 project, was shut down as a result of the reorganization. If there were going to be even more restrictions placed on his research, Kawamoto felt it would be pointless to remain at Honda any longer.

No sooner had Kawamoto received his annual bonus at the end of 1970 than he flew to England to spend the New Years' holidays. He had made up his mind to quit Honda the moment he found an F1-related job in England. Kawamoto approached racing engine company Cothworth for a job. Upon receiving a favorable answer, Kawamoto went to see Kume as soon as he returned from England and told him of his plans to quit Honda. Kume turned to his boss, Kiyoshi Kawashima, for advice.

Kawashima's reply was just what Kume expected. "So Kawamoto wants to quit because he doesn't like it? He's acting just like you did at one time. This sort of thing is like a fever; it'll pass. Just leave him alone and wait and he'll come back on his own accord."

From the very next day, Kawamoto sullenly stopped reporting for work. He stayed home instead, killing time by designing engines for racecars and aircraft. Kawamoto gave up his plans to move to the U.K., but he remained adamant about quitting Honda. He seriously considered working with Soichiro's son, Hirotoshi, to create a new company to build engines for racing cars alone.

During this period, Irimajiri paid several visits to Kawamoto in an attempt to convince him to stay. Kume, too, was worried. Kawamoto stayed out of the office for over two months. Eventually, he calmed down, came back to the office, and started working on the low-emission CVCC engine as if nothing had happened.

This incident had an impact on Kawamoto's career at R&D, which caused him to fall behind Irimajiri in terms of advancement. Although the promotion of a young director in his thirties may simply appear to be no more than an exceptional move that ignored the traditional age-based system, that was only half the truth. The fact was that if, as Kume explained, a director was to be chosen from among the R&D employees, Irimajiri came before Kawamoto, despite the latter being the older of the two.

Irimajiri was promoted to director of Honda R&D in 1974, eleven years after joining the company, and again to managing director in 1978. Kawamoto became director at R&D two years after Irimajiri in 1976. If Kawamoto were made director at headquarters before Irimajiri, it would, in fact, run contrary to the order of priority at R&D. In terms of following the order at Honda R&D, while at the same time reinforcing Honda's youthful image among the public, Irimajiri was the better choice.

Upon assuming his new position, Irimajiri showed no signs of pretense as he commented, "I've been complaining about Honda's management and planning system during my entire time at R&D. I guess they finally thought 'Okay, if you're going to complain about the system so much, why don't you show us what you can do with it?' I believe that's why I was transferred to headquarters."

As far as Honda's other executives were concerned, they were looking to see what a man who had experience in making products could do about selling them. Putting Irimajiri in that position and giving him the title of director would allow the man to display his abilities to the full. And if he didn't measure up, he would simply be asked to take responsibility for his shortcomings. This was the reasoning behind Kiyoshi Kawashima's decision to promote Irimajiri.

When Irimajiri became a director, he took on quite a few additional responsibilities. He became a member of the specialized group on products. If the other directors were unavailable, he took their place in announcing the company's financial statements at the Tokyo Stock Exchange in Kabutocho. When it was his turn, he negotiated salaries with the labor union. In addition to his responsibilities in managing company business in general, Irimajiri also became the member of another group at headquarters that focused on analyzing the North American market. Meanwhile, he still had his old job as managing director of Honda R&D. In short, Irimajiri's plate was quite full.

The promotion completely changed Irimajiri's life. At Honda R&D, his only responsibility had been directing the development of motorcycles. But the job of an executive wasn't quite as simple. The Ohio factory line was already producing motorcycles, and the construction of the automobile factory there was proceeding smoothly as well. As a member of the North American task force, he was charged with visiting the United States to negotiate the planning and marketing of new products with local dealers.

Once Irimajiri rose to executive, he could no longer play himself down with the "I'm still young and inexperienced" routine. He needed to state his opinions clearly to direct Honda's local employees. Irimajiri spent around seven to ten days out of every month in the United States and a good part of the rest of his time handling R&D matters. In between he attended board meetings at headquarters. Irimajiri found himself on the front lines of both engineering and marketing activities. Most of the executives enjoyed a relatively leisurely lifestyle that allowed them come to the office whenever they wanted. As Honda's youngest and newest executive, however, Irimajiri found himself swamped with work.

In talking about business management, Fujisawa often quoted the words of a professional *shogi* player named Kozo Masuda, whose acquaintance he had made when the two had appeared in a magazine interview together.

"I'm at my best in a match when I'm on the edge of victory or defeat. I've made many careless mistakes in my day, and every one of them happened when I felt like I had some slack. Whenever I started feeling like I had some slack, I wasted my energy trying to play with style rather than just to win. It's better for me to feel like my opponent's closing in on me," Masuda had said.

Masuda had been talking about *shogi* but Fujisawa felt it applied just as well to business. He often used Masuda's words to make his point because he felt that such views would be more convincing to listeners if they came from the mouth of someone who made his living winning games, rather than a businessman like himself. Soichiro had been the kind of man who'd try his luck if he had even a one percent chance of success. Both Soichiro and Fujisawa took tremendous pride in the fact that they had been on the edge of victory or defeat and had succeeded in making the Honda Motor Company what it was today. Unconsciously, they expected the exact same attitude from their "kids."

In order to play on the edge of victory or defeat, one has to constantly look further and further ahead. In the world of *shogi,* winning depended entirely on how far ahead you were able to read your opponent's strategy. Reading your opponent's hand was the only way to gain an advantage. If you were shortsighted, you lost.

Fujisawa liked to describe Honda as being a "masculine company." By this he meant that men were capable of taking a long-term view of things, while women tended to take a short-term view. Honda trained its employees to take a long-range view when making decisions. Thus, by his logic, Honda could be called a "masculine company."

Satoshi Okubo, the third chairman of Honda and the father of the term *waigaiya,* supplemented Fujisawa's description with a reference to the company's human dimension.

"At Honda, it's sink or swim," said Okubo. "They don't teach you step-by-step; they just throw you into the pool and let you figure it out on your own. If you don't know how to swim at first, you need to be aggressive to survive.

"This also meant that if things were too peaceful, the directors would be charged with shaking that complacency and tackling a more challenging path. Honda is not a 'tame' company. That's not to say that it's just wild; it means that we are permitted to try out whatever we think we need to take ourselves to the next level. So there's a human, nurturing side to it."

That being said, Honda didn't allow its workers totally free reign, either. "Even if an engineer is desperate to develop a certain product," said Sugiura, picking up where Okubo left off, "there's no way they'll get permission to make it unless it meets some sort of customer need. Honda manufactured a variety of automobiles before the Civic, but nothing except the N360 was a hit. Why? Because the engineers were being totally self-centered. They just wanted to show off their skills. Looking back at it, the only thing that kept Honda alive before the Civic was the existence of enthusiasts who would buy anything Honda made. The engineers were far too dependent on that specialized group of customers. To borrow the words of Fujisawa-san, we were a 'feminine company.' On the other hand, we were totally confident in the Civic because we knew it was just what the customers wanted. That car was Honda's turning point, the time when we started designing our products based one hundred percent on the wants and needs of our consumer base."

President Kiyoshi Kawashima had given a big boost to the concept of maximizing a product to meet customer needs. Kawashima often said that the ideal situation would be to have a development capacity that exceeded sales capacity, and a sales capacity that exceeded production capacity. In other words, the highest priority for a manufacturer needed to be making products that satisfied the needs of the customers. The second priority needed to be establishing a reliable sales network to sell the products. And the third needed to be creating an appropriate system of production to manufacture them. By keeping these priorities in mind, a company would never have to worry about over-investment or dead stock.

When Honda faced business crises in 1954 and 1962, Fujisawa quickly realized the underlying causes—an imbalance between development and sales capabilities in the former case, and between production and sales capabilities in the latter—and managed to save the company by promptly taking the appropriate remedial measures. Kawashima did his best to maintain the correct balance by establishing the order of priority: first production, then development, and finally, sales.

Honda's business appeared to be running quite smoothly during the late 1970s. In reality, however, Honda was forced to make two fundamental changes in its business strategy: updating the Civic, and introducing catalytic converters.

In December of 1973, when Honda first unveiled the low-emission CVCC-equipped Civic, Kiyoshi Kawashima had clearly stated that the Civic was now essentially complete as a basic model and that Honda would not be introducing any new models of the car. When sales in the United States first began taking off, American Honda excitedly contacted headquarters in Japan to inform them that if the trend continued, the Civic had a shot at eclipsing the sales of the legendary Volkswagen Beetle. When it came to the Civic, Kiyoshi Kawashima truly believed that Honda had achieved perfection on all fronts.

Being a relative newcomer to auto manufacturing, Honda lacked experience when it came to introducing new models of car. Although the N360 had been a major hit on the Japanese market, the defect scandal had put an end to the series before any new models could be introduced. Honda's other cars also went out of production before any changes were made to the initial model. Honda's approach was that if customers tired of one product, it was time to dump it and offer a completely new one with a different name. This attitude, a holdover from the motorcycle industry, was firmly ingrained in the minds of Honda employees.

Domestic interest in the "same old Civic" began flagging in early 1976. Japanese sales dropped below the level of export sales. On the other hand, the Civic had been a top seller in America since 1974, thanks in large part to the fact that the Civic swept the fuel efficiency tests conducted by the E.P.A. for four years running.

Honda had produced a total of 1.3 million vehicles, counting its vans, from the introduction of the Civic until the end of 1976. More than twenty million Volkswagen Beetles had been produced over forty years without a single model change. Why not take the same path with the Civic?

Times were changing, however. Automotive technology was rapidly evolving in the wake of the exhaust regulations. Now every manufacturer saw tackling both low emissions and fuel efficiency as a top priority. Even if Honda's engineers believed that they had fully exploited the potential of the Civic design, sooner or later a new product would arrive and knock it off its pedestal.

Generally speaking, automobiles received a model change every four years in Japan. Failure to do so inevitably resulted in a dramatic drop in sales. And like it or not, the Civic was no exception.

In 1975, in light of the sagging sales of the Civic, Honda engineers began work on a car code-named the "SA," designed to be more of a successor to the Civic than a simple model change. Kume had come up with the concept: "as classy as a Mercedes, as fast as a Porsche, and as affordable as a k-car." However, after beginning to develop the project, the engineers found that they were faced with a dilemma. If they managed to realize Kume's concept, the new car would certainly be true to Honda's style and image but it would also risk cannibalizing the sales of the Civic in the U.S. market, which had grown even larger than the domestic market. The potential risk would far lower, they decided, if they didn't deviate too far from the design of the Civic.

No matter how well the Civic was selling in the U.S., manufacturing two completely different types of car at the same time would be totally inefficient from a business standpoint. It would be far smarter to change the company's policy on model changes and introduce the SA as the next version of the Civic.

The original Civic had been popular as the "Japanese version of the Beetle" due to its similar domed shape. The new version, released in the summer of 1979, was larger and somewhat more angular than the original. Honda advertised the car as "the energy-efficient car of the eighties." The retail price was kept at the same level as for the original Civic, which was equivalent to offering a discount: consumers actually got more for their money.

The decision to use a catalytic converter in the new design was the result of a much larger debate within Honda. The Civic had won the title of most fuel-efficient car four times in a row in the United States. But it was impossible to achieve the same level of fuel economy in Japan, due to slower average driving speeds and the stop-and-go nature of driving on Japanese roadways. Consumers wound up dissatisfied with the Civic's handling.

The lean fuel-air mixture of the CVCC meant lower horsepower than a standard reciprocating engine. Lower horsepower meant that a car often ran less smoothly than its driver wanted. Meanwhile, dramatic advances in catalytic converter technology were being made each year. Honda's rivals were eagerly incorporating the new devices into their products, achieving not only lowered emissions and better handling but also improved fuel efficiency in their cars. Honda's engineers began to see the need of introducing catalytic converters in order to improve the CVCC engine's performance as well as fuel efficiency.

Soichiro, however, had been a staunch proponent of tackling the emissions regulations by modifications to Honda's engines alone, without using any exhaust aftertreatment devices. Incorporating a catalytic converter would run counter to his basic philosophy. The Honda kids knew they would have a huge wall to overcome in the form of pressure from Soichiro if they made the decision to use the devices.

Before developing the CVCC, Honda, like its rivals Toyota and Nissan, had actually planned on developing its low-emission engine using a catalytic converter. The project team consisted of a full sixty engineers, representing Honda's top engineers specially chosen to tackle the emissions regulations. The successful introduction of the CVCC, however, signaled a different path for the company. The team found itself downsized year after year as engineers were transferred to other projects. But those who remained doggedly continued their research in spite of the fact that their project remained in the margins.

In 1975, two years after the Civic had first gone on sale, a huge debate over the CVCC erupted at Honda R&D. The main topic was how to simultaneously improve both handling and fuel efficiency. The Civic was, after all, Honda's top product.

Honda's employees took great pride in their company, which they regarded as the original manufacturer of low-emission engines. The majority saw maximizing the potential of CVCC as the only solution, believing that introducing catalytic converters would drown out proponents of the technology and would be tantamount to suicide for the company.

However, the fact remained that other manufacturers were enjoying better and better results from their engines as time went on, while the CVCC showed little if any improvement. If the situation were ignored, it would only be a matter of time before Honda found itself left behind. Advocates for adding catalytic converters approached Soichiro directly and begged him to reconsider his refusal to use auxiliary devices in the CVCC. All of Honda R&D was caught up in the heated debate and so it was decided to hold a thorough discussion the following year in 1976 as to the feasibility of incorporating catalytic converters into the Civic.

More than thirty experts in reduced-emission engines gathered for three days and nights of heated discussion. In the end, a two-thirds majority successfully argued against the inclusion of catalytic converters. Among this group was Yoshitoshi Sakurai, a member of the CVCC development team. Sakurai recalls his feelings on the matter: "The CVCC was our baby. Two-thirds of me wanted to maintain the status quo and continue trying to make a breakthrough with improvements to the engine alone, but one-third wanted to make a go of it with the converter. I was going back and forth."

This is not to say that any of the "CVCC only" advocates actually had an ace up his sleeve where improvement to the technology was concerned. Honda needed to also continue research into the catalytic converter technology as an insurance policy in case the CVCC route didn't work out.

Kume, as the man basically in charge of Honda R&D, watched the discussions intently. At the time, Kume still believed that the use of catalytic converters led to a risk of "secondary pollution." Catalyzing pollutants involved a very sensitive reaction. If the igniters in an engine misfired, the fuel that was supposed to combust during the process would be instead be shunted directly into the catalytic converter and melt the system.

The only way to avoid the problem was to improve the durability and functionality of the carburetor and electronic components of the engine. There was also an urgent need to create a catalytic converter durable enough to last for 50,000 miles of driving.

For these reasons and more, it was obvious that catalytic converters were far from a magic bullet. Kume knew that if he rushed to a decision without thinking things over thoroughly, Soichiro would never let him hear the end of it. Kume truly feared the wrath of an angry Soichiro.

The CVCC had been developed by young engineers, but it was Soichiro who had set the policy that the low-emission engine should be developed through modifications to the engine itself, without the use of auxiliary devices. Even if Soichiro had retired from the front lines of engine design, it was unthinkable for the Honda kids to go against a policy so clearly laid by one of the founders. If R&D were going to decide to use catalytic devices, they needed to have a solid reason, something persuasive enough to make Soichiro understand and agree.

Kume continued to work slowly but steadily at confirming the safety and feasibility of catalytic devices, ordering his young engineers to develop an artificial kidney system to study how catalytic devices work and find out whether they actually did lead to "secondary pollution." He also had engineers study electronic devices—something Soichiro had always had an aversion to.

Meanwhile, Honda continue to uphold its "CVCC only" policy but, as expected, the company found itself running headfirst into a wall. Finally, two years later in 1978, Honda came to the inescapable conclusion that the only way to achieve improved functionality and fuel efficiency would be the use of catalytic converters.

When the emissions regulations had first been enacted, the use of computers to control fuel-injection systems and other parts of the engine was still unheard of. Honda exploited its skill with precision mechanical equipment to create the architecture of the CVCC. The fact that the CVCC managed to meet every requirement with the superior design of its architecture alone formed the basis of the engine's success.

With the arrival of the first oil crisis, however, energy efficiency became a top priority, and the integration density of semiconductors was improved, leading to dramatic advancements in electronic technology. The first microcomputers appeared on the market and this rapid evolution of the computer industry began to show its impact on the auto industry. Manufacturers started replacing carburetors with microcomputer-controlled electronic fuel-injection devices, which allowed greater precision. The first sensors capable of detecting the composition of exhaust gases also appeared on the market. The prospect of combining the sensors with a catalytic converter promised even more efficient engines.

The CVCC remained an undisputed masterpiece of engineering. But if Honda's engineers clung blindly to the design, they would find themselves increasingly marginalized in the coming era of electronics. In fact, it was not only the improvements made to catalytic converters but also the advances in computer control technology that, in the end, led other manufacturers who had licensed the CVCC technology to abandon use of the engine in their cars.

The success of the CVCC as the first low-polluting engine in the world had intoxicated Honda employees. They had essentially shut out any possibility that didn't involve simply tweaking the design. The CVCC had boosted Honda to the top of the worldwide auto industry, but the company found itself falling further and further behind in terms of handling and fuel efficiency. A wise man changes his mind, a fool never, the saying goes. But simply caving in to the status quo would compromise Honda's image as a technological innovator. If the development team wanted to incorporate catalytic converters into Honda engines, they needed before anything else to convince the ever-rational and pragmatic Soichiro and also publicly spin the concept of incorporating the devices into the CVCC as a progressive move.

Realizing that their company was in danger of falling behind, Honda acted quickly. In September of 1978, the company decided to use an oxygen catalyst in the second version of the Civic. The decision came just as the engineers were nearing the final stage of the development of the new car. The CVCC development team, led by Yoshitoshi Sakurai, began a complete overhaul the engine design to accommodate the new device. It was a rush job, but the team managed to complete the modifications before the car went on sale in July 1979.

If the engineers worked around the clock, they could make up for the time lost by not incorporating catalytic converters two years earlier within a year. Regaining the trust of the customers, however, would take double that time. If Honda had protected Soichiro's "honor" by stubbornly refusing to compromise over the new catalytic converter technology, it would never have been able to sell sports cars or larger automobiles later.

Although the second version of the CVCC incorporated a catalytic converter, there remained limits as to the fuel efficiency that could be squeezed from the design. The CVCC was completely abandoned in the third version of the Civic, the Accord, which went on sale in 1983. Today, none of Honda's cars uses a CVCC engine.

The CVCC had been Honda's ticket into compact car industry, but its mission had ended with the onset of the oil crisis. The CVCC had been the perfect answer to car exhaust regulations, but fuel economy proved to be its Achilles' heel. Even for Honda, there was only one way to balance reduced emissions, fuel efficiency, and handling: using computers and other electronic devices.

The CVCC had been, in all aspects, an engine developed to answer the demands of a specific era in the history of automobiles. In the end, abandoning the CVCC didn't affect the public's image of the company, thanks largely to the fact that all of Honda's cars used a front-engine, front-wheel-drive configuration. In the 1970s, the majority of automobiles were front-engine, rear-wheel-drive cars. Faced with the fuel efficiency regulations, however, General Motors opted to switch to a front-engine, front-wheel-drive configuration, which allowed for the creation of smaller, lighter automobiles. The other manufactures quickly followed suit. Honda led the industry in this area and this advantage allowed it to achieve and maintain its reputation as the world's leading manufacturer of compact cars.

5

The second generation of Honda kids, led by Kiyoshi Kawashima, used the fame of their "parents," Soichiro and Fujisawa, to their best advantage. Although the collective decision-making system had taken root over time, the public still regarded Honda as Soichiro's company. The name of the company only reinforced the public's perception that Soichiro was inseparable from the company he had created.

In fact, more than a few people outside of Japan believed that Soichiro was still running Honda even after his official retirement. Even within Japan, quite a few were convinced that Soichiro and Fujisawa continued to run their company from behind the scenes. The more people talked about Honda's incredible sales figures and youthfulness of its executives, the more Soichiro's fame grew, which also meant that the management capacities of the "kids" were in high regard. As such, the kids made no special effort to correct the misinformation about Honda's leadership.

Although Soichiro, as supreme advisor of Honda, had an office in the head-quarters building in Harajuku, he also established his own private office in the Ginza district for use as his base for outside activities. There seemed to be no end to requests for lectures and speeches. Soichiro appeared at headquarters from time to time, but almost never went to his official office there. He would make a bee-line for the "collective directors' room" where the executives worked, speak his mind to the "kids," and leave.

Soichiro's comments were always the same. He reminded them to differen-tiate themselves from Toyota and Nissan. At the same time, he had a great fear of being left behind.

"I read an article in the newspaper about a new car Toyota and Nissan have developed, something with a device called a 'turbo.' I hear they're selling really well. Why aren't we selling something like that? Don't tell me you can't do it!"

Of course, Soichiro never expressed his fears publicly. He made a point of participating in the unveiling of new car designs but never did more than exchange a few words of banter with the executives.

"I was so bored at home that I decided to come down and see what you kids had come up with," he would joke.

By twos and threes, the Honda kids would gather around Soichiro.

"If you're that bored," Kume would say, "maybe we should give you something to worry about. I'm sure we've got some problems for you to tackle."

"Don't bother the man in his retirement now," president Kiyoshi Kawashima would cut in. "The way things are now is best for all of us."

Of course, these exchanges always occurred within earshot of a large number of journalists. They were performances, carefully carried out to reinforce the impression that the founders weren't involved in the day-to-day management of Honda anymore.

"There's no question Soichiro Honda is a genius when it comes to engineering," said Sohei Nakayama, special advisor to the Industrial Bank of Japan, to a retired Honda executive one day. "But what about business management? How were his capabilities as a business manager seen within the company?"

Nakayama was roughly the same age as Soichiro and knew the man fairly well through shared social activities. Nakayama respected Soichiro as an engineer and found his personality charming. But no matter how he wrapped his brain around it, he simply couldn't figure out how Soichiro, with all his child-like innocence and devil-may-care attitude, had actually run the company.

"Soichiro is an engineer. Honda's business affairs were handled entirely by Fujisawa," replied the retired executive.

"Well, that clears it up," replied Nakayama.

Soichiro and Fujisawa's roles didn't change even after their retirements. Soichiro remained Honda's most public figure through his frequent appearances in a wide variety of outside activities. As the guru of the cult of Honda, his role was to recruit fans and make a contribution to society on behalf of his "kids." Fujisawa, on the other hand, remained the man behind the scenes. He never appeared publicly and watched over Honda from the shadows.

Fujisawa basically stayed home for the first six months after his retirement, but after that, he would walk from his house in Roppongi to headquarters in Harajuku once a month in his usual kimono, and spend an hour or so chatting with the Honda kids in the directors' room. Kihachiro Kawashima and Michihiro Nishida, who were close disciples of Fujisawa, were comfortable talking to him on equal terms, but the younger generation of Honda kids felt quite nervous in Fujisawa's presence. All they remembered of him was being shouted at or lectured to. Some executives even went so far as to sneak out the back door when told by the receptionists that Fujisawa had made an appearance. Fujisawa was probably aware of this, which was why he himself would come in by the back door and catch the directors as they tried to leave.

"You're executives of the world-class Honda Motor! Don't act like thieves in the night!" Fujisawa would roar at them.

Whenever the executives found themselves stumped by a business problem, they would send a representative to ask Fujisawa in Roppongi for his advice. They thought of it not so much as consulting the former vice president but making a report to a major shareholder. Even when he had been active in management, Fujisawa hated nothing more than simply being asked what to do. The kids had to describe their own potential solution to Fujisawa first. Those who had worked directly under Fujisawa knew how to communicate with him. If Fujisawa agreed to a decision they had made, he would nod as he listened quietly. If he didn't, he would simply look away.

At the beginning of Kiyoshi Kawashima's presidency, vice president Kihachiro Kawashima and director Michihiro Nishida paid frequent visits to Fujisawa for advice. After they retired, Kiyoshi Kawashima and Kume took over.

Kiyoshi Kawashima and Kume were both engineers who had spent long hours in Honda's factories and at Honda R&D. Talking to Fujisawa helped them realize that Honda owed its existence to more than simply the good products that they had created. Fujisawa patiently instructed Kiyoshi Kawashima and Kume in the true nature of business management and the future of Honda. As engineers trained in logical thinking, Fujisawa's firm belief that everything changes—and that anyone who thrived was also destined to fall—was completely new to them and particularly grabbed their attention.

One might say that Kiyoshi Kawashima had a metaphorical "gilt folding screen" behind his back, supporting his decisions. The sparkling gold face was Soichiro. The plain back face was Fujisawa. Whenever Kiyoshi Kawashima came up with a new strategy, the older employees speculated as to whether it was "Soichiro's will" or "Fujisawa's orders." They felt reassured that the two founders, who had made Honda into the great corporation it was today, still retained a connection to the company's business. Soichiro and Fujisawa acted as moral support for the Honda kids. So long as the folding screen shone behind their backs, the Honda Kids felt secure.

Honda's high export ratio meant that the Honda kids feared nothing more than an escalation in trade friction. If the government stepped in to regulate exports, it would have a large and immediate impact on Honda's business. By 1980, more than seventy percent of Honda's profits derived from exports.

Honda's ascendancy as an international corporation wasn't due to the company's number of exports or the even to fact that it had been first to build a factory in the United States. It was because Honda managed to expand its business without becoming entangled in the growing trade friction with the United States or with Europe.

There was good reason for Honda's high export ratio. Honda's share of the Japanese motorcycle market exceeded fifty percent. Exports were inevitable for further growth. On the other hand, Honda's share of the Japanese automobile market remained quite small. Even though Honda boasted unique cars unlike anything made by its competitors, there remained still a long way to go to beat Toyota and Nissan. And so once again, with automobiles as well as motorcycles, exports were the inevitable answer to the question of how to raise sales.

The motorcycle industry had already undergone a worldwide restructuring. Therefore, even when Harley Davidson's slumping sales became a political issue, Honda's foundations were unshakeable.

The automobile market, however, was a different story. The reason for Honda's growth into the first trillion-yen company of the post-war era was entirely due to rapidly increasing the number of auto exports to the United States.

The fact that the Honda kids were smart enough to look ahead was probably the main factor in their decision to begin local production. Brick by brick, the kids were building on the foundations for the far-sighted, "masculine" company that Fujisawa had envisioned. The announcement of Honda's decision to begin production in the U.S. could not have come at a better time.

In a speech on the White House lawn, President Jimmy Carter openly welcomed Honda's new American factory. Nevertheless, the trade friction between the United States and Japan was not to be resolved by a single Japanese company announcing the start of production in the U.S. In the end, it was only settled when Japanese manufacturers agreed to voluntarily restrict their exports. Douglas Fraser, chairman of the UAW and a strong advocate for the regulation of Japanese imports, sympathized with Honda. Hoping to induct Honda employees into the UAW, he proposed that Honda not be included as a target for the import restrictions, saying that Honda had demonstrated an understanding of the U.S. position.

The high quality of the Civic and Accord, and Honda's corporate image as the first manufacturer to create low-emission automobiles, had been instrumental in making the company a tremendous success on the U.S. market. Now, with the construction of the Ohio factory, Honda received another boost from the perception that it was company making an active contribution to the U.S. economy.

Honda was also the first Japanese company to set foot into Europe. Rather than building a factory, which would have required a tremendous investment, Honda inked a deal with BL (British Leyland; currently Rover) to manage a European business together. BL had been founded jointly by British automakers such as Rover, Austin, and Jaguar with the stated purpose of forming a united front to compete against imported cars from the U.S. and continental Europe. It was also fully backed by the British government.

BL had boasted a fifty percent share of the British market in the early 1970s, but its share decreased year by year as foreign products began to gain a foothold in the British Isles. In 1975, the British government had intervened, backing BL with national capital.

BL then entered into negotiations for a partnership with its French counterpart, Renault, which also was struggling through a business slump. After a considerable number of twists and turns, the negotiations almost culminated in the signature of a contract, before BL's new chairman Michael Edwardes decided to walk away from the table, ending all possibilities of an alliance.

Although BL had decided against teaming up with Renault, it was evident that it needed to find another partner. BL's most pressing problem was the updating of its two main automobile designs—the mid-sized Marina and Allegro— which were already becoming outdated. Due to a shortage of engineers, however, it would take at least four years to launch new models. It was obvious that licensed production would offer a faster remedy.

Increasingly irritated by the glacial speed of BL's attempts to change, a group of young politicians from Britain's Conservative Party issued advised them to enter into a partnership with a Japanese manufacturer. Edwardes chose Honda, whose Accord was selling well in England, as a potential prospect.

At the time, Honda had 33,000 employees, an annual production of 680,000 vehicles, and annual sales of 4.646 billion dollars. BL, on the other hand, had 195,000 employees and an annual production of 785,000. Physically, Honda was a lot smaller than BL, which meant no risk of BL being consumed by its partner. And if BL managed to exploit Honda's sales network in Japan, they could increase their number of exports as well. Edwardes secretly made a visit to Japan at the end of 1978 to suggest a partnership to Honda executives.

The managers of Honda saw Britain as their next-most important market after the United States. But the Japanese government had a "gentlemen's agreement" with the U.K. to ensure that Japanese exports remained at ten percent or less. This meant that increasing exports would be difficult. Because of a late start, Honda's exports to the U.K. remained at less than 30,000 vehicles a year. While it was clear that local production was the only way to increase the number of vehicles sold in Britain, there was, at the time, much more of an urgency to begin production in the U.S.

British labor unions were segregated by job function. Unannounced and unauthorized "wildcat strikes" were commonplace. Although BL was Britain's top manufacturer, its labor force was almost unimaginably large by Japanese standards, in relation to its level of production. BL's products were old-fashioned, its factories decrepit, and its efficiency low. By this point, BL's market share had dropped to twenty-three percent, and the company was in the red.

"I'm only telling you this because you asked for advice," said Soichiro when the kids consulted him on the partnership issue. "It's not just BL. I'm against partnerships with any foreign manufacturer. Do you think we have the resources to bail them out right now? And if you think it's that important to get into Europe, why can't we do it on our own? But you know what? I'm retired. The final decision is up to you."

Soichiro had built his company up from nothing. And he took pride in the fact that Honda had entered the European market by building a motorcycle factory in Belgium all on its own, even though the factory still operated at a loss. The man believed in independence.

Fujisawa had the same take on the situation as Soichiro, but neither nodded or looked away. The Honda kids took that as a tacit "yes." Still, Fujisawa didn't forget to issue a warning:

"Do you really think we've grown large enough to lead a foreign rival? Don't get a swelled head over it."

Since BL was operating in the red, there was no risk of Honda being consumed. However, if BL's offer was simply for capital participation, equal more or less to a financial bailout, Kiyoshi Kawashima intended to turn it down on the spot.

Edwardes made Kawashima an unexpected offer. He said BL was interested in the licensed production of Honda's products. Soichiro didn't like it, but Kiyoshi Kawashima found himself intrigued.

Licensed production didn't pose any risk to Honda. In fact, it had many merits in the form of licensing fees and profit from exported parts such as engines and transmissions. There was also the prospect of allowing subsidiary Honda Engineering to export machine tools to England in the initial stages. It would be great practice, since they were already planning to supply the same tools to the Ohio plant. If licensed production went well, it would be one big step closer to establishing local British production for Honda. The Honda kids saw the deal as a way of killing two birds with one stone.

Honda's automobile line now consisted of three cars: the Civic, the Accord, and the Prelude. Honda was an expert when it came to compact cars, but when it came to mid-sized cars, the company lacked expertise and experience. Honda had an urgent need to create an automobile with an engine larger than 2000cc. While independent development was an important principle at Honda, there was no denying that piggybacking on BL's technology would not only shorten the development time, but also promised far lower costs than developing one on its own. Deciding to ignore the wishes of Soichiro and Fujisawa, the "kids" sat down for negotiations with British Leyland.

Discussions proceeded smoothly, and a basic agreement was reached in May of 1979. The contract was officially signed in December of the same year. The outline of the deal was that Honda would grant BL a license for its newest model of compact car, the "Ballade"; that BL would sell it under its own brand name of "Triumph Acclaim" in the European Community; and that Honda would not sell the same type of car in the region.

Two years later in December of 1981, after confirming the start-up of sales of the "Triumph Acclaim," Honda and BL agreed to cooperate in the creation of a new automobile. It would be more luxurious than an Accord but more accessible to the consumer than a Jaguar. The project team would consist of engineers from both companies. Both companies would share in the responsibilities, and the target date for release of the product was set for 1985.

The cooperation between the two companies only continued to deepen. In 1989, Honda agreed to take a twenty percent stake in BL. In return, BL agreed to take a twenty percent stake in Honda United Kingdom Manufacturing (HUM).

A low-risk relationship had strengthened into a capital tie-up within ten years. The fledgling Honda kids were making steady progress in leaving the protection of their nest.

There are basically two ways for an automaker to enter a foreign market: independently or in an alliance with a local company. Honda exploited both methods to achieve its status as an international corporation. That is not to say that Honda started out with a well-planned global strategy and cleverly applied it in its decisions to enter the U.S. market and initiate a partnership with BL. When it came to advancing into foreign markets on its own, as it had in America, Honda followed its own policy and decisions were always finalized by president Kawashima, using his "four possibilities" method. On the other hand, the company had always been quite passive when it came to alliances with other companies. The case of BL was typical. BL had approached Honda; Honda mulled over the benefits, and made a decision.

Honda had long felt the need to establish a base in the U.K., but knew it would cost far too much to build a factory on its own. BL's offer came at the perfect time. Even afterwards, however, the luxury car co-development project and the capital tie-up originated with BL. Of course, Honda only accepted because it saw the advantage of such an increased cooperation; nevertheless, Honda took a passive role in the relationship when it came to suggesting new ideas.

In contrast, this approach backfired on Honda in its agreement with Ford. In 1973, Honda agreed to sell Ford's products in Japan in exchange for licensing the production of the CVCC to Ford. Honda managed to sell 10,000 Fords over the next six years, but the two companies decided to terminate the partnership in 1980. The fact was that neither company had taken an active role in trying to expand the relationship.

Partnership negotiations are like a game of poker. The side who sits and waits for the other to make an offer would appear to have the advantage. On the other hand, the side who is more proactive with suggestions tends to have an advantage in terms of determining strategy.

BL had approached Honda because it had determined that, unlike Renault, Honda had the products it was interested in, and that the two companies would be able to negotiate as equals, without the risk of BL being swallowed. Sumitomo Bank had suggested a capital tie-up with Mazda to Ford because Mazda needed outside help to survive. Similarly, when Isuzu approached Honda to discuss a partnership for OEM of automobiles and recreational vehicles in 1991, Isuzu had two aims in mind: increasing the operation rate of its American factory and obtaining a product to sell, since it was withdrawing from the automobile industry. Of course, the main reason for the negotiations was the fact that both sides had something to gain. But viewed strategically, Isuzu had the definite advantage.

Playing the passive role in a negotiation may give the impression of strength, but in reality this strength is only superficial. Honda's alliance with United Car and Diesel Distributors (UCDD), a subsidiary of Mercedes-Benz, is a perfect example. At the end of 1980, a year after it had entered into an alliance with BL, Honda formed a partnership with UCDD, a South African company in which Mercedes-Benz had a twenty-seven percent stake. UCDD wanted to strengthen its production capacity in South Africa. Honda wanted a foothold in the African market. Their needs matched. An agreement was reached to co-produce a compact car targeting the public at large designed by Honda at a UCDD factory in South Africa.

Mercedes-Benz had approached Honda with the offer. Small and fuel-efficient automobiles were becoming as popular in South Africa as they were around the world. But Mercedes-Benz was mainly a luxury manufacturer without substantial experience in the design or marketing of cars for the general consumer.

At the time South Africa represented a market for some 400,000 cars a year. Toyota, Nissan, Mazda, and Mitsubishi had already entered the market by outsourcing the local manufacture of their products to local companies. Honda was the last major Japanese automaker to enter the South African marketplace.

Mercedes-Benz also had other factories including those in Brazil, Spain, Nigeria, and Iran. If the partnership in South Africa took off, Honda imagined that it could expect co-production deals at the other factories as well.

The worldwide trend at the time was towards smaller automobiles. Honda executives believed that Mercedes-Benz wanted to exploit Honda's skill at designing compact cars. Honda, for its part, desperately wanted Mercedes-Benz's ability to create successful mid- and large-sized automobiles. And it had been Mercedes-Benz that had asked Honda for cooperation with its subsidiary. The Mercedes-Benz executive in charge of foreign operations had been present at the negotiations with UCDD. Honda's executives were convinced, therefore, that the alliance would lead to a deeper relationship with Mercedes-Benz.

Mercedes-Benz was and is the world's oldest auto manufacturer. That such a prestigious company was asking for help overly excited the Honda kids. They were practically bursting with pride that the great Mercedes-Benz was begging them for an alliance.

In the end nothing came of it. Mercedes-Benz merely selected Honda as their best choice for South Africa. Once they reached an agreement for a partnership there, Honda didn't hear another word. And because the company had taken the passive role in the negotiations, it couldn't very well propose enhanced cooperation from its side.

For foreign manufacturers, including but not limited to Mercedes-Benz, Honda was an attractive company for a partnership. It had know-how when it came to emission standards and fuel efficiency, but remained small enough that a partnership wasn't threatening to the other side.

In spite of the attention Honda was getting from foreign suitors, the specter of Soichiro and Fujisawa in the shadows prevented the Honda kids from taking a more proactive role in forming alliances. The kids wanted to avoid doing anything that could endanger the company their "parents" had built. The more keenly aware they felt this, the less aggressive they were able to be in their relations with other companies. In other words, their hands were effectively tied.

6

The Super Cub motorcycle enjoyed tremendous popularity in both Japan and the United States. In the U.S., it had single-handedly played down the image of the motorcycle user as a "rough rider." That being said, however, the average citizen of both countries still saw motorcycles as somewhat dangerous and perhaps even a little reckless.

However, the economic crunch from the oil crisis gave birth to a whole new type of small motorcycle: the so-called "family motorcycle." The first products hit the market at around the same time that the economy was staging a recovery. The new design countered the previous image of motorcycles, replacing it with one of a convenient and safe vehicle that was simple enough for anyone to drive.

Once again, it was Honda that set off the new trend. The 50cc "Roadpal" went on sale in Japan in February of 1976. Honda aggressively marketed the motorcycle as a tool for daily transportation. The center of their campaign was a television commercial that featured the Italian actress Sophia Loren riding the bicycle-like motorcycle through the streets of Rome. It was a big hit; Honda sold 230,000 Roadpals in the first year alone.

Honda's rivals wasted no time in jumping into the new market. A year after the Roadpal went on sale, Yamaha targeted female consumers with a "step-through" (open frame) motorcycle called the "Passol." The company hired Kaoru Yachigusa, a famous Japanese actress, for its ad campaign. The advertisements centered on the scooter's ease of handling, with Yachigusa declaring, "Even I can drive it!" Both the ad campaign and the ease of handling made the vehicle a popular choice with consumers and showed that there was plenty of profit to be made, even by latecomers. Not to be outdone, third largest motorcycle manufacturer Suzuki released its own version in 1978. It was a boom time for small and lightweight motorcycles.

Domestic Japanese sales of motorcycles had stagnated at 1.1 million annually ever since 1970. Around the time of the oil crisis, rumors began spreading that the motorcycle industry was saturated with too many competing products. The market for "business motorcycles" such as the Super Cub was fully developed. There was profit to be made in regularly updating the basic models, but there wasn't much of a chance of increasing demand for the products. And the mid- and large-size motorcycles preferred by young consumers weren't much of a money-maker either.

Female consumers represented the last untapped market for motorcycles. Prior to the Roadpal, Honda had long tried to target the demographic without success.

Kiyoshi Kawashima saw it as a problem with Honda's development system, which he decided to revamp when he became president of Honda R&D in 1974. Soichiro had long put all research and development under one umbrella. Kawashima divided new product development into three categories: automobiles, motorcycles, and general-purpose products. He assigned the Wako plant to handle research and development of automobiles, while the Asaka plant would handle research and development of motorcycles and general-purpose equipment. At the same time, he separated research from development in each of the categories.

More specifically, he made sure that potential products went through several stages of evaluation before the ones with the highest chance of success were selected for development. All together some 400 employees worked on motorcycles and general-purpose equipment at Asaka.

The first hit product to emerge from the new system was the Roadpal. Just as it had done for automobiles, Honda made sure that both the engineers at Honda R&D and salesmen worked together to develop the new motorcycles. Toshikata Amino, who later became executive vice president of Honda America Manufacturing Inc. (HAM) and head of the Ohio plant, was one of the men selected for the motorcycle development team. Born in the Nishijin textile-weaving district of Kyoto, Amino went to work for a mid-sized company of 600 employees after graduating from university. Tiring of the monotonous work, he was attracted by the high salaries at Honda made the decision to change careers in 1966.

Ten months after joining Honda, Amino was promoted to the head of Honda's local office in Nagano. His work caught the attention of the management, who then assigned Amino to work on the development of the Roadpal.

The concept of the Roadpal was "adapting the motorcycle to the changing face of the Japanese street scene." The team agreed that the product should be as easy to buy as it was to ride. And so they selected the bicycle as the basis for their design.

The Roadpal succeeded at winning the hearts of the ladies. It wasn't just inexpensive and easy to ride. It also gave the rider the pleasure of being in control. And it hit the market at just the right time. Japan was finally recovering from the oil shock, and the economy was growing steadily once again.

Japanese housewives who had been busy with housework and child rearing now found extra time to enjoy themselves. On average, however, the "social range" of a Japanese housewife was limited to houses on the same block. The only way to enlarge this radius would be an easy-to-use form of transportation.

The "family motorcycle" fit the bill perfectly. It gave the housewife mobility and made it possible for her to go out even in the evenings—something that had previously been practically impossible—allowing her to make full use of her day.

The family motorcycle also met the needs of housewives who worked part-time jobs in that they were economical to operate. The motorcycles boasted mileage of roughly sixty kilometers per liter of gasoline, which meant that using them instead of taking the bus to and from the nearest train station would amount to enough savings within a year's time to cover the cost of the vehicle.

In addition to housewives, another demographic was quietly taking a new interest in motorcycles: men in their thirties and forties. Worried about bike gangs, the police paid extra attention when they issued 750cc motorcycle licenses to young men. But middle-aged men, who were seen as more careful drivers, could obtain licenses far more easily. The growing popularity of the motorcycle not only among housewives but also middle aged men re-cast the image of the machines as tools for civic transportation.

In 1976, when the Roadpal debuted, some 1.3 million motorcycles were sold in Japan. In 1977, when Yamaha entered the market for family motorcycles, the number had grown to 1.62 million. And in 1978, when Suzuki unveiled their product, it had risen to 1.98 million. Sales of two million motorcycles a year appeared to be only a matter of time. The increase was due almost entirely to family motorcycles; in fact, the family motorcycle had almost doubled the size of the market in just three years.

Before the appearance of the family motorcycle, Honda had a fifty percent share of the Japanese motorcycle market. Yamaha's share was half of Honda's, while Suzuki's was half that of Yamaha. Kawasaki took the rest. People jokingly described the industry as consisting of "two strong ones (Honda and Yamaha), a weak one (Suzuki), and a total extra (Kawasaki)."

The situation changed in January of 1979, when a market melee lead Yamaha to suddenly overtake Honda in terms of production figures. The reason for this was the Honda had been a step ahead of the others in deciding to adjust its inventory. Yamaha, on the other hand, refused to reduce production, even though it had surplus stock in its warehouses. This led to the reversal of positions for Honda and Yamaha as far as production was concerned.

Yamaha and Honda also had highly disparate views when it came to predicting the future of the motorcycle market. Yamaha's confidence grew from the sheer size of the new potential market. Family motorcycles were gaining popularity among businessmen and students, but the main demand came from women, in particular, housewives.

According to a survey conduced by the Tokyo Metropolitan Police Department, as of the end of 1978 some eight million Japanese women held regular drivers' licenses and two million held licenses for motorcycles of 50cc or less. This represented increases of thirty-eight and seventy-nine percent, respectively, over the previous three years and meant that roughly ten million women were licensed to drive family motorcycles.

On the other hand, total sales at the end of 1978 totaled only 2.2 million. The way Yamaha interpreted the numbers, the motorcycle market appeared poised on the brink of explosive growth in the near future.

Although Honda also recognized the vast potential for further demand, the company took a different stand from Yamaha. The executives at Honda knew that, in the case of family motorcycles, manufacturers needed to actively create demand for the product before consumers would buy it. It was necessary for the manufacturers to advertise the convenience of the family motorcycles through various campaigns, while also contributing to increasing the number of potential users by holding seminars to help consumers obtain licenses and providing opportunities to test-drive the vehicles.

The boom of the last three years, however, was not brought about by the efforts of the manufactures to cultivate demand but was, rather, the result of consumers purchasing the products as part of a new fad. In other words, the manufacturers were not looking at potential demand but actual demand. Cultivating potential demand and turning it into actual demand required time. Honda's analysis predicted that the situation was starting to level off.

By early 1979, it appeared that Honda's analysis was on target. The total number of family motorcycles shipped by Honda, Yamaha, and Suzuki during the first quarter of 1979 was ten percent less than that of previous year. However, the major cause for the drop was the fact that Honda greatly reduced its own shipments by thirty-six percent. Meanwhile, Yamaha and Suzuki hadn't slowed pace at all.

By the beginning of the summer, the gap between the two companies had become all the more visible. Yamaha's share of all motorcycles shipped in June was thirty-nine percent; Honda's was thirty-two percent. For family motorcycles, Yamaha's share was fifty-six percent whereas Honda's was just twenty-three percent. The overwhelming difference pushed Yamaha into pole position.

For products shipped in the period from January to June, Honda barely managed to maintain its share at forty percent, while Yamaha closed in at thirty-six percent, only four percent lower behind Honda. The share of family motorcycles shipped during the same period was forty-nine percent for Yamaha and thirty-four percent for Honda, putting Yamaha in the lead.

"Finally, we have a chance. We're only one step away from overcoming Honda and becoming Japan's top manufacturer of motorcycles!" exclaimed Yamaha president Hisao Koike.

Koike seized on the opportunity to launch his campaign to overtake Honda, and before long, the battle between Honda-Yamaha, or the "HY War" as it was known, had broken out in full force.

The reason for Honda's falling behind was readily obvious. In the spring of 1979, Yamaha had introduced three new products: the Carrot, the Malic, and the Lyric. In contrast, Honda, intent on adjusting its stock, had brought only one new product to market: the Chalet. Honda executives had not anticipated the market for family motorcycles to grow so quickly. Tadashi Kume, president of Honda Research and Development Company, had ordered his workers to begin work on "Project M," a new mid-sized motorcycle. This had reduced the number of engineers available for family motorcycles. Yamaha, on the other hand, introduced one new family motorcycle after another, quickly filling the market with a variety of products.

Honda had not expected that Yamaha would seriously try to oust Honda from its position as top manufacturer in the industry. Both domestically and abroad, the motorcycle industry was basically an oligopoly. There were only four motorcycle manufacturers in Japan. Japan's top manufacturer, Honda, also dominated the market worldwide, and Yamaha, number two in Japan, was also number two in the international marketplace. Although the companies jostled for position, an actual upset was a true rarity.

Being in second place wasn't necessarily disadvantageous. Whenever there was a problem with trade friction, for example, the top manufacturer was inevitably attacked first. The company in second place could easily dodge the problem by "hiding" behind the lead manufacturer. When it came to new products, the second place company could let the top manufacturer test the waters with new products first, study consumers' reactions, and then create their own improved version for a sure-fire hit. Honda had occupied the top slot since around 1960, and Yamaha had fully exploited the advantages of being number two. In fact, they had done it for so long, which was why no one at Honda seriously expected Yamaha to make a play for first place.

Relations between the two companies actually went a long way back. When Soichiro ran Tokai Seiki Heavy Industries during World War II, Kaichi Kawakami, president of Nippon Gakki Co., Ltd., the predecessor of Yamaha, approached Soichiro for engineering assistance. A Nippon Gakki piano factory had been converted to manufacture propellers for fighter aircraft, but the workers' lack of experience meant it took a week to finish a single propeller. Soichiro invented an automatic cutter that drastically shortened manufacturing time to just fifteen minutes. Soichiro's engineering prowess once again drew much praise, and the story also appeared in the newspapers.

Kawakami dubbed Soichiro a "Japanese version of Thomas Edison," and bestowed upon him the title of special advisor for Nippon Gakki. Kawakami portrayed Soichiro as a role model for his engineers, exhorting them to "strive to be even a little like Mr. Honda!"

Their friendship continued after the war, when the propeller factory became the foundations of the Yamaha Motor Company, the subsidiary of Yamaha Corporation, which dealt with engine manufacturing. In fact, Kawakami continued to approach Soichiro for advice whenever he built a new motorcycle factory. One could even say, therefore, that in a way Soichiro was the founding father of the Yamaha Motor Company. Genichi Kawakami, current chairman of Yamaha, is the oldest son of Kaichi Kawakami. While Kaichi had no end of respect for Soichiro, Genichi had something of an inferiority complex about the man, thanks to his father's constant prodding to watch and learn from him.

Genichi hated being compared to Soichiro, but he demonstrated his open-mindedness by hiring Hiroshi Kawashima, Kiyoshi Kawashima's younger brother by two years, to be president of Yamaha Corporation in 1976. The close connection between Honda and Yamaha, both in terms of family ties and company history, led many in the motorcycle industry to believe that the two companies would come to some kind of an agreement to avoid outright competition with one another.

Honda, for its part, regarded Yamaha's campaign to overthrow their company as no more than a rallying cry to inspire the workers at Yamaha. The most pressing matter facing Honda wasn't the motorcycle but the automobile business. Construction work had begun on the Ohio motorcycle plant and the Honda kids now needed to make their final decision regarding local production of automobiles in the United States. The negotiations with BL were proceeding smoothly. And Honda had just launched its new chain of "Verno" auto dealerships in Japan. When it came to the motorcycle business, Honda's first priority was exercising inventory control to optimize profit. Going head to head with Yamaha took a back seat.

In addition, just as Honda had predicted, the market for family motorcycles was leveling off. The only way to expand the market any further was through consumer education rather than new products. Honda's executives knew that simply flooding the marketplace with new products would escalate competition far more than necessary and come back to haunt them in the end.

Along with the increased number of riders came an increase in the number of motorcycle accidents. Motorcycles had finally achieved an image of general safety, but that would evaporate quickly if the manufacturers didn't step in to address the growing number of accidents. If negative rumors began spreading among the housewife set, who made the bulk of family motorcycle purchases, sales of the new motorcycles would sink like a stone.

That being said, the Honda kids knew they couldn't sit back and ignore Yamaha's aggressive new campaign, either. In September of 1979, Honda brought to market its first new product in sixteen months: the "Caren NX50," followed by the "Roadpal S" in November. Honda's share of the market made an immediate rebound to around forty-five percent. The "HY War" appeared to be over. But Yamaha wasn't finished yet.

By 1980, Honda clearly saw that Yamaha was serious about trying to knock their company out of first place. Early in the year, Yamaha president Koike publicly declared the company's aim to sell 950,000 motorcycles a year as part of its strategy to overtake Honda. That summer, chairman Genichi Kawakami suddenly fired Hiroshi Kawashima and took over the presidency himself. The local media explained the situation as arising from someone convincing Genichi Kawakami that the longer Kawashima remained as president, the longer it would take for Kawakami to promote his own son Hiroshi to the position.

The shake-up freed Koike, president of Yamaha Motor Company, to take drastic action. It would have been difficult for him to go all out to defeat Honda, knowing that the brother of the president of Yamaha Corporation, his parent company, occupied the president's chair in the rival company. Now, however, he could do as he pleased.

Koike was ambitious. He wanted to make Yamaha number one. And not just in the family motorcycle market segment. He wanted the markets for mid- and large-sized markets as well. His final aim was to catch up with Honda in foreign markets and unseat them from their position as the world's top manufacturer of motorcycles.

Koike believed that realizing his ambitions was not impossible. He knew that Honda had its hands full with the automobile business: the new plant in America, the partnership with BL, and ironing the kinks out of its new domestic sales network. Koike predicted that this would spread Honda's motorcycle division thin and give Yamaha the opening it needed to strike.

But in the end, it turned out that Koike had judged incorrectly. Honda had grown from the *bata-bata* motorcycles that Soichiro had created in his Hamamatsu garage in the chaos of the post-war era. Soichiro had partnered up with Fujisawa because he wasn't satisfied with a comfortable life in a beautiful suburb. Together they had moved to Tokyo and created a motorcycle company that had grown into the world's largest. And it was thanks to their success in the motorcycle industry that they had been able to successfully expand into automobiles as well.

Honda's automobile sales may have eclipsed that of their motorcycles, but the company still saw motorcycles as its "point of origin." Giving up first place in the motorcycle industry would be equal to abandoning home ground, or to relinquishing the shrine of the "cult of Honda."

The Honda Kids knew only too well what Fujisawa and Soichiro would think. If Yamaha unseated Honda from first place, it wouldn't just tarnish the glory that Fujisawa and Soichiro had worked together to achieve. It would make the man feel that his whole life had been pointless. The executives made up their mind. If Yamaha wanted a fight, it was going to be all-out war.

Honda sold some 1.01 million motorcycles domestically in 1980. During the same period, Yamaha sold 830,000. While Yamaha had not yet met its goal, it had managed to bring the difference with Honda down to a little over 200,000 vehicles. For 1981, Yamaha set it goal at one million units and managed to reach that goal by November. The company appeared to be on the cusp of catching up with Honda.

The final showdown was carried over to 1982.

"We're almost there!" roared Koike during a speech to his workers at the beginning of the New Year. "This is our chance to catch up with Honda! Let's do it!"

7

The Honda kids may have made their decision to go to war, but they remained frustrated by their inability to give their all to the motorcycle industry at the moment. Yamaha might be gaining, but there was no way Honda could simply abandon the automobile business.

Of course, Honda wouldn't just sit back and watch, either. At the beginning of 1980, the company had quietly laid the groundwork for a counterattack with help from the Boston Consulting Group. The Honda kids had prioritized streamlining their manufacturing system as the best tactic to shake off Yamaha.

The kids knew that they needed to enlarge their target audience beyond just housewives to include both men and women in order to expand the market. The way to do that was to increase the variety of products on the marketplace. The Honda kids selected Shoichiro Irimajiri, senior managing director of Honda R&D as well as a director at headquarters and a candidate for the presidency of Honda, to lead the development of new motorcycles.

"Iri-san, I know you need money to create new product, and the current budget for the Asaka motorcycle division of R&D simply isn't enough," said Kawamoto. "I want you to go ahead and use whatever you need from the Wako division's automobile budget for your project. I'm sure we'll hear some complaining from the directors in charge of automobile sales, but this is too urgent to ignore. You can start by making sure all the tool and die manufacturers in Japan are with us, even if you have to stack up sheaves of money to do it. Use whatever resources you need."

Honda's first salvo in the war against Yamaha was a 50cc scooter by the name of "Tact," released in September of 1980. Scooters had been a popular form of transport for the ordinary citizen in the years after World War II, but had largely disappeared from the market with the ascension of k-cars in the late sixties. But the imported Italian "Vespa" had stirred newfound interest in scooters again. The cheapest 50cc Vespa retailed for more than 300,000 yen, but even so, more than a thousand were sold every month.

The Honda kids saw a prime marketing opportunity in scooters. The Tact boasted an automatic transmission with a newly developed toothed timing belt that increased climbing power and acceleration, overcoming the weaknesses of the family motorcycle. In addition, Honda made extensive use of plastic to make the Tact lighter and easier to handle.

Although the Tact was smaller than the Vespa, it featured a large footrest that made it comfortable to ride. The Tact was priced at 108,000 yen. It was a little more expensive than a family motorcycle, but even still only one-third of the price of a Vespa.

The Tact promised great potential and appeared to have a good chance at becoming the biggest hit for the company since the Roadpal. Naturally, Yamaha and Suzuki quickly released their own versions, but Honda enjoyed a head start. The company sold 470,000 Tact scooters in 1981, twice the number that it had sold when it had introduced them the year before, and gained a fifty percent share of the scooter market. Honda only managed with some difficulty to shake off Yamaha that year because it had once again kicked off a new fad.

The success emboldened Honda's executives, who decided to use scooters as their main card against Yamaha. Estimates indicated a demand for 1.6 million scooters in Japan. The plan became to sell one million scooters, or sixty percent of the market, striking down Yamaha in a single blow. Once again, increasing the variety of products was essential in order to expand the market. Honda unveiled the "Lead," a new scooter aimed at male consumers, in February 1982. Shortly thereafter, Honda released another scooter targeting the female market, and then a "luxury scooter" with a retail price of over 200,000 yen.

Senior managing director Koichiro Yoshizawa, who oversaw Honda's motorcycle sales in Japan, supervised the sales operation. Yoshizawa had been president of American Honda, but the outbreak of the "HY War" led Kiyoshi Kawashima to transfer him back to Japan.

At that time, there were about thirty companies that ran motorcycle dealerships in Japan. Yoshizawa bought out their dealership rights at "twice the price they would expect to get" and put the dealers under the direct control of headquarters. Rival companies criticized the tactic as "buying people off," but Honda couldn't afford to listen to such complaints.

"Sixty percent of my mind is occupied by the motorcycle business. The automobile business only takes up forty percent," said president Kiyoshi Kawashima on more than one occasion. Even as the Ohio automobile factory was about to begin production, he made it clear that putting Yamaha in its place was a top priority.

The Yamaha Motor Company was a subsidiary of Yamaha Corporation, the company that had fired Kiyoshi Kawashima's brother. Now Kawashima hated Yamaha and anything related to the company. Although he knew he had to avoid making a public impression that a personal grudge was involved, there was no question that the hate boiled in Kawashima's mind. In fact, he could hardly control his emotions. Soon, Kawashima's goal changed from securing Honda's position in the industry to destroying Yamaha itself.

Competition was severe at the very ends of Honda's sales network: the retail shops. In the last half of 1981, shops in some regions had slashed the price of family motorcycles to as low as half the list price.

"That's unforgivably cheap! Still, we've no choice but to fight back," was Yamaha's position.

"Yamaha started it. Justice is on our side," was Honda's.

Both sides were bent on giving tit for tat, returning like for like. The number of districts selling motorcycles at a loss kept increasing by the day. Eventually, number-three Suzuki cried "uncle" and begged Honda and Yamaha to return to a more realistic pricing structure. Neither listened. In fact, if anything, the competition grew even fiercer.

By 1982, the situation appeared to be developing into a quagmire. Stores were now selling motorcycles for even below half price—in some cases, for less than 30,000 yen apiece. Some shops even started offering four as a set for 100,000 yen, or threw in a family motorcycle for free for customers who purchased high-end bicycles. The war continued to escalate with seemingly no restraints.

Unlike the automobile sales network, the majority of motorcycle dealerships were non-exclusive; many carried both Honda and Yamaha products. In the evenings, it wasn't uncommon for Yamaha salesmen to visit the shops and help the owners clean up—and in the process, move the Honda products to the back while placing the Yamaha ones in the front. The next morning, when the Honda salesmen paid their daily visits, the process would be reversed. These odd little dramas played out in dealerships across Japan.

Wrapped up in a vicious circle, the two manufacturers competed to have shops sell their products by offering huge commissions to the dealers and shop owners. The promise of money only served to heighten the aggressive sales tactics. Some dealers even falsely registered new products so that they would be categorized as "secondhand" and could be sold for even lower prices. As a result, so-called "old but unused" products, a phenomenon unique to the automotive industry, flooded the marketplace. Many of the motorcycles that were given away with other purchases or sold in sets were "old but unused" products.

The rivalry continued to escalate. In 1981, Honda partnered up with the subsidiary of French automaker Peugeot, called Cycle Peugeot, to co-produce 80cc motorcycles. Cycle Peugeot also made bicycles. As part of the agreement, Honda imported the bicycles for sale in Japan.

The agreement infuriated Yamaha, which had been in the final stages of negotiations to sell Cycle Peugeot's bicycles in Japan before being dropped in favor of Honda. President Koike blew his top and flew straight to Cycle Peugeot headquarters in Paris and demanded that negotiations with his company be reopened.

Peugeot employees also began to wonder if it wouldn't be more advantageous to have Yamaha—which certainly had a use for the bicycles in its huge amusement park facilities—market the products instead of Honda, as the latter had no experience in selling bicycles. Such developments only contributed to the overall confusion.

From around the end of spring in 1982, Honda's counterattack against Yamaha went into full gear. Towards the end of the year, Honda continued to introduce one or two new motorcycle models every week. All together, the company released some forty-five different models in that year alone. Yamaha, on the other hand, released only half as many.

Normally, developing a new motorcycle is said to require six months. Bringing so many new products to market in so short a time would seem next to impossible, even for a company like Honda.

Honda's explanation was surprisingly matter-of-fact:

"The six-month standard is old news. We employ innovative development methods and make full use of computer technology; this has allowed us to reduce the required time by fifty percent."

While some people believed the explanation, it was not the entire truth.

Generally, a manufacturer designed roughly double the number of motorcycles that actually went on sale. This meant that if a manufacturer wanted to make five new motorcycles to sell, it designed ten. Honda went ahead and manufactured all of its designs. Needless to say, this still wasn't enough to bring out one or two products every week. So Honda started slapping new façades on the same chassis. The functions were the same, but the motorcycles looked different enough to be sold as a separate model. Irimajiri's motorcycle section could do it, thanks to Kawamoto's improvements to the motorcycle development system. The sheer variety of motorcycles Irimajiri managed to churn out turned the tide towards victory for Honda in the end.

Yamaha wasn't letting up on the foreign front, either. Yamaha saw the U.S. market as its main battleground abroad. The orders for new motorcycles placed at the gathering of American Yamaha dealers at the end of 1981 were the highest recorded in the history of the motorcycle industry. Koike believed Yamaha had a shot at beating Honda in the United States as well as Japan.

Honda's Super Cub had been a major hit in the United States. In the end, however, the market for small motorcycles failed to take off in America as it had in Japan. American dealers imported roughly one million motorcycles a year, which was basically equal to demand in Japan, but focused on larger models. Honda's share was a little less than fifty percent of that figure. Yamaha was quietly amassing inventory in preparation for the next stage of its war against Honda in the United States.

In 1982, Honda released eleven new models of motorcycle. The top-selling product was an 1100cc motorcycle called the GL1100A. The GL1100A was a luxury motorcycle manufactured in Honda's Ohio plant. It included a windshield, trunk, panniers, and a radio as its standard equipment. Options included a stereo, CB, and tape deck.

Honda also unveiled the world's first 750cc motorcycle with a four-cylinder water-cooled engine. Other new products featured short cylinders or a turbo, for use as sports vehicles. Up until the previous year, Honda had sold only five types of motorcycle, none of which featured new engines.

The majority of American motorcycle consumers were young blue-collar workers. The U.S. economy at the time was in a recession and unemployment among blue-collar workers was rapidly increasing. As a result, sales of motorcycles in 1982 remained sluggish in spite of the enthusiasm shown at the Yamaha dealers' gathering. The U.S. was a major market for large motorcycles, but the only way to raise sales during a recession was to lower prices. Manufacturers needed to sell their inventory at any price, lest storage costs began to mount.

Still, neither company could cut prices enough. When the economy is in a downturn, prices need to be slashed dramatically to have any effect. In addition, stricter limitations on credit available to young people worsened the slump. By the fall of 1982, Honda, Yamaha, Suzuki, and Mazda found themselves sitting on more than one million units of trade inventories—equivalent to the total number of exports to the United States in a year.

Yamaha had the largest inventory. The company publicly announced that it had 290,000 motorcycles in stock at the end of October. Industry insiders said otherwise, however. If all Yamaha dealerships were included in the calculation, the rumors went, the company actually had some 490,000 units of trade inventory altogether—a roughly two year supply of product at peak sales levels. Honda, on the other hand, had 30,000 units of dead stock—roughly eight months' worth.

Yamaha planned to manufacture a total of 3.7 million motorcycles—1.5 million for the domestic market and 2.2 million for export—between May 1982 and April 1983. To pull it off, the company had hired about 1,000 new employees.

In a desperate bid to regain a foothold in domestic sales, Yamaha tried using Mazda's automobile sales network to sell their products. But the situation had grown so severe that the measure had virtually no effect. Over the summer, it became clear that Yamaha was clearly losing the battle against Honda. Yamaha's amount of inventory in the U.S. continued to rise. Compounding the situation, none of the company's new products for the Japanese market were selling particularly well. Before long, Yamaha's trade inventory had swollen to 500,000 units. Their aggressive sales and high commission tactics had already been pushed to the limit.

By this point, the only way for Yamaha to take control of the situation was reducing production. Yamaha revised its goals for the second half of the year to 900,000 units for the Japanese market and 1.6 million for exports, a thirty-two percent decrease from initial plans. Goals for the Japanese market alone were slashed by forty-percent. Now Yamaha found itself overburdened by the thousand new factory workers it had hired. In fact, the company was forced to temporarily transfer a large number of workers from its headquarters and factory to its dealerships.

By early 1983, it was obvious to all that Yamaha had lost the battle. The company's inventory loomed large in spite of the drastic production cuts. Yamaha's "war chest" was about to run dry. If the "HY War" continued, there was an increasing danger that it would begin to have a negative impact on Yamaha Motor's parent company. At the end of January, during his company's New Year's press conference, Yamaha Motor Company president Koike publicly announced that his company was throwing in the towel.

"Honda's sales network and ability to develop new products are simply too strong. There is no way we can keep up with it," said Koike.

Immediately after Koike's statement, Kiyoshi Kawashima ordered Irimajiri to stand down. Honda R&D was in the middle of developing not one but two mid-sized motorcycles, the CB400 and CX500. The Honda kids knew the majority of Yamaha's "war funds" were coming from the U.S. marketplace. The two new motorcycles were being specifically designed to deprive Yamaha of further income from that particular market segment.

"The party's over," said Yoshizawa, who oversaw Japanese sales. "No matter how good it may be, nobody will be interested in a plate served after the party. If only we'd served it up a little earlier, we could have ended the HY War at a much earlier stage." Irimajiri couldn't tell if he meant it cynically.

Yamaha put out the white flag in February. Kawashima and Koike met in a dreary meeting room at JAMA headquarters on February 10. The last time they had come face to face was nine years earlier in 1974, when Koike had visited Honda headquarters in Harajuku to congratulate Kawashima on his being named president.

"I'd like to declare the 'HY War' officially over," said Koike, bowing his head to Kawashima in apology.

"You call it a 'war,' but we didn't start it. We'd like to watch and see how Yamaha acts from now on before declaring an end to anything," replied Kawashima.

The meeting ended in an hour. The comment they made to the press after the meeting was very simple. They said:

"Both companies have agreed to stop this unnecessary competition. We have also agreed to resolve our differences in the future through discussions."

Yamaha's April public statement of accounts for fiscal year 1983 was truly miserable. Sales income was down one hundred billion yen compared to the previous year. Ordinary profit had dropped acutely, to two hundred million yen from its 14.6 billion yen record the year before. And what was more, the huge losses incurred by its American dealerships led the company to record extraordinary losses. This put Yamaha sixteen billion yen in red with regards to net profits, forcing it to reduce dividends by four yen. The company instituted drastic financial measures for fiscal year 1984, including a major production cut and suspension of dividends, in anticipation of a twenty billion-yen deficit in ordinary income.

Out of Yamaha's twenty top executives, nine including Koike took responsibility by either resigning or accepting demotions. The move was a reflection of the wishes of Genichi Kawakami, the head of the entire Yamaha group. At the same time, the company also issued a statement that it would "rationalize" the management and organization of 700 of its factory workers in light of the deep manufacturing cuts.

In contrast, Honda's statement for fiscal year 1983 was nothing short of magnificent. Sales income was 1.75 trillion yen, up thirteen percent in comparison to the previous year. Ordinary income was 50.6 billion yen, the highest in Honda's history.

From a numerical standpoint Honda certainly didn't seem to have suffered any ill effects from the "HY War." But in reality, deep wounds lurked under the surface. Honda had spent twenty billion yen in commissions and other payments to dealerships in 1982 alone, when the war was at its peak. The only reason the company was able to report its highest profits in history was due to the tremendous contribution American Honda was making to the bottom line through its dividends.

Honda had received an A1 rating—the highest rating assigned to commercial paper—from Standard & Poor's in 1980 when it decided to begin local production in America. A drop in the rating would have a negative impact on American Honda's international funding, so the company needed to retain its A1 rating at any cost. The truth was that the Honda Motor Company had shored up its statement of accounts for FY 1983 with help from American Honda.

The "HY War" gave Honda a PR boost, but neither Soichiro, Fujisawa, nor any of the Honda kids felt a sense of victory. The foolishness with the price-slashing could well have compromised the consumers' trust of the Honda brand. It had been a lose-lose proposition from the very start. Just as with the outcome of the N360 defect scandal, the victory was a hollow one.

"Of course we were busy with our automobile operation. Still, it was our failure to analyze the situation thoroughly that led things to go as far as they did," said Hideo Sugiura, who had been promoted to chairman the previous year. "I feel bad for Yamaha, but we didn't have any other choice. One of the fundamentals of business management is how quickly a company can respond to changes in the current situation. It's evolve or die." Sugiura's words expressed both a feeling of regret and a resolve to learn from the incident so as never to make the same mistake again.

Hirotoshi Honda, eldest son of Soichiro, offered a levelheaded comment:

"Both Honda and Yamaha fought a foolish war. While it's true that motorcycles are useful as a form of transportation, as the Super Cub has demonstrated, in reality they're more of a hobby product. Lowering prices doesn't automatically result in higher sales. Both sides knew that, but went head to head anyway out of a misguided sense of pride. Honda may have won the war, but only at the cost of the trust of the consumers. I believe we're going to see a tremendous decrease in motorcycle demand."

True to Hirotoshi's words, the end of the "HY War" signaled the beginning of a severe depression for the motorcycle industry, particularly with regard to the motorcycles under 50cc that formed the bulk of Honda and Yamaha's product lines. Some 2.78 million of the machines had been sold domestically in Japan at the peak of the boom in 1982. By 1993, sales were less than one third of this amount, and the number continues to decrease even today.

8

At its shareholders meeting in 1982, Honda announced that it would be amending its articles of incorporation to introduce a new post of "chairman." In Japan, this title is usually bestowed on presidents of companies when they retire, and if the chairman also has representative rights, he can effectively continue to control the company from behind the scenes.

As such, some believed initially that Kiyoshi Kawashima was creating the post for his own sake. But the first person to receive the title was actually Hideo Sugiura, vice president of Honda. Sugiura became chairman in autumn of 1982. At Honda, while the chairman does have representative rights, the position isn't the next step for outgoing presidents.

The executives agreed to define the duties of the post as follows: "The chairman will support the president with regard to outside activities and act as the president's delegate to society at large. The chairman will be a non-regular member of the executive council and only participate those meetings where the agenda includes outside activities." In other words, the chairman of Honda would represent the company but not be involved in business management, focusing rather on outside PR activities on behalf of the president. The chances of Kiyoshi Kawashima taking the post after Sugiura were zero from the very start.

Nine years had passed since Kiyoshi Kawashima had taken the reins of Honda. The long-awaited American automobile factory was set to begin production at the end of the year. Industry gossip held that Kiyoshi Kawashima might use the occasion to officially announce his resignation. But the speculation was wrong.

Kiyoshi Kawashima was only fifty-four years old. If he had worked for Nissan or Toyota, he would have only just reached executive status by now. Nine years was a long time, but Kawashima was just reaching his prime as an executive manager. Since he was not going to become chairman, he wouldn't be actively engaged in *zaikai* activities—lobbying activities to further the interests of the business community. All that remained for him after his retirement was a quiet life of leisure. But Kawashima was simply too young for that kind of lifestyle yet.

Sugiura's acceptance of the chairman post seemed to push off any plans Kawashima had for retirement. But one year later, on October 12, 1983, Kawashima officially announced his intention to retire as president and take on the post of supreme advisor to the board of directors. Just as expected, he named fifty-one year-old Tadashi Kume as his successor.

Ten years sounds like a long time, mused Kawashima, *but it went by in the blink of an eye. Still, I feel tired. The pressure of the founders was a heavy burden to bear. I should have waited and trained Kume for a little longer. For the sake of my health, though, this is something I had to do.*

When Kiyoshi Kawashima met with Fujisawa and Soichiro to tell them of his decision, they had made a single request.

"We're getting old. It's time for us to step down a bit further. We don't mind keeping the title of supreme advisor, but let us retire from being executives. Promote some young ones to fill out the ranks," they told him.

Complying with the founders' wishes, the Honda kids made personnel changes that resulted in an even lower average age for the executive corps. Hiroyuki Yoshino, who had joined Honda the same year as Irimajiri, was promoted to executive at the age of forty-three, becoming the third member of the Honda kids to have been born after 1935. Fifty-six year-old vice president Masami Suzuki, fifty-five year-old managing director Kenjiro Okayasu, and fifty-one year-old Takayuki Kobayashi, also managing director, retired. Combined with the retirement of the two founders from their executive positions and a rejuvenation of the executive corps as a whole, Kawashima's retirement drew all the more attention.

The focus of the attention was on Koichiro Yoshizawa's promotion to vice president and Nobuhiko Kawamoto's promotion to managing director. Kawamoto's rival Irimajiri had been promoted to the same position two years earlier. Now the two finally stood together as equals.

Irimajiri was transferred from the Honda Research and Development Company, where he had been vice president, and sent to head up the Suzuka manufacturing plant. Kiyoshi Kawashima felt Irimajiri needed to build as much experience as possible in anticipation for becoming president in the future. While working at Honda R&D was enough to make one an expert in engineering, it wasn't enough to make someone a top executive. Kawashima wanted Irimajiri to walk the same path that he himself had taken. Kawashima spoke to Irimajiri personally to explain his reasons for transferring the younger man. Irimajiri's career as the "prince of Honda" had begun.

Although Kawamoto had joined Honda at the same time as Irimajiri, Irimajiri had been promoted two years earlier than Kawamoto. In addition, considering that Honda prided itself on youthfulness, few doubted that Irimajiri was next in line for president after Kume.

Kiyoshi Kawashima announced his retirement at a press conference in a Tokyo hotel.

"I've always thought of ten years a my goal for working as president. Anyone in the company can confirm this. We held a huge party in Kyoto on the fifteenth anniversary of Honda. On our twenty-fifth anniversary, the two founders resigned and I became president. This year marks our thirty-fifth anniversary, and I firmly believe the time has come for a changing of the guard at Honda. There are no hard and fast requirements to becoming president. I marked Kume as having potential very early on, and have been quietly watching him until this very day," said Kawashima, revealing his successor for the first time.

Kawashima emphasized that his retirement had long been planned and at the same time, he admitted that he had looked upon Kume as his successor from an early stage. When Kawashima had been promoted to president ten years earlier, he had sworn two things to himself. One was that, in order to make sure the company continued to grow, he would manage based on mutual consent, always respecting the personality and ideas of each one of the executives. Kawashima had felt that the only way to live up to the standards set by the two geniuses who had founded the company was to apply the concept of the "solidarity of the ordinary."

Kawashima's second vow had been to make sure to select the right person for the next president as quickly as possible and to retire at just the right moment. That he had succeeded at both tasks was a great relief to Kawashima.

"I am a firm believer that a former president shouldn't meddle in the business affairs of the current management, even if he thinks he's giving solid advice," concluded Kawashima, ending the press conference.

Kawashima's last words are not to be seen as a criticism of Soichiro and Fujisawa. In fact, Kawashima knew from the very beginning that the Honda kids would continue looking to the founders for advice. Kawashima simply wanted to emphasize that he was not in the position to act as an advisor after he retired. His success at managing the company thus far in the shadow of the two founders, he believed, was not due to his own personal skills but to the mutual consensus of all the executives.

It had under Kawashima's direction that Honda's unique *waigaya* and "collective directors' room" systems took root and flourished. By integrating these systems firmly into Honda's corporate culture, Kawashima had done his best to achieve independence for the Honda kids from their "parents."

In contrast to Kawashima, Kume appeared to be slightly nervous as he announced his plans as new president:

"Up to now, Honda has enjoyed the agility that comes with youth. I'd like now add new some new traits to Honda's personality during my tenure: the tenacity and the vitality to take on and beat any challenge."

Kume was the obvious choice for Kawashima's successor. Soichiro had often said without reserve to both Honda employees and outsiders, "No matter how long Kawashima decides to stay on as president, the next one will definitely be Kume." Fujisawa also praised Kume's tenacity in sticking to his own ideals, as the debate over water-cooled versus air-cooled engines had shown. The choice of Kume as Kawashima successor had, in fact, been so obvious that the personnel changes at Honda received relatively little media fanfare.

Although everyone had fully expected that Kume would become the president, his actual abilities as head manager remained untested and unknown. Kiyoshi Kawashima wasn't really a "second generation" Honda employee; he had shared the ups and downs right alongside Soichiro and Fujisawa. Kume, on the other hand, had been hired after Honda had recovered from its business crisis of 1954. And Kume's long years at Honda R&D meant that the "crises" he had faced were mainly related to the engineering challenges of developing F1 race cars and reduced-emission engines.

In fact, not everyone entirely agreed with Kume's promotion. Yoshio Nakamura, who had supervised Kume as the head of the F1 project, worried about Kume's selection as the next president.

Nakamura had taken responsibility for the death that had resulted from Soichiro's air-cooled F1 racecar in 1968. He had dissolved London-based Honda Racing and submitted his letter of resignation, but Fujisawa and Kawashima managed to persuade him to accept work at a Honda subsidiary in the U.K. instead. As soon as Kawashima became president, however, Nakamura had been transferred back to Japan and promoted first to director and then to managing director before ending up as a special engineering advisor. Some time before Kume's appointment, Nakamura had given a candid appraisal of the man's abilities to Fujisawa and Kawashima.

"We all know Honda was created and thrived based on Soichiro-san's engineering skills," began Nakamura. "But times are changing. I'm an engineer myself, so I know engineers tend to see the world through rose-colored glasses. One reason for this is that we can't develop better products, or improve quality and productivity without an optimistic point of view.

"An president with an engineering background is, so to speak, a figurehead. When a company is growing steadily, there isn't any problem. But when there's a recession, it can be a disaster. He doesn't have any management philosophy that might help him run the business. Engineers aren't trained in business management, so they lack a fundamental grasp of just what it entails. No one knows more than I that Kume is a top-class engineer. But being a great engineer doesn't automatically mean that he'll be a great president as well. I actually think it's cruel at some level to throw an optimistic engineer into a violently changing business environment without any training. I humbly suggest promoting someone with a sales or accounting background who can look at things from a broad perspective instead."

As Nakamura had pointed out, the global automotive industry had entered an age of turmoil in the early 1980s, set off by the rapid increase of exports of Japanese cars. Layoffs at the Big Three led to increasingly large numbers of unemployed laborers in the auto industry, and the Union of Automobile Workers (UAW) found it impossible to cope with the onslaught of imports from Japan.

Claiming that the large number of Japanese imports had seriously damaged the American auto industry, the UAW appealed to the International Trade Commission (ITC) for a remedy in May 1980, just after the the U.S. Department of the Treasury had modified the import duty structure in an attempt to shut Japanese compact trucks from the American marketplace. In August, Ford, whose business had suddenly begun to decline, expressed its support for the UAW. In any event, the only way conceivable "remedies" for the problem would consist of regulating the import of Japanese automobiles.

Contrary to expectations, however, the ITC's decision that November essentially absolved the Japanese manufacturers of responsibility. Although the ITC decision was a positive development for the Japanese manufacturers, there was no question that it also complicated the situation. Shortly thereafter, Ronald Regan was elected President of the United States on a platform of free trade. But the ITC's decision only heightened the criticism of Japan from both the UAW and the U.S. Congress.

Ford's public statement of accounts for 1980 showed a loss of 1.54 billion dollars, the largest deficit in the history of the company. General Motors was in the red for the first time in its history as well. Chrysler, which had headhunted Lee Iacocca from Ford to be its chairman, had barely managed to skirt bankruptcy by securing a seven hundred million-dollar federal subsidy. Chrysler had pinned high hopes on its new "K-car" series, but sales had been only half of expected due to continued high interest rates. As a result, Chrysler ended up having to ask for another government subsidy of four hundred million dollars.

The combined losses of the Big Three companies amounted to four billion dollars. Despite the ITC's judgment, regulation of Japanese imports appeared to be inevitable. President Reagan, who had pledged the return to a strong America during his campaign, could hardly turn a blind eye to the crisis facing the United States' key industry. The governments of Japan and America entered into secret negotiations, with the Japanese agreeing to voluntarily reduce exports by 9.2 percent over the previous year to 1.68 million automobiles after 1981, in order to contribute to the rebuilding of the Big Three. The regulations would continue over the subsequent three years, although the specific amount remained open for discussion each year. Even after the measures were in place, however, the Big Three showed little if any signs of improvement. An extended period of regulation seemed inevitable.

During this period, the biggest of the Big Three, General Motors, was making some complicated moves. In August of 1981, GM suddenly announced that it would take a stake in Suzuki. Isuzu, which was already involved in a capital tie-up with GM, had acted as intermediary for the deal. The truth was that GM chairman Roger Smith had suggested approaching Honda first. Knowing that

Honda would absolutely refuse any form of capital tie-up, however, Isuzu president Toshio Okamoto had recommended Suzuki instead. General Motors planned to use Suzuki k-cars to feed the demand in America.

On March 1, 1982, Smith also held a secret meeting with Eiji Toyoda, president of Toyota, in New York City. The information leaked, making the negotiations public knowledge. But nobody expected the companies to actually reach an agreement; only six months earlier, Toyota had walked out of negotiations with Ford when it became clear that the interests of both sides were not well matched.

Contrary to people's speculations, however, GM and Toyota reached an agreement for American co-production in the spring of 1983. It was the same topic that Ford and Toyota had been negotiating. The alliance between the world's first and second best auto companies shook the industry.

Spurred on by the news, Mazda and Mitsubishi launched investigations into the feasibility of co-production with Ford and Chrysler, respectively, being already involved in a capital tie-up with these companies. Nissan, which prioritized the local production of compact trucks over all else, began considering the manufacture of automobiles at its Tennessee factory as a means of easing the labor conflict.

The backlash against Japanese automobiles was intensifying in Europe as well. Europe had long suffered from an excess of manufacturing facilities. France regulated Japanese manufacturers to ensure that they held no more than a three percent of share of the market. Italy restricted the number of Japanese imports to less than 2,400 vehicles a year. The Japanese share of the British market was set at somewhere between ten and eleven percent. But Japanese automobiles sold like hotcakes in the rest of Europe.

The situation upset the European Committee of Common Market Automobile Constructors (CCMC), which consisted of European firms backed by national capital. Representatives of main member companies—Volkswagen, BL, Renault, Peugeot, Fiat, and Alfa Romeo—assembled in Tokyo in December 1980 for a conference of European an Japanese automakers, where they called for Japanese manufacturers to voluntarily restrict their exports. From this point on, Japanese exports to Europe fell under the jurisdiction of MITI.

One of the by-products of the conference was an agreement for licensed production between Nissan and Volkswagen. Takashi Ishihara, president of Nissan, met secretly with Volkswagen chairman Toni Schmücker not long after the conference, leading to the agreement for licensed production of VW products in Japan.

Nissan had already entered a capital tie-up with a major Spanish truck manufacturer called Motor Iberica in the early spring of 1980. During the summer of that year, Nissan also announced a co-production with Alfa Romeo. And in January of 1981, Nissan made an announcement that it would be building a stand-alone factory in the U.K. at the request of the British government. Those in the auto industry could hardly believe the scope of Nissan's seemingly endless overseas projects.

The surge in automobile exports had saved the Japanese economy from two oil crises, but it had also resulted in serious trade friction. The only way to ease the friction was to curb the number of exports. Honda had taken the initiative by building the factory in the U.S. and setting up the partnership with BL. But there were no guarantees that being first would give the company a long-term advantage.

The Japanese auto market appeared to be maturing. In 1979, the number of automobiles sold in Japan, including k-cars, rose for the first time to a level that had not been achieved since 1973, before the first oil crisis. After the rebound, however, sales stabilized at around five million units a year. Sales in 1980 were at 5.15 million; this dropped to 5.01 million in early 1981, but rallied to 5.13 million by the end of the year, and annual sales in 1982 were 5.26 million. Judging from the figures, the market had by this time reached full maturity.

The figures of car ownership among individuals and households were also clear indications of the maturity of the domestic market. In 1970, only 17.58 million cars were in private hands. This grew to twenty-eight million in 1975 and 37.86 million in 1980. Compared to the early 1970s, when the wave of motorization sweeping the country gave impetus to the increase in private car ownership, the rate of increase was considerably slower in the late seventies and early eighties.

During the same period, the ratio of households with automobiles were 22.1 percent, 41.8 percent, and 56.0 percent, respectively. In the days when motorization was had just taken off, only one out of five households owned an automobile. By the early 1980s, this had grown to one out of two. At this point, eighty percent of new demand was generated by people seeking to replace their cars, rather than by first-time buyers.

Judging from the numbers of automobiles owned and the rate of ownership per household, motorization was definitely reaching a point of inflection. In spite of this, Honda had yet to prepare its national sales network for the increased demand.

On the motorcycle front—the company's main source of revenue—Honda had won the "HY War," but found itself saddled with large amounts of inventory both in Japan and abroad. The company was about to begin reducing production in earnest. In the U.S., Harley Davidson had filed a claim with the ITC alleging that Japanese manufacturers had dumped their products on the American market, effectively hobbling Honda's ability to take drastic measures to increase sales.

Japanese motorcycle and automobile manufacturers were facing a major turning point. Aggressive sales techniques of the sort that had been popular in the 1970s were no longer acceptable in the 1980s, obligating executives to take a broader approach than simply increasing raw sales.

Kawashima and Fujisawa were fully aware of the difficulties facing automakers. In the end, however, Kawashima promoted Kume to the presidency over Nakamura's objections. Kawashima knew full well that both Soichiro and Fujisawa wanted Kume in the position. Even if Kawashima had agreed with Nakamura, there was no way he could go completely against the will of the two founders and choose a successor with a business background.

According to Fujisawa's management philosophy, Honda was essentially a manufacturer of engineered products whose main strengths lay in the technology it was able to offer. The company's mission was to provide society with high quality products at reasonable prices. That was precisely why the president needed to be an engineer. Based on this firm belief, Fujisawa, whose own strengths lay in business management, never thought of taking on Soichiro's position after his partner's retirement.

Fujisawa was more than aware that Kume had not been trained as a business manager.

I want to bet on him, thought Fujisawa. *My dream is for Honda to catch up with and overtake Nissan, making it clear to the world that it has the number-two slot in the industry. Kume is nothing if not tenacious. He has something that the rest us don't have. No wonder Soichiro had a hard time with him—Kume is a man with a backbone. It's true his capacities as a manager are untested, but that just means he has all the more potential. Yoshizawa can handle day-to-day affairs. I made sure to remove any executives who didn't get along with Yoshizawa. Now Kume can play the role of Soichiro, and Yoshizawa can play mine—they can split the work and run the business together. I'm convinced that Kume and Yoshizawa are an unbeatable team. If anyone can make my dream come true, it's these two.*

Honda's net sales income in 1972, just before Kiyoshi Kawashima became president, had been three hundred and thirty billion yen, placing Honda twenty-fourth in the manufacturing industry. Ten years later, net sales had grown to 1.84 trillion yen, pushing Honda into the top ten. Kawashima had increased net sales by 550 percent during his presidency. Kawashima's achievements weren't simply limited to expanding the size of the company. His rapid internationalization of the business had made Honda one of the world's most respected manufacturers, despite its late start in the auto industry.

And yet, Fujisawa remained unsatisfied. If anything, Honda's growth beyond expectations made him even more ambitious. During the first stages of motorization, Fujisawa's goal had been to beat Toyota with a re-purposed F2 racing engine. Soichiro, however, hadn't agreed. Then, as a result of the N360 defect scandal and the enactment of the emissions regulations, Toyota had slipped far beyond Honda' reach. Fujisawa's ambition of overtaking Toyota remained an unrealized dream.

Nissan, on the other hand, began to look like a much closer and easier target. Nissan had launched a variety of large-scale projects overseas, but it would take time for the company to reap the benefits. What was lucky for Honda was that Nissan had been late in deciding to open a local facility in the U.S., where Honda was building a stronger base of popularity year after year. And in the domestic market—Honda's weak spot—Nissan's number of foreign projects was spreading the company thin.

Honda's consolidated net profits already exceeded that of Nissan. In a capitalist economy, the primary goal of a corporation is securing net profit rather than maximizing sales income. In the modern era of rapid globalization and international development, consolidated net profit is viewed as more important than individual sales figures. Honda's predominance in this respect was also reflected in stock prices. On the day Kume took over as president of Honda, Honda shares sold for 987 yen while Nissan shares sold for 710 yen.

In comparison to sales income, however, net profit is based on a multitude of uncertain elements. The fact that Honda surpassed Nissan in consolidated net income was a result of Honda's success in the U.S. market. A strong yen, however, could send profits plunging. The public was fully aware of this and had not yet begun treat Honda as the number two Japanese auto company, even if it's consolidated net profits exceeded Nissan's. Fujisawa wanted to bring Honda within range of Nissan in terms of numbers indicating the size of the business.

The one area where Honda could easily beat Nissan was that of numbers of automobiles exported to the United States. The figure was calculated based on a company's historic number of U.S. sales. This made Honda had a lower export quota than Nissan. But in terms of local production, Nissan had chosen to manufacture compact trucks rather than cars. That meant that once the Ohio factory was in full operation, Honda's numbers would automatically exceed those of Nissan.

Even so Fujisawa remained unsatisfied. He wanted Kume to beat Nissan domestically as well as abroad. By now Fujisawa was more than seventy years old, and he was getting impatient. From day one of his career at Honda, he had always believed that everything changes, that anyone who thrived was destined to wither. When he had run Honda he had done everything he could to stave off the inevitable. The pursuit of Nissan represented Fujisawa's final stand. *Focus on defeating Nissan, run full steam ahead, and Honda will live forever*, thought Fujisawa. *I know Kume and Yoshizawa have it in them.*

Yamaha had doomed itself through the deliberate attempt to overthrow Honda in the motorcycle industry. Honda's blistering counterattack had deflected Yamaha's ambitions and had almost sent the company spiraling into crisis. If Honda openly announced to its employees and to the public that it was going after Nissan, it would only serve to unnecessarily provoke the rival company, and Honda could well find itself in Yamaha's shoes.

Honda was riding high on a string of successes, but Nissan enjoyed a long history and far more experience than Honda. As a post-war startup, Honda still had a long way to go to match that experience. Hardly anyone was more painfully aware of this fact than Fujisawa and the Honda kids themselves.

CHAPTER SIX: THE LAW OF TRANSIENCE

Everyone has their weak points and strong points. That's why we have dif-
ferent personalities. People gravitate towards fields that they feel strongly about,
and help cover for each other's weak points. That's society in a nutshell. We
should utilize the exact same system in our working environment as well.

—Soichiro Honda

Unlike an automobile, a business doesn't have two sets of wheels. I may
have only been vice president of Honda, but I took full responsibility for the
business as if I were the president. The reason for Honda's success is that both
of us were keenly aware of our own weak points.

—Takeo Fujisawa

1

In the years after Nissan's acquisition of Prince Automobile in 1966, the word "merger" all but disappeared from the Japanese auto industry. Nevertheless, Japanese auto manufacturers faced three major turning points after the advent of motorization.

The first of these was the liberalization of capital, which took place around 1970. In a bid for survival, three of Japan's mid-sized auto corporations partnered with foreign companies. Mitsubishi Heavy Industries spun off its automobile division, which partnered with Chrysler. Isuzu and Mazda formed partnerships with General Motors and Ford, respectively.

At the time, the prevailing attitude in Japan held that partnerships with the giant foreign manufacturers all but guaranteed survival in the auto industry. Later, when Japanese automobiles became popular in the United States and Europe, the very same companies that had rushed into partnerships began to reconsider their positions. There was a growing sense that the alliances might actually be hindering rather than fostering future growth.

The relationship between Mitsubishi Motors and Chrysler is a perfect example of the paranoia at the time. When Mitsubishi's executives signed the partnership deal, they hadn't anticipated the inroads that Japanese automobiles would make in the United States. As a result, Mitsubishi willingly signed over the rights to sell its cars in the U.S. to Chrysler. Realizing their mistake some time later, Mitsubishi executives managed to successfully negotiate for a contract revision. But they had lost precious time in the process. By the time the company extricated itself, Mitsubishi had fallen behind Toyota, Nissan, and even Honda in the American marketplace.

Mazda, which had entered into a partnership with Ford in 1979, found itself increasingly irritated by Ford's slumping sales, which had begun almost immediately after they joined hands. Kenichi Yamamoto, who became president of Mazda at the end of 1984, further strained the relationship by publicly announcing that "Mazda will teach Ford how to make small cars" at nearly every opportunity.

The relationship between Isuzu and General Motors was fairly amicable, but even still, feelings of frustration with GM smoldered beneath the surface at Isuzu.

The three companies, Mitsubishi, Mazda and Isuzu had originally forged these alliances as a survival measure. As the relationship between the Japanese and American manufacturers evolved, however, the nature of the partnerships also underwent major change.

Chrysler fell into another business slump in the late 1980s. In order to secure funding, Chrysler not only shuttered the factory it ran in the United States in co-operation with Mitsubishi, it also sold off its shares in Mitsubishi and quickly dissolved the capital tie-up. Chrysler reinvested the income from selling the stock into the development of new automobiles, such as the "Neon," in an ultimately successful attempt to jump-start its business. The break-up fostered a newfound sense of independence at Mitsubishi. Before long, Mitsubishi had surpassed Honda as the top contender for Nissan's number-two spot in the Japanese auto industry.

On the other hand, Mazda wasn't doing well at all. At the height of the "bubble economy," Mazda built five sales networks in Japan, allowing it to grow as large as Toyota and Nissan. Unfortunately, however, the ambitious plan backfired and Mazda found itself facing a crisis. In the end, Mazda was forced to give up half of the stock and the management rights for the factory it ran with Ford on the outskirts of Detroit. Mazda also agreed to install a Ford employee as its vice president with representative rights. In fact, Ford continues to run Mazda's business even today. Although the ratio of stock shares owned by Ford in Mazda has remained the same, Mazda has now been completely absorbed into Ford's global strategy.

When Isuzu fell into business crisis in 1975, it sold its domestic Japanese sales and finance company to General Motors. Isuzu also issued convertible bonds to GM, which increased General Motors' actual share in the company from 34.2 to forty percent. It appeared as if Isuzu had been acquired by General Motors both in name and in substance. However, when GM hit financial trouble in the 1990s, it quickly divested itself of its shares in the sales and finance company as well as the CBs, reducing its share in Isuzu to 37.5 percent. The fluidity of the relationship between these three manufacturers and their foreign partners proves that corporations are like living organisms, undergoing constant flux.

The second turning point centered on emission regulations. The legislation put large manufacturers dealing in a wide variety of automobiles—like Toyota and Nissan—in a difficult position, but even more than that, it pushed smaller k-car manufacturers to the brink of bankruptcy. Suzuki is a prime case in point. At the time, Suzuki exclusively specialized in k-cars with two-stroke engines. No matter what they tried, the company's engineers couldn't devise a way to meet the regulations. Suzuki finally resorted to licensing four-stroke engine technology from Daihatsu to clear the hurdle. But the crisis came with an opportunity as well: Suzuki used the new technology as a stepping-stone into the compact car marketplace.

Keijidosha, or k-cars, especially the passenger car models, are designed to comply with standards unique to Japan. They proved difficult to modify for exhaust regulations, and for the most part could not be sold abroad. These disadvantages are, in fact, the reason for Honda and Mazda's decision to abandon the market segment. In addition, domestic demand was also showing a gradual decline. At the peak of demand in 1970, some 720,000 k-cars were sold in Japan. This dropped sharply to 157,000 in 1975, and floundered between 120,000 and 190,000 in the following years. It was apparent that k-cars had already completed their mission of accelerating the motorization of Japan.

K-cars made a comeback, however, at the beginning of Japan's Heisei era in 1989. The number of k-cars sold that year jumped to 392,000, or 2.5 times that of the previous year. The number continued to rise, and in 1990 sales were 796,000, breaking a record that had stood for twenty years. Sales in 1991 reached 840,000, indicating a full and total recovery for k-car manufacturers. Both Honda and Mazda reentered the market they had previously abandoned.

The revival was largely stoked by the government raising the maximum allowable engine displacement from the original 360cc to 550cc, and further still to 660cc. Other factors were an increase in the number of purchases by female consumers and people living in rural areas. Many of the women purchasing k-cars were "graduates" of family motorcycles who had come to enjoy being in control of a vehicle.

The third turning point centered on the internationalization of the auto business. Japanese automakers needed to internationalize if they wanted to survive in the marketplace of the twenty-first century, and local production in the United States formed the cornerstone of the approach. Being well aware the situation, Toyota broke ground in Kentucky immediately after forming its alliance with General Motors. Mazda, Mitsubishi and Suzuki began local production with the close cooperation of their foreign partners. Lagging behind the others, Isuzu and Fuji Heavy Industries also decided to begin co-production in America, regardless of their capital affiliation. Altogether, eight Japanese manufacturers made the decision to manufacture products in the United States.

Local production in the U.S. was but the first step in a new global strategy for Japanese manufacturers. Once American production was established, the Japanese manufacturers, looking ahead to the EC market integration, began to expand into Europe. It was not difficult to see that, eventually, such "internationalization" would lead to "multinationalization." The question was: how would Japanese manufacturers survive abroad? And how would Japan handle foreign products on the domestic marketplace? The auto industry of the 1990s was shaping up to be even more chaotic than in the decade before.

"Can you look after 'Ame-Kawa' (Kihachiro Kawashima)? I'll take care of 'Euro-Kawa' (Kiyoshi Kawashima)," said Soichiro to Fujisawa over cups of *sake* when Honda had still been a mid-sized corporation.

True to his word, Soichiro trained and groomed Kiyoshi Kawashima to be a top engineer and made him Honda's second president. Fujisawa schooled Kihachiro Kawashima in the ins and outs of business management, making him a perfect right-hand man for Kiyoshi Kawashima. Later, the two Kawashimas continued the tradition. Kiyoshi trained Kume, whereas Kihachiro trained

Yoshizawa.

Together Soichiro and Fujisawa formed the first generation of Honda's management. Kiyoshi Kawashima and his system of managing by mutual consent represented the second generation. During the first half of Kawashima's presidency, Takao Shirai, Kihachiro Kawashima, and Michihiro Nishida—who were known as the "big four" while working side by side with Kiyoshi Kawashima as senior managing directors—formed Honda's "inner circle." During the second half, Kawashima called upon chairman Hideo Sugiura and the three vice presidents, Noboru Okamura, Shigeru Shinomiya and Masami Suzuki, for support. One by one, old executives left and were replaced by fresh young people, like new teeth growing in to replace the old.

When Kume took over the presidency, Sugiura, Okamura, and Shinomiya remained in office, but sooner or later they too would leave the front lines. Yoshizawa was the first "new tooth" to distinguish himself. He played a key role in selling Honda's automobiles on the U.S. market, just as Kihachiro Kawashima had with motorcycles. During the "HY War," Yoshizawa had been in charge of domestic motorcycle sales and was largely responsible for Honda's eventual victory. Noting Yoshizawa's outstanding record, Fujisawa installed him as a supporter for Kume.

Kume's long years at Honda R&D left him with a decided lack of hands-on knowledge when it came to business management. He had joined Honda in 1954 and was sent to work at Honda Research and Development after it was spun off as an independent company. He was promoted to director, then managing director, and senior managing director, before eventually assuming the presidency of the company in 1977. At Honda R&D, all executives, including the president, played a direct role in the technological development process and Kume was no exception.

In 1979, Kume became senior managing director at Honda headquarters, making him one of the board members. His duties still focused on research and development, however, and as such spent most of his time at Honda R&D, rarely showing his face at headquarters in Harajuku. Kume had spent nearly thirty years in research and development without touching upon anything related to overall business management.

Kiyoshi Kawashima and Sugiura were also engineers. The key difference between them and Kume, however, was that they had faced—and had successfully overcome—the challenge of the defect scandal. They had also dealt with the fallout of the car exhaust legislation and learned some valuable management lessons along the way through their dialogue with the public. Kume didn't have any experience of the sort. He had distinguished himself through designing F1 racers and developing some of Honda's best-selling cars.

Fujisawa had hoped that Kiyoshi Kawashima would remain as president for an additional two years. During that time, Kume could be put in charge of automobile operations and would be able to study business management in general. This would also have given Yoshizawa the chance to run Honda R&D and learn more about engineering so as to be better prepared to support Kume. Fujisawa's plans, however, had one major hitch: at roughly the same time that

Honda made the decisions to launch local production in the U.S. and to form a partnership with BL, Kiyoshi Kawashima lost confidence in his health.

In the past, Kiyoshi Kawashima had developed a stress-related stomach ulcer just before the N360 had gone on sale. It had become severe enough to necessitate the removal of his entire stomach. Now doctors had discovered a tumor in the area. If the biopsy proved malignant, he would require immediate surgery to have the tumor removed.

"They say I've got a bit of a tumor in my stomach. I'm thinking to flush it out with a drinking binge," joked Kawashima to Sugiura and his other close colleagues.

Still, the illness was never far from his thoughts and Kawashima's drinking grew heavier every day. *If the tumor does end up being malignant,* he thought, *I'll end up causing trouble for the company.* Kawashima made up his mind to end his ten-year reign as president at the age of fifty-five. No matter what Fujisawa's plans were, Kawashima was under a tremendous amount of stress as president, and the specter of failing health loomed large over him. There was nothing Fujisawa could do to make him stay.

"Get Kume to work at headquarters immediately!" ordered Fujisawa once he understood Kawashima's position. "He doesn't need to be in charge of anything. We just need to get him up to speed about business management."

Kume was ordered to headquarters in 1982. He had stepped down as president of the Honda Research and Development Company the year before, but his successor Sugiura was also vice president at headquarters, which made it impossible for him to commute to the R&D facilities every day. Kume had used this as an excuse to remain at Honda R&D. Now, however, he had no choice.

Kume's working environment at headquarters proved unique. Unlike his fellow executives, he worked alone, in his own room. Kume wasn't given any particular project to supervise. When he was not attending board meetings or executive council meetings, he would while away his time by watching the sky outside his window. Before long, he had earned the nickname of "Kume the hermit." The rumors went that "Kume the hermit is confined at headquarters, just like the warrior Musashi Miyamoto was confined at Shirasagi castle."

Is he really capable of running the company? worried Nakamura. In the end, Kume would become Honda's third president before he ever got a chance to hone his business management skills. Three days after his dramatic ascent to the presidency, more than 10,000 Honda employees filled the grandstands of the Suzuka circuit in a driving rain.

"I'm Kume, the greenhorn president," said Kume, starting his first speech as president with a joke. "Over the last ten years, Honda has grown rapidly even in the face of two oil crises. We could well face similar obstacles in the near future. But I firmly believe that Honda will use its youth and vitality to find a way around them."

At this point, Soichiro took the microphone.

"I was a half-baked, imperfect man. So was Kawashima. Kume is the same. I want all of you to be fully aware that you have an imperfect man as your president! I'm personally asking each and every one of you to work hard and back him up," said Soichiro, concluding the ceremony in his unconventional style.

Fujisawa's first assignment for Kume was catching up with Nissan. Nissan may have fallen far behind Toyota, but it still remained a "tiger" in the auto industry. There would be no way for Honda to face them in a head-to-head competition. Honda's only hope would be through launching and winning a series of smaller battles first.

The first battleground would be the United States, where both Kume and Yoshizawa had full confidence in Honda's sales. *Nissan misjudged the severity of trade friction over automobiles*, reasoned Kume. *They must have decided to produce compact trucks rather than cars locally, not because they lack confidence in automobile production, but because the U.S. raised customs duties on cab chassis to twenty-five percent—the same level as for compact trucks. Nissan chose to concentrate their efforts on addressing this issue. Still, I don't think the voluntary restrictions on exports that the Japanese government agreed to impose will be over after the initial agreed period of three years. Soon or later, everyone—Nissan and even Toyota—is going to have to manufacture cars locally to survive. If that's the case, we should build up a strong U.S. production and sales network while they're still dragging their feet.*

Construction of the Ohio automobile factory proceeded smoothly, and in November of 1982—at the peak of the "HY War"—the factory celebrated its first car coming off the production line. The ribbon-cutting ceremony was held on April 25, 1983, just after the HY War finally came to a close. It was a large-scale celebration with some 500 attendees, including former Ohio governor James Rhodes, his successor Richard Celeste, and many other federal and state officials, parts suppliers, and dealers.

The Ohio factory represented the state of the art in Honda technology and had as its "mother factory" Honda's Sayama plant in Japan. Unlike the Big Three, which utilized separate press and assembly factories, Honda incorporated both into a single factory, just as it did in its Japanese factories. Normally, auto factories employed five press machines, but Honda had reduced the number to four, increasing production efficiency. In addition, other improvements were made in all aspects to allow the company to make a fair profit at 150,000 cars a year.

Since the factory workers were basically still amateurs, Honda decided to begin slowly, manufacturing just 57,000 automobiles in 1983, with the aim of reaching full production by the end of 1984. Honda wasn't aiming for quantity; the goal was to manufacture Accords that matched the quality of those produced at the Sayama plant. Honda decided to supply only thirty percent of required parts locally, giving the workers needed time to get up to speed. In fact, Honda continued to worry about quality control and the technology level of American parts suppliers. As such, the company decided to act conservatively.

In order to make a contribution to the reconstruction of the Big Three, the Japanese government agreed to voluntarily restrict automobile exports from 1981, but a certain level of trade friction between the U.S. and Japan persisted. In fact, immediately after the restrictions began to take effect, a Democratic Congressman from Indiana, Floyd Fithian, introduced a resolution that asked for quotas of

U.S. parts used in cars made by Japanese manufacturers in the U.S. be increased to a maximum of ninety percent. Honda had been proactive about beginning local production, but the tense atmosphere made it obvious that the company could hardly rest on its laurels. To avoid future problems, Honda readjusted its process and raised the ratio of locally supplied parts from thirty to fifty percent.

The Japanese manufacturers kept exports under 1.68 million for the second and third years of the agreement. Just as Kume had predicted, the restrictions weren't lifted after the third year as originally promised although the maximum allowable number of exports was revised upward. In 1984, the quota was raised to 1.85 million cars per year and in 1985 to 2.3 million cars per year. Since the Japanese manufacturers decided to manufacture their cars locally in the U.S., the regulations ended up existing only in name. Nevertheless, the restrictions would remain in place for a total of thirteen years, until they were finally lifted in 1993.

In an attempt to minimize the negative economic impact of the regulations, the Japanese automobile manufacturers gradually shifted focus from economy to luxury cars. They also raised prices drastically year after year. The Big Three also followed suit and raised the prices on their products as well, so that no matter how much the Japanese manufacturers raised their prices, their products did not appear to consumers to be much more expensive than their American counterparts. Somewhere along the line, the regulations had become a system used by both sides to hike their prices.

Honda's automobiles were far and away the most popular Japanese cars on the American market. The second version of the Accord, which was manufactured at the Ohio factory, proved to be a smash hit. The new Accord featured a quiet, four-cylinder, transverse front engine, front wheel drive configuration; a compact chassis; a five-speed transmission; high fuel efficiency of thirty miles per gallon; and an economical price of less than 8,500 dollars. It was superior in every aspect to any of the Big Three's products in the same range.

Demand was so strong that Accords began commanding a premium of up to 2,000 dollars beyond the sticker price. But even at the higher prices, the cars sold like hotcakes. In fact, all of the Japanese manufacturers were turning handsome profits on their products, thanks to an extremely favorable exchange rate of 250 yen to the dollar. Combined revenues for Toyota, Nissan, and Honda swelled to one trillion yen a year.

The three companies chose to spend their windfall in different ways. Toyota poured money into its domestic Japanese sales network. In July of 1982, Toyota Motor Co. merged with Toyota Motor Sales Co., and declared a new goal of securing a fifty percent share of the Japanese market.

Few took Toyota's new goal seriously at first. But the company showed its true strength by keeping its word. By October of 1986, Toyota's spare-no-expense attitude when it came to encouraging dealers paid off with a 53.5 percent share of the Japanese market. In fact, Toyota may have gone a little too far. Before long the company's hard-sell tactics became a magnet for criticism within the auto industry. The company restrained itself somewhat in response, but the message was abundantly clear: Toyota was a force to be reckoned with.

Toyota steadily increased retained profit so that its spare capital, which had been one trillion yen at the time of the merger, had swollen to approximately 2.25 trillion yen by June 1989. This was all according to the plan of Toyota's former chairman, Masaya Hanai, a disciple of Taizo Ishida, "the savior of Toyota," whose penny-pinching style had revived a flagging Toyota in the past. Hanai had set the goal of two trillion yen in extra capital so as to protect his company in the event of misjudged business decisions.

Toyota's rival Nissan, on the other hand, spent most of its money on overseas projects. While Toyota did spend some money to bolster its weak domestic Japanese sales force, the plan only involved buying back sales rights from local dealerships and had almost no direct affect on domestic sales at all.

Then there was Honda. Under Japan's policy of self-regulation, Honda was limited to exporting 360,000 vehicles to America a year. This was later increased to 400,000 and then 450,000 as the policy was revised. Even with the Ohio factory capable of manufacturing 150,000 cars within the United States, Honda found itself unable to keep up with the strong demand for its products among American consumers. The only way to keep up with the flood of orders would be to expand the size of the American manufacturing operation.

Kume and Yoshizawa realized that, with regard to the U.S. market, Toyota was at a disadvantage. Toyota had launched a joint venture with General Motors called New United Motor Manufacturing, Inc. (NUMMI) to manufacture vehicles in the United States, but the finished products would be supplied to GM. There was no way Toyota could increase its share of the U.S. market unless it built a local factory of its own.

It's been a year since the first car rolled off the assembly line. The quality of the American workers isn't as bad as we thought. The ratio of parts supplied locally continues to grow. If we can expand the factory, we may have a shot at beating not only Nissan but Toyota as well, thought Kume and Yoshizawa.

Mitsubishi, which had long aimed for third place in the domestic Japanese market, only exported a small number of cars to the U.S. and had also fallen behind in its expansion into the American marketplace as a result of the limitations imposed by its contract with Chrysler. Nevertheless, the company did profit to a certain extent from the alliance. Mitsubishi spent its profit to improve its domestic Japanese sales network. The investment paid off handsomely after the burst of Japan's economic bubble; it firmly established Mitsubishi's position in third place—and gave the company enough momentum to give Nissan a run for second.

2

Kume made the decision to expand the Ohio factory shortly after taking the reins at Honda. He publicly announced his plans at the company's New Year's press conference in 1984.

Kume's plan involved building another full assembly line within the Ohio factory, increasing production capability for the Accord to 300,000 units a year, as well as building a new factory in Canada capable of manufacturing 80,000 cars a year by 1986. Once completed, the total number of cars Honda would be able to supply to the U.S. market every year through a combination of locally produced products from the Ohio factory and imports from Japan and from the Canadian factory would exceed 700,000.

Honda had already spent some three hundred million dollars in factories for motorcycles, motorcycle engines, automobiles, and other equipment such as lawn mowers in the United States. The company was also investigating the possibility of building an automobile engine factory. The total amount of proposed additional investment, including funding for the Canadian factory, was in the vicinity of five hundred million dollars. The policy of allowing American Honda to retain its income rather than sending it back to headquarters in Japan ensured that there was plenty of money on hand.

Honda's longtime weak point in the U.S. was sales capacity. It was becoming more and more obvious that Honda new needed to tackle the problem, lest it become even more of an issue in the future. It was true that Honda's products were selling well at the moment. But the new factory wouldn't be completed for another two years and there was no guarantee the boom would last. To paraphrase former president Kiyoshi Kawashima, Honda's challenge for the time being was building up "a sales capacity that exceeded production capacity," as quickly as possible.

Approximately 800 dealerships sold Honda products in the United States. It would be unrealistic to expect them to move 700,000 Honda automobiles on their own. The Big Three dealerships, which tended to focus on larger cars, sold somewhere between one hundred and 300 vehicles per dealership each year, but Honda set an annual sales goal of 500 to 600. This meant that Honda needed to increase the number of dealerships to 1,200 by the time the second assembly line in Ohio was completed.

As a brand, Honda enjoyed more popularity in the United States than Toyota or Nissan. Normally, this would make organizing the new dealerships a relatively easy task. Even so, it wouldn't do to just go about the process blindly without a well-thought out strategy.

American Honda knew that the best way to ensure steady, long-term sales growth would be for the dealerships to reinvest a portion of their sales income from selling Honda cars in the company. The chronic shortage of products, however, had all but sapped the dealerships' interest in such a scheme. Instituting a large-scale campaign to create new dealerships would lead to complaints from the existing dealerships for infringing upon on their vested rights.

American Honda came up with the idea of creating a second independent sales network in an attempt to spur the existing dealers to invest. In addition, Honda had already decided to sell its first luxury car—a co-production with BL developed under the codename XX and later sold as the "Legend"—on the U.S. market in 1986. Selling economy and luxury cars from the same network would be too risky.

The Accord had given a tremendous boost to Honda's growth, establishing itself as Honda's flagship car. If Honda sold the Legend through the same network, however, it would effectively bump the Accord from its position. Once that happened, sales would drop.

General Motors had seven independent sales networks: Chevrolet, Pontiac, Oldsmobile, Buick, Cadillac, GMC, and Saturn; Ford had two: Ford and Lincoln-Mercury; Chrysler had three: Prism, Dodge, and Eagle.

Honda's goal of selling 700,000 automobiles per year meant selling as many cars a year as Chrysler did, at least as far as passenger cars were concerned. The Honda kids saw establishing another independent sales network as a matter of course. The prospect promised a variety of side benefits as well. The decision was made, and the new sales network was dubbed "Acura."

The most striking feature of an Acura dealership was the lack of any visual connection to Honda. Even the cars lacked Honda logos. The first products sold through the dealerships were the luxury Acura Legend and a car called the Acura Integra. The Integra had been developed in America and was based on the Civic. Some called it a "younger Accord."

The idea to leave Honda's name out of the second sales network caused quite a stir within American Honda. Many people believe that the reason for the decision was because U.S. regulations required a minimum of ten miles between affiliated dealerships. The truth was that, regulations or no, American Honda had its own ideas about how to proceed with the second sales network.

The idea of removing the Honda name had come from a young American employee who not only knew little of Honda's tradition or history but had not even heard of Soichiro.

"If we want to make the Acura dealerships as efficient as Mercedes-Benz," reasoned the young man, "it might be best to give consumers the idea that we're newcomers. If we use the Honda logo, we won't be able to change anyone's mind about the image, and we'll be saddled with all sorts of other restrictions as well. Leaving off the Honda name instead will give the Acura shops a better outlook for the future."

The comment shocked the management at American Honda. Honda may be an independent brand in the United States, but as far as the Honda Kids were concerned, "Honda" would always equal "Soichiro." Leaving the Honda name off of a Honda car appeared dangerously close to being a rejection of their founder. Yet, the more they listened to what the American employee had to say, the more they came to understand the advantages of such a strategy.

The question was who would tell Soichiro and how. Soichiro was retired; he didn't meddle in the day-to-day affairs of the company any more. But for decisions that affected the very core of the business, his approval was still a must.

Had Fujisawa still been working on the front lines, he could have simply gone and told Soichiro:

"Honda-san, we're dropping Honda's name from the second American sales network. It'll sell better that way."

But that was Fujisawa. The Honda kids couldn't speak to their founder so directly. And of course, they couldn't ask Fujisawa, who had retired from the front lines both in name and in substance, for help. The "kids" felt trapped. Eventually, Soichiro's eldest son, Hirotoshi Honda, volunteered to "bell the cat."

"Dad, it sounds like they aren't going to use the Honda name for the second sales network in the United States," Hirotoshi told Soichiro casually over a game of golf at Pearl Country, the course Soichiro had purchased for himself in Hawaii. "You know, Honda's image there is still pretty strongly tied to economy cars. They're trying to create an all-new image with the Acura name. I'm telling you this on behalf of everyone at Honda. They couldn't bring themselves to tell you personally because they were so worried about how you'd take it."

"So they'll drop the Honda name in the United States? I see. I can understand that. Honda isn't my company anymore. But can they really run the business without the name? That's the only thing that really worries me," replied Soichiro.

The Honda kids had feared that the removal of his name would offend Soichiro. As it turned out, the only thing that worried Soichiro was the future of the company.

After the lengthy debate and discussion, Acura was finally launched as an independent brand name. Although Honda has never made any official statement to the effect, it set a goal of selling one million products per year on the U.S. market. To meet that goal, Honda would have to build another factory in the U.S. One million was possible, but it wouldn't be easy.

Hitting sales of one million didn't mean just getting ahead of Toyota. It meant beating Chrysler as well. In other words, it would mean the birth of a new Big Three consisting of GM, Ford, and Honda. The United States was a huge new market for Honda, much like the New World had been for explorers in the Age of Discovery. At the same time, it was steadily becoming Honda's second homeland.

Now that Honda had established a firm foothold in the United States, its next task as a company was bolstering the Japanese sales network. That Toyota and Nissan were routinely described as Japan's largest automobile corporations was due to the fact that they had built a solid foundation in the domestic Japanese market. Even though Honda's image as a brand was rapidly gaining popularity in the U.S., leading the company's sales in that country to exceed that of Nissan and Toyota, things were different on "home ground." Domestically, Honda was still only vying for third place with Mazda and Mitsubishi.

The U.S. market was open to everyone, and it boasted tremendous depth. The Honda kids had proved that if they played their cards right, they could build Honda into as large a company as they wanted to there. The Japanese market, on the other hand, remained as closed as ever. Toyota owed its success in Japan to its powerful sales network, which it had built up in the tumultuous economic environment just after the end of World War II. Toyota explained to wealthy families and investors all over Japan the potential of the auto industry and convinced them to become Toyota dealers. These dealers were full of entrepreneurial spirit and sold huge quantities of Toyota's cars.

Nissan, on the other hand, had gotten a late start and only managed to secure "second-tier" investors for its dealership network. Mazda and Mitsubishi divvied up the next tiers of investors. When these dealers found themselves losing ground to Toyota, they had no qualms about selling back their dealership rights to the manufacturers. The manufacturers dealt with this by putting up capital and installing their own employees as presidents of the dealerships. While this allowed them to play a more direct role in the business and sales strategies of the dealerships, the tendency of these presidents to slavishly follow the orders of the head company led to a lack of initiative and vitality. This lack was clearly reflected in the companies' sales figures.

Honda, on the other hand, created its automobile sales network by reorganizing and upgrading its motorcycle shops. Honda had a respectable number of dealerships under its belt, but had yet to assign specific sales regions to each store. Furthermore, actual sales for each shop remained quite small.

Such a system might have worked in the days when Honda stuck to selling k-cars. But the market for automobiles was much more sensitive to fashion trends, and Honda could hardly expect to attract any customers with these little shops that didn't even have showrooms to display the products. There was another consideration as well: as Honda introduced more varieties of car, dealers would inevitably focus on the newest models, cannibalizing sales of those already on the market.

In an attempt to address these problems, Honda established a new sales network called "Verno" in Japan in November 1978. Just like Toyota and Nissan, Honda adopted a PMA (primary marketing area) system, meaning that each dealership was assigned a specific target region for sales. The first product sold through the Verno network was a specialized compact car by the name of "Prelude."

Many Verno dealers were "second generation investors," children of the owners of local department stores or gas stations. By becoming Honda dealers, they hoped to gain from Honda's youthful image and pick up hands-on knowledge of the automobile industry in the process.

Verno was based on an unrealized idea known as the "Honda Jidosha Hanbai (Honda automobile sales)" project, which aimed to spin off the company's sales operations into a separate organization. With regard to domestic sales, Honda harbored a feeling of intense rivalry towards Nissan. On the other hand, the company tended to have blind faith in Toyota's business strategies. The Honda kids staunchly believed that, apart from Toyota's historic advantage, the top manufacturer's huge share of the national market was due to the clear division between its manufacturing and sales operations. Honda saw itself as lacking know-how when it came to selling cars in Japan and fixated on Toyota as a perfect role model. So long as Honda copied its *sensei*, the reasoning went, they stood a chance of overtaking Nissan.

"Toyota controls a lion's share of the market not only because it has good products but because it has separate production and sales divisions," pointed out vice president Kihachiro Kawashima. "The two sides have completely different labor requirements. With only one labor union taking care of the both of them, decisions inevitably skew towards the production side. This, of course, has a big impact on the sales section. The current system unnecessarily limits the sales division."

In fact, a group of Honda executives led by Kihachiro Kawashima spent three years starting in 1973 considering the idea of separating the operations. In the end, however, it came to nothing. President Kiyoshi Kawashima judged that having an independent sales division, in addition to the fact that sales and development were already separate entities, would be too difficult to keep a close eye on.

The concept had caused concern for Fujisawa as well from a different angle. Splitting the production from the sales section and putting his beloved "disciple" Kihachiro Kawashima in charge of the latter would almost definitely result in stronger domestic sales. But Fujisawa felt that, as time passed, it would almost inevitably break Honda in two. The idea worried him.

Although the independent sales division concept was abandoned in the end, Honda had accumulated a wealth of ideas during the three-year debate. It was on these ideas that the Verno sales network was built. The initial goal was to have Verno selling 100,000 cars annually within three years.

Unfortunately, however, the Verno network didn't get off to as smooth a start as the Honda kids had expected. The sales point of the Prelude, which some called a "squashed Civic," was its sporty styling. In spite of this, Honda had yet to incorporate catalytic converters in its cars, which created performance issues in the Prelude series. The Verno network paid the price for Honda's tardiness in introducing the devices.

Having only one product to sell was bad enough. If that one product turned out to be not too popular with consumers, the dealers risked going out of business. One after another, Verno dealers gave back their dealership rights. In fact, it would take the introduction of a second version of the Prelude with a catalytic converter and a new car called the "Vigor," a sister model to the Accord, in 1984 to breathe life back into Verno network.

Door-to-door sales had long formed the basis for marketing new automobiles in Japan. With Verno, however, Honda adopted an American-style showroom sales system. Needless to say, the salesmen could hardly just sit back and wait for customers to drop by. Honda relied on "customer surveys," which had been extremely successful in the U.S., and a thorough customer management system to pull consumers into the shops.

Honda specifically selected large cities for the first Verno dealerships. By the time Kume finally became president in 1983, the network had grown to 106 companies and 210 shops.

In 1973, the year the Verno network was launched, Honda's sales, including compact trucks, totaled 254,000. This number grew to 404,000 in 1983—a fifty-nine percent increase in a period of five years. Honda's overall share of the domestic Japanese market, including k-cars, also increased during this period from 5.8 to 7.5 percent.

Meanwhile, Honda's designated rival, Nissan, was in a slump. Their sales figures over the same period showed a decrease from 1.14 million to 1.1 million cars annually. Toyota only showed a small increase: from 1.51 million to 1.59 million. Honda's share of the national market was only one quarter that of Toyota and one third that of Nissan, but considering that, only five years before, it had been just one sixth that of Toyota, and a quarter of Nissan, one could say that Honda had actually done better than any one expected.

Creating an automobile that was good enough to go head-to-head against anything Toyota or Nissan had to offer was Kume's task, but it was Yoshizawa who was responsible for selling as many cars as possible to close the gap between Honda and its rivals.

How can we make Fujisawa-san's dream of catching up to and overtaking Nissan in the domestic marketplace come true? With only our current Honda and Verno, it will be all we can do to move our share into the double digits, let alone catch up with Nissan. In order to achieve our goal, we're going to need a third sales network. But we failed once before with Verno. It's unlikely that we'll find anyone charitable enough to agree to becoming a Honda dealer now. I guess we'll just have to split the current Honda network.

Yoshizawa's concept of "splitting" the original Honda dealership network meant more than simply breaking the network up into two parts. The idea was to select some of the larger of the roughly 2,000 dealers in Honda's network to act as specialty shops. These specialty shops would not sell any k-cars, but focus entirely on selling only compact cars.

The decision was, in some ways, a natural conclusion. Honda had started from scratch as a company and had achieved its first major breakthrough with Fujisawa's "direct-mail project." In order to expand sales of the 50cc Cub motorcycle, Fujisawa had sent personal letters to 55,000 bicycle shops throughout the country and had organized a sales network out of the 13,000 that responded to his call.

When the time came to sell the N360 k-car, Fujisawa again employed the same tactic and sent letters to motorcycle shops, bicycle shops, and auto repair shops. He then selected 25,000 shops and developed a unique dealership sales network that was organized into separate wholesale and retail outlets for motorcycles and automobiles.

Toyota and Nissan executives regarded Fujisawa with awe. The man had a penchant for devising totally novel business strategies to open new markets. So long as Fujisawa was involved in the company, Honda's rivals knew, they could never lower their guards.

Honda now had two networks through which to sell its automobiles—the original Honda sales network and Verno—but the original Honda dealerships were made up of shops of a whole range of sizes, due to their diverse origins and differences in the regions they were assigned to. The Honda kids divided these dealerships into four groups based on their sales figures: L, B, M, and G. For its new network, Honda selected about one hundred dealers from the L group, which had the highest sales. The selected dealers had to allow customers to register new vehicles at the shops, have a showroom as well as a licensed repair facility, have the capacity to sell and dispose of used cars, and employ more than five salesmen per shop. This select network was named "Clio," after one of the nine muses in Greek mythology.

Honda also selected certain shops from the B, M, and G groups based on a variety of factors, such as the existence of official company rules and a monthly closing process, to organize another network. This network was called "Primo," meaning "first," or "number one." Dealerships that failed to meet the requirements were given secondary status as "sub-dealers."

The process of categorizing the dealerships and establishing the new network was completed by 1984. Now Honda had three sales networks. The stage was set for confronting Nissan on the domestic Japanese marketplace.

The foundations of the three-network structure were laid by Masami Suzuki and Takayuki Kobayashi, who represented the last generation of Honda kids that had been schooled in business management by Fujisawa himself. These two men set up the system and then passed the "baton" to Yoshizawa, before retiring from the front lines of the business.

Kume's first shareholders' meeting as president of the Honda Motor Company took place on June 24, 1984. Traditionally, shareholders meetings were chaired by the president. In light of Kume's inexperience, however, and the fact that the meeting was a particularly important one, being the first since a major revision of Japanese Commercial Law, chairman Hideo Sugiura took over the task on Kume's behalf.

Prior to the meeting, Kume had been given a list of seventeen questions from the shareholders. At the meeting, he devoted nearly a full hour to answering them. During the subsequent Q&A session, he was again bombarded with questions from sokaiya. More than three and a half hours had passed since chairman Sugiura had convened the meeting but this was not due to any problems with the proceedings. In fact, the meeting proceeded in a very orderly and amicable manner. At last the subject turned to the final item on the agenda: benefits for retired directors. One participant commented:

"It saddens me to see our founder Soichiro-san retire as a director. I'd like to request that he receives a large benefit in appreciation for all his hard work."

Soichiro and Fujisawa had retired from their roles as executives so were no longer seated on the dais. Soichiro rose from his seat in the first row of the audience and moved to the stage for his farewell speech.

"I'm deeply touched by your kind words. I'll take my memories of all you shareholders and executives with me to the afterlife," he laughed, closing his last official statement for Honda on an unconventionally light note. The sound of thunderous applause marked the end of the era of Soichiro and Fujisawa.

3

In the spring of 1983, after the "HY War" with Yamaha had settled down, Shoichiro Irimajiri was transferred from the Honda Research and Development Company to the Suzuka manufacturing plant, where he took on the role of top factory manager. It was the first time Irimajiri had ever worked in a factory. He showed up at six o'clock every morning and poked his nose into every aspect of factory operations. Whenever he encountered something he didn't understand, he wouldn't hesitate to pull a worker aside for more information.

"Who's the new guy patrolling the factory floor every morning?" the factory workers asked themselves. The mystery man became a big topic of speculation among the workers. It didn't take long for everyone to realize, however, that it was actually their new boss.

Irimajiri was an impetuous man. He wanted to know everything that was going on in the factory as soon as possible. He never missed a morning "patrol," and often worked at his desk often until ten or eleven o'clock in the evenings.

A year later, Irimajiri was transferred again. This time, he was promoted to president of Honda of America Manufacturing (HAM) and head of the Ohio factory, which was considered to be the key element in Honda's global business strategy. The day after Kume's first shareholders' meeting, Irimajiri boarded a plane to Ohio. Honda employees saw this move as proof that process of grooming Irimajiri to become a top executive was nearing its final stages.

As a member of the North American task force, Irimajiri had visited Ohio several times since first being promoted to executive at the age of thirty-nine. In the five years since his promotion, the Ohio factory had undergone major changes. The motorcycle plant, adjacent to the two-story main office building that comprised the main entrance to the site, was now in full gear and exporting products back to Japan. An underground passage connected the office to the new automobile factory, which was also operating at full capacity. And just next to the automobile plant, construction of the second automobile line was steadily under way.

After arriving in his new office and briefly greeting the managers, Irimajiri quickly left for a tour of the factory area. He spoke to the factory workers and listened to their opinions about the production system.

Generally speaking, in American corporate society factory workers have very little, if any, opportunity to converse directly with their president. At the same time, employees are usually more than a little curious about their new president. At the time, the Ohio factory was hiring dozens of new workers every day. Some had just begun to adjust to the new atmosphere at HAM. Others were new and felt insecure. There was a general feeling of expectation and anxiety in the air. As Irimajiri made his rounds, the word rapidly spread among the workers:

"The new boss made a point of checking out the factory himself. Looks like he's on our side."

Irimajiri hadn't planned his actions for the psychological impact of his "tour" would have on the laborers. The truth was that he was as anxious about his new job as they were. Although he had made his rounds every morning at the Suzuka plant during his year there, that was the only experience he had in running a factory. And now, his was in charge of the Ohio factory where his decisions could make or break his company's future. He had simply rushed to the factory floor to ease his own nervousness. Nevertheless, the act made him a virtual hero among the workers from day one.

Several days later, Irimajiri officially introduced himself to the factory workers with a speech. He was a small man, even for a Japanese, but energetic and sincere-looking. He addressed the assembly in his low and steady voice.

"Let me remind you: I'm not your boss. Our customers are the boss. I don't ever want you to forget the customers. That's why I'd like you to call me 'Mr. Iri,' not 'President Iri.'

"Honda has always been about technology. This fact will never change. There are 50,000 Honda employees across the world, and 10,000 of them are engineers. Honda invests five percent of its annual sales income into research and development. When it comes to engineering and technology, this company cannot be beat. That being said, Honda's most important asset isn't technology. Our most important asset is you, the workers.

"I've been involved in motorcycle racing for a long time now. When you enter a race, you enter to win. You enter to win as many races as you can and work your way up to world champion. That's what racing is all about. In order to win, you need the tools and equipment that will allow you to create a fast race car. You also need top-notch drivers, engineers, and managers.

"If we apply this way of thinking to Honda as a company, the tools and equipment would be represented by the factory. But it takes more than a top-notch factory to make good automobiles. You need people to run it. The Ohio factory needs all of you."

Since its launch, the Ohio factory had been managed on the whole by three people: the president and two executive vice presidents—one in charge of production, and the other in charge of management. Former president Kazuo Nakagawa returned to Japan when Irimajiri took over and became president of Honda R&D. Former executive vice president of production Hiroshi Hayano was transferred to Canada to supervise construction of the new factory just outside Toronto. He was succeeded by quality assurance expert Shinsuke Okubo. Okubo had joined Honda in 1961, two years before Irimajiri, and had spent his first ten years in the Suzuka manufacturing plant. After attending a five-month seminar on quality assurance in his second year, Okubo became Honda's first specialist in the field. Of the three top executives, only Shigeyoshi Yoshida, who had been involved in HAM as far back as the property-scouting stage, remained in Ohio.

Under Nakagawa, HAM's primary mission had been easing the burden on the American Honda salesmen. That meant making automobiles with the same quality level as those imported from Japan. The decision to construct the automobile factory had come almost immediately after the motorcycle factory line became operational. There simply hadn't been enough time for the HAM executives to build a dialog with the factory laborers. Now Irimajiri took charge of making HAM into a full-fledged, successful American corporation.

"Don't worry about trying to make the locals like you," advised Kiyoshi Kawashima, then-president of the Honda Motor Company whose decision it had been to build the American plant. He told the Japanese employees the same thing every time he visited the Ohio plant. "Just think about how to make them not hate you first!"

Some 300 employees had been dispatched from Japan to Ohio. That amounted to more than 1,000 Japanese people, including family members and those on short-term assignments. Honda could have built a special apartment compound for them, but creating an isolated "Japantown" wouldn't go far in building goodwill in the community. As such, Honda employees from Japan had no choice but to live among the local population. This meant that they would need to interact with the locals to live comfortably, leading to a sense of community awareness among the Japanese expatriates.

Not long after his arrival and initial meeting with the local employees, in fact, just as Irimajiri began to feel that he was getting a grasp on the situation, tragedy struck. HAM automobile factory manager Bob Watson suffered a fatal cerebral hemorrhage. Watson had played a critical role as the liaison between the workers and the executives. His untimely death meant that a successor needed to be found at once. Whoever it was, he would need to have a certain level of knowledge of the various aspects of the Honda business. Finding someone to fill Watson's shoes would be no easy task.

Irimajiri's hands were full. The automobile factory had just begun full-scale manufacturing. Preparations for expanding the facility also had to be advanced. Irimajiri needed to supervise the purchase of additional land, the ordering of construction materials, the hiring of new workers, and negotiations with local officials, just to name a few of his duties. He simply didn't have the time to devote his full attention on the factory. But if he used the shortage of appropriate human resources as a pretext to take the easy way out and place a Japanese employee in the post, all the efforts to reach out into the local community could be wasted.

Irimajiri spied a potential candidate for a new factory manager in Scott Whitlock, HAM's outside legal counsel. Whitlock worked for a Columbus law firm and had assisted in many of the legal issues surrounding HAM, including the drafting of contracts to purchase new property.

Whitlock also was in charge of taking care of the legal aspects of Watson's sudden death. He postponed a planned three-month holiday to assist both HAM and Watson's family in their time of need.

In Japan, the post of factory manager needs to be filled by someone with a thorough knowledge of engineering. But here at HAM, Honda Japan employees are already covering the engineering side of the operation. The HAM factory manager ensures that the workers are following Honda policy and listens to what they have to say. Scott might just be a perfect fit for the job. Irimajiri contacted the headquarters in Japan to confirm his decision, and then approached Whitlock to see if he was interested.

Whitlock accepted Irimajiri's offer almost at once. *Both my mother and my grandfather on my mother's side were lawyers*, he thought. *But my father worked in manufacturing. I may be a lawyer now, but I've still got manufacturing in my blood. I've spent the first half of my life as a lawyer, and now I could spend the second half in the manufacturing business. Doesn't sound half bad.*

Whitlock's starting salary was higher than Irimajiri's, but even still was less than what he had been making as a lawyer. Whitlock didn't mind. He came on board as factory manager and senior executive vice president.

Now HAM had Whitlock, but Irimajiri still felt that the upper echelons of the company needed more fresh blood. He approached another lawyer at Whitlock's old firm, Susan Insley, to act as executive vice president of public relations. Insley accepted.

Now the management team, consisting of Irimajiri, Okubo, Yoshida, Whitlock, Insley, and HAM's first employee Al Kinzer, began discussing how to run HAM as an American corporation rather than just another factory.

The three Japanese managers explained Japanese customs and Honda's corporate culture to their American counterparts citing various examples. Whitlock, Insley and Kinzer listened closely and digested the wishes of the Japanese managers before they gave their opinion. As long as HAM was going to be hiring Americans to work on American soil, they stressed, it should be run as a one hundred percent American corporation.

In short, the issue boiled down to which would take priority in managing the company, Japanese or American corporate culture? After a heated discussion, the six staff members agreed to manage HAM mainly as an American company. However, they would adopt the best parts of the Japanese work style and create an all-new corporate culture for Honda. They dubbed their new fusion of the two cultures the "Mayflower Project."

Another topic of discussion centered on the future image of the company.

"We understand that in Japan, the company comes before the individual and that even presidents introduce themselves as so-and-so from this-or-that corporation," said Whitlock and Insley. "It's the exact opposite here in America. Take Iacocca, example. He's currently chairman of Chrysler but before that he was president of Ford. But whatever position he may be in, he's recognized as 'Mr. Iacocca,' without the need to add his company name or title. We think the boss of HAM should be the same. We want everyone, not just inside Honda or HAM but also outside the company to recognize you as just 'Mr. Iri.' This is critical to HAM's future here. And to make that happen, you need to be active in external activities."

Whitlock and Insley had heard of Soichiro and Fujisawa but they remained unaware of the unique position that Honda's founder occupied in the company. Interestingly, just as Fujisawa had positioned Soichiro as the guru of the "Cult of Honda," Whitlock and Insley were proposing to make Irimajiri the public face of HAM, i.e., "Mr. Honda," in the U.S. auto industry.

The six shared an ambition to take HAM into the "Major League" of American auto manufacturers. That meant proving HAM's worth as a manufacturer to the rest of the industry. Although the new automobile factory was still under construction, they decided to allow Big Three engineers to visit whenever they asked. At that time, the Big Three looked upon Japanese production methods as something of a mystery. Once word got around about HAM's open-door policy, a steady stream of Big Three engineers came calling day after day. It goes without saying that such measures played a major role in HAM's being accepted as a member of the American Automobile Manufacturers Association (AAMA).

Meanwhile, Insley took a proactive approach in meeting with automotive journalists in Detroit to promote HAM. Her hard work paid off as articles on HAM began appearing quite often in a variety of American news media.

Katsuhiro Nakagawa, chief of the Automobile section of the Machinery and Information Industries Bureau of Japan's Ministry of International Trade and Industry (MITI), was amazed at the frequent and favorable media coverage Honda's U.S. operations were receiving. *Why does HAM get such favorable treatment in America in comparison to other Japanese operations?* he wondered.

Irimajiri's approachable style in greeting the factory workers and his engaging introductory speech helped make him the very symbol of HAM from an early stage. In Japan, Irimajiri's behavior would have been cynically dismissed as mere performance, but the Americans loved it. The positive reception brought out Irimajiri's charismatic side all the more. Still, Irimajiri wasn't a mere symbol just because he had charisma. His true job was running HAM.

One of the basics of quality control and a fundamental aspect of the Japanese production system is having factory employees make suggestions for improvements in production efficiency. HAM also introduced such an open-suggestion system in an effort to support quality control activities.

In Japan, perhaps due to the sheer size Honda's plants, the suggestions were first read by the section chiefs, who passed on what they thought were the most valid to the factory manager, who in turn made his selection to give to headquarters for the final decision. The system had become a somewhat routine affair, however, so that it no longer had the intended effect of allowing direct communication between the factory workers and headquarters.

Irimajiri planned to employ a similar system at HAM, but modified it in an attempt to avoid falling into the same trap. Every month, HAM staff selected roughly one hundred suggestions, including proposals for minor improvements, out of all those submitted by the employees. Irimajiri, Okubo, and Whitlock then walked around the factory to speak to the people in person. A full circle of the factory floor involved a walk of roughly seven kilometers. They spoke to some thirty or forty people along the way, so a single loop took more than four hours. In addition, the Ohio factory employed workers in morning, afternoon, and evening shifts, requiring the managers to make their four-hour circuit three times a day. It was the equivalent in both time and distance to playing three rounds of golf. Irimajiri, who had walked the Suzuka plant every day he worked there, was intrigued by the process and didn't mind the effort in the least.

Some workers embraced the suggestion system at once, enjoying the satisfaction of getting a chance to communicate directly with their boss. But the executives knew that in order to keep the system going over a long period of time, they needed to give the average factory worker more of an incentive. Their answer was the "Top One Hundred Club." At the end of the year, all of the suggestions that had been adopted, including discoveries and inventions as well as suggestions for improvement, were graded according to a point scale. HAM staff put up a list of the names that had suggested the top hundred, and rewarded them with awards and prizes: tickets to the Ford museum in Detroit, gift certificates to local high-end restaurants, and the like. The most popular prize was a free-of-charge car rental.

One of the more unusual prizes consisted of invitations to the gala dinner event at the Automotive Hall of Fame in Michigan, the birthplace of the modern automobile industry. Each year, the Automotive Hall of Fame, Inc., a non-profit organization, recognized and honored individuals who had made contributions to the U.S. automobile industry by inducting them as members of the AHF.

Traditionally, around 1,000 top executives in the automotive industry would gather for the gala celebration, which was held at a luxury hotel in the Renaissance Center in downtown Detroit. Ever since HAM had become a member of the AAMA, it received seven invitations each year. Irimajiri would be attending as president of HAM, but he had the staff give away the other six invitations as prizes for the Top One Hundred Club. The recipients were flown along to Detroit with Irimajiri in a chartered plane, where they had a chance to rub elbows with the elites of the auto industry. Needless to say, HAM was the only company that brought its factory workers to the event.

The prizes proved a great incentive to Honda's factory workers. Construction on the new assembly line had started and HAM was hiring new line workers on an almost daily basis. The workers knew that hard work led to benefits and even to promotion to managerial posts in a short period of time. Spirits were sky-high at the Ohio factory.

The automobiles manufactured at the Ohio factory received an even better reception than expected. Still, Irimajiri couldn't fully shake his anxiety about the future of the factory itself.

We listened to Scott and Susan and started running HAM as an American corporation. The Americans accept us. They even made us a member of the AAMA. But is this really enough? HAM doesn't have any history or tradition. True, HAM is going through its growth phase, and everyone, both Japanese and American, is giving it their all. But the core management team is almost totally composed of employees transferred from Japan and even in the assembly lines, Japanese engineers continue to support the American workers. In other words, it's a two-tiered structure. But such a management structure cannot continue forever. Sooner or later, HAM will be run by Americans alone. Before that happens, though, we should at least teach the American managers all about Honda as a company. Understanding the history and traditions of Honda will make them love their company all the more.

Yoshida and Okubo agreed to Irimajiri's idea. They had, from time to time, told Whitlock and Insley parts of the Honda story but not in any systematic way. Whitlock and Insley had seen Soichiro once before, but had never talked to him for any length of time nor heard the story of how he had created Honda. Fujisawa had never even visited Ohio, so they only knew him as the stern face in his portrait photograph at HAM headquarters. Yoshida had told Whitlock and Insley about the relationship between Soichiro and Fujisawa on numerous occasions, but it didn't mean much to them on a personal level. Now, both Whitlock and Insley expressed an interest in learning more about the birth and history of the company that had given birth to HAM.

Pondering over the question of how best to explain Honda's history and unique business strategies, Irimajiri, Okubo and Yoshida hit upon the idea of creating a textbook, based on their own personal experiences at Honda. The textbook would be organized into various categories such as management, development, production, sales, and so on, and would contain specific examples as well as explanatory comments to help American readers understand unfamiliar concepts. This project was dubbed the "Chrysanthemum Project," in reference to author Ruth Benedict's famed book on Japan, *The Chrysanthemum and the Sword*.

Needless to say, a history of Honda encompassed far too much information for the three of them to handle alone. Fortunately, there was no shortage of Japanese employees dispatched from headquarters at HAM. These people contributed to entries for some of the categories.

Irimajiri, Okubo and Yoshida each drafted their texts for the topics that had been assigned to them. Then Yoshida translated the "prototype" textbook into English and had Whitlock, Insley, and some of the other American executives listen as he read it to them.

Trying to explain "Honda-ism" while integrating the many special terms used only within the company turned out to be a monumental task. The term *waigaya* was a prime example. The term had been coined to refer to the company's unique freewheeling discussion sessions and had no equivalent in English. Irimajiri, Okubo and Yoshida had to begin by explaining the original meaning of the original word *"waiwai-gayagaya"*—chatter in a crowded room—and then supplement their explanation with information about traditional Japanese customs and lifestyle.

"We appreciate what you're trying to do here, Mr. Iri," said Whitlock. "But we still have no idea what the point of this textbook is."

Irimajiri, Okubo and Yoshida knew they needed to make sure that Whitlock and Insley, the two top American executives at HAM, could understand the text before they went any further. They wrote and rewrote, sharing their drafts with the American executives. It took a solid year, but they finally succeeded. The book was titled "The Honda Way." Once the textbook was complete, Irimajiri began holding lectures for the more than one hundred managers at HAM in his spare time, outlining the history of the Honda Motor Company.

Whitlock and Insley were the first Americans to grasp the *waigaya* concept. Until then, due to inevitable differences in customs and lifestyles, not to mention attitude towards the company, there had been a certain lack of communication between the Japanese and Americans executives at HAM. Once the American executives understood the concept of the *waigaya*, however, a new atmosphere of open discussion and debate took root.

HAM didn't have a private office for the president, or even a directors' room. All the executives shared a large room on the first floor with the other office workers. Irimajiri's desk was at the far end of the room, with Yoshida, Okubo, Whitlock and Insley's desks lined up next to his. In the space in front of their desks, there was a small round table, which served as a meeting area. Any one of them could call upon the others for a *waigaya* session at any given time. Once the executives began holding *waigaya* sessions, the practice took root among the employees beneath them and spread through the company as a whole. The Honda Way was steadily taking root in Ohio.

The longer Whitlock worked at Honda, the more curious he grew about the company. He worked closely with Okubo, and Okubo took Whitlock with him whenever there was business at headquarters in Japan, making a point of introducing him to the founders of the Honda ethic. Not surprisingly, Whitlock was particularly intrigued by Fujisawa.

In the summer of 1988, Okubo and Whitlock, along with Kiyoshi Ikemi to act as interpreter, paid a visit to Fujisawa's home in Roppongi.

"Mr. Fujisawa was everything that I expected him to be," recalls Whitlock.

"He told us that when they first started the company, he and Mr. Honda would stay up all night discussing the future of Honda every time they met, even though they lived far apart from each other, with Mr. Fujisawa in Tokyo and Mr. Honda in Hamamatsu. I understand now that Honda started out with a policy, and that this was what led it to develop into the company it is today. I wish I could have listened to more stories from Mr. Fujisawa, but unfortunately he passed away just six months later. I really wish Mr. Fujisawa could have visited Ohio and talked to us here about the Honda Way in his own words."

4

On Sunday, September 22, 1985, the Ministers of Finance and Central Bank Governors of the G5 nations (France, Germany, Japan, the United Kingdom, and the United States) met in New York and reached an agreement which would come to be known as the Plaza Accord. The agreement stated, in part, that "some further orderly appreciation of the main non-dollar currencies against the dollar is desirable."

Starting the very next day, on Monday, each country sold large amounts of U.S. dollars, effectively curbing the overpowering strength of the American currency. The exchange rate of the Japanese yen, which had long remained 250 yen to the U.S. dollar, jumped to 200 yen to the dollar by the end of 1985. The trend continued through the end of 1987, at which time the rate had become 120 yen to the dollar. The yen had doubled in value against the dollar in just two years.

This sudden shift in the exchange rate had a massive impact on the sale of Japanese cars abroad. A doubling in the value of the yen effectively meant that the production costs for the Big Three had been halved in comparison. The only way for Japanese manufacturers to compete would be cutting their own expenses by half. It was impossible by all accounts to slash operating costs so much in so short a period of time. The only way out to cope with the situation was by raising the prices of their products to compensate. Each time the yen strengthened against the dollar, the Japanese automakers were forced to raise their prices; gradually, they all but lost their price competitiveness in the market.

The unprecedented rapid rise in the value of the yen was akin to a direct attack on the Japanese export business. The auto manufacturer that suffered the most was Nissan. In 1985, Nissan had sold 575,000 cars in the U.S., only barely managing to keep ahead of Honda whose sales totaled 552,000. By the following year, however, their positions were reversed; in spite of the exchange rate, Honda's sales grew to 693,000, whereas Nissan's sales dropped to 546,000.

At the same time, Nissan was also experiencing a serious slump in domestic sales. In its midterm settlement of accounts in September 1986, Nissan reported losses in operating income for the first time since its listing on the Tokyo Stock Exchange.

Although the optimum inventory level for imported cars in the U.S. market was considered to be a sixty-day supply, Honda's inventory level was extremely low: a twenty-day supply for the Honda sales network and a ten-day supply for

Acura. It was clear that Honda enjoyed the full benefits of being the first to begin local production. The following year in 1988, Honda sold 738,000 cars, beating Toyota's 628,000 by a significant margin and jumping into place as the top Japanese manufacturer in America. That same year, Chrysler sold just over one million cars. Honda had already swung within range of one of the Big Three.

The Acura network was also off to a good start. Some customers even began trading in a luxury Mercedes-Benz for 40,000 dollars in return for a 30,000-dollar Acura Legend.

"My customer has not only gotten a Legend for his Mercedes, he's also walked away with hard cash!" joked one Acura dealer in the Los Angeles area who accepted a 1986-model Mercedes in just such a trade-in deal.

The reason for these "downtrades" was the stock market crash of October 19, 1987, commonly known as "Black Monday." On this day, the Dow Jones industrial average fell 508 points, or 22.6 percent, marking the largest one-day decline in stock market history. Those in the high-income brackets were the most heavily affected, being consequently obliged to scale down their consumption and spending.

Honda used both the strong yen and Black Monday to its advantage and continued to expand its sales. Honda's sales, in fact, were on the rise with no end to the growth in sight. Encouraged, Honda purchased 8,000 acres of land adjacent to the Ohio factory from the state of Ohio and began construction of a second facility there in the fall of 1987. The new factory would have a production capacity of 150,000 cars per year and would aim to begin operation by the end of 1989. This time, Honda's Suzuka plant would be the "mother factory." Once the second factory was completed, Honda would finally be able to reach its goal of supplying the American market with one million automobiles annually, through a combination of local production and exports from Japan.

"The current factory was designed for 'knock-down' production," Irimajiri explained, demonstrating his enthusiasm for the new facility. "This means that, as local content increases, more and more problems keep popping up. In fact, we've already identified about 3,000 problems that need to be attended to. For our new factory, we will have resolved all these problems. In this respect, it will be a truly unique factory."

Despite the optimistic words, however, Irimajiri's mind was wracked with doubt and worry. *I can't shake the feeling that something's wrong. Honda's cars alone are selling well while every other manufacturer is in slump. One of these days, our cars too may suddenly stop selling.* The constant worry and stress caused Irimajiri to suffer a heart arrhythmia the day before the groundbreaking ceremony for the engine factory. Irimajiri headed to a hospital in Columbus for a thorough medical examination but said nothing to headquarters about his condition at this stage. Before long, his pulse returned to normal.

In contrast to Irimajiri's concerns, American Honda was confident and ambitious about sales. Yoshihide Munekuni, president of American Honda, was energized by the positive news about the Acura dealerships and the decision to build the second factory. If anything, he felt the dream of selling one million cars a year was closer to reality than ever. Munekuni's confidence came largely from the success of the Acura network. Sales of the luxury car Legend had already reached 50,000 per year, equivalent to the combined sales for every model of Mercedes-Benz.

Taking a hint from Honda's success with Acura, Toyota came up with the plans for its "Lexus" stores, while Nissan developed its "Infinity" network. Both were secondary sales networks specializing in luxury cars and both were modeled on Honda's Acura. When it came to the American market, Honda was both leader and role model to the other Japanese manufacturers.

The big question was what would happen if Honda's sales in the United States rose to the same level as the Big Three. In that event, Honda's attitude that "as long as we continue to increase local procurement and make quality products, things should be fine" would hardly be tolerated. Even if Honda enjoyed support from its consumer base, the Big Three and the U.S. Congress would feel threatened by Honda's success and wouldn't miss an opportunity to "bash" their new rival. Honda needed to avoid a mud-slinging situation at all costs.

The only method to truly prevent such Honda-bashing would be making HAM a one hundred percent American corporation. HAM had made great strides in "localization" when it came to human resources, procurement, and financing, but now these efforts needed to be taken one step further.

On the human resources front, some 300 employees from Japan continued to work at HAM, but their roles were changing. Kunio Iwamoto, vice president of labor management, explained, "we're like the American occupation forces in Japan after World War II. Our mission is to select the most capable and talented locals and promote them to positions of authority." In the days following the launch of operations at the plant, the Japanese staff had guided and supported the American workers at every opportunity. As the years went by, however, the expatriates moved back stage and refrained from appearing in the spotlight.

With regard to procurement, HAM had originally set a goal of achieving a seventy-five percent local content rate at the earliest possible stage. Seventy-five percent was higher than the local content rate at Chrysler, and would put Honda in the same league as Ford. Irimajiri strongly opposed to the idea to the end. He worried that rushing to supply parts locally would compromise the quality of the end product. If the quality of Accords manufactured at the Ohio factory were lower than the quality of those imported from Japan, it would taint Honda's entire image. If Honda was going to increase its local content rate, it was absolutely essential that the same level of quality be maintained.

The rate for the 1987 models was fifty-seven percent. HAM decided to raise the ratio gradually every year, aiming to achieve the seventy-five percent goal with the 1991 models. That meant making sure the local suppliers truly understood Honda's commitment to quality beforehand.

"Don't think of it as supplying parts to Honda," said Toshikata Amino to local suppliers whenever he had the chance. "Consider it as supplying the parts directly to the customer. If you look at things that way, you'll maintain quality for sure."

Amino had taken over as vice president of HAM when Shigeyoshi Yoshida was promoted to vice president of the newly established Honda North America

(HNA).

Of the three categories, financing had seen the most extensive "localization." It had always been part of Honda's basic policy that money made in U.S. be spent in the U.S. Ninety-five percent of the capital invested in HAM was put up by American Honda.

The last thing that needed to be done was to "localize" the management of the company. At an informal meeting, Honda president Kume expressed the following vision for HAM's future management structure.

"The localization of HAM is proceeding smoothly. I think that, after two or three more presidencies, HAM should have an American president—someone from the ranks of HAM." Personally, Kume envisioned factory manager Scott Whitlock as HAM's first American president.

Still, the true goal of "localization" was not simply putting an American in charge of the factory. For example, Nissan had built a compact truck factory in Smyrna, Tennessee, and had installed former Ford vice president of sales Marvin Runyon as president. Nissan also kept the number of Japanese dispatched from headquarters low, limiting Japanese employees to the dozen or so who were in charge of financing. None of the factory laborers were Japanese. Nevertheless, no one would consider the management of the Nissan factory to be more "localized" than HAM. In short, the question was how to ensure that a factory built by a Japanese company would be accepted by Americans as a truly American company.

To promote HAM's "localization" from every aspect, Honda founded Honda North America (HNA) in March of 1987.

"HNA's current mission is to supervise Honda's twelve subsidiaries in the United States," announced Yoshida. "However, its primary job is to plan for Honda's future in North America after we successfully establish a system capable of manufacturing and selling one million cars a year in the United States. HNA is essentially a holding company for Honda subsidiaries in North America. However, its objective is not to collect profits from the subsidiaries, but rather to promote understanding of Honda in America.

"We have looked to the French tire manufacturer Michelin as our role model. Although Michelin is funded by the French, it has completely taken root here in the United States. Americans don't feel threatened by the size of Michelin's share of the market. This is what we envision for Honda in the future."

Honda's goal was to provide one million automobiles a year to the U.S. market by 1991. If total U.S. demand were estimated at ten million automobiles, that would mean that Honda would have a ten-percent share of the market. And since the size of the market pie is not likely to see any great increase, Honda could well stand a chance of becoming America's third largest manufacturer behind GM and Ford if it managed to meet its goal.

In the U.S., Honda took all possible precautions and employed a double strategy consisting of offensive measures, i.e., striving towards its goal to sell one million vehicles a year, and defensive measures to protect itself from any bashing. In Japan, on the other hand, the company opted for a completely offensive management strategy.

The domestic Japanese market managed to make a rebound from the temporary recession that had resulted from the stronger yen. By the middle of 1987, it was showing signs of rapid recovery fueled by domestic demand. The GNP for the period from July to September provided proof of the economic recovery: real growth rate was two percent higher in comparison to the previous term, corresponding to a high annualized growth rate of eight percent.

From 1986 to 1987, the Japanese government had implemented a wide range of economic measures. As part of its fiscal and monetary policy, the Bank of Japan had lowered its official discount rate five times during this period to a record low of 2.5 percent in February of 1987. Now the effects of these measures were finally becoming apparent.

Takao Akabane, administrative vice minister of the Economic Planning Agency, officially confirmed the recovery of the economy in a statement on July 31, 1987. "The recession that began in June of 1985 bottomed out in the period from October to December 1986 and has since entered a period of recovery."

Black Monday hit two and half months later in October 1987. The Tokyo markets showed a temporary drop-off in stock prices, but the national economy as a whole was so strong that there was very little impact to the real economy. In the end, the real growth rate for 1987 was 4.9 percent—the highest seen by the country since 1979. The unemployment situation, which had been growing more and more serious during this time, now also took a sudden turn for the better; in fact, some industries were already facing labor shortages.

Exports had been the wind in Japan's economic sails since the end of World War II. Now, for the first time in history, domestic demand was driving the growth of the economy. The first major factor was demand for new homes. The number of new houses built in 1986 had been 1.36 million. The following year, the number jumped to 1.67 million, a level of growth not seen since the "Izanagi boom" of the late 1960s.

The demand for new homes had a large impact on other industries as well. Every house built required kitchen products, consumer electronics, furnishings, and other consumer goods. And houses built in suburban areas increased demand for automobiles.

By this point, Japan was beginning to feel the positive effects of the strong yen. The price of imported goods plummeted, resulting in lower domestic wholesale prices, which in turn led to more stable prices for consumer goods.

This stability in combination with rising salaries resulted in a steady increase of real income. It was a highly favorable environment for auto sales. In 1983, when the Plaza Accord had ushered in the recession, a total of 5.38 million automobiles had been sold in Japan, marking a 2.3 percent increase over the previous year. The number hardly moved over the next two years—5.44 million in 1984 and 5.55 million in 1985—but in 1986, annual sales jumped to 5.71 million. And in 1987, the number of cars sold totaled 6.02 million.

The total number of new automobiles that had been registered, excluding k-cars, was 3.98 million for both 1983 and 1984, 4.03 million in 1985, and 4.09 million in 1986. In 1987, the number suddenly sprung up to 4.31 million. The automobile industry was experiencing the beginnings of the bubble economy—though at the time, of course, none of the automobile manufacturers had any way of knowing this. Honda's attentions were focused on getting its new network of Clio, Primo, and Verno dealerships up and running as quickly as possible. Honda's trump card in this respect was increasing the variety of automobiles in its lineup.

Honda had completely withdrawn from the k-car business in 1974 out of a desire to focus on designing compact cars. The playing field had changed in the years since, however. The government had raised the maximum displacement for k-cars from 360cc to 550cc. In addition, station wagons, dubbed "bonnet vans" in Japan, were enjoying explosive popularity on the domestic market for their ability to haul loads like a truck yet handle like a personal car. The market was completely back on its feet. In addition, the bonnet van's classification as a commercial vehicle meant looser emission regulations, making it cheaper and easier to manufacture than a car.

There was no way Honda could pass up such an opportunity. The company decided to return to the k-car market after its ten-year absence with a new design called the "Today." The appearance of the Today marked Honda's success in establishing a full-fledged line of cars, from k-cars all the way up to the Legend series of luxury cars.

Each and every one of Honda's automobiles enjoyed a unique design, from the "two-box" layout for the Civic and Accord, to the sporty styling of the Prelude and CR-X, and the "tall body" style of the City, which set them apart from the products of manufacturers like Toyota and Nissan. Soichiro had only been directly involved in the N360 and H1300 projects, but his philosophy of creating products that were unlike anything sold by competitors had been passed down through generations of Honda engineers. That being said, Soichiro's retirement marked a fundamental shift in the way Honda created new automobiles.

5

The third version of the Accord debuted in October of 1985. It was revolutionary in both style and structure, incorporating retractable headlights for a smart and sporty look, a double overhead camshaft (DOHC) engine, a double-wishbone suspension, and an increased engine displacement of 2000cc. The success of the car made Honda a first-class international automobile manufacturer.

"Honda has given the world the compact car of the 1990s," announced a confident Kume at the unveiling of the new automobile.

The new Accord stunned Honda's rivals. Looking at it, there was no doubt that Honda was leading the boom for compact cars. Foreign manufacturers took particular note of the car's agile handling, fuel efficiency, and excellent quality in every respect. Although all of the Japanese manufacturers were renowned for the high quality of their products, Honda grabbed the spotlight through its mastery of the front-engine, front-wheel-drive layout.

The Accord received high acclaim from automobile critics as a bold and innovative family car. It became the car of choice for young married couples in their thirties and won the Japanese Car of the Year award for 1985/1986. The Accord was also popular in the U.S. among growing young urban professionals, or "yuppies," who looked on Honda's cars as a perfect blend of style and functionality, thanks to their low cost and good mileage.

Lloyd Reuss, executive vice president of GM and head of the company's North American automotive operations, arrived in Japan in the fall of 1987 for the Tokyo Motor Show. He also paid a visit to the Honda Research and Development Company in Tochigi prefecture, where he told R&D president Kawamoto that Honda's cars were the only products in the world that GM could learn from. Especially with regard to compact car design, GM admitted that it was no match for Honda.

In fact, almost every foreign engineer visiting Japan around the time paid a visit to Honda's Tochigi facilities. Inevitably, the visitors asked the same question:

"Is Honda planning to shorten its development cycle?"

Kawamoto always gave the same response.

"MITI mandates that Japanese manufacturers introduce new models every four years. But even if we weren't bound by the ministry's 'administrative guidance,' we don't have the technology at this stage to shorten our development cycle. I'm afraid you're overestimating us."

It was exactly what the foreign engineers wanted to hear, and they left with a sense of relief. Overestimated or not, in those days, Honda truly owned the market for compact cars.

Auto engineers often use the word "benchmark" to denote car designs that were used as standards throughout the industry. The more engineers visited rival facilities and talked among themselves, the faster information spread through the industry. Engineers naturally incorporated anything they saw and felt would improve their own products, resulting in an increasingly similar look to automobiles sold across companies.

A perfect example can be seen in Chrysler's compact "Neon," which made its sensational debut at the Detroit Motor Show in January 1994. Industry observers believe that Chrysler used the fifth version of the Honda Civic, which went on sale in 1991, as its benchmark. Chrysler has never denied it. In fact, the company hadn't just thoroughly studied the Civic. They had introduced Honda's factory line system as well and had managed to keep the retail price of the Neon below 9,000 dollars. On a related note, Ford's engineers used the third version of the Accord as the design standard for the Mondeo, their second mass-produced car after the Taurus.

Honda took pride in seeing rivals use its products as benchmarks. Whenever Honda introduced a new model, it deliberately integrated the same styling into its entire range of cars, from k-cars to the luxury models. With regard to style, Honda adopted the Accord as the standard so that all the company's other cars were redesigned to look like a "big Today" or a "mini Legend."

While the approach helped create the impression that there were more Honda cars on the streets than there actually were, it also came with the risk that consumers would begin to think that all of Honda's automobiles looked the same. Why, then, did Honda deliberately harmonize the styling of its products? There were two reasons.

One was that Honda decided to use the third Accord as the perfect stepping-stone from niche maker to major manufacturer.

"Back when Honda wasn't recognized as a real auto manufacturer, we needed to keep coming out with one unique car after another to grab attention," said Kawamoto whenever he was asked. "In fact, this worked quite well. These days, however, Honda is a major auto manufacturer. We need to shift focus and concentrate our efforts on our sedans. We standardized our design so that all our cars will reflect our corporate identity."

The second reason for the standardization was a direct request from the sales department. It didn't make sense to sell the same cars through multiple networks. The decision was made to make the Civic and Accord available only through the Primo and Clio sales networks, respectively.

The problem was what to do about the entry-level models. The Primo network had the k-car Today and could expect high-end customers to move on to the Civic. The somewhat more luxurious Clio network, however, lacked a "stepping stone" to either its Accord or Legend. And so Honda created the "City" to meet the need.

The commercials for the first model of the City featured the British rock Madness singing "Honda! Honda!" at the top of their lungs. The ad campaign was a hit with young consumers, and many saw it as a mirror of Honda's corporate image. For two years since it first went on sale, the City sold unbelievably well.

However, the boom didn't last. At its peak, monthly sales of the City totaled 15,000 vehicles. After the second year, the number had dropped to 5,000, and then to 3,000 in the third year. Only truly die-hard fans were buying the cars after that and demand had all but died down.

Yoshizawa, who was responsible for sales of the car, voiced a complaint to Honda R&D.

"I need you to make a car that will sell steadily for four solid years," he said. "A product that sells well for two years and then drops off to nothing for two is too much of a burden on the sales staff. I respect Honda's tradition of creating unique cars, but let's leave those to racing for the moment!

"When sales kick off, the rush of orders means dealers are forced to constantly apologize to customers for shortages and delays. But when the sales drop off after a certain period of time, that puts a burden on the dealers as well. We need cars that will sell steadily rather than cars that have a boom-and-bust cycle."

Yoshizawa's complaint reflected the frustrations of the dealers and retail shops. In response, the R&D engineers redesigned the second version of the City. The new model, which was unveiled in October 1986, had a much lower hood and had a totally different appearance that made it look much more like a specialty car. It was so different, in fact, that Honda enthusiasts felt betrayed.

Nevertheless, engineers at R&D who had worked on the project were quite satisfied with their results.

"The City is the entry-level car for the Clio network, so we made the second version "quieter," with a lower and wider body that mirrors the Accord and Legend. Its predecessor was too tall. This new City won't spoil the high-end image of the Clio name," said Shinya Iwakura, designer of the second City, proudly.

It was true that for the City to serve as an entry-level model for the Accord and Legend, it needed to have a conservative design. Nevertheless, contrary to the ambitions and pride of the development team, the car ended up a miserable failure. Not a single new model was introduced to the series before Honda eventually cancelled production in the spring of 1994.

In any event, Honda had succeeded, at least to a certain extent, in establishing a firm domestic sales structure. Having each of the dealership networks specialize in certain models accentuated the differences between them, which helped enhance the appeal of their products to consumers.

Honda had introduced customer surveys and a customer management system in the Verno network. Now it applied the system to the Clio and Primo stores as well. Honda's style, which utilized dealerships rather than door-to-door sales, began attracting a lot of attention in the industry. Some even called Honda's approach "the future of auto sales."

Meanwhile, Honda's domestic Japanese sales rose to 508,000 in 1986 and 550,000 in 1987. Honda set a goal of 620,000 for 1988. The dawn of the bubble economy led to a shortage of auto salesmen.

The company that felt most threatened by the success of Honda's new sales structure was Toyota. At the time, Toyota's long-term goal was to sell two million automobiles in Japan every year. Toyota used every tool at its disposal to probe Honda in an attempt to estimate the company's potential. Toyota learned that Honda's salesmen were highly trained and that their sales network structure created common goals that unified the dealers. Toyota's executives realized that Honda's potential should not be underestimated.

Even still, the Honda kids were more than aware that they would lose if things came to a head-to-head competition with a behemoth like Toyota. President Kume went out of his way to avoid antagonizing his rivals by humbling himself in public.

"Developing automobiles that meet customers' needs, and selling them in an honest way," he would say. "That in a nutshell is what Honda is all about."

The attitude inside the company, however, was a different story altogether. At an informal meeting of dealers, Honda proposed an aggressive mid-term domestic sales goal of 800,000 automobiles a year.

The figure had been calculated based on Honda's production capability. If Honda operated the Suzuka and Sayama factories at full capacity and on double shifts, it could manufacture 1.3 million automobiles in a year. If the company instituted one hour of overtime every day for a year, total production could be increased to 1.44 million. Of this 1.44 million, 400,000—the maximum allowed by international trade agreements—would be exported to the United States; 120,000 would go to Europe, and another 120,000 to developing countries. That would leave 800,000 for Japan. Such was the basis for Honda's new goal.

Running the factories at full blast would mean increased pay and overtime allowances for the workers. Headquarters would welcome the idea because it promised to lower the break-even point. American Honda too would be happy to have headquarters filling its full export quota. And if Honda succeeded, that is, if it met the goal of selling 800,000 automobiles a year domestically, it would clearly cement Honda's position as the third largest manufacturer in Japan behind Nissan and Toyota.

The dream didn't end there. Honda's target, Nissan, hadn't managed to extricate itself from the business slump it had fallen into as a result of labor and management problems with its London operation. Nissan's domestic Japanese sales dropped to 1.01 million cars a year in 1987. Based on assumptions that Nissan's slump would continue, even the ever-prudent Yoshizawa declared that "the goal of selling one million cars annually in Japan would appear to be realizable by the early 1990s."

In 1985, two years after Honda proposed its mid-term goal of 800,000 vehicles per year, the Honda kids had seriously considered building a new factory in Japan in order to respond to domestic demand. Kume had come up with the idea, but had met with fierce opposition from chairman Okamura and vice president Yoshizawa. Both Okamura and Yoshizawa argued that Honda needed to focus its attention on America for the time being. What was more, they remained unconfident about Honda's domestic sales capabilities.

The chairman and vice president were among Kume's most important supporters; without their backing, he couldn't force the issue. In the end, it turned out to be the right decision. If he had gone ahead with the plan, Honda's second U.S. factory would never have been built.

Honda had started from scratch, building up its foundations as a motorcycle manufacturer and later expanding into automobiles. It would be no exaggeration to call Honda's rapid growth one of the miracles of the world's vehicle manufacturing industries. In fact, of all the auto manufacturers in the world, only two had shown steady growth since the first oil crisis: Toyota and Honda. Although Toyota was aiming for a ten-percent share of the world auto market, it had reached the conclusion that potential for future growth was limited by the maturity of the marketplace. Consequently, Toyota began diversifying into new markets, with a focus on communication.

Honda, on the other hand, had no interest in diversifying at all. It focused on manufacturing motor vehicles, as it always had. Soichiro and Fujisawa shared an ambition to make Honda a large corporation. The Honda kids set a goal of becoming strong enough to compete with any auto manufacturer in the world. In order to realize their dream, it was essential to increase the quantity of products the company produced.

Honda had been the first Japanese company to build a local factory in the United States. That alone put it ahead of Nissan and even Toyota there. Now Honda focused upon catching up with Nissan domestically as well.

In 1983, the year Kume became president, Honda sold a total of 405,000 cars including k-cars in Japan, breaking the 400,000 mark for the first time in its history and overtaking Mazda with a difference of 9,300 vehicles. In 1987, Honda surpassed Mazda in the number of newly registered vehicles (excluding k-cars).

Honda caught up with Mitsubishi with regard to the number of vehicle registrations in 1985. The next year in 1986, Mitsubishi sold a total of 508,208 automobiles in Japan, while Honda sold 508,429. The difference was slight—only 221 vehicles—but there was no denying that the numbers made Honda the third largest seller in Japan after Toyota and Nissan.

Mazda dropped out first from the race for third place in domestic sales, while Honda and Mitsubishi continued to run neck-to-neck. Mitsubishi's sales had been fluctuating since 1980 but Honda had shown a steady increase in its sales every year by roughly 50,000 vehicles, with the exception of 1984. Judging from the trends, Honda was on a roll. It appeared to be only a matter of time before Honda defeated Mitsubishi once and for all. Then it would be time to challenge Nissan for second place.

Still, Mitsubishi Motors was not to be defeated all that easily. The company had the backing of the former Mitsubishi *zaibatsu* firms. What was more, pride refused to allow Mitsubishi Motors to cede victory to a post-war upstart like Honda. In 1987, thanks to support from the Mitsubishi group, Mitsubishi Motors rallied, and exceeded Honda's sales by 4,068 automobiles. The final match was carried over to the following year.

For 1988, Honda set a sales goal of 620,000 vehicles, including k-cars. This was 13.3 percent higher than the previous year and, in fact, the highest growth rate in the industry.

Around this time, Honda's business operations started to show signs of change. Domestic sales was steadily increasing since 1985. During the recession, people had worried that the strong yen would lead to an exodus of heavy industry from Japanese shores, but no longer. Now, surging consumer demand year after year all but erased such concerns. No one realized that Japan was caught up in a bubble economy.

At the beginning of 1988, Honda's cars suddenly began to sell like never before. The number of new Honda cars registered in March had increased 47.2 percent over the same period the previous year, sending waves throughout the industry. Starting with the Civic in February, there were unprecedented waiting lists for many of Honda's cars; in some cases, shortages meant several months between purchase and delivery.

Honda's executives made a decision. Honda had just put the finishing touches on a new auto-painting facility in Suzuka in the spring of 1988. If pressing, welding and assembly lines were added, it could easily be converted into a full-fledged manufacturing plant. In fact, Honda had already signed a contract in 1985 giving them the option to purchase molds and other necessary equipment. All that was needed was the "go" sign, and within one year Honda would have another full manufacturing facility.

At the unveiling of the "Concerto," a new compact car Honda had co-developed with Rover, president Kume casually mentioned that Honda planned to invest twenty-five billion yen to increase the production capability of the Suzuka manufacturing plant.

It would be the first time in twenty-one years that Honda would be adding a new assembly line. The new line would run two shifts and be capable of manufacturing 1,000 automobiles a day, for a total of 240,000 a year. Combined with the two lines already in place, that would raise total production capability for Suzuka to 800,000 per year, making it one of the largest factories in Japan.

The only concern the Honda executives had was that there were never any guarantees as to future demand. The bubble economy had almost reached its peak. When it did, there would be no more room for expansion and the economy could only come tumbling down. Reservations aside, however, Honda knew that enlarging the plant was the only way to deal with the current level of demand.

Experts say that when viewed from a global standpoint, a manufacturer needs to sell more than 2.5 million automobiles a year in order to survive on its own in the highly competitive auto industry. Once an automaker achieved this level of production, it would be able to take the initiative in the event of an industry shake-up, rather than be swallowed by the other party.

Indeed, people have talked of the existence of a "2.5 Million Club" in the world auto industry. Only five automakers—GM, Ford, Toyota, Nissan, and VW—were said to belong to this club. Honda saw the third assembly line at the Suzuka plant as its stepping-stone into this exclusive club.

Honda's sales in 1988 were 610,000 vehicles in Japan, 850,000 in North America, 140,000 in Europe, and 110,000 in developing countries, for a grand total of 1.71 million automobiles. It wasn't even seventy percent of the 2.5 million threshold. How then, could Honda possibly join the 2.5 Million Club?

Honda had laid out a basic plan: it calculated that, when the time came for Honda to join the club, the company would be selling one million cars in North America, one million in Japan, 300,000 in Europe, and 200,000 in developing countries. Yoshizawa had predicted that Honda would be joining the club "by the early 1990s." If Honda's domestic Japanese sales continued to grow by 50,000 cars every year, the company would hit its mid-term goal of 800,000 cars in four years (1992) and would achieve the one million mark in six years (1996). Looking at the rosy speculations, the Honda kids were practically intoxicated by the dream that they too would soon be members of the 2.5 Million Club.

That being said, sticking one's neck out too far was a sure-fire way to get it chopped off. "Honda bashing" began in earnest just as the economic bubble reached its peak. Nissan was the first manufacturer to launch a campaign.

"We cannot allow the Prelude to dominate the entire market for compact specialty cars!" declared Nissan president Yutaka Kume at the unveiling of his company's newest compact car, the Silvia, in May 1988, publicly declaring war on Honda. Nissan was keenly aware of Honda's recent gains and was looking for any opportunity to shake its pursuer. Sales for the Silva picked up the following month, making it the top-selling product in the compact market.

Fujisawa's dream had been to make it clear that Honda was ahead of Nissan, once and for all. Although none of them ever spoke of it, this goal weighed heavy on the shoulders of the Honda kids. While Honda's domestic sales remained in the 400,000-500,000 range, Nissan had paid little heed. But with Honda selling 600,000 cars annually, and apparently striving to hit 800,000, and even one million, Nissan simply couldn't sit back and watch any longer.

No sooner had Nissan resolved to take on Honda than Toyota announced its own plan of attack. Toyota aimed to dominate the market for "luxury" compact cars with engine displacements between 1800cc and 2000cc. In August, Toyota totally overhauled its Mark II, Chaser, and Cresta cars and set a preliminary sales goal of 37,000 per month for the three models combined. At the time, total demand for luxury compacts was 40,000 a month, so Toyota's plan represented an ambitious strategy to capture ninety percent of the market for the cars.

Nissan fought back and introduced its next new car after the Sylvia: the Cefiro. Nissan also overhauled its own luxury compact cars, the Laurel, Maxima, and Skyline, to make them more competitive. Nissan had initiated a boom for luxury cars with its Cima, which had been so successful that the fad was known as the "Cima phenomenon" in Japan. As a result, spirits were high for the time being at Nissan.

Toyota and Nissan were now in an all-out "war" for the luxury compact market. Honda, which had only just began to close in on Nissan when this clash of giants broke out, looked on with apprehension.

Luxury compacts occupied a niche, which in Honda's lineup would have fallen somewhere between the Accord and the Legend. Honda didn't have any cars of this type in its lineup, which would appear to mean that it would be unaffected by the battle between Nissan and Toyota. In reality, however, the competition would undoubtedly result in fierce price slashing among the dealerships, which would inevitably have an impact on the sales of Accord.

Thanks to the strength of the Honda brand name, dealerships were able to move their products without instituting large-scale discounts. But if the competition between Toyota and Nissan escalated, and the prices of luxury compacts were driven down to the level of the Accord, Honda would lose customers for sure. Honda could join in on the price war, ignoring profit to defend its market share, but then its supply capacity would never be able to keep pace.

In the latter half of 1988, manufacturers found that they had to revise their marketing strategies to take into consideration the upcoming introduction of the consumption tax in Japan. The tax was scheduled to take effect on April 1, 1989. At the same time, the 5.6 percent commodity tax would be reduced, which meant that automobile prices would also go down. Realizing that it would be more advantageous to wait for the tax laws to take effect before shopping for a new car, consumers were likely to hesitate from making purchases during the first few months of 1989. The only way to avoid a major drop in sales would be to start slashing prices early.

Mazda took the initiative. In December, when Mazda came out with a new model of the Familia, the company decided to sell the car at a low price that already reflected the planned taxes. As a result, the price war, which had previously been restricted to the luxury compact market, rapidly spread to all types of cars. Toyota and Nissan's dealerships took matters into their own hands and rushed to slash their prices without even waiting to hear from their respective manufacturers. Honda was the last to enter the competition.

Honda also fared poorly with its new "Concerto." The car was developed as a bridge between the Civic and Accord lines and was brought to market via the Clio network. The discovery of defects in early models, however, led to a deluge of customer complaints and as a result, dealers lost interest in the product.

The bubble economy had reached its peak, and consumers were increasingly turning to luxury rather than economy compacts. As a result, Honda's domestic sales in 1988 were 613,000 vehicles—7,000 off of the original goal. It was 240,000 higher than Mazda, but 9,000 lower than Mitsubishi. Honda had dropped back out of its position among the top three after just one year.

6

In August 1985, a shining white, sixteen-story office building went up along Route 246 in Tokyo, diagonally opposite the Crown Prince's Palace in Akasaka. It was Honda's new headquarters and a symbol of the company's rapid growth. After a four-year stint as president of HAM, managing director Irimajiri returned to Japan in August of 1988, just as the bubble economy was driving domestic sales to new heights. Hiroyuki Yoshino, who had joined Honda at the same time as Irimajiri, took over as president of HAM.

Under Irimajiri's watch at HAM, the workforce swelled to 8,000 employees, double the number there had been when he had first arrived in Ohio. Production was going well, and the factory was now capable of manufacturing products that matched those made in Japan in quality, functioning, and almost any other respect. The "Honda Way" had taken root, and was making steady inroads among the laborers at the factory.

In order to make sure that HAM was accepted as an American rather than Japanese company, Irimajiri had followed Whitlock and Insley's advice and had actively interacted with representatives of not only the Big Three but parts suppliers and other members of the automobile industry in Detroit. Before he knew it, Irimajiri had become one of the heroes of the American auto industry. Auto journalists portrayed him as the driving force behind Honda's success in America.

In Japan, everyone recognized Soichiro Honda as the founder of the Honda Motor Corporation. In the United States, on the other hand, his name was only known to a handful of people in Detroit, and not at all outside the auto industry. This wasn't surprising; not many Americans even remembered that the Model T had been created by Henry Ford. In fact, Americans would be hard pressed to connect a speed maniac like Soichiro to the successful manufacturer of family cars.

The "Mayflower Project," which Irimajiri had started with the aim of building a new corporate culture for Honda in Ohio, had proved a great success. Irimajiri became the new face of Honda in the United States. The staff at HAM were sorry to see Irimajiri go, but they believed that their "Mr. Iri" was returning to headquarters in triumph, having proved his worth at the Ohio plant. It was only a matter of time, they thought, before he rose to become president at Honda headquarters in Tokyo.

As Irimajiri's popularity in the U.S. grew, however, so did the number of people at headquarters who looked bitterly upon the success of the new "hero." The reason for this was that a wide gap had formed between Tokyo and Ohio with regard to how HAM should be run. Honda staff at headquarters believed that the fundamental purpose of a factory was manufacturing products, no matter the location. These people felt that Irimajiri's Mayflower Project was taking things too far.

On the other hand, for Irimajiri, who was charged with actually running HAM, involving the American executives and paying heed to their views was the quickest way to make sure HAM was accepted as an American company.

The conflict between headquarters and HAM first came to a head over the issue of whether or not HAM should join the Union of Automobile Workers. When Honda first began production in the U.S., the UAW's membership had been on the decline, due in part to the unprecedented economic slump Detroit was experiencing at the time. Sensing the crisis, UAW president Douglas Fraser established a branch in Marysville and began an aggressive campaign to recruit HAM workers.

From the time the Ohio motorcycle factory first went into operation, HAM's policy had been to postpone joining the UAW for as long as possible, if not indefinitely. When vice president Yoshida had met with labor representatives for the Big Three, every one of them had advised against joining. This was not only because the wages demanded by the UAW were high; unionized workers made factory management much more difficult. Yoshida never forgot how the Big Three representatives had bemoaned the troubles they were having dealing with the UAW. All the HAM executives agreed with Yoshida. *If things are done right, the workers don't need a labor union. A union is only necessary when management fails. As long as we maintain good communication with our workforce, we won't need the UAW.*

As operations at the Ohio plant got into full swing, the advances of the UAW grew more and more aggressive, until finally, cell organizations were set up in the factory. If the management tried to stop the workers from organizing at this stage, it could lead to an open conflict with the UAW.

The HAM executives outwardly adopted a wait-and-see policy, claiming that the decision of whether or not to join the UAW was up to the workers themselves. In the end, a vote was held among the workers. The result was "no." However, a quarter of the workforce joined the UAW as individual members and began to openly try to recruit their fellow workers.

Meanwhile, Honda headquarters had always pushed for HAM to join the UAW ever since the factory began producing its first motorcycles. The leading advocate of this idea was vice president Koichiro Yoshizawa, head of Honda's sales operations.

"We may be able to get by producing motorcycles without the UAW, but automobile production is another story altogether. Do you really think we'll be able to continue operating if we make an enemy of Detroit and the UAW? If the UAW starts bashing us, we'll start losing customers. If things get to that point, it will already be too late," Yoshizawa told first HAM president Kazuo Nakagawa whenever he had the chance.

It was a clear-cut controversy: HAM wanted to put off joining the UAW for as long as possible in order to better focus on its automobile production operations, while headquarters, fearing bashing from the UAW, pushed for HAM to join. Even after Irimajiri took over as president of HAM, the issue remained unsettled. When Irimajiri and Yoshida made a trip back to Japan, they held repeated debates with Yoshizawa and former HAM president Nakagawa. These discussions inevitably followed the same pattern.

Yoshizawa: "The bottom line is that Honda needs to avoid trouble with the UAW in any event. If there's trouble, it will have a negative impact on our sales in the U.S."

Irimajiri: "The top priority for the factory is making the best products we can. To that end, I think it's still too early to join the UAW."

Yoshizawa: "I want you to be flexible. Nakagawa-san, as former president of HAM, what's your take on this?"

Nakagawa: "I think we made the right decision in not joining when we first opened the Ohio factory. But things have changed. We need to look at things from a broader perspective…"

Yoshida: "I see what the two of you are trying to say, but local dealers still prefer automobiles made in Japan to ones manufactured by HAM. We need to establish the factory's quality level first. We are also in contact with the UAW on an informal level. We'll continue making every effort to make sure that our relations with them are good, so I implore you, just give us a little more time."

On one hand, there was Yoshizawa, trying to control HAM from Tokyo, on the other, Irimajiri, doing everything he could to avoid intervention from headquarters. No matter how much time and effort they spent, they seemed to be talking on different wavelengths. Eventually, the UAW abandoned HAM and turned its attentions to Nissan's factory in Tennessee. The issue faded away, without ever reaching a conclusion. Even today, HAM is not a member of the UAW.

The atmosphere within Honda had changed drastically in the four years Irimajiri had spent in the United States. More than anything, Irimajiri was struck by how bureaucratic and impersonal the system had become. Whenever he talked to employees, regardless of which department of section they worked in—the factories, R&D, sales, or management—Irimajiri felt that personal names simply didn't matter anymore. Decisions were no longer made by individuals but by the organization as a whole, which meant that no one needed to take responsibility for them. Understandably, the company was sorely lacking in leaders and heroes.

Since when have Honda employees all become so 'harmless'? Irimajiri wondered. *No wonder headquarters seems so lifeless these days.*

Through most of Irimajiri's early career at Honda, the company had been in its period of rapid growth, an era of chaos and energy. Every branch and department at Honda, from the factories, sales, and management operations, to say nothing of the Honda R&D Company, down even to the affiliated companies had its host of "heroes." While their names may not have rung any bells outside Honda, these people were looked upon with much respect and awe within the company. If an employee's achievements were outstanding, he was accorded a high level of authority, regardless of his age. He would, of course, be held responsible for his decisions, but there was always a second chance if he made a mistake. Fujisawa's basic policy for business management had been based on a large-scale delegation of authority, and this fostered the birth of independent "business heroes" that performed above and beyond their call of duty. In fact, this system was the wellspring of Honda's growth as a company.

The starting point of the Honda Motor Company was a joint enterprise that was actually more like two separate companies working together. The business might just as well have been called "Honda Tech and Fujisawa Trading Company." "Honda Motors," the president's responsibility, would take care of developing the products and running the factories. "Fujisawa Trading" would be responsible for managing the business and selling the products. That the two entities could work together so well as a single company was entirely due to Soichiro Honda and Takeo Fujisawa's shared ambition to make Honda into a top-class company.

As the second president of Honda, Kiyoshi Kawashima inherited the dream. In order to maintain the standards set by the two genius founders as well, Kawashima employed a collective management system based on mutual consent among the top executives.

The "collective directors' room" had been Fujisawa's idea, but it was Kawashima who made sure that the system, as well as its offshoot, the *waigaya* concept, took a firm root throughout the company. By ensuring that all business decisions were made on a collective basis, Kawashima squeezed as much as he could from Soichiro and Fujisawa's public image, while at the same time, making a specific point of minimizing their influence within the actual company. Kawashima deliberately tried to merge the "Honda Motors" and "Fujisawa Trading" aspects of his company's persona into a single, integrated entity. In fact, he had only abandoned his idea of creating an independent Honda sales company because he worried that it would split the company in two.

Honda's third president, Kume, inherited Kawashima's collective management system and took it still further, interpreting collective management to mean decision by consensus.

"From now on," said Kume to the Honda kids, "everything will be decided based on a consensus of all the directors. Once we come to a decision together, it will apply to the entire company."

At best, it was democratic, at worst, mob rule. In the end, only the most conservative decisions, which met with opposition from no one, would remain. The *waigaya* was a useful system for achieving consensus, but if used without restraint, it could lead to confusion and ambiguity about where responsibility rested for the final decisions. Overemphasizing the collective decision-making process would inevitably lead to a phasing out of individual responsibilities.

A typical example was the "2.5 Million Club" plan. Honda executives had done little more than discuss the plan in a few *waigaya* sessions before going ahead with the expansion of the Ohio plant and the construction of a new factory in Canada. A second production line was also under construction in Ohio. Once completed, Honda's annual production capability in North America would soar to 600,000 cars.

Granted, these expansions in North America were necessary to establish Honda's superiority on the American marketplace. However, the decisions to build the third line at Suzuka and the new factory in the U.K should probably only have been made after much more thorough discussions. When the decision had been made to first build the Ohio factory, all the executives above the senior managing director level had "camped out" at an Ohio hotel to debate the pros and cons. The decision was only finalized after the Honda kids had confirmed that, in the even if worst came to worst and they would have to withdraw from the U.S., it would not have a devastating effect on Honda's business as a whole. With the Suzuka line, however, the kids had let their obsession with beating Nissan rush them to an early decision. The fact that the decision was reached by "mutual consensus" made it all the more difficult to reverse track even when problems cropped up later.

Of course, Honda wasn't the only Japanese company to make such mistakes and over-expand its production capacity. Before Honda, Toyota had announced plans to expand into the Japanese island of Kyushu. Nissan too started constructing a second factory adjacent to its existing Kyushu factory, and Mazda also broke ground on a second factory in Yamaguchi prefecture. It was obvious that the new factories would turn out more products than any of the companies were capable of selling, but each blindly believed that it would be the sole survivor of the "manufacturing war." Looking back, it is not hard to see that all the manufacturers at the time were carried away with an incredible sense of optimism that came with the bubble economy.

All the same, when Honda announced its decision to build a factory in the U.K., even fellow automakers were skeptical. Honda had already established Honda of the United Kingdom Manufacturing (HUM) to provide engines to Rover. This time, however, Honda was planning to build a new factory capable of assembling 100,000 automobiles a year. The ambitious plan also called for increasing Honda's capital investment in Rover to twenty percent, with Rover taking a twenty percent stake in HUM. Since Nissan and Toyota had already announced plans to expand into Britain, many of the European countries were starting to complain that Japanese investment was excessively focused on that country.

Even if Honda went ahead with the decision, it needed to clarify the relationship with Rover. According to the proposed plan, it looked like a clear case of redundant investment. Furthermore, it could hardly expect to break even with a production capacity of 100,000 automobiles per year. The prospects of accomplishing a single-year profit any time soon, if at all, were low. While the feasibility study for local production in the United States had been negative as well, there was a major difference. The market of the United States was five or six times that of Britain, promising far greater rewards.

If Honda had an abundance of spare capital as Toyota did, there would have been no problem at all. But Honda lacked the reserves to maintain a battle on three fronts—Japan, the United States, and Europe—at the same time. The Honda kids were so bent on achieving their goal of joining the 2.5 Million Club, that they became blind to everything else and gradually lost self-control.

As an engineer, Kume was first-rate. But his lack of training as a business manager made his decisions rote and obvious. Kume didn't have much in the way of broad social or cultural experience either, which made it difficult for him to come up with an idea like Kiyoshi Kawashima's Indian philosophy-based system of looking at four possible outcomes for every situation. Kume's logic was digital: a simple yes or no. Even if he had wanted to institute a top-down style of decision-making, he simply lacked the resources on which to base his decisions. Believing that the bubble economy would last forever, Kume pushed blindly ahead in the name of "mutual consensus."

The day-to-day aspects of the business were handled by vice president Yoshizawa. However, Yoshizawa was a man who prided himself on being faithful to his duties. He had joined Honda at the same as Kume, which fostered not only a sense of rivalry, but also a certain amount of reserve towards the man. When Kume was president of Honda R&D, Yoshizawa was head of American Honda. As Honda's top managers of product development and sales, respectively, they had passionately debated the types of automobiles that should be sold on the U.S. market. Once they became president and vice president at headquarters, however, things changed. Even when discussion grew heated in the directors' room, in the end, one or the other of the two backed down to avoid a direct conflict. Yoshizawa, for his part, felt he couldn't slight Kume and offer his own views about how the company should be run while the other had yet to provide a clear course of action. *Honda isn't the company it used to be. The scale of the business has simply become too large. We can't tolerate mistakes, even tiny ones, any more. These days, the important thing is not the contribution of individuals, or who succeeded with what project, but harmony. We still need someone to act as the company's face to the public, but don't need any more heroes. As for the company's face, Soichiro Honda is enough.* Putting Yoshizawa's ideas into effect basically called for a bottom-up style of management, leading to even more bureaucracy. Although he never actually voiced his opinions, his way of thinking naturally influenced the atmosphere within the company.

Honda grew bloated and bureaucratic under Kume's leadership. Symptoms of giantism began appearing throughout the company. For example in October 1986, following the example of other manufacturers such as Toyota and Nissan, Honda's factories prohibited the parking of any non-Honda automobiles in the front parking areas. This meant that any Honda supplier with the misfortune to drive another manufacturer's vehicle needed to park in a remote satellite area and walk to the factories. The idea behind this rule was to encourage people to buy more Honda automobiles; it was the plant managers' way of showing their loyalty to headquarters. It was also a PR disaster for the company.

"Looks like Honda's joined the ranks of the big guys like Toyota and Nissan. Guess this means they aren't interested in dealing with anyone who doesn't drive one of their products!" griped one of the Honda's suppliers.

Others complained about changes in procedure.

"We used to just drive into the factory and unload our parts there," said the executive of another supply company. "Now they've got this reception area and make us fill out paperwork detailing our every move!"

All of Japan's auto manufacturers were making a major effort to improve their engineering and manufacturing strategies to keep ahead of their competitors. It was hardly out of the question for Honda to begin keeping track of visitors to its factories. However, the suppliers remembered the "old Honda" and felt the change more keenly. They saw the "new Honda" as having been infested by bureaucrats who weren't interested in anything but rules and formalities.

The symptoms of "corporate bloat" weren't limited to the factories. They were spreading through headquarters as well. Honda's bureaucracy proved as infuriating to the dealers as the suppliers.

"They make us put everything in writing today, even the little stuff we used to take care of by verbal agreement among those in charge. And if the paperwork isn't done perfectly according to the Honda style, they send it back and make us rewrite it. It's like I'm at some government office instead of Honda headquarters. This trend has been getting worse and worse over the last few years!"

"Everything takes way too much time these days. Honda's getting fat, I tell you. In the past, all I had to do was talk to a single sales manager. Now I've got to repeat my story to people all over the company."

Giving younger workers more authority and responsibility had been one of the driving forces behind Honda's rapid growth as a company. Now, however, because of the bureaucratic bloat, these same young workers found themselves cornered and corralled. Seeing their freedom taken from them, they began obsessing over the numbers.

"Now that Honda's gotten so strict about sales results, the young salesmen don't even bother with greetings anymore; they just get straight down to business and leave the minute they're finished. I don't blame them; they've got quotas to fill. But I will tell you that's no way to build a relationship of trust between a manufacturer and a dealer," said the president of a Primo dealership.

The larger a company grows, the harder it gets to avoid bureaucratization. Fujisawa had been convinced that corporate bureaucracy would destroy the company. In fact, this had been one of the main reasons for spinning off Honda's R&D section into a separate entity. Fujisawa hoped that making the R&D section independent would insulate Honda's greatest source of strength from corporate giantism.

In the end, it wasn't enough. As the organization swelled, giantism spread slowly but steadily throughout Honda R&D. In an attempt to curb the trend, president Kawamoto suggested changing all job titles into phonetic representations of the corresponding English language titles. Starting in June of 1987, *shacho* (president) Kawamoto became *purejidento*—president. And *senmu* (senior managing director) Hiroyuki Shimojima became "*shinia manejingu direkuta.*" The list went on.

"I thought making the titles long and hard to pronounce would make people stop using them," explained Kawamoto. "I wanted to encourage employees to call each other by their personal names instead."

Once, Honda employees had affectionately referred to one another using the honorific and diminutive suffixes of -san and -chan. With the number of workers in R&D exceeding 6,000, however, this uniquely Honda tradition had fallen out of style. Now employees referred to one another only by job title, as was typical in most Japanese companies.

The Japanese auto industry had been in a period of turbulent change during the twenty years since Irimajiri joined Honda in 1963 until the outbreak of the "HY War" against Yamaha. If any one of Honda's operations—product development, manufacturing, or sales—had relaxed their efforts, even if only slightly, Honda could well have fallen into the abyss. The independent spirit upon which Honda prided itself also fostered a sense of tension and fear within the company, from headquarters down to the factory floor.

That was the environment in which Irimajiri had been trained. But during his four years in the U.S., Honda appeared to have made a steady change from chaos to order and, in Irimajiri's view, to have become a company that no longer had room for individual heroes.

7

"Even if Honda ever goes under, my company will survive for sure," declared Hajime Matsuo in an informal conversation with journalists—and in the presence of president Kume and chairman Okamura—in 1985. Matsuo had handled Honda's PR under the company's first three presidents, Soichiro, Kiyoshi Kawashima and Kume, and had now been promoted to president of Soichiro's brother Benjiro's company, the Honda Foundry Co., Ltd. At the time, the atmosphere at Honda was still relaxed enough to allow such comments to be made.

"Honda's employees are really lucky," said an incredulous PR representative for a rival company. "There's no way someone in our company could have gotten away with saying something like that."

Honda was a large company with a group system like any other. That being said, Honda employees still enjoyed freedom of speech. Although they respected and followed the decisions of their company, they were openly encouraged to express their honest opinions during the decision-making process so as to avoid any hard feelings.

When I was overseas, Honda looked like a solid fortress, thought Irimajiri. *But now I know why. It's because the company had turned into a bureaucracy. How did this happen? How can we recover the sense of independence and individuality we once had? The company is as good as doomed if we don't make an effort to change now. Is this because the executives failed to articulate any sort of a vision for the company's future to the other employees?*

"Kume-san, you need to come up with a clear vision for Honda's future. Something along the lines of a 'Kume doctrine'," said Irimajiri to Kume.

Irimajiri brought the same request to Yoshizawa. He hadn't discussed the issue with his contemporary, Kawamoto, but he was certain that Kawamoto felt the same way.

"Iri-san, please don't pressure me," said Kume with a pained expression on his face. "I already have Soichiro on my shoulders. So long as he's there, I can't very well do as I please."

Seeing Kume's anguish, Irimajiri began to understand some of the background for the changes that had occurred at Tokyo headquarters.

Meanwhile, Kume too was seriously thinking things over in his mind.

The only thing anyone used to ask of an auto manufacturer was that they made good products. But now we have to think about things from an international perspective, as part of one of the key industries in the world. The era when manufacturers could just keep their heads down and focus on making good products is over.

The question is how can Honda survive on the global stage? The world is testing us. How can we ensure that Honda isn't shunned in the global community? How can we make Honda one of the world's favorite companies?

There's no question that we're facing a crisis. Honda has to somehow find a way to escape such laws of nature as "everything changes" and "inevitable retribution." Old Man Soichiro and Fujisawa have created an amazing system, but no matter how well we tend it, it will inevitably deteriorate as time goes on. As will the power of their personal ideology. How can we restore that?

A master-slave relationship has developed within the company. That's why Honda has turned into a bureaucracy. When we start taking the hierarchical relationship between parent companies and subsidiaries for granted, communication becomes one-sided. That's what makes Japanese corporations so disliked wherever they do business. I want to see a system where parent companies and subsidiaries share open communications and a mutual respect for their unique contributions to the relationship.

The more Kume wrestled with the issue, the more he felt trapped by the rule that "everything changes." Even if Kume was able to identify the specific problems facing his company, he could not articulate a clear vision for Honda's future in the form of a "doctrine," such as Irimajiri had requested. If he did, it would upend the very principles of management laid down by Soichiro and Fujisawa.

Yoshizawa, too, knew that Honda was facing a turning point. Even so, he was still bent on achieving his dream of joining the 2.5 Million Club and could not embrace Irimajiri's suggestion. As far as Yoshizawa was concerned, decisions could wait until the last possible minute.

Soichiro's fame as the Honda "guru" continued to grow year after year. The pressure of Soichiro's reputation weighed heavily on Kume. He felt that he needed to do everything in his power to avoid tainting the business that Soichiro had created. As if that wasn't enough, Kume had to live up to the expectations of the man who had chosen him for the job: Fujisawa. The "Honda myth" needed to be upheld and protected at all costs. As the bureaucracy grew, Kume worried more about how society saw Honda than about the future of the company itself.

Honda's bureaucratization was in part a mirror of the Honda kids' collective inferiority complex. When Honda was still a small company, the market for motorcycles had been considered a niche industry and Honda had been looked down upon by major automobile makers like Toyota and Nissan. In those early days, it wasn't uncommon for Honda employees to hide their company badges when they went out drinking after work. Whenever Soichiro and Fujisawa caught wind of the insecurity of their "kids," it only increased their determination to make Honda a top-notch enterprise as quickly as possible. Both founders were hungry to join the ranks of the elite. Instead of using words like elite or top-notch, however, the two phrased it as aiming to become "world-best."

Honda did, of course, enter the ranks of world's automakers and become a top-notch enterprise in Japan. Being an elite manufacturer meant more of a commitment to the Japanese business world and society at large. The Honda kids, with all their ambition of becoming top-class, also needed to take heed of Fujisawa's warning that "Honda should be more than another big company."

The fact was that the Honda kids had left every outside activity, whether financial, social, or political, entirely in Soichiro's hands. Properly speaking, the Honda kids should have made sure that executives were trained to take over for Soichiro in that field as well. Nevertheless, those on the front lines of the business were simply too busy. When they retired, on the other hand, they were still in their fifties and seen as too young so that they received no offers to take up honorary public office. But most of all, the sheer weight of Soichiro's reputation was enough to make any of the kids hesitate to try and fill his shoes.

Honda's second president Kiyoshi Kawashima retired at the age of fifty-five. After Soichiro's death, he did some work for the Tokyo Chamber of Commerce and Industry but only became vice president in November 1994, a full eleven years after retiring from the front lines. At that time Kawashima was sixty-six years old—roughly the same age as the Toyota president Tatsuro Toyoda and Nissan president Yoshifumi Tsuji. But in that circle of Japan's top business elite known as the *zaikai*, he was still regarded as a youngster.

As Honda gained more and more recognition and public acclaim as a world-class company of the post-war generation, the attention began to have some negative effects on the company. During the push to internationalize at the end of Kawashima's presidency, a decided sense of elitism had taken root. The attitude only intensified during Kume's presidency, when Honda refused to take any position that might compromise its status.

Honda successfully established itself as an international enterprise by expanding into the United States earlier than Toyota and Nissan. Honda's cutting edge design was popular among young people. The functionality of their products was hailed as outstanding. The company had even built itself a shining white building in fashionable Aoyama for a new headquarters.

More and more talented young employees joined the company each year. Most of the executives had chosen, in their day, to work at Honda only after being rejected by Toyota and Nissan. For the younger staff, Honda had been a top-notch company from the start. In fact, one could say that these young recruits only chose to work for Honda for that very reason.

When the elitist attitude spread and began to take root even among the middle-ranking employees who had no experience of Honda's more troubled days, the executives became more restrained and conservative in their decisions. Little by little, Honda lost much of its vitality and strength.

A typical example was Honda's return to racing. The company had withdrawn from international races for both automobiles and motorcycles in order to focus on addressing the defect scandal of the early 1970s and on developing a car to meet the exhaust regulations. The next decade or so might be considered Honda's "dark ages" where racing was concerned.

"It's been ten years since we've withdrawn from the F1. Now that the automobile business is enjoying some stability, why don't we start participating in car and motorcycle racing again? It'll help us keep our momentum," said president Kiyoshi Kawashima to Kume, then president of Honda R&D. The year was 1978 and the specialty car Prelude had just gone on sale. At this stage, neither the president nor the executives were particularly conscious of Honda's status as a top-ranking company.

Hearing the news from Kume, Irimajiri, who was in charge of motorcycles at the time, was overjoyed and immediately launched into preparations for the races. On the other hand, Kawamoto, who was in charge of automobiles, viewed competing in the F1 with nothing but trepidation. If nothing else, the incident served as a clear indicator of the differences between the passionate Irimajiri and restrained Kawamoto.

The Honda motorcycle racing team made its international comeback in 1979. Considering Honda's history of sweeping the Isle of Man TT, most of the employees expected an immediate victory from the moment the Honda team hit the track again. Team leader Irimajiri knew better. *Racing isn't as easy as it looks. Ten years is a long blank spot to overcome. We'll lose for a while until we understand the true worth of victory again: overcoming the obstacles set in front of us.*

Just as Irimajiri had expected, the Honda team ended the season in a total loss two years running. They made some progress in the third year, however, and finally won the championship in 1984, six years after reentering the races.

Now that the motorcycle racing team had its victory, the F1 team was feeling the pressure. *Honda is a top-notch company now. In fact, we're among the best in the world. We've got to be smooth. We've got to live up to expectations.* Kawamoto knew that there would be no way to win the F1 right off the bat. To avoid embarrassment, he entered the Honda team in the F2, which would be easier to win.

Four years had passed since the decision to reenter the F1. It was long enough to develop a solidly performing engine, and the Honda team won sixteen victories in the F2 circuit. With the victories under its belt, the team decided to challenge the F1 in 1983. This time, however, Honda would be participating as an engine supplier.

Kawamoto had made the decision to reenter the F1 at this time because he believed it would be the best way to ensure the success of another project Honda was involved with: the "XX" (Legend) project, a luxury car co-production with Rover (BL). The Legend utilized a V-6 engine very similar to that used in an F1 race car. A victory at the F1 would not only be a great way to publicize the Legend, it would also ensure the car's reputation as a Honda product.

In its first year back in the F1, Honda participated in seven races, with a best result of seventh in the Netherlands GP. The following year, Honda participated in sixteen races, coming in first in the ninth race, the Dallas GP in the United

States. The victory marked the third for the company in its F1 history. Ironically, however, the succession of victories that followed only served to hide the growing problems within Honda, problems that led the company to drag its feet when the bubble economy "burst" shortly thereafter.

Fujisawa began losing interest in Honda shortly after appointing Kume as the third president of the company. Even when Kiyoshi Kawashima, Kume's predecessor, visited him to discuss potential successors to Kume, he failed to show much of a reaction.

"I don't really know Irimajiri or Kawamoto," said Fujisawa. "I just don't have enough information to make a judgment. They're both engineers, so I guess it doesn't matter which becomes president. Soichiro knows them, doesn't he? Why don't you leave the final decision up to Kume and Soichiro?"

In the early years of Fujisawa's retirement, when he had been in good health, he had listened closely and had indirectly given his opinion by either nodding or looking away whenever one of the Honda kids visited him in Roppongi. After Kume took over, however, Fujisawa hardly seemed interested in even hearing regular business reports.

Still, the Honda kids continued their regular visits to update Fujisawa. Fujisawa hadn't personally trained any of the current crop of Honda kids besides Kume and Yoshizawa. It was only natural that his interest was low. Fujisawa listened to the reports in a perfunctory manner and, in his later years, took to asking them to leave after just ten to fifteen minutes.

Another factor in Fujisawa's growing disinterest was his realization that Soichiro's name had grown too large for him to manage. By this point, Fujisawa simply lacked the physical strength to temper the overbearing weight Soichiro's reputation had acquired, as he had in the past. *I did the best I could. Now it's all up to the kids to dodge the "law of inevitable change." But most of all, I don't want to expose my senility to them. I don't want to live until I'm eighty. When I go, I want it to be quick and painless.* Since he had hurt his back sometime after resigning as director, he now needed to use a cane, and this had forced him to abandon his hobby of taking long strolls through the city. He not only stopped paying regular visits to Honda headquarters, he now rarely showed up at all unless there was some unavoidable reason.

Fujisawa met Soichiro only occasionally, when the two showed up at official Honda events, but the two never engaged in any kind of serious conversation.

"Hi. Are you still making those bad paintings?" Fujisawa would ask.

"Yeah. You still listening to that opera and playing that creaky old music of yours? It still mystifies me as to what you see in that stuff," Soichiro would reply.

One thing Fujisawa and Soichiro never discussed was the current state of the Honda business. Soichiro trusted Fujisawa to keep an eye on the kids. Fujisawa, for his part, knew Soichiro didn't understand complex management issues anyway.

Beset by his growing frailty, Fujisawa spent his days at home, listening to Wagner's dynamic operas on state-of-the-art audio equipment. One thing he did worry about was the Ohio factory, which he had yet to see with his own eyes.

Whenever Irimajiri and other HAM executives visited Japan, Fujisawa would invite them to Roppongi for a personal update of the latest news from the American business world.

"The United States appears to be Honda's final battleground, and you seem to be doing quite well. If only my health were better! I would love to see the factory with my own eyes. Unfortunately, I don't think it's possible anymore," said Fujisawa to the HAM executives.

If there was anything Fujisawa regretted, it was his relations with the organization of former Honda dealers that had jumped ship and cooperated with the Japan Automobile Users Union during the N360 defect scandal. The only way to sweep away the accusations had been for Fujisawa and Soichiro to resign together. Since then, none of the former dealers had criticized Honda publicly, but Fujisawa remembered. Perhaps it was by some divine will that in the fall of 1988, just before his death, Fujisawa received a visit from the leaders that had organized the campaign against Honda. After all these years, both sides finally agreed to let bygones be bygones.

Fujisawa suffered a fatal heart attack on the evening of December 30, 1988, leaving this world just as he had wanted: quickly and quietly. The death of the seventy-eight year old signaled the end of an era of Honda history.

"Perhaps it was for the best," said a retired Honda executive. "He wouldn't have been able to rest in peace if he had lived long enough to see the slump Honda has since fallen into."

The death of Japanese Emperor Hirohito just eight days later, on the morning of January 7, 1989, marked the end of the *Showa* era in Japan and the beginning of the current *Heisei*.

Fujisawa's funeral was held on January 27.

"Fujisawa-san," said a mourning Soichiro as he concluded his eulogy, "we burned as brightly as we could and we retired together. I want to thank you for making my life so happy."

For Honda's third president Tadashi Kume, who was in charge of organizing the funeral, the shock of Fujisawa's death was just as great, although in a different sense. Soichiro had been Kume's role model as an engineer, but when it came to being a business manager, Kume depended on no one like he did on Fujisawa. Kume knew that with his ignorance of the business matters, he never would have made it this far as Honda's leader without Fujisawa to serve as the unseen, back side of the "gilt folding screen" behind his back.

Only five days before Fujisawa passed away, he had invited Kume to visit him in Roppongi. The meeting hadn't concerned anything terribly important, but as Kume left the house, Fujisawa had uncharacteristically walked out with his cane to the gate to see Kume off. Kume should have rolled down the window to thank Fujisawa but he had only managed to glance back from the car, after it started to move. He had been surprised to see Fujisawa still leaning on his cane, waving in farewell.

Kume spent his New Year's holidays writing his tribute to Fujisawa. After returning to work, he posted the drafts all over the walls of his office. He spent days reading them aloud and rewriting.

Immersed as he was in Honda's business affairs, Fujisawa hadn't taken part in many external activities. As such, he had barely received any awards or official recognition during his lifetime. For his part, Fujisawa was perfectly content with the situation. He didn't expect anything, and the Honda kids who knew him well didn't make any particular effort to have him honored.

Shortly after Fujisawa passed away, Takao Suzuki, chief of the Automobile section of the Machinery and Information Industries Bureau at MITI, approached the Prime Minister's Office to discuss some sort of official recognition for Fujisawa. Although the office was reluctant at first due to Fujisawa's decided lack of external activities, Suzuki pursued his campaign with great tenacity. Thanks entirely to his efforts, Fujisawa was eventually awarded the Order of the Rising Sun, Gold Rays. The decision came down only three days before the company-organized funeral, illustrating the lengths to which the award was discussed behind the scenes.

8

In 1988, Soichiro went through a period of heaven and hell. His hellish experience took the form of his partner's death. The heavenly experience, on the other hand, was the F1. Williams-Honda had taken the Constructors Championship (a special honor accorded to F1 engine suppliers) for two years in a row in 1986 and 1987. Now, in 1988, another team using Honda engines, McLaren-Honda, won an astounding fifteen out of sixteen races. One of the team's victories had been at the Japan Grand Prix in Suzuka, with famed driver Ayrton Senna at the wheel. It was the first time Soichiro had seen a car with a Honda engine win a race with his own eyes.

The kids have done a tremendous job! thought Soichiro proudly. *Honda had brought honor to its homeland. It's another dream come true for me. The regulations are changing and we won't be allowed to use turbochargers next year. The kids will have to start over again from zero, but I trust them to win again. The point of a race is to win. Honda has to win as many as it can, no matter the obstacles!*

The sixth year after Honda's comeback proved to be the best yet. Honda had reached the top of the F1 and had achieved its major objective.

President Kume and Kawamoto, then president of Honda R&D, quietly discussed withdrawing from the F1 to maintain their glorious record. The string of consecutive victories had raised the bar perilously high for the team. In the end, they came to the obvious conclusion. *The Old Man's dream is winning as many F1 races as we can. Just look at his face! How are we going to tell him we want to quit now? So long as he's alive, we simply can't retire from the F1.* And so a new burden was added to the collective shoulders of the Honda kids.

At the time, the F1 was facing a major turning point. In fact, it was one of the reasons for Honda's string of victories. The beginning of the 1980s, when Honda reappeared on the scene, marked the rise of the turbocharger. In contrast, naturally aspirated engines were on the decline and would completely disappear by 1985.

Turbocharged engines allowed for increased fuel pressure so long as high-octane gasoline was used to prevent knocking. They were tremendously powerful, outputting more than 1000 horsepower. The higher the horsepower, the more pressure was placed on the tires, which necessitated tire changes during races. When naturally aspirated engines had been the mainstay, a blowout usually meant losing the race. In the age of the turbocharged engine, however, stopping for a quick tire change and getting back on the track with new tires lead to better results overall than continuing with worn out tires.

Many felt that the substantially boosted horsepower was jeopardizing the spirit of the F1. The Federation Internationale du Sport Automobile (FISA) attempted to control the spiraling power of the F1 machines. In 1984, it enacted a new rule that limited the amount of gasoline that could be used during a race. If a car ran out of gasoline in the middle of a race, it was automatically retired. The fuel regulations became stricter every year. Although the changes affected every racing team, the real reason for their enactment was to curtail Honda's unprecedented string of victories.

Engines needed to be finely tuned and re-adjusted every year to meet the newest regulations. However, Japanese engineers excelled at this sort of work, and years of research into electronic control technology for consumer cars pushed Japan into the age of the turbocharger earlier than any other country. All the Japanese team needed to do was slightly modify the consumer technology for use in its racing engines.

Although originally intended to cripple Honda, the new fuel regulations turned out to be a blessing in disguise. Honda had already thoroughly analyzed the internal combustion process in the creation of the CVCC engine in the late 1960s. When the engineers discovered that the CVCC created handling problems, they had quickly turned to catalytic converters and electronic control technology instead. Yoshitoshi Sakurai, who had been deeply involved in the CVCC development project, was promoted to the head of Honda's F1 development team in 1985.

Honda had justified entering the F1 for the first time in 1964, on grounds that the cutting-edge technology developed for racing could be applied to consumer automobiles as well. Now, in the age of the turbocharged engine, the situation was completely reversed. Technology developed for consumer cars was being recycled for use in the F1 cars. Honda's huge technological lead in this area proved very attractive to F1 teams and drivers. Williams-Honda signed contracts with star drivers Nelson Piquet and Nigel Mansell, who raced for the team during the 1986 season.

Honda provided the engines. Williams designed the chassis and bodies. The team won nine races and received its first Constructors Championship award in 1986. The team only narrowly missed winning the Drivers Championship. Piquet and Mansell fought hard, but lost the title to Alain Prost of Team McLaren in the end. Piquet and Mansell had split their team's points, allowing Prost to take the lead.

A total of four manufacturers participated as engine suppliers in the F1: Renault, Porsche, Ferrari, and Honda. Renault took a leave of absence from supplying turbocharged engines in 1987 and 1988 to focus on developing new naturally aspirated engines for the 1989 season. This left Porsche and Ferrari as potential rivals, but neither proved capable of coming close to Honda's level in such a short period of time. For the time being, the F1 had become a one-man show for Honda.

Honda set two goals for itself for the 1987 season. One was to cement Honda's reputation in the world of F1 racing. Team leader Sakurai put forth a tremendous effort to approach journalists and increase awareness of Honda in local media. The second goal was to create a solid fan base for the F1 in Japan.

Honda also moved to take over Renault's place in providing engines for the Lotus team. In the era of the turbocharger, nearly every F1 team wanted to get their hands on a Honda engine. Honda selected Lotus, the team that boasted driver Ayrton Senna.

Senna's driving skills were legendary; he was clearly on his way to becoming a new world champion. And Senna had expressed interest in driving a Honda-equipped car to Sakurai on many occasions.

Senna had spent his whole career aiming to be the fastest man on the course. Unlike Prost, who pictured himself ending the race in first place and controlled his driving accordingly, Senna simply focused on driving as fast as he could, even during qualifiers. His pride simply would not abide allowing another driver to get ahead of him. This approach took Senna face to face with danger on many occasions; he saw pushing the limits as a personal duty, even if it meant risking his life in the process. Soichiro was enchanted by Senna's fiery competitiveness, perhaps because it was quite similar to his own. Senna viewed Soichiro with an equivalent amount of respect.

Honda offered its engines to Lotus in exchange for making Satoru Nakajima the second driver for the team. It was hoped that Nakajima's participation in the F1 would kick off a wave of interest in Japan, and Honda moved to promote the race even further by offering to officially host the Japan Grand Prix on the Suzuka circuit. Honda knew that the combination of a Japanese driver and the holding of a race in Japan would create large numbers of local fans. The application was accepted under the condition that the track undergo large-scale modifications. The Grand Prix would return to Japan in 1987.

The first formula race in Japan had been the World Championship of October 1977, held at Fuji Speedway. Its success led to the establishment of an official Japan Grand Prix the following year. Just after the start of the final race of the 1978 Japan Grand Prix, however, one of the most tragic accidents in F1 history took place. Ferrari's car collided with Tyrrell's, actually running onto the latter's rear wheels. Although both drivers managed to escape injury, a large number of spectators had ignored "Keep Out" signs and had pressed their way closer to the track. That was when another race car came crashing in, killing two and injuring seven of the spectators. Having little knowledge of motor sports in general, the mass media used the incident to portray formula racing as inherently dangerous. As a result, the Japan Automobile Federation (JAF) stepped in and banned the sport from Japanese circuits.

The Japan Grand Prix at Suzuka, the fifteenth race of the 1987 season, was the first formula race to be held in Japan since the accident. The qualifier was held on October 30. Williams-Honda and Lotus-Honda won eleven races altogether during the season and had already secured the title of Constructors Champion. Mansell, with six victories under his belt, was also set to receive the title of Drivers Champion. Piquet had won three races, and Senna two. Nakajima, the first Japanese F1 driver, placed seventh in the Brazil Grand Prix and fourth in England, just behind Mansell, Piquet and Senna.

It had been pouring rain on the day of the qualifier, but the finals were held on November 1 to sunny skies. Some 110,000 fans filled the grandstands.

At the time, an odd "jinx" seemed to be in effect. Whenever Soichiro personally attended a race, the Honda teams inevitably lost. When it was decided that the Japan Grand Prix would be held at Suzuka, Soichiro had told everyone that he would me making a point of not going. The closer the date approached, however, the more Soichiro began to regret his decision. Feeling sorry for her husband, Soichiro's wife Sachi finally stepped in the day before the race.

"Why don't you go? You don't have to be so hard on yourself. I've never seen an F1. We can go together." Soichiro agreed. The next day he threw on a pair of blue jeans and headed off to Suzuka with Sachi.

Unfortunately, however, the outcome appeared to prove Soichiro's jinx. Victory went to Team Ferrari. Of the two Honda teams, the best time was marked by Senna, who came in second. Mansell failed to qualify, and Piquet ended in seventh place. The sole saving grace was Nakajima, who placed sixth in the race.

After the race, chairman Okubo and the other Honda executives trudged glumly back to the nearest train station. Kawamoto, who had been responsible for Honda's preparations for the F1, seemed unperturbed and simply commented on how "today was Ferrari's day." Soichiro alone laid into team leader Sakurai.

"What kind of race was that? It's okay to lose once in a while but next time you win. Remember, we're in this to win, not to lose!"

"We'll win next time," assured Sakurai, his face flushed with excitement. "I promise we'll win here at Suzuka next year. Please come back and see!"

"We have to win," Soichiro ordered the kids. "And we have to keep winning."

In an attempt to secure victory, Honda ended its contract with Williams in 1988 and signed a deal with McLaren instead. Until this point, McLaren had used Porsche engines. The team had recently built a new factory for building F1 race cars and had split into two groups: one focusing on development, and the other on race operations. McLaren also boasted a popular designer by the name of John Bernard.

Kawamoto saw a Honda-McLaren collaboration as nothing short of unbeatable. A condition for the partnership was that Senna move to McLaren. Senna, ambitious and aiming for the Drivers Championship, agreed. Honda developed the engines. Bernard incorporated them into the cars he designed. Prost and Senna drove. Thus was forged the strongest team in F1 history.

It would be no exaggeration to call the 1988 F1 a personal showcase for the McLaren-Honda team. They secured fifteen victories out of sixteen races, the only exception being the Italy Grand Prix. That year, Senna counted eight victories, Prost seven. Piquet, who had moved to Lotus even as Senna left, was unfortunately unable to score a single victory, in spite of the fact that he drove a car with the exact same engine used by Senna and Prost.

One of Senna's victories had been at Suzuka, and Soichiro was riding high on the results of his company's team. Fujisawa's death two months later shocked Soichiro out of his reverie. He spent the days and months after Fujisawa's funeral in a daze. Ten months later, however, Soichiro experienced the highlight of his entire career.

Soichiro became the very first Japanese to be inducted into the U.S. Automotive Hall of Fame. Soichiro and Sachi attended the induction ceremony, which was held on Northwood University campus in Midland, Michigan on October 7, 1989. The front doors to the Automotive Hall of Fame traditionally remained closed until the day of the honorees' appearance. This day, they opened for Soichiro. The hall itself featured exhibits and memorials for those who had made an impact on American car history.

The newest corner featured Soichiro Honda's portrait and biography, giving the details of Soichiro's life and career, from his earliest years up until the establishment of Honda as a world-class company. The exhibit also featured five photographs. One captured the instant his car flipped end over end after a collision during the Speed Rally held at the Tamagawa River course just before World War II. Another showed Soichiro posing in front of an F1 car.

In October 1993, two years after Soichiro's death, Sachi Honda dropped by the Automotive Hall of Fame. She removed one of the pictures from Soichiro's display and replaced it with one of his watercolor paintings. Sachi also left his favorite brush and palette. She only had a few of his paintings left; Soichiro had given the vast majority away to friends.

"I happened across the painting when I was cleaning house the other day," explained Sachi. "Maybe he hid it away because he didn't like it. I'm sure he'd be embarrassed if he knew I was putting it up here. But I thought it would be a wonderful way for people to understand the true Soichiro."

Later on, Eiji Toyoda became the second Japanese inducted into the Hall of Fame in the fall of 1994. In addition to a photograph of the groundbreaking ceremony held for the factory his company was building together with GM, Toyoda followed Soichiro's example and also bequeathed a copy of his autobiography *Toyota; Fifty Years in Motion*, a Japanese-language Toyota emblem from its early days, and Toyota's newest logo, which was designed around a letter "T" to highlight the company's new global approach.

The day after his induction ceremony, Soichiro was invited to the Ford Museum in downtown Detroit. He expressed his gratification before the assembled media, which included NBC, ABC, CBS, and all the major American networks.

"I saw my first car when I was only six years old, even before I started going to elementary school. It was a convertible Model T Ford, and it came roaring along a curving, narrow path in the small village where I was born. I ran after it for as long as I could, but it disappeared in a cloud of dust.

After the car had gone, I discovered a spot of black motor oil in a rut. I dropped to my knees and put my nose as close as I could. To me it represented the smell of civilization. That chance meeting with a Ford changed the course of my life. I swore to myself that I'd build my own cars someday. I am deeply touched by the honor you have bestowed upon me today."

The highlight of the celebration was the awards ceremony and gala dinner held at the Westin Hotel in the Renaissance Center in Detroit on October 10. More than 1,000 people from the U.S. automobile industry were in attendance. A tuxedo-clad Soichiro took the stage to thunderous applause, where the chairman of the board of the Automotive Hall of Fame gave him a large, gold medal with the letters "Automotive Hall of Fame" engraved above a picture of the famous doors to the hall.

"My induction into the U.S. Automotive Hall of Fame is truly an honor. I still can't believe this isn't a dream. But it still hurt when I pinched myself, so I guess this is real. I want to thank each and every one of you for making this possible. This represents the pinnacle of my entire life. I am honored that you have made this dream a reality. Thank you. Thank you very much," said Soichiro to a standing ovation.

Interpreter Kiyoshi Ikemi did his best to bring Soichiro's somewhat rough speech to the American audience. Soichiro was a stubborn man, but he truly cared about those around him. No matter how many times he went over the draft for his speech, he fretted about his message reaching the audience. He barely ate in the days leading up to the ceremony.

"Ikemi, do you think they'll understand what I mean by 'pinching myself'? Do you think Americans will get it?" asked Soichiro at one point.

"Don't worry, Honda-san. Just say whatever you want to say. Why don't you make a gesture like you're pinching yourself? That way they'll understand even without the translation," answered Ikemi.

After the festivities were over, Soichiro chartered a plane to Ohio to visit HAM. It was his third visit. He had first come in 1979, when the motorcycle factory was completed, and again in 1982 for the completion of the automobile factory. The expansion of the factory lines led to a massive increase in the workforce. Now almost 10,000 people were employed there.

When Soichiro had visited HAM for the first time, he had walked around the factory and shaken hands with so many of the "associates" (as HAM factory workers were called) that his hand was quite swollen by the end of the day. This time, Soichiro was too weak to walk and greet all of the associates on foot. And besides, his wife was with him. Factory manager Bob Simcox drove the two of them around on an electric cart.

In consideration of Soichiro's health, then-president of HAM Yoshino had given strict orders to drive quickly and make the tour as short as possible. Simcox tried his best, but every time he pressed the accelerator, Soichiro would poke his head out and tell him to slow down. Although Simcox didn't speak a word of Japanese, the meaning was clear enough.

The slower the electric cart went, the more associates came to shake Soichiro's hand. Some had blue eyes. Some had dark skin. Soichiro shook hands with all of them. *It doesn't matter what they look like. They're all Honda kids. And this could well be the last time I ever see them in person. Fujisawa, I wish you were here with me.*

CHAPTER SEVEN: LORD OF THE KIDS

No matter the era, dreams and goals are absolutely necessary in life. And you never reach a point where you can say, "That's enough." Dreams are as limitless as a staircase without end. Honda and I are climbing that staircase to the future, one step at a time.

—Soichiro Honda

You'll never understand the true meaning of a businessman's statements unless you have a firm grasp of the events of the period and see exactly what kind of situation his company was facing. Fragments taken out of context can come to mean something completely different from what was intended.

—Takeo Fujisawa

1

"Human beings begin their journey towards death the moment they are born. In the same way, every company is destined to fall someday. In fact, that 'someday' is usually sooner rather than later."

So began the article in the business magazine *Nikkei Business*. It was entitled "The Fate of a Company."

The article contained lists of the top hundred Japanese companies for each decade between 1896 and 1982. Only one company, Oji Paper, an affiliate of the former Mitsubishi *zaibatsu*, remained in the top hundred throughout the entire period.

A total of 413 companies appeared on the lists. If a company's period of prosperity were infinite, the names would never change. But reality doesn't work this way. A simple calculation yields the average number of times a company appeared on the lists: 2.5. Multiplying this number by the ten-year span of each list shows that a company's glory days could only be expected to last less than thirty years. This is the "Thirty-Year Rule."

Although the comparison is somewhat strained, this figure yields interesting results when applied to the auto industry. Toyota, for example, got started in the car business in 1933, when the Toyoda Automatic Loom Works established its automotive division. At this point the company has a history of more than sixty years.

Toyota's first thirty years, which included World War II, were pure struggle. The second thirty years, which began after the advent of widespread motorization, proved to be Toyota's era of prosperity. Although Toyota remains a first-tier company today, it has already passed its peak.

Nissan's era of prosperity began in the mid 1950s, after the resolution of a severe dispute between labor and management in 1953. It lasted for roughly thirty years, until the mid 1980s, when Katsuji Kawamata—the man who once revived the company's flagging fortunes—and his right-hand man, Ichiro Shioji, fell from power. Ever since, Nissan has been plagued by poor judgment, driving its national production and sales to less than half that of Toyota.

Honda's prosperity began in the early 1960s, after the company overcame its first business crisis in 1954 and sales of the Super Cub began. It lasted for about thirty years, until Fujisawa and Soichiro passed away. Sales figures suggest that Nissan and Honda have both passed their peak and have begun a downhill slide. It appears increasingly improbable that either will manage to defy the "Thirty-Year Rule."

That something had changed at Honda became evident just before the "bubble economy" hit its peak in 1989. National sales had been stagnating since the beginning of the year. People soon began talking about how "the once-invincible Honda has changed."

"The consumption tax has given other companies' luxury cars a boost, and that hurt our sales," said Kume. "When we introduce our new Accord, we'll close the gap for sure."

The much-anticipated fourth-generation Accord debuted in September of 1989. It was sold, as before, through the Clio network, while its "sister product," a new hardtop version of the Vigor, was sold through Verno. In addition, Honda released a new car, the Ascot, for the Primo network, and a spin-off of the Accord, called the Accord Inspire. The Accord series grew from just two cars to four in one fell swoop.

The third-generation Accord had won the Japan Car of the Year award. Everyone in the Japanese automotive press was now focused on the question of just what was new in the fourth-generation model.

The press conference for the new Accord was held at a large banquet hall in the Tokyo Imperial Hotel. President Kume greeted the audience with a short speech, and then yielded the floor to another executive who used a slide show to explain the car's technical specifications. Once the introduction was over, the lights were dimmed and the movable dividers hiding the exhibition area were removed to reveal the new Accord, illuminated by a spotlight. Usually, the audience responded to an unveiling with a bit of a stir. This time, the crowd sat in total silence.

The exhibition area featured ten samples of the latest Accord. They looked nearly identical to the third-generation models.

"It doesn't seem to have changed at all," one of the journalists said to the executives during the subsequent question and answer session. "The design is so subdued it doesn't even look like a Honda."

"Honda no longer wants to jump restlessly from one design to another," countered Kawamoto, who headed the development team. "This is a car that can be enjoyed by young and old alike. We don't want people to drive Hondas when they're young only to switch to Nissan or Toyota when they grow up. That's why we're sticking with a design that isn't flashy, one that you won't get sick of. Drivability is more important than design."

"Honda's sales are driven by handling, not design," agreed Irimajiri. "This new Accord is a natural outgrowth of that."

Honda released the new version of the Accord simultaneously in both Japan and the United States. Toyota and Nissan usually released new models in Japan six months or a year before doing so in the U.S. Both with this model and the one before it, Honda had one-upped its rivals by pulling off a simultaneous release.

The fourth-generation Accord proved to be a strong seller in the United States. Some 783,000 were sold in 1989. This increased to 855,000 in 1990. In fact, sales of the Honda Accord exceeded those of the Ford Taurus for three years running beginning in 1989. The Accord had achieved the triumphant distinction of becoming the top seller in the U.S. market.

Sales in Japan, on the other hand, were miserable. Honda hoped to sell a combined total of 174,000 of the four new automobiles. The company only managed to sell 142,000 in 1990, however, thanks to far lower than expected sales for the Accord and Ascot.

The sales goal for the two automobiles was 102,000. Only 56,000 had been sold. The Clio and Primo networks only managed to sell 31,000 Accords, 46.9 percent of the previous year's sales. New models tended to reinvigorate the sales of a flagging series. Occasionally, they even sold better than previous versions. The Accord and Ascot sold so poorly, however, that the public dismissed them as failures from the very start.

Honda hired two popular actors, Bunta Sugawara and Shinji Yamashita, to star in a TV commercial for the Ascot. The intent was to create a comfortable and homey image for the product, but the commercials ended up feeling dowdy and unfashionable instead. Complaints poured in from the dealers, forcing Honda to pull the commercial far earlier than planned.

The Honda Kids were at their wits' end. American sales were better than ever. But Honda's products seemed unable to gain any sort of foothold in Japan at all. Even longtime fans were complaining:

"Honda's cars aren't interesting anymore."

"Honda just doesn't have the energy it once did."

"Honda's a victim of its own success."

The basic concept of the Accord had been to create a single "worldwide car" for a three-pronged marketing strategy in Japan, the United States, and Europe.

The idea had come from the compact "J-Car," created by GM in the early 1980s. All of GM's subsidiaries and affiliates, including Germany's Opel, Japan's Isuzu, and Australia's Holden, contributed by manufacturing modular parts that could be assembled to create the same automobile anywhere. This interchangeability meant it was easier to manufacture more cars, which promised to reduce overall expenses.

In the end, however, the J-Car was a complete failure. The idea of a "worldwide car" may sound good in principle, but consumers in these diverse markets quickly saw it for what it was: a cost-cutting gimmick that didn't take their respective needs and wants into account.

Unlike GM, Honda didn't focus purely on reducing costs, but the overall concept of global standardization was the same. Honda aimed to develop a car that appealed to markets across the world and manufacture it in Japan and the United States simultaneously. Honda had exhaustively studied and learned from

GM's failure. And in light of the success of the third-generation Accord, the Honda Kids were fully confident they wouldn't repeat GM's mistakes.

Honda executives saw a "worldwide car" as a magic wand for the troubles facing the company. Development of the fourth-generation Accord began just after the spike in the value of the yen from the Plaza Accord. Although the basic car would be the same, Honda still needed to account for differences of taste in Japan, the United States, and Europe. As such the development team incorporated changes appropriate to each market.

The third-generation Accord was the car that convinced the international automobile industry that Honda had started the trend towards smaller cars. This led the Honda development team to decide not to make any major design changes. The development team had become as bureaucratic and conservative as the executives. But this "play it safe" strategy backfired: it led Honda to underestimate completely the widening differences in taste among Japanese, American, and European consumers.

One person did notice this divergence: Norimoto Otsuka, vice president of Honda Research of America, who was involved the development of the fourth-generation Accord at the peak of the project in 1987. Early in the project, he predicted that the new model wouldn't do well in Japan. "In the past, all a manufacturer had to do was build a better car and the world would beat a path to his door," Otsuka had said. "Even just five years ago, we could predict future trends with a high degree of confidence. But now everything is different. It's much harder to read the trends. I can't describe it exactly, but I can tell it's not like it used to be. Is there even such a thing as a car that can sell anywhere? It's clear that advanced technology sells cars, but that alone can't guarantee success."

Unfortunately for Honda, Otsuka's prophecy came true. The worldwide car strategy proved a total failure.

Seen objectively, it isn't surprising that the Accord sold well in America. Honda of America took customer satisfaction surveys very seriously. If a Honda product didn't earn high rankings in the surveys conducted by J.D. Power & Associates, Honda of America made sure to analyze the reasons why. When a product did earn high rankings, Honda would similarly identify which features were responsible and apply that knowledge in subsequent research and development.

During the development of the fourth-generation Accord, the third-generation Accord achieved and maintained bestseller status in the United States. In 1987, five out of the top ten best selling cars in America were Hondas. The percentage of repeat buyers of the Accord grew larger every year. Once an American consumer bought an Accord, he was almost certain to make his next car an Accord. The car enjoyed almost fanatical levels of brand loyalty. This also meant that the average of Accord owners rose every year.

The first Accords had been purchased by customers with an average age in their thirties. In the ten years that had passed since the first version was released, the original customers had entered middle age. Honda had prided itself on the youthful image of its early "two-box" hatchbacks, such as the Civic. Now, Honda found itself moving towards "three-box" cars, i.e. four-door sedans.

The more new models Honda released, the more conservative the company's cars became. The fourth-generation Accord had been developed to correspond almost 100 percent to the requests and needs of repeat customers; Honda of America fully expected the fourth version to outsell the third.

Meanwhile, back in Japan, the bubble economy had drastically changed the tastes of Japanese consumers. Customers there had next to no interest in subdued auto designs.

Unlike Americans, Japanese consumers rarely purchased the same car model twice in a row. The average consumer might buy a sub-compact as his first car, then move up to an affordable compact. Once he had a family, he'd buy a mid-sized sedan. Finally, he would move on to "status symbol" luxury cars such as the Toyota Crown or Mark II. Japanese automakers therefore tried to retain customers by stocking their dealerships with as wide a variety of vehicles as possible.

The huge difference in the tastes of American and Japanese consumers was becoming a thorn in Honda's side. Generally speaking, Americans saw cars as tools of transportation. The period of ownership was relatively long. Mileage at trade-in often exceeded 60,000 miles.

The Japanese, on the other hand, saw cars as fashion items. This kept the period of ownership relatively short; generally, only taxis and other commercial vehicles logged over 60,000 miles before being traded in. Japanese consumers placed a premium on style over drivability and handling. At the peak of the bubble economy, Japanese customers only wanted cars at the cutting edge of trendiness. The Accord proved that scoring a major hit in the United States was no guarantee of achieving strong sales in Japan.

Honda's manufacturing policies were largely based on Soichiro's belief that Honda should "invent new technology on its own, without aping other companies," and Fujisawa's belief that they should "cultivate niche markets in which other companies aren't interested."

As the founders ceded power, however, the idea of niche marketing lost favor. In fact, the original concept of creating unique cars eventually twisted into "never sharing parts among Honda products." Even though the Accord and Accord Inspire were "sister products," they shared barely any parts in common. The new version of the Accord shared only 10 percent of its parts with the previous version. Considering that Toyota and Nissan recycled more than 60 percent of the parts of old models in new ones, it was obvious that Honda's approach was inefficient, which drove production costs even higher.

"We can make 95 percent of a car similar to one by Toyota or Nissan. Just make that remaining 5 percent as unique as possible," Fujisawa would tell the R&D section in an attempt to rein in the engineers. Intoxicated by the bubble economy, however, the R&D section had all but forgotten Fujisawa's admonition. They incorporated new components into every new model, not sharing parts even among closely related automobiles. At one point, Honda created an automobile with a five-cylinder engine, a technological innovation only an engineer would care about. Before long, Honda employees began complaining about the engineers developing their cars: "The R&D section has declared independence, I guess," remarked one.

"Soichiro = motorcycle = speed = F1"

"Civic = CVCC = low-polluting automobile = Accord"

Until the situation in the mid-1970s, Honda's public reputation corresponded quite closely to the actual reality within the company. Honda kicked off its automobile business with the S500, and continued to grow by aiming for niche markets thereafter. Honda always managed to grab the spotlight with innovative auto designs, including the N360, Civic, Accord, Prelude, CR-X, and the City. Nearly all of its cars had debuted to impressive sales, cementing the company's reputation for uniqueness. Honda's strategy had been to cultivate the niche market first, push its products into the mainstream, build the value of its brand name, and only then begin true mass production. The company had flourished as a result, even to the extent of thriving in the U.S.

Niche markets in many ways anticipate the eventual desires of the mainstream. Now, however, head of R&D Kawamoto abandoned the tried and true Honda strategy with his declaration that Honda would no longer restlessly introduce new designs. Honda would focus on conservative sedans like those of Toyota and Nissan. There was now a gap between Honda's image and its reality.

The major reason for Honda's success in the United States was the close match there between the company's image and its reality. Honda of America was a family car company. In Japan, however, Honda's new approach to car marking drove away its customer base. Honda's tragedy was that it couldn't pursue the strategies of global standardization and niche marketing at the same time.

Ironically, just as Honda abandoned its niche-based strategy, Toyota, Nissan, and Mitsubishi introduced a variety of creative new automobile designs. Needless to say, the lack of individuality that marked Honda's latest offerings was related to the bureaucratization within the company.

2

At a June 1989 meeting of the board, two and a half months before the fourth-generation Accord was to go on sale, Kume promoted Irimajiri, Kawamoto, and Munekuni to the rank of executive director. Kume and Yoshizawa had managed the business alone over the past six years. The promotions gave some hint of the management team that would succeed Kume. People both inside and outside the company concluded that the race to be chosen as Kume's successor had now officially begun.

The choice was entirely up to Kume. Whenever he was asked about the next president, he would half-jokingly answer: "It'll be someone who, like me, doesn't want the position."

Many former Honda executives reasoned that if the areas of responsibility the three potential candidates had been assigned were any indication, the smart money was on Kawamoto. Irimajiri was assigned general affairs, management, and production, while Munekuni was entrusted with sales. Kawamoto's promotion meant his stepping down as president of the Honda Research and Development Company, but he had yet to be assigned any specific area of responsibility.

He had, in effect, been given a sinecure.

"Just hang out at the Aoyama headquarters," Kume had told him. It was the exact same assignment that Kume had received from Fujisawa. He had spent an entire year at headquarters without being given a specific task.

Soichiro and Fujisawa had held high hopes for Kume, but he had never once expressed interest in becoming president. Quite the contrary, he didn't want the position. Even after becoming president, whenever things got stressful he would go home, lock himself in his study, and unwind by drawing blueprints of engines that had no hope of ever being made.

Kume was quite serious when he said he wanted to appoint a successor who didn't aspire to the position. Kawamoto appeared to fit the bill. Like Kume, he had spent his entire professional life in engineering. His ten years as an executive at headquarters were concurrent with his nine years overseeing the Honda Research and Development Company. Everybody at Honda knew Kawamoto as the man in charge of the F1 project, but few had any grasp of him on a personal level.

In terms of who had the most impressive résumé, Irimajiri was the prince of Honda. His promotion to head of the Suzuka manufacturing plant in his thirties propelled him out of the ranks of mere engineers. His years as president of Honda of America Manufacturing taught him how to be an effective manager. He was charismatic and kind, with a cheerful personality and a knack for reading people. He seemed to be the perfect candidate to pull the company out of the doldrums.

Irimajiri's rival Kawamoto, on the other hand, was a precise thinker who, as a theorist of engineering, could put any university professor to shame. He also had a bold and larger-than-life personality. His weaknesses were that he often seemed gloomy and had never really played a major role in managing Honda's business as a whole.

After much thought, Kume had picked Kawamoto as his successor. Mimicking his own rise to president, Kume attempted to promote Kawamoto's growth as a manager by freeing him from any specific responsibilities during his "grooming period." Kawamoto, for his part, had no idea about Kume's intentions, and used the time to work as a middleman between the R&D section and manufacturing plants in order to improve the quality of what was being produced.

Irimajiri immediately noticed a change in the mood at the company upon his return to Japan from the United States. Not only had it grown more bureaucratic, but his colleagues had also grown somehow distant. It didn't take him long to realize that the cold reception was due to his having become a "hero" in the United States.

In America, Irimajiri had totally dedicated himself to promoting HAM's growth as a company. His busy schedule occasionally meant he couldn't spare much time for former executives, such as Kiyoshi Kawashima, who came to visit Ohio. Once in a while, he even caught wind of certain nasty rumors that were spreading about him. They followed a similar pattern:

"Irimajiri just loves showing off our factories to the Americans. With him in charge, it's only a matter of time before our manufacturing know-how falls into the hands of the Big Three. Whose side is he on, anyway?"

Or:

"Irimajiri's so Americanized, the only people he listens to are that Scott and Susan. He just ignores everyone else, even Honda of America in Los Angeles and headquarters in Tokyo."

Or:

"I guess Irimajiri wants to make HAM like the Japanese army in Manchuria."

Living in Ohio, he hadn't paid much attention to the rumors. Now that he was back in Japan, however, he was stunned to learn that there were people at headquarters who believed them.

Irimajiri had been offered an honorary doctorate in engineering from Ohio Northern University. Vice President Yoshizawa made Irimajiri decline the offer, warning him "not to stick out too much." Irimajiri was greatly surprised. Declining the degree, in and of itself, didn't bother him; the possible offense it might cause the local community, however, did.

After returning to Tokyo, Irimajiri quickly realized just what Yoshizawa had been driving at. The exalted public image that Fujisawa had cultivated for Soichiro was now taken to be a reality within the company. The executives saw Fujisawa's version of Soichiro Honda as the one and only hero they needed. By this time a number of books treating Soichiro in a reverential light had been published. Furthermore, Soichiro was now more than eighty years old; it was obvious he didn't have much time left.

It was obvious that Fujisawa had personally colored and dramatized many of the Soichiro anecdotes and sayings in order to ensure his place as one of the quintessential self-made men credited with rebuilding postwar Japan. Indeed, more than half of the these stories were fabrications meant simply to prop up the "Cult of Honda."

This imaginary construct was nothing more than an act, but Soichiro quickly grew into the role after his retirement. The older he got, the more people both in and outside the company began to fuss over him, and he always relished the attention. The more splendid the stage, the more desolate one feels when the curtains come down. No matter how ill and feeble he became, Soichiro made a frantic effort to keep the performance up as long as possible.

Towards the end of his life, Fujisawa tried unsuccessfully to rein in the image and return Soichiro back to his true self, his naturally artless and deeply human self. Where Fujisawa had failed, there was no way for the Honda Kids to succeed. Soichiro continued the performance until the end of his life.

Bad news simply wasn't communicated to Soichiro during his final years, and this simply allowed his delusions to swell. By the end, these bubbles of delusion had grown so large that bursting them would only have led to quite pointless confusion and disruption.

Soichiro was born the son of a blacksmith and spent his youth as an apprentice in an automobile repair shop. He firmly believed that apprentices must obey their masters no matter how unreasonable the demands. Soichiro had founded the company, and so he demanded total obedience from the Honda Kids, whom he had practically raised as his own. If anyone ever went against his will, he would spit out, "Get out of my sight! I want your letter of resignation." In the early days, there had been quite a few people who had quit out of sheer frustration with Soichiro's mercurial nature.

Soichiro's temper cooled once he stepped down from the front lines, but he never did shake the hierarchical master-and-apprentice mindset. While Honda cultivated a public image of extreme pragmatism, the reality within the company was quite the opposite; the corporate culture was steeped in a sense of upholding one's personal honor.

The Honda Kids who had joined Honda in 1954—including president Kume and senior managing director Takao Harada—were the last generation of employees that had studied at Soichiro's feet. They knew how to dodge his unreasonable demands and were savvy enough to let Soichiro rage and let off steam before trying to argue a point.

If Kume and Harada, the earliest hires, were like Soichiro's "children," then Irimajiri and Kawamoto were like his "grandchildren." Even parents who go so far as to beat their rebellious children tend to take a softer attitude towards their grandchildren. In fact, if anything, Soichiro actually spoiled these later hires after his retirement. None of them had ever needed to go head-to-head against their mentor.

Soichiro, now near the end of his life, lacked any real hard data with which to decide whether Irimajiri or Kawamoto should be the next president. All he had was his burning desire for victory in Formula One racing. Kawamoto had made this dream come true. Irimajiri, on the other hand, had left Japan for the United States for four years, which distanced him from Soichiro. Kawamoto's work on the F1 project, on the other hand, had brought him closer to the founder.

Until the end, Soichiro never openly expressed an opinion about who should be Kume's successor. Those close to him believed that Kawamoto's victories in F1 gave him the edge. Both the former president, Kawashima, and current president, Kume, had reservations about Kawamoto taking over, but going against the unspoken wishes of the founder was out of the question.

Kiyoshi Kawashima, for his part, had grown disappointed in his own protégé Irimajiri. He felt that Irimajiri had become overly pragmatic. Irimajiri's prodding of Kume for change led Kawashima to question his capacity to lead the company. *As long as the old man is alive,* thought Kawashima, *Honda has to be run by somebody who is selflessly devoted to the company. In that sense, Kawamoto is more suitable than Irimajiri. Irimajiri changed while he was in America. He doesn't understand the true nature of Honda anymore. In that sense, he's just like my younger brother.*

Kawashima's younger brother, Hiroshi Kawashima, had been president of Yamaha. He is currently the chairman of Daiei.

"I've never met Mr. Irimajiri," Hiroshi Kawashima has said, "so I don't know what Kiyoshi meant by 'just like my younger brother.' Perhaps what he and I have in common is the fact that we both became executives at a young age, and worked as executives in the United States. Living in the U.S. naturally makes you more pragmatic. It frees you from the nuisance of worrying about relationships. In America, the bottom line is king, so you don't have spend as much time building consensus the way you do in Japan.

"The harder you try to play the game by the American rules, the larger the gap grows between you and headquarters in Japan. You learn not to pay much attention to what others think of you. Next thing you know, you become complacent. It was only after I quite Yamaha that I realized just how alienated I had become from everyone else in the company."

Soichiro suffered a stroke in the spring of his 79th year. Strict orders were given to keep this a secret, even within the company. It turned out to be a relatively minor stroke, but Soichiro lost much of the use of his left side. Heeding the advice of family members and the Honda Kids, he gave up his driver's license when he turned eighty.

By the time one reaches eighty years old, some signs of senility are inevitable. Fujisawa lived in fear of the prospect. In Soichiro's case, the stroke seemed to trigger the onset. He began mistaking names and telling the exact same story several times in a row. Whenever it was pointed out to him, he would joke, "Well, there's no medicine for stupidity, is there?"

The Honda Kids couldn't bear exposing old Soichiro to the public any more than necessary. Little by little, they cut down his appearances and began setting the stage for his total retirement. At Soichiro's own request, however, he continued participating in the Honda Foundation, which he had established with his own funds, up to the very end.

The Honda Foundation held a symposium in a different country every year, and made a point of inviting that nation's head of state. Soichiro relished the symposia for the chance to meet and converse with people from other countries. Taizo Ueda, executive director of the Honda Foundation, ran everything from behind the scenes. Ueda used his substantial connections to arrange the foreign locations for the symposia. Fluent in English, French, and German, he also acted as Soichiro's personal interpreter during the events.

In addition to the annual symposia, the Honda Foundation held regular gatherings at a Tokyo hotel every two months. The Foundation invited different guest speakers for every meeting, and Ueda personally selected a variety of scholars and journalists (all of whom were, needless to say, sympathetic to the goals of the Foundation) for the audience. After the speech, there was a buffet and reception.

Soichiro never lost his lust for knowledge; he never hesitated to ask questions after the speeches. At the party held just after his stroke, he stayed on his feet for the duration, as though he were perfectly healthy. He even sipped a bit of whiskey and water—something forbidden by his doctor—with the other members of the Foundation.

At the monthly meeting held just after Fujisawa's death, Soichiro shared his reminiscences: "My vice president was an amazing man. I think I'm the only one who really understands his true greatness. He was like a treasure to me. He made me what I am today."

After the loss of his closest colleague and his induction into the U.S. Automotive Hall of Fame, Soichiro rapidly lost both energy and will. Though his passion for Honda never wavered, he never really understood the minutiae of management. And with the Kids keeping any negative news secret from him, he lacked any sense of anxiety about the company's future. As such, when asked about the next president, Soichiro treated it as if the answer were none of his business.

"The next president? That's for the current president to decide," he said. But he couldn't resist adding another comment: "Kume hasn't said a word to me about the matter, but I think I can tell whom he's going to chose."

Kume's inability to ignore Soichiro and Kiyoshi Kawashima's unspoken preferences frustrated him. He saw Irimajiri as the perfect man to guide Honda out of its current malaise. But in the end, Kume based his decision upon Honda's guiding principles: "providing new technology" and "manufacturing unique automobiles."

From that standpoint, the clear choice was Kawamoto. He had led auto development teams ever since joining Honda. Kume had always prioritized engineering over corporate organization during his stint as president. In other words, Kume hoped to use the automobiles themselves to reestablish Honda's corporate identity. Kume and Kawamoto had fought side by side to win the F1. They had shared difficult times as well, including the travails of developing the CVCC. They were only four years apart in age, and in contrast to Irimajiri, both of them enjoyed their liquor.

Another factor was the difference in the candidates' personalities and work experience. Irimajiri had entered Honda during a period of rapid growth for the economy. He had ridden the peak of the economic wave to early success and executive rank. But he had also never experienced the depths of a true downturn. Chances were that he would adopt a highly aggressive business strategy if he took over the company. While Honda did have a record of turning economic recessions into opportunities for growth, Kume worried that the strategy wouldn't always succeed.

Kawamoto, on the other hand, had firsthand experience with trying times and situations. Kume reasoned that he would take a more conservative approach during the next economic downturn.

Kume made up his mind after the New Year's holidays in 1990. He contacted the most important of the former executives, including Soichiro and Kiyoshi Kawashima, to finalize the groundwork for handing power to his successor. Next, he told Vice President Yoshizawa of his decision. Then, after a meeting with the R&D section in Tochigi prefecture, Kume casually mentioned his decision to Kawamoto himself: "Kawamoto, I didn't want this job, you know. And I've decided to give it to someone who doesn't want it, either."

Kawamoto's eyes widened. He simply hadn't seen it coming. Kawamoto had not expected Kume to retire until the middle of his fourth two-year term as president. And he had fully expected Kume to name Irimajiri as his successor instead.

"What? Why the hell do you want me to run the company? I don't know anything but R&D!" replied Kawamoto in shock.

In fact, Kawamoto had already made up his mind to retire alongside Kume.

He had even planned out his life afterwards. He had recently said to his wife, "I'll quit Honda when Kume-san retires. I just want to lead a quiet retirement. I'll take care of whatever you need. We can go on vacations together. And I'd like to get a pilot's license, too. Can you do me a favor and pick up the application forms when you have a chance?"

Kawamoto finally realized why he had been made to "hang out" at headquarters for the last ten months. The following day, he went back to Tokyo and called Koichi Hori, president of the Boston Consulting Group.

"Hori, it looks like they're making me president. They told me informally yesterday. What should I do? Do you have time to get together and talk tonight?"

Hori expected to meet in the private room of a restaurant somewhere, but Kawamoto suggested their usual haunt at the restaurant in the Akasaka Prince Hotel.

Kume planned to make his decision public just after the board meeting to announce Honda's statement of accounts on May 24. Events dictated otherwise, however. The morning after Kawamoto's dinner with Hori, a newspaper wrote that Irimajiri would be the next president. Kume had to nip the situation in the bud. Besides, he had already laid the necessary groundwork for the exchange of power. Kume made the official announcement two weeks early, on May 10.

The rather sudden press conference attracted a large number of journalists to the Palace Hotel.

"I'm Kawamoto, the next president of Honda. I look forward to working with you," Kawamoto said to the journalists, bowing humbly. "I didn't expect this at all. Really, it's like a bolt from the blue. I haven't formulated any specific plans as president yet.

"The important thing is continuity," he continued. "I plan to further develop President Kume's three-pronged marketing strategy in Japan, America, and Europe by creating cutting-edge, high-value cars worthy of the Honda name.

"I will endeavor to predict the future demand for new car designs," he also said, "and rely upon Irimajiri to draw up an outline for that development process."

When Kawamoto became president, Chairman Okubo stepped down to become a permanent advisor. Vice President Koichiro Yoshizawa became chairman. Kume became an advisor to the board of directors. Both Irimajiri and Munekuni were promoted to vice president. It appeared that the new Honda would be governed by a troika, with Kawamoto at the center.

"When Kawamoto became president," recalled Irimajiri, "I saw it as a message to the employees who had joined in Honda in 1963—such as Munekuni, and Amemiya, who was president of Honda of America—to stick together and run the business together."

Soichiro's reign as president of Honda lasted twenty-five years. Kiyoshi Kawashima's lasted a decade. Kume's was only seven. The length of the Honda presidency was growing shorter.

"The rapidly changing times we live in make it almost impossible for any one person to remain president for ten years," said Kume to explain his early retirement.

Kume's comment led the mass media to speculate that Kawamoto would work for two terms (four years), retire at 58 years old just as his predecessor had, and turn the presidency over to the "real candidate," Irimajiri. Kawamoto's promise to rely upon Irimajiri only cemented the impression of the temporary nature of his presidency.

"I guessed right! I assume the choice matched all of your expectations," said Soichiro at a regular Honda Foundation reception, fully satisfied with the decision for Honda's fourth president.

Kawamoto had never been to a Honda Foundation meeting before. He dutifully attended his first regular meeting just after becoming president.

3

The business environment was changing drastically as Kawamoto began his presidency. The economic expansion accompanying the bubble continued even after the Showa era gave way to the Heisei era in 1989, but the growth slowed inexorably every year. On November 10, 1993, the Economic Planning Agency belatedly announced that the economic boom of the Heisei era had hit its peak in April of 1991. They explained that the "Heisei Boom" began in November 1986 and lasted for 53 months until the beginning of a recession in May 1991.

The reason for the delay in the official statement about the economy was the sheer length of the boom. It was the second longest of the post-war era (the longest was the "Izanagi Boom," which lasted 57 months), and there was quite a bit of "residual heat" even after the peak. Furthermore, many companies maintained an aggressive attitude even after the recession began, further obscuring the true nature of the situation. By the time people realized they were in the middle of a recession, it had already grown quite deep.

The increasingly internationalized automobile industry, however, had detected signs of an impending recession even before the bubble economy had hit its peak. The Iraqi Army invaded Kuwait on August 2, 1990, just after Kawamoto became president. The Gulf War broke out in January 1991.

Honda sold 854,000 automobiles in the United States in 1990, 9.1 percent higher than the previous year. Toyota sold 779,000 cars during the same period, a 7.7 percent increase. The numbers broke records for both manufacturers, but the other carmakers saw their sales decline. Nissan's sales dropped drastically from 510,000 to 454,000. Sales of the Big Three declined for the second year in a row. Honda and Toyota's success was due entirely to tremendous sales in the first half of the year.

Japan may have been enjoying the fruits of the bubble economy in the fall of 1990, but the U.S. economy was already showing signs of decline. Almost immediately, the American automobile market went cold. The sales of the Big Three were even worse after the end of the Gulf War. Sales of Japanese automobiles began to slow that fall. The U.S. economy still showed no signs of recovery. Honda sold fewer cars than it had during the fall of the previous year.

For the first time since the enactment of the restrictions on Japanese exports to the United States, the number of the cars shipped to America in 1990 was lower than the previous year. Honda cut its shipment yet again in 1991 and, in a first for the Ohio factory, reduced the production runs there as well. Anxiety began to spread through the company both in Japan and America.

The more time went by, the more the Japanese people realized that the "bubble economy" had been an aberration. Starting in May 1990, when the decision was made to select Kawamoto as Honda's next president, year-on-year domestic sales remained lower for seven months in a row. The situation only worsened. October sales were 20.9 percent lower than the previous year; November sales were 27.9 percent of the previous year. December sales barely cleared those of the previous year, but the numbers dropped off again in the beginning of 1991.

"I'll leave the real work up to Irimajiri and Munekuni and just stay out of their way," Kawamoto had said immediately upon becoming president. He had wanted to isolate himself at headquarters for at least a year to undertake a personal analysis of the problems facing Honda. The rapid drop-off in sales meant he no longer had that luxury. The feeling of crisis continued to grow. Before long, it even started affecting Kawamoto.

"If we don't do anything, Honda will go under for sure. We need to take action and take it now! I'm talking reform. I want a blueprint for changing things around here, and I want it now!" an impatient Kawamoto thundered at his staff in December of 1990.

Irimajiri responded by suggesting that they "hibernate through the winter and wait for the spring." Although considered an aggressive type, Irimajiri's stint at HAM had drastically altered his mindset. Working so close to Detroit had taught Irimajiri the dangers of using a business model that assumed high economic growth. Even after returning to Tokyo, he received regular reports from his subordinates at HAM and had a clear understanding of U.S. market conditions.

Honda's top product, the Accord, continued to sell well in the United States, but not quite as well as it once had. Other manufacturers, including the Big Three, were filling the market with products that equaled the functionality of Honda's flagship product, eroding the company's once-absolute superiority.

Interest in Honda's cars spread from young professionals to the middle-aged demographic. At the time, auto purchases in the United States were driven by a young group that could be called the "Eddie Bauer Generation." These young consumers didn't stand on formality; they favored relaxed fashions such as T-shirts and jeans. The high sales of SUVs and minivans were proof positive that this casual generation had become the mainstream when it came to consumers of new automobiles. And Japanese auto manufacturers had all but failed to pick up on the trend.

Honda's automobiles had long been known as "cutting-edge." As time went on, however, Honda's cars evolved into products for middle-aged consumers. Now the company needed to revise its image again if it hoped for further growth.

Irimajiri watched the market with growing agitation. His "hibernation" plan called for a major shift in production from Japan to abroad. Construction of a third assembly line at Suzuka, capable of producing 240,000 automobiles per year, was completed in the summer of 1989. Construction of a second Ohio factory (known as the East Liberty auto plant), capable of manufacturing 150,000 cars per year, was completed in December of the same year. Yet another factory capable of producing 100,000 cars annually was nearing completion in England. Once these overseas factories were running at full capacity, the demand for finished cars from Japan would drop.

This wouldn't be a problem as long as Honda could sell the automobiles originally intended for export on the domestic market. By now, however, the bubble economy had peaked and national demand was starting to decline. The current exchange rate and issues related to trade friction meant that delaying the planned increases in local regional production was out of the question. U.S. sales might be dropping, but Irimajiri's long experience in the country made him believe that Honda had a real chance at success if it revised its strategy there. Honda lacked a product that appealed to the "Eddie Bauer Generation." Developing some new products for that demographic promised great rewards. Of course, this also meant that the American R&D section would need to take the lead.

That said, there was no way around the fact that reducing exports would result in a cutback in domestic automobile production. Scrapping the old manufacturing facilities before the new assembly line in Suzuka was ready could potentially minimize the damage. Irimajiri began forming a vague plan to shut down the first Suzuka line.

Needless to say, scrapping the old facility was but the first step in Irimajiri's "hibernation" plan. Honda needed to reconsider everything from its overall sales strategy to the structure of the actual sales networks. Conversely, the R&D section had to be expanded and made to expend all of its efforts on developing economical automobiles. In fact, these were the very issues Irimajiri had discussed with Kume in an attempt to clarify Honda's strategy.

In terms of domestic sales in Japan, their plans met with frustration. Honda established a new three-year plan in 1990 that called for selling 800,000 automobiles annually in Japan by the end of 1992, a 20 percent increase over 1989. Specific plans called for sales of 705,000 in 1990 and 720,000 in 1991. Things got off to a shaky start when Honda only managed to sell 679,000 cars in 1990, which despite being 2.4 percent higher than the previous year still fell far short of the goal.

Honda had long maintained its position in third place behind Toyota and Nissan in terms of passenger cars. But when trucks were included in the calculations, Honda trailed Mitsubishi, and if sub-compacts were *not* included Honda trailed Mazda. As a result, when it came to total automobile sales, Honda was in fourth place. Although Honda sold a tremendous amount of product during the bubble economy, the other manufacturers did even better.

Although 1990 sales fell short of expectations, Vice President Munekuni retained his aggressively optimistic outlook: "Now that the third Suzuka line is finally completed, we won't have to worry about supply shortages any more. If we increase our numbers of sales and service representatives, build new dealerships, and enlarge and improve our existing ones, we can maximize in-store sales and meet our three-year middle-term targets."

The concept of the three-year plan had been inherited from Fujisawa, for whom it had been a stepping-stone in his dream to beat Nissan. The only way Kume and Yoshizawa could hope to realize their founder's dream was by stretching the company to the limits. Unfortunately, their plan was predicated on the continuation of the bubble economy. Now, with all signs pointing to the bubble bursting, the plan was beginning to look practically suicidal.

Kawamoto recognized the need for "hibernation" even before Irimajiri suggested it. No matter how he looked at it, the numbers in the three-year plan represented an all but impossible goal. Simply expanding the domestic sales force wouldn't be enough to accomplish it. What the company really needed were hot products for each of the three sales networks. And Kawamoto knew better than anyone that the R&D section simply wasn't capable of delivering that at the moment.

Kawamoto and Irimajiri were in agreement: Honda needed to shut down the oldest of the three assembly lines to ease the burden on the R&D section and give the engineers more ability to focus on developing new cars.

This, however, would require a large-scale reorganization and a transformation of the corporate mindset, from the Honda Kids all the way down to the workers on the factory lines.

Irimajiri watched the situation with growing frustration. *If we don't do something, we're going to lose the ability to take back the lead.* "Honda-ism" is *a wonderful thing, but should we embrace it blindly? Some things need to change, some things need to stay the same. We need to be able to distinguish between what will help this company and what will make it rot from within.*

Kawamoto appointed Irimajiri to supervise the overhaul of the Honda system. When a company makes this sort of decision, it usually puts it into effect on April 1, the first day of the Japanese fiscal year, or on July 1, the day after the annual shareholders' meeting. Kawamoto, on the other hand, arbitrarily picked March 15, 1991: "The earlier, the better."

On the afternoon of the 15th, a special interoffice memo was distributed to every Honda employee. It consisted of twelve pages and was entitled "Establishing a Corporate Structure for Honda's Next Generation: Responding to Rapid Change with Agility." Each section chief convened a meeting to discuss the memo with his staff.

The memo began with a description of how the contributions of individual employees propelled Honda to glory: "In the 42 years since the founding of this company, Honda has always followed its own path. Honda has grown into the company it is today by devising revolutionary technologies to meet the changes and challenges it has faced during every stage of its development. The driving force behind Honda's growth has always been the pursuit and realization of our employees' dreams. The pursuit of these dreams will continue to move Honda forward and build the company's future."

With the company's past glories and shared dreams now addressed, the report moved on to the heart of the matter. "Resources are necessary for a company to move forward. We have to remind ourselves that these resources are the product of our own efforts. We must all reflect honestly on our past work and strive to improve the quality of our contribution. The members of each section must discuss and debate among themselves what exactly their goals are and what they must do, individually and as a team, to make those dreams a reality."

The meaning of this directive, implied in the company's rather distinctive brand of circumlocution, was that although the executives held a great deal of pride in the company's past, they were also willing to do just about anything to reinvigorate the firm in order to realize the corporate dream. But when it came to articulating exactly what that all-important dream was, the memo was far less concrete than Soichiro's rousing exhortation, delivered from the top of a *mikan* crate, to make Honda the best in the world. The executives were lazily telling the employees to come up with a dream on their own.

Some specific reorganization measures were decided. Upon becoming president, Kawamoto had ordered the establishment of four new head offices to represent Japan, the United States, Europe, and developing countries. The Honda business strategy for automobiles consisted of three components: sales (S), engineering (E), and development (D). The four-headquarter concept had been devised to allow the company to quickly ascertain the needs of customers in each region. In reality, however, it simply increased the number of SED meetings for each region, which only created confusion.

Kawamoto soon abandoned this arrangement in favor of creating a single "automotive planning office," which consisted exclusively of the top executives. Kawamoto had final decision-making authority. Honda had once been managed by a "bottom-up" system, whereby the decisions in the SED meetings influenced the executives. Hoping to increase the speed at which decisions were made, Kawamoto instituted a "top-down" system. He also removed the traditional dividing lines in the workplace by giving managers the authority to freely transfer workers throughout the company as needed.

The defining characteristic of Kawamoto's reforms was the abandonment of second president Kawashima's system of group leadership and third president Kume's system of joint responsibility. Kawamoto adopted a totally new system organized into three divisions—passenger cars, motorcycles, and all-purpose vehicles—with himself at the top of the passenger car division in addition to his role as president of the corporation. Irimajiri and Munekuni worked under him as chief of product development and chief of sales, respectively.

All executives were assigned areas of authority and sent to work on site, effectively ending Fujisawa's "common room" system. And without a single boardroom, there would be no *waigaya*, either.

Kiyoshi Kawashima and his fellow executives had created *waigaya* as a tool to allow the Honda Kids to achieve equal footing with the strong-willed founders. Before long the concept blossomed into a unique expression of Honda's unfettered and youthful mindset.

The generation of Honda Kids that had inherited the mantle directly from Soichiro and Fujisawa had no choice but to band together to tear down the obstacles erected by their predecessors. Even before handing over the baton, President Soichiro and his Vice President Fujisawa didn't even come into the office much during the last half of their reign, leaving most of the day-to-day management to the four top executives. When Kiyoshi Kawashima, youngest of the four, became president, Shirai, Kihachiro Kawashima, and Nishida retired, ending the original *waigaya* system.

To borrow Kiyoshi Kawashima's words, *waigaya* was more than just open and clamorous debate: participants freely expressed opinions, analyzed issues from multiple angles using the Indian "four answer" decision-making philosophy, and aimed for the solution offering maximum advantage. Expanding into the American market and entering the partnership with British Leyland, two of the high points of Kawashima's presidency, appeared to have been quite bold decisions. In fact, they were the results of deliberate calculation.

When Kume took over, he threw out all but the framework of the *waigaya* system, essentially rendering it into an extended chitchat where everyone talked and nobody accepted responsibility. Decision-making was rendered faceless.

"*Waigaya* in its true form is an extremely convenient way to achieve consensus. We can fix the *waigaya* system by ensuring that one person makes the final decision," suggested Irimajiri, who had actively adopted the *waigaya* at the Ohio factory. Kawamoto, on the other hand, saw *waigaya* as a fossil of Honda's glory days. His decision to abolish the "large room" was akin to discarding a piece of Honda's cultural heritage.

In August, Kawamoto enacted the "Honda Charter," a guide for the Honda businessman. Soichiro's maxims—now rather stale—were still around, but Honda lacked an actual guide for its employees. Although a handbook had been created along with the founding of the company, it hadn't been updated since and was largely out of date.

As time went on, Soichiro's sayings became like a collection of holy commandments, ones that different people interpreted in their own ways. Signs penned by Soichiro himself hung in every factory that read: "There can be no production without safety." What he meant by this was that motor vehicles were like "rolling weapons" that Honda put in the hands of its own customers. The only way to protect the customers from accidents was by manufacturing safe motor vehicles. The quotation originated from Honda's days as a manufacturer only of motorcycles, but it informed the vigor with which Soichiro fought back against the accusations during the N360 defect scandal.

Over the years, however, the meaning of the saying had changed. Now most people understood it to mean, "Production cannot be increased without focusing on safety and improvements in the working environment."

Fujisawa had his own maxims, for which he claimed a profound dislike. The Honda Kids suggested compiling a book of his sayings as a counterpart to Soichiro's, but Fujisawa responded by saying, "Maxims can take on a life of their own. They don't mean anything without historical context." The book never saw the light of day.

The "Honda Charter" stipulated the minimum standards expected of each Honda employee. Although the rule for placing the customer first could be found in the versions of the charter for each region, Kawamoto changed the versions to reflect the values and conventions of the respective cultures. The charter for the United States, for example, included an article entitled "What Is a Good Corporate Citizen?"

The Honda system had been born from rapid growth and an ever-increasing workload. Irimajiri's proposed "hibernation" would mean reducing that workload. Kawamoto and Irimajiri agreed that Honda's internal system needed to be reorganized to make it work, but they differed as to just what kinds of changes needed to be made.

Irimajiri quickly wanted to move from a collective organization to a functional organization. He advocated replacing the group system with an environment that respected individual achievement. He wanted to return to the kind of workplace Honda had once been, a place where heroes were born. He proposed a new merit-based salary system term limits for executives to help motivate the employees. Irimajiri saw the creation of the charter as the groundwork for a system that fostered individual responsibility and the creation of business superstars. In short, he hoped to revive the old "Honda myth."

Kawamoto, on the other hand, saw the reorganization as a temporary measure. Real change would begin once this interim "patch" started taking effect. Kawamoto's idea of change meant abandoning Soichiro and Fujisawa's carefully crafted "Honda-ism" to create a fresh philosophy for a new era.

"It's impossible to effect the level of change we need in just a year; Honda's too big for that now," Kawamoto and Irimajiri would often say. "That's why we've taken this interim step. We felt the changes needed to begin earlier rather than later."

On the surface, the two appeared to offer a unified front, but as the saying goes, they were "enemies stuck together on the same boat." The two of them didn't imagine at the time that they would have a falling out within the year.

The employees, however, were perceptive enough to sense the subtle differences in their priorities.

"The president and the other top executives seem to be doing their best to change the corporate structure, but down here in the trenches we have no idea what they're trying to do."

Another said, "I guess it's the first step towards making Honda a normal company. We abandoned the *waigaya*, and now the executives limit themselves to their own departments. How is Honda any different from Toyota or Nissan now?"

4

Kawamoto dropped by to visit Soichiro at the supreme advisor's office. Unlike Fujisawa, Soichiro preferred conducting business in his office at Honda's former headquarters in Yaesu rather than at his home. Soichiro was riding high at the time. He had been inducted into the Automotive Hall of Fame the previous year. In December of the year that Kawamoto became president, the Federation Internationale del' Automobile gave Soichiro a gold medal in recognition of his contribution to Formula One racing. In fact, he was only the third recipient after Ferdinand Porsche and Enzo Ferrari. A photograph of a grinning Soichiro standing alongside Ayrton Senna during the award ceremony had appeared in news media all over the world.

"Some 43 years have passed since you founded Honda, and you've left us a great many good things," Kawamoto said when he went to visit the founder. "But there are also aspects that are too outdated to use anymore. I'm thinking to take the plunge and institute some major changes at Honda," Kawamoto added, his expression serious.

Like the earlier corporate memo, the wording of this statement was too abstract and roundabout for Soichiro to grasp the full implications of what Kawamoto was saying.

"I see," replied Soichiro. "Times have changed. Do what you need to do." In his later years, Soichiro lost much of his sense of judgment; he agreed to nearly everything the Kids asked for. Of course, it took more than that to make a formal decision. The current crop of top executives was obliged to discuss any important matter with the retired top executives as well as Soichiro. It was then customary for the retired executives to take the time to explain the issue to Soichiro again. If this second talk went smoothly, the sitting executives took it as a "yes."

Kawamoto's idea of the reorganization was, of course, one of these important matters. But it was obvious that Soichiro didn't fully understand Kawamoto's true intentions. He simply didn't fathom that Kawamoto planned to dismantle the system that it had taken Soichiro and Fujisawa so many years to build.

Although Soichiro tried to maintain the appearance of health, the truth was that disease was quietly ravaging his body. He attended the stockholder meeting held at the end of June as usual. A month later on July 22, however, he was hospitalized at Juntendo Hospital in Ochanomizu. The diagnosis was late-stage cancer. Soichiro's traditional June fishing party was immediately canceled.

The June rainy season, which had been unusually long that year, ended and summer began just after Soichiro entered the hospital. By August, when the sunflowers bloomed and turned their faces toward the sun, his condition took a turn for the worse. On August 4, Soichiro fell into a coma. He passed away with his beloved wife Sachi by his side at 10:48 a.m. the next day. Only three years separated the deaths of Honda's two founders.

Soichiro had left behind strict orders to the Kids not to hold a corporate funeral for him. "A corporate funeral will just create traffic jams!" he had said. "As an auto manufacturer, that's the last thing you want to inflict on the public!"

In keeping with his request, the Honda Kids held a "ceremony of gratitude" at the headquarters in Tokyo and the manufacturing plants in Saitama, Hamamatsu, Tochigi, Suzuka, and Kumamoto instead. Some 62,000 people attended in all.

The ceremony in Tokyo was held at the Honda Hall on the second floor of the headquarters on the 5th, 6th, and 7th of September. Soichiro's various medals, including his Grand Cordon of the Order of the Rising Sun, were on display throughout the crowded hall. His paintings hung on the wall of the lobby. It was more like a one-man exhibition than a funeral. Many of the guests felt as if Soichiro would show up at any minute.

The tenth race of the 1992 F1 was held in August in Budapest, Hungary.

Every member of the Honda-Marlboro-McLaren team, including Ayrton Senna, wore mourning bands as they participated in the race. The team dedicated their victory that day to Soichiro.

The loss of Soichiro, their psychological anchor, set the Honda Kids adrift. Ever since his retirement, Soichiro had thrown himself into the role of public spokesman and representative of the "Cult of Honda." Whether they knew it or not, the Kids were totally dependent on him when it came to things like public relations and philanthropy. His death fully brought home the fact that Soichiro had covered Honda's gaps as a corporation. The dearth of charisma among Honda's top managers was beginning to show in the company's products. The public could tell that Honda had lost its uniqueness as a company.

Soichiro's passing coincided with the bursting of the bubble economy, and before long the auto industry found itself bogged down in a recession. The sense of crisis at Honda was given a new spur. Sales revenue for fiscal year 1990 was 2.8 trillion yen, just a 1.9 percent increase over the previous year. Net profit was 65.4 billion yen, a 34.7 percent decrease. Gross sales for fiscal year 1991 increased 3.9 percent to 2.91 trillion yen, while net profit decreased 17 percent to 54 billion yen. Although gross sales remained steady, net profits continued to slide. It appeared to be time to seriously consider initiating the "hibernation" plan.

Hibernation meant downsizing the Honda business. The first step, reorganizing the national sales network, required urgent discussion. In 1984, Honda established three independent domestic Japanese sales networks with the aim of selling one million automobiles annually. Honda differentiated the networks with separate identities: Primo sold inviting and approachable family cars, including the Civic, Clio sold high-end and luxury cars such as the Accord and Legend, while Verno sold sportier cars such as the Prelude and CR-X.

"Three Networks, Three Identities" had been the slogan. That said, Honda sold its flagship product, the Accord, through both the Primo and Clio networks at first because R&D wasn't able to provide separate products for both. The arrival of the fourth-generation Accord, however, allowed Honda to clearly delineate the networks for the first time. It sold the Accord and Accord Inspire through Clio, the Ascot through Primo, and the Vigor through Verno.

Now that the time had come for "hibernation," the task of reorganizing Honda's sales strategy fell into the hands of Munekuni, former president of Honda of America. Chairman Yoshizawa pledged his full support, and the two decided to apply the sales strategy that had been so successful in America to Japan as well.

The retail automotive industry in America worked along different lines: each carmaker had one dedicated network of dealerships, with each dealership responsible for a single territory. The distributor, who acted as the local agent for the manufacturer, was only involved in the sales process as a wholesaler. Distributors played no role in telling dealers how to sell to their customers. Distributors contributed to sales by adjusting the amount of money spent on advertising. When a product sold well, the distributor would only advertise moderately. When a product sold poorly, the distributor would spend more on advertising it. If that failed to achieve the desired result, the distributor would offer bonuses and other incentives to spur on the dealers. It was analogous to a faucet controlling water, with the water being the flow of automobiles from the factory and the faucet representing the advertising and incentive campaigns. The approach had proven to work well in a large country like the United States.

Honda of America had also used this strategy, but the fact was that Hondas sold like hotcakes even without incentives. Nonetheless, Honda of America didn't allow itself to become complacent. During the building of its sales network, it sent a team of salesmen and engineers to talk with the dealers, read through the results of customer satisfaction surveys, and apply the information to the development of new automobiles. This had been a great success.

In Japan, Honda's sales efforts were focused on dealership walk-ins and targeted sales visits: Every weekend the company sponsored events for the public, handed out door prizes, and gathered contact information. If Honda spotted a potential customer, a representative would follow up later and offer to visit their home to make a sale directly. Headquarters was in charge of the customer satisfaction surveys while dealers handled customer management. Unlike Toyota and Nissan, Honda didn't have any experience in sending "human waves" of salesmen door-to-door, and it didn't plan to adopt the tactic any time soon.

The fact that Honda products sold briskly during the bubble economy despite a shortage of salesmen earned the company high marks for its sales approach. Once the bubble burst, however, the vulnerability of that strategy became apparent. Customers who had tightened their purse strings weren't about to set foot into a car dealership, no matter how much the dealers offered and cajoled.

There was only one way to solve the problem: providing attention-grabbing products to each of the three networks. If there were any letup in sales and marketing efforts, the distribution of popular vehicles among the three networks would grow lopsided.

In the auto business, however, it's just as hard to create a steady stream of hits as it is in the entertainment business. And doing so requires enormous investments in development.

The reality of the situation, however, was that the bursting of the bubble was forcing carmakers to slash costs by restructuring, and the first step in restructuring was to scale back development and reduce labor costs through layoffs and wage controls. In Honda's case, the R&D budget was traditionally 5 percent of the gross sales of the previous year. Strong sales meant a healthy R&D budget while weak sales would call for fairly rapid belt-tightening in the research labs. At one point, sales were so poor that the budget simply wasn't large enough to cover the development demands of all three networks, so headquarters had to temporarily raise the ratio to 6.578 percent of the previous year's gross sales.

Providing solid cars for three sales networks on a tight budget meant sticking to conservative, four-door sedans. Even during the budget crunch, the R&D section continued work on developing a "worldwide" car, but cars for niche markets, long a trademark of the Honda business strategy, had to be put on the back burner.

The drastic reorganization of Honda's sales network meant decreasing the number of products on the market. In order for that to happen, the three sales networks had to be made more efficient by being merged into one. In the mid-eighties Nissan successfully merged its Cherry sales network with other networks in areas of low demand. In the end, Nissan reduced its multiple networks to just four.

The R&D section first proposed the idea of reducing the number of Honda sales networks. The fourth-generation Accord and its derivatives were faring poorly, and the development team felt that providing three or four new products every year to fill the separate networks was inefficient at best.

Any automobile that sells less than two thousand units per month is called a "dead product" in the auto industry. Dead products not only failed to break even for the manufacturer, they were a burden on the distributor as well.

Downsizing to two networks promised to make all aspects of the business—development, production, and sales—more efficient. Kawamoto and Irimajiri were agreed that this was the way to go and one point suggested the idea to then-president Kume and other top executives. They even hired the Boston Consulting Group, at which Koichi Hori was working as president, to analyze the domestic sales system. The report was straight to the point:

"Ideally, domestic sales should be 500,000 cars for each network. Currently, Toyota is the only company that has successfully managed to achieve this. Toyota has five sales networks and a combined sales goal of 2.5 million per year. (In fact, Toyota met this goal in 1990.) Nissan also has five sales networks, but a lack of development capacity has led to a chronic shortage of products. Objectively speaking, Honda does not currently possess the capacity to supply its three sales networks. Two sales networks would be ideal for Honda to sell one million cars a year."

Despite this, Kume flatly rejected reducing the number of sales networks. At the time, Honda had only just succeeded in differentiating the networks with unique products for each, which had contributed to increasing the company's share of the four-door sedan market from 4.2 percent to 9.2 percent.

In the beginning, the basic auto industry sales strategy was to maximize the potential of a single small network to sell the largest number of products. Efficiency was key. As the motorization of society progressed, however, manufacturers established additional sales networks to compete with one another; before long, expansion became the reigning strategy. By suggesting a reduction in the number of sales networks, Kawamoto and Irimajiri were in essence proposing a return to the older model of "profits through efficiency."

After his first year as president, Kawamoto had a sure grasp of Honda's power structure. He had long thought of the president as an almighty figure, but the more he learned, the more he realized that, at least during Kume's presidency, true authority for business management, including domestic and foreign sales, rested with Yoshizawa. The only areas an engineer president could fully control were the development section and the factories. Although final decisions were approved by mutual consent among the top executives, the majority of decisions were actually made in each section.

Yoshizawa was in charge of human resources for all administrative sections, including sales; the only area in which Kume had any real say was R&D. Since decisions were always said to come from "the boardroom," the real distribution of power wasn't clear from the outside.

When Kawamoto took charge he was reminded again of the fact that Honda, which seemed to the world to be a single company, was actually two companies: Honda Kogyo (Honda Tech) and Fujisawa Shokai (Fujisawa Trading Co.). Kume had been the president of Honda Tech and Yoshizawa had been the president of Fujisawa Trading Co. Although Kume and Yoshizawa lacked the charisma of Soichiro and Fujisawa, they did share the same tacit agreement not to meddle in each other's affairs. In fact, they even managed to hide the occasions they couldn't reach an agreement. Kume and Yoshizawa were fully familiar with the way Soichiro and Fujisawa had run the business. Questioning the two-person management structure had never even occurred to them. Even if it had, there was no way to express their misgivings aloud as long as the two founders were alive.

Kawamoto, however, had never been part of the core management team, even after having been promoted to executive. *No matter how I look at it, it just seems strange to have two companies under one umbrella. Engineer or not, the president needs to have a grip on domestic sales and exports to perform his job effectively. The two-company system only worked because of the founders themselves.*

The question then became how to fuse these two halves into a single entity. Kawamoto's concern was that, though he understood engineering inside and out, he knew next to nothing about management. *If only I knew that I would become president back then! I would have made a point to pick Fujisawa's brain for the secrets of running a business...*

But Fujisawa had already passed away. With both of the founders gone, Kawamoto obsessed over the idea of consolidating the president's power by merging Honda Tech and Fujisawa Trading as quickly as possible. Kawamoto laid the foundations for this merger by putting his colleague and rival Irimajiri in charge of general affairs and human resources management in addition to production and development systems. The question of whether the merger was even possible hinged on whether Honda Tech could take control of domestic sales and distribution.

The meeting to discuss restructuring the domestic sales system convened at 4:30 p.m. on Christmas Eve. It was held on the tenth floor of headquarters, which was dedicated to housing reception rooms, meeting rooms, and the "boardroom." There was no worry that an employee would walk in or that the sounds of their voices, no matter how heated the debate, would leak out.

There were six participants: Chairman Yoshizawa, President Kawamoto, Vice President Irimajiri, Vice President Munekuni, Director of National Sales Masaru Miyata, and President Hori of Boston Consulting Group, who was there as an "observer." The chairman of Honda wasn't supposed to attend meetings directly related to business management, but Kawamoto invited Yoshizawa because this wasn't an official meeting and the minutes wouldn't be recorded. More to the point, he wanted to hear about how the company had been run in the past.

Kawamoto had made his decision. If he couldn't convince the others to go along, he was prepared to go down fighting—and take the leadership of Fujisawa Trading Co. down with him.

Hori was the first to speak. He explained that three networks were actually too many in light of current R&D and sales capacity. He concluded with a proposal to address the problem by merging the Verno and Clio networks.

The mood in the room was tense. The friendliness that had marked the *waigaya* was completely absent. In the discussion that followed Hori's report, Kawamoto and Irimajiri expressed their support for the idea. Munekuni and Miyata, the Fujisawa Trading figures at the meeting, argued vehemently against it: "Reducing the number of sales networks to two instead of three is responding to the needs of the company, not the consumers!"

Another one said, "Downsizing the sales network means cutting off the potential for future growth with your own hands. Even if you look at it as 'taking refuge,' it's going to be tremendously difficult to re-expand the network again in the future."

Yet another rebuttal went: "This proposal didn't originate within Honda. It came from a consulting company. Just think about it for a moment. Can you think of a single case of a company following the suggestion of an outside consultant and having it turn out to be a success? If you know of any, please let me know. Honda manufactures and sells automobiles. Consulting companies don't!"

Yoshizawa folded his arms, looked up at the ceiling, and listened quietly. He watched the conversation unfold with a growing sense of shame. Fujisawa's dream of beating Nissan had become a reality in the United States. A majority of Americans, including some of the Ohio factory workers, thought Honda was one of Japan's largest auto manufacturers, on par with Toyota. Some even mistakenly believed it was an American company.

But back in Japan, the reality was that Honda hadn't managed to catch up with Nissan. In fact, Nissan had more momentum and was gradually *widening* the gap between the two companies. Meanwhile, Mazda and Mitsubishi were closing in on Honda; the company found itself struggling even to maintain its number three position. Gross sales revenue was plunging at a rate far faster than anticipated. Reducing the size of the sales network was akin to officially declaring the race with Nissan lost. Yoshizawa wanted Honda to fight for its future.

"I think it's pointless to discuss whether three is better or two is enough. My honest feeling is that I'd like you to end this discussion at once," said Yoshizawa, trying to conceal his growing anger. But Kawamoto and Irimajiri did not back down.

It was just after the winter solstice. It was already dark outside when the meeting had started. The Aoyama section of Tokyo along Highway 246 was bright with neon lights. Since it was Christmas Eve, the lights of the other floors of the headquarters had been turned off by six o'clock. The windows of the tenth floor, however, were still brightly lit.

The clock struck eight and still no conclusion had been reached. A secretary brought coffee and sandwiches. The men crammed the food into their mouths and continued to debate. Why should Honda reduce its number of sales networks to two? The gap between Kawamoto and Irimajiri, the engineers representing "Honda Tech," and Yoshizawa, Munekuni, and Miyata, the businessmen who had come of age at Fujisawa Trading, was too wide to bridge.

Kawamoto and Irimajiri couldn't bring themselves to admit that the R&D section wasn't up to the task of meeting the demands of all three networks. "Efficiency" was the only word they could muster.

Yoshizawa, Munekuni, and Miyata, on the hand, wanted nothing more than to ask if the R&D section had really weakened to the point where it was no longer to keep up with the demand from the sales side. But they knew that such a direct question would only provoke a dangerous confrontation. Their task was to defend and maintain the three sales networks at any cost.

Both sides were aware of the weaknesses in both their own and their opponent's arguments, but neither mentioned them directly. The discussion continued on parallel tracks with no convergence in sight. Before long it was eleven o'clock. Both sides were utterly exhausted.

With a look of bitter resignation on his face, Yoshizawa finally made a compromise suggestion: "It appears that we won't reach a conclusion no matter how much we discuss the subject. I suspect the result would be the same even if we did the same thing tomorrow. I fully realize the difficult situation that Honda is facing and I respect what Kawamoto-san is saying. But the three-network system was a longtime dream for us salesmen. For us to dismantle it ourselves would be like killing our own child with our own hands. We just can't bring ourselves to do it. So perhaps we should leave it up to Kawamoto-san to further investigate what shape our future sales structure is going to take."

By leaving this "further investigation" up to Kawamoto, Yoshizawa was essentially acquiescing to the first exploratory steps in an eventual merger of Honda Tech and Fujisawa Trading.

The mountain has moved! Kawamoto thought triumphantly upon hearing Yoshizawa's proposal. The phrase had been used by politician Takako Doi, head of the Japan Socialist Party, after an electoral victory, and was much in vogue at the time.

5

The Christmas Eve meeting and its outcome remained totally secret, but it was obvious that power at Honda now rested entirely in the hands of President Kawamoto. For the very first time in Honda's history of more than forty years, one man was in charge of everything—development, production, domestic sales, exports, and general administration. Kawamoto's "coup d'état" had been a total success.

He had made up his mind to reduce the number of sales networks from three to two even before the discussion began. As Yoshizawa pointed out, it would be impossible to ask Munekuni and Miyata, who had campaigned so long and hard for three networks, to turn around and remove one. It would be better to appoint somebody more familiar with the R&D section's capacity (or lack thereof) to meet demand. Kawamoto spent the 25th, 26th, and 27th thinking about it, and finally reached a conclusion on the 28th, the final official working day of the year. *Irimajiri is a go-getter: I'll put him in charge of domestic sales for now. Then*

I'll let HAM President Yoshino take over once things get moving. Hiroyuki Shimojima should be the next president of HAM, since he's head of the Saitama plant as well as an executive.

Kawamoto, Irimajiri, and Yoshino had joined Honda at the same time in 1963. They were all seen as promising young men with the potential to grow into future Honda leaders. Irimajiri and Yoshino both came out of the same department at the same university, but Yoshino's quiet personality stood in stark contrast to Irimajiri's flamboyant and dramatic style. Yoshino, however, was second to none when it came to tenacity, thanks to his near-death experiences while evacuating Manchuria in the wake of World War II.

The two of them nonetheless got along very well. Yoshino was promoted to head of the Suzuka manufacturing plant and then took over Irimajiri's position as president of HAM. When Irimajiri made his final speech as president of the Ohio factory, he had introduced Yoshino by pretending as if the two of them were playing catch up on the podium. "My relationship with Mr. Yoshino has been a game of catch like the one we're playing now. This time he's catching my throw here at HAM."

Kawamoto kept his decision to streamline Honda's sales system to two networks to himself, even after New Year's Eve. Since Irimajiri had also advocated that plan and fought alongside Kawamoto at the Christmas Eve meeting to get it accepted, he assumed that he would be put in charge of putting it into effect.

Though it was Kawamoto's own idea to bring Yoshida back from America to take over from Irimajiri, he knew he had to be cautious and time it properly. He had to make sure the transfer wouldn't negatively affect the Ohio factory.

The new East Liberty factory in Ohio was designed for the large-scale manufacture of the Honda Civic. It would soon be running at full capacity, and when it did the first factory would begin manufacturing the new Accord Wagon that had been developed entirely in America. Kawamoto knew that Honda absolutely depended on the success of these two automobiles, and was worried that if Yoshino were transferred too suddenly that success would be jeopardized. The pitfalls seemed potentially endless.

At the same time, auto trade friction between Japan and the United States continued to escalate, which only increased the pressure he was feeling. In June of 1991, a tax issue cropped up between the United States and Canada. Honda, which owned factories in both countries, found itself in the crosshairs.

The friction in the US market was largely due to the extended business slump of the Big Three automakers. GM's 1991 sales figures were 2.9 million, 12.1 percent lower than the previous year, Ford's were 1,630,000, a drop of 15.8 percent, and Chrysler's were 700,000, a drop of 18.4 percent. Altogether, the Big Three sold 860,000 fewer automobiles than the year before.

It was the first time in the postwar era for GM's sales to drop below 3 million. Just before the second oil shock, GM sold 5.4 million automobiles; that number had dropped by 2.5 million in only thirteen years. Chrysler fell behind Honda and Toyota in spite of the Japanese manufacturers' sales being off the previous year, knocking the company to fifth place in the U.S. market.

The Big Three began its campaign against Japanese carmakers around the end of the Gulf War. Chrysler chairman Lee Iacocca initiated it by penning a letter to President George H.W. Bush requesting a reduction in the allowable market share for Japanese manufacturers to 31 percent for 1991.

The executives of the Big Three paid a visit to Washington D.C. to discuss the issue with the president in person. Iacocca expressed the critical nature of the situation by stating that if the Japanese share of the market exceeded 40 percent, Chrysler would go under. He fiercely advocated stricter controls for Japanese automobiles.

There was no question that Chrysler was facing a crisis at the time. Its sales decreased steadily starting with the outbreak of the Gulf War. Revenues dropped precipitously in 1991, throwing the company's balance sheet 795 million dollars in the red.

Despite this downturn, Iacocca was ready to risk everything in a bid to turn the company around. He laid off a large number of employees and invested a billion dollars to build the Chrysler Technical Center, a new headquarters for research and development on the outskirts of Detroit.

Iacocca began divesting Chrysler of its 21.82 percent stake in Mitsubishi in September of 1989, selling off all of the shares by July of 1993. Chrysler had also split the cost of building and running a factory by the name of Diamond Star Motors in Illinois with Mitsubishi. Iacocca transferred his company's right to run the factory over to Mitsubishi in October of 1991.

Iacocca's statements to the president were no exaggeration. Chrysler really was on the brink of collapse. The restrictions that had been placed on Japanese imports had at one point filled the company's coffers; fearing for the future of the automobile industry, Chrysler had made a number of attempts to diversify, but these were mismanaged and ended up being nothing more than a waste of capital; the aircraft maker Gulfstream, which Chrysler acquired and then had to sell off, was one example.

Iacocca's plan for dodging bankruptcy involved lobbying for stricter regulations on Japanese manufacturers, raising prices to increase profits, and pouring the proceeds into the construction of the Technical Center. Iacocca firmly believed that the Technical Center would give him the capability to design cars that could hold their own against the Japanese. But he needed to buy time until it was completed, and it was with that in mind that he made repeated trips to Washington.

GM and Ford, on the other hand, had learned from prior experience that stricter controls on Japanese automakers wouldn't help rebuild the American automobile industry. In addition, a presidential election was on the horizon; the manufacturers knew that President Bush wouldn't risk anything that could have a negative impact on consumers, and were thus halfhearted about any attempts to further tighten import controls.

The one area in which the three manufacturers did fully agree was on the issue of dumping. On May 31, 1991, four months after visiting President Bush, the manufacturers brought a claim before the U.S. Department of Commerce and the International Trade Commission (ITC). Their allegations concerned dumping of Japanese minivans, which had been largely exempt from U.S. regulations until that time.

It was easy to see Chrysler's stake in the matter. Minivans and sport-utility vehicles, in particular the Jeep Cherokee, were Chrysler's sole profitable product line. The relatively limited number of types and models of minivan made it easy to prove a dumping accusation against the Japanese. A finding of guilt would give Chrysler some much-needed breathing room.

The ITC found the Japanese manufacturers not guilty on July 15, 1992. Of course, the Big Three decided to appeal, bringing another case to the Court of International Trade on July 31. The case was dismissed one year later, on July 12, 1993. It was a total wash for the Big Three.

Why had GM and Ford gone along with Chrysler? The reason is that both companies had fallen behind in Corporate Average Fuel Economy (CAFE) standards compliance. Increasing public awareness of environmental and energy-conservation issues promised a tightening of the standards in the near future. In fact, Congress was already considering some ten bills proposing amendments to the regulations.

The bill that appeared to have the greatest potential of passing would oblige manufacturers to increase the fuel efficiency of their cars by 20 percent over the 1988 models by 1995, and 40 percent by 2000. Makers who failed to meet these standards would be fined or even forced to withdraw noncompliant vehicles from the market.

GM and Ford had lent Chrysler a hand during the minivan dispute; all of the Big Three had a shared interested in keeping the new CAFE legislation from passing and so worked together to pressure President Bush to try to block it.

The Bush Administration, for its part, was concerned by the spike in the unemployment rate brought about the deep recession that followed the Gulf War. Bush knew he would need the support of the Big Three to get reelected. Without any sign of economic improvement on the horizon, Japanese automakers made a convenient target. The interests of the Big Three aligned with those of the president. President Bush decided to pay a visit to Japan in the beginning of the following year along with Stempel of GM, Pauling of Ford, and Iacocca of Chrysler.

Automobile issues had become the primary topic of conversation at high-level meetings between Japanese and American officials. The fact that Honda was now outselling Chrysler in America would make it the prime target for attack, a position it had seemed to occupy ever since the U.S.-Canada tax issue had reared its head.

Honda's executives knew the only way to minimize the damage would be a further Americanization of the company. Yoshino was in charge of overseeing the changes at the Ohio factory; transferring him back to Japan during the process would have been extremely difficult. The U.S. market was Honda's lifeline and it couldn't afford the slightest slip-up in its American operations.

When Kawamoto was promoted to president, Irimajiri not only became head of the Honda Research and Development Company but was also made responsible for the production division. Irimajiri also happened to be Kawamoto's right-hand man when it came to general affairs and personnel management. Adding domestic sales to Irimajiri's responsibilities would not only mean a de facto merger of Honda Tech and Fujisawa Trading: it would also mean that, although final authority rested with Kawamoto, much of the actual power would be in Irimajiri's hands.

Kawamoto put a lot of thought into the matter of who should oversee domestic sales, but couldn't come up with a solution. Irimajiri himself felt that, given how the Christmas Eve meeting had turned out, he was the likely candidate. Even though he still hadn't received the nod from Kawamoto as of New Year's Day, he quietly began collecting sales information on Honda's automobiles in preparation.

President Bush arrived at Osaka International Airport on January 7, 1992. He was accompanied by Secretary of Commerce Mosbacher, who also oversaw Bush's reelection committee. A delegation of eighteen prominent business leaders, led by executives from the Big Three, had come along as well.

Reflecting the auto-oriented focus of the summit, the display of a Nissan car in the north wing of the Narita International Airport was hastily replaced with a Pontiac Grand Am in preparation for Bush's subsequent arrival in Tokyo.

"The U.S. economy is suffering. Japan would like to cooperate as much as possible in helping it recover," said Prime Minister Kiichi Miyazawa just before Bush's arrival.

Bush, for his part, said that his primary duty during the trip was the creation of "jobs, jobs, jobs" for American workers. Expectations were high.

Behind the scenes, Deputy Minister Yuji Tanahashi of MITI and Secretary Masahisa Naito of MITI were actively trying to promote the sales of U.S. cars and parts in Japan. In fact, many top MITI officials and auto industry executives had given up their New Year's holidays to put overtime into the issue.

Honda sold some four hundred Chrysler Jeeps in Japan in 1990. MITI asked Honda to triple the number. The absence of SUV-style automobiles in Honda's lineup meant the request wouldn't pose too much of a problem. But buying more American parts was another issue altogether. MITI couldn't force the issue, as Honda didn't have any ties to the Big Three in terms of investment capital.

By passing Chrysler, Honda had muscled in on the Big Three's turf. Honda needed to make a good faith effort to resolve the problem. If it didn't, the brunt of the attacks would fall on its head.

Honda spent 2.77 billion dollars purchasing American-made automobile parts in 1990—the most out of any Japanese automobile manufacturer. MITI wanted Honda to double the number by 1994, but that would have been next to impossible. Honda compromised by proposing a 78 percent increase to 4.94 billion dollars.

Honda would need to put forth a tremendous effort to meet even that compromise goal. It would mean that Yoshino, who was extremely familiar with parts procurement, had to remain in Ohio for the time being. Kawamoto realized that he would have to abandon his initial plan of having Yoshino quickly replace Irimajiri as head of domestic sales. That said, he couldn't leave the post empty, either. Kawamoto was stumped, and time continued to pass.

Irimajiri's grueling workload only got worse after the New Year. He couldn't just show his face and listen to reports at development, production, and management meetings; he also needed to give specific orders to all of his staff. A new incentive-based salary system intended to motivate senior management staff was in the works. If it weren't handled with finesse, however, it could be interpreted as a pay *cut* and send morale plummeting. Negotiations with the labor unions also had to be handled with care.

Irimajiri recalled his first request to the staff upon becoming president of the Honda Research and Development Company: "I'd like you to move towards designs that are easy for both factories and part manufacturers to build."

At the time the R&D section had been too steeped in an ethos of innovation and performance for their own sake to change gears and do things differently. Their overly complacent reports on their progress in this regard sorely tested Irimajiri's patience.

"Before you get so smug," Irimajiri yelled, "get out to the dealerships and see with your own eyes what kinds of cars the customers actually want!"

Since the domestic sales chief had yet to be named by Kawamoto, Irimajiri couldn't go to the dealerships in any official capacity to discuss these matters with the dealers on the front lines. But that didn't stop him from doing so on an unofficial basis.

Whenever Irimajiri had time, he would talk with the salesmen to learn more about the domestic situation. He learned that Honda's late start as an automaker in Japan was responsible for the chronic red ink in domestic sales. The only reason the domestic sales networks had been able to expand at all was because of the enormous profits being made in the United States.

As a Honda Tech man, Irimajiri already had a vague notion that domestic sales were in the red. What shocked him was learning that the losses were largely the result of dealers leaving the Honda fold. If franchise dealership owners wanted to relinquish their right to sell Honda products during a slump, Honda was obliged to buy back the franchise license and sell directly to the consumer through their corporate-owned dealerships. Even during the bubble era, the corporate-owned dealerships racked up bigger losses with each passing year.

In the automobile industry, if twenty percent of the total number of dealerships was operating at a loss, it was seen as being the fault of the dealers. Forty percent meant both the manufacturer and the dealers bore some responsibility. And if more than fifty percent of the dealers were in the red, it was seen as being the manufacturer's fault. In Honda's case, seventy percent of the dealerships were operating at a loss. There was no question that this was Honda's fault.

The cause was the disconnect between R&D and sales; products were provided to the three sales networks very nearly at random. In the old days the man in charge of the Verno network had often bragged to his fellow executives, "All I need to keep my dealerships running are customer satisfaction surveys and customer management files." Now, however, he had changed his tune: "You can't keep a dealership alive on customer satisfaction surveys. And how can you maintain customer management databases if you don't have any money?"

Another problem was that the composition of the domestic sales personnel was lopsided. The head of domestic sales was a former Honda of America president, and somehow the idea that "you're nobody unless you've worked at Honda of America" had spread through the entire staff. The core domestic sales group consisted largely of people who had worked for Honda of America at one time. Over the course of time, the number of people at corporate headquarters who had spent their entire careers in Japan had grown very small indeed.

Domestic sales was considered unglamorous work. Many of Honda's auto dealerships had started off as bicycle shops, then became motorcycle dealerships, then graduated from there to selling cars. Most were relatively small in size. Until the advent of the three sales networks, "roadmen" assigned to particular regions managed everything through face-to-face contact with the dealers in their territories. The roadmen and their dealers had a shared stake in seeing sales rise, and rise they did. Honda's adoption of an American-style sales system, however, did away with these relationships and put all the focus on the bottom line.

How could Honda rebuild its domestic sales division? The company needed to expand its sales force to the same numbers as that of Toyota. But first it needed to readjust the networks themselves. Primo, the smallest network, also had the fewest dealerships in the red. The problem was the Clio and Verno dealerships, many of which were corporate-owned and almost all of which were losing money. The consolidated financial statement of Honda's capital investment arm showed accumulated losses in the billions of dollars.

Irimajiri's discussions with the sales staff led him to believe that Honda needed to put more effort into improving the efficiency of the sales networks. That meant merging dealerships.

The majority of Primo dealerships were small, family-owned shops; their locations were unevenly spread throughout Japan. Some areas had too many shops. Others didn't have nearly enough, in spite of their strategic importance. Furthermore, the display area in each of these tiny dealerships was half or less than that of a corresponding Toyota or Nissan shop.

The only way to solve the problem would be convincing dealers in crowded areas to move to empty ones. Dealers often resisted such drastic measures, however; the manufacturer needed to offer a financial incentive to persuade them.

In addition, if Honda wanted to merge the Verno and Clio networks, it needed to build large "mega-dealerships" that would allow for the strategic display of a wide array of products. It would take twenty billion yen a year for five years—a total of a hundred billion yen—to undertake the remodeling and rebuilding necessary to create the new hierarchy of dealerships. At the time, Honda was spending four billion yen a year on sales. Restructuring would mean spending five times that amount every year. It would be a major undertaking.

Both inside the company and out, more and more people had come to the conclusion that Irimajiri was the only man who could do the job.

6

Just after the burst of the bubble economy, word of a credit scheme called the "M-Fund" spread through the manufacturing industry like wildfire. During World War II, the story went, the Imperial Japanese Army had looted a tremendous amount of treasure from occupied territories and brought it back to Japan for storage. After the war, Major General William Marquat, head of the Allied Occupation Forces' Economic and Scientific Section, had confiscated it for use in financing Japan's postwar reconstruction and recovery. The "M" in "M-Fund" comes from "Marquat."

Rumors of such secret, unused funds intended for the restoration of Japan had circulated endlessly in the years after the war. Reflecting the concerns of the day, these rumors variously described the money as coming from "petrodollars," "secret Imperial Household accounts," or "Ministry of Finance funds." The "M-Fund" became a catchall term to refer to these mythic sources of hidden wealth.

All of the rumors were false. No such hidden riches existed, and the financing schemes claiming to tap into them were frauds. Con artists came out of the woodwork to ply these schemes whenever financial institutions tightened their lending rules. Some estimates held that there were more than three thousand of them.

They came bearing convincingly crafted letters of introduction from powerful politicians, financiers, or government officials. They offered their services to corporations that appeared in need of financing. It was as simple as forging a letter.

No major Japanese corporation was immune to offers of the suspicious funds. Nearly every top management or accounting executive in Japan had met with one of these con artists at one time or another. The ones who could sniff these proposals out as "M-Fund" schemes and turned them down were the ones who tended to rise in the corporate ranks.

The con artists had already approached Toyota, which as Japan's most successful corporation already had nearly two trillion yen in available investment capital, and they didn't hesitate to approach major city banks as well. When financial institutions were targeted, the amount of the "loan" being offered invariably swelled to thirty or even forty trillion yen.

The point of the fraud was to extract a "commission" as collateral before the actual transaction was to take place. Generally speaking, the commission was 1 percent of the total amount of a loan. Of course, even the most gullible marks balked at paying anything before a transaction occurred, in which case the perpetrator would ask the mark to sign a "statement of intent" or some other such agreement. When the loan was inevitably revealed to be a fraud, the perpetrator would request a payment to make the evidence disappear. If the mark refused, the perpetrator would bring the documents to the company and demand money directly.

One famous example involved the president of All Nippon Airways, Tetsuo Oniwa, later to become a major figure in the Lockheed scandal. When it was revealed that Oniwa had signed documents for 300 billion yen worth of financing from an M-Fund scheme, he was forced to resign. Sanae Honda, president of the Maruzen Oil company (currently known as Cosmo Oil) fell into the same trap. And rumor had it that famous actor Jiro Tamiya committed suicide over trouble from an M-Fund scheme.

Even as recently as 1994, Shigekuni Kawamura, president of Dainippon Ink and Chemicals, Inc. and Hiroshi Fujii, vice president of Nissan, were forced to resign over M-Fund scandals. So-called "victimless crimes" such as the M-Fund schemes tend to perpetuate themselves in the shadows.

An older colleague had once warned Irimajiri: "You tend to make reckless decisions. You should take three deep breaths and think things through carefully before doing anything." Irimajiri should have heeded that advice when he was approached with such an offer.

In February of 1992, a former employee of the Honda Research and Development Company asked to meet with Irimajiri for unspecified reasons. Irimajiri would normally have refused to meet anyone who didn't clearly state his business, but he knew the man personally. He figured he could at least take the time to listen to somebody he had once worked with.

The former employee arrived accompanied by an old man, who handed Irimajiri a business card that read: "Tenchi Sora, President, Japanese-Himalayan Botanical Society" ("Tenchi Sora" was obviously a pseudonym, and roughly translates as "The Sky of Heaven and Earth"). Tenchi Sora offered Irimajiri ten trillion yen in financing. It was utterly ridiculous. Irimajiri raised a few questions for the fun of it, then politely asked them to leave.

Some time later, another con artist arrived, this time bearing a letter of introduction written by a powerful acquaintance of Irimajiri. Had Irimajiri known the purpose of the meeting beforehand, he would have refused on the phone. But the man had been intentionally vague, saying he preferred to discuss it in person. Not wishing to offend the friend of an acquaintance, Irimajiri agreed to a meeting. He ended the discussion the moment he realized it was yet another loan scam.

These weren't the first times that con artists had paid such visits to Honda. Usually the chairman or a vice president met them in person and then asked them to leave. In any event, since Irimajiri hadn't fallen for the ruse, there was nothing for him to feel ashamed about. He was in charge of general management, so there was nothing out of the ordinary in his meeting with potential financiers. An honest and open-minded person himself, it never occurred to him to attend these meetings accompanied by a "witness." He felt perfectly comfortable meeting them on his own.

Irimajiri was a thorough and methodical man. He had been extra vigilant about his health since being diagnosed with arrhythmia while president of HAM. He had long avoided both tobacco and alcohol. His daily schedule was to wake up just after five o'clock in the morning, take a little jog through his neighborhood, shower, eat breakfast, and drive himself to arrive at headquarters in Aoyama before eight.

Since he was responsible for so many divisions, he had to hit the ground running like a battlefield commander the second he entered the company doors. He attended one conference after another and made time to speak with employees and visitors. If he had a question about something, he would contact the person in charge of the issue at night and make them explain until he fully understood. He would then take three deep breaths, often to the bewilderment of the person he was talking to, and then hand down his orders. Since he was also president of Honda Research and Development, his weekly schedule included visits once or twice a week to the R&D sections for automobiles in Tochigi Prefecture and for motorcycles in Asaka, Saitama Prefecture to check on the development of new models.

Irimajiri would take work home and read late into the night. He lived on extremely little sleep. Sometimes he'd even wake up in the middle of the night, plagued with anxiety over the company's future.

Honda's finished if we don't do something. Why am I the only one who sees it? How can I return Honda back to its glory days? How can I make it a company that breeds heroes?

It's going to take another massive reorganization. I don't even know if performance incentives and executive term limits will really inspire the middle managers to do their best. Kawamoto and I seem to be mostly agreed on what needs to be done, but still...

No matter how much Irimajiri tried to goad his subordinates into working harder, a group of people who had grown so accustomed to bureaucracy wouldn't change that quickly.

"What's the rush?" they would ask. "A major corporation can't be reorganized that easily," or "Irimajiri, you're rushing things. If we go too fast, it'll hurt the company, not help it."

Irimajiri's restless style caused a lot of people in the company to turn away from him. He became increasingly isolated within the company. He began to sense that people had grown cool towards him, but that only made him push that much harder.

In March, the stress triggered a relapse of his arrhythmia. His doctor ordered him to take a vacation. Much of the stress was due to his frustration at the slow pace of reform, which had practically become a neurotic obsession.

In the midst of it all, Kawamoto caught wind of a rumor that Irimajiri was involved in some sort of financing scheme. The rumor had even been embellished with the bogus detail that Irimajiri had already opened a bank account in preparation for the transfer of funds.

Rumor or not, Kawamoto couldn't ignore it. In fact, the two men had recently had differences of opinion on a number of topics, not just the speed of the reorganization. The crux of the matter was that they had different visions about Honda's future.

Irimajiri had a precise idea of where he wanted the company to go. Kawamoto, on the other had, lacked experience as a business manager; he simply wanted Honda to become a "normal" large corporation, not one that fostered risk-takers and heroes. Ever since becoming president, Kawamoto had begun to feel that the typical "Honda man" lacked common sense. The only way to address that, Kawamoto reasoned, was to make Honda like every other corporation.

Kawamoto summoned Irimajiri to his office on March 16. Irimajiri had grown emaciated from the relapse of his heart condition. He arrived on the tenth floor to find Kawamoto flanked by Chairman Yoshizawa and Supreme Advisor Kawashima. The three looked grave.

"Irimajiri, I know this is sudden, but I'd like you to resign," Kawamoto said bluntly. "And I don't want you to ask the reason why."

Irimajiri refused to be summarily dismissed in such a manner. "What? Please explain yourself."

The three sat silently for a while. Then Yoshizawa broke the silence by hinting at the financing scheme. Irimajiri couldn't believe the stupidity of it all. He explained exactly what had happened.

Perhaps it was careless for me, as a vice president representing the company, to have met them alone. Nonetheless, it's not like it caused the company any trouble or expense. But perhaps this is for the best. If I keep going like this, I'll be flat on my back long before Honda is on its feet. Maybe I should take the doctor's advice and just focus on getting better.

In the end, he readily complied with Kawamoto's request and resigned.

My career as a Honda man is over. Tomorrow I'll have myself admitted to the university hospital and undergo a thorough examination. I can worry about the future once I'm healthy again.

Upon learning of Irimajiri's resignation, a former top executive of Honda commented: "Kawamoto and Irimajiri had different personalities, but they shared one hell of a temper and an inability to compromise. And neither one wanted to share the spotlight. I suppose it was only a matter of time before they went head to head. The financing scheme rumor was just the final straw.

"The sheltered environment of the R&D section tends to create weak executives. Losing Irimajiri could well be the price we pay for having spoiled those two men for so long. In battle, you're supposed to fire at the enemy, but their internal squabbling has simply thrown our side into chaos. They're textbook examples of children who don't know a thing about war."

On May 9, 1992, the finals of the America's Cup began in the waters off San Diego. The finalists competing for the trophy were the United States and Italy. Like the Olympics, the race was held every four years. Hiroshi Hirose, president of Mazda R&D North America, was in attendance with his family. Hirose happened to run into a Japanese acquaintance among his fellow spectators: Hiroyuki Yoshino, president of HAM. Hirose, Yoshino, and Irimajiri were all alumni of the same Japanese university.

"Yoshino, long time no see. What are you doing here?" asked Hirose.

"I'm on my way back to headquarters in Tokyo," answered Yoshino. "There's been a big shake-up."

"You mean Irimajiri? I read about in the papers. He left because of health concerns, it said. He seemed fine when I ran into him at the Tokyo Motor Show last fall, though."

"I don't know any of the details yet. I just got the orders to head back to Tokyo and assume it has something to do with Irimajiri's resignation. Anyway, I figured this might be my last chance to see the America's Cup, so I decided to drop by."

Irimajiri's sudden resignation threw the other executives into turmoil. Chairman Yoshizawa had been planning to step down and become an advisor when he turned sixty, in accordance with the new term-limit rules. He was going to suggest Munekuni as his successor. Before he could bring the idea up, however, Kawamoto asked him to stay on. Kawamoto planned to make Munekuni a vice president at large, and hand general affairs over to Miyata, who had previously been in charge of domestic sales.

Yoshino returned to Japan after the America's Cup, where he received unofficial word that he would be promoted to vice president of headquarters. In keeping with tradition, Yoshino assumed he would be assigned Irimajiri's former responsibilities over development and production. Instead, Kawamoto unexpectedly ordered him to oversee domestic sales. It was an unknown world for Yoshino, whose background was in production engineering.

What in the world happened here over these last six months? Yoshino thought. But he had to rush back to Ohio and couldn't spend any time digging to learn the truth. He had to begin the process of transferring his duties at HAM to Toyoji Yashiki, the manager of the Ohio engine factory. Yashiki was thoroughly familiar with the workings of HAM, and it didn't take long for Yoshino to bring him up to speed.

Irimajiri's departure also vacated the presidency of the Honda Research and Development Company. Kawamoto appointed himself to the role, effectively seizing total authority of the Honda business.

Kawamoto also enacted his proposal obliging executives to be present on site in their respective spheres of responsibility. Now only Kawamoto and a handful of administrative executives remained in the boardroom at headquarters. Furthermore, *waigaya* discussions were no longer being held at any level in Honda. The word itself had become a relic.

Former president Kume vacated the official president's residence in Setagaya, Tokyo, and thereafter entered a life of literal reclusion. Supreme Advisor Kiyoshi Kawashima all but stopped showing his face at headquarters, leaving the special office that had been set aside for him at headquarters unused.

Honda held a conference for U.S. dealers every year. The conferences usually began with a speech from the corporate president focusing on business management policies, then various executives gave reports on their various areas of expertise: sales, development, expansion plans, and so on.

Kawamoto had participated in these conferences as the head of development ever since being promoted to executive. A recent conference had been held at a hotel in Las Vegas, and Kawamoto had turned it into an unexpectedly flashy performance. Las Vegas being a center of entertainment, the hotel was able to accommodate any manner of stage effects. Kawamoto darkened the conference room and threw a rainbow of spotlights on the executives as they walked from their seats to the microphones. Kume, the first speaker, had put his hand to his head in embarrassment as he took the stage. Kawamoto, on the other hand, raised both hands triumphantly and slowly paraded to the microphones when his turn came. The Americans loved the performance, but his fellow Japanese executives could hardly believe it.

"Who does he think he is? Hitler or something?" mumbled Norimoto Otsuka, vice president of Honda R&D America.

"You know, he does kind of look like Hitler. All he needs is the moustache and he'd be the spitting image," chuckled Kume.

Kume started using the new nickname in the R&D section. Before long it had taken root and spread both inside and outside of Honda, creating the impression that Kawamoto was a grim dictator.

Needless to say, the former executives in Yaesu were not amused when word of the nickname got back to them. They defended Kawamoto by praising his hard work through such difficult times.

Domestic sales continued to decrease under Kawamoto's reign. In 1990, when Kawamoto was named president, sales had been 679,000. In 1991, sales dropped to 664,000, then 596,000 in 1992. By comparison, Honda's rival Mitsubishi sold 710,000, 755,000, and 744,000 cars during the same years.

Tomio Kubo, the second president of Mitsubishi Motors, had envied Honda's rapid growth during the mid-1970s. "Honda is a great company," Kubo had said. "It's young, it has vitality. We also happen to share the same bank: Mitsubishi Bank. I'd like to hire Honda employees through the bank so that we can learn more about Honda's management."

Fifth president Toyoo Tachi, who had dedicated himself to extricating Mitsubishi from its "unequal contract" with Chrysler and had managed to get his company listed on the stock market for the first time, cited Honda as a role model as well. "The most difficult task I faced upon becoming president was increasing the momentum of the company," recalled Tachi. "Our employees had become complacent in the lukewarm atmosphere that typified Mitsubishi at that time. Actually, we weren't even allowed to exploit our assets after becoming independent from Mitsubishi Heavy Industries. Our equity ratio was one of the lowest in the industry. Getting listed on the stock market wasn't an easy task at all. Even if we'd set it as a goal, it never would have happened without reorganizing and revitalizing the company. We chose Honda as our role model for that. I read a stack of books that had been written by former Honda vice president Michihiro Nishida and tried to adopt the best parts of the Honda model. Thanks to Honda, Mitsubishi grew into the company it is today."

In the ten years since Mitsubishi's push to reorganize, the roles of the two companies—particularly in terms of domestic sales—had totally reversed. In 1986, the difference in sales between Mitsubishi and Honda was only 221 cars. By 1992, this had dramatically grown to 148,000 cars in Mitsubishi's favor. This trend continued into the following year, when the difference grew to 165,000 cars. By 1994, the gap had grown to 254,000 (reverse-imported automobiles excluded). The long competition for third place in the industry, and the chance to challenge Nissan for second, ended in Mitsubishi's favor by a staggering margin.

A growing gap in profits between Mitsubishi and Honda was becoming apparent as well. Mitsubishi's operating profit exceeded that of Honda in 1990, and ordinary profit exceeded that of Honda in 1993. In addition, Honda's last claim to superiority, the number of products sold in Japan, fell below that of Mitsubishi after Mitsubishi's midterm earnings disclosure in September of 1994. The only thing Honda had over Mitsubishi anymore were the superior numbers on the company's consolidated balance sheet.

Even worse, Honda's final ray of hope, its tremendously successful business in America, had fallen into a slump. Honda's sales in America were clear indicators of a recession. The company sold 803,000 cars in 1991, 6.1 percent off the previous year, the first time in a decade that annual sales had failed to improve on those of the year before. The drop-offs of 1981 and 1982 had been caused by compliance with voluntary regulations on exports to the United States. Honda's hands had been tied. In contrast, the 1991 slump marked a genuine decrease in consumer interest.

Honda's American sales in 1992 were 768,000, the same as four years previous, which put Honda's U.S. sales at the same level as Toyota's. Toyota's 1993 sales were 741,000 units, just 18,000 fewer than the previous year. Honda's sales, on the other hand, were 716,000 units, or 52,000 fewer than the previous year. As a result, Honda ceded its title of No.1 import seller in the United States, which it had maintained since 1986, to Toyota. Honda automobiles had once sold at a premium. Now they were old news. The "Honda myth" was beginning to falter in the United States as well.

The Big Three, on the other hand, were making great strides in revitalizing their businesses. Big Three sales in 1993 beat those of the previous year. Chrysler was doing particularly well. Its sales of 830,000 took it past Honda and Toyota and made it America's third largest seller. Chrysler's minivans were tremendously popular, and the company poured the profits into developing successful new passenger car designs.

Honda slid to fifth place in the American market. Honda of America's profitability also suffered as a result. Acura, the second sales network, had done extremely well at first. Once it had been organized, however, Honda failed to implement any further innovations. The dream of selling one million automobiles annually on the U.S. market had collapsed like a house of cards.

Honda went into litigation over the US-Canadian tax issue. The Big Three didn't miss the opportunity to hint publicly that Honda stood accused of evading taxes. Even after all its efforts to build a positive image in the United States, Honda found itself a target of criticism.

Honda had long believed that as long as it produced quality products, customers would continue buying them. But that logic no longer worked as well as it once had. For one thing, the Big Three makers had greatly improved the performance of their compact cars. For another, the Gulf War had sparked a newfound spirit of patriotism among the American people, who were turning in increasing numbers toward American-made products.

Honda of America's failure to achieve its sales goals put a heavy burden on the Japanese staff. If they didn't sell more cars domestically, it would be difficult to maintain their current production pace. The problem was, nobody thought for a second they could sell a million cars in Japan. The expansion of the Ohio factory meant decreasing the number of exports to the United States. The American market slump drove the numbers down even further. The number of automobiles shipped from Japan to America in 1986, during the period of export regulations, was 450,000. By 1992, this number had plunged to 280,000. If the current dollar-to-yen exchange rate were any indication, there would be no hope of reaching 300,000 again anytime soon. The company had just spent 25 billion yen building a third assembly line in Suzuka. If Honda didn't boost domestic Japanese sales at once, the investment would go to waste.

The factory dedicated to building the luxury sports car called the NSX, located on the grounds of the Tochigi R&D center, had also grown too large to manage efficiently. The NSX was Honda's flagship product. It was a genuine sports car with an all-aluminum body. The NSX had been a major hit; at the height of the bubble, there was a two-year waiting list to purchase one. It sold for a premium in the United States as well (under the Acura brand), with prices exceeding $100,000. The car quickly developed a reputation as the world's most expensive sports car sold by a major manufacturer. Unfortunately for Honda, however, sales dropped sharply both in Japan and abroad once the economic bubble burst.

7

Kawamoto made his decision early in the summer of 1992: "With Honda's current capabilities," he told vice president of domestic sales Yoshino, "I'm convinced that it's impossible to keep running three separate networks. Our best bet is to increase efficiency by reducing it to two."

Thus began the process of reevaluating Honda's sales network. Kawamoto had already taken vice presidents Munekuni and Miyata off of domestic sales. With Chairman Yoshizawa having no real say over day-to-day management, there was nobody left to oppose Kawamoto's will. In a sense, he really had become "Hitler."

The debate among the top executives the previous Christmas Eve had been based on a report prepared by the Boston Consulting Group. The meeting had focused on broad topics and concepts; it hadn't touched on the specific details of the change. Now Kawamoto found himself having to work through all of the possible angles of streamlining the networks so as to understand the potential advantages and disadvantages.

The early process was carried out entirely in secret and with the help of Honda Research & Development. The basic framework was completed by the end of August. Then Honda's sales managers and Boston Consulting Group consultants spent long days and nights ironing out the details. The completed proposal for a two-network system was ready in September.

"Good, let's do it," Kawamoto said. The project was a go. Now all that remained was calling an official meeting to sound out the plan with the biggest dealerships. If everything went smoothly, Kawamoto planned to make an official announcement at the conference of all Honda dealerships at the beginning of the following year.

The plan made the rounds of headquarters without any major objections. In the middle of September, Kawamoto held a final meeting for all domestic sales managers and R&D executives. Munekuni and Miyata were in attendance as well. First Yoshino explained the new system to the assembled staff. Then he turned to address Munekuni and Miyata specifically: "We must streamline the networks to rebuild our domestic sales system. As I've just explained, we will sell our products through two networks from now on: Primo, and a combined version of the Verno and Clio networks. President Kawamoto has approved the plan. We hope to have your support as well."

"Things have gone this far. What choice do we have?" they replied helplessly.

The last remaining obstacle was obtaining Chairman Yoshizawa's consent. Kawamoto saw it as nothing more than a formality, but Yoshizawa wasn't about to give in without a fight. In spite of having been kept largely in the dark about the project, Yoshizawa remained sharply aware of just what was happening inside the company. He had been thinking through his own plan for how to stop Kawamoto's reorganization dead in its tracks.

The ceremony to ask for Yoshizawa's consent was held at headquarters at 7:00 p.m. on October 4. Several of the executives had been on business trips, so the time was pushed back into the evening to give everyone concerned a chance to attend. There were seven direct participants: President Kawamoto, Vice President Yoshino, and Director of Headquarters and R&D Iwakura represented the Honda Tech faction. The Fujisawa Trading faction was represented by Chairman Yoshizawa, Vice President Munekuni, Director Miyata, and Domestic Sales Director Higashizuka. A handful of other executives who had worked on the project waited in an adjoining room in case any of the seven participants required clarification or further explanation. Needless to say, the meeting was held totally off the record.

Kawamoto began by explaining the current state of product development within the company. He concluded his presentation with a proposal to solve the problems facing Honda by shrinking the number of networks from three to two. Next, Yoshino took the floor and explained the actual details of the plan. Yoshizawa watched the ceiling and listened quietly as usual. He let them say everything they needed to say before opening his mouth:

"First of all, let me state that we on the sales side are responsible for the post-bubble slump in domestic sales. I personally bear some responsibility for this as well. For that, I honestly apologize."

Yoshizawa knew full well that Kawamoto had already laid the groundwork for the plan. The only way he could stop it now was to launch a surprise attack, at no small risk to himself. It would have been easy for him to criticize R&D, but he knew that doing so would only create ill will and entrench both sides. Openly admitting the role his sales staff had played in the drop in sales gave him the opening to make his real move.

Yoshizawa continued: "Please try to understand what I mean when I say that domestic sales for us is not just about management theory. For us Fujisawa Trading men, a three-network sales system was a longstanding dream. I'm asking you now not to destroy that dream.

"I understand how hard it is for R&D to supply cars to three different networks, believe me I do. But I think cutting the networks down to two is just too drastic a measure. If R&D can't provide cars for three networks, why don't we just do what Toyota does and simply make cosmetic changes to a single model for each of the networks?"

Yoshizawa paused for a moment to catch his breath and smiled. "Kawamoto-san, what can I say to change your mind? I want us to dream again. I want us to dream big. As long as we have dreams, we can overcome these temporary difficulties."

The last comment was intended to give Kawamoto a way out, a way for him to save face. Although the chairman at Honda held no executive power, Yoshizawa had been Kawamoto's mentor, after all. Furthermore, Kawamoto had long been in charge of the R&D section whose shortcomings Yoshizawa had just pointed out. His words must have cut Kawamoto like a knife.

In spite of that, Kawamoto was in fact pleased. He was pleased because he took Yoshizawa's humble tone as a sign of surrender. Now that the commander-in-chief of the Fujisawa Trading Co. side had effectively surrendered, he calmly withdrew the reorganization plan.

"In light of Yoshizawa-san's comments, I suggest maintaining the current structure of three sales networks," he said. "Let's all do our best to get back on our feet."

The merging of the sales networks had been averted yet again. Soon, people started calling the meeting "The Great Reversal."

The atmosphere within Honda drastically changed after the meeting. Kawamoto and Yoshizawa had a long, candid talk afterwards. That discussion completely changed Kawamoto's attitude toward Yoshizawa. Kawamoto had called Yoshizawa "Yoshizawa-san" in keeping with the Honda tradition of addressing people by their family names. Henceforth, however, he broke with precedent by referring to Yoshizawa by name and title: "Chairman Yoshizawa."

The meeting had the effect of fusing Honda's split personality into a single identity; Honda Tech and Fujisawa Trading Co. became one. Kawamoto stood as the president of this "new" company, with full personnel management authority over everybody, including the sales division. Kawamoto used his authority to officially remove Munekuni and Miyata from domestic sales. His shake-up extended from the lower-ranking executives down to middle management. Kawamoto also replaced Higashizuka with director Riku Iwai, effectively putting Iwai in charge of domestic sales.

Although Fujisawa Trading Co. was absorbed and many of his protégés removed in the process, Yoshizawa took great pride and satisfaction in having successfully defended the three networks to the bitter end.

On September 11, a month before the "Great Reversal," Honda held a press conference to announce the company's official withdrawal from Formula One racing. Rumors of the company's retirement had spread like wildfire throughout the racing world at the beginning of the season that spring.

Kawamoto had flatly denied them, but the rumors sprang from Honda's plunging sales revenues and shortage of capital. F1 expenses, including the development of engines and other related costs, ran some ten billion yen a year. In addition, Honda had to hire more than a hundred extra engineering staff to work on the project. The economic recession only made the F1 an even more difficult burden to bear.

Some three hundred journalists attended the press conference announcing Honda's withdrawal. "Over the last ten years," Kawamoto said, "Honda has dedicated itself to developing the ultimate technology for winning the greatest race series in the world, the F1. Thanks to everyone's hard work, Honda has managed to receive the Constructors' Championship six years in a row. We have reached the goals we set for ourselves. The time has come to withdraw from Formula One racing; the current season will be our last. In fact, we told McLaren of our decision last December."

None of the assembled journalists accepted Kawamoto's explanations at face value. They barraged him with hostile questions:

"What do you think Soichiro Honda would say if he were alive?"

"Can't this be taken as an act of betrayal to Honda's loyal fans and consumers?"

"Many feel that Honda will ruin its image and become just another faceless auto manufacturer if it retires from the F1. How do you respond to that, President Kawamoto?"

Kawamoto kept cool throughout the grilling. He even smiled when he answered. "The old man often said, 'Make sure you win, but don't get bogged down in it, either; the F1 isn't business.' I think I've made the correct decision, and I think he would have respected my decision."

In response to the second question, Kawamoto said, "I admit the decision may be discouraging for Honda fans. It's true that some of our dealers were concerned about the impact on sales and advised against the withdrawal.

"Honda's participation in the F1 is really just a means to an end: it contributes to our research and development, which in turn allows us to make cars that keep our customers satisfied. But it's not good to get hung up on the means. Our products will continue to meet expectations. The engineers who worked on the F1 project will return to Honda R&D, where they're supposed to be, to focus on environmental, safety, and energy issues. Just because we're withdrawing from F1 racing doesn't mean we're going to stop challenging ourselves."

Honda's partnership with McLaren and Ayrton Senna made for the strongest F1 team in the history of the sport. Honda even managed to create a firm base of support for the sport in Japan. The new fans both in Japan and abroad greatly boosted sales of Honda's consumer automobiles.

Honda participation in Formula One racing was essentially as an engine supplier. During the era of the turbocharger, the engine was everything, and this dovetailed nicely with Honda's technological strengths. But in the subsequent era of naturally aspirated engines, the only way to increase horsepower was by improving the entire racecar, including the chassis. More powerful engines wouldn't necessarily guarantee victory, a fact of which Kawamoto was painfully aware. He knew that ensuring victories in the F1 would force Honda to create entire racecars from the ground up. The potential expenses were staggering.

The main reason for banning turbochargers from the sport was to throw a roadblock in the path of Honda's juggernaut of consecutive victories. In an attempt to prove that it could succeed with naturally aspirated engines as well, Honda continued pouring effort into developing new engine designs. The company won ten races in 1989, six in 1990, and eight in 1991. But France's legendary Renault and Italy's shining star Ferrari made rapid technological gains and eventually eclipsed Honda. Honda's record for consecutive victories dropped from the headlines into the history books. In its final season in 1992, Honda barely managed five victories and failed to receive the Constructors' Championship. The only way for Honda to continue with Formula One racing was reappraising the purpose of its participation.

It's fair to say that the history of motor sports and the history of the automobile are practically one and the same. F1 was born in Europe and popular among the aristocracy. In fact, Prince Rainier III traditionally hosted a gala dinner banquet the evening before the Monaco Grand Prix.

As the name implies, winning a Drivers' Championship required extraordinary racing skills. On top of that, however, even the best drivers needed a good car to win. The engine supplier played only a supporting role.

If the Olympics are the ultimate test of an athlete's physical abilities, the F1 racing can be described as an Olympic match with a technical twist. From that standpoint, the F1 is quite similar to the America's Cup. The main difference was that the Japanese team built their own ship and pulled together their own crew for the America's Cup. Japan's only participation in the F1 was as a supplier of engines.

In Japan, Formula One racing only really gained popularity after being broadcast on TV. In Europe, on the other hand, it already enjoyed widespread popularity even before the advent of broadcasting. In fact, many people consider Formula One racing to be an integral part of European culture.

No matter how well Honda's engines did, no matter that Soichiro had been awarded the Gold Medal from the Federation Internationale del Automobile (FIA), Honda's voice remained but a whisper in the world of the F1. The sum total of the company's influence was next to nothing. Honda's withdrawal rated only a back-page article in the European newspapers. A similar announcement by Renault or Ferrari would have made the front page and sparked widespread debate about Formula One's ability to survive. That shows about as well as anything just how much a part of European culture the sport had become.

The FIA ranks at the top of any list of automotive organizations. Its umbrella encompasses the Federation Internationale du Sport Automobile (FISA), which organizes motor sports events, and the Formula One Constructors Association (FOCA), which runs the F1 as an entertainment business. Sensing the growing interest in F1 in Japan, FOCA decided to hold two different F1 races there every year beginning in 1994. When it came to the entertainment side of the business, the era of the F1 as a purely European pursuit was coming to an end. If an F1 race were held in China, for example, the convergence of European and Asian cultures could be said to have taken a major step forward. In such a case, Honda would have the opportunity to expand its role from humble engine provider to being the bridge between Europe and Asia.

In reality, however, both the FISA and FOCA were deeply conservative and exclusive organizations, run by a select handful of people. At the intoxicating heights of the bubble economy, one Japanese company after another poured money into sponsoring F1 teams. Some felt that this "Japanese money" was changing—perhaps even distorting—the real meaning of the F1.

The influx of money allowed owners of top teams to tour the world in private jets, spend holidays on luxury yachts, even build private museums of antique cars. The Paddock Club was founded to give sponsors a place to enjoy champagne and caviar during races. And the vast majority of the money came from the pockets of Japanese corporations.

The supremacy of the sponsors had a tremendous influence throughout the sport, elevating the already high costs of F1 to stratospheric heights. In time, however, Formula One came to be seen as a financial sinkhole. Once the economic bubble burst, the same companies that had rushed to sponsor teams abandoned the sport in droves. Rumors of the end of the F1 spread among Japanese fans; before long, the sport had become something of a symbol for the excesses of the bubble era. Honda's withdrawal only added to this perception.

Honda had staged its F1 comeback by first teaming up with Ralt for the F2. As described earlier, Honda's twelve consecutive victories on the F2 circuit formed the cornerstone of its comeback effort in the F1. Honda's surprising and overwhelming early success in the F2 had the side effect of discouraging many of the other F2 teams. The large number of teams who left the sport led directly to the demise of F2 racing.

"Honda really used the F2 circuit up," recalls one individual who was involved with the F1. "I mean, they really sucked it bone dry. After devouring the F2, they ran off to the F1 and did the same thing there. Honda brought the 'bubble' to the F1. The minute it burst, they abandoned the sport. Formula One is facing a turning point now. I wish Honda had taken the initiative. They could have challenged the conservative organizations running things to demand change and make F1 a real motor sport again." This mixture of criticism and disappointment in Honda was common at the time.

Fearing trouble, Honda left F1 quietly without raising any kind of stir. Although the company's technology had allowed it to dominate the sport competitively, it shied away from potential cultural friction.

Yoshitoshi Sakurai, who had served as racing director since 1984 and had laid the foundation for Honda's consecutive victories, summed up the situation as follows: "Honda's single-minded drive to win in Formula One died along with Soichiro. Honda should have set a new goal for itself after winning for the third time in a row. That goal should have been changing the FIA. The only way to really bridge the cultures of the East and the West would have been venturing into the thick of it, into the core of the organizations that ran the sport. Perhaps Kawamoto-san lost his sense of ambition; he left F1 rather than get into a culture war." Sakurai left Honda shortly after the company left the F1. He currently runs a popular organization called Racing Club International.

"Honda's image in Europe had been that of a motorcycle rather than automobile maker, but our ten-year association with F1 totally changed that," Kawamoto has said. "Honda managed to take Formula One to the next level with its engine technology. When I saw Senna win the Hungary Grand Prix while wearing a badge of mourning for the old man, my decision was made. At that very moment, I realized that we had accomplished what we had set out to accomplish. Ten years is enough time to become complacent about victory. At the beginning, the F1 project members just focused on the job at hand without any thought of winning or losing; by the end they had become like salarymen, complacent and unwilling to challenge themselves. As for Honda taking a leadership position among the governing organizations of Formula One, the thought never even crossed my mind."

The final race of the 1992 season, the Australia Grand Prix, was held in November. McLaren-Marlboro-Honda's Gerhard Berger won, and Honda retired from the sport as promised.

Several days after Honda's withdrawal from the F1, Honda of America president Koichi Amemiya received some terrible news. The situation threatened to jeopardize all of the hard work Honda had put into its American business. He got a call from HAM vice president Scott Whitlock, who was in Washington D.C. on a business trip, that the Alliance of Automobile Manufacturers (AAM) had suddenly expelled HAM from the organization. Amemiya flew into a rage.

This is bullshit! Honda of America has exported more cars out of the U.S. than any maker besides GM. We've made a tremendous contribution to the American economy. We source 82 percent of our Accord parts and 70 percent of our Civic parts locally. We have over ten thousand Americans working in our factories. Any way you slice it, our cars are American-made.

Honda of America has already been a member of the AAM for a decade now. We're even listed on the NYSE! How can they say Honda of America isn't an American company? What the hell more do we need to do?

Still, Amemiya knew anger wouldn't solve anything. After cooling down, he began to consider the situation again. *Honda of America's history mirrors the experience of America's immigrants. Now I understand the difficulties that first- and second-generation Japanese immigrants faced when they arrived here. They endured war and numerous other hardships to get American citizenship. We, on the other hand, breezed into the American market. Perhaps Honda hasn't really taken root in U.S. soil yet. I suppose that's why AAM expelled us.*

Now that I think about it, perhaps we've only been "taking" and not really "giving" anything back. Perhaps the Big Three feel that we've taken all the advantages of being a member without doing our part in return. Without deep roots, Honda of America remains vulnerable to that kind of criticism. And without those roots, we can forget about getting readmitted to the AAM. We're just going to have to try harder.

As it happened, HAM was undergoing another major upheaval right at the same time. HAM president Toyoji Yashiki was getting ready for the regular fall 1992 executive council meeting in Tokyo. Ed Buker, the vice president in charge of quality control, approached Yashiki with the sudden news that he wanted to quit.

"Understood. But let's put off discussing the details until I get back to Ohio," said Yashiki, leaving for the airport without accepting Buker's letter of resignation.

Yashiki was in the middle of checking in at the airport when he received a call from Vice President Al Kinzar, who oversaw the engine factory in Anna, Ohio.

"I need to discuss something with you immediately, Mr. Yashiki," said Kinzar. "It's about my future."

Kinzar was a walking encyclopedia when it came to the Ohio factory. He had worked closely with Irimajiri, Okubo, and Yoshida to promote the spread of the Honda Way throughout the company. He also happened to be Yashiki's right-hand man at the engine factory. BMW had been floating plans to build a factory in South Carolina, Kinzar's home state, and had offered him the position of CEO there. Kinzar had invited Ed Buker to join him, and the pair had decided to leave Honda on the same day together.

Kinzar's mind was made up, but Buker was still wrestling with the decision. He resolved that if Yashiki postponed his trip to Japan and took the time to talk with him, he would reconsider his decision to move over to BMW. Yashiki's response disappointed him. Kinzar and Buker were popular men; in the end, twenty-five employees, including some managers, followed them from HAM to BMW.

"Al's going to leave. He wants a triumphant return to his home state," said former HAM vice president Narumi Yoshida to his fellow executives at Tokyo headquarters. "He might well have stayed if we had made him president of HAM. But with Scott above him, that's simply impossible. I want to warn you that this incident is just the beginning. There will be other people like Al who leave the company. And a good manager always takes quite a few good workers with him when he leaves. You need to be ready for that."

The confrontation over reorganizing domestic Japanese sales, Irimajiri's sudden resignation, Honda's retirement from Formula One racing, the expulsion of Honda of America from the AAM, and Kinzar's resignation: all of it happened in the same year. The chaos within the company had reached a crescendo.

When it lost Soichiro Honda, the strong-willed founder and prophet of "The Honda Way," Honda lost its ability to convey its message both in and out of the company. The Honda Kids were adrift.

8

Shoichiro Irimajiri, now vice president of video game manufacturer Sega, was in the town of Omiya in Saitama Prefecture on May 18, 1994. He had been invited to give a lecture at an event hosted by a newspaper. More than five hundred people attended to hear his hour and a half speech. Had Irimajiri still been at Honda, the title would undoubtedly have been something like "Secrets of Successful Internationalization." But times had changed. The title was "Games and Multimedia."

"Multimedia is already in the mainstream in the United States. But in Japan, where there are still a lot of regulations, it's tough to tell exactly what the future holds," Irimajiri said. His left hand was thrust in a pocket, his right clutched the microphone, and he paced thoughtfully along the narrow stage.

Irimajiri's lecture on the world of multimedia was easy and accessible, as if he were addressing a class of students. He had been at Sega for only one year, but he was already something of a specialist in the field.

Several days later, Irimajiri left for Saipan. He recalled of that business trip:

"It was only at Sega that I realized for the first time that business can be fun. I spent three solid days diving and fishing with the head of an American game software company. We got along very well and I obtained exclusive rights to sell his company's software. Making connections is what business is all about. Now that I think about it, all I ever did at Honda was sit around waiting for people to get things done."

The day after Irimajiri's lecture in Omiya, the Japan Automobile Manufacturers Association (JAMA) held a party at the Palace Hotel in Tokyo after its annual plenary meeting. At the entrance to the hall, Toyota president and JAMA chairman Tatsuro Toyoda stood alongside his fellow JAMA vice chairmen before a folding gilt screen, greeting the arriving journalists, businessmen, and other guests.

Like Mitsubishi and Mazda, Honda usually dispatched its chairman to act as a vice chairman at JAMA. But Yoshizawa had stepped down the previous year and the chairman's seat remained unfilled, so President Kawamoto was supposed to take over the role himself. Kawamoto, however, was nowhere to be seen at the party.

"Kawamoto-san hurt his ankle while fiddling around with his motorcycle," explained a spokesman. "I know he's still on crutches. I assume that's why he couldn't attend today."

Kawamoto hadn't seen Irimajiri in person since forcing his resignation. Irimajiri had asked to meet with Kawamoto once, at the end of 1993, but Kawamoto had turned him down.

Sega was still something of a start-up company, and had been chronically short of skilled manpower. Even after the bubble economy burst and jobs were scarce, Sega had to place want ads in newspapers to find new engineers and middle managers. Some of the applicants were Honda employees. Irimajiri wasn't directly involved in the hiring process, but he did make one request of the person in charge of hiring: "When a Honda employee applies for a job, I want you to make their interview harder. If the decision comes down to a Honda employee and a non-Honda employee, you should probably choose the latter."

Whether executive or not, the mandatory age of retirement for a Honda employee was sixty years old. Regular employees had to retire on their sixtieth birthday, after which they were free to seek another job if they so chose. Honda didn't give them any assistance in this regard, so they had to find any subsequent employment on their own.

Executive-level employees, on the other hand, were allowed to stay on at Honda as paid advisors—in addition to receiving an ample pension—and thus could live out their remaining years in ease and comfort. They weren't allowed, however, to accept employment elsewhere.

One of the men who had worked alongside Irimajiri both in the R&D section and at the Ohio factory retired on December 22, 1993. His final post before retiring was as an executive at one of Honda's subsidiary parts suppliers. Just before his retirement, he approached Irimajiri about the possibility of working at Sega.

Irimajiri had always thought highly of the man, who was several years his senior. Irimajiri received permission to hire him from Sega president Hayao Nakayama. Irimajiri had no ethical problems: Honda and Sega's businesses were completely different, and the man had been an executive at a subsidiary rather than at Honda headquarters.

Irimajiri knew his decision was none of Honda's business, but he decided to make a courtesy call to Kawamoto anyway just so nobody would get the idea that he was trying to steal away Honda engineers.

"The president is currently very busy and can't change his schedule on such short notice. Director Miyata will see you on his behalf," he was told. Although he had worked in that very office a mere two years earlier, the executive assistants wouldn't give him access to the president.

Irimajiri went to the headquarters in Aoyama to visit Miyata and explain the situation. Miyata's response was ambiguous. Irimajiri took it as a "yes."

A few days later, Irimajiri received a letter from Honda. He couldn't believe his eyes. "As of December 21, Honda's regulations for retired executives have been revised. As before, retired executives may not accept employment except at institutions of higher learning. This regulation has now been expanded to include executives at Honda subsidiaries."

Taken at face value, the letter prohibited Irimajiri from hiring his former subordinate. *Why the hell would Kawamoto do something so childish? Honda has really gone off the rails. The company's more bureaucratic than ever.*

Honda's pensions for executives were high even by industry standards, which allowed retired executives to spend their post-Honda years in relative luxury. The amount paid to executives of subsidiaries wasn't nearly as high as that paid to parent company executives, but it was enough to ensure their comfort for several years after retirement. The amended regulation stated that these executives forfeited their pensions if they decided to work for other companies.

Irimajiri wasn't the only one who ran into trouble with the policy. Hideo Sugiura, Honda's first chairman, did as well. As far back as the N360 defect scandal, Sugiura had advocated the need for Honda to involve itself in more philanthropic and outside activities. He followed his own advice, acting as Honda's representative to the Japan Association of Corporate Executives. In keeping with Honda regulations, Sugiura retired as chairman in 1985 to become a special advisor. His term had expired in 1990. Although he could have continued working for Honda under a different title, fate would dictate otherwise.

Six months before the expiration of Sugiura's term, a high school classmate by the name of Seiji Yamazaki contacted him. Yamazaki was the president of a company called Yamatane. "What are you going to do after you step down as an advisor? Just sit around all day? That would be a waste of your talent. Why don't you work for me as an auditor? We're running a rice wholesaling business. We don't have a thing to do with automobiles, so I assume it won't be a problem."

Sugiura answered ambiguously at the time. Just before Yamatane's board meeting in May, however, Yamazaki contacted Sugiura again.

"Sugiura, I hope you remember my request from the other day. We can make an official decision at the board meeting in a few days, and then hold a press conference to announce it," offered Yamazaki.

Sugiura was rattled. Actually, he had all but forgotten about the offer. Becoming an auditor at Yamatane meant getting permission from Honda, and settling the issue of his executive pension. He paid an immediate visit to Chairman Yoshizawa.

"I really wanted to ask you to stay on as a consultant, even after the end of your term as advisor..." Yoshizawa replied.

Sugiura shook off the request and made the decision to join Yamatane.

"It's true that the decision caused some friction," recalls Sugiura, "but I didn't do it for the money. I did it for the sake of my own wellbeing. Living on a pension sounds nice, but the reality is that they just keep you around as an ornament with nothing to do. My salary at Yamatane is enough to pay for my prefectural, municipal, and fixed-property taxes. They also let me give a class—they call it the 'Sugiura School'—to the younger managers from 5:30 to 8:00 one evening a week. I tell them about my experiences at Honda and we have discussions. Actually, I've learned quite a bit from them too."

Retiring at sixty had long been the tradition at Honda. During Kume's presidency, however, the age limits were quietly raised to 67 for presidents, 65 for vice presidents, and 63 for senior managing directors. They even drafted documents to make the new age limits official. In spite of this, the mandatory age of retirement for lower executives remained at sixty. At any rate, the changes were internal and never made public.

The Honda Way called for executives to work hard and exhaust every drop of their fuel before passing the baton on to younger leaders. In spite of the policy allowing the Honda president and chairman to stay until the age of 67, nearly everyone resigned before sixty. Unless they accepted work at another company, retired executive directors, vice presidents, and chairmen were allowed to stay on board as Honda advisors and consultants even after retirement. Sugiura's case would have required another change in the regulations to allow him to accept a position at Yamatane while continuing to work as a consultant for Honda.

Former vice president Kihachiro Kawashima, who had given up his dream of opening a Honda dealership in Los Angeles, returned to Honda as an advisor after he had retired as president of a semi-governmental credit bureau. Of the four top executives who had worked directly beneath Soichiro and Fujisawa, only Kawashima and Michihiro Nishida were allowed to work as consultants indefinitely.

Nishida had a private office in the Takadanobaba section of Tokyo. After returning to the company, Kawashima continued to commute to the former headquarters at Yaesu several times a week. He remarked, "I may have the title of advisor, but I'm basically retired: I've been away from Honda for ten years now. I have no idea what's been going on in my absence. I'm like Rip Van Winkle. That said, I've got to tell you that I'm worried about what I'm seeing at Honda these days. It doesn't seem to have the vitality it once did."

Honda's former executives gathered on the second Tuesday of every month in Yaesu. They listened to a report from a current executive while eating lunch. Their focus at the time was on the slump facing the company.

"We've stayed out of your way in Aoyama," remarked one of the former executives. "But that's only because sales have been so stable up to now. We all know that it's been the tradition for us 'advisors' not to do any advising, and I think it was a good tradition. But things are different now. Can we really keep quiet while headquarters is in trouble? Those of us who are fully retired are a different matter, but those of us who are still advisors or consultants have a responsibility at this juncture to give our advice."

The frustrations of the former executives had been building by the day. Kiyoshi Kawashima, the second president of the company and now the supreme advisor, became the target of their finger-pointing.

"I'm no longer a director, but I am the supreme advisor. Whenever I travel abroad, people always ask me just exactly what my job entails. I always tell them that my job is to give advice directly to the president. That's what I'm trying to do, give Kawamoto the best advice I can," Kawashima replied defensively.

The former executives' dissatisfaction reached a boiling point at the beginning of 1994. Honda had released a modified version of its subcompact Today model just after New Year's. It had released a new version of the compact Integra the previous summer, and a completely overhauled Accord the previous fall. In addition, Honda spun off the sister model of the Accord, the Ascot, to create a new line, and unveiled the Rafaga as a sister to the Ascot, thereby supplying all three sales networks with strong contenders. Despite that, Honda's domestic sales were extremely poor.

Honda sold 24,000 cars in February, 11.5 percent off the previous year. As a result, the company fell to seventh place in the domestic market—not only behind Mitsubishi and Mazda, but also behind the subcompact manufacturers Suzuki and Daihatsu as well. For both the current and former executives, it was an abject humiliation.

The former executives still had no idea about the "Great Reversal" that had taken place at the meeting the fall of 1992. The only thing they knew was that Yoshino, an engineer with next to no sales experience, had been placed in charge of domestic sales, with Iwai, famed for his efforts during the "HY War," working under him.

"There's something wrong with Honda's domestic strategy," complained a former executive during one of the Tuesday lunch meetings. "I kind of understand promoting Yoshino, but the other people assigned to domestic sales have horrible reputations. I can't think of another case where dealers complained like this. They're even writing letters directly to us. I suggest replacing the entire staff."

It was an indirect indictment of Kawamoto's decision-making. Several days later, Kawamoto responded just as indirectly with a message politely suggesting that the former executives refrain from commenting on current management practices.

Things came to a head on January 13, 1994. Kawamoto exploded at a dealers' conference held at the New Takanawa Prince Hotel in Shinagawa, Tokyo.

"We're taking a beating in domestic sales. Why? It's because you aren't working hard enough to sell Honda's products. It's you, the dealers, who have put Honda in the predicament it's in. Since becoming president, I've visited dealerships all over Japan and all I hear you do is badmouth us at headquarters. The dealers who aren't doing what they should be doing have four or five complaints. The dealers who are doing their jobs properly only have one complaint at most. From now on, you're each allowed a total of two complaints. Honda is going to provide you with plenty of good automobiles this year, including a touring minivan and an entry-level car. R&D has been working overtime on it and I want all of you to work overtime as well. I'm well aware that none of you has anything good to say about the director of domestic sales. Do me a favor and stop harping on it. There's nobody right now who can take his place. I don't care what you say about him—he's not going anywhere!"

"I guess that means I get to keep my job," Iwai joked from the corner of the stage. "Please, everybody, stop trying to get me replaced and start working *with* me."

The audience wasn't laughing. Utter silence. More than a thousand dealers were in attendance and they were completely dumbfounded. New Year's celebrations were still underway and a few in the audience assumed Kawamoto's outburst was the result of having drunk too much ritual *sake*. He was in fact completely sober.

Kawamoto's office had prepared an inoffensive speech for the conference beforehand. Kawamoto had never had any intention of reading it. Before getting up to talk he smacked the pages of the speech against the side of the table on the podium and left it there. What came out instead was a venting of long pent-up frustrations.

"I admit that we dealers bore some responsibility for Honda's slump," recalls a senior Primo dealer who had joined Honda back when its flagship product had been the 50cc Super Cub motorcycle. "It would have even been all right for him to point that out directly. But putting himself on a pedestal and heaping all the blame on us was really unacceptable. The lack of talent at headquarters was Honda's fault, the natural result of not bringing new people in and giving them the training they needed. The driving force of Honda's growth in the past was the implicit trust between Soichiro-san and Fujisawa-san and the dealers. No matter how tough things got, they never took it out on us. It's true that Soichiro-san once said something harsh to us dealers at a conference, but there was something about the way he said it that made it impossible for us to hold it against him. At the party afterwards, Fujisawa-san wrote the Chinese characters for 'Thriving Business' on a cardboard square and said to us, 'This is what the president was really trying to say.' The result was that we all vowed to work harder. I've been coming to these New Year's dealers' conferences for forty years now, and let me tell you, I've never been this angry at the company's leadership, or this worried about Honda's future."

"When the old man founded Honda," Kawamoto once remarked, "the prevailing view was that Japanese needed to raise their country from the ashes of war by any means necessary. That kind of Japan-centric thinking doesn't work anymore today. We need to stop treating Japan as the center of the world and begin following international rules of business. This is why we have revised our guiding principles and amended our corporate charter."

Kawamoto's statement appeared to signal his intent to further internationalize the company. Three weeks after the dealers' conference, however, Kawamoto did something that signaled quite the opposite.

On January 31, British Aerospace, the parent company of Rover (formerly British Leyland), made a sudden announcement that it would sell its stake in Rover to BMW. Honda owned a 20 percent stake in Rover and had partnered with the company for over fifteen years. Rover's 800 had been based on the Legend, its 600 on the Accord, and the 400 and 200 on the Concert. Honda also provided the 2700cc engines used in the 800, the 2000cc and 2300cc engines for the 600, and the 1600cc engines for the 400 and 200. Rover, for its part, supplied Honda with body panels for the Accord. On the sales front, Honda sold Rover's Discovery SUV in Japan. The two companies were closely intertwined.

Fully aware of the close relationship between Rover and Honda, British Aerospace approached Honda first when it made the decision to sell off all its shares. Honda counter-offered with a request to increase its stake to 47.5 percent of Rover and install Honda director Takashi Matsuda as vice chairman of the company. British Aerospace didn't budge; it wanted to sell all of its shares of Rover. When negotiations collapsed, British Aerospace turned to BMW. It was later reported that BMW offered 800 million pounds for the purchase.

While aggressive, American-style corporate acquisitions can create hard feelings, this case was different: Honda had been offered British Aerospace's stake on a silver platter. It would have been a golden opportunity for Honda to transform itself into a European corporation.

The Rover brand had prestige; not so long before, purchasing it would have been impossible. Had Honda played its cards right, it could have even bargained the price down to 700 million pounds. It would have been a free ticket to becoming a multi-national corporation—something neither Toyota nor Nissan had ever managed—whenever Honda staged a comeback. The Honda Kids let the opportunity slip through their fingers. Part of it was undoubtedly the fact that they didn't have much capital to spare. The rest could well have been because they weren't confident in their ability to manage Rover.

Honda's Japanese sales continued to lag far behind those of Toyota and Nissan. Fujisawa's dream of beating Nissan drifted far out of Honda's reach once again. Foreign markets were another story. Honda successfully managed to establish its reputation in both the motorcycle and automobile industries abroad. The flip side of its foreign success meant that any mistakes abroad could cause irreparable damage. Perhaps this fear is what paralyzed the Honda Kids.

"I suppose we could have bought Rover," explained Kawamoto, "but corporate acquisitions go against the direction that Kiyoshi Kawashima laid out for the company. Besides, not acquiring the company gave us more money to build factories on our own. Buying Rover would have been a double investment. It just didn't have merit. Internationalizing a company is easier said than done."

Honda had already spent some sixty billion yen establishing factories in England. Viewed from that standpoint, Kawamoto's explanation made perfect sense.

But the former executives were sharply divided on the decision.

"This is quite normal for Honda," remarked the first chairman, Hideo Sugiura. He had been involved in Honda's European business ever since the company had entered the partnership with Rover, back when it was British Leyland. "They rejected the offer because they weren't confident enough. Honda is timid when it comes to joint ventures with foreign companies. At first BL asked us to invest capital, but we weren't confident enough to do that so we agreed instead to cooperate on the sales front. This allowed us to enter the European market smoothly. But we should have terminated the relationship the moment BL was privatized.

"Cutting off the relationship now may cause some problems, but that can't be helped. Look, we just aren't ready to manage Rover. You know, the other day, Fiat chairman Umberto Agnelli wryly remarked, 'Honda is a company that takes everything step by step.' I replied, 'Honda doesn't bite off more than it can chew.' I know such a strategy doesn't reap huge rewards, but it also involves a lot less risk."

Former vice president Kihachiro Kawashima, on the other hand, took a different point of view:

"I don't know why they didn't acquire Rover. We're not the type of company that engages in aggressive takeovers. But in this case, they were asking us to buy them. We need to be a little more forward-thinking here. This was the chance of a lifetime. Honda and Rover had such a close relationship and Honda should have done what was necessary to keep it going—especially when the other option was having Rover run into the arms of the competition.

"The old man has died and we're out of the F1. Honda just doesn't have any momentum today. The foreign business is the driving force behind this company today—even if for no other reason, that's why we should have bought Rover, difficulties be damned."

The withdrawal from the F1 and the separation from Rover pushed Honda further out of the international spotlight. The Honda Kids continued to drift aimlessly.

On March 14, just after Honda and Rover severed ties, federal prosecutors indicted thirteen Honda of America executives on suspicion of bribery.

The scandal had come to light a year earlier. The thirteen were American sales managers, including two senior vice presidents. They had taken nearly ten million dollars in cash and gifts from Honda dealers between 1979 and 1992. The trade journal *Automotive News* exposed the scandal. The *New York Times* and others followed up. It all but ruined Honda's clean image in the U.S. and certainly didn't help sales.

Honda was the first Japanese company in America to have so many executives indicted at once. Eight admitted their guilt; the remaining five went to trial. Needless to say, Honda of America fired the thirteen and initiated legal proceedings of its own against them to obtain compensation for the damage caused.

The primary cause for the incident was Honda's distribution system. In the late 1980's, when the yen was particularly strong and Japanese automobiles began to lose their luster on the American market, Toyota and Nissan began discounting their products. Only Honda's cars continued to enjoy strong sales.

The strong demand for Honda cars led dealers to offer bribes to sales managers so that they would receive preference when new inventory came in. Before long, the sales managers began to demand bribes on their own. One of the more ostentatious of them drove a Rolls Royce and built a mansion in the exclusive suburb of Palm Springs.

The question was whether the Japanese executives in charge of Honda of America knew that this was going on. The American news media argued that they *did* know and had simply turned a blind eye. If that were true, the entire organization was complicit in the crime. Honda came under increasing fire.

"The bribes were a result of our inability to keep up with demand and a lack of checks and balances within the organization," sighed Honda of America president Koichi Amemiya. "We learned of the bribes two years ago. We fired the American senior vice presidents, and replaced the eleven sales managers who were involved. Honda had fallen behind in training younger employees to replace senior ones. We were too busy trying to keep up with demand. Honda has a policy of giving young employees a shot, but it takes time to train them. The bottom line is that these bribes were taken on an individual basis. The company as a whole wasn't involved in any way. If anything, it's another victim of the scandal."

Fujisawa and Soichiro had always insisted that a company should "excavate good workers, sniff them out. They're not something that you 'grow.'" When they were active in running the business, Soichiro and Fujisawa had deliberately screamed at the Kids as a form of training. Those who survived the ordeal were elevated up the ranks. This old-fashioned master-and-pupil approach had worked well when Honda was a small and then a medium-sized company. As the company grew larger, however, the lack of a formal training system became a problem.

In time, the shortage of skilled workers became a ubiquitous complaint. Fukuzo Kawahara, the man Fujisawa had looked up to as a mentor, expressed his disappointment about the situation shortly after signing on as a special advisor to the company.

"Human resources starts with hiring new employees and ends with following through with your retirees. Honda doesn't have a clear policy in terms of personnel management. The lack of any training for the top executives is a perfect case in point."

Shinsuke Okubo, who had worked alongside Irimajiri to promote the acceptance of the "Honda Way" in America, had his own opinion on the matter:

"Honda does have training *after the fact* for people who become section or department managers. But when I got to Ohio and was put in charge of personnel, I was greatly troubled to realize that we don't have any real know-how about how to train people at the beginning so that they're actually prepared for promotion."

Honda's rapid growth even after the retirement of the founders compounded the problems facing the company. Honda being relatively young, more than a few of the company's hires were individuals who had worked for other firms. The company was simply growing too quickly for anyone to spare the time to train employees for their current positions, let alone think about supporting them after their retirement. Honda also failed to provide enough training at its subsidiaries.

As a result, only two of them—Showa, a shock absorber manufacturer, and Keihin Seiki Seisakujo, a radiator manufacturer—became strong enough to go public with their stock.

Honda lacked a large network of related companies that would allow it to redistribute its employees. This meant that restructuring the company in the post-bubble years could only be handled by restructuring headquarters itself. Honda unveiled a new salary system for its executives and new rules governing term limits in June of 1994. The stated purpose was to reduce the number of executives and to cut labor costs. Irimajiri had suggested the policies when he was still vice president of Honda. Kawamoto eventually adopted them as a measure for the company's continued survival.

What did Honda need to do to remain Honda? Kawamoto had yet to come up with an answer.

EPILOGUE: LEGACIES INTONED BUT NOT INHERITED

When I was still president, I believed that wealth meant making money, but now that I've left the workplace, I see that friends are the real wealth of a man.

—Soichiro Honda

The most important thing is what you've actually done in life. I'd like my kids, too, to lead lives that they can relate as legacies.

—Takeo Fujisawa

Autumn 1994—it was three years since Soichiro Honda had become absent from the Suzuka stands. Racing genius Ayrton Senna had died in a shocking accident in May during the third race of the year, the Italian GP; the "Prince of the Sonic" was never to be seen at work again. Japan's first F1 driver, Satoru Nakajima, had already put in what turned out to be his last Japanese race back in the Fall 1991 Grand Prix. And, no matter how many F1 aficionados visited the Suzuka Circuit, they could not expect to see a machine running on a Honda engine. Without Soichiro, Senna, and Honda—the triad that had fueled the F1 boom in Japan— the country's GP race seemed headed for a long winter.

The fifteenth race of the 1994 series, the Japan GP was held at the Suzuka Circuit over three days starting on November 4. The qualifying sessions on the 4th and 5th took place under a cloudy sky. For the race on the last day, despite rainy weather, a massive crowd of over 155,000 turned out to fill the stands.

The rain became a downpour soon after the race began. Ukyo Katayama (Tyrrell-Yamaha) and Takachiho Inoue (Larousse-Ford) crashed in their fourth laps, while Hideki Noda (Simtech-Ford) retired due to engine trouble during his first lap.

Although the Japanese drivers had all been eliminated early, the audience was treated to a battle of a race between Michael Schumacher (Benetton-Ford) and Damon Hill (Williams-Renault), who raised pillars of water as they sped by. It was Hill who finally took the checkered flag, which meant that the champion would not be determined until the very last race of the year, the Australian GP, to take place the next weekend. (Schumacher and Hill collided and both retired in that race, giving Schumacher the championship by the razor-thin margin of a single point.) Though winter had been rumored for the Japan GP, it had fared well even without the stars.

"Whatever the cost, Honda should never have withdrawn from the F1," an employee lamented in the stands as he followed the heated race, not bothering to don rain gear despite the downpour. The fact that Honda had done miserably that year in the French "24 Hours of Le Mans" and the American "IndyCar World Series" deepened his agony; Honda had chosen to compete in those races in lieu of the F1. "If he ever found out that our flagship car NSX was no match for the Porsche 911 in the Le Mans, or that we didn't even qualify for the Indy Race let alone win a medal, the Old Man would yell away at the whole staff, his veins bulging." The Honda R&D engineer who had spent years developing F1 engines, and who was now nearing retirement, looked up at the rainy sky and sighed as though he missed nothing more than the angry face of Soichiro.

Immediately prior to the Japan GP that year, the former racecar driver Tetsu Ikuzawa announced that he was entering the F1. As a young man he had been close to Nobuhiko Kawamoto and Shoichiro Irimajiri; he had helped retool Honda's sport car S600 and was a veteran of many races.

"Japanese makers take a commercialist view of the automotive industry. They lack that sense of automotive culture, so no wonder there's been trade friction. I'm making a machine called the *Ikuzawa*, and I'm putting together a team whose core members will be Japanese, including a Japanese driver. This will be F1 racing by and for the Japanese."

Ikuzawa's project was to be financed out of his own pocket. Noting the resilience of the F1 boom, other automakers—without fanfare and without committing funds—started looking into the feasibility of competing in the race. The Formula One was ceasing to be Honda's patented arena.

After the bursting of the bubble, the Japanese economy had entered into a recession that offered no end in sight. At the monthly cabinet meeting on June 10, 1993, Economic Planning Agency Director General Hajime Funada announced that the recession had bottomed out, but the very next month a surge in the value of the yen took the wind out of a possible recovery.

The recession did seem to be bottoming out indeed by the spring of 1994, but, mindful of its earlier false assessment, the EPA was hesitant to announce that the economy was improving. They managed belatedly to do so in September, and issued an official statement in November that "October 1994 marked the nadir after which regressive trends gave way to ascendant trends."

At the same time, because the exchange rate had crossed the $1=100 yen threshold and looked to remain in the 90s, the agency remained on guard, stating that "there are worrisome factors like the exchange rate's direction." The Heisei Recession had dragged on for thirty months since May of 1990 (just before Soichiro's death) and was declared the second longest in Japan's postwar period (the longest came after the second oil shock and lasted thirty-six months). The recession had perhaps bottomed out, but the recovery portended to be lethargic.

The strong yen marred the balance sheet of automobile exports. Meanwhile, in mid-1994, domestic registration of new cars finally began to surpass year-earlier numbers thanks to stronger consumer spending. The problem, for the Japanese automotive industry, was that the developments did not amount to an overall increase in revenue.

Nissan's autumn interim earnings report for the period ending in March 1995, released before that of the other automakers, was so abysmal that people punned, "Draw *hisan* and you get Nissan." (*Hisan* means "misery," and the alternate reading for the character /Ni/ is /hi/). Sales were 12 percent lower than the year-earlier period and the operating loss a record high of 82 billion yen. On October 28, at the Central Works Council, Nissan CEO Yoshifumi Tsuji stated that "losses for the full year may be the worst ever for a listed company" and requested the union for cooperation in rebuilding the firm.

As for Honda's performance for the same period, revenues were 1.1903 trillion yen, a 5.3 percent decline relative to the preceding year due to sagging domestic sales and exports. Although operating profit was 58.5 percent higher than the year-earlier period, the raw profit was only 14.6 billion yen. That is to say, the rate of profit was just 1.2 percent, a figure one might expect from a general trading company that simply buys and sells goods. Considering that the year-earlier profit rate was 0.7 percent, Honda had merely managed to stay in the black, and the company's image as a high-profit outfit was a thing of the past as far as the hard numbers went.

Ironically, the increase in profit had come thanks to the motorbike and general machinery divisions which Honda had considered burdensome and tried to spin away. Pumps—of which five years' worth of inventory had accumulated—sold especially well of all the general-purpose machines, thanks to an unexpected water shortage, and contributed in no small way to the bottom line.

In the fiscal year ending in March 1993, half the profits had come from motorbikes and the other half from automobiles, while in the 1994 accounting, 99 percent of the profits were due to the motorbike and general machinery divisions. The warped profit structure hadn't changed in the interim report. Were it not for the motorbikes and general-purpose machines, Honda would no doubt have gone into the red. It was due to this difference that Honda managed to post a profit while Nissan suffered huge losses.

The urgent issue for automakers was becoming profitable in the domestic market. Any firm that failed to do so had no chance of surviving.

After the economic bubble burst, businesspeople began to tell each other that "quality trumpets quantity" and that "profit trumps market share," but these ideas did not apply to the auto industry. The structure of the auto industry is one where quantity generates profits and a small market share means unprofitability. Quality and quantity can and have to be pursued in tandem. Just as, in politics, the number of seats a party wins is a crucial matter, the number of vehicles a company is selling is a core auto-industry issue.

After the oil shortages of the 70s, Japanese automakers succeeded in winning market shares overseas. With the high-quality, fuel-efficient compact as their weapon, they proceeded unopposed in a sort of no man's land. It was the constant guaranteed hike in *quantity* that permitted the coexistence of as many as eleven domestic carmakers—a situation not seen in other countries. Yet, trade friction and a stronger yen necessitated internationalization, and while Japanese cars lost their unique competitive edge and the business became less profitable for them, the American Big Three of GM, Ford, and Chrysler revived like phoenixes. In foreign markets, the "Japanese car" myth was beginning to gather moss.

As long as exports had been booming, competition for the domestic market had been relatively relaxed. With a share of over 40 percent (calculated on the basis of new-car registration), Toyota was able to turn a profit purely from the domestic market.

It takes close to 50 billion yen to develop a new car, including the molding and the modifications made to the assembly line. It is impossible to recoup that sum without selling in quantity. Nissan, like Toyota, adopts a full-line policy of producing everything from consumer vehicles to large trucks, but on the all-important matter of revenue, Nissan makes less than half of what Toyota does.

In this sense, for Nissan, product development costs are more than twice the burden that they are for Toyota. In order to become profitable in the domestic market without increasing market share, Nissan can do only one of two things: either cut down on the line of products and manufacture more of each line, or spend less on developing a product line.

The reason Suzuki's balance sheet is relatively healthy is that it is the top maker of light cars. The situation is comparable to that of Honda with its dominance in motorbikes.

The good old days when "a quality product will always sell" are over. In these times, consumers choose manufacturers. Moreover, the wave of price slashing is bound to overtake the auto industry as well. In the days of motorization, manufacturers took the lead in everything from development to sales strategy, but today, in the industry's maturity, the initiative has passed to consumers. Unless an automaker supplies the kind of car that consumers want, it cannot secure the quantity of sales that it needs to turn a profit.

Has Honda caught on to this?

For three days beginning on November 14, a week after the 1994 Japan GP had zoomed past, Honda held a three-day conference with its dealers in a meeting room at a Suzuka Circuit restored to quiet. The 14th and 15th were reserved for the Primo stores, and the 16th for the Clio and Verno stores. The managers of the sales outlets seemed at ease. The "Odyssey," Honda's first SUV, had gone on sale in October and was performing better than expected.

Kawamoto, whose near insolence had raised eyebrows at the New Year gathering, was more composed this time around:

"Honda's global strategy has four poles: Japan, North America, Europe, and the developing world. Everything is on track except for Japan. Yet, without a strong foothold in the domestic market, Honda cannot advance. In that sense, conditions are critical for Honda. This summer, in response to the strong yen, we decided to strengthen our North America manufacturing plants. Our exports will decline as a result. Unless we keep domestic production at a million vehicles per year, we'll see a hollowing out of Honda. Unless we sell 800,000 cars per year domestically, including reverse-imports, we will not survive. In the coming three years, nine of our cars will undergo model-changes, and we will also be putting out six new models. I have absolute confidence in the merchandise. Three years from now, at our fiftieth anniversary, I hope to celebrate having achieved domestic sales in the eight hundred thousands with all of you. Thank you very much."

Kawamoto attended the Primo meeting but skipped the Clio and Verno meeting of the 16th and returned to Tokyo. In his place, Vice President Yoshihide Munekuni presented the plan. He was followed by Director of Domestic Sales Riku Iwai, who stuck his hands in his pockets and uttered what sounded like threats more than anything else. At the post-conference party, Iwai accosted the dealers individually to make sure they were with the program.

"We'll do our best," the dealers replied, having no choice as the weaker party, but in truth they still took a harsh view of headquarters.

A dealer with independent capital who hadn't needed any investment from Honda lambasted the company's ways: "In the summer, I heard unofficially about the plan for domestic sales in the 800,000s. I believe I recall Mr. Munekuni saying then, 'If we don't reach the goal, I'll be asking for the resignation of the Domestic Sales Director. Of course, I'd take responsibility too.' But when those folks resign, they receive executive pensions that'll support them for the rest of their lives. For us, "taking responsibility" means letting the store go bankrupt and flying by night. It means social death. If the Honda brass wants to take responsibility, they can first hand us their retirement money and executive pension as a mortgage. There's nothing as irresponsible as this easy promise that they'll take responsibility."

The total number of automobiles (including k-cars) sold in Japan hit an all-time high of 7.78 million in 1990, at the height of the bubble. By 1994, this was down to 6.5 million. With the economic upturn, it was predicted that the number would start rising again and return to 7.3 million by 1997, three years later.

Honda's capacity for domestic sales was 550,000 vehicles per year. In order to meet the goal, then, Honda would have to win three-tenths of the anticipated new demand. Honda's rivals would be competing for the same with survival on their mind too, and no ordinary effort would suffice.

After Irimajiri's resignation, Hiroyuki Yoshino had taken charge of domestic sales over from Munekuni; however, when Yoshino had been made vice president in the personnel shift of June 1994 and transferred back to development, Munekuni had reassumed the charge. Munekuni's return to sales was a sign that the merger between Honda Tech and Fujisawa Trading Co. was indeed on track.

At the Suzuka dealers' conference, the only vehicles on display were the sister-model compacts Inspire and Vigor, which were scheduled to be remodeled the next spring. The new models were presented in a slide show. No explanations were offered on questions that mattered the most to dealers, such as which cars were to be sold through which channels and in what groupings.

"If we were to take the goal seriously, we'd need to hire more salesmen and even open new outlets. But from what I've heard today, there's no way we can make such investments without being prepared to fly by night. To put it in a stark way, HQ seems to think that they've given us dealers state-of-the-art machine guns, but from our point of view we feel like we've been given spears made of bamboo."

Honda's trail and miraculous growth have been intertwined with the post-war growth of the Japanese economy. Honda's internationalization was also that of the Japanese economy. Today, the recession seems to have bottomed out, but the aftermath of the bubble and the unprecedented appreciation of the yen continue to be worrisome. Honda, which did not indulge in money games, may appear not to have swept up by the bubble mentality, but in truth the bubble economy was the premise of excessive investments and a bad sales system. Without knowing it, the Honda kids had been swallowed up by the bubble too.

It was at just such a time that co-founders Soichiro Honda and Takeo Fujisawa passed away one after the other. Even after they withdrew from the front lines of management, they had been a centripetal force, and a company can become quite fragile when it suddenly loses such a force. If its performance didn't improve, Honda itself could become an instance proving that law of transience. Honda was at an important crossroads.

After the collapse of its myths of growth and development, a company that has fallen can still be pulled up by new management. What such restorers have in common is that they remake by first rejecting the methods of their founders and predecessors.

In terms of the Japanese automotive industry, a good example is Toyota, which nearly went bankrupt in the early post-war years. To ensure its continued existence, founder Kiichiro Toyoda took responsibility for the raging labor dispute and relinquished command, leaving the future of the company in the hands of Taizo Ishida, the head clerk, as it were, of the Toyoda family. Rejecting the "compassion" of Kiichiro, who considered all employees to be family, Ishida made "thrift" the cornerstone of his management philosophy. He implemented a management style that single-mindedly eliminated waste on all levels.

At the same time, Toyota Motor Sales President Shotaro Kamiya, who would later be called "the god of sales," preached at the company that "manufacturing and sales are like the wheels of a car," tickling the vanity of the sales staff and inspiring the division.

Ishida taught all he knew about management to Kiichiro's cousin Eiji Toyoda—who had been in charge of the production floor since the founding of the company—grooming him to lead one day. Ishida also made sure to instill his trademark "avarice" in his trusted protégé on the administrative side, Masaya Hanai (later chairman), while on the technological side he urged Taichi Ohno (later vice president) to move quickly to establish the "just in time" system that had been Kiichiro's dream.

Hanai diligently pinched pennies and set the foundation of Toyota's finances, sometimes described today as "The Bank of Toyota." Ohno, for his part, introduced *kanban* placards and perfected the just-in-time system. These were significant developments as motorization proceeded apace in the 1960's.

During that era of motorization, Ishida returned the "scepter" to the Toyoda family when the former banker who was serving as president died suddenly. After that, the leadership post was assumed by three Toyotas in succession—Eiji, Shoichiro, and Tatsuro—and the company was able to maintain its center of gravity.

In the case of Nissan, it was Katsuji Kawamata, who belonged to the same generation of corporate managers as Ishida, who set the toppling firm aright. Kawamata's management maneuver was to establish a solid cooperative relationship with labor, which he accomplished by teaming up with emerging union boss Ichiro Shioji after their alliance in the Nissan Labor Dispute of 1953.

Giving the union the authority of a second personnel department and a *de facto* role in management, Kawamata not only rebuilt Nissan but grew into Toyota's main rival in the Japanese auto industry. At Nissan, management and labor worked closely on honing technology, increasing productivity, and raising quality. It is not an exaggeration to say that the "typically" Japanese corporate structure based on labor-management unity, featuring life-long employment, salary schemes based on seniority, and in-house unions, was invented by Nissan.

After Takashi "Fighting" Ishihara assumed the presidency and abandoned the cooperative track, however, Nissan, perhaps ironically, embarked on a long period of decline. Domestic market share (based on new car registration), which had constantly cleared the 30 percent mark during the Kawamata era, threatened to dip down below 20 percent.

The extravagant overseas projects that were supposed to put Nissan ahead of Toyota in the consolidated basis did not yield fruits even with an appreciated yen. The consolidated accounting for 1992 showed a loss of a hundred billion yen, and the figure doubled the next year. Nissan's failure to develop a concept to replace labor-management cooperation as the new center of gravity gave it the air of a mammoth being hemmed in by glaciers.

Unlike Nissan, Honda saw its profits rise, on the consolidated basis, thanks to a piggy bank called Honda America, but it had none of the momentum of the old days.

Honda alums one and all said, "Honda must hark back to the founders' starting point." In a nutshell, that starting point was the challenger spirit—the dream, the will. With that spirit, the two founders had taken advantage of the chaotic postwar years and created something out of nothing, the beginnings of a "world-renowned" Honda.

The problem with the management approach developed by Soichiro and Fujisawa was that it could be "intoned but not inherited," something that is generally true when it comes to founders.

The pregnant phrase comes from Masatoshi Ito, who grew a downtown Tokyo clothes shop into Ito-Yokado, the largest and most profitable supermarket concern, while also introducing into Japan the 7-Eleven convenience store developed by the American Southland Corporation. "Successful founders are 'insane' in a way. During those foundational years, doing what everyone else does isn't going to make the company grow. It's only because they do something else, in some different way, that they succeed. In the end, the management approach of a company that becomes wildly successful can only be intoned, but not inherited."

If Honda was able to grow further under its second president Kiyoshi Kawashima, it was because the entire company was still shot through with the spirit of the two founders, who remained active even after their retirement. When their vigor started to wane during the presidency of Tadashi Kume, the myth began to lose luster. Under the fourth president Nobuhiko Kawamoto, with the founders dead, the myth collapsed completely.

Trying mightily to remake the founder-less Honda, Kawamoto was no doubt vexed by the existence of business styles that could be "intoned but not inherited." He said: "My hope is for 'Honda to be Honda always.' That means respecting the Old Man's starting point. But we're in an era of confusion. If you didn't keep your eyes on the road, you could skid and roll. The dream and the will to always be Honda has to be stored away in some safe place until we're past this curve, this era of confusion. At the same time, the Honda banner needs to be raised up for the sake of the future, and I'm more acutely aware of that than anyone else. If a company has a clear banner hoisted up and some lucid catchphrase, it'll naturally have a center of gravity. That was all Honda had, in a way. But to get past this era of confusion, yesterday's Honda and today's Honda need to be rejected once. If we try too hard right now to rally around some banner and catchphrase, we might set off in the wrong direction. That's what I fear most."

How to inherit the will of the founder is a concern common to all companies. Matsushita Electric Industrial Co., child of the "god of management" Konosuke Matsushita, holds an annual New Year meeting every tenth of January to announce management policy in order to foster unity within the conglomerate. The meeting is attended not only by Japanese employees but also by the non-Japanese heads of overseas branches.

Chairman Wasserman and CEO Sheinberg of the American entertainment and movie firm MCA, which Matsushita had acquired, used to get on their private jets to attend the conference all the way from Hollywood (Matsushita later sold MCA).

In his final years, Konosuke's weakened legs made him wheelchair-bound, but he always made a point of turning out on that day. After his death, a huge portrait ten feet high and six feet wide took his place up on the stage.

With the "presence" of the founder in the background, the CEO describes the company's strategy to the 3,500 executives gathered from all over the country and abroad, and the scene is relayed live via satellite to factories and sales outlets in every region of Japan. On the stage flanks, seated on steel-pipe chairs, one could expect to see Chairman Masaharu Matsushita and Masayuki Matsushita, members of the founder's family.

Anyone who was interested in hearing the CEO's presentation could not avoid registering the "presence" that smiled cheerfully above him. While the myth of the founder was usually buttressed by numerous publications brought out by the PHP Institute (Peace and Happiness through Prosperity), on this day Konosuke himself came back to life.

Honda conducts no such rituals. The fact that members of Soichiro and Fujisawa's families didn't join Honda is partly why the founders' presence is fading with each passing year unlike at Matsushita.

It isn't only the kids at the company who're continuing their "chartless journeys." The kids who've retired are adrift, too.

Kiyoshi Kawashima let drop his thoughts regarding the trials of "Honda's drifting children": "All prosperous firms are fated to decline one day. Fujisawa-san tried to defy the law of transience, hoping, 'May Honda be eternal regardless.' These days, I feel that just as any human being's life must come to an end, the life of a company isn't without limit. I wonder which stage Honda's at now…"

Perhaps the Honda kid with the coolest take on the relationship between Honda the man and Honda the company is his literal child, Hirotoshi Honda:

"I may be the eldest son of the Honda household, but I am not a Honda man. What my father always sought was freedom. He was the opposite of the sort of man who's a bully at home but a sheep outside it. At home, he didn't want to be restrained by anybody or anything, and he didn't try to put restraints on any of us, either.

"Maybe because I took after my father, I was terribly bad at group activities like at Sports Day or the School Fair. I didn't want to be constricted by any organization. So since I was little, I knew that I didn't want to join Honda. Even after I graduated from college and got married, I lived like some hippie until I finally struck upon *Mugen*, which manufactures engines for F1 and other races. 'Mugen' means 'without limit' and the message is a hopeful start from zero.

"My father loved to read books about historical figures. Of them the one he had only naked contempt for was the warlord Toyotomi Hideyoshi, who sullied his own final years. Perhaps because he wanted above all else to avoid becoming another Hideyoshi, he never once tried to force me or my late younger brother to join Honda.

"At the same time, he was adamantly proud about 'Honda, the company I built.' While he was still alive, he worried about Honda around the clock. But once you're dead, it's all over.

"From what I can see, Honda's employees have become, by now, regular salarymen and nothing more. I don't know what my father would think of that, but I guess a pundit would say these are our times.

"Kawamoto-san became president in very tough times. I sympathize. But he ought to do as he sees fit without worrying about my late father. The results will be known eventually, ten years from now, or if not, fifty. That's if Honda still exists… Of course, I have no idea if it will."

Perhaps Hirotoshi, too, is one of the drifting children of Honda.

AFTERWORD

It was in the spring of 1973, when Honda's co-founders Mr. Soichiro Honda and Mr. Takeo Fujisawa gracefully retired together upon the company's twenty-fifth anniversary, that I first started covering the auto industry for the business daily *Nikkei*. In this book, I have described the circumstances leading up to it in great detail. Back then, I was still unfamiliar with Honda's history, and reporting on whether or not the two really intended to bow out was a terribly difficult assignment.

No matter how much I pestered Mr. Honda, all he'd say was, "How should I know? Go ask the vice president." He was like the proverbial willow in the wind.

I had no choice but to call on Mr. Fujisawa at his home in Roppongi, Tokyo, and I did so constantly. He was always kind enough to invite me into his living room, but on the crucial matter of their intentions he executed deft parries, instead explaining to me the "law of transience" time and again.

Since these were the fervid times of the *showa genroku*, when I interviewed my sources upon the assumption that, while human lives were finite, "companies were forever," what Mr. Fujisawa had to tell me greatly aroused my interest.

After Mr. Honda retired, and for many years until his passing, I had the opportunity of conversing with him at the meetings and subsequent parties held once every other month by the "Honda Foundation," which Mr. Honda had started with his private funds. Both of us usually made an effort not to bring up Honda's internal affairs, yet, now and then, he would buttonhole me with his honest thoughts and complaints.

My aim in writing a book about Honda Co. was to explore the "life span" of companies, through a specific example, and based on Mr. Fujisawa's conception of "the law of transience."

There are numerous books about Honda in Japan, and if the aim were simply to tell a success story about the founders, both the reporting and the writing of it would have been relatively easy. Unfortunately, I found not one of those books to be satisfactory. Instead, I had to take my time, go to the sources, and redo all the reporting to come up with my own picture of the true faces of the founders.

There is no end to anecdotes about the two men, but some of them "reek" of it. A representative example is the conversation they supposedly had about retiring.

Later, when we met, he motioned with his eyes to come close, so I went to Honda's side.

"Not bad."

"Yes, not bad."

"We've done enough."

"You could say that."

Then Honda said, "We were happy."

"You bet I was. I'll say this from the bottom of my heart: Thanks."

"And thanks to you. It's been a good life."

Thus we decided to retire.

Since Mr. Fujisawa himself put down the above exchange as fact in the company bulletin and in his own book, the countless books about Honda repeat it like some standard number.

It is a moving passage provided that the reader does not know the history of the company and of the two men. It has been handed down until this day as a beautiful vignette accompanying the founders' gracious farewell. The truth is that, prior to their retirement, the relationship between the two men was more hostile than respectful, in no way the idyll of the company bulletin. It was perpetually tense.

Before he passed away, Mr. Fujisawa, lifelong scenarist of the Honda myth, commented to me thus about the anecdote: "Didn't you love that one? My masterpiece. If I painted it that way, neither Honda-san nor I would get tarnished. In fact, it would improve the company's image."

Those Honda children who worked directly under the two founders know the truth behind the retirement drama, so they toe the line that they "haven't read any books about the founders." Yet, with the passage of time, anecdotes that "reek" of it can grow legs of their own to bestride a place. All is good while the company is posting profits, but once the founders are gone and the bottom line fails to bear up, episodes of that ilk lose their luster.

Spring 1995
Masaaki Sato

UPDATE: IN THE TROUGHS OF CONSOLIDATION

Our company will not imitate. No matter how difficult, we'll do it our-selves to become number one in Japan, no, in the world.

—Soichiro Honda

One of the roles of a founder is to bequeath the original management script to successors. It's the founder's duty to make sure the vertical line of manage-ment is kept intact as it's handed down.

—Takeo Fujisawa

1

The Japanese edition of *The Honda Myth* was published in the spring of 1995, four years after Soichiro Honda passed away. There is a Japanese expression, "A decade ago is an age ago." It describes the automotive industry perfectly. Ten years ago, the American Big Three of GM, Ford, and Chrysler were witnessing a new spring, having revived like phoenixes thanks to Japanese automakers' self-imposed caps on U.S. exports, while the strong yen was slamming Japanese cars.

Yet, as another saying goes, "Nothing good lasts forever." The Big Three's prosperity was of short duration. In fact, in 1998, Chrysler merged with Daimler-Benz in what was for all purposes an acquisition by the German maker, and its very name changed to "DaimlerChrysler." The Big Three era of the American automotive industry came to an end, ceding to the era of The Two Bigs—General Motors and Ford.

But that era did not last long, either. In the U.S. market, the main battle-ground of international automakers, GM and Ford have suffered painful setbacks in the past few years. Leader GM accounted for 26 percent and Ford for 17.4 per-cent of the share of 2005 sales, failing to put an end to a trend of long-term decline. Japanese cars, taken together, recorded a 32.2 percent share—a steep increase that put the percentage perilously close to the "trade friction ceiling" of one-third. Yet it looks to be a matter of time before the mark is passed.

In the category of passenger vehicles, Japanese models are going particularly strong. As opposed to GM's 22.1 percent and Ford's 11.8 percent, Toyota had 16.3 percent and Honda 10.6 percent of the sales share. Toyota has completely sur-passed Ford, while Honda is close to outpacing Ford. As far as passenger cars go, the share of Japanese manufacturers is 40 percent: two out of five such cars in the U.S. market are Japanese.

Japanese cars roam the West Coast like they "own" the place. Even in De-troit, seat of the Big Three where twenty years ago one rarely spotted a Japanese car, they've become a common sight. Ford's headquarters are in Dearborn, a De-troit suburb. Even there, in the parking lot for visitors in front of the HQ, one comes across automobiles of Japanese make.

Judging just by the numbers, the American giants not only do not retain any trace of their past glory but are actually in a calamitous state. It was the summer of 2005 when rumors first began circulating on Wall Street that GM intended to file for Chapter 11 of the United States Bankruptcy Code. No matter how much GM denied this, rumor assumed the air of reality as Standard & Poor's warned "it wasn't impossible."

GM's debt is $400 billion, four times that of the telecom company World-Com, which shut down in the biggest bankruptcy in history in 2004. If GM files for Chapter 11, it will truly be the worst bankruptcy: not only is the amount of debt larger, but GM's 300,000 employees—a million workers, if affiliate dealers are also considered—will be affected.

Like GM, Ford posted a loss for its automotive operations for 2005 due to rising health-care and legacy costs and the paucity of hit products. Since, at Ford, the founding family owns a ruling 40 percent of stock, declaring bankruptcy isn't really an option. Detroit has been called the "automotive capital" for more than a hundred years now, but the stronghold is on the brink of collapse under the push of Japanese cars. While the American Big Three have decelerated, the Japanese Big Three of Toyota, Nissan, and Honda have only gained momentum.

Toyota's plan for 2006 is to make and sell nine million vehicles worldwide. If the goal is reached, Toyota will likely surpass GM, reigning monarch of the auto industry for three-fourths of a century, to assume the top seat of "the Earth's largest industry."

Nissan, which suffered a severe management crisis in the late 90s after the bursting of the economic bubble, came under the umbrella of French Renault in April 1999 not long before the coming of the new century. This was Nissan. In the early 80s, when there was stiff competition in the global small-car market, it held its own as one of the top five along with GM, Ford, Volkswagen and Toyota; in the global transformation of the industry, it always counted itself among the buyers.

Now, the protagonist of *The Honda Myth*, Soichiro Honda, was born in November 1906. The publication of this U.S. edition coincides with the hundredth anniversary of his birth. Earlier this year, the Honda children, who inherited Soichiro's legacy, managed to deliver a priceless gift to the founder who rests in peace in Fuji Cemetery overlooking the Fuji Speedway.

The global auto industry's year begins in early January with the North American International Auto Show, which takes place in freezing Detroit (also called "the Detroit Show"). This used to be a minor event until the nineties, but when automakers began displaying their choice products and new technologies at the beginning of the year, the show came to rival the ones held in Tokyo and Frankfurt.

The 2006 Detroit Show opened on January 8. Following the opening ceremony, the North American Car of the Year Awards were announced. Honda won in the passenger car and truck categories with the small car Civic and the pickup truck Ridgeline. Naturally, this was the first time any Japanese manufacturer had won both awards in the same year. The Civic was chosen for its fuel efficiency and refreshing design, the Ridgeline for comfort and drive.

A great accomplishment, needless to say, but Honda's history since the loss of its two inimitable founders has not been one of continuous improvement. Rather the opposite is true. Winning two awards was the outcome of a long struggle along a path that presented one obstacle after another to be surmounted.

In terms of leadership, the presidency was handed down from Nobuhiko Kawamoto, who entered the company in 1963, to Hiroyuki Yoshino of the same generation, then to Takeo Fukui, who joined in 1969. That year, 1969, was an unforgettable one for Honda during which it experienced both heaven and hell.

In May 1969, Soichiro was on top of the world. Honda brought to market his prize sport car H1300, which had an air-cooled 1300cc engine. Meanwhile, Honda's first k-car N360 reached a total of 300,000 in cumulative sales. Yet, not a month later, in June, defects were found in the N360 and the founder tumbled from heaven to hell.

Although Soichiro virtually withdrew from the front lines of management after the defective-car incident, his obsession with the air-cooled engine never really abated. To prove that air-cooled engines were superior to water-cooled engines, he brushed away all objection and entered the F1 race. This only resulted in the death of a driver and Soichiro's gradual isolation.

Fukui joined Honda at such a time. The trio of Kawamoto, Yoshino, and Irimajiri, who all joined the company in 1963—the first two became president while the third left Honda after strategic disagreements—comprised the last generation of Honda men that the unstinting founder had tutored.

By Fukui's generation, Soichiro was an exalted figure whose face they all knew but didn't see often. Few got to converse with him. After retiring in the autumn of 1973 together with his partner, Takeo Fujisawa, Soichiro rarely appeared at Honda headquarters. The two founders started to turn into legends even at the Honda company.

Thus the affectionate words "Old Man" or "Pop" will not come from the mouth of Fukui. When Fukui became president, Honda's future was entrusted to a generation that hadn't experienced the founders' management style, to the great-grandchildren of Honda.

So what happened at Honda in the past ten years? Let us turn the clock back by a decade. Having lost the two founders and the moral support that they offered, the Honda children gambled on expanded production to survive in the domestic market. If they won, the Honda myth would be revived; if they lost, they would immediately be swallowed up by the maelstrom of global M&As.

Made up of former members of "Fujisawa Trading Co.," the sales division hoped to "lift domestic sales up to 800,000 cars by 1998, the company's fiftieth anniversary." With Kawamoto's imprimatur, this became the "Get 80" plan. Since the objective was hatched in 1994, when the figure was at 550,000 vehicles per annum, sales had to increase by 250,000 per annum in four years.

Kawamoto made this seemingly reckless plan his own because, he judged, "Honda will become hollowed out unless it maintains domestic production per annum of a million. The prerequisite for this is domestic sales of 800,000."

Most dealers eyed the target coolly as being "unattainable," but unexpected "divine winds" blew in Honda's favor: the SUV (sport utility vehicle) boom. At the outset, however, Honda was actually behind in that category.

The Japanese SUV boom began with off-road four-wheel-drives, but Honda lacked 4WD technology and could only watch, thumb in mouth, as rivals announced brisk sales. Although Honda R&D began work on 4WD, even its able engineers needed time.

Honda therefore arranged to become Chrysler's dealer in Japan and began importing and selling Chrysler's flagship SUV, the Jeep Cherokee. In addition, for the U.S. market, Honda covered by approaching SIA (Subaru-Isuzu Automotive Inc.), a joint operation in Indiana between GM-affiliate Isuzu and Fuji Heavy Industries that manufactured the 4WD SUV Bighorn.

In the fall of 1994, Honda managed to bring to the domestic market a 4WD of its own manufacture, the minivan "Odyssey." It was followed by the CR-V, the Stepwagon, and the SM-X, all sport utility vehicles that became runaway sellers. Getting every single product to be a hit is a tall order and something of a miracle in the auto industry.

The man in charge of developing these models was Yoshino, vice president of Honda and president of Honda R&D. Yoshino was resigned, in a way. "I leave the business side to Kawa-san (President Kawamoto). He and I joined the same year, so I have no chance of becoming president. But as long as I'm the one in charge of development, I'll see to it that we put out better cars than Toyota or Nissan." Telling himself this, he coaxed and cheered on the young engineers at R&D. At the same time, in preparation for his retirement, he had a new house built sixty miles from Tokyo, in the suburbs of Ito, on Izu peninsula, Shizuoku prefecture. He spent weekdays in the metropolis but delved in gardening at his new home over the weekends.

Honda's SUV-powered charge did not turn out to be of short import. Domestic sales for 1995 reached 617,000, up 12.3 percent from the previous year, and rose again by 21.9 percent in 1996 to reach 772,000. Pleased, Kawamoto issued a directive for the target date to be moved up by one year.

A veteran in the Honda sales department familiar with company potential expressed doubts when the directive was announced. "True, Honda is enjoying tail winds right now. But Honda's SUV series is selling well as a kind of oddity. The sales network itself isn't any stronger, and when the winds die down we'll be back where we started. There is no way Mr. Kawamoto doesn't understand this. Knowing it full well, he issued the directive. That suggests to me he's decided to step down as president in 1998 at the fiftieth anniversary. He probably wants a sales achievement to adorn his retirement."

On the consolidated basis, Honda's performance began to improve after hitting a nadir in 1994. For the fiscal year ending in March 1997, it announced net profits of 221.2 billion yen, breaking its own record for the first time in eleven years. Stocks began to appreciate as a result. At the same time, over 1996 and 1997, a core of Honda alumni mounted a transparent attempt to force Kawamoto into retirement.

The stated reason: "He's past sixty, the company's age limit for executives. He should follow in the footsteps of his predecessors." The high-placed alumni's real argument with Kawamoto was that he systematically rejected the corporate culture that they'd fostered together with the two founders: group leadership, rejuvenating the leadership through early retirement, *waigaya*, putting the directors in one room. Their disgruntlement was only compounded by the unilateral management style of the man who proudly characterized himself as "a dictator like Hitler."

Both Soichiro and Fujisawa had been uniquely charismatic in their own ways, and indeed, in their separate domains, they often acted like dictators. Yet, when it came to management, neither permitted the other to just do as he pleased. The essence of Honda management was for the technology chief and the office boss to run as in a three-legged race. Since one of their legs was tied to the other's leg, trying to dash ahead wildly meant the partner would stumble and fall. The system was set up so that neither half could go nuts without risking a collapse in management.

The preceding presidents, Kiyoshi Kawashima and Tadashi Kume, had loyally inherited the founders' management strategy. Although Kawamoto, too, started out by accepting the framework of group leadership, after the sudden resignation of Irimajiri in 1991, he announced a new policy of one-man leadership and proceeded to jettison, one by one, the fruits of Honda's unique corporate culture.

Kawamoto was worried that sticking to old, sleepy tradition was no way to survive an emergency. Yet, one-man rule, taken too far, would result in a reign of terror with yes-men as the only aides. No new talent would be nurtured, either. The alumni, who were familiar with the difficulties of the founding years, feared such an outcome. The gap that slowly started forming between Kawamoto and his retired predecessors became, in the end, too wide to surmount.

One day in fall 1996, Kawamoto dispatched a close aide to the president's guest room at the old company headquarters in Yaesuguchi, Tokyo, where former board members were gathered. When the aide began to give a detailed explanation of the fiftieth-anniversary ceremony to take place two years hence, one of the former alumni, incensed, cut him off and demanded to be heard. "There's no need to seek our approval for something like a memorial ceremony. The president can plan it as he sees fit. What we want to know is who will be president then [i.e., in the company's fiftieth year]."

The aide was about to say, *Mr. Kawamoto, of course*, but swallowed his words, recalling that Soichiro and Fujisawa had retired suddenly before the company's twenty-fifth anniversary.

On the strength of 1995-96 domestic sales, Kawamoto resolved to put all his efforts into reaching the 800,000 mark during his term. For him to leave his mark as president, the objective had to be attained a year before than originally planned. Even with "divine winds" blowing, it would require some rough tactics to meet the goal in just another year.

Faced with this, the old hands in the sales department who, in their younger days, had been taught by a yelling Fujisawa what it meant to sell something, furrowed their brows. Their consensus: "It goes against Mr. Fujisawa's sales philosophy. We could do the impossible and actually reach the goal, but the after-effects wouldn't be worth it."

From his long experience, Fujisawa had categorized four ways of setting sales objectives. The first was to examine the company's merchandise and marketing muscle and to set a manageable goal, taking into consideration the economic environment. This was the "going-with-the-flow target." It lacked flair; and yet, insecure businessmen were prone to set the goal even lower. Such a "foolish target" was the second category.

The correct method was the third: "add a number reflecting maximum effort to the going-with-the-flow target." A problem arose when entrepreneurs attempted to account for slack and jacked up the figure to make reaching the target doubly certain. This inflated figure was the "stupid target," the fourth category.

How did Honda's 1997 plan size up according to this scheme? The going-with-the-flow target would have been 750,000, roughly equal to the previous year. The foolish target would have been 730,000-740,000, significantly less than the previous year. 800,000 was a good number for the third kind of target. It wasn't a mark that couldn't be attained if headquarters and dealers shared a vision and worked together to bring it to fruition.

But there was also a trap involved. The sales personnel would be prone to add a number x to the goal set for them, thinking that "President Kawamoto's honor hinges on reaching the 800,000 mark." The dealers, for the same reason, would be liable to add yet another number y to the sum when they went to the outlets. The final target would balloon to 800,000 + x + y, an untenable "stupid target."

When Fujisawa was still at Honda, he said once, with much feeling, "The danger of the stupid target is that once salespeople begin to think that the hurdle is too high, you tumble down all the way to the foolish target."

For the dealers, 800,000 vehicles was indeed a high goal. Kawamoto tried to cope with this problem with special commissions. Already in March, in early spring, he let it be known that "for each order received on the 30th or 31st, there will be a special commission of 50,000 yen per vehicle." He had dangled carrots even before they had rounded the first corner, and the effect was immediate. In the last two days of March, there were a whopping 21,000 orders.

In the final stretch of November and December, an incredible 50 billion yen was readied for special commission fees to incite dealers to sell at a discount. The money had been diverted from savings procured in currency exchange thanks to a weaker yen.

With such good-looking carrots dangling before them, dealers took one step beyond selling at a discount, earning commissions by registering as sold cars that hadn't even at a discount. In those months, the job of Honda dealers was not selling cars but registering them.

Industry-wide, domestic sales for November was down 20.4 percent from the previous year. Having sold 72,000 vehicles, only Honda saw an increase, up 6.2 percent from the previous year. In December, too, despite the industry-wide dip of 8.1 percent, Honda sold 85,000 vehicles, a 27.3 percent jump. Honda had beaten Nissan for two consecutive months. In the end, the domestic sales total for 1997 (including American-made Honda cars) was 810,000 vehicles.

On December 24, by when the objective was all but certain to be achieved, not only Honda employees but salespeople at the dealers, servicemen, and workers at affiliate factories—a total of 120,000 people—received from Kawamoto a bottle each of red wine and white wine. A gift timed for Christmas Eve.

But overreaching is never without adverse effect. Time becomes necessary to heal the trauma. In the year 1998, when the winds of the SUV boom died down, domestic sales slumped to 690,000 vehicles, 15 percent down from the previous year and less than the total for 1996. Many dealers lost their touch. Salespeople grew accustomed to giving discounts and registering purchases made by their own firm. The result was a lowering of Honda's brand image in the domestic market.

Before Fujisawa retired, he always made sure to drill into new executives the proper stance of management: "Read three steps ahead, speak about the second step ahead, and shine light on the immediate step ahead." Honda's "Get 80" plan merely prioritized the manufacturer's needs. Without reading ahead at all, it tried to shine light on a spot third steps away.

After the bursting of the bubble in Japan, economists lined up to give their diagnosis that it would take "a decade" for the Japanese economy to be fully cured. Yet, ten years later, the aftershock was still felt. Not so much as a way to recovery had been found. To the extent that Honda never indulged in dubious financial games, it may seem to have steered clear of the bubble mentality, but in truth, weaknesses like domestic overinvestment and retention of an inefficient sales regime were premised on the continuation of the bubble economy.

Yet, on the consolidated basis, Honda continued to impress. For the year ending March 1998, net profit reached 260 billion yen. For the year ending March 1999, despite a serious decline in domestic sales, it announced 305 billion yen in net profit, a company best. The strong showing owed to a robust U.S. economy and weaker yen.

Honda's brand image in the American market is, viewed from Japan, unimaginably high, and no discounts are necessary for brisk sales. Used-car prices are also high in the absence of wholesale deals with rental-car companies (fleet sales) that depress used-car prices. Demand cannot be satisfied by the factory in Ohio even when it is operating at full capacity; imports from Japan are required to meet orders. In 1998, sales in the U.S. market for Honda cars reached 1.01 million, surpassing the long hoped-for mark of a million. The ratio of sales was reversed between the domestic market and the U.S. market.

In June 1998, as widely expected, Kawamoto retired as president to become counselor and director, the success of "Get 80" his trophy. It was the tradition at Honda for the next president to be tapped from among the managing directors, but Kawamoto chose as his successor his vice president Yoshino, who'd joined Honda the same year as himself. In October, Honda saw its fiftieth anniversary. While the twenty-fifth anniversary that followed the co-founders' retirement had been held at Suzuka Circuit, the fiftieth took place at "Twin Ring Motegi," an amusement park in Motegi, Ibaragi prefecture near Honda R&D that had cost more than 50 billion yen to build and was touted to be the largest in the world.

Kawamoto's parting souvenir for Honda was the company's return to F1 racing after a hiatus of seven years. Honda had participated only as an engine supplier, but now it was ready to return as a "Honda Works" operation that would design not just the engine but the machine, from the chassis up, and put together its own racing team. F1 racing was becoming more expensive every year, and going it alone meant an annual expenditure of at least 30 billion yen. The new Honda team was slated to debut in 2000.

On March 9, 1998, shortly before retiring as president, Kawamoto summoned a press conference to announce his plan. Only a year and two months later, however, on May 21, 1999, the new president Yoshino announced that the F1 project would be curtailed drastically. Honda would supply the engine but the chassis would be developed in cooperation with the brand-new British team "British American Racing" (BAR). Honda would enter the races as "BAR-Honda."

Yoshino's reason for cutting back on the plan: "Honda's interest is strictly technological. Any further expenditure is undesirable."

Indeed, while an F1 racing engine provided technological feedback for commercial car design, the chassis offered no applications. For that very reason, European manufacturers like Daimler-Benz, BMW, and Renault limited themselves to the role of engine supplier. Yoshino's revision of Kawamoto's plan was substantial.

Meanwhile, Toyota decided to start participating as an "All Toyota" team beginning in 2002, much as Kawamoto had wanted for Honda. Japanese fans were naturally more hopeful about Honda's prospects than Toyota's. In its previous run, Honda had been constructors' champion for six consecutive years, racking up a total of sixty-nine wins.

But F1 racing isn't a world of fun and games. A hiatus of seven years meant that the winning technology of yore was no longer up to speed. If the new team failed to deliver, Honda would be running negative advertisement about itself. Perhaps afraid of this possibility, Yoshino also limited the contract with the British team to three years. It could be renewed, of course, but the precaution left open a way to avoid a showdown with Toyota.

2

Yoshino's decision to downsize Honda's return to F1 racing was not unrelated to developments in the global automotive industry. Honda had survived the past few waves of worldwide transformation in the industry and managed to retain its independence. Yet, the wave that began to surge in the late nineties loomed far taller than previous ones.

During the late eighties, when the Japanese economy was experiencing a bubble, auto insiders around the world spoke heatedly of the "two-and-a-half million club." In the hyper-competitive auto industry, a manufacturer with an annual production of at least 2.5 million cars could conduct R&D for new models on its own and therefore be on the acquiring rather than acquired side in any storm of industry transformation. Of course, the club itself was fictive.

The only companies that satisfied the prerequisite were GM, Ford, Toyota, Nissan, and VW. At 1.7 million cars, Honda fell short. The Honda children wanted at all costs to join this imaginary club. During the tenure of the third president, Kume, it was decided that Honda must fulfill the requirement "early in the nineties," and all manner of efforts were made to meet the goal.

But the bubble burst, and Honda, unable to get on the SUV bandwagon, started to flounder. Simultaneously, differences within the ranks of management led to the departure of Irimajiri, Kume's all-but-certain successor. Honda lost one of the celebrated trio of Thirty-Eighters who'd joined the company in 1963, the thirty-eighth year of the Showa reign.

Yet, the SUV models that Honda brought to the market late in the day managed to become hit products one and all, a rare feat in the auto world. Domestic sales attained the craved level of 800,000 vehicles. In 2001, Honda finally met the requirement for joining the vaunted 2.5 Million Club. Ironically, by that point, a "qualified" member called Nissan had come under the sway of Renault, proving that belonging to the so-called club wasn't much of a guarantee of anything.

At the height of the bubble era, people spoke of the 2.5 Million Club. In the early years of the twenty-first century, they whisper instead of a 4 Million Club. The idea is the same, with the hurdle 1.5 million vehicles higher. It is easy to pay no heed to the club, but as long as the world's most powerful automakers are all aggressively pursuing scale, Honda of the 3.41 million vehicles (for 2005) cannot simply ignore its imaginary existence.

Since the final years of the twentieth century, the "kill or be killed" drama of global transformation in the automotive industry has only been intensifying. In such a turbulent era, management decisions are of paramount importance. At Honda, where the Kids who studied at the knees of co-founders Soichiro and Fujisawa have retired from the front lines, how have the grandchildren and great-grandchildren, who never learned from the masters, been dealing with the worldwide shock waves of change?

It was on May 6, 1998 that a surprise announcement of a major development shook the global automotive industry: Germany's Daimler-Benz and Chrysler, one of the American Big Three, were merging across borders and indeed an ocean. The two firms had opted for a merger rather than a partnership. The curtain had risen on the final act of industry transformation.

When Kawamoto heard this news, he delivered some frank impressions. "It might be effective, mutually complementing, but I wonder if firms from countries with such different lifestyles and cultures can work well together." In addition to that doubt, he said, "The merger is a pure money game and won't contribute to manufacturing and won't serve customers."

Although Honda is indeed an international firm, successive leaders of the company have been surprisingly un-cosmopolitan. Kawamoto failed to digest the movements and intentions below the surface and ended up turning his back on the drive toward consolidation and cooperation among American and European makers.

In marked contrast, the quickest to respond to the trend was Toyota. When Toyota President Hiroshi Okuda heard of the unprecedented mega-merger, his immediate judgment was that "the merger will ignite a new round of transformations that will involve Japanese makers."

Okuda moved quickly. Three months later, in August, he increased Toyota's capital share in Daihatsu from 34.5 percent to 51.2 percent, making it a subsidiary. He also began to increase Toyota's share in Hino, which was suffering from a glut in the large trucks market. By March 2000, Toyota's share in Hino was 33.4 percent, allowing for veto rights and control over management; later the share was raised to 50.1 percent, making the smaller firm a subsidiary accountable on the consolidated basis.

While affiliated automakers were thus subjected to the law of capital for the sake of overall corporate defense, the major parts suppliers were bound into deeper partnerships through strategic personnel transfers. At the stockowners meeting in late June 1999, three vice presidents who had been supportive of Okuda's presidency were assigned to Denso, Aisin Seiki, and Toyota Industries Corporation either as chairman or vice chairman. All three firms were parts suppliers in Toyota's sphere, but until then the automaker had avoided pushing managers on them out of respect for their autonomy.

If takeover bids and M&A through stock exchanges became standard in Japan, too, there was no guarantee Toyota wouldn't be targeted for acquisition, even if its value in stocks surpassed that of GM, Ford, and DaimlerChrysler put together. If not Toyota, then its parts suppliers could be so raided.

Toyota knew, from bitter experience. In the early nineties, at the peak of the bubble era, President Kitaro Watanabe of Azabu Motor Co., once Chrysler's sales outlet in Japan, teamed up with the American "greenmailer" (i.e. takeover artist) Boone Pickens to buy up the stocks of Koito Manufacturing Company, a Toyota-affiliated manufacturer of lighting appliances. Having succeeded, they demanded a say in its management.

At the same time, a group of speculators backed by a heavyweight politician secretly acquired a large share of stocks in Toyota Industries Corporation, a company that was positioned as a head source vis-à-vis Toyota. By the time Toyota found out, the group was the second largest shareholder after Toyota itself. In the Koito affair, Toyota took an uncompromising stance, rebuffing all of Pickens' demands. In the Toyota Industries case, however, it was forced to buy back all the stock at the speculators' asking price. The Toyota employee who negotiated both deals was Okuda, then managing director in charge of accounting.

As for Toyoda Industries, additional stocks were purchased by companies in the Toyota corporate group until, in March 2006, the total share finally exceeded fifty percent.

Domestically, Toyota's posture may be one of defense, but overseas it is on the offense. Production capacity in North America, its main market, will reach 1.88 million vehicles when the seventh plant currently under construction becomes operative. Commissioned output from partner Fuji Heavy Industries pushes the number up to 2 million.

Toyota's overseas strategy doesn't end with North America. In England, in 1992, it built two factories: one produces 200,000 cars and another churns out 120,000 engines annually. In investment terms, Toyota far outstrips Nissan, which ventured into England first. Moreover, timed with currency unification in Europe, Toyota built its second European auto factory in France, and yet another for small cars in Czechoslovakia, under a partnership with the French Peugeot

Citroen. To bolster its brand image in Europe, Toyota also chose to compete in the F1 races beginning in 2002.

As a symbol of its globalization, in October 1999 Toyota listed its stocks in New York and London. Total investment in overseas projects, starting with the partnership with GM, is in excess of a trillion yen. Toyota's international strategy is an aggressive one that belies its former image as the "hick *daimyo* [lord] of the Mikawa *han* [feudal state]." It is thanks to this aggressive posture that Toyota now has its sights on becoming number one.

All this is in stark contrast with Nissan. It was considered a protagonist in the international consolidation drama, but in the end it succumbed to foreign Renault. Nissan's fate is not something Honda can dismiss as that of a stranger. Let us take a detour through the story of Nissan's fall, whose behind-the-scene details prove that even a major automaker can tumble down into the abyss if it makes the wrong decisions.

It wasn't until 1999 that Nissan was surpassed by Honda in total cars manufactured including overseas production; however, it had been outpaced in terms of net profit on the consolidated basis as early as fiscal 1983, when Honda's American auto plant began operating.

Far from shrinking the gap, Nissan lagged farther and farther behind Honda in profit terms. It was not uncommon for Nissan to lose second place to Honda in a given month even in terms of domestic production and sales.

The chairmanship of the Japanese Automobile Manufacturers Association, which used to alternate between Toyota and Nissan, became open to Honda after 2000 and now circulates among the three. The overseas reputation for Japanese automakers gradually settled into a scheme whereby Toyota was number one, Honda was second, and Nissan third.

Upon learning from news reports in March 1999 that Nissan had come under Renault's control, former president Takashi Ishihara, the "Old Fighter" who was by then ninety years old, grimaced and commented in a ruffled tone, "When I was president, Renault was no more than a target for acquisition. I never even dreamed the great Nissan would come under the control of such a company as that. How did it ever happen?"

The cause of Nissan's poor performance was clearly the failure of the haphazard global strategy pushed through when Ishihara was president, but the old fighter was no longer able to comprehend this.

The added misfortune for Nissan was that Yutake Kume, who took over as president to reconstruct the company in the early bubble years, misread the rosy returns of that epoch for the real thing. He delved deeper into the overseas projects inherited from Ishihara, expanded into new fields of business, and poured money into infrastructure at home.

Kume ceded the president's chair to Yoshifumi Tsuji in 1992, the year the bubble burst, leaving to his successor only a negative legacy of excess infrastructure and massive debt. In fiscal 1992, Nissan was in the red on the consolidated basis for the first time since it was listed on the stock exchange in 1949. During his four years as president, Tsuji failed to get the company back into the black even once and was forced to step down.

All the company's hopes were pinned on "The Last Prince of Nissan," Yoshikazu Hanawa. Upon taking the top job in 1996, he declared to all employees, in an attempt to respond to those hopes, "We'll raise our domestic sales share to 25 percent by 2000." Yet, by then, no employee could believe such words. Indeed, in fall 1997, the first year of his presidency, the insolvency of major financiers such as the Hokkaido Takushoku Bank and Yamaichi Securities came to light. Nissan found itself too busy attending to cash flow problems to be able to present a fundamental restructuring plan.

It could be argued that Nissan's business crisis was twofold. First, while a company must aim to invest in areas that will yield profit in the near term, Nissan poured too much money into those that would only perhaps return the investment, and in the far term. A typical example: venturing into England. The other cause would be the sentiment, which Nissan employees from the top on down could not get rid of, that "Nissan simply couldn't go under," that it was an unsinkable ship, and that the law of the survival of the fittest did not concern them. If the bubble economy of the late eighties had never occurred, the unfeasibility of Nissan's overseas projects would have surfaced earlier. Brisk steps may have been taken to put the company back on track. But that is all in hindsight.

As banks became more and more reluctant to lend after the Japanese financial crisis of fall 1997, Nissan's operations suffered further. Debts on which interest had to be paid rose to 2.5 trillion yen, four trillion on the consolidated basis. When stock prices were high, convertible loans could be turned into stock, but with the stock market in the doldrums, conversion proceeded at a snail's pace and the deadline for their repayment as debt loomed. Borrowing more money to pay up meant getting saddled with more debt and interest. To begin with, financial institutions including Nissan's main bank Nippon Kogyo Ginko (The Industrial Bank of Japan) were balking at making new loans. Upon becoming president, Hanawa called for Nissan to rebuild itself, but at this point he had to face the fact that it was a matter of time before operations would stall due to an insufficiency of funds.

He girded himself: "Nissan cannot rebuild itself. To survive we need foreign capital to come to our aid."

When Hanawa came to this conclusion, Nissan took the first step toward becoming the hottest item in the ongoing global transformation of the auto industry. Hanawa had three possible partners in mind, the former Daimler-Benz, Ford, and Renault.

Renault had contacted Nissan in spring 1997 as though it had foreseen Hanawa's decision. The French automaker desired a partnership with a Japanese counterpart. Bearing a letter from Chairman Louis Schweitzer, Vice President Georges Douin visited Toyota, Honda, Nissan, and Mitsubishi to offer a partnership deal, only to be summarily rebuffed by all but Nissan.

Hanawa had considered the Schweitzer proposal for good reason. Renault, having restructured itself in a short period of time, was seeing its sales rise. After the meeting, Hanawa visited France to inspect Renault's factories and witnessed rational cost-cutting à la Renault. Hanawa's impression was that "Nissan has a lot to learn from Renault." Negotiations, centered on an operational-technological partnership, proceeded at a clip.

Why, in turn, did Renault desire a partnership with a Japanese firm? Though privatized in 1991, Renault is a semi-public manufacturer in which the French government owns a 44 percent stake and makes its will felt. The chairman since 1992, Schweitzer—great-nephew of the philanthropist of the same name known for his medical missionary activities in Africa, and also cousin to the late philosopher Jean-Paul Sartre—took a cool view of the state of Renault from the very beginning: "Every year the figures are worse for Renault's passenger car division. It cannot survive on its own." He moved for a merger with Volvo, but in 1993 the plan crumbled due to opposition from the Swedish automaker.

Immediately afterwards, in order to push through major layoffs, he headhunted Carlos Ghosn from Michelin, the major tire manufacturer. Ghosn promptly put his own formidable business acumen to use and ordered a massive restructuring that included shutting down a factory in Belgium. His measures turned Renault around within a short period of time.

The weak point of Renault's recovery was that it had prioritized layoffs and not new R&D. Renault was inferior in the technological area compared to rival carmakers. It also took a back seat in international competition and remained in a tight spot in terms of long-run survival. Yet, a partnership with any European automaker with which it had long competed was not exactly a palatable thought. And so Renault had turned to the Far East.

In September 1997, half a year after Douin visited Japan and the partnership talks began, Hanawa visited Germany to attend the Frankfurt Motor Show, where, as if lying in wait, Daimler-Benz approached him about the possibility of direct talks with Chairman Jürgen Schrempp. At the impromptu summit, Daimler proposed to acquire Nissan Diesel Motor Co., a Nissan subsidiary that manufactured large trucks. That Daimler was interested in a branch that was deeply in the red was, of course, good news for Nissan.

Daimler wanted Nissan Diesel for two reasons. First, the German company would be solidifying its position as the world leader in trucks. Second, they would be acquiring a bridgehead into the Chinese market, the lynchpin of its Asia strategy.

An agreement was reached in spring 1998. Nissan would sell all its shares in the subsidiary to Daimler. The contract was finished right before the "Golden Week" holidays in early May, and both sides began scheduling for its signing. Then, on May 6, a merger between Daimler-Benz and Chrysler was announced.

The sale of Nissan Diesel was shelved at the last moment. During the entire period, Nissan's bottom line had only deteriorated; its stocks were being sold heavily in the stock market. Unless Nissan announced some countermeasures, delisting was a distinct possibility.

In August, another letter arrived from Schweitzer: "In order to secure our partnership, let us hold shares in each other's firms." Hanawa flew to Paris right away and declined the offer. Nissan's financial situation was too dire; it did not have the monetary luxury to be investing in Renault.

According to calculations that Hanawa asked Nissan's accounting department to make, the sum needed for Nissan's turnaround was 800 billion yen. At that point, the subject of negotiations with Renault shifted from an operational partnership to a capital tie-up in which Renault would invest in Nissan. The conditions that Hanawa brought to the table were fourfold: 1) the company (Nissan) would continue to exist; 2) jobs would be protected; 3) any layoffs would be overseen by Nissan; 4) the CEO would come from Nissan. If any firm was ready to accept these four conditions and whip up 800 billion yen, Hanawa really did not care which.

Renault's reply came in the new year, 1999: "The maximum sum we have available is 400 billion yen." This meant that the negotiations could not go forward.

Hanawa held a hidden ball. In November 1998, just when Renault was scrambling to procure funds to invest in Nissan, Hanawa visited the Daimler-Chrysler headquarters to urge them to sign on the sale of Nissan Diesel. Chairman Schrempp said, "It's not just Nissan Diesel that our firm is interested in. We're considering investing in Nissan itself." Daimler would indeed be an ideal partner: unlike Renault, it had ample funds, and the vanity of Nissan's proud employees would be soothed. Nissan and Daimler entered into negotiations about particulars.

As if his return to Japan had been awaited, now Ford Vice Chairman Wayne Booker visited Hanawa at Nissan's headquarters. Since 1988, Nissan and Ford had been close, joint-developing in the SUV area. At their meeting, Hanawa dropped the hint that Nissan was ready to accept an influx of foreign capital. Ten days later, to put capital tie-up negotiations on the table, Hanawa flew to Detroit to see Booker at Ford's headquarters.

"Ford has a 33.4 percent stake in Mazda, but it's not always easy with such an awkward percentage. When it comes to stock, you need to own a majority…" Booker's offhand remark made Hanawa reluctant to enumerate Nissan's conditions for a capital tie-up. *If Ford acquires a majority share in Nissan, being an American company with its businesslike ways, it will definitely demand the post of CEO. But that's not the problem. They'll pursue total rationalization, including American-style layoffs, and probably sell off all idle properties. It'll amount to nothing less than the disintegration of Nissan. The only possible tie-up partner is Daimler.*

Thus, Hanawa began to have second thoughts regarding a tie-up with Ford. When Jacques Nasser, lined up to be Ford's next president and CEO, received the report of these talks from Booker, however, he had a somewhat different approach.

Ford's ambition was to surpass GM and to retake the position of number one in terms of all the available indicators, from production and sales quantity to revenue and profit. The former champion constantly challenged GM for this purpose; yet, while Ford could indeed compete in profit terms, it could only narrow the gap in terms of sheer scale. But with an impending global shakeup, the company had a good shot at becoming the world's top maker again. Nasser saw a Nissan deal as an ideal opportunity to close the gap with GM.

The problem was that the founding Ford family might object to the damage that taking in Nissan would deal to the balance sheet. Nasser's judgment, nonetheless, was that the Ford ambition couldn't be realized without a tie-up with Nissan. Nasser summoned a special team within Ford to find out everything they could about Nissan's financial status.

Thus, three companies offered themselves as candidates for a tie-up with Nissan, but negotiations didn't proceed as Hanawa might have hoped. The intentions of securities firms, which influenced the negotiations from behind the scenes, complicated the process. Goldman Sachs teamed with Daimler, Merrill Lynch with Renault—they took the stage when the talk turned to assets and stock prices. In response, Nissan signed a consulting agreement with Salomon Smith Barney of Citigroup. A furious information war began under the surface, drawing in the world's mass media. Strategic leaks came not so much from the automakers themselves but from the securities companies and accounting firms.

The maneuvers around Nissan speeded up as the new year arrived. On January 21, Daimler's Schrempp and Robert Eaton, former chairman of Chrysler, the two top decision-makers of the recently merged company, visited Japan with the purpose of promoting the new corporation. After arriving at Narita International Airport, they headed straight to Nissan HQ in Ginza, Tokyo to hold talks with Hanawa.

Despite the enthusiasm Daimler had shown earlier, it now seemed sluggish. The almost feverish passion that Schrempp had shown only two months ago could no longer be felt. At the press conference the next day, the two CEOs merely stated, "We've confirmed that negotiations will continue about matters including possible investment in Nissan itself."

Just three days before DaimlerChrysler's leaders visited Japan, Renault went out of its way to issue a comment that resembled a pickoff play against its rivals: the French automaker was "looking into the possibility of a capital tie-up with Asian partners, including Nissan."

If negotiations with Daimler came to an unfruitful end, Nissan's restructuring schedule would need to be revised. While a tie-up with Renault had its allure—everything other than the sum itself had been agreed to—if the French firm were really able to provide only half of the needed money, Nissan would not be able to push through significant layoffs. Rebuilding the company would take that much longer.

In order to urge Daimler on, Hanawa flew to see its chairman on February 26. He could not but be disappointed by Schrempp's reply: "Our new company is still in the process of harmonizing. May we delay further talks about a tie-up with Nissan?"

Hanawa made only one counter-demand: "Please come to a conclusion by the end of March."

The next day, with heavy feet, Hanawa made a stop in Paris to report the status of Nissan's negotiations with Daimler and his intention to continue them. Schweitzer's expression was clouded as he appealed, "I fully understand that Nissan needs a massive amount of money in order to conduct layoffs. But it is impossible for Renault, given its size, to supply the sum that you seek. Yet, without a partnership with Nissan, Renault will one day cease to be."

It was Hanawa's turn to look depressed. In order to enter into formal talks for a tie-up with Renault, he needed first to sign a "freeze" contract that would bar Nissan from negotiating with other automakers until talks with Renault reached a conclusion.

Schweitzer was persistent about Hanawa signing the freeze contract, but Hanawa could not do so until Daimler came to a conclusion. Hanawa made a counterproposal to Schweitzer, too: "Please wait until the end of March." Because Renault was offering only half the required money, it had no choice but to accept his request.

Nissan had approximately forty days left. A tie-up with Daimler now blinking yellow, Hanawa realized that if he took no action, Renault would be the only candidate left. As soon as he arrived back in Japan, he sent to Nasser, who had just assumed Ford's presidency, a letter saying, "There's a matter I'd like to discuss immediately."

Ford had acquired Volvo's passenger car division for $6.5 billion on January 28. Perhaps Nasser was beginning to feel at ease as top man and replied right away that he would gladly meet Hanawa in Detroit.

The summit between Nissan and Ford was scheduled for February 26. Hanawa arrived in Detroit the day before accompanied only by an interpreter. Vice Chairman Booker also attended the meeting. Hanawa described the state of affairs at Nissan without concealing anything. He also reported that business had gotten worse than feared at Nissan Diesel.

Perhaps sympathizing with Hanawa's sincerity as he gave the unadorned picture of Nissan's torments, Nasser offered a helping hand in the matter of trucks. "We sold our large-truck division to Daimler a few years ago and retreated from that category. But if Nissan is in trouble, I can get you through to the head of Volvo, a Ford ally."

The meeting proceeded in good spirits. Hanawa seized his chance to sound out Nasser: "I'm not really concerned about the percentage. If Ford desires, I don't mind if it exceeds 51 percent..."

Hearing this, Nasser shot back, "Please, not that. Obtaining a majority share in Nissan means making it a subsidiary and shouldering massive debts, with interest. Right now, Ford can't afford to hurt its balance sheet."

Nasser's stance was the opposite of Vice Chairman Booker's. This not only put Hanawa at ease, but also impressed upon him strongly that the world's top automakers had a no-nonsense attitude about the coming wave of consolidations. Hanawa himself held a similar view of the state of affairs.

Nasser finally said, "I understand your needs. Before we enter into formal talks, I'd like a *proposal* from Nissan."

Talks are often waylaid by tricks of language that aren't intended by the involved parties. In the talks between Ford and Nissan, the word "proposal" became the stumbling block. As far as Nasser was concerned, a formal letter from Hanawa requesting a tie-up, simply stating that "Nissan wishes to enter into talks with Ford," would have been helpful in persuading the chairman, Bill Ford, to consider a tie-up that he wasn't bullish about. Nasser expressed this desire with the word "proposal."

Hanawa, meanwhile, understood the word "proposal" literally to mean "a detailed restructuring plan." As soon as he returned to Japan, he dispatched Vice

President Tadahiro Shirai to Detroit. Shirai presented to Booker a business reform plan that had been adopted the previous May. As a result of the two parties having interpreted the word "proposal" differently, more than ten days had been wasted.

On March 8, ten days after his meeting with Hanawa, Nasser visited Sweden to attend an emergency stockholders meeting summoned by Volvo. When journalists popped the question, he freely answered: "I'll gladly listen to M&A offers from any automaker."

It was a message intended for Hanawa. The Nissan president's scenario of switching over to Ford if talks with Daimler didn't go well seemed to be working. The end came sooner than expected.

On the 9th, a day after Volvo's stockholders meeting, Schrempp contacted Hanawa: "Tomorrow afternoon, I'm arriving in Tokyo. I'll tell you what the business is when we meet."

As scheduled, Schrempp arrived in his private jet on the 10th, Japan time, in the afternoon. From Narita airport, he headed straight to Nissan headquarters in the Ginza district. He met Hanawa, stated that Daimler was discontinuing negotiations for investing in Nissan Diesel as well as Nissan, and left Tokyo. He spent only five hours in Japan that day.

Since there wasn't a formal press conference, media people who got wind of this flocked to Hanawa's home in Shinagawa, Tokyo to find out the exact circumstances. Hanawa, who returned home around when Schrempp was arriving at Narita airport, held an impromptu conference in front of his home under the cold night sky. It lasted about a quarter of an hour, and he confirmed that negotiations with Daimler had collapsed. With Ford rather than Renault in mind, he also purported that Nissan would be "exploring a partnership with other foreign firms." The media, which wasn't aware that negotiations with Ford had commenced under the surface, reported with one voice in the next day's papers that the Daimler deal had fallen through and that Renault was the only remaining negotiation partner.

Just as Schrempp boarded his plane, Ford's Asia-Pacific marketing director arrived secretly in Japan and checked into a hotel in Tokyo. His assignment, as Booker's agent, was to explore possibilities of a partnership or joint venture with Asian automakers. The immediate task of his trip was to meet Nissan the following day to schedule partnership negotiations including talks between the firms' heads.

What Hanawa feared most from the collapse of negotiations with Daimler was a demotion in long-term bond ranking. At the end of the year, American Moody's had announced that it was considering lowering Nissan's ranking from the lowest for investment-worthy firms, aa3, to Ba1. Since Ba1 indicated that a firm wasn't an appropriate venue for investment, Nissan would no longer be able to issue debentures if the demotion did occur.

Moody's usually arrived at a conclusion within a month, but in this case it had been following Nissan's negotiations with Daimler closely and reserving its judgment. Hanawa's hope had been that the negotiations' success would stay Moody's hand, allowing Nissan to issue commercial paper (CP) in the U.S. market.

Those hopes had been dashed. Yet, because the media was thankfully making a big deal out of negotiations with Renault, Hanawa gingerly expected Moody's not to go through with the demotion until those talks came to a conclusion.

When he read next evening's *Moody's News*, that hope was cruelly crushed, too. The headline read that Moody's was demoting Nissan Motor Co.'s unsecured debenture to Ba1 given a total of 9.5 billion yen in dollar debt.

MITI was also carefully following Nissan's dizzying moves. Analyzing the day-to-day developments, Minister Kaoru Yosano judged that "bankruptcy was a distinct possibility" and directed the automotive section to look into the effects of such an eventuality.

When Hanawa went to his office the next day on the 12th, he was informed of the results of the meeting with Ford on the previous day. He also received a message from Nasser: "I'm making an unannounced visit to Japan in April. Let's meet directly and decide the framework of the partnership."

Hanawa felt compelled. *Nissan hasn't much time left. If Mr. Nasser is willing, then I can fly to Detroit tomorrow to hold those talks.*

As if he'd read Hanawa's wavering mind, Renault's Schweitzer contacted him that very afternoon. "We've figured out a way to increase our proposed investment. The exact figure will be decided on the 16th at Renault's board meeting. But in order for the board to deliberate upon the matter, there is a condition and that is a freeze contract with Nissan. We would like it to be signed on Saturday the 13th and would appreciate it if you could come to Paris."

News of the termination of negotiations between Nissan and Daimler had reached Renault before noon on the 10th (Paris time). Schweitzer had summoned Senior Vice President Carlos Ghosn immediately to tell him: "Nissan and Daimler failed to arrive at a deal. Just as we expected. This is good news for our firm. To strike up a partnership with Nissan, the minimum condition for us is to provide the monetary sum they've demanded. I'll speak to the government to do something about the money. If the partnership negotiations are fruitful, I'll be asking you to head the reconstruction efforts. You'll be going to Japan, of course."

Unaware of Renault's intentions, Hanawa was completely torn between prioritizing negotiations with Ford and getting on board with Renault's renewed proposal. The night passed without his coming to a decision. The next day, to be on the safe side, he had a ticket secured for "NH205 (All Nippon Airways)," which would be leaving Narita for Paris at 11:50 a.m. on the 13th. He finally arrived at a conclusion just as the date changed from the 12th to the 13th.

It will be Renault. It's not impossible for us to enter into negotiations with Ford, but unless the hands of the clock come to a standstill, it won't be possible to conclude a deal within the month. Nissan directly employs forty thousand people. If we include the parts suppliers, the dealers and their families, we are talking about easily more than five hundred thousand people. While I am president, they will not be cast out onto the streets. The world might say it's an alliance of the weak, but the only way for Nissan to survive is to form a partnership with Renault.

Although it was past midnight, as soon as he came to this decision he made a phone call to Director of Planning Hiroshi Suzuki requesting that he accompany Hanawa to Paris. The president also gave the following instructions to Vice President for Finance Tadahiro Shirai: "Ford's Asia-Pacific marketing director is leaving today. Could you find out what his departure time is and go to Narita? I want you to convey a message to him, as accurately as possible."

The message was a bitter pill for Hanawa himself to swallow: "I seriously considered a partnership with Ford. Unfortunately, because negotiations with Daimler foundered earlier than expected, the situation has changed drastically, including Moody's demotion of our debentures. I have no choice but to prioritize negotiations with Renault. I would like Nissan and Ford to continue as allies nonetheless."

The time difference between Japan and France is eight hours. The flight NH205 carrying Hanawa completed a journey of twelve hours and forty minutes to land at Charles de Gaulle Airport at 4:30 p.m. on the same day. When Hanawa arrived, perhaps thanks to arrangements Renault had made, he was exempted from the usual entry procedures and was escorted by police through a VIP exit. There was a hotel in the airport where the conference was to take place.

Hanawa was being treated like a guest of state. Schweitzer greeted him with a large smile on his face. Keeping the greetings brief, Hanawa looked through the documents Renault had prepared, including the freeze contract. Confirming that there were no mistakes, he signed them without ado. It was the moment when Nissan's fate and Renault's destiny became one.

I've been able to detail the consolidation maneuvers surrounding Nissan because, during the whole process, I served as Mr. Hanawa's confidant, in a personal capacity. Following the ins and outs of the process amounted to getting glimpses of the harshness of the global automotive industry. Once Nissan lost the means to restructure itself, it was nothing more than a doe being devoured by beasts of prey.

3

For many years, Toyota and Nissan were thought of as the Japanese auto industry's east and west *yokozunas*—sumo champs. In the intense international competition over the small-car market that took place in the 1980s, both companies were "winners," joining GM, Ford, and VW on the side of the transformers or consolidators of the industry. For auto insiders who knew the glorious history of Nissan, it was unthinkable for the *yokozuna* of the west, as it were, to succumb to foreign capital. To a French maker, no less—this was also a loss of face for the behemoths, GM and Ford, who reigned in Detroit, capital of the auto industry. The fact that Nissan had come under overseas control gave the impression that the global auto industry was entering an era of turmoil.

Such an era is being ushered in because the situation is changing for the car as such in the twenty-first century. Next-generation technology, including fuel-battery cars and Intelligent Transportation Systems (ITS), requires vast sums of capital. Even the new Big Three of GM, Ford, and Toyota can't hope for further development without cooperation with rival makers. Automakers are embarking upon a new era where, regardless of size, solving crucial issues in the realm of resources, environment, and safety is the ticket for survival.

Given this situation, not even Honda, proud of going it alone, can well afford to turn its back on the waves of consolidation sweeping over the world. No matter how often the "Honda kids" assert that "our engine technology is the best in the world," if other firms don't adopt it, there is no recognition for the fact in the global market. Moreover, as I will later touch upon in greater detail, the design of Honda engines makes it hard for other manufacturers to incorporate them into their own cars.

Honda started out as a manufacturer of motorcycles, but its successes as an automaker began with the low-pollution CVCC engine technology that it developed all on its own. When Toyota, Ford, and other major automakers of the world adopted the technology, Honda's reputation was bolstered in the industry.

True to the teaching of the founders, the Honda children hewed to a track of self-reliance in terms of both capital and technology. But in the new era, with waves of transformation rising across the world, it has become more difficult for Honda, despite its fierce spirit of independence, to shun co-development.

Yoshino, who became Honda's fifth president in June 1998, shortly after Daimler-Benz and Chrysler announced their surprise merger, proposed the catch-phrase "Small is smart." What he meant by this: "If our company continues to bring to market cars that consumers truly want, we can develop steadily, even at a small scale. No matter how high the waves of transformation, we can avoid being swallowed up." Honda's own "Monroe Doctrine," as it were.

His thinking began to shift about a year after he became president. He slowly began to understand that, while the company could perhaps go it alone in terms of capital, it was going to be difficult to keep up with technological advances all on its own. Given Honda's pride, however, even a partnership limited to the technological domain had to be with a firm with top engineering credentials.

To repeat, Honda began to make its presence felt in the U.S. market with the small-car Civic, which debuted in 1972 with a CVCC engine. It won the hearts of female customers—in particular, working women. Exports to the U.S. sky-rocketed, and the luxury car Accord that followed in the Civic's wake recorded dynamite sales with the help of yuppies. Before long, Honda was a company that the Big Three couldn't ignore.

Though Japan's defeat in World War II meant the country had been nearly razed to the ground, one unique company after another rose from those ashes. Most representative of that crop of firms are the technology-driven Honda and Sony. By now, the "HONDA" and "SONY" brands are renowned in all corners of the world.

While the two companies have in common the fact that they made leaps and bounds through their successes in the U.S. market, they accomplished this in very different ways. In the rapidly advancing world of electronics, Sony built up and refined its brand by bringing to market a continuous stream of products— the transistor radio, the portable tape recorder, the Trinitron color TV, the home video deck, the 8mm video, the Walkman, and so on—that no one had thought of and into which it crammed its cutting-edge technology. Sony grew by painting freely on the blank canvas of electronics. The pictures they painted garnered the applause of American customers.

Meanwhile, Honda was faced with the dark canvas that was the mature world of autos. Where no new paint stroke seemed possible, Honda drew the refreshing picture of a family car that the Big Three hadn't ever imagined, punching a small hole in their triopoly. It was in this respect that Sony and Honda were quite unalike.

In the beginning, the Big Three ignored Honda's merely quirky—or so they seemed—cars. As Honda established itself in the U.S. market, however, their cars became uncanny—and gradually, the uncanny became appealing.

In 1973, when Ford's first capital tie-up negotiations with Mazda ended in failure, it was Honda to whom they turned. CEO Lee Iacocca (later Chrysler chairman) personally visited Japan to advance the talks. Unable to break through the strong resistance Honda put up regarding a capital tie-up, he finally had to compromise and go home with a sales partnership, which itself dissolved in due course when the sales of Ford cars in the Japanese market failed to meet expectations.

In the case of GM, too, Chairman Roger Smith explored a partnership with Honda in 1981, when trade friction over autos was intense, but had to give up in the face of strong objections from partner Isuzu's president, Toshio Okamoto. GM pursued Suzuki instead.

In the early eighties, at the outset of the international small-car wars, the minimum annual output necessary for survival was considered to be 2.5 million vehicles. Twenty years later, the number was said to be four million. Honda's leaders knew that there was no factual basis for this imaginary club, but it was also true that they couldn't simply ignore it. The man who grasped Honda's precarious situation before anyone else, Jacques Nasser, became president and CEO of Ford in January 1999.

Shortly after Nissan and Renault announced a capital tie-up, Nasser made a secret visit to Japan. It was mid-April. Originally, the visit had been scheduled for a summit meeting with Nissan, but Nasser had chosen not to cancel his trip. When he was still at Ford Australia, he made frequent visits to Japan and was known at Ford for being a Japan hand. Once he joined the ranks of management at Detroit HQ, however, he was too busy to make frequent trips and was less in tune with developments in the Japanese auto industry. Nasser wanted to survey the newest trends of the Japanese market and auto industry with his own eyes. He also had another, secret purpose. It was to send a signal to Honda President Yoshino regarding a possible partnership.

When he arrived in Japan, to ensure that his message would be conveyed accurately, Nasser spoke to a friend of Yoshino's, choosing his words carefully. "Honda is a wonderful company. Selling Honda cars in the American market is appropriate in a free-market economy. If Honda's productive activities are going to be centered in the U.S., Honda's top man must be much more active in American society. As far as I know, Mr. Yoshino hasn't made any impression in the U.S. since becoming president."

What Nasser said was true. Although Yoshino had visited the U.S. a few times since becoming president, the only places he stopped by was the Ohio factory and the headquarters of American Honda in Torrance, an L.A. suburb. Nasser was pointing out that if Honda really wanted to earn American citizenship as a company, its top man needed to be more active in American society and win its recognition. In sending this message, Nasser wasn't lodging a complaint but rather courting Yoshino. The Ford CEO had come to Japan to make sure his message wouldn't be misconstrued.

In the form of responding to demands by the U.S. government and the UAW (United Auto Workers), Honda became the first Japanese company to build a car factory in America. Once production was on track, Shoichiro Irimajiri, appointed head of the Ohio plant, designated one American after another to important posts, making a conscious effort to localize operations. Honda also joined the Alliance of Automobile Manufacturers. After Irimajiri returned to Japan, however, he clashed with then-president Kawamoto over management issues and left the company, putting an end to the drive to localize leadership. Now, a quarter-century after Honda began producing cars on U.S. soil, model changes can be implemented simultaneously across the Pacific Ocean, but the top man for American manufactures is still being sent over from Japan.

Yoshino had followed the path not of the pitcher, always visible there in the middle of the field, but of the catcher. Though he was tough, he wasn't the born performer that he needed to be to vie for the spotlight against the Big Three. Yet, there was no one at Honda who could take Yoshino's place.

Four months after Nasser's visit to Japan, Yoshino was invited as guest speaker to the University of Michigan's Automotive Management Briefing Seminars, sponsored by Professor David Cole—son of former GM chairman Edward Cole and leading auto industry analyst. Yoshino appeared at Traverse City, a summer vacation spot about two hundred miles from Detroit, on August 3, the night before his lecture. At the empty hotel where the seminar was to be held, he rehearsed his speech relentlessly. The next day he delivered his keynote lecture—"Honda's DNA: Making Small Smart"—in smooth English to an audience of more than a thousand that included businessmen, analysts, and academics.

In the lecture, Yoshino emphasized that a company's success depends not on its scale but on how speedily and accurately it responds to market needs. To do this, it was necessary, indeed, to utilize the merits of size, such as international reach and technological prowess, but also to maintain the characteristics of a small company, such as speed, flexibility, and efficiency. He concluded that for this reason, Honda aimed to keep to its own unique path.

The lecture explained in detail the catchphrase, "Small is smart," that Yoshino had presented upon becoming president. The audience seemed moved by the talk, and Yoshino was surrounded by many members of the press when he descended from the podium. Press interest focused on a single point: "Mr. Yoshino, that was a great talk, but can Honda really stay independent?"

Regardless of Yoshino's philosophy, U.S. media had been dressing Honda up as the protagonist of the next round of transformations. As evidence, at Ford's shareholders meeting in May, there had been a plain question as to "when Ford was going to acquire Honda." Chairman Clay Ford, who presided, responded ambiguously that Ford Motor engaged in various activities in the global market. As for Nasser, he just smiled and answered, "Only God knows."

At the press conference following the shareholders meeting, Nasser gave his own views regarding the transformation of the automotive industry. "I don't have a transparent picture, but certain trends seem to be in place. In the twenty-first century, only those companies that have massive funds, the technology, including for environmental issues, and the ability to supply the world market, can survive. The movement toward consolidation, via mergers and capital tie-ups, will only pick up speed, and ten years from now we'll have, on the one hand, giant groups that sell five million to ten million vehicles per year, and, on the other hand, niche makers that sell a million or two. There will be five or six giant groups, and just two or three niche makers. But car brands will be supervised by the giant groups, so the number of automakers won't decrease all that much. That will be a good thing for customers, too."

If Nasser's predictions had any merit, then Honda's size was too much in between. Annual production in North America was 960,000 cars. Honda also produced cars locally in England, Brazil, China, and Thailand, and planned for a total overseas output of 1.27 million cars for 1999. Domestic output was 1.24 million cars, for the first time putting overseas operations ahead in terms of production.

In the tenth month of his presidency, Yoshino made a decision that would make or break Honda. In April 1999, Honda's third North American plant in Alabama, after the ones in Ohio and Canada, would begin construction; at the same time, one of the production lines at the Suzuka factory would be terminated, dropping domestic production capacity from 1.4 million to 1.25 million vehicles per annum.

The type of car to be produced by the new Alabama plant would be the SUV, for which demand was rising explosively in the U.S. market. $400 million would be invested in a 120,000 vehicles-per-annum production facility. For the year 2002, North American output would be 1.08 million vehicles.

At any rate, the center of gravity of production was shifting from Japan to North America and overseas. Yoshino's predecessor Kawamoto had been apprehensive about building a third North American plant and had avoided coming to a decision during his term; Yoshino, however, made it promptly. Honda crossed the Rubicon.

Familiar with the Ford leaders' remarks and the latest developments at Honda, the press had swarmed Yoshino, but the man they wanted to hear from wore a taut expression. Shaking his right hand in front of his face to fend off questions, he left for the airport without answering them, claiming that he needed to visit the plot in Alabama where the new plant was going to be constructed. Yoshino had maintained his silence for a reason.

On August 1, two days before he appeared in Traverse City, Yoshino arrived at Detroit's Metro Airport after having inspected the Ohio factory. Dearborn, fifteen minutes by car from the airport, is Ford town, and the company's world HQ stands right in the center. Previously, the top of the bluish building had featured the "Ford" commercial logo. When Nasser became president he instructed the sign to be changed to the official company name, "Ford Motor Company."

The twelfth, uppermost floor is reserved for executive officers. President and CEO Jacques Nasser's office was located down the left from the elevator, through the right-hand door at the end of the hallway. Across the hall on the left was the office of Chairman Clay Ford.

Nasser's office was simple, geared to be functional. There was a long, oval table at which a dozen-plus people could be seated; the chairs were upholstered in leather but were made of metal and castered. The office space, behind the table, was a step higher and featured a slender desk several feet long reminiscent of a kitchen counter. Three television sets were encased in the wall up near the ceiling. They showed footage from CNN and other news programs with the sound off. In the right-hand corner was a coffee maker. After asking what suited his guest, Nasser would pour the coffee himself.

It was a presidential office that smacked of a TV studio, but Nasser preferred to work at the table for receiving guests, which was eight inches or so lower than the kitchen-like bureau. When he was alone in his office, he sat at the oval table and worked using his Sony Vaio. If he swung around in the metallic chair, he could easily see the TV screens.

Perhaps thanks to their common Lebanese heritage, Nissan's COO Carlos Ghosn (currently CEO of Nissan and Renault) was invited to come freely into his office. Because Nissan's schedule board often said, "[Date], Detroit, Visit to Ford," there were rumors that Ghosn was planning to join Ford sometime in the future.

Arriving at Detroit's newly renovated Metro Airport, Yoshino headed alone into Ford's HQ, leaving his companions at the Hotel Ritz-Carlton right across the street. The summit was happening at Nasser's request.

There had been furious debate within Honda before the meeting was agreed to. A majority within management asserted that they should turn down Ford's request, given Honda's traditional policy of self-reliance in capital terms as well as technology. Having begun to sense the limit of Honda's Monroe doctrine, however, Yoshino listened to the debate but concluded, "I don't even know what Ford is going to propose. At least I should meet them."

Across the long table the two men, both short of stature, exchanged their opinions about worldwide developments in the auto industry. When the timing was right, Nasser made the following proposal: "We've discussed various matters today. We seem to agree that keeping up with the daily technological progress in autos is too heavy a burden for any one company to bear. So let me suggest this. I've been told Ford and Honda had a sales partnership in Japan years ago. We aren't strangers. Let's engage in a technology exchange this time. If there's something that we can work on together, we can step up to a technological partnership."

Yoshino hesitated for a moment but made a snap judgment. *In terms of applied technology, we're ahead of the Big Three by now, but when it comes to basic technology, Detroit is still superior. A proposal from Ford for a technology exchange—that may be exactly what we need.*

"Okay," he answered. "In terms of technology, both sides have strengths and weaknesses. A technology exchange is something that we desire."

Though limited to the technological area, Nasser had high hopes for an alliance with Honda. As soon as September, he organized a negotiation team headed by the vice president in charge of technology. Honda was informed of the roster. Yet, the negotiation team that Honda put together was composed mainly of mid-career engineers from Honda R&D. It was clear that there could be no meaningful talks between the head of technology, on the one hand, and front-line technicians on the other.

Ford, which saw a technology exchange as the first step toward a more wide-ranging partnership, requested Honda to put in charge of its negotiation team the president of Honda R&D, Managing Director Takeo Fukui (currently Honda president). Both sides were now on an equal footing, and the schedule was set for concrete talks to take place after the Tokyo Motor Show, which would be held in a Tokyo suburb in late October.

Detroit, Tokyo, Paris, Frankfurt, Geneva… The motor shows, held in major cities, are not only the place where new cars and technologies are displayed but a diplomatic venue for the auto world. The negotiations that birthed Daimler-Chrysler got their start when Daimler-Benz Chairman Schrempp visited Detroit in 1998 to attend the North American Motor Show and spoke to Chrysler Chairman Eaton at a hotel near the convention center. The talks bore fruit in a mere four months.

The Tokyo Motor Show of Fall 1999 was attended by the Big Three's top men and by the heads of other major automakers from around the world. In view of the coming round of industry consolidation, they actively engaged in automotive diplomacy behind the scenes. On the day of the preview, when industry insiders and press are treated to the latest before the general public, the "heads of state" mill around to inspect the booths of their rivals rather than their own. Industry etiquette requires saying hello to counterparts who are acquaintances.

God sometimes likes to play tricks. GM Chairman Jack Smith, accompanied by President Richard Wagoner, arrived in Japan the day before the preview and immediately headed to Honda HQ in Aoyama, Tokyo, to pay a visit to Yoshino. There had been a channel between the two companies. As managing director, the preceding president Kawamoto had been friends with GM's chairman Lloyd Reuss, flying a company helicopter on his own to Honda's research facility in Tochigi prefecture to show the chairman around. Since then, the two companies did not enjoy such ties, but GM badly desired contact with Honda. It was Isuzu Chairman Kazuhira Seki who arranged the meeting at the request of GM. Honda Chairman Yoshihide Munekuni had worked at Isuzu Hiroshima prior to joining Honda and knew Seki personally. The same connection had been responsible for the deal where Honda supplied Accords and Isuzu in turn provided Honda with the off-road SUV Bighorn. But the Honda-GM summit, which Seki and Munekuni's friendship helped bring about, appeared only as a sort of ritual to Yoshino himself.

"Honda will be partaking in a technology exchange with Ford." When Yoshino let this drop without much thought, Smith was shaken. What might begin as a mere technology exchange could, with growing trust, develop into a full partnership or even a capital tie-up.

Smith thought quickly on his feet. *If Honda joins the Ford corner, it will make things harder for GM. But if Honda comes to us, we can pull away from Ford in the world market.* Smith left Aoyama, coolly concealing that he was upset. As soon as he returned to Detroit, however, he went on the offensive. He ordered the head of the Tech Center, depository of GM technology, to come up with a technological partnership proposal that would be more beneficial to Honda than to GM. The center responded with a plan to procure engines for 4WDs from Honda.

While it is not widely known, Honda is the world's largest manufacturer of engines—a total of 10 million units per annum for auto, motorbike and general use. It had a good reputation in particular for its low-pollution, high-efficiency engines for automobiles. The Achilles' heel, however, was that Honda engines rotated in the opposite direction from that of rival makers, who understandably thought twice before adopting Honda engines.

Adopting Honda engines meant not just reversing the positions of the engine and the transmission but changing the transmission's structure. Acquiring the transmissions along with the engines solved this problem but signified a jump in cost. While Honda was free to boast that it was "the world's top engine maker," it needed to flip the rotation to match the universal standard if it wanted to get serious about its engine business.

Realizing this at last, Honda issued a policy of gradually flipping the rotation, beginning with its two-passenger sport car S2000, which debuted in spring 1999. The V-6 cylinder engines mounted on the SUVs produced at the Alabama factory naturally conform to the standard rotation.

Just prior to the conclusion of the Tokyo Motor Show, GM informed Honda of its intention to purchase mass amounts of this engine. The move kicked off a technology exchange between the two companies. In December, it was decided that GM would not just be unilaterally purchasing Honda engines but cooperating broadly with the Japanese maker in the engine area. Honda agreed to adopt for the next-generation Civics and Accords produced in England the direct-injection diesel engines that Isuzu (a GM group company) was manufacturing at its Poland factory.

In the spring of 2000, a cooperative agreement was also concluded in the field of Intelligent Transportation Systems (ITS). Specifically, the luxury cars sold via Honda's high-end channel Acura would carry receptors for the "OnStar" information service that GM was implementing nationwide. Employing GPS satellite technology, OnStar reported the location of a vehicle automatically in case of emergencies such as accidents, in addition to providing information to drivers via satellite radio. In May, co-investment and co-development talks began for "XM Satellite Radio," a digital radio system in which GM already owned a stake. Honda also announced its participation in "trade exchange," GM's internet-based parts supplying system.

When Nasser learned about the partnership from the papers, he was indeed angered by Yoshino's actions, which seemed outlandish given their tacit agreement. Yet he never inveighed against Yoshino at Ford. Partnership negotiations between Honda and Ford ended up a mirage with no solid result other than the formation of teams.

It was Charlie Wilson, GM President from 1941, during World War II, to 1953 and later Secretary of Defense in the Eisenhower administration, who trumpeted that what is good for GM is good for the country—"*L'état, c'est GM*" as it were. In those days, GM's domestic sales share was well beyond 50 percent and industry insiders around the world were simply in awe of the company. Those were the days when the concern of GM presidents was that its share was too high, possibly high enough to prompt the government to force a break-up. Half a century later, GM's share has plummeted to nearly half what it was at its peak, and there are few traces of its former glory.

When Nasser became president, it was Ford that had the greater momentum. Yet, many Japanese automakers still harbored illusions stemming from "the world's largest automaker" epithet. Though there was no capital tie-up, in the technology field Honda was in danger of inadvertently becoming a pawn in an old power's grand global strategy.

Honda was not alone in cherishing illusions about GM. In the period between autumn 1998, when DaimlerChrysler was formed, to the end of that year, GM spent 90 billion yen to raise its share in affiliate Isuzu from 35 percent to 49 percent, and in Suzuki from 5.3 percent to 10 percent. Both Japanese companies accepted additional investment with the calculation that deepening their ties with GM secured their future.

From GM's point of view, the best way to halt its downward slide was to place mid-sized automakers under its control and thereby bolster its clout as a group. GM expansionism knew no end. In Europe, after concluding a deal with Sweden's Saab, GM acquired a 20 percent stake in the auto division of Fiat, the largest conglomerate in Italy. Fiat was handed 5 percent of GM stock and went so far as to accept GM's right to propose a hike in share up to and including outright acquisition. Not even GM had the intention of doing the last, but it had insisted on the clause as a pick-off play against DaimlerChrysler.

Indeed, DaimlerChrysler had been the first to make a bid for Fiat. In fall 1999, Chairman Schrempp secretly proposed a unification of management with Fiat. The former Daimler-Benz company's weak point was small cars. It was in order to solve this problem that Schrempp had gone ahead with the Chrysler merger. The American company's know-how, however, wasn't what he had hoped for.

For a period, he considered going after Nissan, which was undergoing a crisis, but the company's poor financial status zapped his enthusiasm. Fiat, on the other hand, specialized in small cars and had a good reputation not just as a manufacturer but for its designs. Fiat's cars would not compete with Daimler's large trucks, luxury cars, and SUVs but rather supplement its line.

Fiat had started out late in the race for globalization and its performance was poor throughout the nineties. Sans a partnership its survival was widely considered improbable. It seemed like an ideal partnership but, contrary to Schrempp's plan, Fiat rejected Daimler's proposal offhand. Honorary Chairman Giovanni Agnelli, who bore the hopes of the founding family, frowned upon a merger with a European company, a German one in particular. While Italy and

Germany were allies during World War II, there was also a vague hostility between the two populations, much the way relatives do not always fancy one another. Regardless of what Daimler and Fiat's respective shares would be, unifying
the management signified a takeover of Fiat by Daimler. For Agnelli, who had
long reigned in the auto industry, it meant nothing other than humiliation.

The largest in Italy though it may be, the sad fact was that Fiat was only
mid-sized in global terms. It could not survive alone. If it did not move quickly,
it was bound to be swallowed up by the rough waves of international consolidation. The partner that Fiat chose was GM. Fiat's leaders flew to Detroit just before
Christmas in 1999 to meet GM Chairman Jack Smith. Direct negotiations led to
a capital tie-up on the spot.

"Dumped" by Fiat, the partner Daimler chose instead was Japan's Mitsubishi Motors. Mitsubishi was a uniquely versatile automaker in that it operated
in the medium, small, and subcompact categories for passenger cars. Conveniently for Daimler, it also produced the whole spectrum from large to minivan
in the truck department as well.

A step ahead of GM, its chief rival Ford had acquired brands like Sweden's
Volvo and England's Jaguar and Land Rover, counting a total of eight brands including Mazda and Ford itself. Fuji Heavy Industries, which had left the Nissan
fold, was a company that GM and Ford competed under the surface to absorb.
Vice Chairman Booker took direct charge for Ford and courted aggressively
through Fuji's major shareholders, Nissan and Nippon Kogyo Bank (currently
Mizuho Corporate Bank). But when Fuji chose as its consultant A. T. Kearney, a
firm with ties to GM, it virtually settled on coming under the GM umbrella. Like
Suzuki and Fiat, Fuji chose, as the Japanese saying goes, "to lean on the large tree
if lean it must," bidding for a secure future.

In Korea, Daewoo, a former GM affiliate that had dissolved the partnership,
suffered a financial crisis and went virtually bankrupt. In an open international
bid in 2005, GM acquired management rights to the company, which was renamed GM Daewoo.

GM thus placed three of Japan's eleven full-fledged automakers within its
sphere of influence. It wasn't before long that the haphazard expansionism ran
aground.

4

Corporate partnerships are a lot like relationships between men and women.
GM's international strategy of the seventies and eighties resulted in tie-ups with
two Japanese makers, the Lil' (= small-scale) Miss Charming (= specialized) Isuzu
and Suzuki. Into this scene came the imposing beauty Toyota. In a real beauty
contest (= business performance), Isuzu and Suzuki were no match, and so GM
and Toyota started dating like true adults.

GM and Toyota found themselves quite attracted to each other. The gist of
a partnership was agreed upon from the get-go: co-production at GM's former Fremont plant in the suburbs of San Francisco. The joint venture promised to be

mutually beneficial. Toyota, which had been coy about moving to the U.S., found a way to reduce the risk of doing so. For its part GM was able to observe to its heart's content the famous "Toyota Production System."

It was a partnership between the world's first and third most prominent players, over the head of number-two Ford. The affair made the automotive industry titter and tremble. Some argued, severely, that the joint venture infringed on U.S. Antitrust Law, but the guardian of that law, the Federal Trade Commission, ruled that "GM and Toyota's limited partnership serves American consumer interests." FTC Chairman Miller's position was clear: the possibility of the joint venture curtailing competition was superceded by the benefits that the American people would derive from having competitive small cars produced locally.

On December 12, 1984, eight months after the FTC's official approval, the first, quality confirmation vehicle came off the line at the joint company called NUMMI (New United Motor Manufacturing). The cooperative venture was finally on track, two years and ten months after GM Chairman Roger Smith and Toyota President Eiji Toyoda (currently supreme advisor) had met secretly in New York.

With this began Toyota and GM's honeymoon. It looked as if the alliance of the strong might usher in a period of stability for the global automotive industry.

More than ten years later, Jack Smith, who had headed GM's negotiation team, became chairman. When Toyota executives visit Detroit, they make a point of dropping by GM headquarters to affirm and deepen ties with the leader of GM. In turn, when the GM top man visits Japan, perhaps for the Tokyo Motor Show, the founding family's Shoichiro Toyoda (president, later chairman, currently director and honorary chairman) invites him over to Toyota's guesthouse "Kioi Ryo," in Tokyo, or to his home in Nagoya.

Still, the two companies are basically rivals. Antitrust caps limit the partnership's scope. What ought, more than anything else, to worry Toyota, whose presence in the U.S. market only makes itself felt the more every year, is the rekindling of trade frictions.

When U.S.-Japan trade friction over autos broke out in 1980, Toyota's reluctance to move production to the U.S. caused the issue to turn political, resulting in self-imposed limits on car exports. Trade friction over autos can occur even if the U.S. is not experiencing a recession because there is a root cause in the widening trade imbalance.

Today, Toyota's fearsome rival is neither GM nor Ford but a reheating of those trade tensions. If another conflagration occurs and develops, again, into a political hot-button issue, it is Toyota that will be affected most deeply. The company needs to make sure the Big Three will not participate in "Japan-car bashing."

The alliance with GM is already more than twenty years old. The content of the partnership, too, has developed, from co-production at NUMMI to joint development of a small car, to be manufactured by NUMMI and imported and sold in Japan as the "Voltz." Furthermore, in 1999, the two companies agreed to conduct joint research into advanced environment-oriented technologies.

Since the partnership between Toyota and GM is mutually beneficial, even if any trade friction arises again it is highly unlikely that GM, champion of free trade, will engage in Japan-car bashing. The same cannot be said of Ford, which assumes the vanguard in criticizing Japanese cars every time economic tensions flare up. If Toyota manages to establish friendly ties with Ford as well as GM, the damage will be minimized in the event of renewed trade tensions.

It was Toyota Chairman Hiroshi Okuda, chairman of the Japanese Automobile Manufacturers Association (also former chairman of the Japanese Federation of Economic Organizations) who was most mindful of this need. Okuda quickly found out that GM was courting Honda since the 1998 Tokyo Motor Show. But he had no fear whatsoever that GM's fling with Honda might diminish the American company's twenty-year-old embrace with Toyota. Urgent, however, was the need to establish friendly ties with Ford.

Okuda's management characteristic is the speed with which he acts on his decisions. At 9 a.m. on July 17, 2000, he was in the CEO's office at Ford headquarters overlooking TPC Michigan where the U.S. pro-golf "Ford Senior Players Championship" had been held until just the day before. Full of commotion ten hours ago, the golf course was returned to its normal quiet. Okuda had boarded his private jet at Komaki Airport, in the suburbs of Nagoya City, in the afternoon on the 16th, Japan time, arriving in Detroit at 7 p.m. on the same day because of the time difference. Given the next day's schedule, the original hotel reservation had been made at the Ritz-Carlton, just across the highway from Ford HQ, but at the last minute the place of stay had been switched to the Townsend Hotel in the suburbs. There had been too much human traffic at the Ritz thanks to preparations for a championship celebration for Ray Floyd, winner of the Ford competition. Okuda would have been too conspicuous at the Ritz because of his robust—i.e., un-Japanese—physique, a memento of his *judo* wrestling days.

Jacques Nasser, who had gotten his start at Ford Australia, and Hiroshi Okuda had known each other since the early eighties, when the Toyota man served as Director for Asia and Australia at the former Toyota Motor Sales. Now, however, they were the top honchos of powerhouses that lorded over the global auto industry; it wasn't quite to rehash their friendship that they were meeting at Ford HQ. They had a mountain load of issues to discuss. The summit lasted well over the initially planned sixty minutes and was wide-ranging—technology exchange, overseas cooperation in Southeast Asia and beyond, alliances between affiliates, finances. The two men promised to "keep in touch" before parting that day.

In the talks with Nissan President Hanawa and Honda President Yoshino, it was Nasser who dominated. But during his Australia days, Nasser had been made to swallow a bitter pill by Okuda, and the trauma of that experience put him on the defensive in the summit with Toyota. The bitter pill in question was the management merger between Toyota Australia and GM Holden in the mid-eighties, prompted by a change in automotive policy on the part of the Australian government and shortly after the unification of Toyota's manufacturing and sales operations (a further policy change by the Australian government eventually led to the dissolution of the merger). Okuda, appointed director at the freshly unified Toyota, was the one who pushed through the international deal. At that time, Nasser assumed that Toyota and GM's partnership was limited to co-production in the United States, so the local merger of his rivals over his head, a dashing maneuver on Okuda's part, stunned him completely.

The past aside, it was more than desirable for Nasser that Okuda had come all the way to Detroit to see him. A Japanese acquaintance who had the inside track on Toyota had given him an important piece of advice before the meeting: "You ought to think about why the busiest economic figure in Japan is making a three-day, one-night trip to visit Ford headquarters right at this time. If the summit meeting ends up as 'just saying hello,' there'll never be another chance for Ford and Toyota to establish an alliance."

When the talks were over, Okuda exited Nasser's office and crossed the hall to the office of Chairman Clay Ford to whom he paid his regards. Then he left Ford HQ and headed straight to the airport to fly back to Japan.

Meanwhile, Nasser called over Vice Chairman Booker, who'd been his boss in Australia, to say the following: "Today's meeting made me see that Ford has as much to gain as Toyota from our getting closer. Right now Mazda gets its k-cars from Suzuki but we'll switch that to Daihatsu of the Toyota Group. Inform Mazda President Mark Fields right away. It will be the partnership's first step. Please come up with a proposal for the mid- and long-term. As soon as it's ready, I'll go to Japan and submit it to Okuda-san personally."

At Ford, there is an annual strategy conference for each geographical bloc. The Asia bloc strategy conference was to be held in Manila that year. Nasser was anticipating a visit to Japan on the way back.

Booker contacted Mazda right away to tell them to get a quote from Daihatsu for k-cars. Daihatsu, which wasn't even aware that the leaders of Toyota and Ford had met, was taken by surprise. Worried that Mazda was just trying to obtain a bargaining chip against Suzuki, Daihatsu offered a marked-up figure. As a result, according to Daihatsu's quote, the cost was going to be 35,000 yen higher per vehicle. In the face of that significant a difference, Mark Fields could not possibly change his supplier. Toyota hadn't imagined that Ford would move so quickly.

Then the misfortune came, suddenly. Shortly after Ford organized a team for fashioning a cooperative framework with Toyota, Ford was beset by a scandal over suspicions that defective tires had been supplied by Bridgestone's U.S. subsidiary Bridgestone Firestone (BFS). Nasser had to cancel his summer vacation to deal with the issue around the clock, and the strategy conference in Manila was postponed.

A rift began to form between Nasser and Chairman Clay Ford beginning with the handling of this scandal. The alliance with Toyota that Nasser had in mind was a full partnership, and the chairman demurred. Clay Ford was worried that Ford Motor, plagued with numerous problems, might not benefit from an alliance with Toyota, which was performing at a stellar level.

Despite Clay Ford's reservations, Nasser's enthusiasm about teaming with Toyota showed no signs of abating. The postponed Manila conference was rescheduled for October, and Nasser arranged to drop by Japan on his way back.

Having received the schedule for Nasser's visit, Okuda started picking the members for Toyota's side. The men he chose were President Fujio Cho, Vice President for Overseas Operations Kosuke Yamamoto, and Tadaaki Jagawa, the chairman's trusted colonel.

The meeting that began after 4 p.m. on November 2 at a hotel in Nagoya had come about thanks to Okuda and Nasser's personal connection, but it was also a formal occasion between two companies. In preparation for the summit to be held in July, both sides brought up issues that seemed amenable to joint efforts.

Ford was most interested in the hybrid technology that Toyota was already using in its products, combining electric motors with gasoline engines. Both companies agreed to have the most likely proposals pursued by their respective administrative personnel.

When the stuffy meeting came to a close, a dinner hosted by Toyota began in the same hotel's banquet hall. Eiji Toyoda's eldest son Kanshiro Toyota, president (currently chairman) of Aisin Seiki, had also been invited. Okuda knew Ford had shown interest in Aisin's transmissions.

The Tokyo Motor Show (mainly featuring business-use cars) had been going on since October 31 in Makuhari Messe in suburban Tokyo, but Nasser, showing no interest, left hastily after dinner and headed to Komaki Airport to take his personal jet back to Detroit.

Negotiations began. In order to maintain the alliance with GM even after entering into a partnership with Ford, Okuda, accompanied by Jagawa, visited Detroit's GM headquarters in December to see Chairman Jack Smith. The purpose was to inform him of the partnership negotiations with Ford.

In addition to Smith, CEO Rick Wagoner awaited them in the chairman's office at GM's HQ building in the downtown Renaissance Center district of Detroit. The scheduled thirty minutes passed by in a flash and the meeting ended up lasting an hour and a half. GM did not say a word about entering into a partnership with Honda. Nevertheless, at the end of the meeting, Okuda announced without fanfare that Toyota was beginning partnership talks with Ford. He left the Renaissance Center without verifying GM's reaction.

In September 2001, almost a year after the partnership negotiations between Toyota and Ford had commenced, Okuda ran into Nasser at the Frankfurt Motor Show. It was the day of the preview, open only to industry and press. Accompanied by Toyota's rep, Okuda was passing by Ford's booth when he saw Nasser. The two men started talking, still on their feet, conscious of their surroundings. A Nasser aide noticed and unobtrusively guided them toward Ford's guest room behind the booth. The two leaders conversed for half an hour—about what, has not been leaked, but it is easy to imagine that they were concerned that the negotiations might go astray now that Nasser's standing within Ford was rapidly worsening.

A month later, towards the end of October, Nasser was at the Tokyo Motor Show in Japan, having arrived shortly after the end of the preview. As if to take advantage of Nasser's absence, back in Detroit, Clay Ford staged a corporate coup d'état. Summarily firing Nasser—mishandling the BFS defective-tire crisis was given as the reason—Ford installed himself as the new CEO while also remaining chairman. Only a family-owned company could pull off such a personnel decision.

With the chief promoter of negotiations with Toyota out of the picture and the chairman, newly empowered as CEO, none-too-eager about a partnership, the alliance seemed dead in the womb. The entire automotive industry thought so. Indeed, after Nasser's dismissal, no new information came from either Ford or Toyota.

Two years later, in late October 2003, two men sipped drinks at a guesthouse in the suburb of Gotemba City, Shizuoka, where they had a great view of Mt. Fuji. The VIP facility belonged to Yazaki Corporation, the major auto parts maker known for its automotive wire harness. The men were Chairman Okuda of Toyota and, in the seat of honor, Nick Scheele, Ford's president and COO.

The auto industry had assumed that the Ford-Toyota talks had died out after Nasser's fall from grace. Not so—negotiations had continued under the surface. A full partnership, however, had been nixed by the chairman. The talks had been limited to hybrid technology.

Okuda and Scheele were sipping at their drinks, gazing at Mt. Fuji as the sun set, because Ford had decided to adopt Toyota's hybrid technology. The partnership was announced half a year later in the spring of 2004. In all likelihood, the negotiations had proceeded more smoothly thanks to the world having forgotten about them.

Citing health reasons, Nick Scheele stepped down in 2004, and Jim Padilla succeeded him as president. Unable to put Ford back on track, in June 2006, he, too, stepped down, and the post was left vacant. The thin thread called the hybrid is what is barely maintaining the Ford-Toyota relationship today.

Nissan also adopted Toyota's hybrid technology, prior to Ford, and Toyota is trying to persuade GM to do the same. If GM goes ahead, the Toyota model will no doubt become the world standard.

At the beginning of this section, I compared consolidations in the automotive industry to love affairs. The aims may have been different, but when Honda grew tight with GM, Toyota made a pass on Ford. When Ford adopted Toyota's hybrid technology, GM forewent Toyota and rushed to co-develop with Daimler-Chrysler. GM is said to have passed on the Toyota technology because the emphasis on electric motors (as opposed to improvements in the engine) leaves much to be desired, manufacturing costs a concern of note. But many in the automotive industry take the shrewd view that GM, king of the auto industry, put itself on the line to keep the Toyota model from becoming the world standard.

It remains the case that Toyota is a couple of steps ahead in the field of hybrid technology. The small passenger car Prius is more popular in the U.S. than in Japan; there is a few months' wait for the model between purchase and delivery. Given new stateside production of the bestselling Camry's hybrid version at the Kentucky factory, Toyota is pulling away from rivals even in the American market.

Low pollution, high efficiency technology used to be Honda's romping ground, yet, in the case of hybrid technology, the firm has fallen far behind Toyota, not just in terms of image, but in actual development, production, and sales. Unlike Toyota, Honda accentuates engine improvement in developing its hybrid technology. As a result, its electric motor is small and can be mounted on 1,000cc-class mass-market cars. Honda is trying to rally and chase Toyota with their help but has hardly begun to catch up. If Soichiro Honda were alive today, he would no doubt fume, "We came in first when they had those emissions restrictions, so how in the world did we come out of the gate late for hybrids? Are you sure you guys weren't feeling complacent?"

The market size for hybrid cars is hard to predict. There is agreement that the real winner in the world of environment-friendly cars is destined to be neither the hybrid car nor the diesel car common in Europe but the fuel-battery car. Toyota and Honda have already begun lease sales of fuel-battery cars, but at a cost of a hundred million yen per vehicle, they are light-years from becoming ubiquitous.

The focus is on when exactly they will start to become common. While manufacturers are speeding ahead with research, the consensus among experts is that at least another ten years are required. Conversely, the era of hybrids will continue for another decade. Betting that the hybrid era will last much longer than that, Toyota plans on raising its ratio of hybrid cars to 10 percent of total output (including overseas production) by 2012—a million hybrids a year.

In terms of the long view, Toyota has been conducting joint research into cutting-edge technological fields with GM since 1999. In March 2006, however, at GM's sudden request, joint research into fuel batteries was terminated. While the cooperative agreement was extended to 2008 for other areas such as ITS preventative safety, GM was breaking a promise a mere month and a half since it had been made. In mid-January, GM Chairman Wagoner and Toyota President Katsuaki Watanabe had met in Detroit to agree on their companies' continued cooperation in advanced technological fields.

The dissolution of the research partnership was not unrelated to GM's deep business slump. Even in tandem with a partner, developing applicable technology for fuel-battery cars requires a vast amount of money. While Toyota can bear the burden, GM cannot afford to be researching fuel batteries when it still needs to develop hybrid cars, engines that run on ethanol extracted from crops like sugar canes, and other technology to cope with the soaring price of oil. GM does not have the luxury to look even a decade down the road.

The company's business performance has grown so poor that bankruptcy seems possible. If GM ever does go under, the single stroke will be enough to destabilize the entire automotive industry. There are already signs that this may happen.

It was in May 2005 that the star investor Kirk Kerkorian spent $870 million to make a TOB and acquire GM stock. Combined with previously owned stock and additional purchases, his share rose to 9.9 percent.

Kerkorian, who controls four-tenths of the casinos in Las Vegas, is a billionaire who is no stranger to the auto industry. In 1995, he teamed with Chrysler's former chairman Lee Iacocca to make a hostile takeover bid against Chrysler. Iacocca, of course, is the famous turnaround artist who rebuilt a Chrysler that had been on the brink of bankruptcy. Headhunting Robert Eaton from GM and appointing him chairman, Iacocca had taken his curtain calls and bid adieu to the auto world. Yet one day, all of a sudden, a man who'd won both fame and fortune, he paired up with a renowned investor to make a hostile bid against his old company, which was still being led by the successor he himself had handpicked. It is as though life must be lived as a Hollywood movie if your name is Lee Iacocca.

Detroit was astounded by the pitiless acquisition play, but in the end, Kerkorian was unable to muster the necessary sum, more than $20 billion, and the bid on Chrysler failed. The same Kerkorian now possessed 9.9 percent of GM stock and demanded a seat as an outside board member, signing a consultant agreement with Jerome York, a former executive at Chrysler and IBM. GM could not rebuff the demand and had to give York the seat in February 2006.

The mammoth became extinct when it could not adapt to changes in the environment. GM, often characterized as the mammoth of the auto world, is also struggling, unable to adapt to changing circumstances. Mammoth GM has only its own survival in mind today and is not able to look after others.

GM's maneuvers since 2005 have made this manifest. First, a stock purchase problem erupted in relationship to Fiat. According to the contract signed in 2000, Fiat was to gain the right to sell its automotive division (Fiat Auto) to GM. The right became available on January 24, 2005, and Fiat demanded that GM acquire all remaining stock.

Yet GM refused, arguing that Fiat was still reorganizing its finances and had received new investment in the interim. Put simply, GM balked at the prospect of shouldering Fiat's massive debt. The deadline for the talks was extended to February 1, but if Fiat, which asserted that the contract was effective, and GM, which asked that it be annulled, could not come to an agreement in due course, the Italian company was ready to bring the matter to court and demand compensation.

The confrontation garnered much public attention in Italy. To put it in somewhat vulgar terms, it was a marital showdown between a husband (GM) who'd become thoroughly fed up with his wife and his wife (Fiat) who, still very much interested in him, needled, "You promised to take care of me for the rest of my life."

A battle in court seemed inevitable, but on February 14 an agreement was reached whereby Fiat relinquished its right to sell its stocks to GM. As a settlement fee, GM had to pay 1.5 billion euros to Fiat and return 10 percent of the stock it held.

The Fiat case made it painfully clear that GM's expansionist global strategy was in shambles. GM's Japanese partners could not afford to think of the Fiat incident as "a fire on the opposite shore of the river" as the Japanese saying goes. Indeed, in December 2005, Fuji Heavy Industries was informed that their capital tie-up was revoked. Of the 20 percent stock, 8.7 percent was sold to Toyota, and the rest was left with Fuji as treasury stock.

In March 2006, GM sold the bulk of its 20 percent share in Suzuki, retaining only 3 percent. Suzuki Chairman Osamu Suzuki groaned, "I had no idea that GM was so hard up on cash." In this case, too, treasury stock was deposited at Suzuki with the understanding that GM would hold it again if its performance improved within a year, but chances of this happening are small.

Immediately after relinquishing that share, GM decided to give up its 7.9 percent stake in Isuzu. This put an end to capital relations between GM and

Japanese automakers. The commotion surrounding the 1966 partnership with Isuzu, which had been likened to the coming of the black ships of Commodore Perry, belongs to a different epoch indeed.

Of course, it is not just in Japan that GM is selling off assets. The Swedish maker Saab will be sold off sooner or later. To wrap up its asset restructuring, GM sold 51 percent of financial subsidiary GMAC (GM Acceptance Corporation) to an alliance of investors headed by the investment firm Cerberus for a sum of $14 billion. In 2005, GM earned $2.5 billion in dividends from GMAC, but income from that source has been halved.

GM's basic strategy, or rather, York's thinking is that bankruptcy must be avoided at all costs. What can be sold is sold so that there will be sufficient capital to restructure the company; GM must regain its footing in North American auto sales, chiefly through the development of a small car that can compete with Japanese brands like the Toyota Corolla and Honda Civic. The time limit has been set at three years. In other words, if GM can't revive itself within three years, it will have to invoke Chapter 11.

Reviving the company is easier said than done. If gas prices stay at their current high levels, GM's 26 percent market share will probably dip down to about 20 percent. GM is in the process of recasting itself so that it will be profitable even if the share drops to such a level. But the lynchpin of the plan, the development of a small car, may not be realistic unless Toyota agrees to supply the engines *en masse*.

Although not a capital tie-up, the partnership with Honda, too, has degenerated into something that is true in name only. As a sort of symbol of the alliance, GM purchases Saturn's V6 engines and transmissions from Honda, but at a mere 50,000 units per year, this amounts to no more than a little engine business. The technology exchange that was supposed to be the crux of the partnership has become so hollowed out that a Honda engineer has openly stated, "We had nothing to learn from GM."

Yet, for the Japanese auto industry, GM is still a special entity. When Toyota's founder Kiichiro Toyoda decided to enter into the auto business, it was the GM Chevrolet that he mimicked. He took apart the engine, sketched its parts, and put it back together with his own hands. Toyota's engines today have a high torque because they still echo the old Chevrolet.

Toyota's American plant was able to get on track quickly thanks to local know-how obtained through cooperation with GM. As for Nissan, in their early days, founder Yoshisuke Ayukawa seriously explored a merger with GM's Japanese branch.

Why did Fuji Heavy Industries choose GM over Ford? Because they believed welcoming "the world's largest automaker" to be their prime shareholder was their ticket to survival. Why did Suzuki, a maker of k-cars, succeed in manufacturing small cars locally in India and Hungary? For no other reason than that it had instant trust as "a GM affiliate."

For a long time, the Japanese auto industry maintained a roster of eleven full-fledged carmakers, but today, after the waves of transformation, only two companies are fully independent in capital terms. They are Toyota and Honda. At the same time, GM has relinquished its shares in Fuji, Suzuki, and Isuzu; Mitsubishi of the DaimlerChrysler group has also been informed, to their chagrin, that the partnership is no more.

Although Toyota has acquired a portion of Fuji stock, it is not large enough for Fuji to be considered part of the Toyota Group. Suzuki, Isuzu, and Mitsubishi bowed to foreign capital in the first place because independence over the long term seemed a difficult proposition. Their position of weakness has not changed, and they will simply have to seek new partners. New trends exist. For instance, the large truck maker Nissan Diesel, formerly part of the Nissan family, has been part of the Swedish Volvo group since March 2006.

Given GM's worse-than-expected performance, the global auto industry's banner of leadership has transferred to Toyota. The industry has entered into a new state of mobility. Yet, Toyota does not share GM's appetite for expansionism. In the words of Chairman Hiroshi Okuda, "Either in Japan or overseas, if the government asks us to step in, it will be hard to say no." In other words, if the U.S. government requests Toyota to supply small-car engines to GM, it will not be easy for Toyota to refuse. If there is a change in leadership at GM before such an overture by the government, Toyota will probably be petitioned directly to aid in the firm's reconstruction.

Either way, it is looking as though the global auto industry will be revolving around Toyota for some time to come, in production, development, technology, and all other fields. If any company has the ability to challenge such a runaway victory, it is Honda. The question is: does Honda have the bravado today to set up a goal like "Stop Toyota"?

5

The pinnacle of auto racing, the 2006 F1 (Formula One) World Championship series, began with the Bahrain GP on March 12.

For Japanese fans, the 2006 series had three points of interest. The first was whether Toyota could win its first championship since its entry in 2002. At the Motorsport Activities report in early March, Toyota President Katsuaki Watanabe signaled his confidence: "This is our fifth year and we'd like to delight you all with our first championship."

The second was the participation of a private Japanese team, with a Japanese driver, in an era when F1 racing had long become a competition among corporate automakers. The racer Aguri Suzuki had come in third at the 1990 Japan GP to become the first Japanese to stand on the winners' podium; he was now returning to the world of F1 racing as an owner.

There is a precedent for Suzuki's example. In 1994, the former racer Tetsu Ikuzawa put together a private team, financing it out of his own pocket. Despite Ikuzawa's enthusiasm, F1 racing proved to be too expensive an endeavor. Just when he was running out of funds and was preparing to give up, Mitsubishi Motors, which was then seeking a partnership with a European counterpart, offered its sponsorship. The negotiations proceeded smoothly and the contract was ready to be signed when a sexual harassment case at Mitsubishi's Illinois plant came to light and brought public scorn on the company. F1 racing was out of the question; Ikuzawa's dream had to die.

The greatest point of interest was that Honda was participating with its own team and with a machine that encapsulated its technology from engine to chassis. Although Honda had returned to F1 racing in 2000 with a machine co-developed with BAR, it had not yet ascended to the top of the winners' podium. Its overall performance for 2005 had been sixth place, behind neophyte Toyota, which had come in fourth. Roused, Honda acquired BAR and was participating as Honda Works for the first time in thirty-eight years.

Soichiro Honda, motorcycles, speed, Formula One: F1 was Honda, and Honda F1. While Soichiro was still alive, F1 racing was Honda's patented strength. Driven by Soichiro's dream to emerge victorious at the pinnacle of world racing, the company participated as an All Honda team during its first run (1964-68) and scaled the winner's podium as champion in just two years. In the second period (1983-92), Honda participated as an engine supplier, and this run, too, became legendary thanks to racing genius Ayrton Senna, prince of the sound of speed. Soichiro exhorted his F1 staff continuously: "In racing, only victory means anything. Whatever you do, win."

Back then, the races were significant as a "running experiment" because the technology developed for the circuit could be applied to commercial vehicles. In contemporary F1 racing, however, the technology involved is so advanced and specialized, from the engine to the chassis, that racing cars have become a thing apart from street cars. Naturally, the role of F1 racing has changed for Honda. Even then, it was indeed sad for the once-glorious Honda not to have snagged a championship a number of years after its return. If Soichiro were alive, he would no doubt have said, "If you can't win, then go ahead and quit."

Honda had trouble winning because the point of participating in the races was unclear. It was Kawamoto, the company's fourth president, who initiated the third run that began in 2000. His plan had been for full participation, as with the first run, but his successor Yoshino immediately curtailed this to an engine-supplier role in the manner of the second run, citing turbulence in the automotive industry. At a press conference, Yoshino gave his frank opinion: Honda's interest was limited to the technological aspects and precious capital couldn't be diverted to F1 racing.

But F1 racing is not a kind world. A seven-year hiatus outmodes previously accumulated know-how. By limiting itself to supplying the engine, Honda was managing risk, but as a result it had a hard time mounting the winners' podium at all, let alone as champion.

Honda has returned to full participation beginning with 2006. While supplying the engine costs 10 billion yen per year, entering as All Honda costs triple that amount. Honda may be doing good business, but it is not easy for the company to funnel 30 billion yen annually into a field whose technological fruits have no product application.

The late-starter Toyota, meanwhile, entered F1 racing to use it as a tool to cultivate the European market. While Toyota is poised to surpass GM to become the world's largest automaker, it is not interested in assuming the throne of number one per se. Rather, Toyota's goal is for its global sales share, which topped 10 percent in 2002, to climb to 15 percent by 2010. The Toyota brand needs to be polished up in the world market for this purpose. F1 racing was deemed effective for boosting the brand in the European market in particular, where share has hovered at a little under 5 percent. The brand image will not improve without a victory, and Toyota is accordingly serious. To prove that it sees F1 as more than just a game, Toyota purchased the Fuji Speedway, where a Japan GP was held in the past, and moreover spent 20 billion yen on a complete overhaul of the circuit. The commitment was duly noted, and it was decided that a Japan GP would be held in October 2007.

What, then, does Honda aim to achieve by participating as an All-Honda team? Fukui, the company's sixth president, has a clear answer: grooming talent. The fact that the president needs to flatly state this reveals what ails Honda. Its business is robust thanks to a strong showing in the U.S. market. Fortunately, Honda was able to stay on the side of the consolidators in the international consolidation drama. Employees are enjoying a sense of security. But there is no guarantee that Honda can stay its course of independence. Fukui himself has a sense of foreboding about the future, but it is difficult to make the rank and file share the feeling when business is so good. How might Honda's technicians be made to undergo ordeals during "peacetime"? Fukui chose F1 racing as the way to temper them.

F1 racing requires the participating team to think about how to win with a limited amount of people, material, and money. To ensure that more than just a few benefit from the experience, the team members are rotated rather than fixed. If grooming talent is the true purpose, then it makes sense to shell out the prohibitive sum and participate as Honda Works. But winning is a different matter. F1 racing is not a kind world.

Indispensable for winning in the races is an engineering genius who is blessed with intuition and inspiration and who can build on the accumulated technology. In Honda's case, multiple teams are working on F1 engines at the same time. Of course, these take more than a year to develop and will not be fully ready for a few years. According to experts, problems in the engines were the reason Honda could not win since its return. The engine used in the 2006 series, however, is already much improved; it is not altogether impossible that Honda will be a regular on the winners' podium. Indeed, in the first entry, the Bahrain GP, Honda barely missed the chance, coming in fourth.

F1 racing may have the effect of motivating the engineers, but it cannot be expected to tighten up the company as a whole. The big problem Honda is facing is that it has become a faceless company. Top management has failed to present a vision for the future.

Today's Honda is not the Honda of yore. Founder Soichiro passed away fifteen years ago; Fujisawa, eighteen years ago. Deceased, too, are the Honda children who studied at their knees when the company was still little more than a town factory, former vice president Kihachiro Kawashima, former chairman Noboru Okamura, former managing director Takao Harada, and others. While

Kiyoshi Kawashima, the second president, and Michihiro Nishida, the former vice president who plays the role of Honda's oral historian, are alive and well, after retiring they have not only made no move to influence management but hardly ever show their face at headquarters.

The decisive difference since the era of the founders is that the company's structure is not amenable to the emergence of a hero. This became evident in the chaotic period when Japan's economic bubble burst and Honda lost its way—when disagreements over how to survive the crisis fomented tension between the fourth president, Kawamoto, and the vice president, Irimajiri.

Kawamoto was sure that "Pops [Soichiro] is the only hero Honda will ever need." Irimajiri, on the other hand, believed that "Honda needs to produce many minor heroes." They were completely at odds, and the more they talked, the more manifest became their management differences. The outcome: Kawamoto assumed total control, while Irimajiri, embroiled in the opaque M Fund scandal, left the company "in a hail of stones." After that, Honda's corporate culture became one that made it difficult even for "minor heroes" to be born.

In truth, it was not the genius engineer Honda, but Fujisawa who was in charge of management that was passionate about creating minor heroes. He never tired of expounding his theory within the company: "Now and in the future, technology is what will keep Honda alive. The president has to be an engineer." Honda started hiring college graduates regularly, and after research and technology was spun off as Honda R&D, Fujisawa made a conscious effort to groom the engineers there for leadership roles.

With the shared understanding that "technology knows no borders," Soichiro and Fujisawa managed Honda with the world market constantly in mind. No matter how small the company, it needed to have a broad perspective and a high aim if it were to compete internationally. If Honda intended to live or die by its technology, it had to make a conscious effort to train engineers who could make the whole world their stage. The first step in their education was to send them overseas, to expand their minds.

Singling out the best young engineering talent, Fujisawa sent them abroad for periods ranging from three months to half a year. What was amazing about his style of personnel management was that, once he decided to send someone abroad, he promoted the employee one rank beyond his "classmates" the year before the trip; then, in the year after, he promoted the same employee by yet another notch. In those days, the average time it took to ascend one rank was five years in speedy cases, and ten years in slower cases.

Fujisawa also considered the age of who was to be sent abroad. He picked employees who were between twenty-seven and thirty-five, with more than five years at the company. Being in the late twenties or early thirties meant that the employee was at the marrying age, or if married, still in honeymoon mode. Rapid promotions at that young age gave the impression all around that the employee was a future executive. Fujisawa's aim was for the promoted man's wife and family to receive that impression as well. Treated by everyone as elite material, the employee would naturally try to meet the high expectations and work extra hours and even weekends. This was during Japan's high-growth years, when "elite engineer" equaled "family-neglecting, die-hard salaryman." The role could not be performed without the family's understanding and support. In order for the wife to see that her husband was on the elite track, the employee was promoted two ranks vis-à-vis colleagues who had joined the same year. Being thus promoted not only tickled the pride of the employee and his family but also entailed the concrete benefits of a higher wage. Fujisawa's was a concerted plan to create "company men."

A typical elite technician was Irimajiri. In the summer of 1973, shortly before the first oil shock, Honda signed a deal with Ford to supply CVCC technology. In order to formulate the program for installation in Ford cars, several young engineers were selected to be sent to Ford's R&D for three months. Put in charge of the squad was Irimajiri, who had just turned thirty-three.

At that time, the Big Three were, not just for Honda but for all Japanese automakers, entities that existed above the clouds. Through his time at Ford R&D, Irimajiri learned that, on all levels, Honda was still not fit to be thought of as a full-fledged carmaker. After the experience, he began to ponder what Honda had to do become a real automobile manufacturer. While Irimajiri was impressed by the depth of Ford's core science of carmaking, he also felt that in terms of engineering—the basis of manufacturing—it was less formidable. *Maybe Japan is better at manufacturing cars. Maybe even Honda can best the Big Three.* This was his intuition, when Honda had just one model, the Civic.

Six years later, in the summer of 1979, Irimajiri was appointed director at Honda at the young age of thirty-nine. The mass media, which was ignorant of Honda's system for grooming executives, announced sensationally, "39-Year-Old Director Born at Honda/Future Candidate for President." In terms of his position at the company, however, Irimajiri had already reached the top rung as a regular employee, and no one at Honda was surprised that he was now joining the ranks of management. This way, a "minor hero" was born.

Irimajiri wasn't the only one who received the elite treatment. Kawamato and Yoshino went through much the same. There was even a case where, following Fujisawa's directive, an employee retired from Honda and joined Benz, there learning in detail how the Mercedes was made; a spy of sorts, a few years later he re-entered Honda. These methods, however, were reserved for technical personnel. Fujisawa did not employ them in the sales-related departments.

After Fujisawa left the front lines of management, Honda ceased to use his elite-grooming measures. They became unnecessary. Honda's expanding operations had begun to attract top talent. Today, Honda technology is top-notch by any measure. The scratch on the pearl is that while the individual engineers are indeed gifted they are not cosmopolitan talents. This is true not just for the mid-career engineers; the bigger problem is that the directors, and even the young technicians, suffer from the ill effects of Honda's Monroe Doctrine.

Both Soichiro and Fujisawa emphasized "Hondaness" in the interests of developing unique products. Over time, this turned into Honda's peculiar Monroe Doctrine whereby outside views were to be shut out. It was a spell cast by the founders.

Unable to break this spell, the directors dwell in "Hondaville" (i.e., the confines of the company). They cannot make business decisions based on a global perspective. Retraining the management has to become an issue for the company.

For many years, Toyota was mocked as the "hick *daimyo* of Mikawa." Taizo Ishida, the rebuilder of Toyota, was given to opining that hanging out in business circles was for those with too much time on their hands. But Toyota has completely transformed itself. After retirement, technicians in production who were involved with the "Toyota Production System" routinely go to work for companies that have nothing to do with autos or auto parts, thus spreading the good word that is "just in time." Many directors engage in various activities for the social benefit after retirement.

After the capital tie-up with DaimlerChrysler was dissolved in 2004, Mitsubishi Automobiles suffered a crisis. The plants were in a shamble after a defective-car scandal and it was even said that quality control would be hard to maintain. Pained by their plight, Toyota Chairman Hiroshi Okuda sent Akihiro Wada, Toyota vice president then Denso vice chairman, to Mitsubishi Heavy Industries, the automaker's parent company, to serve as an outside board member. Wada's task was to put things back on track at Mitsubishi's plant. In just a year, his supervision started showing results. The SUV Outlander, brought to market in fall 2005, and the k-car "i" are selling well, thanks it is said to their good quality. When Wada reported this to Okuda, the chairman grimaced and cajoled, "You taught them too much," but Mitsubishi's cars seem actually to have improved.

Toyota has become a sort of church of the business world, a place to which those in need can flock for aid and guidance. Yukihisa Hirano, former president of the Toyota-affiliated Kanto Auto Works, became president of the Chubu International Airport (Centrair) which opened in spring 2005. When Japan's postal services were turned into a public company in 2003, former managing director Toshihiro Takahashi was greeted as deputy governor. For the commercial company that was set up in accordance with the break-up and privatization of postal services, Toyota Italy Chairman Norio Kitamura was offered and accepted as CEO. In order to promote internationalization, the public broadcasting channel NHK made former Toyota managing director Shin Kanada its new director. As for Sony, which is reorganizing its business, new chairman Fujio Cho was supplied as an outside board member.

In the realm of commercial organizations, too, the pattern holds. Shoichiro Toyoda (third generation) headed the Federation of Economic Organizations, while Okuda, who is not related to the Toyoda family, became the first chairman of the Japan Federation of Economic Organizations when the Federation of Economic Organizations merged with the Japan Federation of Employers' Association. Today it is impossible to imagine a Toyota-less business world in Japan.

In marked contrast with Toyota, Honda's retired directors mostly live private lives of leisure. Honda's company rules state that former directors must not take up post-retirement work except at educational institutions, and this rule is followed by all but a handful (Irimajiri being one of the exceptions). Bound by this rule, most distinguished Honda alums do not attempt to use what they learned in business to give back to the world as their counterparts at Toyota often do.

After resigning as president, Soichiro was active in such circles. Foisting all that on the founder, the Honda children left the company one by one. Soichiro had been the whole gamut of Honda's non-corporate activity.

Still, the post of vice chairman of the Tokyo Chamber of Commerce, which Soichiro had occupied with some great passion, remained a designated post for Honda presidents. Soichiro was succeeded by Kawashima, then Kawamoto, but neither of the successors was truly active in the role. Since Honda became a powerhouse, its leader was routinely invited to accept the vice chairmanship of the Federation of Economic Organizations, the Mt. Olympus of Japan's business world. Yoshino did assume the post but only in name, doing very little.

The exception is Munekuni, who served as chairman of the Japanese Automobile Manufactures Association for two years beginning in 2003. Placing more weight on the association's chairmanship than on his Honda chairmanship, Munekuni arbitrated within the automotive industry and worked to raise its relative profile in the business world. The great job he did was recognized, and after his term was over, the Tokyo Stock Exchange requested him to become chairman. But he hardly had the time to even consider the proposal when active and retired directors objected and he had to decline.

Not only former presidents, but most former directors forego engagement in any form of public activity. When one of them set up a business consultancy, wordless pressure from Yaesu (the old headquarters, where the counselors' room is found) and Aoyama (the current headquarters) forced him to shut it down in a blink of time.

In contrast, retired personnel from the sales side who did not advance beyond department manager and are not bound by Honda law tend to be quite active. The Japanese distributors for GM, Ford, VW, and Porsche have all been headed by former Honda employees. Others have joined the ranks of management at DaimlerChrysler and BMW. Honda is an important source of talent for foreign car dealers.

An example is Eiji Iwakuni. After serving as president of Honda Clio in Saitama, he retired from the company to become president of Ford Japan. He was impressive enough there that DaimlerChrysler scouted him to become vice president of domestic sales for Mitsubishi Motors. There is also the case of Toshiro Kurosawa, president of Porsche Japan, whose six-year contract at an annual salary of 60 million yen rivals that of Honda president.

Fujisawa had said: a Honda executive should burn out completely. Soichiro and Fujisawa had indeed given their all before withdrawing from the world of management. The founders assumed that their "children," too, would burn out and then resign. The founders set up a generous pension system for former directors so that they could retire and live in leisure without taking up new work. In reality, what happened was that without really having burned out, the "kids" convinced themselves that they probably *had* burned out, interpreting their predicament to suit them. They enjoyed early retirement packages that were thus bereft of their true meaning.

Few of the directors actually retired after burning themselves out. As far as the presidents go, apart from Soichiro, the only ones who left the company satisfied are the second president Kawashima and the third president Kume. The fourth president Kawamoto and the fifth president Yoshino resigned under circumstances that were not fulfilling for them in the same way.

Nonetheless, Kawamoto did strew petals over his path to retirement by channeling the disoriented post-bubble energy within the company into domestic sales and achieving the mark of 800,000 vehicles sold in a year. As for Yoshino, when the mass-market small car Fit that he had helped develop as vice president started selling explosively upon hitting the streets in 2001, he was seized by a domestic-sales dream much like Kawamoto. *At this rate, we could beat the Toyota Corolla in domestic sales.* Exhorting the sales force with the directive to "overtake the Corolla," Yoshino pushed the Fit hard. Just as, late in his reign, Kawamoto resorted to desperate measures to meet his "Get 80" objective, a huge sum was prepared for commissions and dealers were urged not only to sell at a discount but to aggressively self-register unsold product. For the year 2002, domestic sales for the Fit reached 250,000, making it the bestselling car of the year. 226,000 Corollas had sold. There was surprise all around that the Fit had beaten the leader of thirty-three consecutive years. Total vehicles sold for the year surpassed 900,000, breaking the Kawamoto-era record. "In 2005, we'll sell a million cars," the encouraged Yoshino blustered at the press conference held on New Year's Day 2003.

But pushing the sales force too hard always produces unwanted side effects. The dealers were worn out. Worse, it got out that taxes had been inflated in cases of dealer self-registration, and a warning was issued by the Automobile Fair Trade Council. The organization's chairman was the JAMA chairman, Munekuni. In other words, in a rare event, Council Chairman Munekuni had issued a warning against Honda Chairman Munekuni.

"Honda will not pursue quantity in domestic sales. We will compete in terms of quality." At a press conference held in March 2003, Fukui, just selected *de facto* to be Honda's sixth president, shot down Yoshino's trumpeted goal of selling a million cars domestically. Yoshino had curtailed his predecessor Kawamoto's F1 plans upon becoming president. This time, the sitting president's objective was being negated by the president-to-be. All this suggests that the top executives aren't communicating well and that there is no continuity in management.

Kawamoto served as president for eight years and retired at the age of sixty-three. After five years, Yoshino followed suit and became director and advisor as well. Both of them became obsessed with boosting domestic sales in the end. Although they managed to meet their ambitious goals, they had to bow out, reluctantly. Neither could fend off alumni voices that had menaced them since their sixtieth birthday: "Quit as soon as you can, you must be burned out…"

Then Fukui, too, set about to reform domestic sales. In fall 2005, he made the important decision to merge the three-channel regime of Verno, Clio, and Primo into one beginning in April 2006.

The question of unifying domestic sales was discussed on Christmas Eve in 1991, the year Soichiro passed away. The chairman, president, vice president, senior managing directors, and others held a heated discussion and settled at last on maintaining all three channels. The outcome of the meeting seemed, on the surface, like a come-from-behind victory on the part of the sales faction (Fujisawa Trading Co.), which argued successfully against giving up a channel and reducing the front. In truth, however, through this meeting Kawamoto and Irimiajiri's engineering faction (Honda Tech), which had pressed for retreat, gained the upper hand within the company. It was the moment when Fujisawa Trading Co. and Honda Tech underwent a merger and Kawamoto from Honda Tech became the new president (i.e., seized all power).

History is full of ironies. Kawamoto could not have achieved the "Get 80" goal a year ahead had not all three channels been retained back then. Yoshino, too, mobilized the Fit to interrupt the Corolla's winning streak, which ended at thirty-three years. Both men left their mark in domestic sales, not their field of expertise, to retire as presidents who had accomplished something for the company.

Current president Fukui, meanwhile, castigated as "going too far" Kawamoto and Yoshino's obsession to expand domestic sales and decided, without any apparent doubt, to whittle the channels down to one. When a retired sales veteran heard of this decision, he yelled angrily, "The one channel idea is just wrong. It's like speeding on a highway with a huge engine. What Honda needs to do now is develop a sales scheme that's different from those of Toyota and Nissan and others. We must change lanes. If Mr. Fujisawa were alive, that's what he'd do."

Domestic sales are at a saturation point, and all the automakers are considering shrinking their sales network. Immediately before entering into a tie-up with Renault, Nissan slimmed its original five channels down to two, Blue and Red. Although CEO Carlos Ghosn accepted the two-channel scheme as a premise, he is pushing through a plan to trim it down to virtually one channel by having both dealers handle all car types.

Honda's unification of channels will predate Ghosn's measure. The mass-production models of major products like the Odyssey and Fit are already being sold on all three channels. Some within the Honda company take the optimistic view that the unification will have no real effect since it has, in a way, happened already.

But that view is simplistic. Honda's sales outlets started out as town shops that sold motorbikes. When these were organized, they became the Primo stores. Because these stores are small, relatively few cars are on display and most models are subcompacts and mass-market cars. The Verno and Clio stores, on the other hand, sell mass-market cars but also luxury sedans and sport cars. While most of the Primo stores operate with indigenous capital, the Verno and Clio stores are 70 to 80 percent owned by the automaker. The natural course of things would be to unify these two channels first, as proposed fifteen years ago. Honda's strength is the strength of the weed, which the Primo stores retain. The Clio and Verno channels are more like elegant boutiques.

In order to increase domestic sales, at all its outlets Nissan sells subcompacts that Suzuki manufactures by commission. But at the Nissan dealers, the subcompacts are treated on a par with the accessories. Small cars could suffer a similar fate at the Clio and Verno stores. Meanwhile, the Primo stores, given their paucity of floor space, cannot display the models sold originally at the fancier outlets.

When the sales veteran called for "changing lanes," what he meant was that instead of unifying all the channels, Honda should combine the Clio and Verno shops and adopt a two-channel scheme, and in the meantime reform its overall sales tactics. No matter how powerful an engine (a single channel) they mount, Honda sales does not stand a chance against Toyota's five channels on the highways. The result of Fukui's unification will soon be evident.

6

Times may change but it is never easy to resurrect a system that has been abolished once. For some time now, *waigaya* has been something of an archaism at Honda—the fourth president Nobuhiko Kawamoto effectively did away with that intangible cultural asset of the company. There is still a large common room for the directors at the headquarters building in Aoyama, Tokyo, but perhaps due to the firm's increased size and clearer delimitations of directors' area of oversight, few of the them can be found at headquarters at any given time. The common room is an artifact whose meaning has become lost. Most of the directors spend their time not in Aoyama but in a private office at the operational center over which they have been assigned responsibility.

Slowly but surely, Honda became a "mere" sterling company with faceless management. After the Japanese economic bubble burst and the company was in dire straits, former chairman Hideo Sugiura said with much feeling, "Pop (Soichiro) and Uncle (Fujisawa) had the right idea when they didn't let their children join Honda, to avoid hereditary rule by the founding families. But when a company faces a crisis, you need some kind of banner to maintain a center of gravity. If, as the symbol of the founding family, Hiro-chan (Soichiro's eldest son Hirotoshi Honda) had become maybe one of the auditors and become the banner, there might have been more cohesion." But since Soichiro hadn't wanted his son to join Honda and Hirotoshi had no intention of doing so either, asking for this was like pining after some elixir.

It was Hirotoshi who caused an incident that tarnished the image of Honda and its founder Soichiro. In 1973, with funding assistance from his father, Hirotoshi set up Mugen (the word means "infinity") to develop and manufacture car racing engines. Though Honda the company did not own any shares, it looked after Mugen, at times openly and at times discreetly, while Soichiro was still alive. Mugen entered the F1 races in 1992 and performed brilliantly, a machine bearing its engine winning four races including the Monaco Grand Prix. However, after Soichiro's death, Mugen and Honda gradually began to drift apart and, with the passage of time, became fairly distant.

Honda's own retreat from F1 racing only helped widen the gap. When orders from Honda plummeted, lackadaisical business practices at the firm became a liability, and Mugen reported a loss for 1996. Since the company had been set up by the founder's scion, Honda could not afford to look the other way. Shortly after Mugen took its plunge into the red, Kawamoto summoned Hirotoshi to Aoyoma headquarters and announced that they were cutting ties:

"Hiro-chan, whatever you do, you're the oldest son of the Old Man who founded Honda. There's no capital relation between Honda and Mugen, but the world won't swallow that. This time, Honda is bucking your losses. But Honda is taking this opportunity to cut ties with Mugen, people-wise too."

Honda shouldered his losses, and Hirotoshi was indebted to the company. Thus the second act began. In 1998, having lost confidence in his own management skills, Hirotoshi chose as his confidant Norio Hirokawa, who had served as Mugen's auditor via a transferal from Honda in the past. Hirokawa was now rejoining Mugen, once again as auditor.

Within the Honda company, Hirokawa did not have a good reputation. He was passionate about accumulating personal wealth and was given to telling his colleagues that his motto was: "My life is about money." In fact, Hirokawa was on the notorious side. He retired from Honda as soon as his transferal to Mugen expired and, for a while, managed a cram school. Until the incident occurred, aloofly enough, Honda headquarters had not even learned that Hirokawa had reassumed the post of auditor at Mugen.

In July 2003, the Saitama District Prosecutors Office charged that Hirotoshi and Hirokawa had conspired to conceal 2.8 billion yen in income through fictive materials expenses over a period of three years beginning in 1998 for the purpose of issuing a false loss report, evading approximately 1 billion yen in taxes. The prosecution gave as Hirotoshi's motive an attempt to obtain funds to pay Honda family estate taxes and to build a Soichiro Honda Memorial Hall. "The tax evasion was for personal gain," the prosecutor's charging statement denounced, "with a view to securing funds for the payment of estate taxes in the future. The principal suspect Honda requested accomplice Hirokawa to help him devise a tax evasion scheme."

While there was an actual plan to remodel the Honda home in Nishiochiai into a foundation-run "Soichiro Honda Memorial Hall," it was a peculiar plan according to which the building would not become open to the public. The whole idea did have the appearance of a tax evasion scheme.

Hirokawa asserted his innocence throughout the trial, claiming, "I was simply following Mr. Honda's orders. The prosecution is confusing inaccurate accounting with tax evasion. I never once intended the latter."

Hirotoshi also asserted his innocence. His lawyer said in the final disquisition: "The crime was committed solely by Hirokawa, who attempted embezzlement, never informing the principal suspect of the actual movement of funds."

Hirokawa and Hirotoshi were tried separately, but the prosecution requested for them both a sentence of four years and a fine of 300 million yen for the corporation Mugen.

At the final disquisition, Hirotoshi pleaded with tears in his eyes, "I swear upon heaven and earth that I did not commit the dishonor of using ill-begotten funds to construct a memorial hall for my great father, whose record was unblemished. Your honor, please believe me."

The truth will probably never be known, but Hirotoshi, like his father, was insouciant about money matters. He left in the hands of specialists not only the management of Honda family assets but Mugen's financials and tax reporting. He had entrusted to Hirokawa the seals and bankbooks of all affiliated operations.

If one may give Hirotoshi the benefit of the doubt, he relied on Hirokawa as his right-hand man, but Hirokawa—unlike Fujisawa, whom Soichiro trusted from the bottom of his heart—lacked not just business acumen, but ethics. Hirotoshi would still not be without blame. Though he came to resemble his father physically as he advanced in years, his personality was the opposite of Soichiro's. Whereas Soichiro had been larger than life, Hirotoshi was timid. Right after his father passed away, Hirotoshi described his dream as follows: "My dream isn't to expand the company (Mugen) but to make sure the fortune I inherited from my father hasn't decreased by the time I bequeath it to my daughter." This modest dream was crushed by Hirokawa.

Parallel to the criminal trial, Hirotoshi brought a civil suit against the company run by Hirokawa, demanding that it return the 2.6 billion yen "in funds that were diverted from Mugen." In May 2005, the Tokyo District Court ordered Hirokawa's company to return the whole sum as requested by the plaintiff. In April 2006, the Tokyo High Court, which heard the appeal, supported the district court's judgment. Hirokawa appealed again. Even if the Supreme Court concurs with the lower courts and settles the judgment, there is no guarantee that the sum would be returned to Mugen. In 2004, soon after the incident came to light, all of Mugen's operations were transferred to a different company and Hirotoshi is no longer involved in them.

The criminal trial's verdict was delivered on May 23. The judge gave Hirokawa a sentence of three years without a stay of execution, stating that "the crime is of a malignant nature. The guilty continuously directed (Mugen's) employees and others to cook the account books." The reading of the judgment lasted five hours and included the following statement on the issue of Hirotoshi's complicity: "The written agreement exchanged with Hirokawa contains no clauses that are premised on tax evasion. There are passages in Hirotoshi Honda's memos that would not make sense if he were indeed aware of the fictive and inflated expensing. There is no proof of his complicity."

Two days later, on May 25, the verdict on Hirotoshi and Mugen was delivered in that same court room. Hirotoshi was found innocent, but the judge ordered Mugen to pay a fine of 240 million yen. After the verdict, Hirotoshi commented, "I'm disappointed that Mugen was found guilty, but I highly commend the verdict in that I was proven to be clean just as I've asserted from the beginning. I'm relieved that today's verdict has put an end to three years of torment."

Soichiro's wife Sachi lives alone in the house in Nishiochiai that was about to be turned into a memorial hall. Ever since Hirotoshi's trial, the Honda children have more or less stopped visiting her. After the verdict cleared her son, she spoke the following words to her late husband's altar: "Soichiro, our son was found innocent, but now there's a blot on both the company's name and yours. I can't tell you how sorry I am. You weren't a believer, so there is no tablet in the altar. When I want to meet you, I have to go to the cemetery at the foot of Mt. Fuji. I'm too old to go there often. Instead I have to speak to you here. What shall I do? Tell me, Soichiro."

Having cut all ties with Mugen during Kawamoto's presidency, Honda was in the dark about the truth of what had happened. Even though Hirotoshi was found innocent, there was no question that he had smeared the good name of his father, the great founder. The Honda company and the Honda family became estranged as a result.

On May 17, about a week before the verdict, Honda President Takeo Fukui decided important policy that would affect the company's future. He held a press conference and let it be known that Honda was building an advanced production system in Japan, strengthening its overseas growth structure, and stepping up environment-related R&D. "Accelerated shoring up of the basics to make further leaps and bounds," said the press release.

After the demise of the founders, Honda had gradually become overcautious, "knocking on the stone bridge before crossing it" as the saying goes, more so than Toyota ever did when it was still the hick *daimyo*. Honda had come to eschew adventure. In Honda's early years, it had tirelessly challenged itself to do new things. When, boldly, Honda became the first Japanese maker to manufacture cars locally in the U.S., Soichiro told the press with chutzpah, "GM didn't start out as the world's number one automaker, either. One day, Honda might overtake GM. Local production in the U.S. is the first step."

Although it was Honda that took the plunge first, over the years the basically stronger Toyota caught up and overtook Honda regarding U.S. production. Toyota, in fact, has already surpassed GM itself in terms of profit and overall stock value. It is also poised to do so in terms of scale—global sales and revenue—and to assume the top seat of "the largest industry the Earth has birthed" (i.e., autos). The fact GM may be dragged off the throne worries the star investor Kirk Kerkorian, who owns nearly a tenth of GM's stock. The 89-year-old gentleman sent his aide Jerome York into GM as a board member and, in June 2006, wrote a letter to GM urging it to partner with Nissan/Renault.

In Europe, too, Honda has not been able to build on its F1 reputation or local production in England. It missed the bandwagon initially in the SUV boom. Thanks to its brand-new Odyssey becoming a huge hit, Honda made up for its late start and even ignited the minivan boom that still continues. Yet, while Honda was playing desperate catch up in the SUV field, Toyota was stealing its thunder in environmental technology, developing hybrid cars that run on electricity and gasoline, and fuel-battery cars. In Honda's patented arena of F1 racing, too, Toyota is bearing down rapidly.

In the turbid world of consolidations that is the global auto industry, Honda continued to reject M&As and stayed its own high way, yet grew large enough to become one of the "New Big Six" along with GM, Ford, DaimlerChrysler, Toyota, and the Nissan-Renault alliance. Honda is a company of rare excellence and could rightly be called one of the miracles of the auto industry. At the same time, the image of Honda as a forward-looking venture firm—the image built by the founders—is growing fainter every year.

Now approaching 2008, its sixtieth anniversary, Honda is conducting its largest infrastructural investment since the founding days. The highlights are new plants in Saitama prefecture and North America and bolstered production capacity in China, India, and Brazil—the "BRIC" countries other than Russia—for a projected annual output of 4.5 million vehicles for 2010. The total cost of expanding their capacity will be $1.27 billion.

Japan's domestic auto market is already mature, and the number of finished cars exported to developed countries is being depressed every year in order to forestall trade friction. Overseas local production having taken the place of exports, not one new auto plant has been built in Japan since the bursting of the bubble. Just as no new furnace—that symbol of the steel industry—has been commissioned in the last forty years, the prevailing view has been that no new auto plant can possibly be built in Japan.

Flaunting the conventional wisdom, Honda acquired 800,000 square meters of land in the town of Yorii, 35 kilometers from its Sayama plant, for a new full-assembly factory that will cost $636 million. When it is completed, annual domestic production will jump from 1.3 million to 1.5 million vehicles. It will be Honda's first new auto plant in forty-six years since the one at Suzuka was built. Forty-six years ago, motorization was just beginning to lap Japan's shores.

The new plant's aim is not just an increase in production capacity; it will be used to implement cutting-edge technology developed by Honda R&D. Production technologies, such as quality improvement, that are fermented at the plant will be transposed to other production centers scattered around the globe.

Approximately $400 million will be poured into the new North American plant, which will be located in Indiana, where Toyota already has a factory that manufactures SUVs and pick-up trucks. Honda's facility is scheduled to become operational in 2008 with a production capacity of 200,000 vehicles per annum. In addition, near its Canada factory, Honda is building a $140 million engine plant that will be turning out 200,000 units per year. The overall aim is to increase the percentage of locally supplied parts and thereby to strengthen Honda's production base in North America, where the company generates more than half of its revenue on the consolidated basis.

Honda's current North American production centers are in Ohio (two plants), Alabama, Ontario, and Jalisco in Mexico, making the new Indiana center its sixth. For fiscal 2005, North American sales was 1.68 million vehicles, while local production capacity was only 1.4 million vehicles. Sales for fiscal 2006 are projected to be higher due to high gas prices—1.76 million vehicles. The Sayama and Suzuka plants are getting old and there is a limit to the exports they can handle.

That leaves increasing local production overseas. Honda is boosting its North American production capacity for the first time in eight years. After the founders' deaths, Honda has shown an almost cowardly level of caution about investing in new infrastructure. Ten years ago, faced with the same problem, Honda would have prioritized and built either the domestic or the North American plant before the other. Fukui, however, did not choose that path and commissioned both plants simultaneously, forking king and rook as it were.

As for the Chinese market, where demand is certain to rise, Honda promptly switched to local production, as it had done in the U.S., and still maintains a lead over its Japanese rivals Toyota and Nissan. In India, second only to China in terms of potential new demand, the production capacity of the plant that manufactures the Fit Aria will be raised to 100,000 vehicles per year by 2007, three years earlier than originally envisioned.

What merits attention about Honda's new initiative is not just the largest expansion of production capacity since the company's founding but the hunkering down that it plans in the field of hybrid cars, where it has been outrun so far by Toyota. The hybrid system that Honda developed independently was installed in quick succession in the two-passenger Insight in 1999, the Civic in 2001, and the Accord in 2004. Yet cumulative sales for all three models amounted to a paltry 133,000 vehicles at the end of 2005, far outstripped by Toyota's Prius alone (170,000 vehicles sold). Honda, whose sell has always been technology, cannot tolerate such a state of affairs.

In order to rectify the situation with one stroke, Fukui made a defiant statement at the May 17 press conference: "In 2009, we will be selling a hybrid-exclusive model that will be superior to gasoline-fueled cars in terms of affordability as well." The touted product will be a small car that is expected to sell a total of 200,000 vehicles per year, 100,000 in North America, 50,000 in Japan, and 50,000 in other regions. The minimum price for the Civic Hybrid is about $20,000, but if the hybrid exclusive is successfully mass-produced it should be priced at significantly below that figure.

Although Honda's first hybrid car, Insight, came in first place in the Ministry of Transportation's "Best 10 Gasoline-Efficient Cars," its high price pushed down sales every year after its debut. In 2005, only 800 cars sold, one-seventh of its peak sales, and it will no longer be available on market in 2007.

The number of hybrid cars sold worldwide in 2005 was a mere 48,000, less than 2 percent of total sales. However, with the help of the hybrid-exclusive car that will contend with Toyota's Prius, sales is projected to rise to 300,000 vehicles, 6 to 7 percent of the total, for 2011.

Honda's new hybrid system "IMA (Integrated Motor Assist)" is characterized by its light weight, compactness, and relatively low cost. Toyota, which is ahead of Honda in hybrid technology, plans on a full-range installation across all categories, while Honda is planning to limit installation to models smaller than the Civic.

Toyota, of course, isn't sitting back and doing nothing in this area where it currently leads. It has managed to set a timetable for developing a third-generation hybrid system with improved fuel efficiency. Toyota plans to install the system in 1 million cars annually beginning in 2010. At any rate, the hybrid market, which Toyota has so far dominated, will soon be welcoming a tough contender in Honda. There will be more competition, but also, more hybrids relative to gas-fueled cars on the streets.

In addition to the hybrid-exclusive car, Honda is also developing a diesel engine that will meet new U.S. emissions standards that mandate nitrogen oxide levels equal to that of gas-fueled cars. By 2009, a model with a four-cylinder engine will be going on sale. A V6 diesel engine has also entered the development phase and will start to be installed as soon as it is ready.

In Europe, the sales share of diesel cars is above 50 percent, but in the U.S., where gas prices are low, the share is a mere 3 percent. But because diesel engines are fuel efficient, if gas prices stay high, the market for them is expected to grow rapidly. From 2009 onwards, Honda's strategy will be "small hybrid cars and large diesel cars."

At the press conference, Fukui concluded, "By continuing, Honda-like, to hone our drive for innovation and providing moving experiences, we intend to become the world's number one automaker." Fukui was not saying that Honda would one day lead in quantity, one imagines, but rather that the company aims to become the most influential automaker in the world through quality, or technology.

Honda rose from the ashes of World War II. All it had then was Soichiro's engineering genius and Fujisawa's business acumen. In the founding days, Fujisawa, in his own words, "tried everything short of robbery and fraud for the sake of money," so tough were his fundraising efforts. Yet, in the end, the motorcycle maker that they created out of nothing grew, in a short period, to become the world's best.

The second and third presidents Kiyoshi Kawashima and Tadashi Kume, the Honda kids personified, had it beaten into them by Soichiro that becoming "the world's best" mattered, while they learned from Fujisawa "the law of transience." Their response was to make Honda a reputed world-class maker not just of motorbikes but of automobiles. During the Kawashima-Kume era, when some conundrum arose, the two supreme advisors were always there to be consulted.

The change occurred toward the end of Kume's presidency when Fujisawa died, and Soichiro soon after as if to follow suit. Nobuhiko Kawamoto and Hiroyuki Yoshino belonged to the last generation of Honda men to be baptized by the founders and were in that sense the Honda grandchildren. The founders were no longer of this world and could not be approached for advice. Older hands who had assumed posts as counselors made it clear that they, too, would absent themselves from the management process: "A Honda counselor is someone whose counsel isn't sought." The later presidents had to make all business decisions on their own. When disputes arose over which way to take the company, it ended in internal strife. It was the reason why Honda floundered for a period. When Kawamoto emerged from that conflict as the *de facto* and *de jure* chief executive, he abolished *waigaya*, the directors' commons, and other unique aspects of Honda corporate culture to lead the company out of the wilderness.

"Everything that receives life in this world must perish. How might a company elude that law and develop forever?" Fujisawa's answer: "By continuing to grow." Honda's successive presidents bear this burden—the founders' curse, so to speak. Although there were ups and downs during Kawamoto's reign, the legacy of his predecessors, namely North American production, helped the company post huge profits for the U.S. market. The profits were plowed lavishly into domestic sales to subsidize the long-sought goal of selling 800,000 cars at home over a year. During his successor Yoshino's reign, the small car Fit beat the Corolla to become the top selling model, if only for one year. While Fujisawa's dream of "beating the Corolla at all costs," which he mouthed as a sort of habit before he finally passed away, was granted, the streak in domestic sales eventually came to an end, and Toyota simply pulled away farther than before.

Honda's great-grandchildren, Fukui's generation, did not ever have wrenches hurled at them by Soichiro, nor did they ever listen to Fujisawa intone the law of transience. What was business management all about? They missed that lecture, too. Honda's business methods could be "intoned but not inherited" so they had to devise their own management vision in order to keep developing the company. The goal Fukui has set is "most influential automaker in the world," with technology at the core; the business direction for its realization, "an accelerated shoring up of the basics." The genes of the co-founders, who ceaselessly pursued growth, seem, after all, to be present in the grandchildren and great-grandchildren as well as the children.

Suddenly, in the summer of 2006, plans were floated of a triangle partnership between GM and Nissan/Renault, but the era of glory via M&A is already over. Looking back on the Big Three's strategy, it is not an exaggeration to say that the M&A way is bankrupt.

Fate is curious. In 1931, the year GM beat Ford to become the world's largest automaker, Toyota founder Kiichiro Toyoda produced a small four-horsepower gasoline engine that he had modeled on the American Smith Motor engine. Seventy-five years later, Toyota surpasses GM to take the throne of number one. And now Honda, which came into the world in the postwar years when Toyota nearly went under from a shortage of funds, prepares to become the homegrown giant's antagonist.

7

What this book needs to touch upon as its closes is the subsequent story of the hero of the first chapter, Shoichiro Irimajiri, "The Prince of Honda" who left Honda at the young age of fifty-two.

There was no way the automotive industry was going to leave alone a talented engineer like him, and indeed, after he left Honda and his health recovered, GM tried to headhunt him just as he was wondering what to do with his new lease on life. The offer was a good one and Irimajiri was ready to accept it, but he was seduced by the words of an old acquaintance of his, Boston Consulting Group President Koichi Hori, who, much like the proverbial devil into the other ear, cautioned that GM just intended to use and cast him aside. In the end Irimajiri joined Sega Enterprises, a game maker with no ties to the auto industry, as vice president.

At Sega, as the man in charge of research, development, and production, he supervised *Sakura Wars*, a game software released in 1996 for the Sega Saturn platform. When it became a hit series, he received the credit and was promoted in 1998 to president. The next step was to challenge the dominance of Sony's home game system Playstation with Sega's next-generation platform, the Dreamcast.

Fortune and misfortune came simultaneously. The fortune was that, in 1999, Delphi Automotive Systems (the GM parts division had spun off to become an independent company) invited Irimajiri to become an outside board member. Since his GM days, Delphi Chairman and CEO J. T. Battenberg III regarded Irimajiri very highly. *Well, if it's just as an outside board member.* Irimajiri accepted the invitation lightly, but every time he looked through the piles of papers that Detroit sent him, his heart danced. *Autos are so much fun.*

The misfortune was that the Dreamcast, which Sega had a lot riding on, failed on all fronts, plunging the company into the red for fiscal 1999 for the third year in a row. Taking responsibility, Irimajiri withdrew to the post of vice president in June, and half a year later, in December, quit the company, washing his hands clean of the game industry.

After leaving Sega, he set up an office with the somewhat peculiar name of "Shoichiro Irimajiri, Inc." As expected, many companies came to seek the advice of the now independent Irimajiri: the mapmaker Zenrin, the major toymaker Bandai, the PR consultancy Fleishman-Hillard of the American Omnicom Group, and so on. In order to secure free time for himself, Irimajiri avoided involvement at the core management levels, opting instead to participate as director of an affiliated company or as advisory board member.

It was in autos that Irimajiri could put his talents to greatest use. His role at Delphi was not just advising business decisions but helping sell product (auto parts) to Asian automakers including those in Japan.

What struck him every time he visited Delphi's factory in Detroit was the yearly waning respect for manufacturing in the United States. Naturally, this had effects on the ground, at the factories. Japan, meanwhile, remained robust in that regard. Ideas for further rationalization and quality improvement, typified by the Toyota Production System, bubbled up incessantly from the factories. Every time he visited Detroit, Irimajiri could not but think: *The era of the Big Three has ended.*

While the U.S. auto industry may have been in decline, his title as outside board member of Delphi was powerful. Irimajiri had a free pass to meet the head of GM, Delphi's parent. He hit it off with former Ford top man Jacques Nasser from the very beginning, and the two speak freely as friends over the phone.

Auto-related work came in one after another. Courted in person by Timothy Collins, owner of RHJ International—which, as Ripplewood, had acquired the insolvent Long-Term Credit Bank of Japan in 2003 and turned it around as the Shinsei Bank—Irimajiri signed an industrial partner agreement. RHJ had acquired Asahi Tech, an auto parts maker, and Irimajiri's first task was to revive the company as director with representative rights.

Thanks to Irimajiri's connections, Asahi Tech found new clients, and this combined with thorough rationalization put the company back in the black for fiscal 2005 on both the independent and consolidated bases. Through his work at Asahi, Irimajiri also befriended the head of Korea's Hyundai. It was not so much Irimajiri bowing to Hyundai to gain a client, but his promising to teach manufacturing to them in exchange for getting their business.

At one point, the world-class outer parts maker Ogihara requested him to become chairman, but this did not come to pass because Daiwa Secruities SMBC, RHJ's rival, offered its support to Ogihara. Becoming a board member of an auto-related company was difficult given Irimajiri's contract with RHJ; becoming an advisor was not a problem. When he took up such a post at Toyota Industries Corporation, the head source as it were of Toyota, Irimajiri started gaining friends among Toyota's engineers.

Perhaps because the Irimajiri office is in Shinbashi right in the center of Tokyo, it receives an endless stream of visitors. Most come for work-related meetings, but now and then, old acquaintances, executives at Suzuki and the motor-bike maker Yamaha, whom Irimajiri got to know during his Hamamatsu plant days, show their faces. They all ask the same question: "I'm approaching retirement. I'd like to take up the kind of work you're doing…" At such times Irimajiri becomes a consultant about life itself.

Time healed the wounds that Irimajiri suffered when he had to leave Honda against his will. As new men have assumed Honda's presidency, Irimajiri's relationship with his old company has been restituted. Although he rarely sees Kawamoto, Irimajiri has reclaimed his friendship with Yoshino, with whom he golfs. The current president, Fukui, worked directly under Irimajiri in Hamamatsu and occasionally seeks the advice of his former superior.

Irimajiri, Kawamoto, and Yoshino, who all joined Honda in 1963, are facing a turning point in their lives. Irimajiri had been the favorite to become Honda's fourth president, but if he had, neither Kawamoto nor Yoshino would have assumed the post after him. Both Kawamoto and Yoshino have resigned as president and are living out their golden days. It is Irimajiri who is still active, traveling inside and outside Japan, absent from Tokyo half of the month to engage in business.

What Irimajiri wants to do more of now is to tell primary and secondary school students that science and technology rock. The desire was ignited when he gave a lecture to an industries-oriented vocational high school. Hearing that the students were industry majors, Irimajiri pictured male students. As it turned out, four-fifths of the faces in the audience belonged to young women.

One of them asked him during the Q&A period, "What should I study if I want to design F1 chassis?"

Though completely flabbergasted, Irimajiri answered with care. "The big premise for winning in F1 is having a top-quality engine. The chassis on which that engine is mounted has to pursue functionality to the extreme. You don't start out with a design for the chassis. When you pursue functionality, you end up with the design that's common. In order to pursue functionality, you have to be well-versed in science and technology."

Unfortunately, the female student who asked the question failed to grasp Irimajiri's point. It worried him. *F1 is a motorsport, but from the perspective of the constructors, it's a pure distillation of technology. If Japanese science declines, F1 racing will be the least of problems. What I want elementary and middle school kids to get interested in is perhaps basic science, even more than technology. Science and technology set you dreaming. If I can tell kids my experiences, maybe they'll understand some of that dream.*

And so, while it is still only a few times a year at this point, Irimajiri gives talks at Japan's elementary and middle schools. Irimajiri's favorite word is "dream." He always ends his talks with the dream he nourished.

"I became fascinated by airplanes and wanted to make them, so I studied airplanes in college. But back when I graduated, Japan wasn't allowed to make airplanes. So I channeled my dream into racing instead and joined Honda. At first it was motorbike racing. When we were winning one race after another, I learned that Honda was going to try its hand at F1 racing, and I nearly jumped up and down with joy. My dream turned from motorbikes to F1 cars. I plunged headlong into it, and after much effort, we were able to get to the top of the winners' podium. We put our knowledge to use in our passenger cars, and Honda became world-class not just in motorbikes but in automobiles too. A dream will always come true if it's focused and if you strive after it. It's because you have a dream that you can try so hard."

At the end of March 2006, Irimajiri resigned his board seat at Delphi, which had entered into a tailspin. Today, 70 percent of Irimajiri's activity is still auto-related, but he plans on decreasing his workload. He wants to speak of his dream to schoolchildren more often.

Soichiro Honda, who lived a kind of dream life, burned himself out and left the world of business when he was sixty-six. Shoichiro Irimajiri was the little hero that the genius technician certified as being "the best engineer in the world." Having experienced both glory and squalor, Irimajiri has been liberated at last from the spell of Honda. At sixty-six now, he shines as a common soldier.

* * *

The co-founders Soichiro Honda and Takeo Fujisawa continue to live on in HONDA. I, for my part, can almost hear the banter that they're exchanging in heaven.

Soichiro Honda: Hey, Vice, it's thirty-three years since we withdrew from Honda management. When we quit together, the world auto industry was a rigmarole fretting to meet the emissions restrictions that Representative Muskie had proposed. I developed the CVCC engine then and created our foothold in four-wheelers. If it weren't for those emissions restrictions, Honda wouldn't be what it is today.

Takeo Fujisawa: Honda-san, don't you agree the auto industry's situation today is a lot like the one back then? It's very much in flux. What hasn't changed is that, without the technology, you can't survive. I'm so glad I had the technicians succeed you as president. If we administrators had headed the company, it wouldn't have grown so large.

H: When we were active, the American Big Three were a breed apart.

F : Oh yes. But then you always used to say, "GM didn't start out as a huge company. One day we'll outpace them."

H: I did, but no one took me seriously.

F : And GM looks like it's slipping off the throne of number one.

H: What, really? Who beat them?

F : Toyota, who looked after you during the war years when you were at Tokai Seiki Heavy Industries.

H: Yeah, Ishida-san took good care of me. But in those days, Toyota couldn't build a car worth the name. So I ask you, Vice, if we beat Toyota, our company's the top carmaker in the world?

F : Why not? But if you care to know what I think, Toyota didn't assume the throne because of what it did. It's rather that GM and Ford fell into that old trap of the law of transience and declined. Even if Toyota becomes number one in the world, there's no guarantee it won't fall into the same trap. If the company that you and I built continues to grow, one day it's destined to become the world's top carmaker. I believe it. But if the active boys haven't the guts to go for number one, they won't escape the law that nothing is eternal.

H: Well, how about F1 racing? If you can't stand at the center of that winners' podium, "world's top carmaker" is just a dream within a dream.

F : Honda-san, want to hear some good news? We were up there just recently.

H: Is that a fact? When was that?

F : At the Hungary GP in August 2006, the thirteen race of the year. For the first time in fourteen years, Honda stood at the center of the podium. Last time before that was the Australian GP in 1992. Actually, we designed both the engine and the chassis this year, and winning all on our own isn't something that's happened since the Italian GP in 1967 when you were in charge.

H: Well done! You enter the F1 to win. From now on, we'll just keep on winning.

F : You were born on November 17, 2006, so if you were alive, you'd be a hundred years old. In January, Honda won the "2006 North American Car of the Year Award" in two categories, passenger and truck. And then the F1 win in August. It's got to be a hundredth anniversary gift from the boys down below. Let's entrust the future of Honda to the kids we raised, and to the grandchildren and great-grandchildren that our kids raised.

H: Hey, Vice, you're right. Let's root for them from where we are. After all, we haven't much of a choice!

Midsummer 2006
Masaaki Sato

ABOUT THE AUTHOR

Masaaki Sato simply has no peer when it comes to reporting on the Japanese auto industry, his prominence dating back to the 1980's when he was on the auto beat for *Nikkei* (the Japanese *Wall Street Journal*). Currently an executive at Nikkei Business Publications, he is the author of highly regarded histories including one on the early days of home video technology (i.e., VHS vs. Betamax) that has been adapted to the big screen. His most recent book is *The House of Toyota*.